introduction to

Basic
Legal
Principles

introduction to

Basic
Legal
Principles

REED T. PHALAN

Associate Professor of Business Law
College of Business Administration
The Pennsylvania State University

INTERNATIONAL TEXTBOOK COMPANY
Scranton, Pennsylvania

To Mother and Dad

Preface

There is unanimous agreement that college education for business should include some study of law, legal reasoning, and legal institutions. Courses designed to meet this need, usually titled with some variation of the term "business law," have long been included in business administration curricula. In more recent years, a further need for basic law courses has been developing. Recognizing that the law is one of the most important of the social sciences, more and more educators are seeking a basic law course for undergraduates as a social science or general education elective, a course for students in all curricula.

Basic survey courses offered for students from other specialties are an essential part of the college scene, and the general purpose of such survey courses is well understood—namely, *to show how the discipline under study* (physics, chemistry, geology, economics, law, or some other course) *fits into and affects the social order, thus enabling the student, as an educated person, to better understand, adjust to, and contribute to his social environment.* No one will claim that completion of a basic physics course will make the student a scientist or enable him to carry on scientific research. A man does not become an economist with one course in economics or a historian after having a survey course in history. Equally limited in purpose and effect are basic law courses offered to college undergraduates, whether business administration majors or not. Such courses, therefore, should be general education or social science courses, rather than sets of rules for "do-it-yourselfers." The primary purpose is not to teach rules of law or to enable students to handle their own legal affairs, but rather to introduce the law as a social institution.

When it comes to determining the course content for an undergraduate survey course in law, the following factors provide helpful guidelines:

1. The law is the chief agency for social control.

2. The law achieves social control through weighing and adjusting the conflicting interests of individuals and of groups, and then recognizing and defining legal rights and enforcing legal obligations.

3. The conduct of business—the buying and selling of goods, land, and services—is the principal nonpolitical activity of society.

4. The bases for most private or nonpolitical legal rights and obligations involve the two main fields of the law, torts and contracts.

Therefore, for a basic law course to adequately picture the law and legal reasoning in action, it should briefly describe courts and lawsuits, and then consider some of the basic policy factors which have shaped the law and continue to shape it in the fields of torts, contracts, and general business operations and transactions.

If a survey course in any field is to achieve its proper objectives, the manner in which the course is presented is of vital importance. A student taking a basic physics course will not concentrate on memorizing formulas for momentum, falling bodies, intensity of light, and so on. Rather, he will examine the basic principles from which the formulas are derived. Such an approach is especially necessary for an undergraduate law course in order to emphasize clearly the most important feature of the law as a social institution—namely, that a rule of law is a statement of what is considered to be sound, wise policy (fair, reasonable, and practical) under certain particular circumstances.

I should like to outline the manner in which this book attempts to achieve the foregoing objectives.

1. The book begins with a general introduction to the nature of law, to legal systems and courts, and to basic legal procedure, followed by a general introduction to the basic principles involved in the fields of tort and contract law.

2. Following this general introduction, certain specific topics are presented to introduce students to the general plan of the law as applied in greater detail to common business operations and transactions.

3. Where applicable, the basic policy decisions written into the Uniform Commercial Code are indicated and illustrated.

4. A considerable amount of case material is included in the examples and problems. The examples demonstrate the interplay of policy factors and the application of legal principles in resolving disputes. The problems stimulate the student in analyzing fact situations, recognizing legal issues, thinking in terms of basic legal factors, and applying fundamental principles to resolve disputes.

5. On the whole, the approach for most topics is analytical rather than merely descriptive, emphasizing the policy factors which underlie the basic rules of law. I believe that by means of this "policy" approach, not only will a student become somewhat familiar with the basic everyday rules under which society operates, but, what is more important, he will observe the legal process in action—the weighing of conflicting interests in the determination and formulation of what are believed to be the soundest policies and the wisest rules.

My selection of legal topics and the space allocated to each has been guided by the objectives for which this book has been prepared. Admittedly, certain topics are very briefly referred to (for example, crimes and gifts); others are covered in summary fashion (for example, partner-ships and corporations); and some are presented only in outline form (for example, real property, and wills and estates). Even the discussions which go into greater detail make no pretense of covering topics thor-oughly or providing solutions for all conceivable situations. I am con-fident, however, that, with my general objectives in mind, no reader will be misled into taking my discussions for more than they are intended to be—basic surveys of some of the more important legal topics which affect the day-to-day activities of society.

In the field of general contracts, a text discussion must present the two parallel bodies of law—the Uniform Commercial Code applying to sales-of-goods contracts and the non-Code, common law applying to other contracts. In doing this, I have taken advantage of the basic Code changes to illustrate some of the policy factors which are at work in shaping today's rules of law. For the separate topics of sales of goods, commercial paper, and financing transactions, however, it is extremely confusing to speak to students in the antiquated, obsolete language and thought patterns of the Uniform Sales Act, the N.I.L., and so on. While an instructor might welcome a comparative discussion of pre-Code and Code rules for his own study, there is little reason to emphasize changes to undergraduate, nonlegal students who come into class with no pre-vious knowledge of what the law was before it was changed, and no reason to study this aspect of legal history.

Even if an instructor favors a comparative approach, however, his presentation should be guided by the fact that the states in which the Code has been adopted contain an overwhelming majority of the coun-try's population. Therefore, the Code should be covered *first*, and then, if he wishes, the instructor may give details of the pre-Code law as a short appendage.

A considerable amount of disagreement has existed among instructors concerning whether an undergraduate book of this type should contain longer text discussions with cases presented as examples and problems or, instead, shorter text discussions supplemented by actual court opinions. This debate, however, is no longer evenly balanced. An instructor who favors using court opinions will find himself considerably handicapped by the general adoption of the Uniform Commercial Code and the dearth of cases decided under the Code. In any situation covered by the Code, most pre-Code court opinions will be expressed in obsolete, pre-Code language and thought patterns, useful to lawyers, but confusing to un-dergraduate, nonlegal students.

My case material consists almost exclusively of examples and problems, thus achieving the advantages of the case approach while avoiding the confusion arising from the use of pre-Code court opinions—and also avoiding the waste of student and class time which so often results when undergraduate, nonlegal students plod (and stumble) their way through the unfamiliar language of court opinions.

REED T. PHALAN

University Park, Pennsylvania
April, 1964

Acknowledgments

Of the many persons at The Pennsylvania State University whose suggestions, criticisms, or encouragement have aided me greatly, I should like to mention particularly Dean Ossian MacKenzie, Associate Dean David H. McKinley, and Professors Joseph F. Bradley, Lynn Christy, Franklin H. Cook, Ralph H. Wherry, and (Professor Emeritus) Sheldon C. Tanner. I should also like to express my appreciation to Professor Lon L. Fuller of Harvard Law School for graciously permitting me to use his excellent discussion of "The Adversary System," and to the American Law Institute and the National Conference of Commissioners on Uniform State Laws for permission to quote from the explanatory comments (copyright 1963) which accompany the Uniform Commercial Code.

Some of the problems which appear at the ends of the chapters are accompanied by the notation, "A.I.C.P.A.," an abbreviation for the American Institute of Certified Public Accountants. Twice a year the Board of Examiners of the Institute prepares questions which are adopted and used by the accountant examining boards of all states, territories, and the District of Columbia. I am grateful to the Institute for granting me permission to use its questions.

REED T. PHALAN

Contents

xiii

book III
The Basic Law of Business Organization

book V
Survey of Basic Property Principles

introduction to

Basic
Legal
Principles

book *I*

Introduction to Law

Reason is the life of the law; nay, the Common Law itself is nothing but reason.

Sir Edward Coke, 1552-1634

chapter *1*

The Legal System

In any society persons can be expected to act primarily for their own interests, with friction and conflict resulting from the competition of various self-interests. To restrain such friction and conflict within tolerable limits, rules for the control of people have been essential from the very dawn of civilization, rules which set the framework or pattern within which all human activity is carried on. The chief repository for such rules is the law. The *law* can be defined, therefore, as a body of rules for human conduct, enforced by a governing power, as the means by which the control of society is achieved. (The term *society* includes the neighborhood, town, state, nation, and, to the extent control among nations is achieved through law, the world.)

The rules of law that exist today are the result of a process of gradual evolution over centuries of social progress, a process which continues unabated. The remote roots of any legal system can be traced back to early tribal life. As disputes arose within a tribe, rules for the conduct of the tribal members were gradually formulated. In a primitive hunting society disputes like that given in the following example probably arose frequently.

Example: A and B, both members of the same tribe, were hunting separately. B grievously wounded an animal and was in pursuit when A, not seeing B nearby, intercepted the animal, killed it, and took possession of it. Tribal rules forbade combat within the tribe. Therefore to settle the disputed ownership, A and B requested a decision from the chief.

Whichever way the chief decided, he would necessarily be stating a rule that would apply in the future should the same kind of dispute arise again. Through the process of deciding day-to-day disputes, rules for conduct were gradually built up.

It is interesting to note that the primitive rule favored the party who first took possession of an animal; during centuries of social progress in conceptions of justice, methods of proof, and knowledge of mortal and nonmortal wounds, the rule gradually changed. In a case which arose in 1914, the Wisconsin Supreme Court said:

"It is conceded that if the plaintiffs had substantially permanently deprived the wolf of his liberty—had him so in their power that escape was highly improbable, if not impossible, before defendant appeared on the scene, and, with his gun pointed so as to reach within some 3 feet of the animal, delivered a finishing shot, it had become the property of plaintiffs, and was wrongfully appropriated by appellant [the defendant]. Such is according to the prevailing rule. The instant a wild animal is brought under the control of a person, so that actual possession is practically inevitable, a vested property interest in it accrues, which cannot be divested by another's intervening and killing it. . . . Such is the law of the chase by common-law principles, differing from the more ancient civil law which postponed the point of vested interest to that of actual taking."[1]

The legislatures of some states have felt that a codification (definite statutory rule) either repeating or changing the common-law rule is desirable. For example, the Pennsylvania statute deviates from the modern common-law rule and returns somewhat to the ancient rule, saying: "When a mortal wound has been lawfully inflicted on any game, but the same is not killed immediately and continues in flight, and is thereafter lawfully shot by another hunter who inflicts a mortal wound, thereby stopping the flight of such game and killing it, enabling such hunter to take possession of the carcass, the ownership of the carcass shall be deemed to be in the hunter whose fatal wound stopped the flight of such game and enabled him to take possession of the carcass." Apparently the legislature believes that a rule awarding game to the person who delivers the killing blow and takes possession is simpler and easier to apply than the common-law rule and therefore a more desirable rule.

At first the Roman law underwent such a gradual evolution. Then with the Roman penchant for centralized government and for detailed logical classification, various codifications and texts appeared, culminating finally in the sixth century with the promulgation by the Roman Emperor Justinian of a complete code of law, frequently referred to as the Justinian Code. By this time however, the breakup of the Roman Empire had already begun. With the further disintegration of the Empire, together with the breakdown of trade and commerce that followed the Moslem conquest of Northern Africa and Spain, Europe regressed to a disorganized, rural society, and the Roman Code, no longer necessary, sank into obscurity. Europe's emergence from the Dark Ages spurred interest in the study of Roman law. As Europe developed economically and politically and centralized governments began to emerge, the Roman Code provided the framework for the expanding legal systems needed by the increasingly complex society. Various revisions of the Roman Code were made, and finally in 1804 the most famous recodification was promulgated by Emperor Napoleon. The Napoleonic Code (also called the French Civil Code or Code Napoléon) has become the basis of the legal systems in the countries of continental Europe, and in areas settled under continental European influence—including all of the nations on the American continents, except the United States and Canada; in these two nations, only the state of Louisiana and

[1] *Liesner v. Wanie*, 156 Wis. 16, 50 L.R.A.N.S. 703 (1914).

the province of Quebec, both settled by the French, base their legal systems on the Napoleonic Code.

No such complete codification occurred in England. Although the Norman Conquest of 1066 brought centralization of government at a much earlier date than on the continent, the Norman political system had not yet developed the concept of detailed legislation. Instead, beginning in the twelfth century, centralization of justice was begun by the King's improving and expanding the jurisdiction and authority of the King's Court. The judges of the King's Court, whether holding central court at Westminster, or traveling on circuit and holding court throughout the country, formulated the legal principles which they felt should be applied to the controversies brought before them. These principles were based largely on the customs and rules that had gradually evolved over the centuries. When these customs differed among the various communities, as they frequently did, the King's judges decided which should stand as the common law of the land, thus gradually developing the English common-law system. Even as late as the thirteenth century the quantity of legislative or enacted law in England was very slight. Most of the legal principles were formulated by the judges in the process of settling controversies brought before them. Such judicial lawmaking is the chief characteristic of the English legal system from which the American common-law system developed, as opposed to the Roman code-law system (also called the civil-law system) which is based on legislative law.

As indicated by the foregoing discussion, rules of law can be broadly subdivided into legislative law and decisional law. *Legislative law* consists of rules enacted and promulgated for the future conduct of all persons, according to the legislative authority's conception of the public good. A *decisional rule of law* is a rule formulated by the decisional authority (usually a court) in the course of settling a particular dispute between two parties. In deciding the outcome of a particular dispute, a court may simply be required to select the proper legislative rule and apply it to the facts of the dispute. Frequently under the common-law system, however, no applicable legislative rule exists. Since the dispute must be resolved, the court must function as a lawmaker, determining and formulating what it feels to be the proper rule to apply from the standpoint of sound public policy. The American legal system today consists of legislative law (constitutions, statutes enacted by legislatures, and regulations and ordinances promulgated under statutory authority) and also of a considerable body of decisional law.

It should be emphasized that rules of law, whether legislative or decisional, are reflections of what is considered sound public policy, from the standpoint of fairness, reasonableness, practicality, and consistency with previously declared rules. As Justice Holmes has written in his memorable book, *The Common Law:*

> The life of the law has not been logic: it has been experience. The felt necessities of the time, the prevalent moral and political theories, intuitions of public policy, avowed or unconscious, even the prejudices which judges share with their fellow-men, have had a good deal more to do than the syllogism in determining the rules by which men should be governed. The law embodies the story of a nation's development through many centuries, and it cannot be dealt with as if it contained only the axioms and corollaries of a book of mathematics. In order to know what it is, we must know what it has been, and what it tends to become. We must alternately consult history and existing theories of legislation. But the most difficult labor will be to understand the combination of the two into new products at every stage. The substance of the law at any given time pretty nearly corresponds, so far as it goes, with what is then understood to be convenient; but its form and machinery, and the degree to which it is able to work out desired results, depend very much upon its past. . . .
>
> A very common phenomenon, and one very familiar to the student of history, is this. The customs, beliefs, or needs of a primitive time establish a rule or a formula. In the course of centuries the custom, belief, or necessity disappears, but the rule remains. The reason which gave rise to the rule has been forgotten, and ingenious minds set themselves to inquire how it is to be accounted for. Some ground of policy is thought of, which seems to explain it and to reconcile it with the present state of things; and then the rule adapts itself to the new reasons which have been found for it, and enters on a new career. The old form receives a new content, and in time even the form modifies itself to fit the meaning which it has received. . . .
>
> The very considerations which judges most rarely mention, and always with an apology, are the secret root from which the law draws all the juices of life. I mean, of course, considerations of what is expedient for the community concerned. Every important principle which is developed by litigation is in fact and at bottom the result of more or less definitely understood views of public policy; most generally, to be sure, under our practice and traditions, the unconscious result of instinctive preferences and inarticulate convictions, but none the less traceable to views of public policy in the last analysis.[2]

In short, law is policy. Conceptions of policy and circumstances which shape policy change. If a rule of law is a viable rule today, it must have sound, present-day policy reasons for its existence. In seeking present-day reasons, one should bear in mind that the promotion of certainty and stability in the law is itself a desirable and necessary objective. The law must not only determine the effect of past conduct but must also give assurances as to a person's future rights and obliga-

[2] Holmes, Oliver Wendell, Jr., *The Common Law* (1881; Cambridge: Harvard University Press, 1963), pp. 5, 8, 31-32.

tions. A necessary legal principle therefore is expressed by the term *stare decisis*, Latin for "let the decision stand." Under this principle, once a decisional rule of law has been formulated, it is applied to similar disputes in the future, until the court is clearly convinced that the rule has become obsolete or is wrong.

An excellent example of the common-law system in operation, with the court reasoning from prior decisional law to form new decisional law, is provided by the case of *Summit Hotel Co. v. National Broadcasting Co.,* 336 Pa. 182 (1939). The citation for this case shows that the lawsuit was brought by the hotel as the plaintiff against (versus) the broadcasting company as the defendant, and that the court's written *opinion*— statement of the court's conclusion and its reasons for reaching that conclusion—is published in volume 336 of the Pennyslvania Supreme Court reports at page 182.

Example: The lawsuit in the Summit Hotel case developed from a statement made during a radio broadcast. In 1935 the Shell Oil Company sponsored an NBC radio program starring Al Jolson. One program featured Jolson interviewing a golf champion. The prepared script, which was followed exactly during rehearsal, had Jolson asking, "But tell me, Sam, what did you do after you got out of college?" and the golf champion answering, "I turned golf professional and in 1932 I got a job at the Summit Golf Club in Uniontown, Pennsylvania." During the actual broadcast, Jolson at this point ad libbed, "That's a rotten hotel." The Summit Hotel Company sued NBC for $15,000 damages for the defamation.

The question was whether a radio company should be held liable for a performer's unexpected remark. This exact question had never before been litigated, and at that time no applicable legislative law existed. The closest analogies which had already developed in the courts involved newspaper publishers and owners of public halls. In reference to these, Jolson of course would be liable for his slanderous statement. If Jolson as a columnist had made the statement in a newspaper column, the newspaper publisher would be liable. In some states the decisional rule is that a newspaper publisher is absolutely liable for defamatory statements; the rule in some other states is that a publisher is liable if he has failed to take all reasonable measures to assure that a published statement is true. Under either rule, the publisher's liability is based upon his opportunity to control what is printed. On the other hand, if the owner of an auditorium with a public address system rents it to a lecturer, the owner is not liable for defamatory statements which the lecturer is able to spread through use of the hall and equipment.

The court decided, from the standpoint of fairness, reasonableness, and practicality, that the radio case more nearly resembled the auditorium case. Although the radio broadcaster had a control booth, the sound engineer with his switches and dials was merely assuring the technical quality of the broadcast and was not in the position of a censor. He had no opportunity to cut off Jolson's remark; it was made and broadcast before the engineer could act, unlike the publisher who has ample opportunity during the preparation of a newspaper to delete defamatory material.

An essential part of the concept of law is enforcement by a governing power. Without enforcement a rule actually is not law. Force is obvious in a criminal law action; after being apprehended and adjudged guilty, a wrongdoer is punished. Force is equally a part of the non-criminal law (usually called civil law). For example, a seller sells and delivers certain goods to a buyer who promises to pay $500 in thirty days. The goods are of proper quality but the buyer fails to pay. The seller sues the buyer and the court determines that the buyer owes the seller $500 and has no valid excuse for not paying. The court's conclusion is called the *judgment* in the case, and in effect is the court's stamp of approval on the seller's claim for $500. If the buyer fails to pay the amount of the judgment, the court will at the seller's request, order the sheriff to seize property belonging to the buyer, sell it at public auction sale (sheriff's sale), and turn over to the seller the proceeds, up to $500 plus certain expenses; any money remaining is paid to the buyer. This force which can be used if necessary—in this example seizure and sale of the buyer's property—stands behind every civil dispute.

UNIFORMITY OF LAWS AMONG THE STATES

The United States Constitution grants to the Federal government the general power to regulate businesses and commerce which cross state lines (generally termed *interstate commerce*) or which affect interstate commerce. This means that the Federal government has the power to establish rules of law applying to most businesses. This power extends even to businesses which do not themselves sell and ship across state lines, because although not directly a part of interstate commerce, the activities of such businesses may nevertheless "affect" interstate commerce. The Federal government has exercised its power by establishing rules of law for working conditions in businesses which affect interstate commerce (minimum wages, maximum hours, labor relations, etc.), and by establishing freight rates and other rules for transportation affecting interstate commerce.

Congress has not yet considered it desirable as a matter of policy for the Federal government to exercise completely its powers over matters affecting interstate commerce. Rather, Congress has left to the states the function of declaring and enforcing rules of law for many matters involving the conduct of business. Particularly, the formation and enforcement of agreements or contracts are still ruled by state law, even though many of the contracts involve the sale and shipment of goods across state lines.

There is a tendency for rules of law to vary somewhat from one state to another. These variations are the result both of varying economic, geographic, social, and political conditions, and also of varying opinions as to desirable policy from the standpoint of fairness, reasonableness, and practicality. Such variations appear both in legislative law and in decisional law. When a business transaction involves persons and businesses in more than one state, the rules of law which will apply are those of the state in which the contract is formed and is to be carried out, even though these rules may differ from those of the state in which a lawsuit is brought to enforce the contract. Thus if a contract formed and to be performed in Michigan is sued on in Ohio, the Ohio court will apply Michigan law to the dispute. Suppose that a buyer in Pennsylvania orders goods from separate sellers in New York, Ohio, and Michigan. Usually each seller's shipment of the goods will form a contract and begin performance. Each of the buyer's three contracts therefore will be controlled by the law of a different state. If the states were to have differing rules of law, a cautious buyer would want to familiarize himself with all of the varying rules before entering into the contracts. An immense saving of time and of money results when rules of law are made uniform so that the same rules apply regardless of the state in which contracts are made and are to be performed. Smooth, efficient conduct of business requires that rules of law be stable and uniform throughout the multistate business community.

Several organizations, composed of prominent lawyers, judges, and law teachers, and aided by many businesses, have been working for some time to promote uniformity of state laws, both legislative and decisional laws. The two most important and effective of these organizations are the National Conference of Commissioners on Uniform State Laws, and the American Law Institute. The National Conference, composed of members from all states (usually appointed by the governors) was first organized in the 1890s. It determines topics upon which uniform statutes among the states seem desirable, studies and discusses drafts of such statutes, and recommends the completed drafts to the state legislatures. In this way, uniform statutes covering various phases of business transactions have been prepared and enacted into law by the legislatures in most of the commercial states. The most important of these uniform statutes are the Negotiable Instruments Law (covering checks, notes, and drafts), the Sales Act (covering sales of goods), the Conditional Sales Act (covering installment purchasing by consumers), the Trust Receipts Act (covering credit purchases of inventory by dealers), the Bills of Lading Act, the Warehouse Receipts Act, and the Stock Transfer Act. The

American Law Institute was organized in the 1920s by a number of prominent lawyers, judges, and law teachers, aided by grants of money from charitable foundations and other sources. It has been mainly concerned with nonstatutory or decisional rules of law. The Institute studies, consolidates, and publishes concise statements of decisional rules of law, using the title, "Restatement of the Law." Topics covered by such studies include contracts, agency, torts, property, and many others. These restatements are very often used by courts as convenient and authoritative sources of decisional rules of law.

In recent years both of these organizations have cooperated in the preparation of the *Uniform Commercial Code*, a complete restatement and codification of the rules of law applying to commercial transactions. The objectives of the code are to modernize the rules of commercial law and to present them as a unified whole, rather than in a series of separate statutes. The Conference and the Institute both feel that just as a business transaction is a unified whole, involving the interrelation of sale, shipment, financing, payment by check (or note or draft), etc., so too should the rules of law be unified and interrelated. The Code is recommended by these organizations to the state legislatures for enactment into law, replacing all of the previous uniform commercial statutes. Sometimes the Code rules are the same as the rules under the uniform statutes; sometimes the Code makes changes and additions.

Preparation of the Code has taken a number of years, has cost hundreds of thousands of dollars, and has involved thousands of hours of study and conferences by a number of legal and business groups. The history of the common law has never before seen anything like such a sweeping codification and rewriting of the law. As can be expected with such a sizable undertaking, involving policy decisions on numerous controversial points, the Code has both advocates and opponents.

On the side of the Code's advocates, the late Judge Herbert F. Goodrich, Chairman of the entire project, has written in his forward to the 1957 Official Edition of the Code:

> Neither the Institute nor the Commissioners can claim perfection for this Code. No group of people, however careful, can use words that will be perfectly clear in their meaning to all other people. No group can make rules for the whole broad field of commercial law and have every rule which is written completely satisfactory to all who read it. There are interests to be balanced between parties whose desires conflict. What can be said for the Code is that the language has been worked over with care and the ideas embodied in the rules likewise worked over with care to get a fair balance of interests for all concerned.

Opponents challenge some of the policy decisions embodied in the Code as being unfair, unreasonable, impractical, or overly partial to certain business interests, and also argue that some of the language is so general as to be confusing and ambiguous, inviting differing interpretations by courts in various states, and thus actually reducing the desired uniformity of commercial laws.   Obviously the best measure of the Code is how it works in actual practice.   In states in which it has been enacted, the Code seems to be working very satisfactorily.

The Code is divided into ten Articles entitled as follows:

Article 1 General Provisions
Article 2 Sales
Article 3 Commercial Paper
Article 4 Bank Deposits and Collections
Article 5 Letters of Credit
Article 6 Bulk Transfers
Article 7 Warehouse Receipts, Bills of Lading and Other Documents of Title
Article 8 Investment Securities
Article 9 Secured Transactions; Sales of Accounts, Contract Rights and Chattel Paper
Article 10 Effective Date and Repealer

LEGAL RIGHTS, DUTIES, AND REMEDIES

Rights and Duties

The method by which the law achieves the control of society is through recognizing legal rights, imposing legal duties to observe such rights, and providing remedies if the rights are violated and the duties breached.   For every legal right there is a correlative legal duty.   The driver of an automobile has the right to be secure from injury caused by the careless acts of other drivers.   All drivers have the duty to act carefully so as not to cause injury.   If carelessness causes injury, the injured person has as a legal remedy a procedure to recover money from the careless person, money for his expenses (for hospital and doctor, repair of damaged property, etc.), money to make up for lost or reduced income (for time from work, temporary or permanent disability, etc.), and money to compensate for any pain suffered.   A lawsuit or legal action between persons (the injured person as the plaintiff against the wrongdoer as the defendant) is called a *civil action*.   Its main purpose is to compensate for injury sustained through the violation of an individual legal right.   Generally, punishment of a wrongdoer is not a proper objective of a civil action.

Society (that is, the community—city, county, state, and nation) has the right to remain at peace, undisturbed by wrongful conduct. To continue the example used in the preceding paragraph, careless driving may be so reckless as to be considered a disturbance of the peace—a crime. Society has as a legal remedy a procedure to punish the wrongdoer, by fine, imprisonment, or some other deprivation of rights—for example, a reckless driver may have his driver's license suspended or revoked. A lawsuit or legal action brought by society against a wrongdoer (State, Commonwealth, or United States against the wrongdoer as the defendant) is called a *criminal action*. Generally its main purpose is to punish, not to compensate an injured person. Any fine that is collected goes to society as a whole and cannot be used for the benefit of the injured person. The proper objectives of punishment are to deter both the wrongdoer and others from committing such acts, to reform the wrongdoer, and when necessary for the protection of society, to segregate the wrongdoer from society either for a time or permanently.

If certain conduct violates both individual and community rights, both a civil action (to compensate the injured person) and a criminal action (to punish the wrongdoer) may be brought.

Individual rights are of two main types:

1. Rights possessed by all persons in society. These include the rights to be secure or free from wrongful injuries to the body, to property (both personal property and real estate), to reputation, etc. A violation of such a right is called a *tort* (discussed in Chapter 2).

2. Rights arising out of agreement or contract. Consider a typical sales contract in which a seller agrees to sell and deliver certain described standardized goods, and a buyer agrees to receive the goods and to pay $500 as the purchase price. The law accomplishes enforcement by recognizing that, arising from the agreement, the seller has a right to receive $500 in exchange for the goods (and the buyer a corresponding duty to pay), and the buyer a legal right to receive the goods in exchange for his money (and the seller a corresponding duty to deliver). If the seller fails to deliver, the buyer has as a legal remedy a procedure to recover the money loss he sustains from the seller's wrongful act. Likewise should the buyer default, the seller can recover his resulting money loss from the buyer.

LAW AND EQUITY REMEDIES

The usual individual remedies available in a lawsuit are:

1. An action for money damages; or

2. An action by the owner of certain property to recover its possessions when it is wrongfully withheld from him.

At an early date in the development of the English law, situations arose in which the law-court remedies were not adequate. Aggrieved persons appealed directly to the king for special relief, the king referred these petitions to one of his advisers, called the chancellor, and eventually a system of courts was set up called chancery or equity courts. Their purpose was to give remedies when ordinary remedies available in the law courts were not adequate, and otherwise to handle matters not considered by the law courts.

The legal system known as *equity* is, therefore, a system of remedies available for situations where the ordinary legal remedies (available through law procedure as distinguished from equity procedure) are not adequate. Originally the equity system was administered through separate equity courts. In most states now the law system and the equity system are both administered by the same courts. Whichever remedy is appropriate for the dispute determines which system—law or equity—is to be applied.

Example: By written contract, a seller agreed to sell and a buyer to buy 1,000 bushels of a specified grade of potatoes at $2 a bushel, to be delivered on a specified date. Without excuse the seller refused to deliver on that date. To obtain the same grade of potatoes on the market, the buyer had to pay $2.50 per bushel. He bought 1,000 bushels, paying $500 more than he would have paid if he could have obtained the potatoes from the seller according to the contract.

The buyer could sue the seller and recover $500 as damages suffered through the seller's breach of contract. The $500 would compensate the buyer for the seller's breach of contract, would put the buyer in about as good a position as he would have been in if the seller had performed as agreed. Should the seller refuse to pay the judgment, the buyer could obtain the $500 through a sheriff's seizure and sale of the seller's property. The buyer's remedy in this example is obtainable in a law action rather than through an equity action.

Example: The owner of an auto, driving negligently, ran into and injured a pedestrian who had been walking carefully. The pedestrian incurred hospital and doctor bills, lost time from work, suffered pain, and sustained a permanent disability.

The pedestrian could sue the driver and recover money damages to compensate for his injuries. So far as the pedestrian can be compensated at all, money will do it. This would be a law action.

Example: By written contract a seller agreed to sell and a buyer to buy a described plot of land at a stated price. The seller thereafter refused to transfer the land.

Land is different from the potatoes of the preceding example inasmuch as the same plot of land cannot be procured elsewhere. Therefore money damages ordinarily will not compensate a land-contract buyer; he wants the described plot of land, not another. Since the ordinary legal remedies would not be adequate, the buyer could seek relief in equity. He could ask the court to decree or order the seller to carry out the contract—that is, to specifically perform the contract (the equity remedy of specific performance). If the seller still refused, he would be disobeying a direct order of the court, would be guilty of contempt of court, and could be punished by fine, imprisonment, or both. And if his refusal persisted, the court could transfer the land to the buyer who would obtain the seller's title by authority of the court proceeding. This would be an equity action.

Example: As part of the written agreement for the sale of a grocery business and its goodwill, a seller agreed with a buyer not to open a similar business within a radius of one mile, during the next five years. A few months after making the agreement, the seller began preparations to open another grocery store within the proscribed area.

The amount of loss sustained by the buyer as a result of the seller's competition would be speculative, since the profits of a business are affected by many factors. Also, if the buyer sued for money damages, he would have to estimate into the future, bring a series of lawsuits, or wait until expiration of the five years. An action for money damages for breach of the contract, therefore, would not give adequate relief. The buyer could ask for an equitable remedy—a court order or decree prohibiting the seller from opening the competing business; this would be an *injunction*. A person who disobeys an injunction can be punished for contempt of court, and other means of enforcement are available. This is an *equity lawsuit*.

Example: A landowner procured a quantity of dirt and had it dumped on his land to bring it up to street level so that he could have a driveway constructed. The owner did not have a retaining wall built and everytime it rained some of the loose dirt washed down onto his neighbor's adjoining land.

What the owner did (or hired to be done) was wrongful and constituted a trespass to his neighbor's land. (A *trespass* is a wrongful entry or intrusion upon another's land.) The neighbor could sue for damages but after he recovered a sum of money for restoration of his property, future rains would bring more of the loose dirt. To require the neighbor to wait until he suffered damages and then to bring a series of lawsuits would not afford the neighbor a complete and adequate remedy for the owner's wrong. The neighbor could sue in equity and, in addition to recovering for the damage already done, he could obtain an order or decree requiring the owner to stop his wrongful act by having a retaining wall constructed. This would be an equity action.

The principal (but not the only) equity remedies are 1) an injunction, 2) a decree of specific performance, and 3) a decree ordering rescission or cancellation of a contract. Note that the equitable remedies are available *only* when the ordinary remedies available in a law action are not adequate.

LAWSUITS

A dispute between two persons will involve either a disagreement over facts (that is, a disagreement as to exactly what has occurred between the parties), a disagreement over rules of law (that is, a dispute as to the legal effect of the facts), or a disagreement over both facts and rules. Settling disputes therefore requires a procedure for determining facts, for formulating rules applicable to the particular facts, and for enforcing the rules. The law fulfills its dispute-settling function through court hearings or lawsuits in which the disputing parties appear, present evidence as to what has happened, argue their differing contentions as to the proper rule of law, and obtain a decision. A lawsuit usually involves the following steps: commencement of the lawsuit, the pleadings, and a trial which results in a verdict and judgment. The lawsuit may also involve an appeal, and require steps to enforce the judgment.

Commencement of the Lawsuit

For a court to have power to validly settle a dispute, the court must have jurisdiction over 1) the type of case and 2) over the parties involved. The jurisdiction which the various courts have over types of cases is discussed later. A court obtains power over the plaintiff's rights in a dispute when the plaintiff brings the lawsuit in that court. Usually the court obtains power to adjudge the defendant's rights in a dispute when an officer of the court (usually the sheriff, a deputy sheriff, or a comparable official) gives to the defendant a written notice of the general nature of the lawsuit and of the time within which the defendant must present in court any defense he may have. Such a notice is frequently called a *summons*. With some exceptions the summons must be served on the defendant while he is within the geographical area (usually a particular county) over which the court has the power to operate. Cases in which it is possible for a court to obtain power over a defendant without a summons being served within its territorial jurisdiction include:

1. Accident claims against nonresident motorists. A court in the state where an auto accident occurs can obtain jurisdiction over a nonresident driver even though he is not served with a summons within that state; usually this is accomplished by serving the summons on a state official designated by statute, and sending a certified mail notice to the nonresident defendant.

2. Claims against nonresident owners of local property. If a plaintiff sues in a county where some of a nonresident defendant's property is located (either personal property or real estate) the plaintiff may have that property attached and subjected to his claim even though no summons is served on the defendant within that state.

If, after a court obtains jurisdiction over a defendant, he thereafter fails to appear before the court and present his defense, the court may enter a judgment by default against him and in favor of the plaintiff. Such a default judgment is just as effective as a judgment after a full-scale trial.

Pleadings

The pleadings are the formal written statements which the parties file with the court, alleging what each party believes to be the true facts upon which he bases his claim or defense. By comparing the plaintiff's and the defendant's statements, it is then possible to isolate the fact questions upon which the parties are in dispute and avoid wasting time on points that are not disputed.

Trial

The purpose of a trial is to determine the facts in the case, to decide from the evidence what actually occurred as to the point or points upon which the parties are in dispute. If the parties to a lawsuit are in agreement as to the facts, but disagree as to what legal rights and liabilities result from the facts, no trial is necessary. Instead, the lawyers for the parties present to the judge oral and written arguments concerning the disputed legal question, and the judge then reaches a conclusion as to the correct rule of law and gives judgment accordingly. If facts are in dispute so that a trial is necessary, the parties sometimes agree to have the judge determine the facts. Otherwise the facts are decided by a jury of twelve persons with the conduct of the trial refereed by the judge. The referee is necessary to assure that the parties comply with the standard rules prescribed for the presentation of evidence, rules which are designed for more quickly and accurately deciding disputed facts.

During the course of the trial it is not unusual that the testimony of one person will differ in certain respects from that of another. This does not necessarily mean that one or the other is deliberately lying; not infrequently a person is honestly mistaken in his recollection of events.

At the end of the trial, after all of the evidence is seen and heard by the jury, the judge instructs the jury as to the rules of law which apply to the dispute. The twelve jurymen go off by themselves, discuss the evidence as they remember it, and vote to determine their conclusion on the disputed fact or facts. When they all agree, they report their verdict to the judge. A jury does not often fail to reach an agreement. However (under the common-law rules which still prevail in most states) if the jury cannot agree unanimously one way or the other, they so report to the judge, and if the failure to agree persists, the judge will declare the trial ended with no settlement of the dispute. To obtain what he is seeking the plaintiff will then have to bring the dispute to another trial with a new jury.

If the jurymen agree on a verdict which in the opinion of the judge is supported by believable evidence, the judge enters a judgment accordingly. A decision of the disputed facts in favor of the defendant and a judgment to that effect expresses the court's conclusion that the defendant is not liable to the plaintiff. On the other hand, if the jury and the court decide that the defendant owes the plaintiff a certain amount of money, the judge will enter a judgment in favor of the plaintiff for that amount, plus interest and court costs.

The court costs usually do not include the expenses of the plaintiff's lawyer. Suppose that a plaintiff has a legal right to collect $2,000 from a defendant and that because of the defendant's refusal to pay, the plaintiff has to spend $500 in lawyer fees to obtain a $2,000 judgment against the defendant. It is certainly arguable that the plaintiff should have the right to collect $2,500 from the defendant, the original obligation plus the expense of obtaining the judgment. Likewise, if after initiating a lawsuit a plaintiff is unable to prove his case so that judgment is entered in favor of the defendant, it is arguable that the plaintiff should compensate the defendant for the lawyer expenses which the plaintiff's lawsuit required the defendant to incur in defending the action. Whether the losing party should be required to pay the fees of the winning party's lawyer is entirely a question of policy as to what society considers to be fair, reasonable, and practical under the circumstances. Early in its development the English common-law system began the practice of permitting the winning party to recover reasonable lawyer fees from the losing party, and the English courts have continued the practice. After the American Revolution, the practice was not considered to be desirable policy in the United States and was gradually abandoned, so that in most cases under the present American system lawyer fees in any substantial amount cannot be collected by the winning party. The chief reasons given for the American view can be summarized as follows:

1. The purpose of a civil lawsuit is to compensate a plaintiff for the damages he sustains as the result of the defendant's wrongful act.

a) Litigation expenses are indirect. Even though the defendant may be guilty of the alleged wrong, the expenses of the plaintiff's attorney are not a direct result of the defendant's wrong. In the words of the Connecticut Supreme Court:

> Now the expenses of litigation are never damages sued for in any case when the action is brought for the wrong itself, not even if the tort [wrongful conduct] be wanton or malicious. They are not the

"natural and proximate consequence of the wrongful act," . . . but are remote, future and contingent.[3]

b) Engaging in litigation is not of itself wrongful. If there is reason to be doubtful of a defendant's actual liability, it should not be considered wrongful for a person, either as plantiff or defendant, to insist upon a lawsuit to determine this doubtful question. Since, therefore, bringing or defending a reasonably disputed lawsuit is not wrongful conduct in itself, no damages should be awarded either way for the expenses required by the litigation.

2. Under the constitutional provision that no person can be deprived of his property without due process of law, a person clearly has the right of access to the courts for a determination of his legal rights and liabilities. Certainly a person should not be penalized for exercising a constitutional right, and it is arguable that to require a litigant to pay for his opponent's lawyer as well as for his own would in a sense be penalizing him for bringing about the litigation.

3. The time, effort, training, and experience required of a trial lawyer varies so considerably from one lawsuit to another that no fixed scale of fees can be drawn up with any accuracy or fairness. On the other hand, granting the winning party a right to be reimbursed for his lawyer fees without any restraint on the amount of the fees would in effect be giving the winning party's attorney a blank check at the expense of the losing party. Therefore any system for recovering lawyer fees would require court supervision of the fees in each individual case, increasing the time and effort involved in each lawsuit, and imposing on lawyers some of the restraints which result from any system of price regulation.

The American rule developed during what was primarily a frontier era, when ready access to the courts was considered highly desirable. Present-day society, organized about a metropolitan rather than a frontier economy, is much more complex, and overcrowded court calendars delay the settlement of disputes. Some legal scholars suggest that, in order to encourage compromises and diminish litigation, the American rule and the factors supporting it should be reexamined alongside the experience and practice of the English system in which the recovery of reasonable lawyers fees is permitted.

Even under the American rule, when a lawsuit is brought about through the serious and intentional wrong of one party, the policy picture changes, and a more persuasive argument can be made in favor of the innocent party's recovering his lawyer fees. Under such circumstances statutes in some states permit at least a limited recovery of lawyer fees.

---

[3] *St. Peter's Church v. Beach,* 26 Conn. 355 (1857).

Appeal

Just as a person is entitled to a court hearing before a decision is made concerning his rights and liabilities, so too he is usually entitled to have the conduct and result of that hearing reviewed by another court called an appeal or appellate court. Because this is not a second trial, a jury is unnecessary. In an appeal the several judges of the appellate court read the written record of what was done and said in the trial court, consider the oral and written arguments of the lawyers representing the litigants, and determine as a matter of law whether or not there was error in the trial and judgment. An appeal in a civil case is usually so expensive in lawyer and court costs that a losing party will take an appeal only if he firmly believes: 1) that the trial judge through error permitted certain evidence to be presented which under the established rules for trials was very misleading to the jurymen and should not have been considered by them, or 2) that the rule of law applied by the trial judge was not the correct rule of law, or 3) that the verdict of the jury is not supported by any believable evidence.

When the appellate court judges finish considering and discussing the appealed case among themselves, they vote as to their conclusion. If a majority believe that prejudicial error occurred during the trial, they declare that the judgment of the trial court is canceled or reversed. With the reversal, if it is clear that all evidence has been presented and only one conclusion may properly be reached, the appellate court will enter judgment for the other party. This is the final judgment of the dispute, unless in turn reversed by a higher appellate court. If the appellate court feels that the evidence must be reweighed before the dispute can be settled, it will send the case back to the trial court for a new trial. The plaintiff can then quit; if he still feels he is entitled to a judgment against the defendant, he can obtain it only by initiating and winning another trial. If the appellate court concludes that no prejudicial error was involved and that the judgment of the trial court is correct and binding, the appellate court will affirm the judgment.

Example: A buyer in Erie, Pennsylvania, wrote a letter ordering from a seller in Chicago, Illinois, a stated quantity of a specified kind, grade, and size of lumber for $2,000, payable thirty days after shipment. The lumber which the seller promptly shipped in response to the order was delivered at the railroad siding in the buyer's lumber yard. After inspecting the shipment, the buyer notified the seller that the lumber was not of proper contract quality, that the buyer did not want to keep it, and that the seller should make arrangements to take the lumber away. The seller's answering letter asserted that the lumber did conform to the buyer's order. About a week later, while the parties were still haggling, a fire and explosion occurred in an adjoining factory and the flames quickly spread to the buyer's lumber yard, destroying a quantity of lumber, including the railroad cars and lumber received from the seller. The seller demanded that the buyer pay $2,000. When the buyer refused, the seller sued the buyer. For the sake of this example, assume that the buyer did all he reasonably could to prevent the destruction of the lumber and that it was customary for the buyer's fire-insurance coverage not to extend to lumber as yet unloaded from railroad cars. The seller's lawsuit would involve the following basic steps:

1. *Commencement of the Lawsuit.* Assuming that the buyer did no traveling and owned no property away from Erie, the seller as plaintiff would have a lawyer file a lawsuit in the Court of Common Pleas of Erie County, Pennsylvania, and have the sheriff (or his deputy) serve a summons on the buyer as defendant.

2. *Pleadings.* The plaintiff frequently combines his pleading with the first step. The seller's statement would describe the buyer's order, the seller's alleged shipment in conformity with the order, and the buyer's failure to pay. The buyer's statement would describe the alleged defective quality of the lumber, the buyer's offer to return the lumber, and its accidental destruction. The pleadings would thus disclose the fact question in dispute to be whether or not the lumber was of contract quality.

3. *Trial.* Assuming that the parties did not agree to waive a jury trial, a jury would be called together to decide the disputed fact in question. Under oath to tell the truth, the seller would present to the jury the buyer's written order and describe the lumber that he shipped in response to the order. Any of the seller's employees who worked on the shipment could also testify under oath. Upon completion of the seller's evidence, the buyer, under oath to tell the truth, would describe to the jury the lumber received from the seller. Any employees of the buyer could also testify. If the buyer had an impartial inspector examine the lumber (a wise precaution when a dispute concerning quality arises), the inspector would testify. When both parties finished presenting their witnesses, the judge would summarize the evidence for the members of the jury and instruct them that if they believed the lumber to have been of contract quality the seller should collect the agreed price plus interest, but that if they believed that the lumber was not of contract quality, the seller should not collect anything.

4. *Verdict and Judgment.* Assume that after considering the evidence the jury decided that the lumber did conform to the contract. On the basis of this verdict the judge would announce judgment for the seller and against the buyer for $2,000, plus interest and court costs (which would *not* include the expense of the seller's lawyer).

5. *Appeal.* Assume that the buyer believed the verdict and judgment to be erroneous. The buyer could have his lawyer file an appeal with the Pennsylvania Superior Court for the conduct and result of the trial to be reviewed. In actual practice, usually the buyer's lawyer would first urge or make a motion that the trial judge enter judgment in favor of the buyer, notwithstanding the verdict (sometimes called "judgment n.o.v."), or that the

trial judge grant a new trial; upon the trial judge's refusal to grant either motion, the appeal could be taken.

6. *Enforcement of the Judgment.*   Assume that the seller won the appeal but that the buyer still refused to pay.   The seller would have his lawyer obtain a court order directing the sheriff to seize or levy on property belonging to the buyer, and (after proper time and notice) put the property up for public auction (sheriff's sale).   After deducting the costs of the sale, the sheriff would pay to the seller the proceeds received from the sale, up to the amount of the judgment and interest.   Any balance remaining would be returned to the buyer.

Judgment by Confession

Unless a claimant has a lien (such as an ownership interest, a mortgage, or some other security interest) on some item of his debtor's property, the claimant usually has no right personally to take any of the debtor's property, or to interfere with it in any way.   As an unsecured creditor, the claimant has only the usual collection remedy—namely, to sue and obtain a judgment against the debtor, and after obtaining the judgment to have the sheriff attach and sell property belonging to the debtor.   Note that to obtain satisfaction the creditor must first obtain a judgment against the debtor.   A creditor usually obtains a judgment in the manner previously described and illustrated—by commencing and successfully completing a full-scale lawsuit against the debtor.   However, if before trial a debtor should voluntarily admit or confess to the court that he is liable for the amount claimed by the plaintiff, further litigation would become superfluous, and a judgment could be entered against the debtor without a trial.   If a defendant wishes to confess his liability, he can do so personally, or instead through an agent whom he authorizes to act for him, and for whose authorized act the defendant would therefore be bound.   As the practice of judgment by confession has developed at common law, such an authorization can be given to a certain named attorney or instead can be given to any person in general, or to any person of a certain class (such as any lawyer); and the authorization to confess liability in the defendant's name is effective whether the authority is granted before or after the start of a lawsuit against the defendant.

In states in which this common-law practice is still followed, confession-of-judgment provisions are frequently included in many types of standard form contracts, such as promissory notes and contracts for either purchasing or leasing real estate or goods.   A confession-of-judgment note in common use is reproduced on page 404.   The following promissory notes illustrate simplified versions of authorizations to confess judgment.

Form 1.

Philadelphia, Pa., [Date]

Two years after date I promise to pay to the order of Charles Carter $1,000.

And further, if this note is not paid at maturity, I authorize any attorney of any court of record of the United States or elsewhere, to appear for me and confess judgment against me for the above sum.

(signed) Donald David

Form 2.

Philadelphia, Pa., [Date]

Two years after date I promise to pay to the order of Charles Carter $1,000.

And further I do hereby authorize any attorney of any court of record of the United States or elsewhere, to appear for me and confess judgment against me for the above sum.

(signed) Donald David

Pursuant to such an authorization, any attorney (usually the same one who is serving as the plaintiff's attorney) can submit the defendant to the jurisdiction of the court (without the necessity of service of summons on the defendant and therefore even if the defendant is a nonresident), and in the defendant's name admit or confess his liability for the stated or claimed sum. The judgment which is thereupon automatically entered is as effective as one obtained after a full-scale lawsuit; it can form the basis for a sheriff's attachment and sale, and must be accepted as a valid judgment by the courts of other states. By having a confession-of-judgment paragraph inserted in the debtor's contract, a creditor is able to obtain a quick and inexpensive judgment against his debtor.

There are two types of confession-of-judgment provisions in common use:

1. A provision authorizing confession of judgment if the specified obligation is not paid when due, as in Form 1 above.

2. A provision authorizing confession of judgment at any time, even before the specified obligation comes due. Usually this latter type of provision is written in one of two ways. The authorization to confess judgment may expressly state that it can be exercised at any time; a common phrasing for this is "as of any term." Or instead, the authorization to confess judgment may be expressed in the present tense with no time stated. In Form 2 above, while the obligation evidenced by the note does not come due until the time stated (two years), the creditor can obtain judgment against the debtor as soon as the note is signed or any time after that.

If a creditor has a judgment confessed and entered before maturity of the related obligation, he cannot collect on the judgment (through sheriff's levy and sale) until the obligation matures. Nevertheless many creditors desire such a provision because as soon as a judgment is entered on the record (even though the related obligation is unmatured) the judgment is a lien on real estate owned by the defendant in that county. The effective date of the lien is the date the judgment is entered rather than the date the related obligation matures.

Sometimes, as illustrated in the following example, creditors have misused the power to obtain judgments by confession.

Example: Through fraudulent misrepresentation a dealer induces a buyer to puchase certain goods, and has the buyer sign a written contract, agreeing to pay the purchase price of $500 at a stated future time and authorizing a confession of judgment for that amount. When the buyer discovers the fraud, he tenders return of the goods. When the dealers refuses to take back the goods, the buyer says that he thereafter holds the good for the dealer, makes no further use of them, and upon contract payment date, refuses to pay.

The buyer would have a good defense should the dealer sue for the agreed $500. However with the confession-of-judgment provision, the dealer can obtain a judgment without giving the buyer an opportunity to present his defense. The buyer would then have to initiate a legal proceeding to have the judgment canceled on the ground of fraud. The burden of starting a lawsuit is thus shifted. Instead of waiting for the dealer to sue and then presenting his defense in the dealer's lawsuit, the buyer must take the initiative in starting a lawsuit.

The legislatures of a number of states feel that the practice of obtaining judgments by confession gives too much power to creditors or is otherwise unfair, and should be restricted or abolished. Close to twenty states have altogether abolished judgments by confession, while about fifteen states restrict the use of such judgments. In some states the restrictions are minor; some other states impose major restrictions. One common type of minor restriction attempts to warn a debtor of the presence of a confession of judgment provision by requiring the provision to be written or printed separate from other parts of the contract and separately signed. A common major restriction voids confession-of-judgment provisions in contract forms, by providing that such a provision is not effective unless signed *after* maturity of the obligation to which it relates. On the other hand, some states place no restrictions at all on confessed judgments. In these states confession-of-judgment provisions are commonly included in most standard contract forms.

The Adversary System

In the English and American legal systems, a lawsuit is conducted as a debate. Each side of a legal dispute is represented by a lawyer whose duty is not to be impartial, but rather, in an entirely partisan manner, to present and argue his client's side as vigorously and skillfully as he can. The decision is then made by an impartial court (judge and jury, judge alone, or group of judges) on the basis of the evidence and arguments produced and developed by the partisan lawyers. This manner of deciding disputes, frequently referred to as the *adversary system,* has been described and explained in the following manner by Professor Lon Fuller of Harvard Law School:

> The philosophy of adjudication that is expressed in "the adversary system" is, speaking generally, a philosophy that insists on keeping distinct the function of the advocate, on the one hand, from that of the judge, or of the judge from that of jury, on the other. The decision of the case is for the judge, or for the judge and jury. That decision must be as objective and as free from bias as it possibly can. The Constitution of Massachusetts provides—in language that in its idiom calls at once to mind the spirit of a great age, the Age of the Enlightenment and of the American and French Revolutions—that "It is the right of every citizen to be tried by judges as free, impartial and independent as the lot of humanity will admit." If the judge is to perform that high function—a function which the Constitution recognizes may put human nature to a severe test—then the rules of procedure that govern a trial must be such that they do not compel or invite him to depart from the difficult role in which he is cast. It is not his place to take sides. He must withhold judgment until all the evidence has been examined and all the arguments have been heard.
>
> The judge and jury must, then, be excluded from any partisan role. At the same time, a fair trial requires that each side of the controversy be carefully considered and be given its full weight and value. But before a judge can gauge the full force of an argument, it must be presented to him with partisan zeal by one not subject to the restraints of judicial office. The judge cannot know how strong an argument is until he has heard it from the lips of one who has dedicated all the powers of his mind to its formulation.
>
> This is the function of the advocate. His task is not to decide but to persuade. He is not expected to present the case in a colorless and detached manner, but in such a way that it will appear in that aspect most favorable to his client. He is not like a jeweler who slowly turns a diamond in the light so that each of its facets may in turn be fully revealed. Instead the advocate holds the jewel steadily, as it were, so as to throw into bold relief a single aspect of it. It is the task of the advocate to help the judge and jury to see the case as it appears to interested eyes, in the aspect it assumes when viewed from that corner of life into which fate has cast his client.
>
> This is in general what we mean by the adversary system when we apply that phrase to the trial of controversies before courts. . . .
>
> Let me begin with that aspect of the adversary philosophy which is most puzzling—not to say, most offensive to the layman. . . .
>
> The rule I am discussing is one which says that without impropriety a lawyer may, if he sees fit, defend a man he knows to be

guilty. Not only that, but the lawyer may render this service for a fee; he may, without qualms of conscience, accept compensation for appearing in court to plead the cause of a man he knows to be guilty. . . .

The purpose of the rule is not merely to protect the innocent person against the possibility of an unjust conviction, precious as that objective is. The purpose of the rule is to preserve the integrity of society itself. It aims at keeping sound and wholesome the procedures by which society visits its condemnation on an erring member.

Why have courts and trials at all? Why bother with judges and juries, with pleas and counterpleas? When disputes arise or accusations are made, why should not the state simply appoint honest and intelligent men to make investigations? Why not let these men, after they have sifted the evidence and resolved apparent contradictions, make their findings without the aid of advocates and without the fanfare and publicity of a trial?

Arrangements tending in this direction are not unknown historically. One of them has at various times and in various forms been familiar on the European continent. This is the institution of the investigating magistrate, *le juge d'instruction.* . . .

No such office or institution exists in the countries of the common law, including the United States. Why do we reject an arrangement that seems so reasonable in its quiet efficiency? In answer I might simply draw on the European experience and quote a French observer who remarked that in cases where the *juge d'instruction* reaches the conclusion that no prosecution should be brought, it is usually with a tinge of regret that he signs the necessary documents. European experience also suggests that political interests are often involved in charges of crime and that it is desirable in order to prevent abuse that every fact bearing on guilt be tried in courts open to the public.

But publicity is not of itself a guarantee against the abuse of legal procedures. The public trials of alleged traitors that nearly always follow violent revolutions are a sufficient testimonial to this fact. What is essential is that the accused have at his side throughout a skilled lawyer, pledged to see that his rights are protected. When the matter comes for final trial in court, the only participation accorded to the accused in that trial lies in the opportunity to present proofs and reasoned arguments on his behalf. This opportunity cannot be meaningful unless the accused is represented by a professional advocate. If he is denied this representation the processes of public trial become suspect and tainted. It is for this reason that I say that the integrity of society itself demands that the accused be represented by counsel. If he is plainly guilty this representation may become in a sense symbolic. But the symbolism is of vital importance. It marks society's determination to keep unsoiled and beyond suspicion the procedures by which men are condemned for a violation of its laws.

The lawyer appearing on behalf of an accused person is not present in court merely to represent his client. He represents a vital interest of society itself, he plays an essential role in one of the fundamental processes of an ordered community. The rules that govern his conduct make this clear.

It is a fundamental principle of the lawyer's canons of ethics that he may not state to the judge or jury that he personally believes in the innocence of his client. He may say, for example, "I submit that the evidence fails to establish the guilt of my client." But he may not say, "I personally know my client to be innocent," just as he may not be asked by the judge or jury whether he believes his client to be guilty.

These rules concerning the lawyer's conduct in court are not only important in themselves, but also for the spirit that lies back of them. They make it clear that the lawyer is present, not as an individual with all of his likes and dislikes, beliefs and disbeliefs, but as one who plays an important role in the process of social decision. At no time is the lawyer a mere agent of his client. If he disapproves of his client's conduct during the trial, he may—though this is often a painfully difficult decision—withdraw from the case. Obviously, he may not participate in the fabrication of testimony, just as he may not, to free his client, cast suspicion on innocent persons. . . .

I have so far emphasized chiefly the role of the lawyer in the defense of criminal cases. But the need for an adversary presentation, with both sides vigorously upheld, is also present in civil suits. For one thing, there is an element of social condemnation in almost all adverse legal judgments, so that the considerations that apply to criminal cases are also relevant to civil controversies. To be found guilty of negligent driving or of breaking a contract does not carry the stigma of a criminal conviction, but in these cases, too, society must be concerned that even the qualified condemnation implied in an adverse civil judgment should not be visited on one who has not had a chance to present his case fully.

More important in complicated controversies is the contribution that an adversary presentation makes to a properly grounded decision, a decision that takes account of all the facts and relevant rules. In a statement issued recently by a committee of the American Bar Association, it was pointed out how, in the absence of an adversary presentation, there is a strong tendency by any deciding official to reach a conclusion at an early stage and to adhere to that conclusion in the face of conflicting considerations later developed. In the language of the committee:

"What generally occurs in practice is that at some early point a familiar pattern will seem to emerge from the evidence; an accustomed label is waiting for the case and, without waiting further proofs, this label is promptly assigned to it. It is a mistake to suppose that this premature cataloguing must necessarily result from impatience, prejudice or mental sloth. Often it proceeds from a very understandable desire to bring the hearing into some order and coherence, for without some tentative theory of the case there is no standard of relevance by which testimony may be measured. But what starts as a preliminary diagnosis designed to direct the inquiry tends, quickly and imperceptibly, to become a fixed conclusion, as all that confirms the diagnosis makes a strong imprint on the mind, while all that runs counter to it is received with diverted attention.

"An adversary presentation seems the only effective means for combating this natural human tendency to judge too swiftly in terms of the familiar that which is not yet fully known. The arguments of counsel hold the case, as it were, in suspension between two opposing interpretations of it. While the proper classification of the case is thus kept unresolved, there is time to explore all of its peculiarities and nuances. . . ."

I have only a few minutes to touch on an expanded sense of the adversary system that applies its philosophy to decisions reached by less formal procedures, let us say, decisions reached in the course of operating an industrial or educational enterprise. In the conduct of any human enterprise, collective decisions must always involve a compromise of interests that are at least partially divergent. For example, in the operation of a factory one may distinguish among the following groups: 1) those whose primary objective is to produce a maximum of goods, 2) those whose primary interest is in developing a satisfied work force, working under conditions of complete dignity and impartial justice, and 3) those whose main urge is to improve the product, even at the cost of some present inefficiency. Each of these interests is a legitimate and proper one, yet each must be qualified by a recognition of the legitimate demands of the others.

An effective consensus cannot be reached unless each party understands fully the position of the others. This understanding cannot be obtained unless each party is permitted to state fully what its own interest is and to urge with partisan zeal the vital importance of that interest to the enterprise as a whole. At the same time, since an effective consensus requires an understanding and willing cooperation of all concerned, no party should so abandon himself in advocacy that he loses the power to comprehend sympathetically the views of those with different interests. What is required here is a spirit that can be called that of tolerant partisanship. This implies not only tolerance for opposing viewpoints, but tolerance for a partisan presentation of those viewpoints, since without that presentation they may easily be lost from sight. . . .

In the end, the justification for the adversary system lies in the fact that it is a means by which the capacities of the individual may be lifted to the point where he gains the power to view reality through eyes other than his own, where he is able to become as impartial, and as free from prejudice, as "the lot of humanity will admit."[4]

FINALITY OF JUDGMENTS

In most cases the time for taking an appeal or otherwise correcting the action of a trial court varies from a few weeks to a few months, depending upon the type of lawsuit. If the proper time has passed without a reversal or correction, a civil judgment is usually considered final and conclusive as to the rights and liabilities involved in the dispute,

[4] Reprinted with permission from Harold J. Berman (ed.), *Talks on American Law,* (New York: Vintage, 1961), chap. 3.

and usually will not be dissolved or changed by later action, either of the same court or of some other court.

This is a policy rule, necessary for the protection of honest litigants. Suppose that long after a trial and decision the losing party was able to have the issue reopened by claiming that he had newly discovered evidence not available to him at the time of the previous trial, or by claiming that the previous judgment was obtained by perjured testimony. Such claims might be false but the successful party might be unable to disprove them, if his witnesses had forgotten or died or certain essential documents had been lost or destroyed. Also (even more than is regrettably true at present) ultimate victory might go to the litigant able and willing to spend the most money on litigation. The fact that in a few cases the rule for conclusiveness of judgments will reward a perjurer is usually considered as overbalanced by the protection which the rule gives to honest litigants. Accordingly in most states cancellation of a judgment is usually limited to the rare situations in which the court process itself has been tampered with in such a way as to completely prevent it from functioning fairly—as for example when the winning party bribed a juror or bribed the losing party's attorney to "throw" the case, or through a trick the winning party kept the losing party from attending the trial.

Example: A seller sold and delivered certain goods to a buyer on credit. After making various payments from time to time, the buyer contended that he had paid the price in full and refused to pay anything further. The seller contended that a balance of $800 remained unpaid and sued the buyer to recover that amount. At the trial the buyer and a witness for the buyer both testified that the buyer had made payments in addition to those admitted by the seller. The jury returned a verdict in favor of the buyer and judgment was entered for the buyer and against the seller—in other words, the seller lost the lawsuit. About two months later the witness signed a confession that he had testified falsely. The buyer and the witness were both indicted for the perjury involved in having given false testimony in the seller's lawsuit. The witness pleaded guilty, the buyer was tried and convicted, and both were sentenced to prison. The seller then brought an action to cancel the judgment previously entered against his $800 claim.

In a similar case, the Pennsylvania Superior Court held[5] that since the time for correction had passed, the seller was not entitled to have the adverse judgment canceled. The court pointed out that during the original trial the seller had full opportunity to challenge the buyer's testimony and to disprove his defense of alleged payments. Since the issue of the alleged extra payments was tried and decided, the court felt that as a matter of policy the dispute should be considered settled.

[5] *Powell* v. *Doyle*, 77 Pa. Super. 520 (1921).

Generally a judgment is conclusive not only in the state where it is obtained but also in all other states. The United States Constitution expressly requires that each state give full faith and credit to the judicial acts of other states. If a New York court, with proper jurisdiction over the parties and over the matter in dispute enters a judgment in favor of a plaintiff, that judgment will have the same effect in California as it has in New York. If the defendant owns property in California, the plaintiff through the simple procedure of suing for a California judgment on the basis of the New York judgment, can in effect have the judgment transferred to California, and can proceed to have the defendant's California property levied on, without the needless burden of retrying the merits of the case in California.

COURT SYSTEMS

Within any state in the United States, two court systems have jurisdiction: 1) the courts of that particular state, and 2) the Federal courts. Although the courts in the various states differ somewhat among themselves and also from the Federal courts in the names by which they are known, they all follow the same general pattern, classifiable into trial courts and appeal courts.

State Court Systems

Trial Courts

Most states have two types of trial courts: 1) courts of limited jurisdiction, for the trial of less significant cases and cases involving smaller amounts of money, and 2) courts of unlimited, general jurisdiction.

Courts of Limited Jurisdiction. The typical state court at the lower end of the hierarchy of trial courts is the justice of the peace court. In larger communities, courts of limited jurisdiction are frequently called magistrates' courts, or municipal or city courts. Very often justices of the peace and magistrates are not required to have legal training. This is a holdover from much earlier times when there was a shortage of men schooled in the law, and travel was slow and difficult. To settle minor local disputes it was necessary to vest judicial authority in men whose lack of legal knowledge, it was hoped, could be compensated for by sound judgment and common sense. While justices of the peace served usefully under these early conditions, experts in judicial administration feel that since such conditions no longer exist, any system which vests judicial functions in persons without legal training should be discarded. However, although they have become quite obsolete, justice of the peace courts cannot be easily or quickly abolished, both because the incumbents have political strength, and also because the court systems of many states are prescribed by their constitutions, and constitutional amendment is slow and difficult.

Frequently a jury is not used in a trial before a justice of the peace or similar judicial official, both the determination of facts and the application of law to the facts being made by the justice or magistrate. Also, procedure is much less formal than in trials conducted before legally trained judges. Although a person has the right to be his own lawyer in any case, considerable knowledge of law and legal procedure is required for adequate presentation of a case in the more formal trial courts, while less technical knowledge is required for simpler cases before a justice of the peace or magistrate. Nevertheless a litigant before one of these minor courts is well advised to seek legal assistance if he is the defendant, or if the dispute is at all complex or involves more than an insignificant amount of money.

Frequently no word-for-word record is made of the testimony of witnesses during a justice of the peace trial. Because of this, an appeal from the decision of a justice court is frequently not merely a review of the previous trial but instead involves a new, full-scale lawsuit and trial in the next higher court.

Courts of Unlimited Jurisdiction. Cases before trial courts of general or unlimited jurisdiction are easily classifiable into three types. In many states separate courts are provided for each type. Although known by a variety of names in the different court systems, these courts, *in function,* are: 1) criminal courts, 2) estate courts (having jurisdiction over the estates of deceased persons, the guardian of minors, and the like), and 3) general civil courts.

Appellate Courts

Every court system has an appellate court which hears appeals from the decisions of the various trial courts. Because of the great number of appeals, many states, in addition to a final appellate court, have one or more intermediate appellate courts to consider appeals in less important cases or cases involving less than a certain sum of money (for example $5,000 in Pennsylvania). However, even if a state has both an intermediate appellate court and a final appellate court, a litigant usually has a right to only *one* appeal. If a case involves less than $5,000 (or whatever sum is fixed in the system as the dividing line between the jurisdiction of intermediate and final appellate courts) so that the appeal goes to the intermediate appellate court, a person has no *right* to have a second appeal in the final appellate court. The latter court may at its discretion allow a further appeal if the court feels the case warrants it, but the decision as to whether or not to hear a second appeal is entirely up to the higher appellate court.

FEDERAL COURT SYSTEM

The Federal district courts are the trial courts in the Federal system. The appellate courts are the courts of appeal (of which there are ten for the entire country) and the United States Supreme Court.

The Federal courts have *exclusive* jurisdiction of crimes punishable under Federal statutes and of cases arising on navigable waters, or under bankruptcy, postal, or Federal banking laws. *Concurrent* with state courts, the Federal courts have jurisdiction in cases in which 1) the amount in dispute exceeds $10,000 *and* 2) a Federal question is involved, that is a) a question under the United States Constitution, laws, or treaties, or b) a dispute between citizens of different states. For example, if a seller in Chicago has a $12,000 claim against a buyer in Philadelphia, the seller can at his option sue in the Federal District Court for the Eastern District of Pennsylvania, or in the state trial court of general civil jurisdiction for Philadelphia County. If the amount claimed is less than $10,000, the seller has no choice—he can bring the action only in the state court. Whether the action is brought in a state or in a Federal court, the same rules of law will be applied in deciding the dispute.

The United States Constitution provides that Federal laws are the supreme law of the land, and that the Federal judicial power extends to all cases arising under the United States Constitution or laws. One result of these provisions is that while a state court has no power over a case properly in Federal court, a Federal court can take control over some types of cases in the state courts. This supremacy of Federal courts appears mainly in three types of situations.

1. Before trial, a lawsuit begun in a state court may be transferred to a Federal district court upon prompt request by the defendant, if a) the case involves an amount in excess of $10,000; *and* b) either it concerns a right arising under Federal laws or Constitution, or it involves parties who are citizens of different states, with the defendant a nonresident of the state in which the case starts.

2. After trial and appeal in the proper state courts the losing party may request the United States Supreme Court to hear a further appeal if the case involves a right arising under the United States Constitution or statutes. Whether or not it will hear such an appeal is left to the discretion of the United States Supreme Court; it may grant or deny the requested appeal. One of the most important provisions in the United States Constitution in regard to Federal-state relationships is the guaranty

to a person that no state shall deprive him of life, liberty, or property without due process of law. For example, if it is claimed that a state criminal conviction is based upon a confession forced involuntarily from the accused, a Federal question is raised upon which the accused may request an appeal to the United States Supreme Court. If a dispute in a state court does not involve Federal rights, there is no basis upon which to request an appeal to the United States Supreme Court. Most civil disputes in state courts do not involve Federal laws or issues. If a state court follows proper judicial procedure but the losing party claims that the court's decision is erroneous because of a mistake as to applicable state law, a Federal issue is not raised. The losing party is considered to have had the benefit of proper judicial due process as guaranteed to him by the United States Constitution. The interpretation and application of state law is left to the state courts, the United States Supreme Court having no general right to supervise such local matters.

3. After exhausting all available rights of appeal, a person imprisoned under state authority may ask a Federal district court to inquire into his imprisonment and order his release, if shown to be in violation of his rights under the United States Constitution.

ARBITRATION

ARBITRATION BY AGREEMENT

Settling a dispute by arbitration rather than through a lawsuit is growing in favor with many businesses. To settle a dispute in this way, the parties agree to submit their dispute to an arbitrator (or group of arbitrators) for decision, *and* to abide by the decision. Such an agreement for arbitration can be entered into after a dispute arises, or it can be included as a contract provision when the parties are negotiating their contract. Such an arbitration agreement will be enforced by the courts. If a plaintiff starts a lawsuit in violation of his agreement to have disputes arbitrated, the court will grant the defendant's motion to dismiss the action; the plaintiff must comply with the agreed arbitration procedure if he wishes to have the dispute settled. If after completion of an arbitration proceeding, the losing party refuses to abide by the decision or award, the winning party may obtain a court judgment based on the award, without the necessity of a court trial of the dispute.

For many business disputes, arbitration offers various advantages over court settlement including the following:

1. The formality of court procedure and overcrowded court calendars frequently combine to cause considerable delay in court actions. Appeals increase the delay so that it is not unusual for a year or two to pass between the start of a lawsuit and final satisfaction of the judgment

thereby obtained. On the other hand, arbitration can be quite speedy.

2. Technical knowledge is often required in deciding a business dispute. Technical words in a contract, trade practices and customs, or particular production and operational techniques may be involved. In such a case a court trial is further delayed by the need to impart the necessary technical knowledge to the judge and jury, and sometimes their lack of technical background may result in an inaccurate consideration of the entire problem. However, arbitrators are usually selected from men already quite familiar with the techniques of the particular trade involved.

3. Discontinuance of further business relations between the parties is frequently an outcome of a dispute which goes into a lawsuit, whereas this is not as likely to follow a dispute settled by arbitration.

4. Court proceedings are public, whereas arbitration proceedings can be private, avoiding public disclosure of operations and information which businesses might prefer to keep private.

COMPULSORY ARBITRATION

In recent years, Pennsylvania has inaugurated a successful experiment (which is being closely watched by many other states) requiring compulsory arbitration of all lawsuits (except those involving title to land) in which the amounts in dispute do not exceed $2,000. Under this plan, a lawsuit is initiated in the usual way. Then, when the case is ready for trial, instead of going to a court trial, the case is switched to a board of arbitrators consisting of three lawyers selected by the clerk of court from an alphabetical list. A separate board is appointed for each case. The board holds a hearing, considers the evidence, and reaches a conclusion deciding the dispute. This decision becomes the binding judgment in the case unless the losing party promptly files an appeal in court. The compulsory-arbitration system is in effect in most of the more populous counties under a Pennsylvania statute which authorizes all county courts at their option to adopt the system. Since the inauguration of the compulsory-arbitration system, relatively few arbitration decisions have been appealed; the system has been quite successful and is popular with lawyers, judges, and litigants alike.

PROBLEMS

1. Suppose you read or heard the following statement: The doctrine of *stare decisis* is archaic, smacks of ancestor worship, and should have little application in today's modern, rapidly changing society. Would you agree with the statement? Explain.

2. In many states any number of persons, or only one person, may lawfully own all the stock of a business corporation. In such a state the stock of a particular corporation was owned by three persons, B, C, and S, with B owning 45 percent, C 47 percent, and S 8 percent. S entered into a legally binding contract with B under which S agreed to sell and deliver his stock to B and B agreed to pay a certain stated price. When the time came for performance of the contract, B tendered the agreed amount of money to S but S said he had changed his mind and refused to take the money or to transfer his stock to B. Explain what legal remedy or remedies B would have. If you were B, what would you do? (Modified from A.I.C.P.A., Nov. 40-12 and May 56-3.)

3. A produce dealer in Buffalo, New York, ordered in writing from a New York City produce wholesaler 500 crates of apples at $10 per crate, the order specifying grade and shipment date. The wholesaler promptly accepted the order in writing and promised to ship the goods as ordered. However, when the shipment date arrived, the market price for such goods had risen and the wholesaler, without legal justification, refused to ship. The market rise was such that the same grade of apples purchased elsewhere would cost the dealer $1,000 more than the contract price. The dealer learned that the wholesaler had on hand more than a sufficient quantity of the proper grade of apples to fill the dealer's contract and that the wholesaler was retaining them, hoping for an additional increase in the market price. The dealer sued the wholesaler for specific performance and requested the court to order the wholesaler to ship the agreed apples to the dealer. Should the court decree that the wholesaler specifically perform the contract? Explain.

4. Determining the inferences which may properly be drawn from certain evidence often involves consideration of the rules of law and of logic. Some persons suggest that in this modern age of specialization, the jury system should be abolished and that instead cases should be tried and facts determined by trained legal logicians. What do you think of such a suggested change?

5. B, owner of a large business in Cleveland, Ohio, operated a small branch in Erie, Pennsylvania. For the Erie branch, B ordered and received a certain specially designed machine from S of Erie, B agreeing to pay $6,000 in 30 days. Shortly B complained to S of unsatisfactory operation, discontinued use of the machine, and offered to return it to S. S refused to accept the return of the machine, asserting that it was not defective, and when B refused to pay for the machine, S sued B in the Erie County court. The court instructed the jury that if the machine was defective as B claimed, B could return it and have no liability to pay S anything; but that if the machine was of contract quality, S could recover the agreed purchase price. From conflicting evidence as to the condition of the machine, the jury returned a verdict that the machine conformed to the contract, and the court entered judgment for S and against B for $6,000 plus interest and costs. B appealed the judgment to the Pennsylvania Supreme Court. There being sufficient evidence to sustain the jury's verdict, and the trial judge's statement of the applicable rule of law being correct, the Supreme Court found no reason to reverse the judgment and therefore affirmed it. Upon being advised of the outcome of the appeal, B resumed use of the machine and shortly it broke

down completely. A thorough inspection conclusively showed that the cause of the breakdown was the very weakness about which B had complained. An inspection thorough enough to disclose this type of weakness could not prevously have been made without wrecking the machine. B refused to pay the $6,000 judgment. Each of the following is a separate fact situation.

a) B promptly brought an action in the Erie County court to have the judgment canceled, and offered as evidence the thorough inspection described above (conclusively showing that the machine had been defective ever since received). Should the judgment be canceled? Explain.

b) The assets of the branch not being sufficient for collection of the judgment (assume that B made no attempt to have the judgment canceled by the court which entered it), S sued B in Cuyahoga County, Ohio (Cleveland area), on the Pennsylvania judgment. B offered as evidence the thorough inspection described above (conclusively showing that the machine had been defective ever since received). Was S entitled to recover in the Ohio lawsuit? Explain.

6. B of Philadelphia purchased and received certain goods from S of Chicago, for which B promised to pay a certain price in thirty days. After unpacking and inspecting the goods, B decided that they were defective, put them aside, and never used them. He advised S that he would not pay and asked for instructions as to how S wished to have the goods returned. S refused to permit return, asserted that the goods were not defective, and when B still refused to pay, sued B for $15,000 damages.

a) S started the lawsuit in the Federal District Court for the Philadelphia area. Explain whether this court would be a proper court for S's lawsuit.

b) Assume that S brought the lawsuit in the proper state trial court for the Philadelphia area. After a close trial involving conflicting expert testimony, the jury concluded that the goods conformed to B's order and returned a verdict in favor of S and against B for $15,000. The trial court entered judgment accordingly, and on appeal the Pennsylvania Supreme Court affirmed the trial court's judgment. B then asked his lawyer about further appealing the case to the United States Supreme Court. On these facts, explain whether any basis existed upon which the United States Supreme Court could be requested to consider a further appeal.

chapter *2*

Torts

Covering, even in summary, the general law of torts is beyond the scope of this book. All that is intended here is 1) to summarize some of the reasoning behind tort law, 2) to indicate the role tort law plays in forming the legal environment within which all of society functions, and 3) to warn the reader to be "legally sensitive" to the rights of others.

As is mentioned in Chapter 1, a tort is a violation of an individual, noncontractual right, for which the law gives a remedy. Generally, the remedy is money compensation for loss or injury sustained from the conduct classified as tortious.

In formulating any rule of law, courts and legislatures balance conflicting interests and weigh various factors to determine, from the standpoint of fairness, reasonableness, and practicality, what seems to be the best policy rule to follow. This interplay of various factors is especially apparent with the rules of law pertaining to torts. If a person is obliged to compensate for injuries which his conduct causes, then to that extent such conduct is made more costly and sometimes is discouraged altogether. What conduct should in this way be prohibited, only somewhat restricted, or totally uninhibited (in other words, which injuries are compensable and which are not) constitutes the policy question to be decided according to what is best for the individuals involved and for society as a whole. The control of traffic in play areas presents a simple example of this balancing of interests. Many children, in the excitement of play, thoughtlessly run into the street and are injured or killed by carefully driven cars. The number of such accidents would be considerably reduced if all automobiles were required to have governors preventing speeds in excess of 15 miles per hour. In modern society such an overall restriction on speed would result in incalculable harm both to individual drivers and to society as a whole, harm which would not be justified even by the injuries and deaths thereby prevented. The conflicting interests are balanced and a compromise is reached with the rule that drivers must slow down in school and play areas.

The policy factors most important in the formulation of the rules of tort law include the following:

1. The social value or utility of the particular activity in question
2. The intent or mental attitude of the doer of the act

3. The likelihood that the act will cause injury
4. The possibility of avoiding injury while still substantially accomplishing the purpose of the act
5. The type or nature of the injury threatened
6. The ease or difficulty of supervising or enforcing a restraint upon the particular activity

During its centuries of evolution, tort law did not develop as a unified system. Rather, until relatively modern times, the rules pertaining to different torts developed somewhat independently from each other in connection with the varying procedural rules that were applicable in different types of lawsuits. For this reason, any present-day attempt to consolidate and systematize tort rules lacks precision and exhibits considerable overlapping.

Any system of classifying torts usually starts by considering the intent of the wrongdoer and subdividing torts into those which are intentional and those which are unintentional. The concept of intent as developed in tort law goes beyond the malicious or evil motives usually looked for in criminal law. It is possible for a defendant's act to be classed as intentional even though he neither desires nor reasonably expects that his act will interfere with the legal interests of another. On the other hand, a defendant's act can be unintentional even though it occurs as a result of his intentional conduct. If a defendant strikes a plaintiff with a baseball bat, clearly the defendant's act should be classed as intentional if his desire or purpose is to strike the plaintiff. If the defendant is merely swinging the bat for exercise, without any desire or expectation of hitting anyone, then, although the defendant's act of swinging the bat is a voluntary and intentional act, his striking the plaintiff should clearly be classed as unintentional.

Suppose that a farmer, mistaken about his boundary line, cuts down his neighbor's tree, honestly and reasonably believing it to be his own tree. Although the farmer does not intend to trespass on his neighbor's property, his purpose is to cut down that particular tree. Since cutting the tree is an intentional act, the farmer would be classed as an intentional wrongdoer. Suppose further that the farmer cuts up the tree into a load of fireplace logs, which he sells to a householder. The householder's burning of the logs is an intentional act. Without the original owner's permission, it is a wrongful act. Although wholly innocent of any malice and therefore not guilty of any crime, the householder would nevertheless be classed by tort law as an intentional wrongdoer.

After the basic subdivision into intentional and unintentional acts is made, torts are usually further subdivided according to the general nature of the plaintiff's injury. The following is a brief classification of the principal torts:

1. Intentional misconduct.
   A) The defendant's intentional conduct involves physical violence or action.
      1) The defendant's act causes physical injury to the plaintiff or to his property.
         a) The injury is caused by direct contact with the defendant or with something set in motion by the defendant.
         b) The injury is caused indirectly—that is, while the act itself does not involve physical contact with the plaintiff, it disturbs him mentally or emotionally to such an extent as to cause him to suffer physical injury. For example, although the defendant's aim is poor and his gunshot misses the plaintiff, he frightens the plaintiff into having a heart attack.
      2) The plaintiff sustains no physical or property injury.
   B) The defendant's intentional conduct consists of offensive or disturbing words.
      1) The defendant's words injure the plaintiff's reputation.
      2) The defendant's words make public disclosure of information or facts which the plaintiff desires to have kept private.
      3) Although the defendant's words neither injure the plaintiff's reputation nor invade his privacy, they disturb him mentally or emotionally to such an extent as to cause him physical injury.
2. Unintentional (negligent) misconduct.
   A) The defendant's act causes injury (personal injury or property damage) by coming in physical contact with the plaintiff or with his property.
   B) Although not involving physical contact, the defendant's act disturbs the plaintiff mentally or emotionally to such an extent as to cause him to suffer physical injury.

INTENTIONAL MISCONDUCT

Physical Act, Direct Injury

The chief examples of this type of misconduct include a defendant who, without excuse or justification, 1) strikes the plaintiff (battery), 2) takes or damages goods or land belonging to the plaintiff (conversion or trespass), or 3) through physical force or threat of force against the plaintiff or his property imprisons the plaintiff or otherwise limits his freedom of motion (false imprisonment). In affording the plaintiff a remedy for torts such as these, the law is recognizing and protecting the plaintiff's right to be secure in his person and in his property from unjustified interference by others.

Note that the defendant's act is wrongful only if not legally justified; if the defendant acts with justification, he commits no tort. For example, the defendant is justified if the plaintiff consents to the defendant's act (players participating in a football game consent to physical violence within the rules of the game), or if the defendant in self-defense does what is reasonably necessary to protect his person or property from wrongful acts of the plaintiff. It is considered sound public policy to limit the right of self-defense to what seems necessary for the defense of person or property; a person has no right to use force in retaliation for past injuries or for present verbal abuse. Since an owner of property has the right to do what is reasonably necessary to protect his property, a retail store owner has the right to detain a customer for investigation if the retailer has reasonable grounds to believe that the customer is guilty of shoplifting. That the investigation which follows the detention proves the customer innocent does not retroactively nullify the right which the retailer exercised in detaining the customer, provided 1) the retailer had reasonable grounds to be suspicious and 2) the detention was reasonable in manner and extent. Since a jury can be expected to sympathize with an insulted and humiliated customer, a retailer should be extremely cautious. It is advisable for a retailer to consult with his lawyer about the circumstances which will constitute reasonable grounds for detaining a customer and about the proper procedure to follow.

Physical Act, Indirect Injury

The most common example of this type of wrong is the tort of assault. An assault is an attempt to commit a battery. It consists of an intentional, unjustified act by the defendant which reasonably leads the plaintiff to expect an immediate blow or offensive touching. Note that the legally protected right is to be free from fear or expectation of an *immediate* blow or touching from a wrongful *act*. The tort of assault is not committed by a threat alone; the threat must be accompanied by an act attempting to carry the threat into effect.

Physical Act, Recoverable Damages

An intentionally wrongful act is more reprehensible than an act which is careless but not intended, and as a matter of policy should be attended with greater liability. Thus the victim of an intentional wrong can recover for all his actual injuries, even those that are quite unusual and could not have been anticipated. In addition, the plaintiff can recover for his pain, suffering, humiliation, and any other emotional distress.

Naturally, no definite price can be placed on pain, suffering, or emotional disturbances, just as no money value can be placed on sight or hearing. However, to the extent that an injured plaintiff can be compensated in any way for pain and emotional disturbances, money will do it. He is, therefore, entitled to recover a sum of money reasonably related to the degree of his pain, suffering, humiliation, and any other emotional distress. Furthermore, when a defendant is guilty of intentional misconduct, the plaintiff is permitted to recover for humiliation or shock even though he sustains no real injuries. For example, a person who without justification is intentionally struck and knocked down may sustain no actual injuries, perhaps not even be bruised. Nevertheless, most courts consider it sound policy for the plaintiff to have a right to recover money damages from the wrongdoer in an amount commensurate with the plaintiff's humiliation and indignity.

Since it is considered sound policy to award money damages for pain, humiliation, and other such intangibles, it is not wholly unrelated to say that the amount of money damages should also be influenced by the degree of malice displayed by the wrongdoer's conduct. Therefore, even though the the general purpose of a civil lawsuit is to compensate for injuries and not to punish (punishment being the purpose of a criminal action), it is sometimes considered sound policy in assessing damages to take into account the wrongdoer's maliciousness. This element of recoverable money damages, called "exemplary" or "punitive" damages, is admittedly for the purpose of punishing the wrongdoer and deterring him and others from committing similar acts. Punitive damages in an amount reasonably related to the wrong can usually be awarded for acts done with a bad motive or with reckless indifference to the rights of others.

Defamatory Words

Just as the law has opposed physical violence since early in the evolution of legal rights (and therefore has recognized that a person has a legal right to be free from injury or disturbance through the wrongful, unjustified physical acts of others), so also has it opposed intentional and unjustifiable injuries to reputations. The tort involved is called *defamation*. There are two types, *slander* (oral defamation) and *libel* (written defamation). In defining the legally protected right to be secure in reputation, the law has developed certain policy rules, principally the following:

1. There is no defamation unless the defendant communicates the defamatory words to one or more third persons. What the defendant thinks of the plaintiff, or tells, or writes to him, cannot affect the plaintiff's

reputation unless the defendant permits his words to be heard or read by some third person. No particular number of third persons is required; the tort of defamation is committed whether the defendant libels the plaintiff in a newspaper article read by thousands or in a letter addressed to the plaintiff's business office, which, as the defendant has reason to expect, is opened and read by the plaintiff's secretary. The number of persons to whom the defendant spreads the defamatory words is merely a factor in determining the extent of injury to the plaintiff and the amount of damages he can recover.

2. The words used must actually injure the plaintiff's reputation or have a strong likelihood of doing so. In many states, the law of defamation makes a distinction between an impermanent, oral statement and a more lasting written statement. If the oral statement falsely accuses the plaintiff of committing a crime or of having a loathsome disease, or is such as to injure the plaintiff in his business, trade, or profession, the plaintiff can recover commensurate damages without proving actual injury to his reputation. For other oral statements the plaintiff can collect substantial damages only if he can prove some actual injury to his reputation. No such distinction is made with written defamation; the plaintiff is entitled to recover commensurate damages in any case. Of course, the reputation protected is only that to which the plaintiff is entitled. Generally, telling or writing the truth about a person is not defamation, although such conduct may constitute another tort (invasion of the right of privacy), which is discussed next.

PUBLICATIONS INTRUDING UPON PRIVACY

In fairly recent years the law has recognized that a person has a right to have certain of his acts and circumstances kept private. This right does not extend to circumstances or incidents which are of legitimate public interest (such as news stories) or to persons who strive to catch the public eye (such as politicians and theatrical stars). It should be emphasized that no attempt is made here to cover completely, or even in a general way, the activities or incidents which the law encloses within the protective curtain of the right of privacy.

Example: Davis owed a garageman a past-due debt. After unsuccessfully attempting to collect the obligation and warning that publicity would be given to unpaid bills, the garageman placed the following sign in his show window:

NOTICE

Davis owes an account here of $49.67, and if promises would pay an account, this account would have been settled long ago. This account will be advertised as long as it remains unpaid.

For emotional distress and humiliation resulting from the sign, Davis sued the garageman and recovered a verdict for $1,000 damages.

On appeal, the Kentucky Court of Appeals held that the defendant was guilty of a tort, namely, an invasion of the plaintiff's right of privacy.[1]

NONDEFAMATORY VERBAL ABUSE

The law has been very hesitant to grant protection against abusive language which neither injures reputation nor invades privacy. The policy factors involved in this reluctance include the following:

1. The wide prevalence of bad manners. Short tempers and offensive words being so common, the courts fear that if they were to open the doors to all insulted and humiliated victims, cases would be too numerous for the courts to handle. Even more important than the threat of an avalanche of cases, the courts feel that because offensive words are so common the use of such words and their normal effect on the ones being castigated should be regarded merely as an unavoidable result of community living, to be tolerated just as people are expected to tolerate a normal amount of other annoying noises, such as barking dogs, honking horns, pneumatic jackhammers, etc.

2. The infrequency of actual injury and the risk of faked claims. Only in recent decades has medical science proven a direct causal relationship between mental disturbance and physical maladies. To paraphrase the old adage, physical injury is much more likely to result from throwing sticks and stones than from throwing offensive words. Also, since proof that certain physical harm has resulted from offensive words is likely to be indirect and often conjectural, it is more easily faked.

Because offensive language is not so commonly used toward business customers, there is a growing feeling that a customer should have a right to expect not only goods or services of contract quality but also courteous treatment, especially from businesses which are obliged to serve the general public, such as carriers and hotels.

The field of liability for offensive language is one of the frontiers of the law and is still in the early stages of development. There is a trend toward the view that if a defendant's language causes such severe emotional distress to a plaintiff as to result in physical injury and if the defendant's conduct is not only intentional or reckless but also extremely outrageous, the defendant is guilty of a tort and is liable to the plaintiff for damages.

NEGLIGENT MISCONDUCT

Negligence, the antithesis of intentional misconduct, is inattention or carelessness. As a general proposition it seems fair to say that a careless

[1] *Brents v. Morgan*, 221 Ky. 765, 299 S.W. 967, 55 A.L.R. 964 (1927).

person should be required to compensate for injuries which his carelessness causes to other persons. However, various factors argue that a defendant's liability for negligence should be limited to some extent. Some of these factors are:

1. In comparison with cases involving intentional misconduct, evidence of whether or not a defendant has been careless is frequently less clear-cut, with a proportionate increase in the possibility of mistaken and faked claims.

2. Jurymen often tend to favor a seriously injured plaintiff even though the question whether or not the defendant exercised adequate care is arguable.

3. The seriousness of a plaintiff's injury may be unexpectedly enhanced by his peculiar characteristics and weaknesses. While it seems quite clear that an *intentional* wrongdoer should be liable for *all* injuries that result, it is not so clear that a negligent defendant (whose only wrong is his inattention or neglect to use sufficient care) should be liable for highly unusual injuries which could not reasonably have been foreseen.

4. A single careless act may set in motion a lengthy chain of events. Here again the policy question arises whether it is fair to hold a negligent defendant to the same liability as an intentional wrongdoer for remote injuries which could not reasonably have been foreseen. Suppose that a defendant is driving carelessly and, as a result, collides with a properly driven car. Certainly the careless defendant should be held liable for damages to the other car and for injuries to its occupants. Suppose, further, that the defendant's car rams the other car into a pole, knocking the pole over and causing it, or some wires, to fall on a nearby pedestrian. It seems fair to hold that the careless defendant should be liable to the pedestrian also. But suppose that the collision with the pole causes an electric wire to fall on a hunter 500 yards away from the scene of the collision. Should the defendant be held liable to the hunter? Suppose that the electric shock causes the hunter (through no fault of his) to discharge his rifle and, by rare chance, the bullet injures a passenger riding in the car with which the defendant originally collided. While it is fair to hold the defendant liable for injuries caused by the collision of the cars, is it fair to hold him liable for the totally unexpected gunshot wound of one of the passengers?

The question of when a person should be held liable for injuries resulting from his carelessness and when liability should not be imposed requires (as with all law) the legislatures, and especially the courts, to decide and declare what they consider to be sound policy from the standpoint of fairness, reasonableness, and practicality. In a case before the Wisconsin Supreme Court, the question was whether a driver who carelessly ran down and killed a little girl should be held liable for physical injuries sustained by the girl's mother as a result of witnessing the accident. In deciding against liability, the court explained that its decision was entirely one of policy, saying:

> Human wrongdoing is seldom limited in its injurious effects to the immediate actors in a particular event. More frequently than not, a chain of results is set up that visits evil consequences far and wide. While from the standpoint of good morals and good citizenship the wrongdoer may be said to violate a duty to those who suffer from the wrong, the law finds it necessary . . . to attach practical and just limits to the legal consequences of the wrongful act. . . . The answer to this question cannot be reached solely by logic, nor is it clear that it can be entirely disposed of by a consideration of what the defendant ought reasonably to have anticipated as a consequence of his wrong. The answer must be reached by balancing the social interests involved in order to ascertain how far defendant's duty and plaintiff's right may justly and expediently be extended.[2]

In determining the scope of negligence liability the courts must weigh various policy factors, the chief of which are commonly identified by the name tags 1) carelessness, 2) causation, 3) injury, 4) physical contact, 5) foreseeability of injury, 6) plaintiff's contributory misconduct, and 7) burden of proof.

CARELESSNESS

A person should always be attentive and careful in his associations with others. In attempting to define more particularly the degree of care which a person should exercise, the law creates a hypothetical "reasonable man" as its standard. The English wit and playright, A. P. Herbert, has written the following humorous and picturesque description of the role which the reasonable man plays in the common-law system:

> The Common Law of England has been laboriously built about a mythical figure—the figure of "The Reasonable Man." In the field of jurisprudence, this legendary individual occupies the place which in another science is held by the Economic Man and in social and political discussions by the Average or Plain Man. He is an ideal, a standard, the embodiment of all those qualities which we demand of the good citizen. No matter what may be the particular department of human life which falls to be considered in these Courts, sooner or later we have to face the question: Was this or was it not the conduct of a reasonable man? Did the defendant take such care to avoid shooting the plaintiff in the stomach as might reasonably be expected of a reasonable man? . . . Did the plaintiff take such precautions to inform himself of the circumstances as any reasonable man would expect of an ordinary person having the ordinary knowl-

[2] *Waube* v. *Warrington*, 216 Wis. 603, 258 N.W. 497, 98 A.L.R. 394 (1935).

edge of an ordinary person of the habits of wild bulls when goaded with garden-forks and the persistent agitation of red flags? . . .

I need not multiply examples. It is impossible to travel anywhere or to travel for long in that confusing forest of learned judgments which constitutes the Common Law of England without encountering the Reasonable Man. He is at every turn, an ever-present help in time of trouble, and his apparitions mark the road to equity and right. There has never been a problem, however difficult, which His Majesty's judges have not in the end been able to resolve by asking themselves the simple question, "Was this or was it not the conduct of a reasonable man?" and leaving that question to be answered by the jury.

This noble creature stands in singular contrast to his kinsman, the Economic Man, whose every action is prompted by the single spur of selfish advantage and directed to the single end of monetary gain. The Reasonable Man is always thinking of others; prudence is his guide, and "Safety First" . . . is his rule of life. All solid virtues are his, save only that peculiar quality by which the affection of other men is won. For it will not be pretended that socially he is much less objectionable than the Economic Man. While any given example of his behavior must command our admiration, when taken in the mass, his acts create a very different set of impressions. He is one who invariably looks where he is going and is careful to examine the immediate foreground before he executes a leap or bound; who neither star-gazes nor is lost in meditation when approaching trapdoors or the margin of a dock . . . who never mounts a moving omnibus and does not alight from any car while the train is in motion; who investigates exhaustively the *bona fides* of every mendicant before distributing alms and will inform himself of the history and habits of a dog before administering a caress . . . who never drives his ball till those in front of him have definitely vacated the putting-green which is his own objective . . . who in the way of business looks only for that narrow margin of profit which twelve men such as himself would reckon to be "fair," and contemplates his fellow merchants, their agents and their goods, with that degree of suspicion and distrust which the law deems admirable; who never swears, gambles, or loses his temper; who uses nothing except in moderation and even while he flogs his child is meditating only on the golden mean. Devoid, in short, of any human weakness, with not one single saving vice, sans prejudice, procrastination, ill nature, avarice, and absence of mind, as careful for his own safety as he is for that of others, this excellent but odious character stands like a monument in our Courts of Justice, vainly appealing to his fellow citizens to order their lives after his own example.

I have called him a myth; and insofar as there are few, if any, of his mind and temperament to be found in the ranks of living men, the title is well chosen. But it is a myth which rests upon solid and even, it may be, upon permanent foundations. The Reasonable Man is fed and kept alive by the most valued and enduring of our juridical institutions—the common jury. Hateful as he must necessarily be to any ordinary citizen who privately considers him, it is a curious paradox that where two or three are gathered together in one place they will with one accord pretend an admiration for him; and when they are gathered together in the formidable surroundings of a British jury, they are easily persuaded that they themselves are, each and generally, reasonable men. And without stopping to consider how strange a chance it must have been that has picked fortuitously from a whole people no fewer than twelve examples of a species so rare, they immediately invest themselves with the attributes of the Reasonable Man and are, therefore, at one with the Courts in their anxiety to support the tradition that such a being in fact exists. Thus it is that while the Economic Man has under the stress of modern conditions almost wholly disappeared from view his Reasonable cousin has gained in power with every case in which he has figured.[3]

Writing in a more serious vein, Justice Holmes says in his book, *The Common Law:*

> The ideal average prudent man, whose equivalent the jury is taken to be in many cases and whose culpability or innocence is the supposed test, is a constant; and his conduct under given circumstances is theoretically always the same. . . .
> The standards of the law are standards of general application. The law takes no account of the infinite varieties of temperament, intellect, and education which make the internal character of a given act so different in different men. It does not attempt to see men as God sees them for more than one sufficient reason. In the first place, the impossibility of nicely measuring a man's powers and limitations is far clearer than that of ascertaining his knowledge of law, which has been thought to account for what is called the presumption that every man knows the law. But a more satisfactory explanation is that when men live in society a certain average of conduct, a sacrifice of individual peculiarities going beyond a certain point, is necessary to the general welfare. If, for instance, a man is born hasty and awkward, is always having accidents and hurting himself or his neighbors, no doubt his congenital defects will be allowed for in the courts of Heaven; but his slips are no less troublesome to his neighbors than if they sprang from guilty neglect. His neighbors accordingly require him, at his proper peril, to come up to their standard; and the courts which they establish decline to take his personal equation into account.[4]

In short, a person should exercise the care expected of an average, normal person under like circumstances. If a person is handicapped (blind, deaf, etc.), he must use care sufficient to compensate for his disability. However, the law properly allows for the immaturity of children. A child is expected to use the care of an average child of like age, intelligence, and experience. An extremely young child (in many states a child under the age of six or seven) is considered unable to

[3] Reprinted from the fictitious case of *Fardell* v. *Potts*, published in A. P. Herbert's, *The Uncommon Law* (London: Methuen, 1952), with permission of the author, the Proprietors of *Punch*, and the publisher.

[4] Holmes, Oliver Wendell, Jr., *The Common Law* (1881; Cambridge: Harvard University Press, 1963), pp. 86, 89.

recognize the dangers inherent in certain of his acts and is, therefore, not guilty of negligence and not liable for injuries caused by such acts.

The obligation of a businessman to exercise reasonable care and thereby to keep his premises in reasonably safe condition extends not only to his building and equipment but also to all other conditions on the premises, including the behavior and conduct of other persons. If a businessman knows of a disturbance or of the dangerous conduct of other persons, or if in the exercise of reasonable supervision over his establishment he should know of the disturbance or danger, he is obliged to take reasonable steps to correct the condition. He is expected to try to stop a fight and to call for police assistance, when necessary. If the businessman fails to do what he reasonably can to quell the disturbance and as a result an innocent bystander is injured, the businessman is liable for the injuries.

Business operations involve many hazards. Large numbers of people are daily sustaining a wide variety of injuries, and there are many people who will not hesitate to allege false or faked claims. A wise businessman relieves himself of the burden of numerous disputes by carrying liability insurance. Of course, having insurance does not relieve a property owner from his moral obligation to do what he reasonably can to protect others in their persons and property.

CAUSATION

For a careless defendant to be held liable, his carelessness must have been a substantial factor in causing the injury in question.

INJURY

The injury for which a careless defendant is liable must be an actual physical injury or actual property damage. When a defendant is a careless wrongdoer rather than an intentional wrongdoer, a plaintiff usually cannot recover for fright, shock, or other emotional disturbance which does not result in harmful physical consequences to the plaintiff.

PHYSICAL CONTACT

In addition to actual injury, courts in a few states also require that the injury be associated in some way with an actual physical contact with the plaintiff or his property. In the absence of such a contact, these courts hold that the defendant is not liable for a physical injury resulting solely from the plaintiff's emotional disturbance. The policy reasons followed by these courts are quite similar to those discussed previously in connection with nondefamatory verbal abuse—the courts feeling that to permit a plaintiff to recover for physical injury not associated with physical contact would produce a multitude of lawsuits and often would raise evidence questions which would be very difficult to supervise and too easily faked. Especially in recent years, most courts in which the question has arisen have concluded that the drawbacks are not overwhelming and permit recovery for actual injuries, in spite of a lack of physical contact, if all of the other negligence elements are present.

Example: The defendant carelessly failed to provide an adequate enclosure for his cattle and thus some of his cattle frequently trespassed on the plaintiff's farm, trampling and eating the plaintiff's crops. On one occasion, several cows and a bull belonging to the defendant came onto the plaintiff's land. Without noticing the bull, the plaintiff approached to drive the cows off her land. The bull charged, and as the plaintiff turned to run, she suffered a heart attack and collapsed. The bull was driven off before reaching the plaintiff. The plaintiff sued the defendant for damages. The trial judge held that, as a matter of law, the plaintiff could not recover for her heart attack and its resulting physical consequences because of the lack of physical contact. The Pennsylvania Superior Court affirmed by a four-to-three decision. On further appeal, the Pennsylvania Supreme Court affirmed by a five-to-two decision.[5]

In a very persuasive dissenting opinion, Justice Musmanno of the Pennsylvania Supreme Court pointed out that if the bull had touched the woman, even slightly, or if in running to escape, the woman had stumbled and bruised her knee or twisted her ankle, then under Pennsylvania decisions she could have recovered full damages, not only for the contact injury but also for the heart attack and consequent impairment resulting from her fright and shock.

Courts in most other states would probably differ with the majority decisions of the Pennsylvania courts and permit the woman to recover full damages.

FORESEEABILITY OF INJURY

For a defendant to be held liable for an injury resulting from his carelessness, the possibility of such an injury must have been reasonably foreseeable as to 1) the place or area where the injury might occur and 2) the type of injury.

Area of Danger

Although the presence and injury of a particular plaintiff or of his property need not have been foreseeable, the plaintiff or his property must be within the zone of apprehended danger, that is, within the area in which persons or property would, as a matter of policy, be considered

---

[5] *Bosley* v. *Andrews*, 393 Pa. 161, 142 A.(2d) 263 (1958).

as unduly jeopardized by the defendant's carelessness. To such persons and their property, the defendant would be considered as owing a duty to use proper care.

Example: After a train which had been stopped at a station began to move, a man ran across the station platform and jumped onto the moving car. The man was carrying a small package wrapped in a newspaper. The package contained fireworks, but its appearance gave no notice of its dangerous contents. After jumping onto the car, the man seemed unsteady, as if about to fall. A trainman who was holding the car door open reached forward to help the man and a station employee pushed the man from behind. The pulling and pushing knocked the package from the man's hand. When the package fell on the rails, it exploded. The concussion of the explosion caused some crates stacked at the other end of the platform to fall on a woman who was standing beside the crates, injuring her. The injured woman sued the railroad for damages.

These were essentially the facts in one of the classic cases in the evolution of the law of negligence, decided by the New York Court of Appeals in 1928, with the court's opinion written by Justice Benjamin Cardozo, an outstanding legal scholar. In the course of the opinion which denied the woman's right to recover, Justice Cardozo wrote:

"The conduct of the defendant's guard, if a wrong in its relation to the holder of the package, was not a wrong in its relation to the plaintiff, standing far away. Relatively to her it was not negligence at all. Nothing in the situation gave notice that the falling package had in it the potency of peril to persons thus removed. . . . One who jostles one's neighbor in a crowd does not invade the rights of others standing at the outer fringe when the unintended contact casts a bomb upon the ground. The wrongdoer as to them is the man who carries the bomb, not the one who explodes it without suspicion of the danger. Life will have to be made over, and human nature transformed, before prevision so extravagant can be accepted as the norm of conduct, the customary standard to which behavior must conform. . .

"The argument for the plaintiff is built upon the shifting meanings of such words as 'wrong' and 'wrongful,' and shares their instability. What the plaintiff must show is 'a wrong' to herself, i.e., a violation of her right, and not merely a wrong to someone else, nor conduct 'wrongful' because unsocial, but not 'a wrong' to anyone. . . One who seeks redress at law does not make out a cause of action by showing without more that there has been damage to his person. If the harm was not willful, he must show that the act as to him had possibilities of danger so many and apparent as to entitle him to be protected against the doing of it though the harm was unintended. . . ."[6]

Another court has summarized Justice Cardozo's reasoning in the following language: "The defendant's act cannot be negligent as to the plaintiff unless some harm to the plaintiff or the class to which he belonged was foreseeable; the orbit of danger as disclosed to the eye of reasonable vigilance is

---

[6] *Palsgraf* v. *Long Island Railroad Co.,* 248 N.Y. 339, 162 N.E. 59 A.L.R. 1253 (1928).

the orbit of the duty, and no duty is owed to one who is outside such orbit of danger."[7]

In the previously posed hypothetical case of a power line falling on a hunter, it is arguable that the hunter was outside the zone of danger—he was not the type of person who was unreasonably jeopardized by the defendant's careless driving—and therefore could not recover from the defendant for his injuries.

Type of Injury

If the injury which a defendant's carelessness inflicts upon a plaintiff within the zone of danger is of the general type threatened by the defendant's conduct, the plaintiff should be able to recover even though the exact manner in which the injury occurs may be unexpected or unusual.

Example: A mining company owned and operated a private, narrow-gauge railroad line. The narrow-gauge track crossed the tracks of the Pennsylvania Railroad Company (PRR), curved in a semicircle, and recrossed the PRR tracks again, the two intersections being about 650 feet apart. On one occasion, an inexperienced engineer was operating the narrow-gauge engine, backing toward one of the crossings, pushing a loaded car. Because of large slag piles, it was impossible for anyone nearing this crossing on the narrow-gauge line to see trains approaching on the PRR line. The narrow-gauge engineer failed to sound the whistle and failed to have an adequate watch at the crossing. When the narrow-gauge engine had almost reached the crossing, the engineer saw, for the first time, a PRR train already at the crossing. The narrow-gauge engineer applied his brakes, then reversed his engine; and when he saw he would be unable to avoid a collision, he shut off the steam and jumped. The narrow-gauge car collided with the rear car of the PRR train, derailing one set of the latter car's wheels. The PRR train made an emergency stop, at which time it was partly across the second narrow-gauge crossing. The impact of the collision jarred the narrow-gauge engine, opening the throttle. With the controls already in reverse and nobody in the cab to change the controls, the narrow-gauge engine ran around the semicircle of track and struck the middle coach of the PRR train at the second crossing, injuring a passenger. The passenger sued the mining company.

The passenger could recover damages. Careless operation of the narrow-gauge engine constituted an unreasonable risk of injury to anyone on the PRR train or any person or property near the crossings. The injured person was within the zone of foreseeable danger, and his injury through a collision of the trains was not unexpected, even though the exact manner in which the accident occurred was quite unusual.

[7] *Dahlstrom v. Shrum*, 368 Pa. 423, 84 A.(2d) 289 (1951).

On the other hand, even though a plaintiff is within the zone of danger and therefore a person to whom the defendant owes a duty to use proper care, the plaintiff cannot recover for a particular injury resulting from the defendant's carelessness if it was *highly extraordinary* that such a type of injury would result. In the hypothetical case of the power line and the hunter, it is arguable that a bullet wound as a result of careless driving is so unusual that the defendant would not be liable for such an injury. (The wounded passenger, of course, could not recover from the hunter either, since the hunter was not at all careless or at fault.)

Plaintiff's Contributory Misconduct

Even though a defendant's careless act results in an injury to a plaintiff, if the plaintiff is also somewhat at fault, it may not be fair, as a matter of policy, to require the defendant to pay full compensation for the plaintiff's injury. This policy question arises most often when the injured plaintiff has himself been careless or has been trespassing on the defendant's property.

Contributory Negligence

Even though a defendant's negligence causes an accident resulting in an injury to a plaintiff, the injured person generally cannot recover if his own failure to use proper care is a contributing cause of the accident. Many legal writers and judges have, with good reason, soundly criticized this contributory negligence rule. Suppose that a careless driver runs into a careless pedestrian, resulting in damages in the amount of $10,000 to the pedestrian (medical expenses and lost and impaired income) and damages in the amount of $100 to the driver's car (bent fender and broken headlight). In most states the pedestrian's contributory negligence will prevent him from recovering anything at all. Since both are at fault, it certainly does not seem fair that the pedestrian should bear the full $10,000 loss while the driver bears only his $100 loss. One suggestion is that the entire damages be totaled and split equally. This would permit the pedestrian to recover $5,050 from the driver. An objection frequently raised to this solution is that in many cases the parties are not equally at fault. Accordingly, another suggestion is that the total loss be adjusted in proportion to the relative degree of the negligence of each. However, degrees of negligence (such as slight, ordinary, and gross) are difficult to define and still more difficult for juries to apply in the multitude of varying factual situations that commonly arise in negligence cases. Moreover, accidents—especially automobile mishaps —frequently involve more than two participants and often include several victims, further complicating any formula for sharing losses. The well-known tendency of juries to sympathize with grievously injured persons is also an important factor, throwing doubt on a jury's ability to administer or apply any formula for sharing losses. While the civil-law system (as distinguished from the common-law system) and the English and American admiralty-law systems, which are derived largely from the civil law, do not hold that contributory negligence bars recovery, any relaxation of the contributory negligence theory in common-law jurisdictions has been only by statute, and that very slow and slight. In most states the contributory-negligence theory remains quite inflexible; even though a plaintiff is only a little careless while a defendant is extremely careless, most courts will not attempt to compare the relative degrees of negligence, but instead will rule that the plaintiff cannot recover from the defendant at all.

It should be noted, however, that a plaintiff will not be classed as contributorily negligent unless he is guilty of negligence in the eyes of the law. Thus an extremely young child can recover from a negligent defendant, even though the child's injury is caused not only by the defendant's negligence but also by the child's conduct—conduct which in an older child or in an adult would be classed as contributory negligence sufficient to prevent the older child or adult from recovering from the negligent defendant. Also, although the courts reject any comparative negligence theory, the plaintiff's negligence will not cancel a defendant's liability if the defendant's misconduct is worse than carelessness. If a defendant is guilty of reckless indifference to consequences (sometimes called willful and wanton misconduct) or of intentional wrongdoing, the injured plaintiff can recover even though his own negligence contributed to the happening of the incident which caused his injury. In defining wanton misconduct, the Pennsylvania Supreme Court has said:

> It must be understood, of course, that wanton misconduct is something different from negligence however gross—different not merely in degree but in kind and evincing a different state of mind on the part of the tort-feasor [person guilty of a tort]. Negligence consists of inattention or inadvertance, whereas wantonness exists where the danger to the plaintiff, though realized, is so recklessly disregarded that even though there be no actual intent there is at least a willingness to inflict injury, a conscious indifference to the perpetration of the wrong.[8]

Many states ease the strictness and rigidity of the contributory negligence rule by allowing a plaintiff to recover full damages if the plaintiff's negligence preceded that of the defendant by a sufficient interval of time so that, after discovering the position of peril into which the plaintiff has negligently placed himself, the defendant, through the exercise of

[8] *Kasanovich v. George*, 348 Pa. 199, 34 A.(2d) 523 (1943).

reasonable care, could have avoided injuring the plaintiff. This rule is usually called the "last clear chance doctrine" or the "doctrine of discovered peril." Some states limit this rule considerably or refuse to follow it altogether.

Example: A customer in a supermarket was pushing a shopping cart through the aisles of the store. At one point, she was walking beside the cart while scanning the tops of the shelves for a particular commodity. Suddenly she tripped and fell over a full bucket of scrub water, which was on the floor near the shelves. One of the employees had been using the scrub bucket while cleaning some shelves and had been called away to assist another customer. The injured customer sued the owner of the market for injuries sustained in the fall.

The storeowner was not liable. A businessman is required to keep his premises in reasonably safe condition for persons whom he can expect will enter to trade. However, although the storeowner (through his employee, for whose acts he was responsible) was negligent, the customer was contributorily negligent in not looking where she was walking, and therefore could not recover.

Example: P, driving north on North Street, approached the intersection of North and West Streets, where a police officer was directing traffic. The officer made the proper hand signals to stop vehicles on West Street and permit vehicles on North Street to move through the intersection. At the officer's signal, the driver ahead of P drove through the intersection. Dividing his attention between watching the traffic officer and the car ahead, P drove into the intersection. Suddenly D, driving west on West Street, entered the intersection on P's right, completely disregarding the traffic officer's signals, and collided with P, damaging P's car and injuring P. P sued D for damages.

P was held guilty of contributory negligence and barred from recovering, even though D was negligent. A person is justified in assuming that others will act carefully and properly. However, this assumption should not be made blindly; a person is careless if he fails to give even cursory attention to the possible carelessness of others. Even though P had been signaled ahead by the traffic officer, he should have looked for oncoming traffic before committing himself to the intersection. With a brief glance, P could have noticed that D was not preparing to stop and could have and should have avoided the collision. Therefore, P could not recover.

Trespass

A *trespasser* is a person who comes onto another's property without express or implied permission. A trespasser is not completely outside the protection of the law—there is never an "open season" on trespassers—but he is entitled to less protection than is accorded an invitee. In most states the possessor of a tract of land is not liable for negligent injuries sustained by a trespasser, but he is liable for intentional injuries and injuries resulting from the possessor's willful, wanton, or reckless conduct. Even though prior experience would reasonably lead a possessor to expect trespassers on his property, he generally owes no duty to take affirmative steps to make the premises reasonably safe, unless the trespassers are children. The law recognizes children's consuming curiosity, their delight in playing with unusual devices and in unusual places, their inattention to their surroundings while playing, and their inability to recognize many possible dangers. On the other hand, the law wishes to avoid imposing unreasonably burdensome duties on property owners and possessors. As a compromise (sometimes referred to as the "attractive nuisance" doctrine), the courts feel that it is sound policy to hold a property possessor liable for injuries to trespassing children if all the following conditions are present:

1. The possessor knows or reasonably should know that children are likely to trespass.

2. The possessor maintains a structure or device which he realizes or should realize offers an unreasonable risk of serious injury to children.

3. The children, because of their youth, are unaware of the danger.

4. The cost of removing the danger or of rendering the structure or device reasonably safe is slight when compared with the risk to young children.

BURDEN OF PROOF

In most negligence lawsuits, the burden is on the plaintiff to present sufficient evidence to prove that the defendant has been negligent. If the plaintiff fails to do so, he will lose the lawsuit and judgment will be given in favor of the defendant. In other words, the law will not presume or infer that the defendant is guilty of negligence or of any other wrongful conduct merely because an accident occurs in which the plaintiff is injured. However, if whatever is involved in injuring the plaintiff or his property is entirely within the control of the defendant and if the incident causing injury is one which experience has shown rarely occurs unless the defendant has been careless, then the happening of the accident supports a presumption or inference that the defendant has been negligent. In such a case, in order to escape liability, the defendant has the burden of presenting evidence to show that he exercised proper care.

Example: The defendant's automobile skidded and collided with the plaintiff's auto, causing a total of $5,000 damages to the plaintiff and to his car. The plaintiff sued the defendant for that amount.

These facts alone would not be sufficient to show that the defendant was at fault. Unless the plaintiff introduced evidence from which it could be fairly concluded that the skidding was caused by the defendant's negligent driving, judgment would be given in favor of the defendant.

Example: The plaintiff, a passenger in a railway coach, was injured in a train wreck and sued the defendant railway company. The only evidence the plaintiff presented was the fact of the train wreck and the extent of his injuries.

Unless the defendant railroad presented evidence showing that the accident was not caused by any negligence of the railway, the plaintiff would be entitled to recover for his damages. For this type of accident, the burden of presenting evidence of what happened would be on the defendant.

NUISANCES

If a defendant comes onto a plaintiff's land without permission, he violates the plaintiff's legally protected right to have exclusive and undisturbed possession of his land and is guilty of the tort known as trespass to land. A defendant's nontrespassing conduct (acts which the defendant performs on his own land) may also interfere with a plaintiff's use and enjoyment of his land. Examples include air pollution, water pollution, and vibration. All such disturbances are not necessarily wrongful. What a defendant should be permitted to do on his own land without incurring liability for disturbing his neighbor is, like other aspects of tort law, a question of policy. If a particular act of the defendant's is considered wrongful, his tort is termed a *nuisance*.

Factors important in determining what a defendant is permitted to do on his own land and at what point he incurs liability for disturbing his neighbor include the tort policy factors discussed at the beginning of this chapter; most important are the following factors:

1. The nature and extent of the harm threatened by the defendant's act
2. The social utility of the defendant's act and its suitability to the particular locality
3. The expense or burden of performing the act in a way that will eliminate or reduce disturbance to others

Example: A homeowner lived in an area partly devoted to manufacturing operations. A manufacturer bought the vacant corner lot adjoining the homeowner's house and constructed a manufacturing plant. Heavy machinery was installed on the side of the plant nearest the homeowner's land. When production began, the machinery caused considerable vibration to the homeowner's land and house and interfered with his rest and sleep. When the homeowner complained, the manufacturer offered to buy the homeowner's property. The homeowner refused to sell and sued for legal relief. In the lawsuit, the evidence conclusively showed that neither in the construction nor in the operation of the factory was it important that the machinery be located along one side rather than another.

Under the circumstances, the manufacturer's conduct was considered unreasonable and he was held guilty of maintaining a nuisance. The homeowner recovered money damages and obtained a court order requiring the manufacturer to move his machinery to the other side of his building, even though the evidence also showed that moving the machinery would cost more than the value of the homeowner's property and would force suspension of manufacturing operations for several weeks.

If the position of the machinery where originally installed had been a significant factor in the efficient operation of the manufacturing plant, the court would probably have declared the manufacturer not guilty of maintaining a nuisance and the homeowner would have lost the lawsuit.

LIABILITY WITHOUT FAULT

The usual grounds or bases for legal liability are either agreement (contract) or wrongdoing (tort). If a person's conduct is not in violation of any agreement and he is not committing a tort, he usually is not liable, no matter how much he injures others. However, in a few limited situations the law considers it sound policy to hold a person liable for damages which he causes, even though he is not at all blameworthy or at fault in causing the damages. The use of explosives is one of the most common examples. No matter how carefully explosives are used, the results are not fully predictable and may cause injury to adjoining property owners. On the other hand, prohibiting their use would be very unwise; they are necessary to accomplish purposes highly useful to society. The law, therefore, makes a policy compromise. Engaging in such ultrahazardous activities is not prohibited, but one engaging in such activities is liable for *all* damages which may result, regardless of his care or lack of fault.

The theory of liability regardless of fault, which the common law applies to a limited number of ultrahazardous situations, has in most states been extended to industrial accidents by workmen's compensation statutes. These statutes provide an excellent illustration of the continuing evolution of the law to reflect changing conceptions of public policy. After more than a century of industrial development, the conviction spread that the conventional tort rules were hopelessly inadequate for the mounting toll of industrial accidents. Under the conventional rules, the liability of employers to injured employees was based upon fault. An employer was not liable unless the injured employee could prove 1) that his injury was caused by his employer's negligence, 2) that the employee was not himself guilty of contributory negligence, and 3) that the injury was not associated with risks which theoretically the employee was being paid to assume, including the risk of the ordinary hazards involved in the type of work undertaken and the risk of possible negligent conduct of fellow employees. Most workmen's compensation statutes abandon the conventional theory that liability should be based

on fault, and instead adopt a policy of compensation regardless of fault.
Under these statutes, the employer (and through him, society) is liable
for industrial injuries, regardless of the care or lack of care shown by the
employer, by the injured employee, or by fellow workers. Compensation
payments are made from insurance funds, the premiums for which are
paid by employers, who in turn pass the cost along to the consuming
public. In the early days of workmen's compensation statutes, many
state appellate courts, and the United States Supreme Court as well,
were called upon to consider the purpose and theory of such statutes and
invariably upheld the statutes as a valid exercise of the governmental
power to legislate for the public welfare. In 1916 the Montana Supreme
Court wrote:

> With the increased hazards consequent upon the use of high ex-
> plosives, complicated and dangerous machinery, and the powerful
> agencies of steam and electricity, the percentage of injured employees
> having justiciable claims rapidly increased until relief was sought in
> liability statutes which modified or eliminated some or all of the
> common-law defenses. But whether remedy was sought at common
> law or under an employer's liability statute, the actionable wrong . . .
> for which the master was liable . . . was the gist of the claim for
> damages and the basis of any right to recover. Experience demon-
> strated that more than one half of all industrial injuries resulted from
> inevitable accident or from the risks of the business for which no one
> could be held responsible; that neither the common law nor em-
> ployers' liability statutes furnished any measure of relief to more than
> 12 or 15 per cent of the injured and that further appreciable im-
> provement from the modification of existing laws could not be expected
> so long as the element of negligence was the foundation of legal
> liability.
> Workingmen's insurance and compensation laws are the products
> of the development of the social and economic idea that the industry
> which has always borne the burden of depreciation and destruction
> of the necessary machinery shall also bear the burden of repairing the
> efficiency of the human machines without which the industry itself
> could not exist. The economic loss from vocational disease, industrial
> accident, old age, and unemployment was a subject of serious inquiry
> among the constituent German states before the days of the Empire,
> but the credit for crystallizing the sentiment into workable laws will
> always remain with Bismarck. From the enactment of the sick insur-
> ance statute in Germany in 1883 and the fundamental law in 1884,
> the idea of compensation based only upon the risks of the business and
> the impairment of earning efficiency spread to other European states,
> and finally penetrated to this country. . . . The fundamental differ-
> ence between the conception of liability and compensation is found in
> the presence in the one, and the absence from the other, of the element
> of actionable wrong. The common law and liability statutes furnished
> an uncertain measure of relief to the limited number of workmen who
> could trace their injuries proximately to the master's negligence.
> Compensation laws proceed upon the theory that the injured working-

man is entitled to pecuniary relief from the distress caused by his injury, as a matter of right, unless his own willful act is the proximate cause, and that it is wholly immaterial whether the injury can be traced to the negligence of the master, the negligence of the injured employee or a fellow servant, or whether it results from an act of God, the public enemy, an unavoidable accident, or a mere hazard of the business which may or may not be subject to more exact classification; that his compensation shall be certain, limited by the impairment of his earning capacity, proportioned to his wages, and not dependent upon the skill or eloquence of counsel or the whim or caprice of a jury; that as between workmen of the same class who suffer like injuries, each shall receive the same compensation and that, too, without the economic waste incident to protracted litigation, and without reference to the fact that the injury to the one may have been occasioned by the negligence of the master and to the other by reason of his own fault.[9]

Some legal writers feel that, in the present motor age, the numerous and costly injuries inflicted upon persons and property through the operation of millions of motor vehicles should be treated the same as industrial injuries; that, instead of liability dependent upon fault, the theory of recovery should be changed to one allowing compensation regardless of fault; and that all persons suffering injuries or damages from motor-vehicle accidents should be compensated according to a statutory scale, regardless of who was at fault in causing the accident and even though no one was at fault. In 1946 the Canadian province of Saskatchewan made a limited beginning in this direction by requiring compulsory insurance and providing for a scale of varying payments to be made to all who suffer injuries from auto accidents, without regard to fault. The Saskatchewan plan, however, supplements rather than replaces the conventional tort approach which ties liability to fault; although an injured person will receive a payment according to the statutory scale, his conventional tort remedies remain. If the injured person can prove that his damages were caused by the negligence of another and that he himself was free from contributory negligence, he can sue the party who caused the accident and recover the amount by which his actual damages exceed the statutory insurance award already paid to him.

PROBLEMS

1. After D, a retailer, conducted an advertising campaign to introduce a new type of product into his community, P, the owner of a competing store, acquired some similar items which he advertised at a lower price. Although P's advertising in no way misled customers into confusing the item P was selling with the item D had advertised, it was clear that P was taking advantage of the market demand which D had developed by his advertising

---

[9] *In re Application of Lewis and Clark County,* 52 Mont. 6, 155 P. 268, L.R.A. 1916 D 628 (1916).

campaign. Quite angered, D wrote to P saying among other things, "Your practices are fraudulent and dishonest, and you are no better than a thief." P sued D for damages for defamation.

a) No one other than P (and, of course, D) read the letter. What should be the result of P's lawsuit against D? Explain.

b) P was the first person (other than D) to read the letter. After reading it, P gave it to his secretary to read and had her send it to P's lawyer. What should be the result of P's lawsuit against D? Explain.

c) D dictated the letter to his secretary. After she had typed the letter, D signed it and had her mail the letter. After the letter left D's office, no one other than P read it. What should be the result of P's lawsuit against D? Explain.

d) As D knew, P's standard office practice was for his secretary to open all mail not marked "personal." Personal mail the secretary would put on P's desk unopened. No one (other than D) read the letter before it arrived in P's office. 1) D did not mark the envelope "personal," and P's secretary opened and read the letter before giving it to P. What should be the result of P's lawsuit against D? Explain. 2) Although D marked the envelope "personal," P's secretary overlooked that notation and opened and read the letter before giving it to P. What should be the result of P's lawsuit against D? Explain.

2. On the way home from school, an eleven-year-old girl stopped in the book department of a large department store. The girl was carrying a brief-case in one hand and a box of popcorn in the other hand. While looking at some books, she put the box of popcorn in her briefcase. After spending a few minutes at the book department, the girl went to the ladies' rest room. A woman detective employed by the store, having noticed the girl putting something in her briefcase, followed the girl into the ladies' rest room and asked the girl where she had put the books she had taken from the book counter. When the girl began to cry, the detective took hold of the girl's arm with one hand and took her briefcase in the other hand. Two women shoppers who were also in the rest room protested the detective's actions and all four (the girl, the detective, and the two shoppers) went to the manager's office. When it was ascertained that the girl had not taken any books, she was escorted to a bus stop and put on the bus which she usually used to go home. The girl was quite nervous, upset, and became ill, and through her parents sued the store for damages.

a) On what grounds could the lawsuit be brought? Explain.

b) What would be the result of the lawsuit? Explain.

3. The trustees of a nonprofit hospital decided to establish a nursing school to be operated in conjunction with the hospital. A fund-raising campaign was initiated, appealing to all persons and businesses in the community for contributions for the nursing school. A number of businessmen signed pledges agreeing to pay amounts ranging from $100 to $5,000, payments to be completed by the middle of the year. In the fall, the nursing school began operation. Shortly thereafter a full-page newspaper advertisement was published

by the trustees in space donated by the local newspaper. The advertisement read in part:

> We acknowledge with justifiable pride in our community the generous support given our community hospital nursing school. The nursing school, which will be of inestimable value to the community, would not have been possible without the generous support of the following community-spirited business establishments:

Name of Business	Immediate Payments and/or Pledges Payable by June 30 of this year	Total Payments Actually Made up to October 1
Ace Athletic Store	$1,000	$1,000
Barton Bakery	500	None
Carter Car Sales	750	600

[The advertisement continued in the same way, listing the names of about forty other businesses.]

A further report will be made to the community at the end of the year.

> Board of Trustees
> Community Hospital

a) The information concerning Barton Bakery was true. Nevertheless, Barton Bakery sued the trustees for damages. On what grounds and with what result? Explain.

b) A business in the community, known as the Allen Auto Sales, had declined to contribute anything to the nursing school fund, and the preceding advertisement made no mention of the Allen Auto Sales. The Allen Auto Sales sued the trustees for damages. On what grounds and with what result? Explain.

4. One evening a woman was annoyed by her neighbor's loud playing of his radio and complained to the police. The following day the woman was sitting on the back porch of her home with a friend and the friend's two children when the neighbor came home from work. Seeing the woman, the neighbor came to the fence between the two properties and in a loud voice profanely called the woman various abusive names. The woman was considerably shocked, upset, and humiliated, and remained nervous and physically upset for several days. The woman sued the neighbor for damages. Assume that under the circumstances it was clear to any hearer that the words used by the neighbor were not intended to have their literal meaning and that the neighbor therefore was *not* guilty of slander. Do you think the neighbor committed a tort for which the woman should be able to recover damages? Briefly state a few policy arguments on both sides of the question, and explain your decision whether or not the woman should collect.

5. A bill collector called at a woman's home to collect a $10 debt she owed his employer. The woman was alone at the time, and when she truthfully said that she was unable to pay at the moment but would be able to pay a few days later, the bill collector profanely called the woman various abusive

names. The woman was considerably shocked, upset, and humiliated, and remained nervous and physically upset for several days. The woman sued the bill collector. Would your policy arguments in this case be any different from your arguments in Problem 4? Explain.

6. While driving north on a through highway at a moderate rate of speed, D slowed, upon approaching an intersection. As a result of an incident [described further on in Parts (a) and (b)] occurring at the intersection, D's car went out of control. After his car was out of control, D did all he reasonably could to bring it under control. In spite of D's efforts, the car mounted the curb, striking and seriously injuring P, a pedestrian, who was using proper care when he was injured. P sued D and proved damages of $5,000. D did not have any liability insurance.

a) D's car went out of control as a result of a collision with another car. Although using proper care, D was unable to avoid the collision. The other car was driven by a person who, without stopping at the stop sign, entered the intersection from D's left. Following the collision, while D was still dazed, the other driver drove away and the police were unable to locate or identify him. Was P entitled to judgment against D? Explain.

b) D's car went out of control as a result of skidding on some spots of oil on the road. D did not see the oil at the intersection, and a driver exercising reasonable care could not have seen the oil in time to avoid skidding on it. Was P entitled to judgment against D? Explain.

c) Other facts remaining the same, assume that at the time of the accident, D had an insurance policy under which the insuring company agreed to pay any amount, up to $10,000, for which D might become legally obligated because of personal injuries to others resulting from D's operation of an automobile. With the fact of D's insurance added to the previously mentioned facts: 1) Would your answer to the situation in Part (a) now be the same as, or different from, the answer you had given? Explain. 2) Would your answer to the situation in Part (b) now be the same as, or different from, the answer you had given? Explain.

7. On June 1, S, a retail appliance dealer, entered into a written contract with B, a customer, under which 1) S sold and delivered a described TV set to B for $400, 2) $50 of the price was payable upon signing of the agreement, the balance in monthly installments of $50 each, starting July 1, 3) until the entire $400 was paid, title to the TV set was to remain with S, and 4) if B defaulted in the agreed payments, S was to have the right to repossess the set from B's home at any time. B made the $50 down payment and the July 1 payment, but by the middle of August had paid nothing further. S called on B at his home, and when B said he was then unable to pay anything further but would be able to pay $100 on September 1, S said he intended to repossess the TV set. When B protested, asking for more time, S swung his arm in a backhand motion against B's head, pushing B out of the doorway. S, thinking B was feigning when he seemed to sustain great pain from the push, entered the house and removed the TV set. S's backhand motion was more of a push than a blow. However, the impact on B's ear was sufficient to aggravate and spread an ear infection, causing a more serious

infection and a partial loss of hearing in that ear. B's wife, who was seven months pregnant, was also present. S did not threaten her in any way nor come near her, but her fright and shock at seeing S's conduct caused her to collapse in a hysterical condition and to suffer a miscarriage.

a) B sued S for a substantial amount for the serious results sustained from S's backhand motion. S conclusively proved that he had no knowledge of B's ear infection and, through the exercise of reasonable care, could not have suspected the existence of the infection. S also proved that, under ordinary circumstances, his backhand motion would have caused no injury to B at all. What should be the result of B's lawsuit? Explain.

b) B's wife sued S for the damages which she sustained. What should be the result of the wife's lawsuit? Explain.

8. a) D, a former resident of a small town, returned to that town for a short visit after an absence of several months. When D resided there, Sassafras Street, running north and south, was a two-way, through street with stop signs to halt traffic before entering Sassafras Street. During D's absence from the town, Sassafras Street was made a one-way through street for southbound traffic only. The first day of his visit, D (with a new, quietly operating car) drove west on 25th Street, stopped at the intersection, and then, not noticing the small one-way sign with an arrow pointing south, turned north (the wrong way) on Sassafras Street. As D, driving north on Sassafras Street, approached the intersection of 24th Street, D saw P, a pedestrian on the sidewalk walking west toward Sassafras Street. When P reached the intersection of 24th and Sassafras Street, he stopped on the curb for a moment and then suddenly stepped into the street only 10 feet in front of D's car. Although D was driving at a reasonable speed, he could not avoid hitting P. P sued D for the injuries sustained. At the trial, P testified that, before stepping off the curb, he had looked toward the north (looking for southbound traffic) but had not looked toward the south and therefore did not see D's car. Explain 1) the reasoning upon which P might attempt to collect, 2) the reasoning upon which D might attempt to defend, and 3) who should win the lawsuit.

b) Other facts remaining the same, assume the following changed facts: At the time of the accident, Sassafras Street was, and always had been, a two-way street. P, looking toward the north but not toward the south, did not see D approaching from the south. Because D was driving unreasonably, but not recklessly, fast, he could not avoid hitting P. P sued D. Answer the same questions asked in Part (a).

9. A merchant owned and operated a small two-story department store, the second floor being reached by a staircase at the rear of the store. When the building was constructed, there were railings on each side of the staircase. After a time, the railings became loose and the railings and brackets were removed. One day a woman customer was shopping on the second floor. As she was going down the stairs, the heel of one of her shoes came off. As the woman felt herself falling, she grabbed for the wall. Because there was no railing and the wall was smooth, she was unable to avoid falling. This was the first time the heel had come off; it had not previously appeared loose.

The woman sued the merchant for damages for injuries which resulted from the fall.

a) Explain 1) the reasoning upon which the woman might attempt to recover, 2) the reasoning upon which the merchant might attempt to defend, and 3) which party should be given judgment.

b) Would your answers be the same if the staircase had never been equipped with railings? Explain.

10. P was driving slightly over 40 miles per hour along a two-lane, concrete highway when he was unexpectedly blinded by the bright headlights of an oncoming car. Because the other driver failed at any time to switch his lights to the lower beam, P's vision remained obscured until the other car passed, during which time P's car traveled about 150 feet. Immediately after the blinding lights had passed, P saw, for the first time, the rear of a truck 30 feet ahead. P had not seen the truck sooner because the truck body was dark in color and had no rear lights and no illumination or reflectors of any kind. The truck was heavily loaded with coal and moving at a very slow speed, whereas P's car was traveling about 40 miles per hour. After seeing the truck, P did all he reasonably could, but was unable to swerve sufficiently and crashed into the rear of the truck, causing considerable damage to his own car. P sued the truck driver. What would be the result of the lawsuit? Explain.

11. State Street was a one-way street for westbound traffic only; North Street was a north-south street open to two-way traffic; and East Street, one block (200 yards) east of North Street, ran parallel to North Street. D, driving north on North Street in a negligent manner, collided with M, who was driving west on State Street with proper care. The force of the collision knocked M's car into the porch of A's frame house located on the northeast corner of the intersection. A fire immediately broke out in M's car. M managed to struggle clear from his car before the gas tank exploded, spraying burning gasoline onto A's porch. A's porch quickly joined the conflagration. The fire spread to the remainder of A's house and, in spite of firemen's efforts, to B's house just east of A's house. The draft created by the growing fire accelerated its spread and all the buildings in the block were destroyed or badly damaged by the fire before it was finally put out. Included, in addition to a number of intervening buildings, was C's retail store building on the northwest corner of State Street and East Street. A, B, and C each filed a separate lawsuit against D. Explain 1) the reasoning upon which the plaintiff in each lawsuit might attempt to collect, 2) the reasoning upon which D might attempt to defend the lawsuits, and 3) which party should be given judgment in each lawsuit.

12. A construction company was under contract to install curbs and sidewalks and repave a certain street. Alongside the street ran the tracks of the Community Transit Company. The tracks were embedded in concrete and the company's streetcars were of a new type, relatively noiseless in operation. P, an employee of the construction company, on an errand to the toolhouse, was walking west along the westbound track not more than 18 inches from the north rail. P was negligent in walking with his back toward the east, the direction from which streetcars would come on the westbound track. (This was so clearly negligence that a jury could not reasonably conclude otherwise.) A streetcar motorman, a little behind schedule, was taking advantage of the slight downgrade and driving his westbound streetcar about 30 to 35 miles per hour. The motorman first saw P walking beside the track when the streetcar was about 200 feet away from P. Although P continued to be clearly visible to the motorman from that time on, the motorman did not sound his bell, slow down, or apply the brakes until after the right front of the streetcar struck P a severe and crippling blow. P sued the transit company for damages. Explain 1) the reasoning upon which P could attempt to recover, 2) the reasoning upon which the transit company could attempt to defend, and 3) which party should be given judgment.

13. A manufacturer owned a piece of land upon which was a factory and along the edge of which was a small, unused, brick stable, one and one-half stories high. The east wall of the stable was three feet from the west wall of a factory located on an adjoining property. Desiring to construct an addition to his factory, the manufacturer contracted with a builder for demolition of the stable and construction of a new building. Since the stable and the land immediately surrounding it had not been previously used by the manufacturer, children had always used the premises as a playground. During demolition of the stable, children gathered to watch. On the third day of demolition, a heavy rain began about 3 p.m., forcing the builder's workmen to quit work. The rain lasted an hour, after which the builder decided to do nothing more that day and sent his men home. At that time, all that remained standing of the stable was a section of the east wall about 10 to 15 feet high. During the process of demolition, bricks had fallen or been thrown into the narrow space between the east wall of the stable and the west wall of the adjoining factory. When the rain stopped, a number of children returned to the area to play. After they had been playing awhile, three boys were standing on top of the section of wall which had not been demolished; P, 14 years old, was standing at the bottom of the wall. Suddenly the wall collapsed, almost burying P in a mass of bricks. P sustained serious and permanent injuries and through his father sued the builder for damages. Experts on building demolition testified that the wall collapsed because of a combination of the following factors: 1) the builder's workmen had already chipped and weakened the wall near the bottom, 2) rain water was absorbed by the bricks piled in the narrow space between the wall and the adjoining factory, causing them to exert pressure against the wall, and 3) the rain had weakened the exposed mortar in the wall. The experts also testified that the presence of the three boys on top of the wall had nothing to do with the collapse of the wall. Explain 1) the reasoning upon which P could attempt to collect, 2) the reasoning upon which the builder could attempt to defend, and 3) which party should be given judgment.

chapter *3*

Crimes

In accomplishing its function of controlling society, the law not only defines and protects the rights of individuals but also recognizes that certain legally protected rights are vested in society as a whole. The definition and enforcement of society's legal rights are accomplished by means of the criminal law and criminal procedure.

CRIMINAL PROCESS AND CIVIL DEBTS

Just as the compensation of injured persons and not the punishment of wrongdoers is the objective of the civil law and its remedies, so the role of the criminal law is to punish wrongdoers and not to provide relief for their victims. As is further discussed in Chapter 7, a person is usually guilty of duress or extortion if he uses or threatens to use a criminal proceeding to collect a civil claim.

An exception in which punishment is made a legitimate part of a civil lawsuit (namely the allowance of punitive damages) has been referred to in Chapter 2. There are also a few exceptional situations in which the criminal law assists an injured person to secure compensation. The most important of these situations concern 1) the restitution of stolen property, 2) the refusal of installment buyers to account, and 3) bad checks.

RESTITUTION OF STOLEN PROPERTY

In some states, when a criminal court is prescribing the punishment for a defendant convicted of stealing, the court is permitted to include an order that the defendant return the stolen property to its owner or, if that is not possible, that the defendant pay to the owner the value of the stolen property.

REFUSAL OF INSTALLMENT BUYERS TO ACCOUNT

Suppose that a dealer sells and delivers a TV set to a customer who 1) agrees to pay the purchase price in stated monthly installments and 2) agrees that, although the customer will have the set in his home, the dealer will continue to own the set (or have a security interest in it) until the full price is paid. If the customer defaults in making the agreed payments, the dealer has the right to repossess the set. Occasionally when a customer defaults, the dealer then discovers that the particular customer is not only a poor credit risk but also dishonest. The customer may dishonestly assert that he no longer has possession of the purchased item, and may refuse to disclose where it is or to give any further information. (The dishonest customer may have turned the purchased item over to a friend or relative who will return it to the customer when the dealer gives up trying to collect.) Of course, the customer still owes the unpaid balance of the purchase price and the dealer can obtain a judgment against the customer for that amount. However, the dealer may be unable to find any property belonging to the customer upon which the sheriff can levy, and in many states wages while still in the hands of an employer are, at least to some extent, exempt from attachment by an employee's creditors.

Similar fact situations sometimes arise between banks (or other lending institutions) and dealers. If a bank makes a loan to a dealer which is secured by goods in the dealer's possession, the bank runs the risk of a dishonest dealer defaulting on his loan obligation and also hiding or refusing to account for the collateral security.

Such dishonesty is practically the same as stealing and is expressly made punishable by criminal statutes in many states. As a typical example, a Pennsylvania statute provides that if such a debtor (that is, one in possession of goods in which his creditor owns a security interest) "maliciously or fraudulently sells, injures, destroys, conceals, abandons, or defaces identifying marks on such goods, or otherwise disposes of such goods under claim of full ownership," he shall be guilty of a misdemeanor, and on conviction shall be sentenced to pay a fine not exceeding $500 or undergo imprisonment not exceeding one year or both.

In a state having such a statute, a dishonest debtor may be persuaded to account for secured goods by having his attention directed to the statute. However, the creditor's mention of the criminal statute should be carefully worded so that the creditor will not himself become criminally liable for compounding a crime or for extortion, nor civilly liable for malicious prosecution, in the event he later initiates the threatened criminal action. It is wise for the creditor to have his lawyer write the form letter to be used.

BAD CHECKS

All states have statutes which define the crime of dishonestly passing a bad check and prescribe appropriate punishment. Under most of these statutes a drawer (the person who makes out or draws a check on a certain drawee bank) commits the crime when he negotiates a check 1) with *knowledge* that his account or credit arrangement with the drawee bank is insufficient for payment of the check, and 2) with an *intent* to defraud. If a drawer has no account at all in the bank upon which he draws a check, then (unless he mistakenly used the wrong check form) the drawer obviously has knowledge that his check will not be paid. However, if the drawer actually has an account and the drawee bank refuses to pay because the balance in the account is less than the amount of the check, it is quite difficult to prove the drawer's actual knowledge and intent. A drawer can always claim that he is poor in arithmetic and made a mistake in calculating his bank balance. For this reason, most bad-check statutes authorize the making of certain presumptions or conclusions in regard to a drawer's knowledge and intent.

Actually, since intent is a state of mind and can never be directly proven by microscope or test tube, it can only be presumed to exist by reason of the existence of other, proven facts. A brief excursion into the general field of legal presumptions or conclusions will be helpful. In one sense, presumptions or conclusions can be subdivided into 1) natural or obvious presumptions and 2) statutory presumptions. A natural or obvious presumption is one which is made from certain facts because any other conclusion would be so highly unusual as to be illogical, unreasonable, or absurd. On the other hand, a statutory presumption is not so obvious or inevitable. Instead, it is a presumption or conclusion which, for purposes of public policy, is authorized by statute for a certain situation, even though another conclusion would also be reasonable or logically possible.

Example of Natural Presumption: As the defendant drove past a group of persons at a labor rally, he fired several shots, killing one of the demonstrators. When brought to trial for murder, the defendant claimed that he had not intended to kill, but only to fire over the heads of the demonstrators to frighten them.

Courts frequently say, "Every person is presumed to intend the natural and probable consequences of his acts." If the jury did not believe the defendant's claim, the fact that the defendant intended to kill could be found as a natural presumption, an obvious conclusion which a jury could reach without any special statutory authorization.

Example of Statutory Presumption: A foot patrolman saw a car drive through a red light. The car did not stop and all the evidence the patrolman had was the license number, which showed that the car was owned by Martin Morton. The state prosecuted Morton for driving through the red light.

Ordinarily, when a person is accused of a crime, the burden of presenting evidence is on the state. In the words of the well-known rule, "A person is presumed innocent until he is proven guilty." Thus, in the absence of a special statute, the state would have to prove not only that Morton's car was driven through the red light, but also that Morton was driving at the time. It is quite common for persons to loan their cars to others. Therefore, it would not be naural or obvious to conclude from the fact of ownership alone that Morton was driving.

However, to achieve certain socially desirable ends, society sometimes in effect shifts the burden of presenting evidence to the defendant. This occurs when a jury is authorized to make a conclusion which, although probable, falls short of being the *only* natural or logical conclusion that can be reached from the proven facts.

In the interests of adequately controlling traffic, statutes in some states provide that when an automobile is involved in a traffic violation, the registered owner is presumed to have been driving unless he presents evidence to prove that someone else was driving. Thus, if the state in which Morton was prosecuted had such a statute, the jury would be authorized to presume that Morton was driving, unless he proved otherwise, and therefore to find him guilty.

Most bad-check statutes make use of either of two types of statutory presumptions. Under the statutes of some states, if a drawee bank refuses to honor (that is, pay) a check because of insufficient funds, a jury can presume or conclude from this fact that the drawer had guilty knowledge and guilty intent when he negotiated the check. The statutes in many other states require a notice to be given to the drawer before the presumption can be made. Under this latter type of statute, if a drawer is notified that the drawee bank has dishonored his check because of insufficient funds, and the drawer thereafter fails to make good on the check within a stated period of time (ten days in most states), the jury can presume or conclude that the drawer had guilty knowledge and intent when he negotiated the check. It should be emphasized that neither type of statute makes nonpayment of the check *conclusive* proof of the drawer's guilt. The statutes merely authorize a jury to make a presumption in the absence of contrary evidence; a drawer still has a chance to raise a reasonable doubt in the jury's mind. However, unless the drawer can raise a reasonable doubt concerning either his guilty knowledge or guilty intent, the jury can presume that he acted wrongfully and find him guilty.

In a state with a notice-type statute, a drawer is under a strong inducement to pay the amount he owes on a dishonored check before the expiration of the statutory period, in order to avoid a criminal prosecution. Such a statute not only permits but actually encourages a holder to threaten a criminal action in order to collect the amount due on a dishonored check. To avoid misusing the statute, the holder of a bad check should consult his lawyer for the proper wording of the notice which should be sent.

Courts in the various states disagree as to whether a person who dishonestly gives a bad check for a *preexisting* debt can be said to have an intent to defraud. Some courts hold that a person has no intent to defraud unless he intends to obtain something of value with his bad check. Courts of many other states, however, recognize that there is a difference between the *specific intent* to obtain something of value by false pretenses (which is usually a more serious crime) and the *general intent* described by the expression "intent to defraud," which indicates no more than a dishonest state of mind. These courts therefore hold that if a person with no honest purpose in mind gives a check which actually or presumably he knows is bad, he evidences an intent to defraud and is guilty of the crime of passing a bad check, even though the check is given for a preexisting obligation.

REQUIRED QUANTITY OF EVIDENCE

The quantity or persuasiveness of evidence required for a decision against a defendant differs between civil and criminal lawsuits. When evidence is conflicting, a defendant may be found *civilly* liable if the believable evidence weighs more heavily toward liability than toward nonliability, while in a *criminal* case, the weight of evidence must be stronger, sufficient to leave no reasonable doubt of guilt.

CRIMINAL INTENT

The intent requisite for liability is frequently less in civil cases than in criminal cases. Suppose that an employee working at his job drives his employer's truck recklessly and injures a pedestrian. It is fair to say that since the employer's interest is being advanced at the time, he is *civilly* liable for the injuries. The employee himself can also be found criminally liable for reckless driving (or for manslaughter if the pedestrian is killed). However, the employer has no criminal liability, since he does not personally have the requisite degree of guilt, knowledge, or intent.

For some crimes, however, intent is unimportant. The interest of the community in controlling certain activities requires that a person be declared guilty and punishable regardless of his actual knowledge or intent. Examples include the sale of liquor to minors and the sale or handling of certain food products.

Example: The owner of a small restaurant innocently bought from a dishonest supplier merchandise which was wrapped and labeled as butter but which was actually oleomargarine. The restaurant owner was prosecuted for violation of the following statute: "It shall be unlawful for any hotel, restaurant, public dining room, or public boarding house to serve to customers, or to have on the premises, any oleomargarine, butterine, or similar substance, made or colored so as to look like yellow butter. Every person, firm, or corporation, and every officer, agent, servant, and employee of such person, firm, or corporation, who shall serve to customers, or be in possession of oleomargarine, butterine, or similar substance in violation of any of the provisions of this act shall, upon conviction thereof, be sentenced to pay a fine of not less than sixty dollars nor more than one hundred dollars and costs, and in default of payment of such fine and costs, shall be sentenced to undergo imprisonment in the county jail for not more than thirty days."

Since the statute omits any reference to a restaurant owner's knowledge or intent, the owner would be guilty and punishable, even though he was completely innocent of any guilty knowledge and was unable to analyze or test incoming products.

PROBLEMS

1. The plaintiff complained to his neighbor, the defendant, about the latter's dumping trash at the back of his property in such a careless manner that some fell onto the plaintiff's property. The defendant became angered and without justification hit the plaintiff, knocking him to the ground and breaking his glasses (costing $25) and a dental plate (costing $75). The plaintiff was not otherwise injured. The plaintiff swore out a warrant against the defendant for the crime of assault and battery. The defendant was arrested, tried, and convicted as charged. He was sentenced to pay a fine of $100 and court costs, which he paid. The plaintiff then demanded that the defendant pay for replacing the plaintiff's glasses and dental plate, and when the defendant refused, the plaintiff sued the defendant for $100. In defense the defendant protested that he had already been tried and had fully paid for his wrongful act. Would the defendant's defense be effective to prevent the plaintiff from recovering a judgment for $100? Explain.

2. G, a resident of Chicago, cashed a check for $100 at a Philadelphia hotel where he was staying. The check was G's personal check, drawn on a Chicago bank in the amount of $100 and naming the hotel as the payee. A few days later G checked out of the hotel and paid his hotel bill of $75 by indorsing and giving to the hotel a check for $75 which named G as the payee. The check was drawn on a Philadelphia bank by a local businessman. On the following day the $75 check was returned to the hotel by the bank on which it was drawn, marked "insufficient funds." The hotel immediately notified G in Chicago. G had no previous knowledge that the Philadelphia businessman's check was bad. G promptly mailed his own personal check to the hotel in the amount of $75. A few days later, both of G's checks were returned to the hotel marked "insufficient funds." The hotel notified G and demanded payment of the full $175. G failed to make good on the checks and after two weeks, when G was in Philadelphia again, the hotel caused a criminal prosecution to be initiated against him. State whether there was sufficient evidence to convict G a) as to the $100 check, b) as the $75 check. Explain.

book *II*

The Basic Law of Contracts

Briefly stated, a *contract* is an agreement involving a promise or a set of promises which the law will enforce. While modern society is absolutely dependent upon the making and performing of promises, no legal system in the world enforces *all* promises which people make. The task of the law therefore is not only to enforce promises (that is, to provide adequate remedies to persons who are injured when others fail to perform their promises) but also to formulate rules for determining as a matter of public policy, just when, under what circumstances, and to what extent promises should be enforced.

Under various statutes (commonly called Statutes of Frauds, further discussed in Chapter 9), certain types of agreements must be in writing or otherwise corroborated in order to be enforceable. Unless an agreement is of the type to which such a statute applies, the agreement need not follow any particular form to be an enforceable contract. The parties need not expressly state in words all of the terms of their contract. Terms can be implied from the conduct of the parties, and the actual making of the agreement itself can be implied from conduct.

Example: S said to B: "I hereby offer to sell you the following goods (describing them) for $100." B promptly replied, "I accept your offer," thus forming an enforceable contract.

Since neither party expressly stated otherwise, it would be presumed (or implied) that both parties intended delivery and payment to be made in the usual or customary manner. Delivery and payment at the customary time and place would, therefore, be enforceable obligations, undertaken by the parties when they formed their agreement without specifying other terms.

Example: Wishing to buy bread, a buyer went to a grocery store where he had a charge account. Seeing that the grocer was busy waiting on another customer, the buyer picked up a loaf of bread, and waved it at the grocer. The grocer nodded his head and the buyer left the store.

The grocer and the buyer thus entered into a contract under which the buyer agreed to pay the usual price at the usual time. Since nothing was stated expressly in words, the contract would be classified as an implied contract, both the formation of the agreement and its terms being implied from the conduct of the parties.

In addition to determining the existence and scope of contractual promises, the law finds it useful to borrow from contract rules and apply their ideas in certain situations, even though an actual contract does not exist. The theory, called quasi-contract, is one of the most common examples.

The Latin term *quasi* means "as if" or "analogous to." The term *quasi-contract* is a tag or label for a theory which provides for recovery in a situation in which, although there is no actual agreement between parties, not even an implied agreement, it would be unfair and unjust to deny recovery. In the early development of the law, the form in which a lawsuit was brought was of vital importance. If a plaintiff could not fit his case into one of the recognized forms, he might be unable to obtain relief. If it seemed too unfair to deny recovery, the law would grant relief to a plaintiff by pretending that he was a party to a contract, permitting him to recover in a quasi-contract action, "as if" there were a contract.

Example: From time to time Davis incurred obligations to Carter. On one occasion when Davis was paying various of his creditors, he erroneously thought that he owed Carter $200 and paid him that amount. Although Davis was not indebted to Carter at that time, Carter honestly thought that there was an outstanding obligation and accepted the payment. When the parties discovered their mistake, Davis demanded return of the money and upon Carter's refusal, sued Carter to recover $200.

When cases such as this first arose, tort law had not developed to the point of considering that Carter's retention of the payment might constitute a tort. However the law permitted Davis to recover on the theory that, to prevent unfairly and unjustly enriching Carter at Davis' expense, the situation should be treated "as if" there were a promise by Carter to repay the $200 to Davis.

Example: When a bus was involved in an accident, a passenger suffered a serious head injury, and was rushed to a hospital in an unconscious condition. A surgeon performed an emergency operation in a reasonable attempt to save the injured person's life, but the patient died without regaining consciousness.

Since the passenger was unconscious all of the time, he was unable to form an actual contract with the surgeon. Nevertheless, a patient of sufficient means is expected to pay for medical services. When the injured passenger was found to have left a sizable estate, the surgeon was able to recover from the estate for the reasonable value of his medical services—on the theory of quasi-contract, "as if" there were a contract.

chapter *4*

Formation of Agreements

For a legally enforceable contract to be formed, two (or more) persons must indicate that they are in agreement on a certain proposition—they must consent or assent to something which binds or commits them in some definite way. The mechanics by which two persons form a contractual agreement is, almost invariably, for one person to make a definite proposal or offer to the other and for the other to acquiesce in or accept the offer. Suppose that the owner of a rare book remarks to a companion, "I'm thinking of selling this book. I'd like to get $300 for it," to which the companion promptly replies, "I'll give you $300 for it." Suppose further that after thinking a moment the owner answers, "No, I've changed my mind. I guess I won't sell now," whereupon the companion insists that a legally enforceable contract has already been formed. The question thus raised is whether or not the parties have mutually assented to a binding commitment. Clearly the answer is not to be found by asking either the owner or his companion what he actually intended or what he believes the rights of the parties should be. Any system for deciding disputes must utilize provable and impartial measuring devices. In contract law as in tort law—in fact for all human activity—the law's chief yardstick is "the reasonable man." In the above-described rare-book dispute, the companion certainly agreed to commit or bind himself to something definite—to buy the book for $300. The only question is whether the owner bound himself to sell—whether a reasonable man would conclude from what was said that the owner intended to be committed as soon as the companion might acquiesce and without any chance to bargain or discuss the matter further. Analyzed in this way, the owner's statement clearly does not form a sound basis for considering him legally bound. The law expresses this conclusion by saying that the owner did not make an offer, and therefore, although the companion acquiesced, no contract was formed. In this manner the law uses the concepts of offer and acceptance as the measuring instruments for analyzing a fact situation and determining, from the standpoint of the reasonable man, whether a contractual agreement has been formed.

OFFERS

A person who makes an offer is usually referred to as the offeror, while the person to whom the offer is made is the offeree. When a person makes a proposal expressing an intent as to the kind of contract he is willing to make and the terms by which he is willing to be legally bound, the expression of intent is an offer if it would lead a reasonable man in the position of the offeree to believe that the one who is expressing his intent means to be bound or committed to the stated proposition as soon as the offeree indicates his consent, without any further bargaining or discussion of the matter. If a reasonable person would not conclude that the maker of the statement is making such a commitment, no offer is made. This question whether a statement of intent is or is not an offer most commonly arises in connection with statements made in jest or under strong emotion (such as anger or fear) and with statements made to invite or attract persons to buy or to deal.

Joking and Emotional Exclamations

A statement of intent may appear to be seriously meant and therefore may constitute an offer even though the maker of the statement is excited, angry, fearful, or joking. Such agitation or jocularity is merely a circumstance to be considered with all of the other surrounding circumstances in determining whether a reasonable person would be justified in believing that the statement is seriously meant.

Example: A few days after an old harness owned by the defendant and worth about $15 disappeared from the defendant's barn, a boy found a portion of the harness in the plaintiff's berry patch. The defendant and the plaintiff recovered that part and brought it to the plaintiff's blacksmith shop, where the defendant gave the boy a quarter and promised him a dollar if he found the remainder of the harness. At the same time, the defendant angrily exclaimed to the plaintiff and other men who had gathered around, "I'll give $100 to any man who will find out who the thief is and $100 to a lawyer for prosecuting him, and I won't get a cheap lawyer but a good one," accompanying his statement with rough language and epithets concerning the thief. Shortly afterwards, a neighbor told the plaintiff about seeing Smith, who was the village halfwit, carrying a harness on the day of the theft. The plaintiff watched Smith that night and saw him hiding the remainder of the harness. When the plaintiff told the defendant of this, they obtained a search warrant and recovered the remainder of the harness from Smith's house. The plaintiff then demanded the $100 reward and sued when the defendant refused to pay.

The plaintiff could not recover. On similar facts, the Appellate Court of Illinois said[1] that under the circumstances (swearing and boasting, the trifling

[1] *Higgins* v. *Lessig*, 49 Ill. App. 459 (1893).

amount paid and promised to the boy, great disproportion between the amount of the "reward" and the value of the harness), a reasonable man in the position of the plaintiff would not have been justified in believing that the owner seriously intended to offer a $100 reward.

Example: A man and his wife lived on the fourth floor of an apartment hotel. At a time when the husband was away but the wife was known to be in the building, a fire started. After the fire had been raging for about thirty minutes, the husband arrived on the scene in great excitement and declared, "I will give $5,000 to any person who will bring the body of my wife out of that building, dead or alive." Hearing this statement, the plaintiff entered the building at great personal risk and brought out the dead body of the wife. When the husband later refused to pay the promised reward, the plaintiff sued for $5,000.

Whether a reasonable person would be justified in believing than an offer was really intended would depend upon all of the surrounding circumstances, including the husband's manner of speaking, his seeming ability to pay such a sum (judging from his appearance and the type of residence involved), etc. In the case upon which this example is based, the jury concluded that under the circumstances, as disclosed by the evidence presented during the trial, the husband reasonably appeared to have a serious intent, and therefore an enforceable contract was formed.

INVITATIONS TO DEAL

Statements intended to invite or to attract persons to buy or to deal are made in circular letters, advertisements, catalog listings, and other announcements concerning items for sale. Again the reasonable man serves as the guide for determining whether or not such statements are offers. The statement is an offer only if, under all of the circumstances, a reasonable person would be justified in concluding that the one making the particular statement intends to be bound or committed as soon as the offeree indicates his consent and without any further bargaining or discussion. Factors important in resolving this question include the following:

1. The definiteness or indefiniteness of the language used:
    a) As to the person to whom the statement is made.
    b) As to the quantity of the commodity available.
2. Otherwise (in addition to definiteness or indefiniteness), the appropriateness of the language to indicate or express a commitment.
3. The customs of business.

Suppose that a retailer displays in his store window a radio bearing the tag, "For Sale, $95." Rather than being directed to any particular person, this statement is made to anyone who happens to look into the window. Two or more persons might simultaneously enter the store and, speaking to different clerks, each say that he will buy the radio displayed in the window. If the window display is considered to be an offer, then a contract would arise as soon as each customer agreed to buy. If the retailer's supply were limited, he could become bound by more contracts than he would be able to fill. It would not be reasonable, therefore, to say that when the retailer displayed the radio, he was committing himself to sell without any further expression of assent on his part. Unless a retailer clearly indicates that he intends to commit himself, his window display is not an offer but rather is an invitation for customers to enter his store and offer to buy. The retailer can then accept or reject such offers as he wishes. Although retailers will usually sell according to their published advertisements in order to maintain customer goodwill, a retailer does not owe potential customers any legally enforceable obligation to sell even one advertised or displayed item. Such a retailer may, however, incur a criminal liability. Although the courts have uniformly held that false advertising statutes do not apply to "come-on" advertisments, a few state statutes go further. For example, one such statute provides that a person is guilty of a misdemeanor punishable by not more than six months' imprisonment, $1,000 fine, or both, if by any means he advertises something for sale to the general public with no intent to sell at the advertised price. The statute adds that unless the price is erroneously stated (through a typographical error or some other innocent mistake), a refusal to sell at an advertised price is prima-facie evidence (that is, sufficient evidence without the necessity of more proof) of such an intent not to sell, unless the advertisement also states the limited quantity that is available for sale. Note that although this statute prohibits conduct which the legislature feels constitutes an unfair business practice, the statute does *not* create a contract where one would not otherwise exist, nor in any other way change the *civil* effect of the retailer's conduct.

Just as it is unreasonable to conclude from a window display that a seller intends to bind himself to an unlimited number of persons, so also is it unreasonable to assume that, without any further expression of assent on his part, a seller who announces goods for sale intends to bind himself to sell an unlimited quantity. It is possible for a seller to commit himself to sell whatever quantity a buyer may order, but this is so unusual that such an intent must be clearly stated.

Example: A wholesale salt dealer wrote to a quantity salt buyer: "In consequence of a break in the salt trade, we are able to offer Michigan fine salt in full carload lots of 80 to 95 barrels, delivered at your city, at 85 cents per barrel, to be shipped per the C&NW Railroad only. At this price it is a bargain. We shall be pleased to receive your orders." On receipt of this letter, the buyer promptly telegraphed to the dealer: "You may ship me 2,000 barrels of Michigan fine salt as offered in your letter." Two thousand barrels was a reasonable quantity for the buyer to order, and not in excess of what the dealer, from his knowledge of the buyer's business, might reasonably expect to be ordered. The dealer refused to ship and the buyer sued for damages for breach of contract.

Under similar facts, the Wisconsin Court held[2] that no contract was formed and that therefore the buyer could not recover. Although the word "offer" was used, the indefiniteness of quantity made it unreasonable to assume that the dealer was committing himself to sell any quantity that might be ordered, or even any quantity he might reasonably expect would be ordered. The indefiniteness of quantity also indicated that probably the same communication was sent to a number of potential buyers. The dealer's letter was a circular-type letter, inviting buyers to offer to buy; a dealer could reject any or all such offers, without any liability.

A statement concerning the price of certain described goods may be definite both as to the person to whom made and as to the quantity of goods, but nevertheless business custom may weigh against the statement being construed as an offer. A common example is a price quotation in response to an inquiry. Sellers frequently receive letters asking for their prices for certain quantities of goods. It is a common business practice for a potential buyer to send the same inquiry to several different sellers. Moreover, it is not unusual for the one who makes such an inquiry to decide not to purchase from anyone. For these reasons, a seller who answers such an inquiry is not expected to set the described goods aside or to hold them available on the slim chance that the inquirer might order. Therefore, although a seller's reply to an inquiry is definite both as to person and quantity, it is usually not reasonable to consider it an offer.

Example: On December 15, a buyer wrote to the owner of a vacant lot, saying: "If you have not sold, I of course am the logical purchaser, as your lot is worth more to me than to anyone else. I hope I shall have the pleasure of hearing from you shortly." On December 16, the owner wrote to the buyer: "If you should be interested in this lot, I would be glad to hear from you. Size of lot, 20 feet by 100 feet, price, $1,000." Two days later the buyer telegraphed to the owner: "Will accept your proposition of $1,000." However, the owner decided to sell the lot to another person and so notified the buyer on December 23. The buyer thereupon sued for a decree of specific performance to require the owner to transfer the lot to the buyer.

Under similar facts, a New York court held[3] that the buyer could not recover. Generally a mere statement of the price at which property is held for sale is not a commitment or offer to sell at that price.

Example: On April 20 a buyer wrote to a seller: "Please advise us the lowest price you can make us on our order for ten carloads of Mason green

[2] *Moulton* v. *Kershaw,* 59 Wis. 316, 18 N.W. 172 (1884).
[3] *Patrick* v. *Kleine,* 215 N.Y.S. 305 (1926).

jars complete with caps, packed one dozen in a case, either delivered here or f.o.b. cars your place as you prefer.   State terms and cash discount." On April 23, the seller wrote to the buyer: "Replying to your letter of April 20, we quote you Mason fruit jars complete in one-dozen boxes, f.o.b. cars at our plant, as follows: pints $4.50, quarts $5, half-gallons $6.50, per gross, for immediate acceptance and shipment not later than May 15; sixty days credit or two percent off for cash in ten days.   Please note that we make all quotations and contracts subject to the contingencies of agencies or transportation, delays or accidents beyond our control."   On April 24, the buyer wired the seller: "Your letter 23d received.   Enter order ten carloads as per your quotation.   Letter specifying sizes follows."   The seller wired the following reply on the same day: "Impossible to book your order.   Output all sold."   When the seller refused to deliver the ordered jars, the buyer sued for damages for breach of contract.

The Kentucky Court of Appeals concluded[4] that seller's reply was an offer and that the buyer's order was an acceptance, thus forming a contract. This is a borderline case; another court could easily have decided just the opposite, and said that the seller's reply was not an offer.

Argument for the Buyer: By using the expression "for immediate acceptance" the seller showed an intent to be bound upon the buyer's immediate or prompt acceptance.   Therefore since person and quantity were sufficiently definite, the seller's reply constituted an offer.   Although quantities for various sizes were not fixed, the seller's reply could be construed as an offer to sell the stated quantity in whatever assortment of the three specified sizes the buyer might later select.

Argument for the Seller: The word "quote" is usually not considered as expressing a commitment to sell.   Likewise a reply to a price inquiry is usually not construed as an offer.   Although the total quantity was definite, the quantity of each size to be delivered was indefinite.   The phrase "for immediate acceptance" was merely a form expression meaning that the stated price was a current price quotation.   The seller did not offer to sell; rather, the buyer's order was an offer to buy.   The buyer's offer was rejected and no contract was formed.

When a businessman is involved in a legal dispute, he incurs expenses and loses goodwill even if he wins the lawsuit.   Certainly he should do all he reasonably can to prevent disputes from arising.   In connection with his invitations to deal (that is, advertisments, circular letters, catalog listings, price quotations, and the like) a businessman can minimize the possibility of disputes by including a provision clearly showing that he is not making an offer.   Such expressions as the following are commonly used: "This is not an offer," "All quotations are subject to prior sale," "All prices are subject to change without notice."

[4] *Fairmount Glass Works* v. *Grunden-Martin Woodenware Co.,* 106 Ky. 659, 51 S.W. 196 (1899).

ACCEPTANCES

An offer can be called a conditional commitment—that is, a commitment which is conditioned or dependent upon the offeree's expressing his acquiescence by accepting in the manner requested by the offer. If the offer requests an act in exchange for the offered promise, the offer is accepted and a contract is formed when the offeree performs the requested act. Since the contract thus formed does not require the offeree to do anything further, it is termed a unilateral (one-sided) contract; it consists of a promise on one side only (the promise of the offeror), for which the offeree, as his acceptance, performs the requested act.

Example: Bernard Barton writes to a seller: "Please ship to me the following goods [describing them] for which I will pay you $500 one month after delivery. (signed) Bernard Barton."

When the seller promptly ships the requested goods, a unilateral agreement is formed. The agreement consists of the promise of the buyer to pay $500 for the goods which the seller, in accepting the offer, has shipped.

If an offer requests a promise from the offeree in exchange for the promise offered by the offeror, the offeree's making the requested promise forms a bilateral contract—so called because the contract consists of promises on both sides.

Example: Barton writes to a seller: "Please enter my order for the following goods [describing them] to be shipped to me two months from this date, for which I will pay you $500 one month after delivery. (signed) Bernard Barton."

When the seller promptly writes to the buyer promising to ship the ordered goods, a contract is formed. The contract consists of promises by both parties, the promise of the seller to ship and that of the buyer to pay.

It is not unusual that after one party makes a proposal, the other party replies suggesting certain changes, to which the first party suggests further changes, and so on until they finally reach an agreement. In such a case there are a series of offers, with each party in turn being an offeror until one party finally expresses satisfaction with and thus accepts the other party's latest proposal. Negotiating back and forth in this way while bargaining over a myriad of details can become quite involved. The terms of the offer that are finally accepted may be spread over several communications, so that all of them must be read together to determine exactly what the parties have agreed to. Sometimes the parties expect that after they finally reach an agreement a single contract form will be prepared and signed by both parties. This is usually intended to provide convenient evidence of the agreement; unless it is clear that the parties do not intend to be bound until this contract form is prepared and signed, they form a binding contract as soon as they reach an agreement, even before preparation and signing of the formal contract.

Example: Desiring to build a warehouse adjacent to his factory, a manufacturer advertised for bids for construction according to certain written plans and specifications. Several builders submitted written bids and were present when the bids were opened. When he determined which bidder had submitted the lowest bid, the manufacturer said to that builder that the contract was his, asked him to start work at once, and instructed him to have the formal contract written, sign it, and send it to the manufacturer for signature. The builder accordingly began construction, including subletting a portion of the work, and had a contract drawn embodying the plans and specifications and the agreed price. The builder signed the contract but the manufacturer refused to sign, saying that he had changed his mind and that the builder should proceed no further with the work. The builder sued for damages for breach of contract. Since the manufacturer had not signed the contract form, he argued that an enforceable contract had not yet been formed between the parties, and that his only liability was on a quasi-contract theory for expense incurred by the builder at the manufacturer's request prior to the stop-work order.

There was an enforceable contract between the parties. If all essential terms are agreed upon and all that remains is to incorporate the agreement into a formal writing, an enforceable contract is formed when the parties first reach their agreement, unless they also manifest an intent that they not be bound until the formal writing is signed.

For an offeree's response to an offer to constitute a binding acceptance, his response must comply with certain requirements which can be summarized as follows:

1. The offeree must have knowledge of the offer.

2. The offeree's response must manifest unequivocal agreement with the offer.

3. The offeree's response must become effective while the offer is still open.

4. The offeree's response must comply with the terms of the offer.

First Requirement: Knowledge of Offer

Obviously a person cannot accept an offeror's proposition unless he knows of the offer at the time of his alleged acceptance. Furthermore, no offer exists in respect to a particular offeree (and thus he has no power to accept and form a contract) unless and until the offer is communicated to him by the offeror or by the offeror's authorized agent.

Example: An owner who lost a wallet containing considerable money, cards, and valuable papers advertised a $100 reward for its return. The person who found the wallet ascertained the owner's name and address from the cards and returned the wallet and contents to the owner. The owner said, "That's fine. I guess you're entitled to the reward I advertised." The finder replied, "Oh, was there a reward? I didn't see the ad." The owner then refused to pay and the finder sued.

The finder could not recover. The finder could not accept an offer and become a party to an agreement if he was ignorant of the offer. Therefore no contract was formed and the owner would have no obligation to pay the advertised reward to the finder.

SECOND REQUIREMENT: UNEQUIVOCAL AGREEMENT

In order to form a contract, an offeree's acceptance must indicate that he clearly and definitely agrees to the offer. If the offeror intends a bilateral contract, the offeree's acceptance must manifest a commitment sufficient to bind the offeree himself to an enforceable obligation. In other words, the acceptance must be clear and definite enough to justify a reasonable person in concluding that the offeree is in full agreement with the offer, and is committing himself as requested in the offer, without reservation and without any intent to delay final commitment until some further expression of assent by the offeree. Thus a reply, "We have received your order and it will receive our prompt and careful attention," has been held not to be an acceptance. The offeree is really only saying, "We will think about it," and not necessarily saying, "We will ship the ordered goods."

Example: On May 4, B sent to S a written order for 8 carloads of lumber. The order specified grade, size, price, and delivery in stated installments beginning June 15. By letter of May 9, S acknowledged receipt of the order but instead of accepting it, wrote: "This being our first business with you, it is only proper for us to have an understanding as to terms." S then stated his terms for time and manner of payment, and listed certain contingencies (such as rail strike and the like) which would excuse S from any contract obligation to deliver. S concluded his letter by writing: "If the above conditions are satisfactory, we will be glad to begin shipment as requested in your order. Please let us hear from you on the subject." On May 15, B wrote to S: "We have for acknowledgment your letter of May 9 regarding our order for 8 cars to be delivered as specified in our order, beginning June 15, all of which is in order." On May 24, S wrote to B: "We have previously written you on the subject of terms and manner in which we wish the stock to be paid for and not hearing from you in reply to our letter, we take for granted that you do not wish the material and are therefore canceling your order." B in turn wrote to S: "Replying to your letter of the 24th, we refer to our letter of the 15th replying to yours of May 9, in which

we advise that the terms, etc., as given in your letter were all in order."
When S refused to ship, having canceled the order and sold the goods elsewhere, B sued S for damages for breach of contract.

On somewhat similar facts, the Pennsylvania Superior Court held[5] that
no contract was formed between the parties, and that therefore B could not
recover. S made a counteroffer in stating the terms under which he was
willing to contract. The expression B used in referring to S's counteroffer,
"all of which is in order," was not a clear-cut expression of acceptance
sufficient to bind S to his proposal.

One judge dissented, stating that in his opinion B's May 15 letter was a
sufficient agreement to S's proposed terms.

Whichever view is taken of B's reply, it certainly violates a cardinal
principle of good letter writing—that a business letter should state clearly,
simply, and exactly the meaning and intent of the writer.

THIRD REQUIREMENT: EXISTENT OFFER

Certainly no agreement can arise through an offer and an acceptance
if the offer has ended or terminated before the offeree tries to accept it.
An offer will terminate or come to an end in any of a variety of ways,
the most common of which are: (1) lapse of time, (2) revocation by the
offeror, (3) rejection by the offeree, and (4) death or insanity of either
party before acceptance.

Termination by Lapse of Time

It is quite unreasonable to assume that an offeror intends the conditional commitment he makes in his offer to bind him for an extended
period. Therefore the law concludes that an offer will end upon the
expiration of the time specified in the offer, or if no time is specified,
upon the expiration of a reasonable time.

Expressly Stated Duration. Sometimes the duration of an offer is
indicated by a request for a reply by "return mail." This expression
should be given a reasonable interpretation. It does not necessarily
mean the very next mail which leaves after the offeree receives the
offer. In a large city with mails leaving frequently it might be impossible
for an offeree to get a reply on the very next mail train. Usually the
term "return mail" means that the reply should be on its way the same
day that the offer is received; if there is no mail shipment which the
offeree can reasonably reach that day, then the reply is sufficiently prompt
if it is in the first reasonably available mail shipment the following day.

If an offeror requests a reply within a specified number of days, a
question will sometimes arise as to when the specified period should
begin. Suppose that a seller offers to sell a described plot of land for a

[5] *Coastwise Lumber & Supply Co. v. Stitzinger*, 81 Pa. Super. 554 (1923).

stated price, and in his offering letter to the buyer says, "You have ten days in which to accept." Under the standard "reasonable man" test, the offeror should be bound by what a reasonable man in the position of the offeree would assume is the offeror's intent, regardless of what the offeror actually means. Under this approach there are three possible theories as to when the ten-day period begins to run:

1. Since the offeror has no way of knowing exactly when the offeree receives the offering letter, it is reasonable to assume (unless clearly stated otherwise) that the offeror intends for the ten-day period to start from the date of his offering letter.

2. Since no offer is actually in existence until it has been communicated to the offeree, the ten days begins to run from the date upon which the offeree receives the offering letter.

3. The third theory is a modification of the second. If the offeree knows or has reason to know of some unusual delay in the delivery of the offering letter, the ten-day period should be counted from the time when the offeree would ordinarily have received the offering letter.

Surprisingly few cases have involved this point. While it is arguable that the first theory is the most reasonable, one of the few courts faced with the question (the West Virginia Supreme Court) adopted[6] the second theory, even though in the case before the court, an error of the postal authorities delayed delivery of the offering letter for three days beyond normal delivery time. If an offeror wishes to specify a duration for his offer, he should avoid ambiguity by indicating a certain date by which the offeree must accept. For example, instead of saying, "You have ten days in which to accept," the offeror should say, "This offer is subject to your acceptance by [a specified date]," or "This offer is subject to my receipt of your acceptance by [specified date]."

Implied Duration. If an offeror fails to specify a time period for his offer, the offer will be considered as lapsing after the expiration of a reasonable time. The duration of this "reasonable time" will depend upon the circumstances of each case, with the following factors being particularly important:

1. The time needed to do whatever is indicated as an acceptance. If an offer calls for an act as acceptance, the expected duration of the offer will at least be long enough for performance of that act.

2. The method used to communicate the offer. Sending an offer by telegraph indicates urgency; if an offering telegram is received near the close of business hours, an attempt to accept early the following day will usually be too late. Likewise, if an offer is made orally during a conversation, it will not extend beyond that immediate conversation unless the offeror expressly agrees to a longer time.

[6] *Caldwell* v. *Cline*, 109 W. Va. 553, 156 S.E. 55, 72 A.L.R. 1211 (1930).

3. The stability in value of the subject matter involved. If an offer concerns a commodity whose value fluctuates rapidly on the market, the duration of the offer will be much shorter than for an offer concerning an item of stabilized value.

4. The customs of the particular business involved.

Termination by Revocation

The word *revocation* is applied to the termination of an offer by the offeror's withdrawing it. While a revocation is usually accomplished by a direct notice to the offeree, an indirect revocation is possible. Suppose that after offering to sell certain land to an offeree, the offeror sells and transfers the same land to someone else. The offeror's disposal of the offered property does not automatically terminate the offer. If the offeree accepts before he learns of the sale, the offeror will be bound by a contract, and since he can no longer perform the contract, he will be liable for damages for breach of contract. However, if before the offeree tries to accept he learns of the offeror's disposal of the land, the offeree's knowledge of the offeror's change of mind would serve to terminate the offer. Obviously, it is risky for an offeror to rely on the uncertainty of an indirect revocation to terminate his offer.

Time of Revocation. Usually a revocation notice becomes effective either when it is received by the offeree, or when it is received at the place to which the original offer was sent, whichever occurs first. If an offeree denies ever receiving a revocation, it may be difficult (but not impossible if the jury believes the offeror's testimony) for the offeror to prove that he revoked the offer if all he has is his own testimony, plus the presumption that if a letter is mailed with correct address and postage it is usually delivered. In matters of any importance it would be wise for the offeror to revoke by a means which would be easier to prove, such as telegraph or certified mail.

Right to Revoke—In General. By its very nature a contract is considered a two-sided proposition. This is not inconsistent with the idea of unilateral contracts. Although a unilateral contract consists of a promise on one side only, it is given in exchange for the other party's performance of an act. The promise is legally enforceable because the promisee has already done something or given something which is binding upon him. On the other hand, if nothing is done or given in exchange for a promise, the promise is not legally enforceable, unless some other factor is present which makes it desirable policy for society to enforce the promise. This legal principle—that usually both parties must in some way be bound or obligated or no contract exists—is customarily expressed in terms of *consideration* and *equivalents of consideration,* which are further discussed in the next chapter.

While by definition an offer is an expression of a binding commitment, it is a conditional commitment. The offeror is not bound to anything until the offeree agrees and binds himself by accepting the offer. Since an offeror is not bound before acceptance, it logically follows that the offeror can withdraw his offer at any time before the offeree accepts it. Sometimes, however, in addition to making an offer, an offeror also agrees or promises that he will not withdraw the offer for a certain period of time. Following the reasoning that an offerer is not bound until the offeree binds himself in some way, the common law has formulated the generally accepted rule that despite an offeror's promise to hold his offer open, he can nevertheless withdraw the offer anytime before it is accepted. If on the other hand the offeree binds himself in some way, for example by paying to hold the offer open, then the offeror is also bound and cannot terminate his offer. This type of transaction is usually called an *option agreement.*

Example: On June 3 a buyer received from a seller a letter dated June 1 stating: "I hereby offer to sell you the following land [describing it] for $20,000 and agree that this offer will remain open until June 30. To be effective your acceptance must reach me by June 30." On June 22 the buyer received from the seller a letter dated June 20, stating, "I hereby withdraw my offer of June 1." On June 27 the seller received from the buyer a letter dated June 25, stating, "You agreed that your June 1 offer would remain open and I hereby accept it."

The offeror could terminate his offer anytime before acceptance. Since the offer was revoked, the attempted acceptance would not form a contract.

Example: On June 3, after preliminary negotiations, a seller signed and gave to a buyer a letter dated June 1, stating: "In consideration of your payment to me of $1, receipt of which I hereby acknowledge, I offer to sell you the following land [describing it] for $20,000 and agree that this offer will remain open until June 30. To be effective your acceptance must reach me by June 30." Assume that revoking and accepting letters were written and received just as in the preceding example.

A contract would be formed on June 27 when the seller received the buyer's accepting letter. In this type of offer or option the agreed money is paid for the offeror's holding the offer open for the time stated and makes the offer irrevocable for that period. (The money paid and received for an option is not considered as a part payment of the purchase price, unless the parties expressly so agree; therefore, if the offeree decides not to accept he is not entitled to return of the money which he paid for the option.)

Sometimes an offeree will sustain a monetary loss if an offeror is permitted to renege on his promise to keep his offer open. For example, in order to decide whether or not to accept, an offeree may have to make some preliminary surveys or research, and he may be willing to undertake this expense only because of the offeror's assurance that the offer will remain open. Or in reliance on an offer, an offeree may make a further contractual commitment to some third person. While an offeree can make an offer irrevocable by entering into an option agreement with the offeror, this is not always convenient or even practical. A number of years ago, therefore, some businessmen began to think and speak of certain offers as being "firm" and irrevocable. Following the lead of the business world in recognizing a need for irrevocable offers other than options, the New York legislature adopted a "firm offer" statute in 1941, and the Uniform Commercial Code contains a similar provision. Writing about the Code provision, Professor Corbin has said:

> This section recognizes a growing custom among merchants in both Britain and America, to differentiate between two kinds of offers. Knowing that offers are generally revocable by notice, at the will of the offeror, there is a felt need for a type of offer on which the offeree can rely, for a reasonable time or for a definitely stated time. More and more frequently, offerors are making what they describe as a "firm offer," understanding by that term that the offer so described shall be irrevocable for a limited time. Sometimes the offer is made in this form at the special request of the offeree, and sometimes by the offeror's own motion in order to make it more attractive to the offeree and to induce his serious consideration. Unless the law gives effect to the intention of the parties in these cases, an offer represented to be "firm" and "irrevocable" becomes a trap to the offeree and a special advantage to those offerors who are willing to be guilty of bad faith.
>
> It is only three quarters of a century since a very learned author could write that "an irrevocable offer is a legal impossibility." No doubt, the statement was incorrect when made; but theory and practice alike have grown continually more opposed to it.[7]

The Code provision states:[8]

> An offer by a merchant to buy or sell goods in a signed writing which by its terms gives assurance that it will be held open is not

---

[7] 59 *Yale L.J.* 821 (1950).

[8] U.C.C. Sec. 2-205. A basic tenet of the Code is that, for certain situations, greater business competency and a higher standard of reliability are expected from merchants than from nonmerchants. Accordingly, although Article 2 of the Code applies to *all* sales-of-goods transactions whether the parties are merchants or not, some special rules are expressly stated as applying only to merchants. Some of these special rules (like the one involving firm offers) apply to merchants in general— meaning any person, partnership, or corporation engaged in business to such an extent as to be presumed to be familiar with common, nonspecialized business practices— while a few of the special rules are expressly limited to merchants who are dealers in goods of the kind involved in the transaction in question.

revocable, for lack of consideration,[9] during the time stated or if no time is stated for a reasonable time, but in no event may such period of irrevocability exceed three months. . . .

In summarizing the legal pattern which has developed in regard to the right to revoke offers, it will be helpful to distinguish between bilateral and unilateral contract offers and then to consider offers for auction sales separately.

Revocability of Offers for Bilateral Contracts. Initially a distinction must be made between 1) offers which say nothing as to their duration, and 2) offers which expressly state that they are irrevocable or firm, or which otherwise indicate that they will be held open. Clearly, offers of the first type can be revoked at any time before acceptance. On the other hand, the revocability of offers of the second type depends on additional facts, which can be summarized as follows:

1. If the offer involves something other than the sale of goods, it can be withdrawn at any time before acceptance, even though the offeror has assured the offeree that the offer will remain open for a longer period (unless the promise to keep the offer open is paid for or supported by a recognized equivalent of payment as explained in Chapter 5).

2. If the offer involves the sale or purchase of goods, then

a) If the offer is made by a nonmerchant, or is made by a merchant whose assurance to keep the offer open is oral, the offeror's right to revoke is the same as for an offer which does not involve the sale of goods.

b) If the offer is made by a merchant who in a signed writing assures that the offer will remain open, the offer is irrevocable for the duration stated (but not exceeding three months), even though the offeree pays nothing to hold the offer open. Should the specified duration exceed three months, the offer is irrevocable for only three months (unless the offeree makes a payment or its equivalent to hold the offer open). If the merchant's written assurance that the offer will remain open specifies no time period but merely states that the offer is irrevocable or firm, the offer will be irrevocable for a reasonable time—which of course would never exceed three months and usually would be considerably shorter than that.

Example: On June 3 a buyer received a letter dated June 1, written by a seller who was a businessman, stating: "I hereby make a firm offer to sell you the following goods [describing them] for $1,000. To be effective your acceptance must reach me by June 30." On June 22 the buyer received

[9] The term "consideration" refers to the concept, explained in Chapter 5, that a promise is not legally enforceable unless something is given in exchange for the promise or unless there is some other good reason for enforcing the promise.

from the seller a letter dated June 20, stating, "I hereby withdraw my offer of June 1." On June 27 the seller received from the buyer a letter dated June 25, stating, "You agreed that your June 1 offer would remain open and I hereby accept it."

There would be a contract between the parties.

Example: On June 3 a buyer received a letter dated June 1, written by a seller who was a businessman, stating: "I hereby offer to sell you the following goods (describing them) for $1,000 and agree that this offer will remain open for six months from the date of this letter. To be effective your acceptance must reach me by December 1 of this year."

Since no payment or equivalent of payment was made to hold the offer open, the offer would be an irrevocable firm offer for only three months and, until accepted, could be revoked any time after expiration of the three-month period.

Revocability of Offers for Unilateral Contracts.

An offer for a unilateral contract is one which is to be accepted by the offeree's performing a certain act. If such an offer is a firm offer under the Uniform Commercial Code, it is irrevocable. As to offers which do not come under the Code's firm offer theory, a very vexing problem is presented when the offeree, intending to accept, begins performance of the requested act, and then before completion of the offeree's performance, the offeror gives notice revoking his offer. To hold that there is no contract would deprive the offeree of compensation for what he has already done; on the other hand to argue that there is a contract suggests that the offeror should be bound before he receives what he requested as an acceptance.

It is certainly sound policy for the law to avoid this vexing dilemma, if possible. Therefore if an offer does not clearly indicate that it can be accepted only by performance of a certain act, the courts will usually interpret it as acceptable either by the offeree's performance of the act or by his promise to perform the act. The Uniform Commercial Code expressly adopts this view for sales-of-goods offers.[10]

If the offer is not ambiguous, if it clearly specifies that it can be accepted only by performance of a specified act, many courts use some variation of the irrevocable offer concept to prevent the unfairness which would result from a revocation after partial performance. Basically, these courts hold that unless an offer expressly states otherwise, the act of the offeree in promptly beginning performance, with reasonable notice thereof to the offeror, has the effect of making the offer irrevocable for the time reasonably necessary for completion of the performance. In applying this theory, the courts will distinguish between preparation to begin performance and the actual commencement of performance; thus, if an offer specifies the payment of a stated sum of money as the ac-

[10] U.C.C. Sec. 2-206.

ceptance, the offeree's assembling the necessary currency, and even starting toward the offeror's place of business with the money, would usually be classed as preparatory only, rather than commencement of performance.

Revocability in Auction Sales. As the law in regard to auction sales gradually evolved from early common-law days, two rules emerged as expressions of what society considered to be sound policy.

The first auction rule is that neither an announcement (or advertisement) that certain property will be sold at auction to the highest bidder, nor putting the property up for auction and receiving bids, should be construed as an offer on the part of the seller or auctioneer. This rule is based on the general policy conclusion that although there is definiteness both as to the property to be auctioned and also as to the manner for determining the person to whom the property will be sold (namely the highest bidder), there nevertheless appears little reason for treating either the advance announcement or the commencement of the auction as any different from a retailer's advertisement or window display. Therefore when the auctioneer asks, "What am I bid?" he is not offering to sell to the highest bidder but rather is inviting offers. A bid is an offer to buy. The first time that an offer appears in the transaction is when a bid is made, and no binding contract is formed until the auctioneer announces that he accepts a particular bid, either by the fall of his hammer, by saying "sold," or by other customary manner.

The second auction rule is that if the auctioneer expressly states that the auction is "without reserve" (meaning that the auctioneer relinquishes both the right to set a certain minimum price and also the right to withdraw an item from the sale after bidding begins) the auctioneer binds himself to sell to the highest bidder. The "without reserve" term therefore is a firm or irrevocable commitment to sell to the highest bidder. Under the generally accepted common-law theory, a without-reserve auction is just like a with-reserve auction except that the auctioneer has a binding obligation to accept the highest bid. Thus each bid is an offer and no contract is formed until, upon completion of the bidding, the auctioneer accepts the highest bid. Some legal scholars have suggested a different theory, arguing that a without-reserve auction should be considered as involving a series of contracts successively formed and canceled. Under this proposed theory, putting goods up for sale in a without-reserve auction would be construed as an irrevocable, firm offer, and a bid would be an acceptance, thus forming a contract— conditioned, however, on no higher bid being made. Each time a higher bid would be made the contract with the previous bidder would be automatically canceled and a new contract would be formed with the new bidder. Although an earlier, tentative version of the Uniform Commercial Code adopted this suggested theory, the common-law theory won out in the final draft of the Code, in the absence of any sound policy reason for making the change or for having the rule which applies to goods different from the common-law rule which still applies to land-auction sales.

Thus the Uniform Commercial Code provides:

> A sale by auction is complete when the auctioneer so announces by the fall of the hammer or in other customary manner. . . .
>
> Such a sale is with reserve unless the goods are in explicit terms put up without reserve. In an auction with reserve the auctioneer may withdraw the goods at any time until he announces completion of the sale. In an auction without reserve, after the auctioneer calls for bids on an article . . . that article . . . cannot be withdrawn unless no bid is made within a reasonable time. In either case a bidder may retract his bid until the auctioneer's announcement of completion of the sale, but a bidder's retraction does not revive any previous bid.
>
> If the auctioneer knowingly receives a bid on the seller's behalf or the seller makes or procures such a bid, and notice has not been given that liberty for such bidding is reserved, the buyer may at his option avoid the sale or take the goods at the price of the last good faith bid prior to the completion of the sale. This subsection shall not apply to any bid at a forced sale.[11]

Notice that a seller's secretly having someone bid an item up is considered dishonest and the usual common-law remedies are restated in the Code.

Example: A seller wished to have an old building removed from his land to make way for a new structure. The seller advertised that the old building would be sold at public auction, the successful bidder to remove the building within a stated time. On the day of the auction sale, bidding progressed until the amount of $675 was bid by A. B then bid $680. The auctioneer told B that $5 was too small an increase for his bid to be considered. When B failed to make a higher bid, the auctioneer announced that the building was sold to A for $675. B protested and tendered $680 to the seller. The seller refused the tender and made out a written contract of sale to A for $675. B then sued the seller for damages for breach of contract.

Since the auction was not announced as being "without reserve," the seller (through the auctioneer as his agent) was free to reject B's bid. Thus no contract was formed with B, and B was not entitled to recover.

Rejection

Different from a revocation (which is a withdrawal of an offer by the offeror), a *rejection* is a refusal or turning down of an offer by the offeree. If the offeree reasonably leads the offeror to understand or

[11] U.C.C. Sec. 2-328.

assume that the offeree does not intend to accept and is no longer considering the offer, the offer is terminated, and the offeree cannot afterwards change his mind and accept the offer. Suppose that upon receiving an offer the offeree promptly replied that he was not interested in buying. If the offeror should afterwards change his mind about selling, he would not consider it necessary to give notice of revocation to the offeree, who had already said that he was not interested. It would not be fair, therefore, to consider an offer still open after the offeree rejects it, even though time remains during which the offer would still be open had it not been rejected.

Example: Assume that each letter in this example was delivered the day after it was written. On June 1 a seller wrote to a buyer: "I hereby offer to sell you my land [describing it] for $20,000. You have thirty days from the date hereof to accept. To be effective your acceptance must reach me by June 30."

1. Assume that on June 5 the buyer wrote to the seller, "I do not want to buy your land for $20,000." To this the seller made no reply and on June 10 the buyer wrote again to the seller, saying, "I have changed my mind and will buy your land for $20,000 as offered in your letter of June 1." The seller however had changed his mind and refused to sell.

There would be no contract. When the buyer rejected the offer, the seller was reasonably justified in concluding that the buyer was no longer interested. The rejection terminated the offer.

2. Assume that on June 5 the buyer wrote to the seller, "In reply to your letter of June 1, I'll give you $17,000 for your land." To this the seller made no reply and on June 10 the buyer wrote again to the seller, saying, "I have changed my mind and will buy your land for $20,000 as offered in your letter of June 1." The seller refused to sell.

There would be no contract. From the buyer's counteroffer of June 5, the seller would be reasonably justified in assuming that the buyer was not interested in buying for $20,000. The counteroffer therefore implied a rejection and terminated the original offer.

3. Assume that on June 5 the buyer wrote to the seller, "In regard to your June 1 letter, will you take $17,000 for your land?" On June 6, the seller replied by letter, "In reply to your June 5 letter, I will not sell for $17,000." On June 10 the buyer wrote again to the seller, "I will buy your land for $20,000 as offered in your letter of June 1." The seller however refused to sell.

There would be a contract. The buyer's June 5 letter was not a counteroffer; the buyer was inquiring about possible better terms but was not offering to buy for $17,000. Since the buyer did not clearly indicate that he was no longer interested in the seller's June 1 offer, the offer was still open when the buyer accepted with his June 10 letter.

4. Assume that on June 5 the buyer wrote to the seller, "In regard to your June 1 offer, I'll think about it but if you wish to close the deal im-

mediately, I'll give you $17,000 for your land." On June 6 the seller replied by letter, "In reply to your June 5 letter, I will not sell for $17,000." On June 10 the buyer wrote again to the seller, "I will buy your land for $20,000 as offered in your letter of June 1." The seller refused to sell.

There would be a contract. Although the buyer made a counteroffer, he indicated that he was still considering the seller's original offer. Therefore the seller's June 1 offer was still open when the buyer accepted with his June 10 letter.

Termination by Death

A person's death does not automatically cancel all of his existing contracts; only those contracts that require his personal performance are affected. For example, suppose that B engages A to perform services which depend upon A's special abilities or qualifications. Since B cannot without his consent be required to accept performance by some person other than A, such a contract would be classified as requiring personal performance by A. In other words, the continuation of A's ability to perform would be a necessary condition for enforcement of the contract. Should A die, the contract would be considered as automatically canceled.

Most contracts do not require personal performance. Thus, in a contract for the sale of either land or goods, it is usually immaterial who actually makes delivery, so long as the buyer obtains the land or the goods described in the contract. Likewise, to whom the property is delivered is immaterial so long as the seller receives the agreed price. In such an impersonal contract, death of one of the parties or of both parties will have no effect on the continued enforceability of the contract. When a party to a contract dies, a court will appoint a personal representative (an administrator or executor) for the decedent's estate. The administrator or executor takes over the decedent's property in order to collect obligations owed to the decedent and to complete the decedent's outstanding commitments.

Even though the death of either party or of both parties *after* the formation of an impersonal contract will have no effect on the life of the contract, sometimes the death of a party *before* an offer has been accepted will automatically terminate the offer and prevent a contract from being formed. Usually the effect that death will have on an unaccepted offer depends upon whether the offer is revocable or irrevocable. If an offer is irrevocable (either because contained in an option agreement or made as a firm offer), it is considered as vesting in the offeree a legally enforceable right to form a contract by accepting within the irrevocable period. This right is something of value which the offeree owns, in much the same way as he owns his car or his house. It cannot be taken away from him without his consent, and like most of his other impersonal rights, it can be transferred by him to someone else, who thereby obtains a right to accept the offer and form a contract with the offeror. Since the offeree's right to accept is not personal to the offeree, and cannot be affected by any act of the offeror, the offer is not affected by the death of either the offeror or the offeree. Therefore (assuming, of course, that the offer contemplates an impersonal contract) if an offeree has an irrevocable right to accept, he can still accept and form a contract after the offeror dies. Likewise, if the offeree dies, his personal representative can accept and form a contract binding upon the offeror (or upon the offeror's estate if the offeror is also dead).

On the other hand, if an offer is revocable so that it can be taken away from the offeree at any time without his consent, he cannot be considered as having an ownership interest in the offer. Without an ownership interest there is nothing which the offeree can transfer or which will remain after his death. All that the offeree has is a power to form a contract by accepting while the offer is still open. The exercise of this power is dependent upon the offeror's continuing intent to form a contract, an intent which he manifests by refraining from withdrawing the offer. After an offeror dies he cannot be said to continue to manifest any intent. Therefore most courts hold that if an offer is revocable, the death of either the offeror or the offeree will automatically and immediately terminate the offer so that it cannot afterwards be accepted.

Termination by Insanity

An offeror or offeree's becoming mentally incompetent to handle his own affairs, has the same effect on an outstanding offer as the incompetent party's death would have.

Fourth Requirement: Compliance with Offer

An offer states the terms and conditions upon which the offeror is willing to contract. Since different terms cannot be imposed upon him without his consent, an enforceable contract can be made only on the offeror's terms and conditions.

Offers for Unilateral Contracts

If an offeror proposes a unilateral contract (that is, if what the offeror requests as an acceptance is the actual performance of an act), the offer is not accepted by the offeree's promising to perform the requested act.

Example: A creditor held a mortgage on a debtor's land. On April 4 the balance remaining unpaid was $5,450, payable in installments of $250 every three months. On April 4 in reply to an inquiry from the debtor, the creditor wrote: "I hereby agree to accept cash for the mortgage and will allow you a discount of $780 providing said mortgage is paid on or before May 31 of this year." In the latter part of May the debtor went to the creditor's house and knocked on the door. Without opening the door the creditor asked who was there. The debtor identified himself and said, "I have come to pay off the mortgage." The creditor replied that he had sold the mortgage. At the debtor's insistence, the creditor partly opened the door. The debtor then exhibited the cash he had brought ($5,450 less $780) and said that he wanted to pay off the mortgage according to their agreement. The creditor repeated that he had disposed of the mortgage to another investor. The new mortgage holder refused to allow a discount. Since the debtor had already contracted with a buyer to sell the land free from the mortgage, the debtor had to pay the full amount of the mortgage to the new mortgage holder, and consequently sued the creditor for $780 as damages for breach of contract.

The New York Court of Appeals held[12] that the owner could not recover. As the acceptance of his proposal the creditor requested that the money be "paid on or before May 31." Had the debtor written to the creditor promising to pay, the promise would not have constituted an acceptance. The word "paid" means either actual payment (which involves the creditor taking the money) or at least a presentation or tender of the money for the creditor to take it. Until the door opened, the debtor was unable to present the money to the creditor. Without a presentation of the money, the debtor's statement that he had come to pay was not a tender of payment. Before the debtor made a tender of money, the creditor said that he no longer owned the mortgage, thus giving notice sufficient to withdraw his offer. Therefore since the offer was revoked before it was accepted, there was no contract.

Deviation from Requested Act. Sometimes the act performed by an offeree in apparent acceptance of an offer fails to comply exactly with what the offeror has requested. The common law has adopted the policy view that usually no contract rights or obligations can arise except on the offeror's exact terms, that any deviation in the offeree's performance from what the offeror requests will prevent a contract from being formed.

Example: A publisher advertised a contest in which he offered a prize of $1,000 to the person submitting a list containing the greatest number of words which could be made from the letters in the word "determination." Among the published rules for the contest was the following: "Do not use obsolete or foreign words, abbreviations, contractions, reformed spelling, prefixes and suffixes, or proper nouns or adjectives." The two contestants submitting the largest number of words were A and B. A submitted a list of 3,938 words, B 1,428 words. Of A's words 2,481 violated the above quoted rule, leaving 1,457 correct words. The publisher awarded the prize to B. A sued the publisher, contending that since he submitted the largest number of correct words he was entitled to the prize.

[12] *Petterson v. Pattberg*, 248 N.Y. 86, 161 N.E. 428 (1928).

In a case presenting substantially these facts, the Iowa court held[13] that since the publisher's offer specified certain terms and conditions, a contestant's entry could not be an acceptance if it failed to comply with the stated conditions.

When this fundamentally sound common-law rule is applied to modern commercial transactions, the results are sometimes unfair. Suppose that in response to a buyer's order for certain first-quality goods, a seller shipped the correct quantity of what appeared to be first-quality goods; however, in due course the buyer discovered the goods to be of second quality rather than of first quality. If the buyer sued the seller for breach of contract, the seller could point out that since the only communications between the parties consisted of the buyer's order and the seller's shipment, the only acceptance could be the seller's act of shipping. From this the seller could argue that if the goods which were shipped were actually not first quality, then under the common-law rule the seller never accepted the buyer's order, and no contract was ever formed between the parties. On the other hand, the buyer could argue that the seller manifested an intent to accept the offer, when he made a shipment without advising the buyer that the shipment differed from the order; that in doing so the seller reasonably led the buyer to believe that a contract was formed; and that therefore it would be unfair to permit the seller to deny the existence of a contract. Under circumstances such as these, it seems fair and reasonable to decide that a contract exists and to hold the seller liable for breach of contract. The task of the law is to formulate a practical and workable rule to reach this desired conclusion, without undermining, unduly weakening, or confusing the whole structure of admittedly sound and desirable contract rules.

To resolve such situations, the authors of the Uniform Commercial Code have formulated the following rule, which (with the economy of words characteristic of the Code) is combined with the rule relating to offers which are ambiguous as to the method for accepting:

> Unless otherwise unambiguously indicated by the language or circumstances . . . an order or other offer to buy goods for prompt or current shipment shall be construed as inviting acceptance either by a prompt promise to ship or by the prompt or current shipment of conforming or non-conforming goods, but such a shipment of non-conforming goods does not constitute an acceptance if the seller seasonably notifies the buyer that the shipment is offered only as an accommodation to the buyer.[14]

[13] *Scott* v. *People's Monthly Co.*, 209 Iowa 503, 228 N.W. 263, 67 A.L.R. 413 (1929).

[14] U.C.C. Sec. 2-206.

This is certainly a model of brevity; some people feel that here the authors of the Code have been too stingy with words. However, stating the rule with greater exactness would be quite difficult and perhaps unnecessary. Certainly if a seller ships five refrigerators when a buyer has ordered five stoves, no one should contend that the seller is manifesting any agreement concerning the order for stoves. If a seller ships glass tumblers when a buyer has ordered plastic tumblers, any question as to whether the seller is thus forming a contract for the plastic tumblers ordered by the buyer would seem fairly to depend upon a number of variable factors concerning the buyer's needs, expectations, and subsequent conduct. Suppose that knowing of the seller's shipment but unaware that the tumblers are glass instead of plastic, the buyer makes further plans or commitments on his own part in the expectation of receiving plastic tumblers. The one who creates the problem is the seller when, without disclosing the fact, he ships something different from what has been ordered. Fairly the burden should be on the seller to absolve himself, to show that under all of the surrounding circumstances a reasonable person in the position of the buyer would not be justified in assuming that his order has been accepted.

Regardless of whether this Code provision should be interpreted broadly or narrowly, it certainly serves as a warning to sellers in respect to substitute shipments. Some sellers, when they are unable to ship goods which have been ordered but have similar goods on hand, occasionally (to increase customer goodwill or sometimes merely to make a sale) will ship the similar goods without first ascertaining if the buyer is willing to accept the substitute. Under this Code provision, unless the seller explains that his act means something else, his act of shipping goods in response to the order will sometimes be considered as an acceptance of the order and an agreement to be bound by its terms. If so construed, the buyer not only could reject the substitute goods (since they fail to conform exactly to his order) but also could hold the seller to a contract to deliver as ordered. If a seller does not wish his shipping substitute goods to obligate him to deliver as ordered, the seller should, with the shipment or in advance of it, explain to the buyer that it is a substitute shipment sent as an accommodation to the buyer. If the seller so explains, then his act of shipping does not form a contract between the parties, but merely makes a counteroffer. If the buyer rejects the counteroffer, the only loss to the seller will be his own shipping and handling expenses; he will not be obliged to ship the originally ordered goods.

Notice of Acceptance. If an offer requests performance of an act as the acceptance, a contract is formed as soon as the offeree performs the requested act, even though the offeror is unaware of the offeree's performance. It is not fair, however, for the offeror to be kept in ignorance of the acceptance. Therefore if the act which has been performed is not likely soon to come to the offeror's attention, the offeree must notify the offeror within a reasonable time that the accepting act has been performed. Otherwise the contract formed upon performance of the act will automatically lapse or terminate.

Example: A seller was unwilling to extend credit to Bernard Brown. At Brown's request, G, on June 1, signed and mailed to the seller the following: "[Date] If you will sell goods to Bernard Brown on sixty days' credit, I will guaranty his payment up to $500." The seller received the guarantying letter on June 2 and on the same day sold and delivered certain goods to Brown for $475 due in sixty days. On June 3, the seller received a letter from G revoking his letter of June 1. Although the seller had not previously intended to notify G of the sale, he immediately replied to G's revoking letter, telling of the June 2 sale to Brown. When Brown defaulted in payment, the seller sued G.

The seller could recover. When the seller made the June 2 sale to Brown, he performed the requested act, thus accepting G's offer and forming a contract with G. The seller's June 3 letter was notice within a reasonable time and prevented the contract from lapsing.

Offers for Bilateral Contracts

Deviation from Requested Promise. If an offer requests a certain promise as an acceptance, obviously a different promise will not constitute an acceptance and therefore will not form a contract. However, in determining the effect of a reply which includes terms not expressed in an offer, it should be borne in mind that an offer seldom states all of the terms and provisions which are intended to apply to the proposed contract. For example, an offer to sell certain described goods at a certain price may say nothing about the time for delivery and payment. The offeror is presumed to intend the customary terms and provisions when he does not state otherwise. Delivery within a reasonable time and payment upon delivery are therefore implied terms of the offer. If in reply the offeree says, "I accept provided delivery is to be within a reasonable time and payment is to be made upon delivery," the offeree is merely expressing what is already implied by the offer. Since the offeree's reply neither changes nor adds to any of the offered terms, the reply would be a valid acceptance and would form a contract.

Example: A seller wrote to a buyer offering to sell a described plot of land for $2,000. The buyer promptly wrote to the seller, "I accept your offer on condition that you can convey good title to me."

If an offer to sell property says nothing about any mortgages or other liens against it, it is assumed that what is offered is a good title clear of all liens.

Therefore the buyer's reply, "on condition that you can convey good title to me," merely expressed what was already implied, did not add or change any terms, and so was an unconditional acceptance and would form a contract between the parties.

Sometimes an offeree's reply in response to an offer is so ambiguous that it is difficult to determine exactly what intent the offeree means to express. Suppose that a seller offers to sell certain property to a buyer for $1,000, payable on delivery, and that the buyer replies: "I accept your offer and will buy the property for $1,000. I will pay $500 on delivery and the balance one month after delivery." This ambiguous reply raises a question as to the buyer's intent—or, more accurately, as to what a reasonable man would be justified in concluding is the buyer's intent. Is the buyer primarily interested in buying for $1,000, and willing to pay on delivery if he has to, or instead is he primarily interested in deferring a portion of the payment and definitely not agreeable to paying the entire price in cash? The rule which gradually evolved at common law is a fairly simple and clear-cut rule, related to the policy view that if an offeree wants to accept and form a contract with an offeror, the offeree must clearly and unequivocally indicate that he is in complete agreement with the offer. Thus under the common-law rule, the legal effect of an offeree's reply is determined by the total intent which he expresses. If in its totality, the offeree's reply differs from the offer, the offeree's reply is not an acceptance and no contract is formed. In the above-quoted reply ("I will accept your offer and will buy the property for $1,000. I will pay $500 on delivery and the balance one month after delivery.") the total intent expressed by the buyer differs from the seller's terms. Under the common-law rule, therefore, the reply is not an acceptance but rather a counteroffer, and no contract would be formed unless the seller in turn accepts the counteroffer.

However, when this fundamentally sound common-law rule is applied to modern commercial transactions, the results are not always satisfactory, especially in the type of situation which is frequently dubbed "the battle of the forms." Large business establishments commonly use printed forms in ordering and in accepting or acknowledging orders. The forms used by each business are prepared with the help of its legal staff and incorporate the terms and conditions under which the business intends to make its contracts. As can be expected the terms stated in one form will frequently differ from those in the form used by another business. Sometimes the differences are trivial, sometimes substantial. Employees who use such forms usually do not diligently compare, item for item, the form received from another business establishment with the form sent or being sent out by their own establishment. Confusion also may arise when representatives of businesses negotiate a sales agreement through a number of oral conferences or by a series of letters and then, as frequently occurs, one (or both) of them sends a formal acknowledgment or memorandum stating the agreement. Especially when the acknowledgment or memorandum has gone through the legal office of the sender, it may include some added items that were not previously discussed; again the employees involved may not diligently compare the formal writing with the previous negotiations. In most such cases the goods in question are shipped and paid for and no question is raised. If, however, a dispute arises and the common-law rule is applied, the legal staffs of the businesses, and the courts as well, have a vexing problem in determining whether a contract actually exists, and if so what its terms are.

The authors of the Uniform Commercial Code feel that for sales-of-goods transactions, the common-law rule should be somewhat modified into a more modern rule which they state as follows:

1) A definite and seasonable expression of acceptance or a written confirmation which is sent within a reasonable time operates as an acceptance even though it states terms additional to or different from those offered or agreed upon, unless acceptance is expressly made conditional on assent to the additional or different terms.

2) The additional terms are to be construed as proposals for addition to the contract. Between merchants such terms become part of the contract unless:

a) the offer expressly limits acceptance to the terms of the offer;

b) they materially alter it; or

c) notification of objection to them has already been given or is given within a reasonable time after notice of them is received.

3) Conduct by both parties which recognizes the existence of a contract is sufficient to establish a contract for sale although the writings of the parties do not otherwise establish a contract. In such case the terms of the particular contract consist of those terms on which the writings of the parties agree, together with any supplementary terms incorporated under any other provision of this Act.[15]

This Code rule reflects the willingness and ability of the more mature legal system of modern times to undertake complex tasks of analysis and interpretation. In distinction to the common-law "total intent" rule, the Code rule can be called a "principal intent" rule. If the main or primary intent which the offeree expresses is to accept and form a contract as offered, the offeree's reply has the desired effect; it is an acceptance and forms a contract on the offeror's terms, even though the reply includes different or changed terms. On the other hand, if the offeree's principal intent is to form no contract except on his own terms, then the offeree's reply is a counteroffer and not an acceptance. Note that the determinant is the principal intent of the offeree as disclosed in the language he uses,

[15] U.C.C. Sec. 2-207.

without regard to the importance or unimportance of the changes suggested by the new or changed terms. If the offeree's principal intent is
to accept, a contract is formed on the offeror's terms; in also adding new
or changed terms to his acceptance, the offeree is offering or proposing
an amendment to the contract which the principal part of his reply
has already formed. The original offeror can in turn accept or reject the
offeree's proposed amendment. If the offeror makes no reply to the proposed changes, only then does the importance of the changes become
relevant. If the original offeror and offeree are both merchants, and
also if the proposed changes are minor, then if the offeror fails to write
to the offeree rejecting the changes, the offeror's silence constitutes an
acceptance of the change. If the proposed changes are material, or if
both parties are not merchants, the offeror's failure to object is not an
acceptance of the changes. The authors of the Code suggest that
changes in terms are material if they would cause surprise or objection,
or would result in hardship if considered a part of the contract without
both parties being expressly aware of them. Examples include negating
a standard warranty, or requiring 100 percent deliveries when some
deviation is usual in the type of commodity and trade involved. Minor
differences are such as would cause no undue surprise. Examples include: fixing within customary limits a certain time for return of defective
items with no claim or return permitted after such time; providing for
interest to accrue on overdue money obligations; stating situations under
which a seller would be excused from performing and including only
those which customarily excuse a party, or only slightly enlarge on the
customary excuses.

Example: On June 1 B sent S a written order for certain described goods
costing $800, one-half of the order to be shipped on the following August 1,
the remainder on September 1; terms for payment were stated as 2/20, net 60
(meaning 2 percent discount for payment within 20 days after shipment,
the net amount due in 60 days).

1. On June 2 S replied in writing: "I hereby accept your order of June 1
and agree to ship at the times stated. Terms for payment: net 20 days."
B did not reply and on August 1, S made the first shipment which B received
without complaint or qualification. At the expiration of 20 days, S demanded
payment. B refused, asserting that he had an additional 40 days in which to
pay. On September 1 S refused to ship the second installment of goods,
contending that he was excused from shipping because of B's continuing
failure to pay for the first shipment. B assured S that payment would be
made within the 60-day period, and when S persisted in demanding payment
before making the September 1 shipment, B sued S for damages.

It is strongly arguable that the contract between the parties gave B 60
days in which to pay, and that therefore 1) B was not in default for refusing
to pay within 20 days, 2) S was not excused from making the second ship-

ment, and 3) B could recover damages for S's refusal to ship on September 1. The principal intent of S's June 2 reply (it is strongly arguable) was to accept B's offer on B's terms, and at the same time to further offer to amend the contract thus formed, in order to change the terms for payment from "2/20, net 60," to "net 20." This would be a material change. Even if B were a merchant, his failure to object to the change would not make it a part of the contract. His acceptance of the shipment would not show that he was agreeable to S's terms because (as is strongly arguable) there was already a contract on B's terms.

2. On June 2 S replied in writing: "Subject to your agreement to the terms and conditions on the reverse side hereof, I hereby accept your order and agree to ship at the time stated . . ." On the reverse side of S's communication was written (or printed): "Terms for payment: net 20 days."

The principal intent of S's June 2 reply was not to accept, but rather to make a counteroffer; no contract would arise between the parties unless B in turn agreed to the counteroffer.

3. Suppose other facts as in Part 2 of this example, except that S's June 2 communication read: "Subject to the terms and conditions on the reverse side hereof . . . ," omitting the phrase "your agreement to" which appears in Part 2 immediately after the words, "Subject to."

It is arguable that without the omitted phrase ("your agreement to") S's reply would not be (in the language of the Code) ". . . expressly made conditional on *assent* to the additional or different terms," (emphasis added), and that therefore S's reply would be an acceptance on B's terms. Although this argument is weak, it would be unwise for S to omit some statement requiring B's agreement to the new terms.

4. Assume the same facts as in Part 2 of this example, plus the following: B never replied to S's June 2 communication, and on August 1, S shipped one-half of the ordered goods. B received and retained the goods without any comment. Twenty days later S demanded that B pay.

The principal intent of S's June 2 letter was to make a counteroffer. B's failure to reply to the counteroffer would usually not be construed as an acceptance. However, S's shipment was a renewal of his counteroffer to sell on S's terms, and B's retention of the goods was an acceptance; a contract was thereby formed, and the terms would be S's terms.

Communication of Promise—in General. Certainly a legally enforceable obligation cannot arise from a person's making an uncommunicated promise to himself. Thus for an offeree to make a promissory commitment requires some kind of communication, some conduct which as a matter of policy will be considered sufficient to manifest the offeree's commitment to the offeror. In addition to a promise made in the usual way through spoken or written words, a promise to the offeror may under certain circumstances be made by the offeree-promisor's conduct, and occasionally by his inaction or remaining silent.

Promise Communicated Through Conduct. Even though an offer requests a promise rather than an act as an acceptance, it frequently is possible for the offeree to make the requested promise by conduct instead of by words. If the conduct of the offeree reasonably leads the offeror to believe that the offeree is agreeable to the offer and is committing himself accordingly, the offeree's conduct makes and communicates the requested promise and forms a contract. Thus if an offeree accepts goods which he should reasonably know are not intended as a gift, the offeree by his conduct of accepting the goods makes a promise to pay the requested price according to the stated terms. If no price is stated, the offeree is obligated to pay a reasonable price on customary terms. An example of a contract formed in this way is shown in Part 4 of the preceding example. A person who continues to accept delivery of a periodical after his subscription has expired is likewise, through his conduct, promising to pay.

Promise Communicated Through Failure to Act. Usually it is not fair to assume that a person is agreeing to a certain proposition merely because he remains silent or inactive after learning of the proposal. Therefore silence is usually not construed as an acceptance.

Example: Upon opening a package received by parcel post, the recipient found a book which he had not ordered or requested. Included with the book was a letter identifying the sender, describing the book, stating the price, and adding. "If you do not wish to buy this book, return it to us and you will have no further obligation." The recipient put the book aside and did not use it, pay for it, return it, or communicate with the sender in any way.

The recipient did not accept the offer and no contract was formed. If the recipient had used the book (more than merely for examination) or otherwise had acted as an owner toward it (even by giving or throwing it away when he had sufficient storage space) he would be doing something more than merely remaining silent and his conduct would constitute acceptance.

Suppose, however, that not only does an offer indicate silence or inaction as the method by which it is to be accepted, but in addition the offeree remains silent with an intent to accept. If thereafter, contrary to the offeree's expectation, the offeror should assert that no contract has been formed, persuasive arguments can be made for either side of the dispute. It is not surprising, therefore, that in the few cases which have involved this point, the court decisions are not in agreement.

Example: A seller says to a buyer, "I'll sell you this book for $5. It is such a good bargain that unless you say 'no' in ten seconds, I'll assume that you accept."

1. The buyer says nothing, but does not intend to accept. There is no acceptance and no contract. Usually a person cannot be forced to reply at the risk that if he does not, he will be assumed to have accepted a certain proposition.

2. *Intending to accept, the buyer makes no reply.* Although the offeree's remaining silent is doing exactly what the offeror requests as an acceptance, some courts tend toward the view that since the offeree's remaining silent is not a definite manifestation of an intent to bind himself, his mere silence is not sufficient to bind the offeror on the offeror's promise; and that therefore even though an offeror specifies silence as an an acceptance, an offer for a bilateral contract is incapable of being accepted by the offeree's silence, unless accompanied by some additional conduct manifesting the offeree's intent to be bound.

Admittedly some other conduct on the part of the offeree, when added to his silence, may constitute a sufficient manifestation of the offeree's intent to bind himself, and thus also serve to bind the offeror. The courts are not in agreement as to what such "other conduct" may consist of. Only a few courts have said that if an offeree induces the offeror to make an offer, the offeree's remaining silent and failing to promptly reject the offer thus solicited by him constitutes an acceptance. On the other hand, many courts have held that if through prior dealings the offeree has led the offeror reasonably to believe that the offeree will respond promptly to an offer, then the offeree's failure to act promptly is sufficient to constitute an acceptance and to form a contract binding on both parties.

Example: On June 25, a man signed an application directed to the X Insurance Company, applying for a 20-payment $2,000 life insurance policy payable to the applicant's estate, and paid $4 as a deposit on the first premium. The agent to whom the application and money were given was not authorized to issue insurance policies, not even temporary binding agreements; he was merely an agent to solicit applications. The applicant was thereafter contacted by agents from other life insurance companies but was not interested in their proposals because of his application to the X company. On August 24 the applicant was accidentally killed. Up to that time the X Company had failed to give notice of its action on the application. The applicant's administrator sued the company for the amount of the policy, contending that by holding the application for so long a period, the company had accepted it. The company in turn tendered return of the applicant's $4 initial payment.

Under somewhat similar facts the Pennsylvania Supreme Court said[16] (as would courts in many other states) that the failure to reject was not an acceptance and that the company's only obligation was to return the $4. Which party took the initiative was immaterial—whether the company's agent first contacted the applicant and induced him to apply for the insurance, or whether the applicant sought out the agent.

Example: During the seven-month period preceding August 23, a wholesale grocer gave a series of orders to the district salesman of a meat packing company. The orders were accepted and the goods shipped not later than

[16] *Zayc* v. *John Hancock Mut. Life Ins. Co.,* 338 Pa. 426, 12 A.(2d) 34 (1940).

one week after the date of each order. On August 23 the wholesaler gave the salesman an order calling for the prompt shipment of a certain quantity of shortening at 7½ cents per pound. As had the previous order forms, this form stated: "This order is subject to acceptance by the packer at the point of shipment." Not receiving the shortening nor hearing from the packer within one week, the wholesaler inquired as to when the shipment would be made. In a reply received by the wholesaler on September 4, the packer said that the order was rejected. By that time the price of shortening had risen to 9 cents per pound, and the wholesaler sued the packer for damages for refusal to ship at 7½ cents per pound.

The Mississippi Supreme Court said[17] that there was an enforceable contract at 7½ cents per pound, that through his past conduct the offeree led the offeror to reasonably assume that silence or inaction following receipt of an offer was intended as acceptance, and that therefore failure to promptly reject the August 23 order constituted an acceptance. Courts in some states would agree with this conclusion, while courts in some other states would not.

Promise Communicated Through Words. Although the offeree can make his acceptance promise by conduct or occasionally through silence, an offeree usually makes the requested promise in words (such as "I accept"), which indicate that he is agreeing to the offeror's proposal and willing to be bound by it. If the parties are not talking directly to each other, either face-to-face or by telephone, but instead the offeree expresses his acceptance by letter or telegram, there is a delay or time lag between the offeree's expression of his intent and the offeror's receiving and learning of the acceptance. If during this time lag the offeror attempts to revoke his offer, or if one of the parties dies (automatically revoking unaccepted offers), it immediately becomes essential to know at what point of time the acceptance becomes effective, if at all, so as to know whether or not there is a contract.

Since the offeror is initiating the proposed offer, he may specify whatever he wishes as an acceptance. He may, for example, specify that the acceptance must be communicated in a certain way or delivered to a certain place, and the offeree cannot accept unless he meets these conditions. Most offers, however, fail to specify particular conditions for acceptance; for such offers reasonable rules have evolved as to when an acceptance is considered communicated and effective. The chief fact situations can be classified as to whether transmission is 1) through the offeror's personal agent or 2) through an independent agency.

1) Transmission Through Offeror's Personal Agent. If the offeree delivers his acceptance to the offeror's personal agent who is authorized to receive such communications, the acceptance should certainly be con-

---

[17] *Ammons v. Wilson & Co.*, 176 Miss. 645, 170 S. 227 (1936).

sidered communicated and effective when given to the agent. For example, if the offeree takes his written acceptance to the offeror's office, the acceptance is considered as communicated and effective when the offeree gives it to a suitable employee in the offeror's office, even though the offeror himself is not available. Likewise, suppose that in communicating an offer the offeror uses his own employee as a messenger, instructing him not only to deliver the offer but also to wait for an answer; the offeree's acceptance in reply to the offer would be communicated and effective as soon as given to the offeror's messenger, although the messenger would still be on the offeree's premises.

2) Transmission Through Independent Agency. Usually the offeree delivers his acceptance to some independent transmission system, such as the postal system or the telegraph company, for transmittal to the offeror. To have a workable rule, the law must indicate some pinpoint of time as the moment when an acceptance can be said to become effective. There are two possible choices: either the time when the acceptance is delivered to the transmission system, or the time when the transmission system delivers the acceptance to the offeror's address. Which of these two the law should select is entirely a matter of policy— of fairness, reasonableness, and practicality under the circumstances. In deciding the question, the law has concluded that although the postal or telegraph system is not actually a personal messenger employed by the offeror, it is sufficiently similar to justify applying the personal messenger rule. The chief policy factors leading to this conclusion are demonstrated by comparing the results of each of the two possible choices. If the acceptance is effective when mailed, then sometimes the *offeror* will be unaware of when he becomes bound by a contract or whether there is a contract at all. The offeror could avoid this disadvantage by specifying in his offer that an acceptance will not be effective until received. On the other hand, if the acceptance is effective only when received, then sometimes the *offeree* will have the disadvantage of not knowing when he becomes bound by a contract or whether there is a contract at all. The offeree could reduce this disadvantage by using a means of transmission, such as a telegram or certified mail, which would enable him more easily to determine the time his acceptance has been delivered. Thus whichever rule is followed—acceptance effective when sent or not until received—one or the other party will sometimes be at a disadvantage. The law considers it fair to pick the offeror as the one to bear this disadvantage since he can so easily avoid it when he initiates the offer (by specifically requiring receipt of the acceptance), and since by selecting a certain medium for transmission he to some extent assumes the risks which that medium entails, such as loss or delay in transit, etc.

As a matter of policy, therefore, the rule has become well established that if an offer does not specifically require that the acceptance must be received to be effective, an acceptance sent in a way authorized by the offeror is effective when started on its way (that is, depending on which means is authorized, when dropped in a mail box or given to a clerk in a telegraph office) properly addressed, with charges prepaid. On the other hand, if an acceptance is sent in an unauthorized way, it is not effective until received—provided the offer is still open at that time.

The medium that is authorized for transmitting an acceptance is the way specified in the offer. If none is specified, the medium used to transmit the offer is impliedly authorized for transmitting the acceptance. If the medium which the offeree selects for transmitting his acceptance is not expressly specified in the offer and also is different from the medium used to transmit the offer, but is nevertheless reasonable under the circumstances, then 1) if the offer concerns something other than sale of goods, some courts say that the different but reasonable medium is not authorized, some say that it is authorized; 2) if the offer concerns a sale of goods, the Uniform Commercial Code states[18] that in the absence of a contrary express requirement, any medium reasonable in the circumstances is authorized. A medium of communication is reasonable if it is in common use and also is as fast or faster than the medium used to transmit the offer.

Example: A nonmerchant offeror sent an offer by regular mail, giving ten days to accept, not specifying a medium for replying, and not stating that the acceptance would be effective only when received. In reply the offeree mailed an acceptance on the sixth day, properly addressed and stamped.

1. Assume that the offeree's accepting letter was received by the offeror on the eighth day. The contract would be considered as formed on the sixth.

2. Assume that the offeree's accepting letter was delayed in transit (through no fault of the offeree) and not delivered until the fifteenth day. The contract would be considered as formed on the sixth.

3. Assume that the offeree's accepting letter was lost in the mail (through no fault of the offeree). If the offeree's testimony that he properly mailed an acceptance on the sixth is believed, a contract would be considered as formed on the sixth.

4. Assume that the offeree changed his mind and (as is possible under postal regulations) obtained return of his accepting letter from the postal system so that it never was delivered to the offeror. If the offeror could prove these facts, a contract would be considered as formed on the sixth.

5. Assume that the offeree's accepting letter was mailed on the sixth and received by the offeror on the eighth day, but that on the seventh day, the offeree had received from the offeror a communication revoking the offer. The contract would be considered as formed on the sixth. Since the offeree

---

[18] U.C.C. Sec. 2-206.

effectively accepted before receiving the revocation, the revocation would not be effective.

6. Assume that after mailing his acceptance on the sixth, the offeree, on the seventh, telegraphed that he had changed his mind and that his accepting letter should be ignored; the offeror received the telegram on the seventh, and the accepting letter on the eighth. The contract would be considered as formed on the sixth, and the offeree could not undo or cancel the contract without the offeror's consent. The telegram of the seventh would be construed as an offer to cancel, and the recipient's failure to reply usually would not be construed as an acceptance of this proposal.

Example: A nonmerchant offeror sent an offer by regular mail, giving ten days to accept, not specifying a medium for replying, and not stating that the acceptance would be effective only when received. On the fifth day the offeree mailed a letter rejecting the offer, but on the sixth day, the offeree changed his mind and mailed a letter (properly addressed and stamped) accepting the offer. The offeree's rejecting letter was received on the seventh, his accepting letter on the eighth. When the offeror denied that there was a contract, the offeree sued, arguing that since a rejection is not effective until received, the offer was still open on the sixth and that therefore a contract was formed on the sixth when the accepting letter was mailed.

To avoid such an unfair result, the law would say that the offeree's conduct suspended the ordinary rule of an acceptance being effective when mailed. If an offeree sends both an acceptance and a rejection, knowing that the rejection might arrive first (and the rejection contains no reference to any previous acceptance), then the acceptance will be effective only if the offeror actually receives it before he receives the rejection. If the rejection arrives first (and contains no reference to any previous acceptance), the acceptance arriving later will not be effective to form a contract.

Example: A nonmerchant offeror sent an offer by regular mail, giving ten days to accept, not specifying a medium for replying, and not stating that the acceptance would be effective only when received. In reply, the offeree telegraphed an acceptance on the ninth day, properly addressed and with charges prepaid. Transmission of the telegram was delayed through fault of the telegraph company and the telegram was not delivered to the offeror until the twelfth.

1. Assume that the offer concerned the sale of goods. Under the Uniform Commercial Code, if reply by telegram was reasonable (as it usually would be), it was an authorized medium of communication, and a contract would be considered as formed on the ninth.

2. Assume that the offer concerned something other than sale of goods— such as land, personal services, or a loan. Some courts would say that the use of the telegraph was unauthorized, that the acceptance could not be effective until received (on the twelfth) by which time the offer had expired, and that therefore no contract was formed. Other courts would follow the same rule as the Code adopts for sales-of-goods offers.

PROBLEMS

1. A retail clothier contracted with the publisher of a newspaper for the following advertisement: "Special in furs. Large animal scarfs, taupe, brown, and black. Satin lined. For three days only. Special price, $15." When the advertisement appeared in the newspaper, it erroneously stated the price as $5. Since no proof sheet of the advertisement was submitted to the retailer, he did not see the error until the newspaper was published. The retailer sued the publisher for $480 damages for breach of contract and proved that after the advertisement was published, 48 persons came to the retailer's store, mentioned seeing the advertisement, and demanded and were each sold a scarf for $5.

a) Was the retailer entitled to judgment against the publisher for $480? Explain.

b) Suppose that the advertisement reading $5 was what the retailer had ordered published, but that the retailer had thereafter changed his mind and did not want to sell for less than $15. Unaware of the retailer's change of mind, a customer who had read the advertisement came to the store and told the retailer that he wanted to buy for $5. When the retailer refused to sell for less than $15, the customer accused the retailer of breaking a contract. Was the customer correct? Explain.

2. B. Brown received the following typewritten letter, dated February 2, from S. Smith: "Dear Mr. Brown: We have Mason green jars of one quart capacity complete with caps that we can offer you at this time for immediate acceptance at $8 per gross, delivered in your city. Terms 60 days or less, 2 per-cent for cash in 10 days. Awaiting your orders, we are yours truly, (signed) S. Smith." B promptly replied by telegraph as follows: "Your February 2 letter just arrived. Enter order for 500 gross complete goods." The February 2 letter had not been in response to any inquiry from B. Five hundred gross was a reason-able quantity for B to order and not in excess of what S, from his knowledge of the business of B, might reasonably expect B to order. S answered by tele-graph: "We can enter order for only 250 gross." B sued for breach of contract for S's refusal to ship 500 gross of jars.

a) Was B entitled to judgment? Explain.

b) Explain how, if at all, S could have avoided the possibility of this dispute arising, without further limiting his freedom of action.

c) Other facts remaining the same, assume the February 2 letter was printed and the salutation read: "Dear Customer." Was B entitled to judgment against S for refusing to ship 500 gross? Explain.

3. On March 10, Brown Seed Company received the following letter from S. Smith, a farmer residing at Lowell, Nebraska: "Brown Seed Co., Omaha, Nebraska. Gentlemen: I have for sale about 1800 bu. of millet seed of which I am mailing you a sample enclosed with this letter. This millet is recleaned and was grown on sod and is good seed. I want $2.25 per hundredweight for this seed, f.o.b. Lowell. (signed) S. Smith." The same day B Company sent S the following telegram: "S. Smith, Lowell, Nebraska. Sample and letter received. Accept your offer. Millet like sample two twenty-five per hundred. (signed) Brown Seed Co." S received the telegram the same day it was sent. S. refused to sell, having found another buyer and B Company sued S for damages.

a) Explain 1) the reasoning upon which B Company could attempt to collect, 2) the reasoning upon which S could attempt to defend, and 3) which party should be given judgment.

b) Explain how, if at all, S could have avoided the possibility of this dispute arising, without limiting his freedom of action.

4. S of Detroit, Michigan, was the owner of a piece of property, well known as the Table property, located in Sharon, Pennsylvania. B of Sharon told S's sister that he was considering purchasing the property for $40,000. S's sister told S of this conversation and on July 11 S wrote B: "In reference to the offer you recently quoted to my sister ($40,000 cash) for the sale of the Table property, I am pleased to accept your offer. Please write me and let me know when it would be convenient for us to get together in Sharon to close the deal." In reply, B wrote S, July 13: "I am enclosing an option which you are to sign in which you agree to sell this property, clear of all liens, for $40,000. I want the sixty days mentioned in the option in order to try to raise enough money to purchase the property myself. If I am unable to do so, I feel certain I can interest somebody in Sharon at this price." In reply to this letter, S wrote B, July 18: "I am returning the option which I do not care to sign. However, if at any time you have raised the money and wish to close the deal, I shall be glad to do so. Let me hear from you soon." On August 21, B wrote S: "I hereby accept your written offer of July 18 to sell me the Table property for $40,000." When S refused to sell, B sued S for a decree of specific performance which would order S to transfer his interest in the property to B for $40,000. S contended that there was no offer which B could accept by his August 21 letter, because a) any offer S had made had lapsed, and b) S really had made no offer. Was B entitled to the requested decree? Explain.

5. B was in the business of exporting crude petroleum to France, his trade amounting to about 100,000 barrels a year. S, an oil refiner, contacted B, suggesting that B purchase his requirements of oil from S and further suggesting that B attempt, by a visit to Paris, to increase his export trade. To assist B on his trip, S on March 1 signed and gave B a letter reading in part: "In accordance with our interview, I am willing to enter into a contract with you for the furnishment of Pennsylvania crude oil for a term of two years in the amount of 400,000 barrels of 42 gallons each, per year, at the following price . . . [specifying a price and details of transportation and handling charges]. I extend to you a refusal of making the contract on the above basis for the term of four months from this date. Should it not be accepted in writing on or before that time the above is to become null and void and without effect between us." B traveled to Paris at his own expense and after some negotiations succeeded in entering into contracts with various French refiners to supply them with crude petroleum totaling 400,000 barrels a year.

a) Thereafter, S sent B the following: "May 23. I wish to advise you that I withdraw my offer of March 1. You will therefore consider the same canceled." To this B replied: "May 24. I hereby notify you that I accept and will fully carry out the option and contract you gave me by your letter of March 1. I hereby repudiate your attempted withdrawal of said option." Each letter was received by the respective addressee the day following the date of mailing. Upon S's refusal to deliver oil to B, B sued for damages for breach of contract. Was B entitled to judgment against S? Explain.

b) Assume facts the same as in Part (a) of this problem, except that the date of S's letter to B was June 23 and the date of B's answering letter to S was June 24. Was B entitled to judgment against S? Explain.

6. A state government advertised for bids for the construction of a public building. A merchant sent an employee to the state capitol to look over the building plans and specifications and calculate the total amount of linoleum required for the building. The employee underestimated the total yardage by about one-half the proper amount. On December 24, in ignorance of the mistake, the merchant sent to about thirty builders likely to bid on the job, an offer to supply at a specified price all the linoleum required in the specifications for this particular building. The offering letters concluded saying: "We are offering this price for reasonably prompt acceptance after the general contract has been awarded." B, a builder, received one of the offering letters on December 28, used the linoleum figure in calculating his bid, and the same day submitted the bid to the proper state office together with the usual money deposit. On December 29 the merchant discovered the error and telegraphed all the builders to whom the offering letters had been sent, withdrawing the offer and saying that a new offer would be sent at about double the amount of the old one. Upon receiving the telegram, B did not withdraw his bid because there was not sufficient time to submit another bid, the linoleum was a trifling part of the cost of the whole building, and withdrawal of the bid would have resulted in forfeiture of the money deposit. On December 30 the state awarded the contract to B. On January 2 B sent to the merchant an acceptance of his December 24 offer. When the merchant refused to supply linoleum at that price, B sued for damages. Explain 1) the reasoning upon which the merchant might attempt to defend, 2) the reasoning upon which B might attempt to recover, and 3) which party should be given judgment.

7. On December 8, in reply to an inquiry S telegraphed to B: "Will sell you 2,000-5,000 tons of 50 pound iron rails for $54 per gross ton, cash, f.o.b. cars our mill, March delivery. If offer accepted, expect to be notified of same prior to December 20." Assume that under the particular circumstances this constituted an offer. On December 16 B telegraphed S: "Enter order 1,200 tons rails as per your wire of December 8." On December 18 S telegraphed B: "Cannot book your order of 16th at that price." On December 19 B telegraphed S: "Enter order 2,000 tons as per your wire of December 8." S received this telegraph on December 19 but did not reply until January 19 when, after repeated inquiries from B, S stated that he would not ship the rails. B sued S for damages for breach of contract. Explain 1) the reasoning upon which B might attempt to collect, 2) the reasoning upon which S might attempt to defend, and 3) which party should be given judgment.

8. On February 1 B, a manufacturer of refrigerator cases, sent to S, a supplier, a written order for 300 latches of a certain style called "spring lock" at $2 per latch, f.o.b. shipping point, 2/10 net 30. This was S's first order from B, and S desired to obtain B as a customer. However, S had no spring lock latches on hand and could procure them only at a price which, with S's normal markup, would make S's selling price $3 per latch. S had on hand a quantity of "roll-lock" latches on which S's normal selling price was $2.15 per latch. As S knew, many manufacturers had found the roll-lock latch as satisfactory as or superior to the spring lock latch. In response to B's order and without any further communication, S, on February 3, shipped to B 300 roll-lock latches invoiced to B at $2 apiece. On tender of delivery B noticed that the latches were roll-lock latches and refused to receive delivery. The railroad returned them to S on S's payment of the freight charges. B demanded but S refused to ship any other latches.

a) If S sued B for the loss resulting from B's refusal to receive delivery, could S recover? Explain.

b) If B sued S for the loss resulting from S's refusal to ship other latches, could B recover? Explain.

c) How if at all could S have shown that he desired to serve B promptly and still have avoided the dispute and lawsuit? Explain.

9. S wrote to B: "I hereby offer to sell you my land [describing it] for $2,000, transfer to be made in one month." Assume that under the circumstances this constituted an offer. B promptly replied in writing: "I hereby accept your offer and agree to buy your land for $2,000, on condition that you can convey to me a good title. Terms shall be $500 on delivery of deed, the balance in two months." S did not reply. The following day, still within a reasonable time, B wrote S: "I accept your offer and will pay $2,000 on transfer of the property." S did not reply within a reasonable time.

a) Assume that B changed his mind and decided he did not want to buy. Was there a contract which S could enforce against B and if so what were its terms? Explain.

b) Assume that S changed his mind and decided he did not want to sell. Was there a contract which B could enforce against S and if so what were its terms? Explain.

c) Other facts remaining the same, assume that the subject matter of S's offering letter was certain described goods, and that after B's second communication, S decided he did not want to sell. Was there a contract which B could enforce against S and if so what were its terms? Explain.

10. B Company sent to S Company a signed printed purchase order form reading in part: "Please enter our order for the following described goods," followed by a typewritten description of the goods ordered and prices. The form contained no reference to strikes. In reply S Company sent to B Company a signed printed form titled "Purchase Memo," the pertinent part of the printed form reading: "This acknowledges receipt of your order for the follow-

ing described goods, which we accept, subject to the terms and conditions on the reverse side hereof." The description of goods and prices were typewritten on the S Company form, as copied from the B Company's purchase order. On the reverse side of S Company's purchase memo form, among other things, was printed: "S Company will not be liable for any delay in delivery or failure to deliver, resulting from labor trouble or strike." B Company did not reply.

a) Before S Company could ship the ordered goods, its plant was closed by a strike. B Company sued S Company for damages for nondelivery. Assume that the ordinary rule concerning strikes (see Chapter 11) would apply, that is, that a seller's labor trouble will not excuse him from his contract obligation to deliver unless his contract expressly contains a strike excuse or escape provision. Explain 1) the reasoning upon which B Company might attempt to win the lawsuit, 2) the reasoning upon which S Company might attempt to defend, and 3) which party should be given judgment.

b) Receiving no reply from B Company, S Company shipped the ordered goods with reasonable promptness. B Company had decided not to purchase (without informing S Company of this fact), and refused the shipment. S Company sued B Company for damages for breach of contract. What result? Explain.

11. On November 9 B wrote to S, a manufacturer, ordering certain described packing materials, at a stated price, one-tenth of the total quantity ordered to be shipped as soon as possible, and the remainder to be retained by S until requested by B, since B had no storage space; the goods were to be billed only when and as shipped on B's instructions and B was to give shipping instructions for all the ordered goods within the next four months. On November 12 S replied that he could not store and ship in that way without charging an extra 5 percent for the accommodation. On November 15 B wrote S refusing to pay an extra 5 percent, stating that B had dealt under those terms with other manufacturers, and hoping that S would reconsider and enter B's November 9 order. Without further correspondence, S began to manufacture the described material and on December 15 shipped the one-tenth portion requested in B's November 9 letter, billed "as per your November 9 order," at the price in the original order. Assume that under the circumstances this shipment was "as soon as possible," within the meaning of B's November 9 order.

a) B refused the shipment and S sued B for damages for breach of contract. Explain 1) the reasoning upon which S might attempt to recover, 2) the reasoning upon which B might attempt to defend, and 3) which party should be given judgment.

b) B accepted delivery and paid as billed. Shortly afterwards B wrote to S that no further shipments would be accepted. By that time the manufacture of all of the packing material was completed. After repeated vain attempts during the next four months to induce B to accept more of the packing materials, S sued B for breach of contract. Answer the same questions as are asked in Part (a).

12. A stationery supply store voluntarily and without request by the accountant, delivered by messenger to the accountant's office, a package of analysis paper, together with a sealed envelope containing a letter stating that the paper was either to be paid for at the price stated, or returned within 10 days. The package and letter were accepted as a matter of routine by the accountant's reception clerk who did not know, and had no way of knowing, their contents. The accountant put the package aside but made no reply to the store. One month later the store demanded payment for the paper. Was the accountant obliged to pay and if so how much? (Modified from A.I.C.P.A. Nov. 38-5.)

13. Effective April 1, an insurance company issued a $25,000 one-year policy of fire insurance to a businessman covering certain described buildings owned by the businessman. This was the first insurance the businessman ever obtained from this particular company. On March 15, of the following year the businessman received a letter from the company saying that the policy would be renewed for the same buildings and amount, for a further term of one year from April 1, and that the company would bill the businessman for the annual premium on May 1, unless the businessman notified the company that he did not want the insurance renewed. Intending to have the insurance renewed, the businessman filed the letter and made no reply. On April 20 the buildings were totally destroyed by an accidental fire. When the businessman filed a claim with the insurance company for $25,000, the company asserted that the buildings were not insured. The businessman sued the company for $25,000. Explain 1) the reasoning upon which the businessman could attempt to collect, 2) the reasoning upon which the company could attempt to defend, and 3) which party should be given judgment.

14. On April 7 S mailed a letter to B, offering to sell two carloads of specified goods for a stated price, and saying nothing as to the method of replying to the offer. The letter containing the offer, was delivered to B in due course at 10 A.M., April 9. B replied as described in (a) or (b) below. At 9:30 A.M. on April 9, S dispatched a telegram to B reading "Disregard my letter of April 7. Have sold goods elsewhere." B received this telegram at 10:55 A.M., April 9. B maintained that there was a contract, S denied this and refused to deliver. The market price for such goods having gone up, B sued S for damages for breach of contract.

a) Assume that at 10:30 A.M., April 9, B mailed to S a letter of acceptance. The letter was postmarked 11 A.M., April 9 and delivered to S. 10 A.M., April 11. Was B entitled to judgment in his lawsuit against S? Explain.

b) Assume that at 10:30 A.M., April 9, B dispatched to S a telegram of acceptance. The telegram was delivered to S, 11:30 A.M., April 9. Was B entitled to judgment in his lawsuit against S? Explain. Would your answer be different if through the sole fault of the telegraph company, the telegram was delayed and not delivered to S until 5 P.M., April 12? Explain.

c) Explain how, if at all, S could have phrased his letter to avoid the possibility of such a dispute as arose here.

15. At 10 A.M., March 10, S of Philadelphia sent an air-mail letter to B of Portland, Oregon. Under the crcumstances, the letter constituted an offer to sell certain described goods to B at a stated price f.o.b Philadelphia. The letter concluded by saying: "You have three days in which to accept." B received the letter in due course at 10 A.M., March 12. At 4 P.M. March 14, B mailed by regular mail a letter accepting S's offer. S received the accepting letter in due course of mail at 10 A.M., March 17. Learning of a chance to sell to someone else at a higher price, S refused to ship to B and B sued S for damages. Explain 1) the reasoning upon which S might attempt to defend, 2) the reasoning upon which B might attempt to collect, and 3) which party should be given judgment.

16. S decided to replace a machine in his factory with a more modern design. Recalling interest in the machine previously expressed by his friend B, owner of a small machine shop, S, on a Wednesday, dictated a letter to his secretary offering to sell the described machine to B for $400. After the letter was typed, S sent his secretary out to deliver a folder in another building, and before she returned S had to leave for a business conference. He signed the letter containing the offer to B and left it on his secretary's desk, together with a separate note that he would be out the remainder of the day. After the secretary returned, she began working on some files in an adjoining room. A few minutes later B came into the office to see S. Noticing that the letter on the secretary's desk was addressed to him, B read it. Also seeing the note that S would not be back, B left without seeing S's secretary.

a) Before leaving, B wrote on the bottom of S's letter, "Accepted. Thanks a lot" and signed it. Was a contract formed and if so, when? Explain.

b) Assume that although B read S's letter, he wrote nothing on it. At 5 P.M. S's secretary mailed the letter and it was delivered to B the following morning (Thursday) at 10 A.M. Late Wednesday afternoon B wrote a letter to S accepting the offer made in the letter B had seen in S's office. B mailed his accepting letter at 6 P.M. and it was delivered to S Thursday morning at 11 A.M. By this time S had changed his mind and at 11:30 A.M. Thursday he phoned B that the deal was off. B sued S for breach of contract. Was a contract formed, and if so, when? Explain.

17. S offered by mail to sell B a described farm for $10,000. S's letter was mailed on July 5 and received by B on July 8.

a) Assume that B wrote S on July 9, inquiring: "Won't you take less?" S replied by letter on July 13, "No." B then mailed a letter to S on July 14, stating "I accept your offer of July 5." S refused to have any further dealings with B. Assuming that July 14 was (under the particular circumstances) a reasonable time within which to have replied to the offer of July 5, was there a valid contract between S and B for the sale of the farm? Explain.

b) Assume that B, on July 9, sent a telegram to S in which B accepted the offer of July 5. S never received the telegram. Was a valid contract formed between S and B for the sale of the farm? Explain.

c) Assume that B was not interested in S's offer and gave S's letter to P telling P to accept it if he were interested. P sent a letter to S in which he said, "I accept your offer of July 5." When S refused to transfer the property to P, P sued S. Was P entitled to recover? Explain. (Modified from A.I.C.P.A., Nov. 52-3.)

d) Assume that on July 10, B mailed a letter to S in which B accepted the offer of July 5. Unknown to B, S had suffered a heart attack on July 9 and died the same day. When B's letter arrived, it was turned over to the executor appointed for S's estate. The executor refused to transfer the land to B and B sued S's estate and the executor. What result? Explain.

e) Assume that on July 10, B mailed a letter to S in which B accepted the offer of July 5. Unknown to B, S suffered a heart attack on July 12 and died the same day. When B's letter arrived on July 13, it was turned over to the executor appointed for S's estate. The executor refused to transfer the land to B and B sued S's estate and the executor. What result? Explain.

18. After exchanging telegrams not constituting offers, relative to the price of Puerto Rico potatoes for prompt shipment, B, on Friday, February 2, sent to S, an importer, a telegram reading "Ship 150 barrels Puerto Ricos today at your quoted price. Wire car number." S replied by telegram the same day, "Will ship Monday." The potatoes were not shipped on Monday, and B wired S on Wednesday, February 7, "When are you going to ship potatoes? Booked shipment. Answer quick." By "Booked shipment" B meant that he had in turn already entered into a contract to sell the potatoes to someone else. Upon receiving this wire on February 7, S did not reply, inasmuch as he had written and mailed a letter to B on February 6, explaining that he was unable to ship on account of weather conditions. Assume that this reason would not excuse a person from performing any contract he may have entered into. S shipped the potatoes on February 10 and wired B at the time of shipment, giving the car number. On February 14, when the potatoes arrived in due course, B refused to accept them. S sued for damages for breach of contract. Was S entitled to judgment against B? Explain.

chapter *5*

Consideration and Equivalents of Consideration

The mere fact that two parties have reached an agreement—one party making a proposal and the other party accepting the proposal—does not necessarily mean that the parties have formed a legally enforceable contract. One outstanding type of promise which the law will almost invariably refuse to enforce is a social arrangement. Suppose, for example, that the annual golf tournament of a county real estate association has been scheduled for a certain afternoon, and that realtor Davis has promised that he will stop at realtor Porter's house right after lunch and give him a ride to the golf course. Suppose further that Davis forgets, and it being too late for Porter to make other arrangements, he has to take a taxi to the golf course. Should Davis be required to pay Porter's taxi fare? Although admittedly the parties reached an agreement, it seems clear that the agreement should not be treated as a legally binding, contractual agreement. Even if he had given Porter the promised ride, Davis could not reasonably expect to be compensated. Would it be fair to hold Davis legally obligated to perform a favor for which he would have no legal right to be paid? It seems better policy to say that if a person is not entitled to payment for some promised performance, he should not be obligated to render the performance—unless something else is present of sufficient importance to justify legal enforcement of the promise. Of the multitude of legal scholars who have expressed this concept in various ways, the following is a limited sample:

> There can be no doubt that from an empirical or historical point of view, the ability to rely on the promises of others adds to the confidence necessary for social intercourse and enterprise. But as an absolute proposition this is untenable. The actual world . . . is not one in which all promises are kept, and there are many people—not necessarily diplomats—who prefer a world in which they and others occasionally depart from the truth and go back on some promise. It is indeed very doubtful whether there are many who would prefer to live in an entirely rigid world in which one would be obliged to keep *all* one's promises instead of the present more viable system, in which a vaguely fair proportion is sufficient. Many of us indeed would shudder at the idea of being bound by every promise no matter how

foolish, without any chance of letting increased wisdom undo past foolishness. Certainly, some freedom to change one's mind is necessary for free intercourse between those who lack omniscience.[1]

When one receives a naked promise [that is, a promise for which nothing is given in exchange] and such a promise is broken, he is no worse off than he was. He gave nothing for it, he has lost nothing by it, and on its breach he has suffered no damage cognizable by courts. No benefit accrued to him who made the promise, nor did any injury flow to him who received it. Such promises are not made within the scope of transactions intended to confer rights enforceable at law. They are lightly made, dictated by generosity, courtesy, or impulse— often by ruinous prodigality. To enforce them by a judgment in favor of those who gave nothing therefor would often bring such imperfect obligations into competition with the absolute duties to wife and children, or into competition with debts for property actually received, and make the law an instrument by which a man could be forced to be generous before he was just.[2]

There is a social interest in being able to rely upon any promise that any person may make. Our social order would be a better social order if people could always rely upon every statement that others might make. Human beings would be happier if all of them always told the truth. Under these circumstances it may be wondered why the law has not made contracts out of all promises. The reason why it has not is probably a reason of public policy. Some promises are not of enough importance to make it worth while to make contracts out of them. The legal enforcement of all promises is expensive. No more expense should be incurred for the enforcement of promises than the needs of our social order make imperative. There is a social interest in personal liberty; and personal liberty, even the personal liberty to lie, ought not to be delimited unless the social interests of other people are thereby injured enough so as to warrant the delimitation of personal liberty. Self-control is also a matter in which there is a social interest. If social control was applied to all promises there would be very little opportunity left for self-control. So far as it is possible the making and performance of promises should, therefore, be left to personal liberty.

Yet some promises are of such importance that social control must be applied to them. Not all promises can be left to self-control. Wealth in a commercial age is largely made up of promises. An important part of everyone's substance consists of advantages promised by others. There is a demand of society that some promises, at least, be kept. Hence, our Anglo-American law, much as all systems of law have done, has compromised between enforcing all promises and enforcing no promises, and as a result we have special classes of promises to which this form of social control is applied and which are contracts.

[1] Cohen, "The Basis of Contract," 46 *Harv. L. Rev.* 553 (1933).

[2] *Davis & Co.* v. *Morgan*, 117 Ga. 504, 43 S.E. 732, 61 L.R.A. 148, 97 Am. St. Rep. 171 (1903).

Our problem, therefore, simmers down to a problem of determining these different classes of promises.[3]

Through centuries of evolution in which the mechanics of the English legal procedure were gradually adapted to meet the needs of a growing commercial economy, a rule termed the *consideration rule* was forged as the chief measuring device with which the Anglo-American law separates agreements into those which are legally binding and those which are not. The word "consideration," as it is popularly used by non-lawyers, has various somewhat related but different meanings. One meaning refers to "thoughtful contemplation or meditation," another meaning to "thoughtfulness or kindness," and still another to "the reason or basis for a conclusion or action." The law of contracts uses the word in this last sense.

It cannot be too strongly emphasized that the rule of consideration is entirely a rule of policy. It is felt to be sound public policy that every promise which a person makes should not necessarily be legally enforceable, that there must be "something" in addition to the fact that a promise is made and an agreement reached, for the promise to be deemed enforceable in the courts. This "something" which policy indicates should be present to make a promise legally enforceable, usually (but not always) consists of an exchange given or received for the promise. Modern theory applies the term *consideration* to this exchange. In addition, it is also felt to be sound public policy that certain other circumstances should be deemed sufficient to justify legal enforcement of promises, even though consideration in the usual, exchange sense is not present. These other circumstances are frequently referred to as "equivalents of consideration." To summarize, therefore, unless a promise is accompanied either by consideration in the exchange sense, or by a legally recognized equivalent of consideration, the promise is not legally enforceable. The task, then, is to define "consideration" and to spell out the special circumstances which should be accepted as "equivalents of consideration."

Part 1   CONSIDERATION

The modern concept of consideration involves two main ingredients, 1) agreed exchange, and 2) detriment or benefit. In order for something to be construed as legally sufficient consideration for a promise, it must be given or received as the agreed exchange for the promise (that is, as the price bargained for and paid for the promise), and also it must involve either a legal benefit acquired by the promisor or a legal detriment sustained by the promisee. While detriment and benefit are usually both present in an enforceable agreement, both are not necessary; either legal detriment *or* legal benefit will be sufficient to constitute consideration.

[3] Willis, "Rationale of the Law of Contracts," 11 *Indiana L.J.* 227 (1936).

AGREED EXCHANGE

When consideration is defined as the *agreed exchange* for a promise, both of these words are meaningful.

Agreement. Something upon which the parties have not agreed cannot be consideration for a promise. Since the agreement of the parties is expressed by one party making an offer and the other party accepting the offer, the consideration is necessarily a part of the offer and acceptance. For example, if consideration is present in a unilateral agreement, it is found in the performance of the act which the offered promise requests as an acceptance.

Exchange. Something done by a promisee, even if requested by the promisor, cannot be consideration unless it appears to have been given or paid for the promise. As Justice Benjamin Cardozo has said:

> "Nothing is consideration," it has been held, "that is not regarded as such by both parties. . . ." The fortuitous presence in a transaction of some possibility of detriment, latent but unthought of, is not enough. . . . Promisor and promisee must have dealt with it as the inducement to the promise.[4]

Elaborating on this same point, Justice Holmes has written in his book, *The Common Law:*

> But although the courts may have sometimes gone a little far in their anxiety to sustain agreements, there can be no doubt of the principle which I have laid down, that the same thing may be a consideration or not, as it is dealt with by the parties. This raises the question how a thing must be dealt with, in order to make it a consideration.
>
> It is said that consideration must not be confounded with motive. It is true that it must not be confounded with what may be the prevailing or chief motive in actual fact. A man may promise to paint a picture for five hundred dollars, while his chief motive may be a desire for fame. A consideration may be given and accepted, in fact, solely for the purpose of making a promise binding. But, nevertheless, it is the essence of a consideration, that, by the terms of the agreement, it is given and accepted as the motive or inducement of the promise. Conversely, the promise must be made and accepted as the conventional motive or inducement for furnishing the consideration. The root of the whole matter is the relation of reciprocal conventional inducement, each for the other, between consideration and promise. . . .
>
> Both sides of the relation between consideration and promise, and the conventional nature of that relation, may be illustrated by the case of the cask. Suppose that the truckman is willing to carry the cask, and the owner to let him carry it, without any bargain, and that each knows the other's state of mind; but that the truckman, seeing his own advantage in the matter, says to the owner, "In consideration of your delivering me the cask, and letting me carry it, I promise to carry it," and that the owner thereupon delivers it. I suppose that the promise

[4] *McGovern v. New York*, 234 N.Y. 377, 138 N.E. 26, 25 A.L.R. 1442 (1923).

would be binding. The promise is offered in terms as the inducement for the delivery, and the delivery is made in terms as the inducement for the promise. It may be very probable that the delivery would have been made without a promise, and that the promise would have been in gratuitous form if it had not been accepted upon consideration; but this is only a guess after all. The delivery need not have been made unless the owner chose, and having been made as the term of a bargain, the promisor cannot set up what might have happened to destroy the effect of what did happen. It would seem therefore that the same transaction in substance and spirit might be voluntary or obligatory, according to the form of words which the parties chose to employ for the purpose of affecting the legal consequences.[5]

Example: A tramp came to a householder's front door asking for something to eat. The householder said, "If you go around to the back door, I'll give you a piece of pie and a cup of coffee." The tramp promptly went around to the rear of the house, but in the interim the householder decided to discourage vagrancy, and upon reaching the back door told the tramp, "Beat it or I'll call a cop."

If the tramp should sue for the value of the promised food, he would not recover because there was no consideration for the householder's promise. Under the circumstances, a reasonable man would not be justified in concluding that the requested act was the price or exchange for the promise. The tramp's going to the rear of the house was not an agreed exchange for the promise, but instead was merely a condition for the promised gift. The fact that a condition was stated and performed did not change the promise from what it essentially was, a promise to make a gift.

LEGAL DETRIMENT AND LEGAL BENEFIT

UNILATERAL CONTRACTS

A person sustains a legal detriment if he does something which he previously was not legally obliged to do; a person acquires a legal benefit if he obtains something to which he previously was not legally entitled.

Example: An uncle promised to pay his nephew $500 if the nephew obtained a grade of "A" in his basic law course. The nephew applied himself and earned an "A" (it *is* possible). The uncle however refused to pay and the nephew sued.

The uncle asserted that his promise was not enforceable because it lacked consideration, and supported his assertion with two arguments:

1. The nephew did not sustain a detriment, but instead really acquired a benefit in developing better study habits, increasing his knowledge, and obtaining an excellent grade on his record.

Answer to the Argument: The nephew was under no legal duty to the

[5] Oliver Wendell Holmes, Jr., *The Common Law* (1881; Cambridge: Harvard University Press, 1963), pp. 230-232.

uncle or to anyone else to work harder for the excellent grade or even to pass the course. Even though he may have acquired an actual benefit, the nephew sustained a *legal* detriment in doing something he was not previously legally bound to do.

2. The nephew was a good student and would have worked hard and obtained the excellent grade anyway.

Answer to the Argument: For the performance of an act to constitute consideration for a promise, it is not necessary that the promise be the sole motive or only reason for performance of the act. If the parties bargain or agree on the act in exchange for the promise, and if in performing the act the promisee is doing something he previously was not legally bound to do, the act is consideration for the promise.

Therefore the nephew could recover the promised $500.

Example: On June 1, without any exchange bargained for, an uncle promised that he would pay his nephew $500 on the following July 1. The nephew expressed full agreement with the idea. When the uncle defaulted on his promise, the nephew sued.

The nephew argued that his acquiring $500 would be a legal benefit to which he was not previously legally entitled, and that the uncle's paying would be a legal detriment, the uncle doing something he was not previously legally obliged to do.

The nephew could not recover. There are two fallacies in the nephew's argument:

1. The argument goes around in a closed circle, it declares that if a certain promise is enforced, then its performance constitutes the act sufficient to make it enforceable. Under this argument all promises would be enforceable without anything more. Consideration for a promise must be something *separate* from the promise itself.

2. The argument reverses the direction in which benefit and detriment must go. The following diagram shows that the promise is *out* from the promisor and *in* to the promisee, and in exchange for the promise there must be something *in* to the promisor or *out* from the promisee—an *in* for an *out*. Of course the same thing can be and usually is both detriment to the promisee and benefit to the promisor.

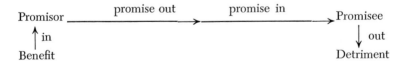

Example: A debtor owed his creditor a past due debt of $1,000. A guarantor wrote to the creditor, "If you will give the debtor six months longer on his $1,000 debt owed to you, I will guaranty payment." The creditor replied that he agreed and waited six months without trying to collect from the debtor. After expiration of the six months, the debt was still unpaid and the creditor was unable to collect from the debtor because he had become insolvent. The creditor demanded payment from the guarantor and on his refusal to pay, sued the guarantor.

The guarantor argued that he had received nothing in exchange for his promise. Whether or not the creditor received any benefit is immaterial. Either detriment *or* benefit is sufficient to constitute consideration. In waiting six months the creditor did something he was not legally obliged to do in exchange for the guarantor's promise, and the creditor thus sustained a legal detriment. This constituted consideration for the guarantor's promise and the guarantor's promise would be enforceable.

Example: An owner owned a vacant lot across which his neighbor habitually drove as a shortcut, ignoring the owner's frequent requests to desist. Hoping to break the habit, the owner said to the neighbor, "If you will refrain from driving across my lot for one month, I'll pay you $10." The neighbor ceased his trespassing for one month, claimed $10, and sued when the owner refused to pay.

Since there was no consideration for the promise, the neighbor could not recover. Although the neighbor sustained an actual detriment in exchange for the promise, it was not a legal detriment—he did only what he was already legally obliged to do. Although the owner acquired an actual benefit, it was not a legal benefit; he acquired nothing more than he was already legally entitled to—that is, to have the neighbor cease trespassing.

Example: An owner sent ten shirts to a laundry and in due course received them back together with a bill for the usual charges. Printed on the bill was the statement, "All claims for damages must be made within ten days after return of goods." The owner read this statement and then paid his bill without protest. This was the owner's first experience with that laundry. Two weeks later when the owner for the first time unfolded the tenth shirt in the pile, he discovered that it had been badly torn through negligence of the laundry. When the owner notified the laundry and claimed payment or replacement, the laundry refused to make any adjustment because the owner had not presented his claim within ten days. The owner sued.

The owner could collect. Since the owner had no prior dealings with the laundry he was unfamiliar with the ten-day limitation until his shirts were returned. Therefore it was not an implied term of his original contract.

The laundry would argue that since the owner knew of, and acquiesced in, the time limitation when he accepted return of his shirts, he thereupon agreed to the limitation. This is correct, but there was no consideration for the owner's agreement. The laundry was already under a legal duty to return the shirts. It sustained no legal detriment, the owner acquired no legal benefit, thus there was no consideration, and the owner's agreement to the ten-day limitation was not enforceable.

If the laundry wished to hold customers to the ten-day limitation it should have made the limitation part of its original contracts. Added afterwards, it would have to be supported by additional consideration in order to be enforceable.

BILATERAL CONTRACTS

In a unilateral contract a promisee's doing something (consisting of either legal detriment to the promisee or legal benefit to the promisor) as the agreed exchange for a promise, constitutes the consideration necessary to make the promise enforceable. In a bilateral contract the promisee's legally binding *promise* to do the agreed thing can be just as effective as his actual *doing* of the thing to constitute the necessary consideration for the promisor's promise.

Suppose that a seller delivers a requested book to a buyer and in exchange the buyer promises to pay the price of $5 in seven days. The seller's act of delivering the book, which he was not previously obligated to do, is a legal detriment and constitutes consideration for the buyer's promise to pay. If instead of delivering the book immediately, the seller promises to deliver the book in thirty days and the buyer promises to pay $5 within seven days from the date of the contract, each promise is given for the other. The buyer is promising to pay in advance of time for delivery, and in exchange for his promise he obtains the seller's promise to deliver the book in thirty days. Previous to making the agreement the seller had no obligation to deliver the book. When the seller assumes such an obligation, the buyer acquires a legal right which constitutes consideration sufficient to make the buyer's promise enforceable. Therefore, the seller can collect from the buyer after expiration of the seven-day period. Should the seller promise to deliver in seven days and the buyer to pay in thirty days, then the buyer could enforce the seller's promise to deliver, even though (as provided in the agreement) the buyer would not yet be required to pay anything.

NOTE that the requirement of consideration does *not* mean that unless some *money* is paid a sales contract is not enforceable. If so agreed, a legally binding *promise* to pay is just as effective a consideration as an actual payment would be.

Mutuality of Obligation

In a bilateral contract the promise of each party is given in exchange for, and constitutes consideration for, the promise of the other party. For this reason, there must be mutuality of obligation, each party must be bound to something which involves legal detriment, or neither party is bound. Whether or not there is mutuality of obligation becomes a pertinent question if the promise of one of the parties is to do one of two or more things in the alternative, with the promisor reserving to himself the right to choose which alternative he will perform. If any one of such alternatives does not involve legal detriment, then the promise of that party is not consideration for the promise of the other party, and therefore the promise of the other party is not enforceable.

The principal types of contracts in which the question of mutuality has arisen are 1) contracts which provide that one party has a right to cancel the contract, and 2) contracts which provide for delivery of an indefinite quantity of goods.

1) *Right to Cancel.* If a contract expressly gives one party an unlimited right to cancel, then in reality that party is not binding himself to do something involving legal detriment, and there is no consideration for the other party's promise. If, however, a party's right to cancel is limited to certain conditions or can be exercised only in a certain way, then that party is limiting his freedom of action to some extent and is thus sustaining some legal detriment, which constitutes consideration for the other party's promise.

Example: A contract for the sale and purchase of certain described goods at a stated price expressly gave the seller a right to cancel, the cancellation provision reading as quoted below. Although the seller did not cancel, the buyer repudiated the contract and refused to receive the goods or to pay when the seller tendered delivery according to the contract. The seller thereupon sued for damages for breach of contract.

1. The cancellation provision read: "The seller reserves the right to cancel this contract at any time the seller may deem proper, by giving ten days written notice thereof to the buyer."

The seller would have a right to recover damages for the buyer's breach of contract. According to the contract, the seller could perform either 1) by delivering goods according to the contract, or 2) by giving to the buyer the described notice of concellation. The first alternative would obviously involve legal detriment. So also would the second alternative—before making the contract the seller had no legal obligation to write the described notice to the buyer. Since even the second alternative involved legal detriment, its value (that is, the value or worth of the seller writing a letter ten days before delivery time) would be immaterial. This was the exchange agreed upon between the parties for the buyer's promise. The buyer's promise therefore was supported by consideration and would be enforceable.

2. The cancellation provision read: "The seller reserves the right to cancel this contract at any time the seller may deem proper."

Some courts would say that if the seller decided to cancel, he could do so by taking no action whatsoever, that by doing nothing at all the seller could fully perform his promise, and that therefore since the seller could select an alternative which would not involve legal detriment, his promise would not be consideration for the buyer's promise and the buyer's promise would not be enforceable. Some other courts would say that any cancellation provision implies the affirmative act of giving notice and that therefore this cancellation provision should have the same effect as that quoted in Part 1 of this example.

2) *Indefinite Quantity.* Sometimes an agreement is entered into under which a seller promises to sell and deliver whatever quantity of certain described goods the buyer may order, up to a stated maximum. Whether there is consideration for the seller's promise depends upon whether or not the buyer binds himself to do something involving legal detriment. The reverse type of agreement also is possible, with a buyer promising to buy whatever quantity the seller delivers, up to a stated maximum.

Example: On March 1 a seller dated, signed, and sent to a buyer two copies of the following: "I hereby offer to sell to you all the wheat (specifying the grade) that you choose to order at $3 a bushel, not to exceed 10,000 bushels. If you wish to accept this offer, sign and return one copy of this letter. Upon your acceptance of this offer, the contract will continue in effect for six months from date hereof." On the same day the buyer wrote "Accepted" at the bottom of one copy, signed it, and returned it to the seller. During the next four months the buyer ordered, received, and paid for 5,000 bushels. At the beginning of the fifth month the buyer ordered 1,000 bushels. The seller promptly replied rejecting the order and stating that he canceled the March 1 agreement. The buyer protested and ordered an additional 2,000 bushels. When the seller refused to deliver any of the 3,000 bushels, the buyer sued for damages for breach of contract.

The buyer could recover damages for nondelivery of 1,000 bushels but would not have an enforceable contract for the other 2,000 bushels. All that the buyer gave in exchange for the seller's promise to sell for six months was a promise to buy what he chose to order. The buyer's promise would not be broken if he chose to order nothing or bought elsewhere. Since the buyer's promise contained an alternative which did not involve legal detriment, it was not consideration for the seller's promise, and therefore the seller's promise to sell at $3 for six months was not an enforceable contract. The seller's promise was merely an offer which the seller stated would remain open for six months. As a firm offer under the Uniform Commercial Code, the offer would be irrevocable for three months and revocable afterwards. The buyer ordered 1,000 bushels before the seller revoked the offer and thus formed an enforceable contract for 1,000 bushels. The seller then terminated his offer so that no contract was formed when the buyer ordered 2,000 bushels.

If as the requested exchange for the seller's promise, the buyer had promised to buy all of the wheat he needed in his established milling business for the next six months, the buyer's commitment not to buy his requirements elsewhere would be consideration for the seller's promise and the seller's promise would be fully enforceable.

Or if as the requested exchange for the seller's promise, the buyer had agreed to buy some specified quantity (for example 1,000 bushels), the buyer's promise would be consideration for the seller's promise to sell all that the buyer chose to order, up to 10,000 bushels. An enforceable maximum–minimum contract would thus be formed, with the buyer obliged to buy at least the minimum (1,000 bushels) and the seller obliged to sell any additional quantity the buyer wished to purchase, up to the agreed maximum.

Adequacy of Consideration

To say that consideration is something given in exchange for a promise does not mean that the value of what is given must be substantially equal to the value of the promise. If *anything* regardless of value is actually bargained for and given in exchange for a promise, this will usually be sufficient. In bargaining, the parties express their conclusion as to the value of what is given, and the courts will usually not attempt to usurp the opinion of the parties.

Example: A buyer (B. Brown) paid a seller $1 and the seller signed and gave to the buyer the following: "In consideration of $1 in hand paid, receipt of which is hereby acknowledged, I hereby offer to sell to B. Brown my land [describing it] for $25,000 and agree that this offer shall remain open for six months." A few days later the seller notified the buyer that the option was terminated and tendered return of the buyer's $1. The buyer refused the $1 and sent a written acceptance of the seller's offer. When the seller refused to transfer the land on the buyer's tender of $25,000, the buyer sued.

The buyer could recover. The seller might argue that $1 was ridiculously inadequate for a six-month option on property worth $25,000. Nevertheless that was the price the parties had placed on the option, there was consideration, and the offer would be irrevocable.

If several items or promises are involved, the courts will usually not inquire into adequacy of consideration by attempting to allocate or divide portions of consideration among the items or promises. What is given is consideration for *all* that is received, what is received is consideration for *all* that is given.

Example: A creditor (C. Carter) refused to make a requested $1,000 six-month loan to a debtor (D. Davis) unless someone with a good credit rating guaranteed the debtor's repayment. Accordingly a guarantor dated, signed, and gave to the creditor the following: "In consideration of C. Carter's loaning D. Davis $1,000 due six months from date, I promise that if Davis does not repay the loan when due, I will pay Carter." At the same time the creditor loaned $1,000 to the debtor, the latter dated, signed, and gave to the creditor the following: "Six months from date I promise to pay C. Carter $1,000." When the debtor defaulted, the creditor sued the guarantor.

The guarantor argued that the creditor's loan was consideration for the debtor's promise and that there was no additional consideration for the guarantor's promise. However, the creditor bargained for both promises. What the creditor gave was consideration for *all* of the bargained exchange, and the creditor could recover from the guarantor.

There is an exception to the rule that the courts will not inquire into the relative value of what is given in exchange for one or more promises. If a bargain concerns things identical in nature (especially money for money) to be exchanged at the same time and place, value is already so fixed and clear that the bargain cannot be said to involve any individual opinion of the parties. The identical items will be canceled out; something additional must be given for any additional promise. Contract forms used by some businesses and even by some lawyers begin: "In consideration of $1 each to the other in hand paid, receipt of which is hereby acknowledged, the following agreement is hereby made. . . ." The swapping of dollar bills even if actually done is ridiculous and not consideration for anything. If nothing further is given by one party, there is no consideration for anything further promised by the other party.

Example: Wishing to bind himself to give his nephew (N. Norton) $1,000 in one year, an uncle requested and received $1 from the nephew and dated, signed, and gave to the nephew the following promissory note: "In consideration of $1 in hand paid, receipt of which is hereby acknowledged, I promise to pay N. Norton $1,000 one year from date." Upon maturity of the note the uncle defaulted and the nephew sued.

There was consideration for the uncle's promise. This is a promise of money for money, but not at the same time and place. The parties in effect have valued the use of $1 for one year at $999, and the court will not usurp the parties' judgment as to value. The uncle's promise however would not be enforceable for another reason—interest at an excessive rate is usury and cannot be collected (see Chapter 8).

Although something inadequate in value can be sufficient consideration for a promise, a court may refuse equitable remedies if the disproportion in value is considerable. A person has no *right* to equity remedies, he may obtain relief in equity only if fairness and justice so indicate.

Example: A decedent was survived by his wife, an adult son, and other relatives. The decedent's will was probated and the court appointed an executor to take over the decedent's assets, pay his debts, and distribute the remainder according to the will. The decedent's assets included a $900 judgment against the son, and the decedent's will left a bequest of $1,300 to the wife. After some negotiations involving the executor and all of the heirs, the wife and the executor reached an agreement, the executor agreeing to transfer the $900 judgment to the wife and the wife agreeing that $900 be deducted from her $1,300 bequest. A few months later the executor prepared the papers which had to be filed in court to carry out this agreement. When the wife refused to sign, the executor brought an action in the name of the decedent's estate against the wife for a decree of specific performance, to require the wife to sign the papers necessary to effectuate the agreement. Evidence in the lawsuit showed that the son was completely insolvent, his debts considerably exceeding the total value of his assets, so that there were no assets from which the $900 judgment could be collected at that time.

The Pennsylvania Superior Court refused to issue a decree of specific performance, saying: "We must not lose sight of the fact that this is not an action at law for damages for breach of the contract, nor is it a distribution of the estate . . . in the orphans' court; it is a proceeding in equity to specifically enforce the contract according to its very terms. . . . There was no question that the consideration was sufficient to support the contract as a binding obligation in a court of law. . . . We are of the opinion that this contract was upon the part of the widow so exceedingly improvident that a chancellor [that is, the judge in the equity lawsuit] ought not to be called upon to enforce it according to its terms; the parties should be left to their remedy at law."[6]

PERFORMANCE OF PREEXISTING CONTRACTS

Sometimes a party to an existing contract makes a new promise adding to or modifying his obligation under the existing contract. If what the promisee of such a promise does or promises to do in exchange for the new promise is no more than what he is already obliged by the existing contract to do, there is usually no consideration for the new promise.

Contracts Under the Uniform Commercial Code

Sales-of-Goods Contracts.   An agreement modifying a contract for the sale of goods needs no consideration to be binding.   The Code considers[7] the existence of the original contract a sufficient equivalent of consideration to make enforceable any agreed modification of the contract.

Other Contracts.   In addition to sales of goods, transactions to which the Code applies include storage and shipment of goods, borrowing on goods, negotiable commercial paper (checks, notes, and drafts), issuance and sale of stocks, and some other types of transactions.   As to any such transaction, the Code provides:

> Any claim or right arising out of an alleged breach can be discharged in whole or in part without consideration by a written waiver signed and delivered by the aggrieved party.[8]

The preexisting obligation together with putting the waiver or renunciation in writing constitute an equivalent of consideration sufficient to make the waiver or renunciation enforceable without actual consideration.

Example: A seller sold, indorsed, and delivered to a buyer (B. Burns) a certificate for ten shares of stock in a certain corporation, for which the buyer paid to the seller $200 and agreed to pay the seller $1,000 more in sixty days.

[6] *Spotts* v. *Eisenhauer*, 31 Pa. Super. 89 (1906).
[7] U.C.C. Sec. 2-209.
[8] U.C.C. Sec. 1-107.

After the obligation was overdue, the buyer paid the seller $750 and the seller signed and gave to the buyer the following: "Received from B. Burns $750 in full satisfaction of the $1,000 still owed to me for the purchase of stock, and I hereby release him from said debt." The seller afterwards changed his mind and sued for the $250 balance due.

The seller could not recover. His waiver of rights would be enforceable without consideration.

Contracts Not Under the Uniform Commercial Code

Transactions to which the Code does not apply include contracts involving the sales of land, construction of buildings, performance of services by employees and others, and loans of money (unless the loan happens to be evidenced by a negotiable promissory note).

Example: The owner of a plot of land contracted with a builder for construction of a house according to certain plans and specifications for $25,000. When the house was partially completed, labor and material costs increased. The builder said he could not finish unless the owner would agree to pay $2,000 more.

1. The owner promised that upon completion he would pay $2,000 in addition to the original contract price. However, when the building was completed, the owner refused to pay more than the original price, and the builder sued for the additional $2,000.

Courts in most states would hold that the builder could not recover. In exchange for the owner's promise, the builder did only what he was already under contract obligation to do. Therefore the builder sustained no legal detriment, the owner acquired no legal benefit, there was no consideration, and the owner's promise would not be enforceable.

2. The parties entered into a second contract expressly canceling all prior agreements, and agreeing that the builder would build according to stated plans and specifications (identical with those of the original contract) and the owner would pay $27,000 ($2,000 more than in the original contract). When the building was completed the owner refused to pay more than the original price and the builder sued for the additional $2,000.

As in Part 1, the question is whether there was consideration for the owner's agreement to pay the additional $2,000. The builder would argue that the old contract was canceled and a new, enforceable contract formed. The theory of canceling the old contract and substituting a new contract would apply if the parties actually did just that—that is, if they actually canceled the old contract so that both, even for a moment, were free from any contract obligation. If both were freed, if the builder could then have refused to sign the new contract and walked off with no further obligation to continue building, then the builder's promise to build would be consideration for the owner's promise to pay the price in the second contract. However, parties will seldom wish to risk fully releasing each other. Here, since the cancellation provision was a part of the new contract, neither party was free at any time from the obligation of the first contract. Therefore, whatever the parties would call it—a promise to pay additional compensation or a cancellation of the old contract and the formation of a new one—there would be no consideration for the additional $2,000, because the builder was agreeing to do only what he was already bound to do.

3. In requesting the additional $2,000, the builder offered to add a breezeway not included in the original plans if the owner would agree to pay the additional $2,000. The owner agreed and the builder completed the building according to the original plans and also added the agreed breezeway. The owner paid only $300 more than the original contract price and when the builder sued for the remaining $1,700, the owner presented evidence conclusively showing that the breezeway increased building costs by not more than $300.

The builder would collect the $1,700 for which he sued. The builder was not previously obliged to include a breezeway. His doing so in exchange for the owner's promise would be sufficient consideration to bind the owner on his promise to pay the additional $2,000, regardless of the actual cost or value of the breezeway.

Sometimes a creditor will agree with his debtor to accept less than full payment in complete satisfaction of a debt. If the creditor later changes his mind, the question arises whether, in spite of his agreement, the creditor can collect the balance of the debt. Possible fact situations can be classified as follows:

1) The debt is past due (matured) when the debtor and creditor enter into their new agreement.

a) The amount of the debt is definite and not disputed (sometimes called liquidated).

b) The amount of the debt is not definite, or is reasonably in dispute (sometimes called unliquidated).

2) The debt is not yet due when the debtor and creditor enter into their new agreement.

Matured Debt, Definite and Not Disputed. Generally if a debt for a definite amount is matured, not reasonably in dispute, and not evidenced by a negotiable promissory note, the creditor's promise to accept a smaller sum as payment in full is not supported by consideration and is not enforceable.

Example: In an obligation not coming under the Uniform Commercial Code, a debtor named D. Davis owed his creditor, C. Carter, $2,000 due February 1.

Part I. On February 7 the debtor paid the creditor $1,500, in exchange for which the creditor dated, signed, and gave to the debtor the following: "Received from D. Davis $1,500 which I hereby accept as payment in full of his $2,000 debt owed to me, which came due February 1." A month later the creditor changed his mind and sued the debtor for the $500 balance of the debt.

The creditor could collect the $500 for which he was suing. The debtor would argue that the creditor had promised to accept the part payment as payment in full. However, in exchange for this promise the creditor received nothing more than he was already legally entitled to receive and the debtor paid no more (in fact $500 less) than he was already legally obliged to pay. Thus there was no legal benefit or detriment, no consideration, and the creditor's promise would not be enforceable.

Part II. On February 7 the debtor sent to the creditor a check for $1,500, payable to the creditor; on the check the debtor wrote, "Payment in full of all claims to date." The creditor crossed out this statement, indorsed and cashed the check, receiving $1,500, and then sued the debtor for $500 as the balance claimed due on the debt.

The creditor could collect the $500 for which he was suing. The check was an offer by the debtor to settle the debt for $1,500. As the offeree, the creditor could not use the check and refuse the conditions under which it was tendered. Although the creditor was attempting to reject the offer by crossing out the statement, his conduct of cashing the check constituted his acceptance. By cashing the check the creditor in effect promised to accept the $1,500 as payment in full. However there was no more consideration for this promise than there was in Part I of this example. Therefore, the creditor's promise would not be enforceable.

Part III. On February 7 the debtor signed and gave to the creditor a one-month negotiable promissory note in the amount of $1,500 naming the creditor as payee, and the creditor agreed to accept the note as full satisfaction for the $2,000 debt. A few weeks later the creditor changed his mind and sued for the full $2,000. (Since the debt had not previously been evidenced by a negotiable promissory note, the creditor's agreeing to release the debtor from a portion of the debt would not be a release of rights arising under the Uniform Commercial Code and therefore would not come under the provision, referred to on page 128, that such a waiver can be enforced without consideration.)

The courts of the various states do not agree as to this type of situation:

1. Courts in some states would say that the creditor could recover nothing until maturity of the note and then only the face amount of the note ($1,500). The note was itself something of value; it is easier to sue on an obligation when it is evidenced by a negotiable note, and a negotiable note can more easily be transferred than can a debt not evidenced by a note. Under this view, when the creditor received the $1,500 note, he received something to which he was not previously legally entitled (legal benefit), the debtor gave something he was not previously obligated to give (legal detriment), there was consideration for the creditor's promise, and the promise to accept the note as full payment would be enforceable. This reasoning—concerning the debtor's giving a negotiable *note*—is not inconsistent with the reasoning in Part II of this problem which involves the debtor's giving a negotiable

check for a lesser amount. A note is used when the parties intend to delay payment, and therefore is a contract separate and different from payment itself, while a check is merely a way to make a present payment of money.

2. Courts in some states would say that there is no difference between a debtor's note for $1,500 and his cash (or check) payment in that amount, that the giving of the note would not be consideration for the creditor's promise to accept its amount as full payment, and that therefore the creditor would be entitled to collect the full $2,000 debt.

Part IV. On February 7 the debtor and creditor dated and signed the following agreement: "C. Carter hereby agrees to extend for six months the $2,000 debt owed to Carter by D. Davis, which originally came due February 1, and Davis hereby agrees to pay the debt six months from date hereof, with interest at the rate of 6 percent per year." Several weeks later the creditor changed his mind, decided not to wait the full six months, and on April 1 sued the debtor for $2,000 with interest to that date.

The courts of the various states do not agree as to the solution of this situation.

Creditor's Argument: Even if the original debt does not provide for interest, interest accrues and is payable at the legal rate (for example, 6 percent per year in some states) on any overdue obligation. Since the debtor was already bound to pay interest until the debt was paid, his promise to pay interest imposed no additional legal obligation on him. There was no legal detriment or benefit, no consideration, and the creditor's promise would not be enforceable. The courts of some of the states have adopted this view.

Debtor's Arugment: It is true that interest accrues and is due at the legal rate on any overdue obligation. However, unless he agrees otherwise a debtor may at anytime stop further interest from accruing by paying his overdue obligation. In the quoted agreement the debtor bound himself to pay interest for six months longer, thus surrendering his right to terminate his interest obligation by paying before then. Thus the debtor was undertaking an additional legal obligation and the creditor was acquiring an additional legal right (namely interest for the six-month period, not subject to reduction by the debtor's paying earlier), there was consideration, and the creditor's promise would be enforceable. This seems to be a sounder argument and is followed by a majority of the state courts.

Part V. The debtor was indebted to various other creditors in addition to Carter and was unable to pay them all in full. On February 7 the debtor explained his financial situation to Carter, and Carter dated, signed, and gave to the debtor the following: "To Whom It May Concern: This is to certify that in consideration of $1,500 to be paid to me by D. Davis three months from date, I will accept said sum in full satisfaction of his $2,000 debt owned to me which originally came due February 1." The debtor showed this writing to some of his other creditors and obtained their agreements to settle for part payment. When the three-month period expired, Carter changed his mind, refused the debtor's tender of $1,500, and sued for the entire $2,000.

Carter would not be able to recover. A creditor who joins in such an agreement (called a composition of creditors) does so because other creditors have joined or are expected to join in similar agreements. This mutual action, or expectation of mutual action, is a recognized equivalent of consideration and makes each participating creditor's promise enforceable without actual consideration, even though the arrangement does not include all creditors. The form of the composition agreement is not material. Frequently all joining creditors sign one paper; sometimes a condition is stated that the agreement does not become effective until a stated number of creditors join.

Matured Debt, Indefinite or Reasonably in Dispute. A debt is indefinite in amount if the debtor has engaged work to be done without any agreement, either express or implied, as to the price he will pay. The debtor's resulting obligation is to pay the reasonable charge for the work done. If the parties cannot agree, a court must eventually determine what amount is reasonable.

A debt may be disputed even though a definite amount has been agreed upon by the parties. If goods shipped under a sales contract fail to conform to the contract, the buyer can either reject them altogether, or, if he wishes, retain them. If he retains the goods, his obligation is to pay the contract price less damages resulting from the failure of the goods to conform to the contract. If a buyer honestly and reasonably believes that goods do not conform to his contract, then, whether he rejects or retains them, his obligation to pay is "reasonably in dispute," even though court action might later determine that the goods exactly conform to the contract.

If the amount is either indefinite or reasonably in dispute, a debtor is not obliged to pay any specific sum until a court determines whether he has any obligation at all, and if so, the exact amount of his obligation. In paying anything at all in advance of such a court determination, the debtor is doing something which he is not at that time legally obliged to do. Such a payment therefore constitutes legal detriment and is consideration for any promise made by the creditor.

Unmatured Debt. If a debtor makes a payment prior to the date his obligation comes due, the debtor is doing something he is not legally obliged to do, and the creditor is obtaining money before he is legally entitled to it. The early payment therefore will be consideration for the creditor's promise to accept a smaller sum as payment in full, *if* the earliness of the payment is agreed to by both parties as the exchange for the creditor's promise, or at least if the earliness of the payment appears presumably to be in the contemplation of both parties as a significant element of the new agreement.

Performance for Third Party.   Suppose that at a time when a debtor's obligation to his creditor is past due, a third person promises to give the debtor some specified item if the debtor will pay this debt.   Courts of the various states are not agreed as to whether the debtor's paying (or promising to pay if a promise is what the third person requests) can be consideration for the third person's promise.   Some argue that in paying his creditor, the debtor is doing only what he is already legally obliged to do and thus is giving no consideration for the third person's promise.   Others argue that the obligation is owed to the creditor not to the third person, and that if for the third person or at his request the debtor makes payment to his creditor (or promises to do so), the third person is obtaining something to which he himself was not previously legally entitled; and that the third person thus obtains a legal benefit which is sufficient consideration to make his promise enforceable.

Part 2   EQUIVALENTS OF CONSIDERATION

An *equivalent of consideration* is a fact situation which, as a matter of policy, is felt to justify the legal enforcement of a promise without actual consideration.   Amendments or waivers involving contracts under the Uniform Commercial Code, and compositions of creditors are two equivalents of consideration which have already been referred to.   In addition to these two situations, the principal equivalents of consideration are found in connection with promises made for past obligations or performances, promises upon which promisees rely, promises under seal, and promises expressly stated to be legally binding.   While all such promises are not automatically enforceable, *some* of these types of promises are, under certain circumstances, deemed to be enforceable without actual consideration.

PROMISES FOR PAST ACTS

After one person has completely performed an act, another person will sometimes make a promise to pay a certain amount to the one who has performed.   Since the act has already been performed, there is, of course, no exchange of the act for the promise, and therefore the past act cannot be actual consideration for the present promise.   However, under certain circumstances it is felt to be sound policy to enforce such a promise even though there is no actual consideration.   The principal fact situations involving present promises for past acts may be classified as follows:

1) *Promises Related to Some Legal Liability of the Promisor.*

a) *Past liability no longer enforceable.*   Such a situation occurs when the promisor was at one time legally obligated on a debt but its enforcement is barred by a statute of limitation[9] or by the promisor being discharged from his obligation through a bankruptcy proceeding. The fact that there once existed a legally enforceable obligation is recognized as an equivalent of consideration, so that a new promise to pay the obligation is legally enforceable without any new consideration.

b) *Presently enforceable, unliquidated liability.* An unliquidated or indefinite liability can arise in a number of ways. For example, if nongratuitous services are performed at the request of a person who has not in advance agreed on the amount of compensation to be paid, the recipient of the services will be obliged to pay whatever amount the court may determine to be the reasonable value of the services. Suppose that before court action the recipient promises to pay a specific amount for the services, later reneges on his promise, and the resulting lawsuit determines that the reasonable value is less than the promised amount. Courts in some states say that the promisor is obliged to pay the promised amount, that the existence of the enforceable but unliquidated liability is sufficient as an equivalent of consideration to make the promise to pay the specified amount enforceable. The Uniform Commercial Code adopts[10] this view if the promise to pay the specific sum is evidenced by a negotiable promissory note. If a negotiable note is not used, some courts hold that the promisor is only obliged to pay the reasonable value of the services, that the promise to pay a specific sum is evidence of value but is not itself an enforceable promise without additional consideration.

2) *Promises Not Related to Any Previous Legal Liability of the Promisor.* If the recipient of certain, nongratuitous performance has requested the performance, he certainly has an actual contractual obligation to pay. On the other hand, if he does not request or permit the performance, no actual contract arises. The classic example is the case of the painter who mistakenly paints the wrong house. If the homeowner is aware of the painter's mistake and stands by without saying anything, when he reasonably should know that the paint job is not a gift, the homeowner's conduct amounts to an acceptance of the painter's offer and forms a contract. If however the house is painted in the owner's absence, no actual contract ever arises. If such an unrequested act is of necessary or vital importance to a person, some courts have found

---

[9] A statute of limitations is a statute fixing a period of time within which a lawsuit must be brought. Its purpose is to prevent enforcement of stale claims after passage of so long a period of time that proof of any defense could become impossible through loss of evidence and witnesses. Under the Uniform Commercial Code, for example, lawsuits must be brought within four years (unless the time is shortened by the contract of the parties) for claims involving sales of goods (U.C.C. Sec. 2-725). Statutes of limitation are further discussed in Chapter 11.

[10] U.C.C. Sec. 3-408.

a quasi-contractual obligation to pay. But if an act has not been requested or voluntarily accepted, and is not of vital importance, the recipient of the performance is not bound to pay; he has neither a contractual nor a quasi-contractual obligation. Suppose, however, that such a person agrees to pay a certain amount for what has been done for him. In many states the promise will not be legally enforceable against the promisor. In some states, however, if an unrequested benefit is substantial, it will be deemed an equivalent of consideration, sufficient to make a promise to pay enforceable without actual consideration. Note that this equivalent of consideration applies only when the promisor was not previously under a contractual obligation; the theory, therefore, cannot be stretched to cover a promise to pay more than had been originally agreed for certain contracted performance.

RELIANCE ON PROMISES

In practically every contract lawsuit which is brought following a defendant's failure to perform his promise, the plaintiff has sustained the damages for which he is suing only because he has to some extent relied on the defendant's promise. To say that such reliance should automatically make the defendant's promise enforceable would completely reverse the policy of the law so long recognized as sound, that consideration or other good reason is necessary for a promise to be legally enforceable. On the other hand there is a limit to how far society can permit a promisor to mislead others. It is certainly sound policy for *some* promises to be declared enforceable solely because promisees have substantially relied on them. This policy view has given rise to a theory, usually called the promissory estoppel or *detrimental reliance* theory. Under this theory, the combination of the following three conditions will constitute an equivalent of consideration, sufficient to make a promise enforceable without actual consideration:

1. From the nature of the promise in question and the circumstances under which it is made, the promisor should reasonably expect that the promisee will rely on the promise and act in some definite and substantial way (or to a substantial degree give up or refrain from some definite action).

2. The promisee does so act (or refrain from acting).

3. Substantial unfairness or injustice will result unless the promise is declared enforceable.

When a promise to contribute to a charitable institution is deemed to be enforceable, it is usually on the basis of the detrimental reliance theory. If the institution relies on a promise and makes binding commitments (for building, expansion, or whatever is contemplated), the promise is enforceable. That other persons contribute (or promise to contribute), induced by the promise of an earlier contributor, is held by courts in some states to be sufficient to make the earlier promise enforceable, even before the charity takes any action. Courts in some other states however say that the promise is not enforceable until the charity itself acts in reliance on it.

One distinguished court has suggested that the detrimental reliance theory applies only to gift promises, that is, promises (like charitable subscriptions) for which no exchange is expected. Another court has doubted that the theory should be restricted only to donative promises. However, even if not limited to donative promises, the detrimental reliance theory does *not* apply to the majority of promises that are made. Notice especially the terms used in stating the detrimental reliance theory: "reasonable expectation," "substantial action," "substantial unfairness and injustice." Such vague, flexible terms, incapable of exact definition, should warn a person that he is taking a great chance on his promisor's good faith if he relies on a promise not otherwise enforceable against the promisor.

PROMISES UNDER SEAL

Under the common law, a written promise to which the promisor has added his seal needs no consideration to be enforceable. Thus a seal is deemed to be an equivalent of consideration, making the promise enforceable without actual consideration. No particular form is required for a seal. A seal can be any mark the signer uses for that purpose. Nowadays usually only corporations have distinctive seals and even some corporations dispense with the formality. In most sealed documents, the seal consists of the word "seal" or the letters "L.S." (abbreviation for a Latin term meaning "place of seal"), and a person (or corporation acting through its agent) who signs beside the word "seal" or the letters "L.S." is deemed to adopt the word or letters as his personal seal.

The historical reason for this common-law rule goes back hundreds of years and no longer prevails. When an ordinary person signs a contract form, it is usually immaterial to him whether the line on which he signs is followed by the word "seal" or is blank. If the average person who signs beside the word "seal" does not attach any significance to the word, it is certainly arguable that the law should not assume otherwise and therefore should not treat a sealed contract as any different from an unsealed one. Pursuant to this reasoning, the legislatures in most states have completely abrogated the common-law rule, and the Uniform Commercial Code does likewise with respect to negotiable commercial paper (notes, drafts, and checks), and sales-of-goods offers and contracts.[11]

[11] U.C.C. Secs. 2-203, 3-113.

PROMISES EXPRESSLY STATED AS BINDING

Sometimes a person who promises to make a gift, desires to make the promise legally binding upon himself or upon his estate after his death. Some legal scholars believe that as a matter of policy the law ought to provide a way for this to be done, and several states have adopted statutes accordingly. One such statute is the Uniform Written Obligations Act (drafted under the auspices of the Commissioners on Uniform State Laws), which has been adopted by a few states. Under this statute, a promise or release is binding without consideration if *all* of the following three conditions are present:

1. The promise or release is in writing.
2. The writing is signed by the one promising or releasing.
3. *In addition* to the promise or release, the writing contains (in any form of language) an express statement that the signer intends to be legally bound.

PROBLEMS

1. S. Smith advertised that he wished to sell a plot of vacant land known as the Smith Farm for $25,000. B. Brown wrote to S, "I would like a three-month option to buy the Smith Farm for $25,000." In reply S wrote to B, "July 1. To B. Brown: I hereby give you a three-month option to buy the Smith Farm for $25,000. If you choose to exercise this option, I shall expect to hear from you by October 1." On July 9 B wrote to S, "Enclosed is my check for $100 which I feel is a fair price for the three-month option you gave me in your letter of July 1." On July 16 S wrote to B, "I have decided not to sell the Smith Farm and therefore hereby return your $100 check sent to me on July 9, and withdraw the option previously given you." On July 27 B wrote to S, "Enclosed is the $100 check you returned to me with your letter of July 26. You gave me a three-month option on the Smith Farm and I hereby give notice that I am taking up the option. I hereby agree to buy the Smith Farm for $25,000, which I will pay you upon delivery to me of the deed." When S tendered return of the $100 check and refused to sell, B refused the check and sued for a decree of specific performance. The evidence showed that $100 was a fair price for such an option. Assume that each of the above letters was properly addressed and signed, and received by the respective addresses on the day following the date of the letter.

a) What would be the result of the lawsuit? Explain.

b) Other facts remaining the same, assume that starting with B's July 9 letter, the parties were dealing with $100 in cash. Explain whether your answer would be the same as in Part (a).

2. On July 1 B, a doctor, signed in duplicate a printed order form furnished by S. Smith, a car dealer, reading in part: "To S. Smith: I hereby order you to equip and deliver to me at Scranton, Pennsylvania, as soon as reasonably possible, the following described motor vehicle which I agree to

accept at the price and according to the terms set forth below and on the reverse side hereof." Appropriate spaces on the front of the order form were filled in with the make, model, and price of the car B wanted. On the reverse side was printed: "It is agreed that the seller will not be held liable for any delay or failure to make delivery through any cause whatsoever." On the same day, S dated and signed both copies of the form after the printed word, "Accepted," and delivered one copy to B. On July 10, before S had tendered any car to B, B notified S to cancel the order. On July 15, which was a reasonable time for delivery of a car ordered on July 1, S tendered to B a car exactly complying with the description in the order form. When B refused to accept delivery, S sued B for damages for breach of contract. Explain 1) the reasoning upon which B might attempt to defend, 2) the reasoning upon which S might attempt to collect, and 3) which party should be given judgment.

3. a) A trucker who owned and operated several trucks for short distance hauling was negotiating with a distributor of petroleum products. On January 28 the distributor wrote to the trucker the following, which under the circumstances legally constituted an offer: "I hereby offer to sell you Star Brand Motor Oil, SAE 20 at 60 cents a gallon and Star Brand Regular Gasoline at 15 cents a gallon, in such quantities as you may order, delivery to be made within 5 days after order, payment within 30 days after delivery, 2 percent off for ten days. Upon acceptance by you of this offer, the agreement will continue in effect for six months from February 1." Receiving two copies, the trucker wrote on the bottom of one copy, "Accepted, January 30," signed it, and returned it to the distributor. During February, March, and the first part of April the trucker ordered, received, and paid for various quantities of gas and oil from the distributor. On April 15 the trucker sent an order, received by the distributor April 16, for 5,000 gallons of gasoline. On April 17 the distributor wrote a letter received by the trucker April 18, saying: "I regret I will be unable to deliver your April 15 order or any further orders at the previous prices. Our costs have advanced sharply and I'm sure you will understand my position. I shall be happy to fill your April 15 order and any further orders in any quantities you wish, at my current prices of $1 a gallon for oil and 25 cents a gallon for gasoline of the grades you have previously been buying." The trucker protested but the distributor remained firm and refused to deliver at the January prices. On April 22 the trucker sent an order received by the distributor April 23 for 1,000 gallons of oil, the trucker specifying that he was ordering under the January agreement. The distributor refused to deliver. On May 6 the trucker sent an order, received by the distributor May 9, for 3,000 gallons of gasoline, the trucker specifying that he was ordering under the January agreement. The distributor refused to deliver. These three orders conformed in quantity and frequency with the trucker's orders during the previous two and a half months. Each time the distributor refused to deliver, the trucker purchased the same grade elsewhere at the lowest obtainable prices of 80 cents a gallon for oil and 20 cents a gallon for gasoline. The trucker sued the distributor for damages consisting of the amounts the trucker had to pay over the prices in the

January agreement, namely 1) $250 on the April 15 order, 2) $200 on the April 22 order, and 3) $150 on the May 6 order. Disregarding court costs and interest, state how much, if anything, the trucker was entitled to recover. Explain.

b) Other facts being the same, assume that the three orders were dated May 15, May 22, and June 6 and that the distributor's letter first giving notice of the price increase was dated May 17, received May 18. Disregarding court costs and interest, state how much, if anything, the trucker was entitled to recover. Explain.

4. On May 16 a salesman for a manufacturer of farm machinery solicited an order from a farmer for a certain type of farm machine at a stated price. The order form signed in duplicate by the farmer concluded by stating: "This order is not subject to countermand. No verbal understanding of the agent is to affect this order, all conditions under which this order is given are specified herein. All orders are subject to approval of the manufacturer." The order form contained no warranty of any kind. The salesman sent the signed copies of the order form to the manufacturer. On May 23, before anything further had been done about the order, the farmer notified the manufacturer canceling the order and stating that he would not accept the machine. On May 26 the manufacturer wrote on both copies of the order form: "Accepted, will ship today, May 26," signed both copies, and mailed one copy to the farmer. Assume that under the circumstances this was within a reasonable time. The manufacturer shipped the machine to the farmer on May 26, but the farmer refused to receive it from the carrier. The carrier returned the machine to the manufacturer, who again reshipped it back to the farmer. The salesman then on June 30 induced the farmer to receive delivery and permit the machine to be installed, the salesman expressly warranting in the manufacturer's name that the machine would operate in a certain way. The machine did not perform as warranted and the farmer demanded that the manufacturer remove it. The manufacturer refused and sued the farmer for the purchase price.

a) Was an enforceable contract between the manufacturer and farmer formed on May 26? Explain.

b) Was an enforceable contract between the manufacturer and farmer formed on June 30? Explain.

c) Was the manufacturer entitled to recover the purchase price from the farmer? Explain.

5. S sold and delivered a certain machine to B. S expressly warranted satisfactory operation for six months and B promised to pay the agreed price in twelve equal monthly installments. Eight months later the machine broke down, and B, who had been paying according to the agreement, refused to pay any more. S proposed that if B would pay the remainder of the price at once, S would repair the machine at no cost to B. B agreed and paid S the balance of the price. S then refused to repair the machine, and B sued S for damages. Explain 1) the reasoning upon which S could attempt to defend and 2) whether B should recover from S.

6. D owed C $1,000 in a transaction that did not come under the Uniform

Commercial Code. On the due date, February 1, C requested payment from D. D said he was unable to pay the entire debt but would pay $300 if C would extend the balance six months longer. C said he would not extend the debt unless another person guaranteed payment. D suggested G, a friend of his, and C acknowledged that G's credit was satisfactory. On February 6 the three parties got together. As a favor to D and without compensation, G signed and delivered to C the following writing, dated February 6: "To C: If you will agree with D to give him six months longer on his debt to you, not to exceed $700, I will guaranty his payment." D paid C $300, and C signed and delivered to D and G the following writing, dated February 6: "At the request of D and G, I hereby agree to extend until next August 6, D's obligation to pay the $700 balance of his debt to me."

a) Assume the following additional facts: D failed to pay on August 6, or thereafter, and C, unsuccessful in attempting to collect from D, demanded payment from G. G refused to pay on the ground that he had received nothing for his promise. Could C recover from G? Explain.

b) Instead of (a) above, assume the following additional facts: On April 6, C changed his mind about waiting until August for his money and sued D for the $700 balance. Could C recover from D in the April lawsuit? Explain.

7. A mare named Grace, owned by O, was entered in the Kentucky Futurity Race to be held in connection with the meeting of the Kentucky Trotting Horse Breeders Association in Lexington, Kentucky. The mare was to be driven by D, a driver of great skill and experience, who was then in the employ of O. This race was one of the most noted races among trotting horsemen in the United States, and the winning of it greatly increased the value of the sire, dam, and brother and sisters of the winning horse. The purse offered in the race was $14,000, division of which included $10,000 to the owner of the winner and $300 to the owner of the dam of the winner. At this time and for many years prior, F owned and managed a stock farm near Lexington. Among the race horses owned by F were the sire, dam, and brothers of the mare Grace. Before the race, F agreed with D to give D $1,000 if, with him as driver, the mare Grace should win the race. D agreed and the mare driven by D won the race. Thereafter F paid D $200 but failed to pay the balance and D sued F for $800. Explain 1) the reasoning upon which F could attempt to defend, 2) the reasoning upon which D could attempt to collect, and 3) which party should be given judgment.

8. On June 22 a retailer orally ordered from a manufacturer 60 dozen shirts of stated sizes, colors, and styles at $4.75 per dozen, and the manufacturer orally accepted the order. On August 11 the manufacturer wrote to the retailer: "Due to labor increases as effected by a new contract signed by the garment industry with the clothing workers' union, we are compelled to add a surcharge of $2.50 per dozen on existing shirt orders now in the process of manufacture, among which yours is included. We ask your permission to add the surcharge as listed above to existing orders, and will await billing any additional merchandise for your account until we receive your permission to do so. If you are unwilling to pay this additional charge which is right and proper from every angle, we will be willing to accept cancella-

tion on that portion of your order to which the surcharge would be applicable. In view of the replacement costs which are much higher than our price plus surcharges, we would strongly advise that you accept the merchandise under these conditions." On August 14 the retailer replied by letter: "In answer to your letter of August 11, we ask that you please rush the shirts on back order, and add the $2.50 surcharge." On August 18 the manufacturer shipped the 60 dozen shirts which the retailer had ordered. The retailer paid $285 (the price of 60 dozen at $4.75 per dozen). When the retailer refused to pay any more, the manufacturer sued for $150 as balance due. Assume that under the circumstances a shipment on August 18 was reasonably prompt for the June 22 order.

a) Explain 1) the reasoning upon which the manufacturer might attempt to recover, 2) the reasoning upon which the retailer might attempt to defend, and 3) which party should be given judgment.

b) Would your answer be different if the retailer's reply of August 14 had been made orally by long-distance phone? Explain.

9. A debtor sends a $100 check to his creditor with a letter stating, "This is payment in full," and the creditor cashes the check. Later if the creditor sues the debtor to recover a balance allegedly still due, it will be important for the trial court to determine whether the original debt was liquidated or unliquidated. Explain concisely why this is so. (Modified from A.I.C.P.A., Nov. 55-6a.)

10. A homeowner engaged a plumber to do certain work, with no agreement as to the amount to be charged for the work. Upon satisfactory completion of the work, the plumber sent the homeowner a bill for $163. The homeowner objected that the bill was too high and requested an itemized bill. The itemized bill the plumber sent to the homeowner totaled $175.06. A few weeks later, the homeowner phoned and told the plumber that he was going to send a check for $100 in full settlement. The plumber replied that he was unwilling to settle for that amount. Nevertheless, the homeowner sent the plumber a check for $100 marked on the face and back "Payment in full for all claims to date." The plumber crossed out the quoted words and indorsed and cashed the check, receiving $100. The plumber then sued the homeowner to recover $75.06 as the balance due. The court concluded that the reasonable charge for the work was $170.

a) Did the plumber make a promise to accept $100 as payment in full? Explain.

b) How much could the plumber recover from the homeowner? Explain.

11. M. Morton desired to have his auto engine overhauled, including reboring cylinders, reseating valves, and replacing piston rings. M discussed what he wanted with a garageman. At M's request, the garageman prepared a written statement detailing all that would be done, and stating that the job would cost $350. The garageman prepared the statement in duplicate, signed both copies, gave one copy to M and retained the other copy after having M write on the bottom of the paper, "I hereby engage the above-named garageman to do the work described above and agree to pay the above price within 30 days after completion of the work. (signed) M.

Morton." The garageman completed the work satisfactorily and returned the car to M on June 1. About two weeks later M's neighbor had the same work done on his car by another serviceman for $250. The neighbor's car was the same make, model, and year as M's, and had been in approximately the same condition. When M questioned the garageman about the amount of his bill, the garageman replied that his price for the work done was as stated, $350. Thereupon, on the date stated below, M wrote to the garageman that he thought he had been overcharged, would not pay $350, but was willing to pay $275 for the work, and enclosed his check for $275 marked, "In full payment for all work done on my car to date." The garageman crossed out this statement, cashed the checked, and sued M for $75 as the balance claimed due. In the lawsuit it was proven through impartial witnesses that the work done on the two cars (the neighbor's and M's) was exactly the same in kind and quality. In the lawsuit for $75, explain 1) the reasoning upon which M might attempt to defend, 2) the reasoning upon which the garageman might attempt to collect, and 3) which party should be given judgment, if:

a) The date of M's letter and check was July 25.

b) The date of M's letter and check was June 25.

12. A public accountant rendered professional services to a businessman, without advance agreement as to the amount of the fee. Upon completion of the work, the accountant told the businessman that the fee for the work was $2,000, which according to local custom was payable in thirty days. The businessman accordingly signed and gave the accountant a thirty-day note for $2,000, naming the accountant as payee. Two weeks later the businessman had the accountant's work appraised by three disinterested experts, all of whom agreed that the fair value of the services was $500. When the businessman offered this amount as full payment, the accountant refused the offer and sued the businessman on the note. What defense could the businessman present, and would the defense be good if 1) the note was negotiable in form? 2) if the note was nonnegotiable in form? (Modified from A.I.C.P.A., Nov. 30-3.)

13. A number of identical new homes were built fronting on Roger Road. T, owner of a newly constructed house at 1452 Roger Road, obtained a quotation of $500 from P. Porter, owner and operator of the Porter Paving Company, for blacktop paving of T's driveway and breezeway area. After obtaining other quotations, T phoned the Porter Company giving his name and address and requesting that the paving be done immediately. In the absence of the regular secretary, one of the field men took the message, writing on a slip of paper which he turned over to one of the paving foremen. The address was so sloppily written that it looked like 1462 Roger Road. At that address was another new home recently purchased by D who had not yet moved in. D had also obtained a quotation from Porter for similar paving but had done nothing further. After checking the file copy of Porter's estimate for 1462 Roger Road, the foreman took his men, materials, and equipment and paved the driveway and breezeway area at 1462 Roger Road. Upon discovering the error, Porter wrote to D explaining what had

happened and saying that he thought as a matter of fairness D should pay at least $250 for the job.

a) D refused to pay anything and Porter sued D. What result? Explain.

b) D replied by letter that he believed $250 a fair price and would pay Porter that amount within sixty days. When D failed to pay, Porter sued D. What result? Explain.

14. A public accountant was engaged by a businessman to make an audit of the latter's books, at specified per diem rates. During the course of the audit, the accountant uncovered a defalcation whereby the businessman saved $25,000. After the audit was concluded and the accountant rendered his report, the businessman promised to pay the accountant an additional fee of $5,000 for uncovering the defalcation. Later the businessman paid only the specified per-diem charge for the audit and refused to pay more. The accountant sued for the additional $5,000 promised. Could the accountant recover? Explain. (Modified from A.I.C.P.A., Nov. 30-6.)

15. The trustees of the Presbyterian Church in a small town planned to have a new church constructed. To raise the necessary funds, they prepared and circulated the following subscription paper written on the church letterhead paper: "I, the undersigned, hereby subscribe and promise to pay to the trustees of the above-named Presbyterian Church the sum set opposite my name, for the purpose of raising $50,000 for the building fund of the new Presbyterian Church which the trustees are to have erected at the corner of Beaver Avenue and Frazier Street. Said sum is to be paid within one month after the trustees give notice that at least $50,000 has been promised by the signers hereto." C and D were early signers, each agreeing to contribute $1,000. Before the subscription list was completed, C became a Catholic and notified the trustees that he withdrew his subscription, and D died. After more than $50,000 was subscribed, the trustees had the new church constructed and brought lawsuits against C and against D's estate.

a) What result? Explain.

b) Could the trustees have worded the subscription promise differently to make collection easier? Explain.

16. D and B were partners operating a clothing store in a building leased from L, landlord, for a term of four years at a stated monthly rental. Two years later D desired to withdraw from the clothing business and start a different kind of business in another locality, but only if he could be free from all obligations of the clothing business. D explained his desire to L. L said, "So long as you are withdrawing from the business, I release you and am satisfied to look to B alone for the remaining payments under the lease." D and B then entered into an agreement under which B bought out D's interest in the partnership, B agreed to be solely liable for the remainder of the lease, and the partnership was terminated. D notified L of the agreement, B continued operating the clothing store, and D started a restaurant in the same town. A year later the clothing store began falling behind in rent payments, and upon expiration of the lease period owed $1,500 overdue rent. It is a rule of law that a person who was a partner at the time an obligation was undertaken continues to be personally liable on that obligation even

after termination of the partnership, unless the creditor makes an enforceable agreement releasing such a person. L sued D and B.

a) Explain 1) the reasoning upon which L might attempt to hold D liable, along with B, 2) the reasoning upon which D might attempt to defend the action, and 3) whether L should obtain judgment against D as well as against B.

b) Briefly explain how, if at all, D could best have prevented this dispute from arising.

c) Other facts remaining the same, would it make any difference if L had said to D: "If you withdraw from the business, I will release you"? Explain.

17. A debtor borrowed $5,000 from a creditor, promised to repay the loan in five years, and, as security, gave the creditor a mortgage on certain property belonging to the debtor, consisting of a house (valued at $15,000) and the land on which erected (valued at $2,000). The debtor had a fire insurance policy covering the house. At the debtor's request the insurance company added a mortgagee provision to the policy, so that, in case of fire loss, the proceeds of the policy would first be paid to the creditor to the extent of his interest and then the remainder paid to debtor. A few years later the debtor sold the house and lot to a buyer. The premises remained subject to the mortgage, but since the buyer did not specifically promise to pay the amount of the mortgage debt, he did not become personally liable to the creditor for the debt. The buyer took out a fire insurance policy payable entirely to the buyer. The policy did not mention the mortgage. The creditor also took out a $5,000 fire insurance policy on the house, payable to himself. Shortly afterwards the creditor and buyer met on the street. During their conversation the buyer mentioned having fire insurance on the house. The creditor said that the policy should have a mortgagee provision. The buyer replied that on the following day he would have the creditor's name as mortgagee added to the policy. After this conversation the creditor canceled his own policy. Unknown to the creditor, the buyer neglected to have the mortgagee provision added. About a month later the house was completely destroyed by fire, through no fault of the buyer. When the proceeds from the buyer's fire insurance were paid entirely to the buyer, the creditor sued the buyer claiming the amount of the mortgage as damages for the buyer's failure to have a mortgagee provision added. Explain 1) the reasoning upon which the buyer might attempt to defend, 2) the reasoning upon which the creditor might attempt to collect, and 3) which party should be given judgment.

18. M. Martin, the owner of a small manufacturing business, did not have a pension plan and had never mentioned any arrangements for retired employees. However, when E. Edwards, one of M's long and faithful employees reached the age of 65 years and retired, M promised E to pay him $100 per month for the remainder of his life. The promise was made in the manner described below. After continuing such payments for three years, M ceased further payments although E was still alive and not gainfully employed in any manner. E sued M for the promised pension.

a) M made the promise to E during a conversation between the two in M's office. Explain 1) the reasoning upon which M might attempt to defend,

2) the reasoning upon which E might attempt to collect, and 3) which party should be given judgment.

b) M made the promise to E at the conclusion of a speech at a banquet given in E's honor by M and attended by all of M's employees. Explain whether your answers in Part (a) will also apply here.

c) M dated, signed, and gave E the following writing: "To E. Edwards: In consideration of and appreciation for your long and faithful service in my business, I hereby agree to pay you $100 per month for the remainder of your life, payments to begin one month after date hereof. (signed) M. Martin." Explain whether your answers in Part (a) will also apply here. (Modified from A.I.C.P.A. May 33-1.)

19. After several years employment by a manufacturing company, F was promoted to the position of a department foreman at a salary of $125 per week, and D was promoted to the position of chief draftsman at an annual salary of $8,500 payable in monthly installments. As was also true with F's former positions with the company, no particular period of time for F's employment as a department foreman was named. D's employment was on a one-year contract running from May 1. On June 1 the company obtained an important defense contract, to be completed by January 1, of the following year, and on June 15 announced to all employees: "The Board of Directors has decided that for the purpose of inducing employees to continue with the company and refrain from accepting employment elsewhere until after completion of the current defense contract, the company promises all employees now in its employment that upon completion of the defense contract the company will pay to each employee as a bonus a sum of money equal to one month's salary of each such employee who continues in the company's employment until completion of the said defense contract." The defense contract was completed on time, but shortly thereafter the company began to feel the pinch of a recession and was unable to pay the announced bonus without borrowing money, an act which the directors wished to avoid. The company therefore announced: "Because of present economic conditions, the company cannot at this time pay the bonus announced on last June 15." F and D each sued the company for the promised bonus. In each lawsuit impartial witnesses proved that the salaries paid to F and D were reasonable and fair compensation for the type of work they were hired to perform.

a) As to F's lawsuit, explain 1) the reasoning upon which the company might attempt to defend, 2) the reasoning upon which the plaintiff might attempt to collect, and 3) which party should be given judgment.

b) As to D's lawsuit, would any of the answers be different than the answers given in Part (a)? Explain.

20. L. Lucas and T. Thomas, as landlord and tenant respectively, entered into a written lease agreement under which L leased certain described premises to T for one year from June 1, of a specified year, and as rental for that period T agreed to pay L the sum of $600, payable monthly in advance. The lease agreement also provided: "During the duration of this lease, L. Lucas hereby gives T. Thomas an option to purchase the rented premises for $20,000." On the following February 1, L notified T in writing that L no longer wished to sell the property and that the option was terminated as of that date. On March 1, along with his March rental payment, T notified L that T wished to exercise the option and purchase the property. On March 15, T tendered $20,000 to L and demanded a deed for the property. When L refused to deliver a deed, T sued for a decree of specific performance.

a) What result? Explain.

b) Other facts being the same assume that the conclusion of the lease agreement read: "In witness whereof the parties have hereunto set their hands and seals on the date above written. (signed) L. Lucas SEAL. (signed) T. Thomas SEAL." The word "seal" was typed twice as indicated when the lease agreement was being prepared for the signatures of the parties. How would your answer compare with the answer in Part (a) above? Explain. (Modified from A.I.C.P.A., May 47-1.)

chapter *6*

Parties of Limited Contractual Capacity

Part 1 MINORS

Basically all persons should be considered as having equal rights and equal obligations. Equality under the law is certainly an essential concept for any system worthy of being called a system of justice. However, the concept must conform to reality; the law cannot validly require a standard of conduct which is an absolute impossibility. Therefore, although a person is entitled to full legal protection from the moment of his birth, a tiny baby obviously cannot be held legally responsible for his conduct. The law delays holding persons legally responsible until they can be considered actually aware of the nature of their acts. What age this should be depends upon the act in question and the needs of society.

In a very simple, primitive society, persons were considered adult members at a fairly young age, sometimes as soon as they had reached the age of puberty. As society became more complex, it was necessary gradually to delay the age of full maturity. The introduction of heavy armor in the days of knighthood forced considerable delay in contrast with other notions of maturity current at that time. Necessarily, knighthood (and the burden of a hundred pounds of sheet metal) could not be conferred on a young man until he had reached his full physical growth and strength, and as the eminent historians of English law, Pollock and Maitland, point out:

> . . . here again we have a good instance of the manner in which the law for the gentry becomes English common law. The military tenant is kept in ward until he is twenty-one years old; . . . Gradually . . . the knightly majority is becoming the majority of the common law.[1]

Thus the rule developed under the English common-law system that a person is not considered a mature, adult member of society until he reaches the age of twenty-one years. (A few states have lowered this age somewhat by statute.) A person under twenty-one is termed by the law an *infant*. To apply this term to twenty-year old marines, construction workers, and college students is certainly giving the term a

---

[1] Sir Frederick Pollock and F. W. Maitland, *History of English Law Before the Time of Edward I*, Vol. 2 (2d ed.; Boston: Little, Brown, 1899), p. 438.

broader meaning than is popularly held. The term *minor* is more appropriate. The period of minority can itself be subdivided into three periods:

1. Infancy (using the term in its popular sense)—from birth through (usually) six years. Until a person reaches what is commonly called the age of reason, he is not held legally liable for any of his acts.

2. Childhood—from seven through thirteen years. Upon reaching the age of reason, a child is expected to conform to the most basic, elementary rules of society. Thus the average twelve-year old in modern society can usually be expected to know that deliberately killing another is wrong, while for him criminal slander may not be considered a wrong at all.

3. Adolescence—from fourteen through twenty years. An adolescent can usually be expected to conform to the standard moral code of adult society. Thus he is practically an adult in the eyes of the criminal law— but not in the eyes of contract law, since contracts usually contemplate more complex and mature thought processes than are involved in understanding and applying the universally accepted moral code. As Professor Sheldon Amos has written:

> . . . in England, criminal irresponsibility ceases at an earlier age than civil, while an absolute presumption of irresponsibility in respect to crime is only admitted for the first seven years of human life. . . .
>
> The absolute incapacity of forming an *intention* attributed in all cases to the early years of infancy, is extended, in all systems of law, to a later age in respect of the generality of the more unfrequent acts, of which nothing but time and experience could teach the immediate consequences; and even to the time of early manhood in respect of all those acts to which an extremely complex condition of civilization has annexed consequences in all respects artificial and arbitrary [such as contractual agreements].[2]

MINORS' CONTRACTS

Because a minor frequently lacks the experience and sound judgment necessary to protect himself from unwise and wasteful agreements, the law considers it desirable policy to afford minors some protection. Prohibiting all minors from making contracts or declaring their contracts completely void would be too extreme and unnecessary a remedy. Instead, the protection takes the form of recognizing the validity of minors' contracts but at the same time permitting minors to disaffirm (that is to cancel or avoid) most of their contracts.

In thus protecting minors, the law recognizes an exception to the

[2] Sheldon Amos, *The Science of Law* (New York: D. Appleton & Co., 1874), p. 106.

usual requirement (see Chapter 5) that contract obligations must be mutual, that usually both parties must be bound or neither is bound. Unless a minor is guilty of dishonestly inducing an adult to enter into a contract by fraudulently misrepresenting his age, the adult is fully bound by the contract, while the minor may, as he wishes, either disaffirm the contract or enforce it against the adult.

To spare the courts the impossible task of attempting to appraise the competency of each individual and analyze every agreement, the law extends its protection *generally*—to *all* minors and for *all* contracts (with some exceptions). Therefore a minor's right to disaffirm a contract is not dependent on proof that the particular agreement is unfair or unwise, nor that the particular minor lacks sound judgment. The degree of a minor's independence is not important; a minor freed from parental control, even one married and supporting his own family, is protected.

But, a dissenter might object, if the protection is applied generally, is it not possible for a minor who is a shrewd bargainer to speculate as to future business conditions or prices, enjoy all the advantages of a fair and reasonable contract, and at the same time shift the risk of possible loss to the adult contracting party? The answer is yes. Admittedly the protection which the law extends to minors is at the expense of adult parties to contracts, and at times will be quite unfair to the adults. This is another instance in which the law balances conflicting interests and, entirely as a matter of policy, decides to throw a loss upon one of two equally innocent parties. Once society decides as a matter of basic policy 1) that while it is socially desirable for minors to be free to enter into contracts, it is equally socially desirable to protect them in their contracts, and 2) that it is impossible as a practical matter to administer protection by testing each individual minor and appraising each individual contract, then the result is unavoidable—there will be a certain amount of unfairness and injustice to adults. How much unfairness should be tolerated, what price adult society should pay for protecting minors— or in other words, how much protection should be given minors—is entirely a question of policy, in which the need for protecting minors and the desirability of having a workable rule of general application is weighed against the resulting unfairness to adults. And as with almost any question of policy, the courts and legislatures of the different states have reached varying conclusions, some states giving only limited protection and other states giving fairly extensive protection.

In summarizing the status of minors' contracts, it will be helpful to classify the contracts into three types, 1) ordinary contracts which do not involve necessaries, 2) ordinary contracts involving necessaries, and 3) special contracts in which society as a whole possesses an overwhelming interest in the subject matter of the contract.

ORDINARY CONTRACTS NOT INVOLVING NECESSARIES

In general, a minor's contract which is not for a necessary or strongly tied to the public interest can be disaffirmed, provided the contract has not already been ratified.

Ratification

Affirmance or ratification of a contract consists of any manifestation by a contracting party, *after* he comes of age, that he considers the agreement binding. After an ex-minor effectively ratifies his contract, he cannot disaffirm it. An effective ratification can be either expressly stated, or instead implied from conduct. Thus an ex-minor impliedly ratifies his contract if (*after* coming of age), he sells or uses the item obtained under the contract or otherwise accepts a benefit under the contract, or even if he retains the item without use for longer than is considered reasonable for giving notice of disaffirmance.

Sometimes an ex-minor may be unaware of his right to disaffirm contracts. This is entirely immaterial. If the enforcement of legal rights and obligations were made dependent upon actual proof that the parties involved were aware of the applicable rules of law, the legal system would be entirely unworkable. In recognition of this, courts frequently repeat the well-known axioms, "Ignorance of the law is no excuse," and "Every person is presumed to know the law." Thus an ex-minor's words or conduct can form a binding ratification, even though at the time he spoke or acted he was unaware of his legal right to disaffirm.

Disaffirmance

A minor can disaffirm his contract at any time during minority and for a reasonable time after coming of age, unless previously (but *after* coming of age), he effectively ratified the contract. (Under the common law with some exceptions, a person could not, during his minority, disaffirm a contract involving the sale of land but had to wait until he came of age to disaffirm the contract.) When a minor or ex-minor effectively disaffirms, then:

1) "Extensive-protection" states: The minor cancels or avoids his own further contract obligation and can recover whatever he gave or paid under the contract, or its value. The only obligation imposed upon the minor or ex-minor is to return what he received under the contract, if he still has it, in whatever condition it is in at the time he disaffirms. He is not liable for depreciation, wear and tear, damages, or the value of his use. If whatever the minor or ex-minor received under the contract is no longer in his possession, if he has consumed, discarded, or sold it, he can still disaffirm and is not required to account for any proceeds received from his disposal of the item. A minor's failure voluntarily to disclose his age is not dishonesty or fraud, and he can still disaffirm. In extensive-protection states, a minor's lying about his age has no effect on his right to disaffirm his contract nor on his right to recover what he paid. However, a minor who fraudulently misrepresents his age is committing a crime equal in gravity to stealing, and, through a criminal prosecution, he can be punished with a substantial fine, jail sentence, or both.

2) *"Limited-protection" states:* The usual limitation affects the amount which a disaffirming minor or ex-minor can recover. In some states, if the contract was fair and reasonable, the value of the minor's (or ex-minor's) use of the item he is returning, or the amount of damages or depreciation, will be deducted from what the minor paid or gave, and he can only recover the difference. For example, in many limited-protection states if a minor buys and pays $100 for a radio, but after the radio has depreciated to $60 disaffirms the contract and returns the radio, he can recover only $60 rather than the $100 which he originally paid. Some states which grant extensive protection to honest minors limit the protection if a minor has dishonestly lied about his age. Some of these states prohibit disaffirmance altogether, some other states permit the dishonest minor to disaffirm his contract but require him to pay for damages or depreciation or deduct this amount from what he can recover.

Rationale

At first glance it may seem only fair that a disaffirming minor or ex-minor should be charged for depreciation, damages, or use. However, a strong argument can be made for the view of the extensive-protection states, in which a minor can recover all that he paid without any deduction. The granting of any protection at all to minors is based on society's conviction that, as a result of their lack of experience, maturity, and sound judgment, they may enter into unwise and wasteful agreements. To the extent that a minor who has purchased an item is charged for use, depreciation, or damage, to that extent he is being charged for the exercise of his immature judgment, the very thing against which society has decided to protect him.

Example: A seller sold a horse, harness, and wagon to a minor who was 18 years old, was married, and had one child. The minor had no use for the outfit except driving for pleasure. He disposed of the harness and wagon, and the horse became so emaciated and disabled, either by disease or neglect, that it was shot on order of agents for the Society for Prevention of Cruelty to Animals. When the seller sued for the unpaid balance of the purchase price, the minor disaffirmed the contract and sued for the amount already paid to the seller.

In approving the trial court's decision in favor of the minor, the Rhode Island Supreme Court said: "The law gives to a minor the right to disaffirm his contracts on the ground of the disability of infancy. This has been provided as a protection to him from the consequences of his own improvidence and folly. It is the same lack of foresight that in most instances leads to his dissipation of the proceeds of his voidable contracts. To say that he shall not have the protection of disaffirmance with which the policy of the law seeks to guard him, unless he has had sufficient prudence to retain the consideration of the contract he wishes to avoid, would in many instances deprive him, because of his indiscretion, of the very defense which the law intended that he should have against the results of his indiscretion. . . . Not infrequently, even in cases where the infant still has the consideration and returns it to the other party to the contract, such other party is far from being placed in *status quo* [the status he was in before entering into the contract]. It has been said that the right of an infant to avoid his contract is absolute and paramount to all equities."[3]

But how about the dishonest minor who lies about his age? Certainly a system of justice should never deliberately prefer a dishonest defrauder over the innocent victim of the fraud. Nevertheless, a strong policy argument can be made to support the rule in the extensive-protection states that a minor's fraud should not effect his right to disaffirm and to recover all that he paid. When a court in an extensive-protection state permits a defrauding minor to disaffirm his contract and make full recovery, the court is *not* saying that society should overlook the minor's dishonesty or that society should protect the minor from the consequences of his deliberate lie. If the defrauded adult will swear out a warrant against the minor, the court will be most happy, in a *criminal* action, to have the minor prosecuted and, if convicted, fined or jailed for his crime. The law's paying no attention to the minor's fraud in a *civil* action is largely a result of the law's taking a practical and realistic view of people, both jurymen and litigants. A rule of law may actually be sound and wise, and may clearly be the best policy rule to follow when considered within the entire framework or pattern of society, yet at the same time the rule may seem unreasonable and unfair if considered alone, separated from this societal pattern, and divorced from related fact situations. More specifically, some persons, especially if they are adult businessmen, may take a narrow view, condemn as archaic the rule protecting minors, and strongly believe that minors should be bound by their fair and reasonable contracts. Suppose that a group of such men form the jury when a minor disaffirms his contract and sues to recover what he paid. So long as the facts are undisputed, the judge can direct

[3] *McGuckian v. Carpenter,* 43 R.I. 94, 110 A. 402 (1920).

a verdict and prevent the jurymen from ignoring the accepted rule of law. However, if the defendant-seller sees a way of beating the case and saving himself a substantial sum of money, he may be the type of person (of which unfortunately too many exist) who is willing to lie under oath if he thinks he can "get away" with it. The seller will be tempted to testify falsely that the minor lied about his age, if under the law of that state the minor's dishonesty would affect his right to recover. This would then raise a question of fact upon which the jury would have to decide. The jurymen might actually believe that the minor was honest and did not lie about his age, but if the jurymen also stubbornly insist that a minor should not be able to recover, in spite of what the judge tells them is the correct rule of law, the jurymen are offered an easy way to achieve their desired result. They can pretend that the minor lied about his age and thereby prevent the minor from recovering. The ease with which jurymen who disapprove of certain rules of law are able surreptitiously to ignore them, has been described by Professor Henry J. Abraham, who writes:

> On the basis of the somewhat questionable assumption that the jury fully comprehends the judge's instructions concerning the applicable substantive legal rules, it is usually required to return a *general* or *over-all* verdict in favor of one party or another. Theoretically . . . this jury verdict is based on the *facts* of the case, the judge himself having determined the rules of *law*—although it is not always possible to separate facts and law. In practice, however, the general verdict permits the jury to do what it pleases; it gives no details, simply reports its decision, and no one either really knows or may safely predict just what facts a jury found from the evidence.[4]

Thus to the extent that the state law limits the right of a defrauding minor to recover, adult parties are tempted to perjure themselves and make fraud an issue in every case, and jurymen (who, of course, are always adults), even though unconvinced of a minor's dishonesty, are enabled to tamper with the law and illegally restrict the rights of minors to recover. In extensive-protection states the *criminal* law is used to control dishonest minors; dishonest litigants and stubborn jurymen are not enabled to subvert the protection which society believes should be accorded to minors.

Contracts Between Minors

If both contracting parties are minors, either one or both may disaffirm the contract. Relatively few cases have litigated the point, but the practical effect of a double disaffirmance would seem to be that 1)

---

[4] Henry J. Abraham, *"The Judicial Process,"* (New York: Oxford U.P., 1962), p. 117.

either party can avoid his further obligation under the contract, and 2) either party can recover whatever property or money he gave or paid under the contract, but only to the extent such property or money is still in the other party's possession. A minor who is no longer in possession of what he received under a contract has no obligation to repay its value. This has been held to apply to money, with the result that if a minor-buyer pays for goods received from the minor-seller, the buyer can recover what he paid only if the seller has the identical pieces of currency that he received from the buyer.

ORDINARY CONTRACTS FOR NECESSARIES

A minor is obliged to pay the reasonable value for necessaries he actually receives. This is really not an exception to the rule that permits a minor to disaffirm his contracts. The rule as to contracts not involving necessaries and the rule as to necessaries are both based on the welfare of the minor. Usually protection of the minor is accomplished by permitting him to avoid his contracts. But in some situations it is of more benefit to the minor that he be able to bind himself. Suppose a minor supporting and maintaining his own home and family buys and pays for a loaf of bread which he and his family eat. If he could then recover his money from the grocer, most grocers would be unwilling to undertake the risk and would refuse to sell food to the minor. Thus the minor is benefited by being able to bind himself for the purchase of his necessaries.

That the rule as to necessaries is for the benefit of minors provides a guide for defining necessaries. *Necessaries* are those things which, as a matter of policy, are considered essential or of sufficient benefit to the minor in question, that the law will help him to obtain them. The position and station in life of a particular minor are considered in determining what are necessaries for him. Even if an item is of a type considered essential (which would certainly include food, clothing, shelter, medical services, and elementary or vocational education), it is not a necessary if the particular minor already has a sufficient supply or has a parent or guardian able and willing to supply him with his needs. Necessaries are usually limited to the person of the minor (and of his wife and children if any). Items considered useful or even essential for the maintenance of a minor's property or for the operation of his business, are usually not necessaries, even if the business is the minor's sole support.

If an item is held to be a necessary, the minor's obligation is to pay the reasonable value to him of such an item. This can be less than the price which the minor agreed to pay. Also, the minor's obligation is to pay only for necessaries he actually receives. He can disaffirm any unperformed portion of a necessaries contract.

PUBLIC SERVICE CONTRACTS

In some situations the interests of society are considered as overriding any desire or need to protect minors. Contracts which a minor cannot disaffirm include enlistments in the Armed Forces and marriages.

MINORS' TORTS

TORTS NOT RELATED TO CONTRACTS

Minor's Liability

A minor is fully liable for damages resulting from his torts if a contract is not involved. Of course, the age of the minor may prevent his conduct from constituting a tort at all, as for example when a baby swings his bottle and breaks the eyeglasses of a person bending over the baby carriage.

Parent's Liability

Under the common-law rule followed in many states, a parent is not liable for injuries caused by his child's torts unless the parent's connection with the child's wrongful act involves more than merely being the parent of the child and the owner of the property being used by the child. For a parent to be liable, usually either of the following situations must exist:

1. The parent himself is guilty of a tort which is a substantial factor in causing the injury in question. Thus a parent will be liable if he puts a dangerous object into the hands of his child, knowing that the child will not use proper care, or if the parent fails to use proper care to supervise and control his child.

2. The child's tort which causes the injury in question is associated with a master-servant relationship existing between the parent and the child *at that time*. As is more fully discussed in Chapter 12, the relationship beween an employer and his employee is commonly termed by the law a master-servant relationship. Although a parent has the general right to control and discipline his child, a master-servant relationship does not exist between the parent and child except when the child is performing some service for his parent and under the parent's control. When a master-servant relationship does exist (either between a parent and child or between an employer and employee), the law considers that as a matter of fairness the master should be held liable

for the torts which are committed by the servant while he is engaged in advancing the interests of his master. In connection with automobile accidents, for example, a master-servant relationship arises if an owner permits someone to drive his car while the owner rides as a passenger; the presence of the owner in the car usually gives him the right to control the manner of driving, regardless of who is being benefited by the trip, and thus makes the driver the owner's servant, with the result that the owner is liable for the driver's negligence. If an owner permits another person to drive his car and the owner is not present in the car, a master-servant relationship exists only if the driver is on an errand for the owner. Compulsory insurance statutes in effect in many states usually do not change the ordinary master-servant rules. The typical statute will usually provide that in case of an accident caused by a person driving with the owner's consent, if the owner does not have insurance (or a statutory equivalent) covering the accident, his auto registration will be suspended for a time while the possibility of an actual master-servant relationship can be litigated. However, unless an actual master-servant situation is found to exist, the owner will not be liable for the driver's negligence.

In some states the rules for liability in automobile accidents have been extended beyond the ordinary master-servant rules, either 1) by permissive driving statutes, or 2) by the family-purpose doctrine.

1) Permissive Driving Statutes. Statutes in New York and some other states provide that if the owner of a car permits another to drive, the owner is liable for the driver's negligence even though 1) the owner is not present at the time of an accident, and 2) the driver is not on an errand for the owner. It should be noted that liability is determined according to the law of the place where an auto accident occurs. If an auto owned and registered in Pennyslvania is involved in an accident in New York State, New York law will apply. The owner with whose permission it is being driven will be liable for the driver's negligence, even though the circumstances are such that the owner would not be liable had the accident occurred in Pennsylvania.

2) Family-Purpose Doctrine. In some states the courts consider that it is sound policy in connection with automobiles to broaden the ordinary master-servant rules by a theory called the family-purpose doctrine. Usually a family automobile is purchased and intended for use by the family while title is taken in the name of the head of the family. The family-purpose doctrine provides that the head of the family is liable for any negligent driving which occurs while the car is being used for the usual family purposes. A son's taking his girl friend to a dance is a common use of the family car. In some of the states which follow this doctrine, the father would be liable for his son's negligent driving while on his date. Some other states, even though following the family-purpose doctrine, would not extend it to the son's using the car for his dance date. In many other states the courts feel that the family-purpose doctrine is not desirable policy and do not follow it.

Torts Related to Contracts

In some states which afford extensive protection to minors, a minor is not liable for a tort if it is so related to a contract, that to hold him liable for the tort would be the same as enforcing the contract.

Example: Falsely saying that he was twenty-two years old, a minor induced a seller to sell and deliver certain goods to the minor, for which the minor agreed to pay the purchase price of $200 in thirty days. Through the minor's fault the goods were destroyed. When the obligation matured, the minor refused to pay and disaffirmed his contract. The seller sued the minor for damages resulting from his tort of fraudulently misrepresenting his age.

The seller could not recover in an extensive-protection state. However, although the minor would have no civil liability, he could be punished in a criminal proceeding.

CRIMES

A minor is fully liable for criminal acts which a person of his age and experience should be expected to know are wrongful. As previously indicated, a minor who falsely states that he is an adult in order to purchase goods commits the crime of obtaining something of value by false pretenses. This crime is similar in seriousness to stealing and is severely punishable by a fine, imprisonment, or both.

RECOMMENDATION

In view of a minor's limited liability both for contracts and also for torts related to contracts, the practical question arises as to what a businessman should do in dealing with a minor or with a youthful-appearing person. Relying on the customer's word is not safe since he may be lying about his age. If a businessman wants to avoid the risk of possibly sustaining a loss should a youthful customer actually be a minor and later disaffirm a contract, the businessman should do either of the following:

1. Refuse to deal with the youthful customer. Instead, have him bring in a person known to be an adult with whom the businessman may then safely contract. Whether the adult promptly gives the purchased item to the minor is of no concern to the businessman, since the adult cannot disaffirm his contract.

2. Accept the minor or youthful person as a customer only after he brings in an adult of satisfactory credit, who will sign a guaranty agreeing to pay the businessman the amount of his loss if the minor later fails to pay or disaffirms the contract.

Part 2 OTHER PERSONS OF LIMITED CONTRACTUAL CAPACITY

With some variations, contracts of the insane or drunk have about the same status as minors' contracts.

Under the common law, married women had quite limited contractual capacity. Statutes in most states now accord to married women the same rights to enter into contracts as married men have.

PROBLEMS

1. B, a minor, without misrepresenting his age, entered into a written contract with S, an adult, under which S agreed to sell to B, and B to buy at a stated price, certain described merchandise not constituting necessaries. When the time came for performance, B, still a minor, tendered the price but S refused to deliver on the ground that B was a minor.

a) S was aware of B's age at the time of entering into the contract but was not cognizant of the law pertaining to minor's contracts. B sued S for damages resulting from S's refusal to deliver. Was B entitled to judgment against S? Explain.

b) After entering into the contract, S for the first time learned that B was a minor. B sued S for damages resulting from S's refusal to deliver. Was B entitled to judgment against S? Explain. (Modified from A.I.C.P.A., Nov. 37-5.)

2. B, who had just celebrated his twentieth birthday, bought and received from S, an appliance dealer, a stereo radio-phonograph for $300. B paid the entire price in cash upon receiving the instrument. B made no statement as to his age, and since it was S's practice to require proof of age from youthful-appearing customers only in credit sales, S did not hesitate selling the instrument to B. After six months B tendered return of the instrument, stated that he was disaffirming his contract, and demanded return of the $300 he had paid. S refused and B sued S for $300. S proved that the value of the instrument had depreciated to $100. Was B entitled to judgment against S, and if so, for how much? Explain.

3. B who looked older than his actual age, lived with his parents but had a full-time job and was permitted to retain all his earnings. B's birthday was June 18. On April 1, B, then twenty years old, falsely stated that he was twenty-four years old, and entered into a contract with S, an adult, under which S sold and delivered to B a certain car, not a necessary, for $800, B paying $200 in cash and signing a two-month note for the balance of $600.

a) On April 3 S learned of B's actual age, offered to return to B $200 in cash and his note, and demanded return of the car. When B refused, S sued B to recover possession of the car. What result?

b) Assume that the facts under (a) above did not occur. Two and a half months after purchasing the car, B, on June 15, considerably damaged the car by carelessly driving into a concrete abutment. After the collision the fair value of the car was $100. 1) B offered to return the car to S, said that he was disaffirming the contract, and demanded return of his $200. When S refused, B sued S. What result? 2) Assume that after the June 15 collision B did not return the car to S but instead, on the date stated below, sold and delivered it to P for $100, its fair value. On June 22 S who had heard nothing concerning the car since selling it to B, demanded payment of B's $600 note, then three weeks overdue. B in turn told S that he was disaffirming the contract and demanded return of $100 of the $200 he had paid, saying that as a matter of fairness he would consider the $100 received from P as for the benefit of S. When S refused this arrangement, B sued S for $200. S filed a counterclaim again B for $600, the amount of B's note. a) The date of B's sale and delivery of the car to P was June 16. 1) What would be the result of B's lawsuit and S's counterclaim? 2) Suppose S sued B's parents. What result? b) the date of B's sale and delivery of the car to P was June 20. What would be the result of B's lawsuit and S's counterclaim?

4. M who looked older than his actual age of twenty years owned an automobile which was not a necessary. M lived with his parents but had a full-time job and was permitted to retain all that he earned. Falsely stating that he was twenty-two years old, M left his car with a garageman for a complete motor overhaul, including grinding valves and reboring cylinders. When the work was completed and the bill submitted to M for the reasonable value of the work, M refused to pay and demanded return of his car. The garageman refused to surrender the car and cited the following state statute: "When, pursuant to a valid contract with the owner of goods, a repairman takes possession of and performs work upon said goods, and the contract between the repairman and the owner contains no provision for the extension of credit to the owner, the repairman shall have the right under said contract to retain possession of the said goods until the owner shall have paid to the repairman the contracted price for the work or if no price shall have been agreed upon, the reasonable value of the contracted work." M sued to recover possession of the car and proved that he was only 20 years old. What result?

5. B looked older than his actual age of nineteen years. Falsely stating that he was twenty-two years old, B entered into a contract with S, an adult, to buy a radio from S for $400. B paid $25 at the time of the purchase and agreed to pay the balance in monthly installments of $50 each. After B used the radio for two weeks, it was accidently broken, through no fault of B's, so that it no longer worked. B returned the damaged radio to S and asked for return of his $25. S refused and sued B for damages for tort. S proved that when returned, the radio had a fair value of $50.

a) Did B commit a tort against S? Explain.
b) Could S recover tort damages from B and if so, how much? Explain.

6. A nineteen-year-old self-supporting orphan was employed as a book-keeper. He subscribed for a noncancellable correspondence course in accountancy for which he agreed to pay a stipulated amount. He completed half of the course, paid one-quarter of the stipulated amount and thereupon, at the age of twenty years, refused to continue the course or to make further payments. What were the rights of the parties? Explain. (Modified from A.I.C.P.A., Nov. 35-3.)

7. An adult merchant sold a suit of clothing to a buyer who said he was twenty-two years old when in fact he was only twenty. The agreed price for the suit was $100, payable in thirty days. However, the fair market value of the suit was only $75. After the thirty days had expired, the buyer refused to pay, offered to return the suit, and said he was disaffirming his contract. Since a used suit was of no value to the dealer, he refused to accept the return of the suit and sued the buyer. What result? Explain. (Modified from A.I.C.P.A., Nov. 50-1.)

8. B, twenty years old, owned and operated a lumber yard by means of which he supported himself, his wife, and his one-year-old baby. B regularly purchased lumber from S on thirty days' credit and regularly paid promptly. The price of lumber suddenly dropped at a time when B still had intact in his yard the last carload of lumber obtained from S. Since B had not yet paid for this lumber, he notified S that he was disaffirming the contract because of his minority and offered to return the lumber to S. S refused to take back the lumber, and sued B for the agreed price. Explain 1) the reasoning upon which S might attempt to collect, 2) the reasoning upon which B might attempt to defend, and 3) which party should be given judgment.

9. Upon graduating from the state university at Collegeville, D, the twenty-year-old daughter of O, returned to her parents' home 200 miles from College ville, and immediately obtained a job. Before starting on her job, D asked to borrow O's car in order to drive to Collegeville and bring home her winter clothes and other personal belongings she had left at her aunt's home in Collegeville. Since D was to be accompanied by two girl friends, O consented to the trip and had his car lubricated and gassed in preparation for the drive. O also gave D sufficient money for the drive and instructed her to drive carefully. While returning home from Collegeville, D was driving negligently and collided with the car of P who was driving with proper care, injuring P and damaging his car. P sued O for the damages. Explain 1) the reasoning upon which P might attempt to recover, 2) the reasoning upon which O might attempt to defend, and 3) which party should be given judgment.

10. D, eighteen years old and a high-school senior living with and supported by his parents, had a date for the senior prom. F, D's father, consented to D's using F's car the night of the prom. While returning from the dance late that night, D, driving negligently, ran into the car of T. Although he was using proper care, T was unable to avoid the accident. The next morning, after D told F of the accident, D, F, and T went to the garage to which T's car had been towed. T did not threaten arrest or

suit, but asked F what he was going to do. F said, "Have your car repaired and I'll pay the cost of the repairs." Later the same day, and before T had ordered work to begin on his car, F called T and said that he had changed his mind, did not consider himself responsible, and would not pay for any damage. F had no liability insurance. T had his car repaired and, upon completion, sued F for the expense of the repairs.

  a) Was F liable for D's tort? Explain.
  b) Was F liable on his promise? Explain.

chapter 7

Reality of Consent, Representations, and Warranties

Although through an offer and an acceptance two parties give the appearance of consenting to a proposition, the consent manifested by the parties may not be actual or real enough to form an agreement which society is willing to enforce. *Reality of consent* may be lacking for any of a variety of reasons, principally the following:

1. Indefiniteness in expressing essential terms of the agreement;
2. Duress forcing a person to enter into the agreement; or
3. Mistake on the part of one or both parties as to some fact, such that had the truth been known, the mistaken party or parties would not have entered into the agreement. Some mistakes are caused by something one party to the agreement does or says, either deliberately (fraudulent misrepresentation), carelessly (negligent misrepresentation), or innocently (innocent misrepresentation). Also, under certain circumstances, a representation may become an enforceable provision or term of the contract between the parties—in other words, a warranty.

Part 1 INDEFINITENESS

The terms of an agreement must be reasonably definite or certain in order for the agreement to be considered an enforceable contract. This does not mean that all of the terms must be expressly stated. When the parties to an agreement do not expressly indicate otherwise, it is presumed that they are contracting according to the usual or customary terms, and such terms therefore become an actual part of their contract. However, if the parties show that they are not following the pattern of what is usual or customary and at the same time they fail to indicate the essential terms of the agreement with reasonable clearness, no enforceable contract is formed.

Practically all contracts involve a sale for a price—a sale of goods, of lands, or of services. The elements of a contractual agreement consist of what each is to give or to do under the agreement, and when and where the contract is to be performed. Usually no difficulty arises when an agreement is silent as to the "when" or the "where." *As to when:* it is presumed that the seller is to deliver or to perform at the usual time (that is, within a reasonable time), and that the buyer is to pay at the usual time (on delivery or completion of performance). *As to where:* with sales of goods not involving a shipment, the usual place of delivery is the seller's place of business, or his home if he has no place of business. In service contracts, the place of performance is usually determined by the nature of the services to be performed. *As to what:* if an agreement is silent as to how much a buyer is to pay, it is presumed that he is to pay the usual or reasonable charge. If, however, the parties expressly exclude reasonableness as the measure of an indefinite bargain, they never form an enforceable agreement. For example, an employment agreement which provided for a specified salary plus "a liberal share of profits" was held to be too indefinite for the employee to collect more than the specified salary. On the other hand, an agreement for cost plus "a reasonable profit" did not exclude reasonableness as the test, and so constituted an enforceable agreement for whatever the court determined to be a reasonable profit under the circumstances.

Sometimes when entering into an agreement the parties expressly state that omitted details will be supplied by a later agreement. At common law an enforceable contract does not exist until the later agreement is entered into, and if the parties are unable to agree at the specified later time, no contract ever exists. For sales-of-goods contracts, however, the Uniform Commercial Code rejects this common-law view that "an agreement to agree is never enforceable." Instead, the Code attempts to give greater effect to the intent of the parties. If the parties show an intent to form an actual contract, the law will cooperate as much as it can in defining and enforcing their intent. In accomplishing this liberalization of contract theory, the Code provides:

> Even though one or more terms are left open a contract for sale does not fail for indefiniteness if the parties have intended to make a contract and there is a reasonably certain basis for giving an appropriate remedy.[1]

In partial explanation of this provision, the authors of the Code have written:

> If the parties intend to enter into a binding agreement, this subsection recognizes that agreement as valid in law, despite missing terms, if there is any reasonably certain basis for granting a remedy. The test is not certainty as to what the parties were to do nor as to the exact amount of damages due the plaintiff. Nor is the fact that one or more terms are left to be agreed upon enough of itself to defeat an otherwise adequate agreement. Rather, *commercial standards* on the point of "indefiniteness" are intended to be applied,

[1] U.C.C. Sec. 2-204.

this Act making provision elsewhere for missing terms needed for performance, open price, remedies and the like.[2] [Emphasis added.]

As the authors point out in the last sentence just quoted, the Code goes on to draw various guidelines for interpreting the meaning of an agreement in which certain terms are left open, both the commonly omitted terms such as time and place for delivery, and time, place, and manner of payment, and also terms such as price, duration of a contract, and to some extent quantity, as in output and requirements contracts or in contracts giving a buyer some choice as to quantity.

For example, in respect to an open price term, the Code provides (in part):

> (1) The parties if they so intend can conclude a contract for sale even though the price is not settled. In such a case the price is a reasonable price at the time for delivery if
> (a) nothing is said as to price; or
> (b) the price is left to be agreed by the parties and they fail to agree; or
> (c) the price is to be fixed in terms of some agreed market or other standard as set or recorded by a third person or agency and it is not so set or recorded.
> (2) A price to be fixed by the seller or by the buyer means a price for him to fix in good faith.
> (3) When a price left to be fixed otherwise than by agreement of the parties fails to be fixed through fault of one party the other may at his option treat the contract as cancelled or himself fix a reasonable price.[3]

Notice how this provision clarifies the status of agreements which state that the price is to be the seller's list price on the date of shipment. Under the Code, if the parties intend to be *presently bound,* their agreement forms an enforceable contract for a price reasonably and in good faith fixed by the seller at the stated future time.

The Code's liberalized approach also clarifies the law with respect to another fairly common type of contract, one in which a buyer is given a choice within stated limits, with the price to vary according to the buyer's choice.

Example: A seller agreed to sell and a buyer to buy 5,000 gallons of a specified brand of motor oil, with the buyer to specify from SAE 10 to SAE 70 weight at stated future delivery dates, and with the price to vary from 21 cents to 31 cents per gallon depending upon the viscosity of oil selected by the buyer.

Before the Code, some courts said that such an agreement was not definite enough to be enforced, while other courts (taking the view now written

---

[2] Comment to Sec. 2-204.
[3] U.C.C. Sec. 2-305.

into the Code) decided more reasonably that since the parties manifested an intent to form a contract, and since there was a reasonably certain basis for estimating damages (that is, the buyer was obliged to take at
least the lowest-priced item or pay damages for not doing so), there would
be an enforceable contract.

Part 2   DURESS

Under sufficient torture, most people can be induced to agree to
practically anything. Obviously an agreement obtained through wrongful pressure (duress) should not be considered as legally enforceable.
On the other hand, it is equally obvious that *every* type of pressure should
not be condemned and considered as sufficient reason to excuse a person
from an agreement which he is thereby induced to make. Most people
live under a variety of economic and social pressures which shape,
direct, or influence their conduct. Only if the pressure to which a person
is subjected is *wrongful* will it constitute duress.

Example: A landlord, owner of a house in Philadelphia, leased it to a
tenant for one year at a yearly rental of $960, payable in monthly install-
ments of $80 on the first of each month. In the latter part of the leasehold
year, the tenant fell behind in his rental payments. He began paying smaller
amounts on account whenever he was able, but he failed to keep an accurate
record of his payments. A few days before the expiration of the leasehold
year, the tenant went to the landlord to make another partial payment on his
overdue rent obligation. When the tenant told the landlord that he intended
to move out the following day, the landlord demanded that the entire balance
of overdue rent be paid immediately and asserted that the amount still
owed was $253.75. When the tenant replied that he was unable to pay
the entire sum, the landlord asked the tenant to sign a one-year note for
$253.75. The landlord threatened that if the tenant refused to sign, the
landlord would have all of the tenant's household belongings seized the
following morning before the tenant could move out. As the landlord knew,
the tenant's wife had been sick for some time. The tenant signed the note
because of the landlord's threatened action and its possible adverse effect
on his wife's health. When the tenant failed to pay the note upon its maturity, the landlord sued for $253.75, the amount of the note. The landlord
could, of course, recover whatever amount of rent was still due; the question
raised was whether the landlord could recover the specific amount of the
note.

Under the common-law remedy for overdue rent, which is still followed
in some states (including Pennsylvania), a landlord has the right, without a
prior lawsuit, to seize goods on the premises and have them sold in order to
secure the rental money due him. Since the landlord was merely threatening
to do what he had the legal right to do, he was not exerting wrongful pressure.
His demand that the tenant sign the note before moving his household effects

from the premises was not oppressive, not an abuse of the landlord's rights, and therefore not duress. The note could be enforced.

If an agreement is obtained under duress, it is not enforceable. The victim of the duress can avoid (that is cancel or disaffirm) any such agreement, and he can also recover whatever he has been forced to pay or give, provided he paid more than he actually owed. As to this proviso —even though a payment is obtained by duress, a debtor cannot recover his payment if it is made for a definite, undisputed, legally enforceable obligation. Permitting recovery of such a payment would accomplish nothing; the creditor could still enforce his claim and reobtain the amount paid. However even if the debtor is for this reason unable to recover the amount he is forced to pay, he can still recover damages for any tort the creditor may commit in wrongfully inducing the payment.

The word "pressure" in reference to duress means any act or threatened act which causes a person to agree to a proposition to which he otherwise would not have agreed. Pressure which is considered as wrongful usually involves either 1) personal violence, 2) criminal prosecution, or 3) interference with property or contract rights.

PERSONAL VIOLENCE

Actual or threatened violence either to the person who is thus induced to enter into an agreement, or to a close relative of his, is clearly wrongful pressure.

CRIMINAL PROSECUTION

Sometimes a person is induced to enter into an agreement because of threats that he or a close relative will be criminally prosecuted. The criminal law is for the protection of society as a whole. In a few exceptional situations referred to in Chapter 3, criminal proceedings may properly be threatened to assist the collection of civil claims. Except for such situations, an individual who uses or threatens to use the criminal process to induce settlement of a civil claim, is misusing the criminal process, and thereby exerting wrongful pressure or duress. Threatening criminal proceedings for personal gain would seem to be a misuse of the criminal process (except for the situations noted), regardless of the guilt or innocence of the threatened person. However, courts in some states hold that such a threat is duress only if the threatened person is actually innocent of the crime for which imprisonment is threatened.

In addition to the risk that his threat constitutes duress, there are further reasons for a creditor to be extremely wary (and to seek legal advice) before threatening criminal proceedings in order to induce a civil settlement. By making such a threat, a creditor may himself incur a civil liability for the tort of malicious prosecution, and he may incur criminal liability for extortion and/or for compounding a crime. A creditor's attempt to collect by threatening to accuse his debtor of a crime has been held by courts in some states to constitute the crime of extortion or blackmail, even though the debt involved is definite, undisputed, and past due, and even though the debtor is actually guilty of the crime which the creditor threatens to expose. As to the possible offense of compounding a crime: a creditor is guilty of this offense when he agrees to accept something of value for stifling information concerning the "compounded" crime.

Example: A corporation's business included dealing in trading-stamp books. The treasurer's daughter was employed by the corporation as a clerk. One day the treasurer was called to the office of the corporation's president where he found, in addition to the president, the corporation's lawyer, and three directors. The lawyer told the treasurer that his daughter was accused of stealing trading-stamp books. After some discussion the lawyer demanded $2,500 from the treasurer as settlement for his daughter's theft. After further discussion, the lawyer reduced his demand to $1,500 and said that if the treasurer failed to pay within a week his daughter would be arrested and put in jail. The demand and warning were repeated during the week. The treasurer was considerably upset and agitated for the next few days, and was seen actually to be crying at various times. During the week the treasurer paid $200, and by the end of the week an additional $500 which he obtained by borrowing on his life insurance. For the $800 balance the treasurer signed a promissory note. When the note came due, the treasurer refused to pay and asserted that his signature had been obtained through duress.

Some courts have said that vague, indefinite references to the possibility of arrest will usually not constitute duress. In the case upon which this example is based,[4] although criminal action had not been started, the threat was clear that such an action would immediately result if the treasurer failed to make the demanded settlement. The court held that the note was signed under duress and therefore was not enforceable against the treasurer.

INTERFERENCE WITH PROPERTY OR CONTRACT RIGHTS

Taking, retaining, or injuring a person's property or threatening to do so:

1. Is wrongful if done without legal process or right. Interfering with another's property without legal process or right is clearly wrongful; it is tortuous and frequently criminal.

2. Is wrongful if done under legal process or right but in such a way

[4] *Ortt* v. *Schwartz*, 62 Pa. Super. 70 (1916).

or under such circumstances as to constitute a misuse of the process or right. A claimant who threatens an ordinary lawsuit is bringing some pressure on the other party to induce him to settle or compromise in order to avoid the various detrimental results (expense, inconvenience, and adverse publicity) which frequently accompany a lawsuit, even a lawsuit which the defendant ultimately wins. Such pressure is not duress. Even greater pressure is exerted if the lawsuit is the unusual type which can be initiated by attaching some of the defendant's property at the start of the lawsuit, as, for example, when the lawsuit is initiated in the state where the property is situated, and the defendant is a nonresident of that state. This pressure is usually not duress, even though the plaintiff attempts to induce a settlement by securing a court attachment of the defendant's property in an amount which clearly exceeds what is reasonably necessary for the plaintiff to pursue his proper legal remedies. Usually a grossly excessive attachment does not of itself constitute duress, because the defendant is considered sufficiently protected by his usual legal remedy, namely applying for a release from the attachment. However if a plaintiff deliberately has a grossly excessive attachment made when the defendant has insufficient time to secure relief through legal process, when any such delay will result in irreparable loss to the defendant, the plaintiff will be considered guilty of misusing the legal process and exerting wrongful pressure.

Sometimes after a contract has been formed, one party attempts to force the other to agree to an amendment by threatening to breach the contract if it is not amended. Usually the ordinary legal remedies for breach of contract are considered sufficient to protect the innocent party from any threatened loss. Therefore (and consistent with the general policy of not interfering with the freedom of contract unless clearly necessary), a threat to breach a contract is usually not considered wrongful pressure. However, under special circumstances such a threat may be so oppressive that it will be considered as wrongful pressure and therefore duress.

Example: For steel previously sold and delivered, the seller (a steel producer) had a claim against the buyer (a steel distributor) for the agreed purchase price. However, because of alleged defects in the shipment, the distributor reasonably disputed the amount of this obligation. To avoid litigation, the parties agreed to compromise the disputed obligation for a lesser sum, which the distributor then fully paid. Sometime afterwards the producer and distributor entered into another contract for the sale of a certain quantity of steel to the distributor, to be shipped by a certain date. The distributor in turn contracted with a refrigerator manufacturer to sell and deliver this steel to him. However, on the date agreed upon for shipment to the distributor, the producer refused to ship unless the distributor would pay the full amount which the producer had claimed in their prior dispute. The producer persisted in his refusal even after the distributor explained that he had already contracted to resell the steel. Because of an unusual demand for steel at the time, there was a reasonable likelihood that the distributor could not obtain steel elsewhere in time to perform his resale contract. Therefore, to obtain the steel he needed for his other contract the distributor, under protest, paid the producer the amount he demanded. After obtaining the steel and filling his resale contract, the distributor sued the producer.

In a somewhat similar case a court held[5] that the producer was guilty of duress and permitted the distributor to recover the additional payment. The case presented these unusual circumstances:

1. The producer's demand was oppressive. Because of the prior compromise agreement, the producer knew that he had no grounds whatsoever for his claim.

2. The producer knew of the distributor's urgent need to obtain prompt shipment in order to avoid liability for substantial damages on his resale contract.

3. The producer knew that it was practically impossible for the distributor to obtain the needed steel elsewhere.

4. At the time he made his involuntary payment the distributor could reasonably fear that his ordinary court remedies would not be adequate to save him from sustaining a substantial loss.

Part 3   MISTAKE

Sometimes a person's decision to enter into an agreement is based largely on a mistaken assumption or understanding concerning something connected with the agreement. When the mistake is discovered, if the other person nevertheless wants to enforce the agreement while the mistaken party wants to cancel it, society must then decide what effect the mistake in question should have on the validity of the agreement. All mistaken agreements are not automatically invalid. When persons enter into agreements, they are frequently taking chances or making assumptions concerning possible existing facts or future expectations. To permit an agreement to be canceled every time one party makes a mistaken assumption would unduly weaken the stability of contracts. On the other hand, justice requires that some mistaken agreements be canceled. The effect which a particular mistake should have on the validity of an agreement is, therefore, entirely a matter of policy—of what seems fair, reasonable, and practical under the circumstances.

The chief types of mistakes which may possibly affect the validity of agreements can be classified in the following way:

1. A mistake concerning the language or words used in expressing the agreement in question.

[5] *Pittsburgh Steel Co.* v. *Hollingshead & Blei,* 202 Ill. App. 177 (1916).

A) A mistaken interpretation of words—that is, a mistake in understanding the meaning of words that are used.

B) A mistaken expression of intent—that is, a mistake in choosing words, so that as a result the intent of one party or of both parties is not accurately expressed.

1) The intent of both parties to the agreement is mistakenly expressed;

2) The intent of one of the parties is mistakenly expressed,

a) Through his own fault or through the fault of one of his employees,

b) Through the fault of an independent transmission agency.

2. A mistake concerning extrinsic facts—that is, although the intent of the parties is accurately expressed, one or both parties enter into the agreement because of a mistaken assumption or understanding concerning certain surrounding facts.

MISTAKES AS TO LANGUAGE USED

Mistaken Interpretation of Words

Since many words have varying shades of meaning, the courts are frequently called upon to interpret the meaning of certain terms used in an agreement. The best guide is reasonableness. If the parties to an agreement do not expressly define the meaning of their terms, they are presumed to be using words in their customary manner. If the parties are not both members of a particular trade or vocation, the customary meaning of the words in question is taken to be the meaning commonly given such words by the general public. On the other hand if both parties to an agreement are members of a certain trade or vocation, they are presumed to be using whatever particular meaning such words usually have in that trade or vocation.

Before entering into an agreement a person should request an explanation of any words or terms which he does not understand. He will not be excused from an agreement merely because he assumed in his own mind that certain words had a different meaning than their customary meaning, or merely because he was ignorant of the customary meaning of such words.

Sometimes certain words used in an agreement are capable of different meanings or applications, each of which is equally reasonable under the circumstances. If one party has one such meaning in mind and the other party is using the other meaning, they never actually reach an agreement at all and therefore no enforceable contract is formed.

Example: A seller and a buyer contracted for the sale and purchase at a stated price of 125 bales of a specified grade of cotton which was to arrive in Liverpool on the ship "Peerless" from Bombay. Unknown to the parties at the time of their agreement, there were two ships by that name both carrying cotton from Bombay, one to arrive in October the other in December. The buyer was thinking of the October ship, while the seller's cargo was on the December ship. When the October ship arrived, the buyer demanded that the seller deliver the agreed cotton. The seller refused since none of that cargo belonged to him. When the December ship arrived with the seller's cargo, the buyer refused to accept the cotton tendered by the seller, and the seller sued the buyer for damages for breach of contract.

The seller could not recover. Since the seller attached one meaning to the word "Peerless," and the buyer another meaning, and since both meanings were equally reasonable, there was no agreement and no enforceable contract between the parties.

Mistaken Expression of Intent

Sometimes although there is no misunderstanding concerning the meaning of words, a mistake arises through the selection or use of wrong or inaccurate words in expressing an agreement. If both parties make the same mistake in expressing their agreement, the case is relatively simple. Thus if the parties to a written contract mistakenly sign a contract form which, because of an error in wording, fails to state correctly the agreement which both parties intended to make, either party can obtain a court order reforming or restating the written agreement so that it will conform to their actual intent.

Example: A seller owned Lots 2 and 3 in Block 1 in a certain residential area. On Lot 2 was the seller's house. Lot 3 was vacant. Deciding to sell Lot 3, the seller advertised and interested a buyer who agreed to buy the vacant lot for $4,000. A written contract was typed but the typist struck the wrong key so that the contract read "Lot 2, Block 1" instead of "Lot 3, Block 1." Without noticing the error the parties signed the contract form. When the error was discovered, the buyer tendered $4,000 and insisted on a literal enforcement of the written agreement.

Since $4,000 would obviously not be the price for the lot upon which the house was erected, the seller could prove what the parties actually had intended, and the court would correct the written contract accordingly.

A much more difficult case arises if only one of the two parties to an agreement inadvertently uses the wrong word and mistakenly expresses his intent. Of course, if the other party knows of the error before a contract is formed—knows, for example, that the offer he has received is not the sender's actual intent—then certainly the erroneous communication cannot form the basis of an enforceable contract. Proof of actual knowledge is often difficult, sometimes impossible. Therefore, even though the recipient of a communication may deny knowing of an error, the fairest approach is to assume that all persons are reasonable, and possess the knowledge and form the conclusions of reasonable people. If under the circumstances the error in question would have been apparent to a reasonable person, then the recipient is treated as though he had actual knowledge of the error—and he cannot form a contract on the basis of the erroneous communication. If, on the other hand, the recipient is unaware of the error, an enforceable contract will *sometimes* be formed. Situations involving this type of error—that is, an erroneous expression of one party's intent—can be subdivided into 1) those in which the error arises through the fault of the sender of the erroneous communication or through the fault of his employee for whose acts it is fair to hold the sender responsible, and 2) those in which the error arises through the fault of an independent transmission agency.

1) Mistake by Sender or His Employee. Frequently the courts will hold a sender to what he personally or through his employee leads the other party reasonably to understand is meant. Thus if an offeror misstates his price and the offeree accepts without knowing of the error, many courts will hold that an enforceable contract exists from that moment on. On the other hand some courts have shown a tendency to permit a contract to be canceled if the error is quite substantial and is discovered early enough so that canceling the contract will restore both parties to the position they were in before forming their contract.

2) Mistake by Independent Transmission Agency. If an error is made by an independent transmission agency, the courts in some states hold that the erroneous communication will nevertheless form the basis of an enforceable contract, but the courts in most states have reached the opposite conclusion.

Example: A lumber dealer in Bangor, Maine, delivered to the telegraph office in Bangor a message addressed to a buyer in Philadelphia, containing the following offer: "Will sell you 500 M laths delivered at your wharf two ten net cash. July shipment. Answer quick." When the message was delivered to the buyer it read, ". . . two net cash . . ." the "ten" having been omitted through the telegraph company's negligent transmission of the message. The buyer was unaware of the error and under the circumstances a reasonable person would not have suspected the error. The buyer immediately replied by telegraph, "Accept your telegraph offer on laths." Through subsequent correspondence the parties learned of the error before the laths were shipped, and the question immediately arose as to whether or not a contract had actually been formed.

Argument for the Buyer: The seller knew that his message would be recopied in the course of its transmission by telegraph, and in selecting the telegraph system he assumed the risks involved in that medium of transmission.   Generally an offeror is bound by what he leads the offeree reasonably to understand is meant, and no sound reason is present to deviate from this general rule here.   Some courts therefore would hold that an enforceable contract was formed for the sale of the laths at $2 per thousand.

Argument for the Dealer: Since the dealer had no control over the selection of telegraph company personnel and no right to supervise their work, there was no master-servant relationship between the dealer and the telegraph company.   The message delivered to the buyer was not the message sent by the dealer.   Neither the dealer nor a person for whose conduct he was responsible led the buyer to believe that the offered price was $2 per thousand.   Therefore, many courts would hold that the exchange of the quoted telegrams did not form a contract.

Regardless of which view a particular court might follow, the telegraph company would be liable to whichever of the parties sustained damages as a result of the company's failure to transmit the message correctly.   However, recoverable damages might be inadequate, inasmuch as a contract between a sender and a telegraph company usually contains a provision limiting the company's liability.   For example, one standard form of telegraph blank in common use states on the reverse side: "The Company shall not be liable for mistakes or delays in the transmission or delivery . . . of any message received for transmission at the unrepeated message rate beyond the sum of five hundred dollars . . ."

MISTAKES CONCERNING EXTRINSIC FACTS

Although an agreement correctly states the intent of the parties, one party or both parties will sometimes be mistaken as to certain facts concerning the subject matter of the contract, the mistake being such that had the truth been known the mistaken party or parties would not have consented to the agreement.   A mistake by one party only is frequently called a "unilateral mistake," the mistake of both parties a "bilateral mistake."   When litigation arises because of the mistake, a very basic policy question is presented.   To what extent can relief from mistakes be given without unduly weakening the stability of contracts?   For contracts to have any value in society, they must be quite stable, not easily changed or overturned.   It is not unusual for one party to a contract to become disappointed and dissatisfied, and wish to cancel his contract.   Many people are not above pretending that they made some mistake if doing so would help them to escape from a burdensome contract.   The overall stability of contracts would be seriously jeopardized if people could easily cancel contracts with which they had become displeased.   On the other hand it would be quite unfair to rigidly enforce all contracts regardless of very serious mistakes which the parties may have made.   In weighing (on one side) the desirability that contracts be stable, against (on the other side) considerations of fairness and reasonableness, one of the chief guides used by the courts is to evaluate the relationship which the particular mistake in question bears to the risk of misjudgment present, at least to some extent, in every contract. Another factor also considered is the severity of the loss threatened by the mistake and the possibility of avoiding such loss.

Risk Evaluation. When entering into any contract both parties are guessing or estimating as to the value of what each is to give in exchange for what he will obtain. Since value is based on a number of variable factors, it seems fair to say that each party is assuming (consciously or unconsciously) the risk of possible error in his opinion as to value. Certainly the occurrence of the very error upon which a party takes a chance should not justify canceling his contract, whether the mistake is unilateral or bilateral. Also (different from knowingly taking advantage of another's mistaken expression of intent, which is clearly unfair), it is usually not unfair for a nonmistaken party to take advantage of the other's unilateral mistake or ignorance concerning value. Parties to sales contracts are usually said to be dealing at "arm's length," meaning that usually neither party is obliged to share all that he knows with the other party. However, if one person induces a mistake through misrepresentations, the picture changes. A person should not be permitted to take advantage of a mistake which he himself has caused. Mistakes caused by one party's misrepresentations, therefore, are classified differently from other mistakes and will be discussed later.

During the process of evaluating the relative risks which contracting parties assume, some courts rather needlessly involve themselves in semantical difficulties. These courts say that a mistake in the *value* of the subject matter of a contract is not grounds for canceling the contract while a mistake as to the *existence* or *nature* of the subject matter *is* grounds for canceling a contract. When the rule is stated in this way, there remains the very difficult problem of distinguishing between the "value" of the subject matter and its "nature," or "existence," since a mistake can directly affect value and nevertheless seem to justify canceling the contract. It is easier and more accurate, therefore, to state this policy factor simply in terms of assumed risk. Thus even though a mistake affects value, if it concerns a matter totally unexpected, a matter assumed by the parties to be stable and not subject to variation, it is a matter regarding which they are not assuming the risk of error. Stability of contracts is not too greatly weakened when relief from such mistakes is permitted.

Example: A seller sold a certain tract of land to a buyer for $5,000 which the buyer paid upon receiving the deed. Unknown to the seller, oil had been discovered on adjoining land and the actual value of the tract at the time of the sale was $10,000. When the seller learned of this, he sued to have the transfer canceled.

1. Assume that at the time he purchased, the buyer was also unaware of the oil discovery.

In estimating value each party assumed the risk of error. That the assumed risk occurred would not be reason to cancel.

2. Assume that at the time he purchased, the buyer was aware of the discovery of oil and knew that the seller was ignorant of the presence of oil.

So long as the buyer was not guilty of any actual misrepresentation or misstatement of fact, the seller could not cancel.

Example: A seller agreed to sell and a buyer to buy for $10,500 a tract of land described by its exact boundaries. Both parties believed that the described tract contained about 200 acres. When the parties later learned that the tract actually contained 175 acres, the buyer attemped to cancel the contract.

The contract would be enforceable as made. Since the agreement did not call for a survey, size as well as other factors affecting value was something both parties were estimating. That they might be in error was a risk both were assuming, and therefore not grounds to cancel the contract.

Example: A seller and a buyer had a tract of land surveyed. The surveyor reported that the tract conatined 200 acres. The seller and buyer then contracted for the sale and purchase of the specified tract at $30 per acre. The buyer paid the agreed down payment of $100, gave his note for $5,900 (the balance of the purchase price), and received a deed for the land. Later the parties learned that the surveyor had made a mistake, and that the tract contained only 175 acres. The buyer paid $5,150 which added to his down payment paid for 175 acres at $30 per acre. When the seller demanded the remaining $750 due on the buyer's note, the buyer refused to pay, proposing that the seller should either consider the land fully paid for or instead return the buyer's money and cancel the transfer. The seller refused both suggested alternatives and sued to collect the $750 unpaid balance of the buyer's note.

The seller could not recover. In entering into the contract the parties believed that the survey was accurate. The mistake in size was totally unexpected and unforeseeable, and not a risk that the parties were assuming. For such a mistake the original contract could be canceled.

Loss Evaluation. In addition to considering the risks assumed by contracting parties, some courts also consider 1) the loss which would result from enforcement of the contract as compared with the loss if the contract is canceled (disregarding of course any gain resulting solely from the mistake itself), and 2) the possibility of restoring the status quo—that is, considering the particular mistake in question and the time it is discovered, whether it is possible to prevent a substantial loss by restoring the parties to the positions they were in before making the contract. If a mistake is unilateral, the courts in some states give little weight to the possibility of restoring the status quo and instead say rather rigidly that a mistake of one party only is never (or almost never) grounds for canceling a contract.

The entire field of extrinsic mistake is quite complex and fixed guidelines cannot be found which will apply with equal effect in all cases. The ultimate objective is to achieve justice while at the same time maintaining stability of contracts, but both of these are variable concepts. While the two most important factors to be considered are the risks assumed and the losses threatened, these factors must in some cases be further subdivided and other factors also considered. From the standpoint of risks assumed, some risks are more consciously and completely assumed than are certain other risks. To illustrate, consider the following example of builders A and B.

Example: Builder A contracted to construct a certain building for $48,000, and builder B a different building for the same price. Before entering into their respective contacts, A and B each calculated construction costs at $40,000 and added 20 percent for profit and overhead (depreciation of equipment, etc.).

A's Contract. From the normal test boring pattern, A assumed the existence of a certain underground rock formation. However, on the day after A entered into the contract an accidentally heavy dynamite explosion occurred on a nearby road construction job. The resulting surface subsidence of nearby land disclosed the existence of an unsuspected underground rock cavern, a portion of which extended under the lot where A was to build. This would increase A's costs to $50,000, and A requested cancellation of his contract.

B's Contract. In calculating his costs, B mistotaled a column of figures, putting down $40,000 instead of the correct total of $50,000. On the day after B entered into the contract he discovered his error in arithmetic, and requested cancellation.

Clearly A's mistake would be classified as an extrinsic mistake, and so would B's. B made no mistake in expressing his intent. At the time he expressed his intent, he intended to build for $48,000, he said what he meant and meant what he said. Although both contracts involve extrinsic mistake, B's argument for cancellation would be stronger than A's. A's mistake was so clearly the very type of risk that any builder is assuming that his argument would arouse little sympathy. On the other hand, while B's mistake was his own fault, it is not so obviously the type of risk which a builder consciously assumes or should be considered as assuming. A builder takes a chance on increased material and labor costs, on bad weather, and on a myriad of other conditions and occurrences that might adversely affect construction—including the subsurface land pattern. Any such event usually will not excuse the builder from his contract. But a builder does not to the same extent assume the risk of clerical or computational errors, and if such an error causes no loss to the other party, why should not the builder be relieved from it? Although B's argument is strong, this does not mean that he should be excused or that most courts would excuse him. Other factors are also involved. For example, in approaching such cases the law can never lose sight of the possibility that B found his contract unprofitable for some other reason, and made up the appealing story of being a good-faith contractor who was just poor in arithmetic, in order to escape from his contract. Some courts would excuse B, some other courts would not. The latter courts would argue that merely because a contract has recently been formed and performance not yet begun is no reason to permit the contract to be canceled, and that to excuse a person on the ground of computational error would undermine the practice of awarding contracts by secret bids. It would tempt a builder to shave his costs very closely and then, should he find his bid substantially lower than all the rest, claim mistake and excuse, thus almost completely defeating the purpose of having sealed bids submitted.

Part 4   MISREPRESENTATIONS

During contract negotiations, parties often make various statements of fact concerning the matters being negotiated. A statement of fact which is influential in bringing about an agreement is called a *representation*. A false statement is called a *misrepresentation*. A person who is induced to enter into a contract through a misrepresentation is acting under a mistake of fact caused directly by the other party to the contract, that is, by the representer who made the misrepresentation. The fact that the representer has led the other party into mistakenly entering into the agreement is certainly sufficient reason to cancel or invalidate the agreement, without further inquiry into the relative risks assumed by the parties or the other factors discussed in Part 3 of this chapter.

In connection with the effect of misrepresentations, the law makes an important distinction between fact and opinion. A person forms a variety of opinions as a result of many influences, including intangible feelings and personal idiosyncrasies; persons can be expected to hold radically different opinions on the same thing. Usually it is not considered sound policy, therefore, to hold a person legally liable for entertaining erroneous opinions, nor for expressing them, and a mistake as to another's opinion is usually not considered sufficiently important to affect the validity of a contract. Thus for a misrepresentation to justify the cancellation of a contract, it must concern some actual fact rather than the representer's opinion as to a certain fact.

The law sometimes encounters difficulty in classifying a certain statement as to whether it concerns fact or opinion. A statement describing past occurrences is usually a statement of fact, while a statement of what can be expected to occur in the future is usually merely the representer's opinion. However, a statement of future expectations or an expression which the representer clearly states is only his opinion, may nevertheless imply the existence of certain facts. To that extent, such a statement constitutes a representation of certain facts, although it may be expressed in the form of an opinion.

Example: A seller owned a block of 100 shares of stock in the Star Corporation. In inducing a buyer to buy, the seller said, "Dividends you will receive for this stock in the next five years will equal what you are paying for the stock."

Although the seller's statement was an expression of opinion, it implied that he was unaware of any *fact* which would make the occurrence of what he predicted practically impossible. Suppose that the buyer could prove that when the seller made the quoted statement, he knew that the corporation was hopelessly insolvent. In such a case, the seller could be found guilty of misrepresenting a fact.

Suppose that when a person enters into a contract with a representer he is acting on the faith of a statement of fact which the representer previously made to someone else. In order to avoid the unacceptable proposition that a person can be held liable to everybody, everywhere, and for any amount, the courts have usually limited cancellation or other liability for misrepresentation to situations in which the representer *directly* misleads another person into making a contract. In other words, usually the only person who can hold a representer liable for a misrepresentation of fact is the person to whom he has directly made the misrepresentation in question, plus the other persons (if any) whom he actually intended would rely on the misrepresentation.

Misrepresentations of fact can be classified in the following way, according to what the representer indicates is his intent or state of mind:

1) Dishonest Misrepresentations (otherwise known as "fraudulent misrepresentations"). This type of misrepresentation is a tort and usually also a crime. It occurs when the representer does not honestly believe that the fact represented is true, either because he knows that his statement is false or because he is aware that he lacks the knowledge which he manifests in making the statement.

Example: While attempting to sell a suburban lot, a salesman was asked by a prospective buyer whether the city water main had been extended to the area. Although the salesman did not know, he answered, "Yes" instead of saying, "I don't know but will check and find out." Actually city water was not available in the area.

The salesman would be guilty of a dishonest or fraudulent misrepresentation.

2) Honest Misrepresentations. This type occurs when the representer honestly believes that the fact he states is true. Such misrepresentations can be further subdivided according to whether the representer's belief is reasonable or not. To say that his belief is not reasonable is another way of saying that the representer has failed to use reasonable care to assure the accuracy of his representation. This is sometimes called a negligent misrepresentation.

FRAUDULENT MISREPRESENTATIONS

Types of Fraud

Fraudulent misrepresentations can be made in several ways, principally by an express lie, by giving partial information, by conduct, and sometimes by nondisclosure of facts.

Express Lie. The representer states in words that a certain fact exists, when he knows either that the fact does not exist or that he has no knowledge as to whether or not the fact exists.

Partial Information. While appearing to state all of the facts pertaining to a certain matter, the representer states only a part of the facts and deliberately refrains from disclosing the remainder of the facts.

Example: A seller moved to a town about 300 miles away from a 160-acre plot of land which he owned. When the seller moved, there were several producing oil wells in the neighborhood. About two years after the seller moved, a new, deeper well was drilled on adjoining land and began producing oil in considerably greater quantities than the previous wells. A buyer called on the seller and offered to buy the 160-acre tract. During the course of their conversation the buyer told the seller how the existing wells were producing and of various neighborhood occurrences, but the buyer said nothing about the new oil strike, of which the buyer knew the seller was ignorant. The seller agreed to sell and delivered a deed for the land to the buyer. A few days later the seller learned of the new oil discovery and sued to cancel the sale because of fraud.

The transfer could be canceled. The buyer was not obliged to give the seller any information, but once he started to tell of happenings, he was obliged to give a complete picture. The buyer was guilty of fraud in deliberately omitting one important fact while appearing to tell about all of the important occurrences since the seller moved away.

Acts or Conduct. Sometimes a person will act in a certain way in order to assert that a certain fact situation exists when actually the true facts are otherwise. For example, although he says nothing, a used-car dealer who daubs grease over a crack in the engine block before showing a car to a prospective buyer is through such conduct asserting a fact which is not true.

Nondisclosure. Everyone has a natural inclination to try to obtain the best bargain he can for himself. It is usually considered better overall social policy to leave this natural inclination fairly unrestricted, and to accord to each person full freedom to negotiate advantageous contracts, so long as he avoids actual dishonesty. Usually therefore, a person with certain knowledge concerning the subject matter of an agreement, is not required to disclose what he knows to the other party, and his nondisclosure does not constitute fraud. As the Georgia Court of Appeals has remarked:

> We are aware that neither courts of law nor courts of equity maintain as high a standard of business and commercial integrity and honesty as is demanded by moral obligation. The doctrine of the Roman law, strongly approved by that great orator and lawyer, Cicero, that it is the duty of every man to disclose all facts to another with whom he is dealing which are material to his interest (Cic. de Offic. Lib. 3, Ch. 13),[6] is not generally enforced in courts of justice, either in England or America. . . . While principles of justice and sound morals may require the most scrupulous good faith, candor, and truth, in all dealings whatsoever, the courts of law and equity take a more practical and commercial view of the question, and assign limits to the exercise of their jurisdiction, short of these principles. The well-established rule of the common law, that men who trade trade at arm's length, is applicable to business transactions, in the absence of any special fiduciary relations between the parties. This rule is not based on a high standard of business morality, but appears to be the outgrowth of practical business exigency.[7]

And as the Kentucky Court of Appeals has said:

> If any other rule were adopted, it would have a depressing tendency on trade and commerce by removing the incentive to specula-

[6] Cicero wrote (to quote from the Walter Miller translation, 1913): "The following are problems of this sort: Suppose, for example, a time of dearth and famine at Rhodes, with provisions at fabulous prices; and suppose that an honest man has imported a large cargo of grain from Alexandria and that to his certain knowledge also several other importers have set sail from Alexandria, and that on the voyage he has sighted their vessels laden with grain and bound for Rhodes; is he to report the fact to the Rhodians or is he to keep his own counsel and sell his own stock at the highest market price: I am assuming the case of a virtuous, upright man, and I am raising the question how a man would think and reason who would not conceal the facts from the Rhodians if he thought that it was immoral to do so, but who might be in doubt whether such silence would really be immoral.

"In deciding cases of this kind Diogenes of Babylonia, a great and highly esteemed Stoic, consistently holds one view; his pupil Antipater, a most profound scholar, holds another. According to Antipater all the facts should be disclosed, that the buyer may not be uninformed of any detail that the seller knows; according to Diogenes the seller should declare any defects in his wares, in so far as such a course is prescribed by the common law of the land; but for the rest, since he has goods to sell, he may try to sell them to the best possible advantage, provided he is guilty of no misrepresentation."

Cicero then summarizes what Diogenes and Antipater might say to each other if they were discussing this case, and as his own opinion writes: "I think, then, that it was the duty of that grain dealer not to keep back the facts from the Rhodians. . . . At all events he would be no candid or sincere or straightforward or upright or honest man, but rather one who is shifty, sly, artful, shrewd, underhand, cunning, one grown old in fraud and subtlety. Is it not inexpedient to subject oneself to all these terms of reproach and many more besides?"

[7] *Marietta Fertilizer Co. v. Beckwith,* 4 Ga. App. 245, 61 S.E. 149 (1908).

tion and profit that lies at the foundation of almost every business venture.[8]

At an earlier date the same court said:

> From those who have reason to expect information from us the truth should not be withheld, but such as look not to us for information and expect no disclosure from us, have no cause to complain of our silence, and to reproach us for not speaking, with having suppressed the truth.[9]

If a certain specialized fact situation exists, the courts follow a different rule and impose upon a person a legal obligation to make a full disclosure of facts. The most important of these special situations include the following:

1. When the undisclosed fact involves a matter concerning which the contracting parties are not assuming the risk of error: in other words, the undisclosed fact is such that a contract would be cancellable if both contracting parties were mistaken concerning that fact. If the fact is of this type, a party who knows the truth concerning the fact in question is obliged to disclose what he knows to the other party, and his failure to make a full disclosure constitutes fraud.

2. When the nondisclosing party is already under an obligation to be loyal to the interests of the other contracting party, as for example when the nondisclosing party is an agent for the other party or when the parties are copartners.

3. When the failure to warn of hidden conditions unreasonably jeopardizes the health or physical safety of the other contracting party.

4. When the nondisclosing party goes further than merely remaining silent and actively attempts to conceal a fact. Such a case is more properly classified as a species of misrepresentation by act or conduct.

REMEDIES FOR FRAUD

A person who is induced by a fraudulent misrepresentation to enter into a contract usually has a choice between either of two remedies, namely:

1) Rescission. The defrauded party can rescind or cancel the contract, return the property he received under the contract, and recover what he gave or paid. Also he can usually recover for any consequential damages he has sustained, such as personal injuries or actual expenses.

2) Affirmance and Recovery of Damages. Instead of rescinding, the defrauded party can affirm the contract (that is, retain what he received under the contract) and recover as damages the loss sustained as a result

---

[8] *Hays* v. *Meyers*, 32 Ky. 832, 107 S.W. 287, 17 L.R.A.N.S. 284 (1908).
[9] *Taylor* v. *Bradshaw*, 6 T.B. Monroe (Ky.) 145, 7 Am. Dec. 132 (1827).

of the fraud. In measuring the amount of this loss, the courts in the various states use either of two theories, 1) the out-of-pocket rule, or 2) the loss-of-bargain rule. Under the out-of-pocket rule the loss recoverable by the defrauded party is determined by subtracting the actual value of the purchased property from the contract price the defrauded party was induced to pay. The loss-of-bargain rule is the same rule that is applied in measuring damages for breach of warranty, discussed later in this chapter. Under this rule, the amount of recoverable loss is determined by subtracting the actual value of the purchased property from the value it would have had if the representation had been true.

Example: Through fraudulent misrepresentations a seller induced a buyer to purchase a tract of land for $10,000. Upon discovering that he had been defrauded, the buyer decided to retain the property and sue the seller for damages. The evidence showed that the actual value of the land at the time of the purchase was $8,000, and that if the seller's misrepresentations had been true, the land would have been worth $13,000.

The out-of-pocket damages would be $2,000—the $10,000 paid by the buyer minus $8,000, the actual value.

The loss-of-bargain damages would be $5,000—$13,000, the value if the misrepresentation had been true, minus $8,000, the actual value.

As discussed in the chapter on torts (Chapter 2), a plaintiff's contributory negligence does not bar him from recovering if a defendant is guilty of an intentional tort. By definition fraud is an intentional tort. Therefore the fact that a defrauded party has relied on a misrepresentation instead of making his own investigation of facts certainly should not bar him from recovering, nor should a defrauded party's failure to use proper care to protect his own interests (contributory negligence) bar him from recovering—except when maintaining the stability of *written* contracts (discussed next) is added as a policy factor.

ORAL REPRESENTATIONS VERSUS WRITTEN CONTRACTS

During the course of negotiating a written contract, parties frequently propose and discuss various possible provisions before they agree on final terms and enter into a contract. Later if one of the parties is disappointed with the contract, he may dishonestly assert that the parties actually agreed on additional or different terms than those stated in the writing. Or a person may honestly believe that the agreement included other than the written terms. One of the chief reasons for putting an agreement in writing is to minimize disputes and to protect both parties from the need for (and uncertainty of) future litigation to determine the actual terms of their agreement. Also if a writing purports to be a statement of the entire agreement, it seems reasonable to expect that a person will refuse to sign until the writing completely states the agreement. Based both upon the diligence expected of a reasonable person (to have his written contract completely and accurately state his agreement), and upon the known inclination of a person to try to escape from what has later proven to be a bad bargain, the law considers it to be sound policy to say that if persons put their agreement in writing and the writing appears to be a complete expression of the agreement, then the writing is their *entire* agreement up to that point. Any other provisions that were discussed during the negotiations but were not included in the writing are not part of the agreement. In other words, the terms of the agreement cannot be altered or qualified by oral or written evidence of terms allegedly agreed to *before* or *with* the signing of the agreement. This rule of policy is commonly called the "parol evidence rule." (Note that this rule and the policy factors that give rise to it do not at all apply to a case in which one party alleges that *after* the written contract was signed, the parties orally agreed on a modification or cancellation.)

Suppose that after a written agreement has been signed, one of the parties claims that his consent was obtained through fraudulent misrepresentations of certain facts. Although he may not directly claim that any terms different from those expressed in the writing were actually agreed upon, his assertion will sometimes indirectly involve the parol evidence rule. The most common fact situations can be classified in the following way:

1. Assume that proving the alleged fraud will not change or qualify in any way what is stated in the written contract.

a) Assume further that the other contracting party made or authorized the fraudulent misrepresentation. If these assumptions can be proved, the defrauded party should certainly be entitled to relief from the contract. He can either rescind the contract or affirm the contract and recover damages.

b) Assume that the fraudulent misrepresentation was made by the agent of one of the parties and was neither authorized by nor participated in by the agent's employer or principal. If the defrauded party wishes to rescind, he should be permitted to do so, in order to prevent the other party from enjoying the benefits obtained by his agent's fraud. If, however, the defrauded party wishes to affirm and recover damages instead of rescinding, the courts are not agreed. In most states if the misrepresentation concerns a matter about which an agent might be expected to give information, the principal, although himself innocent, will be held responsible for his agent's conduct and liable for the damages sustained by the defrauded party. A few states apply a narrower rule (as further explained in Chapter 12), holding that a defrauded party cannot recover damages from the other party when the latter neither authorized nor participated in his agent's fraudulent statement.

Example: A seller resided in a town some distance from a tract of vacant farmland which he owned. The owner of an adjoining tract of farmland went to the seller's home with an offer to buy the seller's land for $400. When the seller confessed ignorance of land values in the area, the buyer said that he was familiar with the values of such lands, that the seller's tract was poor pasture land worth about $400, and that the buyer desired the land only because it would give him more convenient access to some of his own farmland. The seller gave the buyer a deed transferring the land to the buyer for $400. The deed said nothing concerning value or the buyer's intended use. Several months later the seller learned that at the time of the transfer the buyer knew of a valuable granite deposit under the seller's land, that the buyer desired the seller's land for the purpose of opening and operating a quarry, and that because of the granite the value of the land when transferred was $15,000 rather than $400. When the buyer refused to return the land upon the seller's tender of $400, the seller sued to rescind the transfer.

Land contracts and deeds usually do not contain any provision concerning value or intended use. Although the writing was a complete expression of the agreement, proof of the fraud would not change or qualify any term of the deed and therefore the seller could have the transfer canceled. Note that the buyer was guilty of an express lie rather than mere nondisclosure.

Suppose that an agent for the buyer made the fraudulent statement without the buyer's knowledge or consent. Since the seller wished rescission rather than damages, the seller could rescind even under the narrower rule.

2. Assume that proving the alleged fraud will change or qualify some provision in the written contract. Most such cases involve the effect which should be accorded to an oral-representation-waiver provision such as the following:

> This writing contains the entire agreement of the parties. No statements, representations, or promises, not included herein, shall be binding, valid, or of any effect between the parties.

Should such a provision immunize the contract from the effects of an oral fraudulent misrepresentation? If the fraud was practiced by the other contracting party, either personally or through his authorized agent, the oral-representation-waiver provision will usually not be effective to shield the defrauding party. The innocent party will be entitled to relief from the contract, either through rescission or through affirmance and recovery of damages. On the other hand, if the oral fraudulent misrepresentation was entirely the idea of the other party's agent and was neither authorized nor participated in by the agent's principal, the case is not so clear cut. On one side it can be argued that even though the principal is innocent of his agent's fraud, it is not fair to permit him to retain any benefit (including the contract) obtained by means of the fraud. On the other side is the argument that if a person gives clear notice that his agent lacks authority to make any representations, he is justified in assuming that no person will enter into a contract in reliance on any representations of the agent, and that therefore a contract negotiated through the agent should be binding and enforceable according to its terms. Of the usual remedies for fraud (rescission or affirmance with recovery of damages) courts in some states say that the defrauded party is entitled to either remedy, courts in a second group of states say that because of the oral-representation-waiver provision, the defrauded party has only the first but not the second remedy, and courts in a third group of states say that he has neither remedy, that the contract is valid and binding—unless in addition to making the fraudulent misrepresentation the agent also, by a dishonest trick, prevented the representation from being included in the written contract. For example, if the innocent party explains that he is unable to read the contract form (because of eye, language, or literary deficiency) and the agent misreads or misstates what the written contract says, the agent is fraudulently preventing inclusion of the misrepresentation in the written contract, and the defrauded party may rescind the contract even in a state falling into the third group (assuming that the defrauded party can prove these facts).

Example: A company in the business of furnishing advertising services, supplied its agents with printed order forms to be signed by dealers wishing to subscribe for the service. Signed forms would then be sent to the company for acceptance. The forms contained the following waiver provision: "Neither party will be held responsible for any provision or representation not embodied in writing herein." One of the company's salesmen contacted a dealer who operated a heating and plumbing supply business, and induced him to subscribe for the advertising service. To obtain the dealer's agreement, the salesman fraudulently stated that the company had a business connection with a cooperative buying association, that if the dealer subscribed for the advertising service he would become a member of the buying association, that through the association he could buy heating and plumbing fixtures at 12½ percent below jobbers' prices, and that he could become a member of the association only through subscribing for the advertising service. As the dealer could see from reading the printed order form, it contained no reference to any buying association. The dealer signed the order form agreeing to pay $260 for certain described advertising materials, and shortly afterwards received notice of the company's acceptance of the order. Later the dealer learned that there was no such buying association as the agent had described, and refused to accept any of the contracted advertising materials from the company. The company had had no previous notice of the salesman's fraudulent tactics, and sued the dealer for $260.

Although the dealer's consent was obtained by means of the agent's fraud, the principal was innocent of the fraud. Therefore in some states the dealer could not rescind. Under the facts in this example, the Pennsylvania Superior Court held[10] that the advertising company could fully enforce the contract.

NEGLIGENT MISREPRESENTATIONS

Before discussing the status of contracts obtained by means of negligent misrepresentations, it will be helpful to consider the general overall liability of negligent informants.

GENERAL LIABILITY FOR DAMAGES

Chapter 2 discusses the way in which the law interposes certain policy limitations on a person's liability for careless conduct. Beyond such limits a careless person is not held liable even though his carelessness does cause additional damages. Such policy limitations apply whether the defendant is driving a car without proper care or is giving information without taking proper care to assure its truth and accuracy.

The results of applying such policy limitations to negligent misrepresentation cases can be summarized by classifying the cases according to the relationship between the parties (whether personal or impersonal), and also according to the type of harm threatened (whether bodily or merely monetary). A relationship is impersonal when an informant makes a negligent misrepresentation to the general public; the relationship is personal if the negligent misrepresentation is made to a specific person. If an informant is under contract to supply information to a specific person, certainly the informant should be held liable for losses which that person sustains as a result of negligently erroneous information. The courts are reluctant to extend liability much further than this. Thus a negligent informant will usually not be held liable to a person with whom he has no contract to supply information, if nothing more than money or property loss is involved. On the other hand, even when the relationship is impersonal, if bodily injury is foreseeable as a result of erroneous information, liability is frequently extended to any person who is thus threatened with injury.

Example: Through a jeweler's carelessness, a clock in his window labeled "Correct Time" is thirty minutes slow. A person relies on the clock and misses an important appointment (or misses a train or the like) and sustains a loss.
The jeweler would not be liable.

Example: Through a publisher's carelessness, information given in a newspaper is erroneous (but not defamatory). A person sustains a loss through relying on such information.
The publisher would not be liable.

[10] *Lloyd & Elliott, Inc.* v. *Lang*, 118 Pa. Super. 190, 180 A. 74 (1935).

Example: An accountant was engaged by a businessman to conduct a complete audit of the latter's business and to submit a report to the businessman. Because of the accountant's carelessness, his audit report inaccurately pictured the business as being in good financial condition when actually it was practically insolvent. The businessman showed the audit report to a bank and obtained a substantial loan. When the businessman became insolvent and unable to repay the loan, the bank investigated, discovered the inaccuracy of the audit report, and sued the accountant for the amount of the loan.

The accountant would not be liable to the bank. If an informant's carelessness does not involve possible bodily injury, it is usually not considered sound policy to hold the careless informant liable to an unlimited number of persons for an infinite variety of kinds and amounts of money or property loss.

If an accountant's misstatement is intentional or reckless (as, for example, when he certifies something as true of his own knowledge although he fails to make any investigation) courts have held the accountant liable to a third party for money loss sustained in relying on the erroneous audit.

Example: A manufacturer engaged a boiler inspector to inspect the factory's steam boiler. The inspector was careless in his inspection and gave to the manufacturer a report inaccurately certifying the boiler as safe to a certain pressure. Shortly afterwards, while under pressure much less than that certified as safe, the boiler exploded, injuring a homeowner who resided near the factory. The injured homeowner sued the boiler inspector.

Since the inspector's carelessness involved a foreseeable risk of bodily injury to third persons, the court held the boiler inspector liable to the injured homeowner, both for bodily injury and also for property damage.

VALIDITY OF CONTRACTS

Suppose that through a representer's negligent misrepresentation, a person is induced to enter into a contract with the representer. Usually a distinction is made between the two standard misrepresentation remedies—1) affirmance of the contract and recovery of damages, and 2) rescission of the contract.

1) Affirmance and Recovery of Damages. As previously indicated in discussing overall liability for negligent misrepresentations, the expresser's liability for damages is a question of policy, depending upon whether under the circumstances the representer should be considered as owing to the injured party a duty to use proper care. At the present stage of legal evolution such a duty is usually not recognized (and therefore a negligent misrepresenter is not liable for damages), unless the misrepresentation involves either an unreasonable risk of bodily harm, or a *contract* obligation to give information to the injured party.

2) Rescission. Regardless of whether or not the representer would be liable for damages, the misled party will usually have the right to rescind the contract and recover all that he paid or gave, if the misrepresented fact was at all material in his deciding to enter into the contract; the representer should not be permitted to retain a benefit obtained through a mistake which he has induced. *However,* the previous discussion, Oral Representations Versus Written Contracts, must be kept in mind. Under the circumstances indicated in that discussion, a misled party may be denied *any* right to cancel a written contract.

INNOCENT MISREPRESENTATIONS

An innocent misrepresentation differs from a negligent misrepresentation in that not only does the representer honestly believe the truth of the fact he represents or expresses, but also his belief is reasonable. Nevertheless, since the representation is not true, it is classed as a misrepresentation. Again a distinction is made between the two standard misrepresentation remedies.

Affirmance and Recovery of Damages. A person who makes an innocent misrepresentation is not guilty of wrongdoing and has no tort liability for damages, although—as is discussed as the next topic in this chapter— the expresser *may* under certain circumstances have a contract (breach of warranty) liability for damages.

Rescission. If the misrepresented fact is at all material to the contract the misled person usually has the right to cancel the contract; the representer should not be permitted to retain the benefit of the other party's mistake when the representer, however innocently, has caused that mistake. Note, however, that the qualification in regard to certain written contracts, previously discussed in this chapter as Oral Representations Versus Written Contracts, applies here; under the circumstances indicated in that discussion, a misled person may have no right to cancel at all.

Part 5 WARRANTIES

As has been previously discussed in this chapter, a person who enters into a contract in reliance on an express misrepresentation 1) may recover damages if the misrepresentation is dishonest, and sometimes if the misrepresentation is negligent; or 2) may rescind the contract and recover what he has given or paid under the contract, whether the misrepresentation is tortious or innocent. For various historical and policy reasons, the law concerning the effect of misrepresentations developed along divergent lines for different types of contracts. In connection with contracts involving the sale of goods, rules of law gradually developed which permit a misled person to recover damages even for an honest and reasonable misrepresentation, and even if the misrepresentation is made impliedly through conduct rather than expressly in words. Such obligations are called *warranties*.

The warranties discussed here are those pertaining to sales of goods. Principles pertaining to land warranties differ in many respects from sales-of-goods warranties, for various reasons including 1) different historical developments, land warranties having developed from landholding under feudal tenure; 2) the requirement that all land transfers must be in writing (Chapter 9); and 3) the principle that when a land transfer deed is accepted by a buyer, it constitutes the entire agreement between the parties, any provisions in their preceding agreement being considered as waived or superseded if omitted from the deed (Chapter 10). Warranties accompanying sales of land are usually studied as a part of the law of real estate and will be discussed in Chapter 20.

EXPRESS WARRANTIES

A person is free to make any contract he wishes—so long as it is not against the law or otherwise opposed to public policy. If he so desires, he may make a contract that a certain thing will happen or exist in the future, and the contract obligation will be fully enforceable against him, even though the contracted event is dependent on factors over which he has only partial control or no control at all. When a person enters into a contract that is dependent on a future event which he cannot fully control, he is in reality agreeing that he will pay for any damages or losses sustained if the contracted future event does not occur. Thus if a paint manufacturer enters into a contract that his paint will never fade or peel, he is not promising to do something after he makes a sale to prevent the paint from fading or peeling. Rather he is agreeing that if the paint does fade or peel, he will pay money damages for any loss that could reasonably be expected to result. The manufacturer's contractual promise or assertion concerning the condition or quality of the paint is called a "warranty." If what is promised or asserted is not true or does not occur, the warranty is considered as breached.

The formation of a legally enforceable warranty agreement does not require any particular formula of words. Suppose that in inducing a buyer to buy paint, the manufacturer as the seller makes one of the following three statements:

1. "I agree that if this paint fades or peels, I will pay whatever damages you sustain."

2. "I agree (or promise or warrant) that this paint will not fade or peel."

3. "This paint will not fade or peel."

Reasonably interpreted, the manufacturer undertakes the same contractual obligation, whichever one of the three statements he makes.

Warranty liability is not restricted to manufacturers or producers who know or should know the quality of the goods they sell. Any person who sells goods, whether he is a producer, a wholesaler, a retailer, or a nonmerchant, may undertake a binding warranty liability. Compare for a moment the relative bases of tort liability and contract liability. Modern tort liability is almost always based on some sort of wrongdoing or fault —usually the defendant's intentional misconduct or unreasonably careless misconduct. On the other hand, contract liability arises if a defendant voluntarily agrees to perform in a certain way or agrees that a certain event will occur, and then fails to perform as agreed or the event fails to occur, whether the failure is the defendant's fault or not (so long as performance is not prevented by the other party to the contract). Thus, as discussed in Chapter 11, increased costs, shortages, and even the impossibility of obtaining the goods in question ordinarily will not relieve or excuse a seller from his contract obligation to deliver as agreed. In modern theory a warranty is usually considered as a part of a contract, so that warranty liability is a type of contract liability. Therefore when a seller warrants goods in certain respects he will be liable for breach of warranty if the goods are not as warranted (in other words, because the contract agreement is not fully performed), even though the seller honestly and reasonably believes in the truth of what he asserts in his warranty. Suppose that a retailer enters into a contract to sell a quantity of paint of a certain type, grade, and color. If he unexpectedly cannot obtain from his distributor the paint he intended to deliver in fulfillment of the contract, he is not relieved from the contract obligation which he voluntarily assumed. He must obtain the described paint elsewhere, paying a higher price if necessary, or be liable for damages for failure to deliver. Likewise with quality; a retailer may honestly and reasonably believe that the paint is colorfast and will not peel, perhaps because the manufacturer has said so. Nevertheless, if the retailer asserts colorfastness, and after delivery to the buyer the color fades, the seller is liable for breach of this term of his contract—that is, for breach of warranty.

The basic principles applicable to express warranties are stated in the Uniform Commercial Code as follows:

> 1) Express warranties by the seller are created as follows:
> a) Any affirmation of fact or promise made by the seller to the buyer which relates to the goods and becomes part of the basis of the bargain creates an express warranty that the goods shall conform to the affirmation or promise.
> b) Any description of the goods which is made part of the basis of the bargain creates an express warranty that the goods shall conform to the description.

c) Any sample or model which is made part of the basis of the bargain creates an express warranty that the whole of the goods shall conform to the sample or model.

2) It is not necessary to the creation of an express warranty that the seller use formal words such as "warrant" or "guarantee" or that he have a specific intention to make a warranty, but an affirmation merely of the value of the goods or a statement purporting to be merely the seller's opinion or commendation of the goods does not create a warranty.[11]

IMPLIED WARRANTIES

Frequently the parties to a contract do not expressly state all of their contractual provisions, but rather leave some details to custom or understanding. Suppose that an agreement between strangers for the sale and purchase of goods says nothing about the time and manner of payment. It is certainly safe to assume that if they mean to extend credit, they will say so. The purchase price therefore is to be paid on delivery of the goods. Cash on delivery is an implied term of the contract, "implied" because not expressly stated, but a very real term of the contract because payment with delivery appears to be the intent of the parties.

Consider another example. A homeowner is approached by a boy, a stranger, who solicits a lawnmowing job. They agree that if the boy will "mow the lawn," the owner will pay him $2. The boy tries to cut 16-inch swaths with a 14-inch lawnmower, leaving ridges of uncut grass in regular rows over the entire lawn. Although it was not expressly stated that the grass should be cut uniformly and without ridges, no one (with the possible exception of the boy himself) will seriously contend that the $2 has been earned. Before he is entitled to the $2, the boy must "mow the lawn." Since the parties do not specifically define the word "mow," they are attributing to the word its common or usual meaning. The boy might argue that this is the way he always mows lawns, and therefore that this is what he means by the word "mow" in the agreement with the owner. But the boy is bound by what he reasonably leads the owner to understand is meant. Not having stated otherwise he is taken to mean the usual or customary lawn-mowing job. In other words, it is an implied term of their understanding that the usual or customary job be done. Whether it includes trimming would be a matter for more serious argument.

Implied Warranty of Merchantability

Suppose that a buyer wishes to secure from a dealer, not himself a publisher, a new copy of a certain book. Besides stating author and

[11]U.C.C. Sec. 2-313.

title, the buyer's order might specify that the pages be bound, and that there be no reverse, double, or smeared printing. When the dealer accepts the order, a contract is formed. If the dealer ships a book which contains defective printing, the dealer breaches his contract; he fails to ship the quality of book which he *expressly* agreed to ship. The book may be in the original wrapper in which it came from the publisher and the defects may be unknown to the dealer. Nevertheless, since the dealer fails to perform the contract obligation which he expressly and voluntarily assumed, he will be liable for damages. On the other hand, suppose that the buyer merely orders a copy of the specified book without expressly mentioning the quality of printing. It is clear that he means "book" as the term is usually or customarily used—just as the homeowner in the preceding paragraph meant "mow the lawn" as that term is customarily used. Books usually do not have reverse, double, or smeared printing and are usually bound. Therefore, one free of these defects and bound is what the buyer actually (by implication) orders, and what the dealer agrees to sell when he accepts the order. It is *implied* that the book be of standard, usual, or marketable quality—that is, merchantable. In other words, from the normal meaning of the words used in the contract, the law finds that the dealer has impliedly agreed to a warranty of merchantability.

The basic principles applicable to implied warranties of merchantability are stated in the Code as follows:

> 1) Unless excluded or modified . . . , a warranty that the goods shall be merchantable is implied in a contract for their sale if the seller is a merchant with respect to goods of that kind. . . .
> 2) Goods to be merchantable must at least be such as
> a) pass without objection in the trade under the contract description;
> b) in the case of fungible goods are of fair average quality within the description;
> c) are fit for the ordinary purposes for which such goods are used;
> d) run, within the variation permitted by the agreement, of even kind, quality and quantity within each unit and among all units involved;
> e) are adequately contained, packaged, and labeled as the agreement may require; and
> f) conform to the promises or affirmations of fact made on the container or label if any.[12]

Example: A customer went to a grocery store for a loaf of Star brand bread. The grocer sold to the customer the bread he requested, wrapped in a sealed package as it had come from the Star Baking Company, the baker. The grocer made no statements concerning the quality or fitness of the bread. Unknown to the parties, a pin had accidentally fallen into the dough during

[12] U.C.C. Sec. 2-314.

its preparation and this particular loaf had been baked with the pin concealed within the bread. The pin seriously injured the customer's mouth while he was eating the bread, and an infection resulted requiring the removal of two teeth. The customer sued the grocer for the damages sustained.

The customer could recover. When the customer requested a loaf of bread, he meant what usually comes in the market under that name—in other words merchantable bread. By selling the bread to the customer the grocer asserted that it was bread of the usual quality. Bread does not usually come with pins baked in it. Therefore the grocer did not perform his contract with the customer and for his breach of contract (that is, for his breach of the implied warranty of merchantability) the grocer would be liable for any loss or injury resulting to the customer.

Implied Warranty of Fitness for Particular Purpose

As part of his sales contract, a seller may agree that the goods he sells are appropriate or fit for some particular purpose. He may expressly so state and there will be no question as to his contractual liability. Or he may through his conduct impliedly assert the fitness of the goods for a particular purpose—and such an implied term will be just as real a part of the contract and as binding as if expressly stated.

Suppose that a buyer, not by trade a painter, enters a seller's paint store, says that he intends to repaint his baby's crib and requests some nonpoisonous paint. The seller states as to a particular type of paint that it contains no poisonous substances and sells a can to the buyer. Clearly the seller's assertion is a part of his contract, and there is no difference whether the seller says, "I warrant that this paint contains no poisonous substances," or merely, "This paint contains no poisonous substances." If the paint actually contains substances poisonous to a baby chewing on it, the seller has not delivered to the buyer the kind of paint he has contracted to deliver and will be liable for any resulting damages. And as previously discussed, it is immaterial that the seller may honestly and reasonably believe that the paint is safe. He has made a contract and his nonperformance is a breach of contract, even though the nonperformance may be the result of circumstances unknown to him and beyond his control.

Suppose, however, that the seller makes no express statement about the ingredients in the paint, but sells a can of paint to the buyer in response to his request for a nonpoisonous paint to repaint his baby's crib. By the act of selling, the seller accepts and agrees to the terms stated by the buyer; in other words, the seller contracts that the paint is nonpoisonous paint.

Now suppose that all the buyer says when he enters the seller's paint store is that he wants some white paint to repaint his baby's crib.

Although the buyer does not add that he wants a nonpoisonous paint, the inclination of babies to chew on cribs is well known. The buyer is relying on the seller as a dealer to select paint suitable for the announced purpose. By the mere act of selling, the seller asserts that the paint is suitable for the buyer's purpose. Although not expressly stated, the implied assertion is a real part of the seller's contract. When the law holds the seller liable if the paint is poisonous and the baby becomes ill from chewing on it, the law is enforcing the agreement which the parties by their conduct show that they intend to make. That this is the actual intent of the parties can be easily verified. Suppose that in response to the buyer's request for paint to repaint his baby's crib, the seller presents a can, states the price, and adds "I don't guarantee this is nonpoisonous." Of course the buyer will immediately refuse to buy. The buyer states his purpose because he wishes to buy paint suitable for that purpose.

Note that the bases for this implied warranty (fitness for a particular purpose) are twofold: 1) that the seller knows the buyer's purpose, and 2) that the buyer relies on the seller to select something suitable. If the seller is a dealer in goods of that type and the buyer is unskilled, it is usually clear that the buyer is relying on the seller's superior knowledge. The Uniform Commercial Code states these basic principles as follows:

> Where the seller at the time of contracting has reason to know any particular purpose for which the goods are required and that the buyer is relying on the seller's skill or judgment to select or furnish suitable goods, there is unless excluded or modified . . . an implied warranty that the goods shall be fit for such purpose.[13]

IMPLIED WARRANTY OF TITLE

Generally, by his conduct of selling certain goods and not saying otherwise, a seller is impliedly asserting that he owns the goods, and has the right to sell them and to transfer good title, free from any outstanding claims. This assertion or implied warranty of title becomes an enforceable part of the sales contract.

There is no such implied assertion or warranty if circumstances clearly show that the seller is not claiming title or is selling only whatever limited title exists. Suppose that a sheriff levies on the property of a debtor and sells the property at a sheriff's auction sale. Clearly he is only selling whatever title the debtor has; the sheriff is not, through his conduct of selling, asserting that there is good title.

These basic principles are stated in the Code as follows:

[13] U.C.C. Sec. 2-315.

1) Subject to subsection (2) there is in a contract for sale a warranty by the seller that

a) the title conveyed shall be good, and its transfer rightful; and

b) the goods shall be delivered free from any security interest or other lien or encumbrance of which the buyer at the time of contracting has no knowledge.

2) A warranty under subsection (1) will be excluded or modified only by specific language or by circumstances which give the buyer reason to know that the person selling does not claim title in himself or that he is purporting to sell only such right or title as he or a third person may have.[14]

EXCLUSION OF WARRANTIES

EXPRESS WARRANTIES

By definition, an express warranty is based upon some statement made by the seller. Obviously then, a seller can avoid an express warranty by not making or agreeing to any express promise or assertion of fact. In this connection, oral sales are a frequent source of disputes. A buyer may assert that the seller made certain oral statements of fact while the seller denies having made any such statements. If the parties cannot agree as to exactly what was said and done, a jury (or a judge if the case is tried without a jury) must determine the correct facts. It is wise for the parties to eliminate this source of dispute by putting their agreement in writing and having the writing state that it is the complete agreement of the parties. Then under the parol evidence rule, no express warranty accompanies the sale unless stated in the agreement. (This applies to express warranties. As explained under the next heading, the parol evidence rule does *not* exclude implied warranties.)

IMPLIED WARRANTIES

The entire field of limitations of warranties and exclusions of warranties has been considerably complicated by the growing use of standardized, form contracts. Admittedly such contracts play a vital role in the present-day mass distribution of goods; problems arise from the fact that usually the forms are drafted and printed by sellers, who can be expected to slant the contract provisions in their own favor. When form contracts become shockingly unfair, the courts will refuse to enforce them. To this effect, the Uniform Commercial Code provides for sales-of-goods contracts:

If the court as a matter of law finds the contract or any clause of the contract to have been unconscionable at the time it was made the court may refuse to enforce the contract, or it may enforce the re-

[14] U.C.C. Sec. 2-312.

mainder of the contract without the unconscionable clause, or it may so limit the application of any unconscionable clause as to avoid any unconscionable result.[15]

Explaining this provision, the authors of the Code have written:

> This section is intended to allow the court to pass directly on the unconscionability of the contract or particular clause therein and to make a conclusion of law as to its unconscionability. The basic test is whether, in the light of the general commercial background and the commercial needs of the particular trade or case, the clauses involved are so one-sided as to be unconscionable under the circumstances existing at the time of the making of the contract. . . . The principle is one of the prevention of oppression and unfair surprise . . . and not of disturbance of allocation of risks because of superior bargaining power.[16]

Some "rugged individualists" might argue that a basic dogma of the free-enterprise system is freedom of contract, that if persons have agreed to a certain proposition, it should be enforceable whether the contract is individually negotiated or filled in on a printed form, and that if a person signs a written contract, he is bound by its terms, whether or not he has read and understands the contract—including small-print provisions which cannot be read without a strong magnifying glass. A quick answer is that society has *never* been willing to enforce *all* agreements. Agreements obtained by duress or fraud certainly should not be enforced, and likewise oppressive agreements which are clearly against the best interests of society should not be enforced. As Professor Morris Cohen has written:

> To put no restrictions on the freedom to contract would logically lead not to a maximum of individual liberty but to contracts of slavery, into which, experience shows, men will "voluntarily" enter under economic pressure—a pressure that is largely conditioned by the laws of property. Regulations, therefore, involving some restrictions on the freedom to contract are as necessary to real liberty as traffic restrictions are necessary to assure real freedom in the general use of our highways.[17]

And as Chief Justice Hughes has written:

> We have had frequent occasion to consider the limitations on liberty of contract. While it is highly important to preserve that liberty from arbitrary and capricious interference, it is also necessary to prevent its abuse, as otherwise it could be used to override all public interests and thus in the end destroy the very freedom of opportunity which it is designed to safeguard.[18]

[15] U.C.C. Sec. 2-302.

[16] Comment to U.C.C. Sec. 2-302.

[17] *Law and the Social Order* (New York: Harcourt, 1933), p. 105.

[18] Dissenting opinion in *Morehead* v. *New York*, 298 U.S. 587, 56 S. Ct. 918, 80 L. Ed. 1347 (1938).

In a landmark case decided in 1960,[19] the New Jersey Supreme Court wrestled skillfully and at length with two very formidable questions: 1) should a contract provision amounting to an almost complete disclaimer of liability[20] be effective to exclude an implied warranty of merchantability in connection with the sale of a complex and potentially dangerous machine such as an automobile, and 2) should a manufacturer be considered as impliedly warranting to the ultimate consumer that an automobile is safe. The court's views as to this second question will be noted later in this chapter. In answering the first question, the court said, in part:

> The traditional contract is the result of free bargaining of parties who are brought together by the play of the market, and who meet each other on a footing of approximate economic equality. In such a society there is no danger that freedom of contract will be a threat to the social order as a whole. But in present-day commercial life the standardized mass contract has appeared. It is used primarily by enterprises with strong bargaining power and position. "The weaker party, in need of the goods or services, is frequently not in a position to shop around for better terms, either because the author of the standard contract has a monopoly (natural or artificial) or because all competitors use the same clauses. His contractual intention is but a subjection more or less voluntary to terms dictated by the stronger party, terms whose consequences are often understood in a vague way, if at all." . . .
>
> "In recent times the marketing process has been getting more highly organized than ever before. The standardized contract with its broad disclaimer clauses is drawn by legal advisers of sellers widely organized in trade associations. It is encountered on every hand. Extreme inequality of bargaining between buyer and seller in this respect is now often conspicuous. Many buyers no longer have any real choice in the matter. They must often accept what they can get though accompanied by broad disclaimers. The terms of these disclaimers deprive them of all substantial protection with regard to the quality of the goods. In effect, this is by force of contract between very unequal parties. It throws the risk of defective articles on the

[19] *Henningsen v. Bloomfield Motors,* 32 N.J. 358, 161 A.(2d) 69, 75 A.L.R.(2d) 1 (1960).

[20] The printed contract form contained the uniform warranty of the Automobile Manufacturers Association which stated that the seller "warrants each new motor vehicle . . . to be free from defects in material or workmanship under normal use and service. Its [the seller's] obligation under this warranty being limited to making good . . . any part or parts thereof which shall, within ninety (90) days after delivery . . . or before such vehicle has been driven 4,000 miles, whichever event shall first occur, be returned . . . and which its examination shall disclose to its satisfaction to have been thus defective; this warranty being expressly in lieu of all other warranties expressed or implied, and all other obligations or liabilities on its part, and it neither assumes nor authorizes any other person to assume for it any other liability in connection with the sale of its vehicles. . . ."

most dependent party. He has the least individual power to avoid the presence of defects. He also has the least individual ability to bear their disastrous consequences."

The warranty before us is a standardized form designed for mass use. It is imposed upon the automobile consumer. He takes it or leaves it, and he must take it to buy an automobile. No bargaining is engaged in with respect to it. The form warranty . . . is the uniform warranty of the Automobile Manufacturers Association. Members of the Association are: General Motors, Inc., Ford, Chrysler, Studebaker-Packard, American Motors, (Rambler), Willys Motors, Checker Motors Corporation, and International Harvester Company. . . .

The gross inequality of bargaining position occupied by the consumer in the automobile industry is thus apparent. There is no competition among the car makers in the area of the express warranty. Where can the buyer go to negotiate for better protection? Such control and limitation of his remedies are inimical to the public welfare, and, at the very least, call for great care by the courts to avoid injustice through application of strict common-law principles of freedom of contract. . . .

Courts keep in mind the principle that the best interests of society demand that persons should not be unnecessarily restricted in their freedom of contract. But they do not hesitate to declare void as against public policy contractual provisions which clearly tend to the injury of the public in some way. . . .

Public policy at a given time finds expression in the Constitution, the statutory law and in judicial decisions. In the area of sale of goods, the legislative will has imposed an implied warranty of merchantability as a general incident of sale of an automobile by description. The warranty does not depend upon the affirmative intention of the parties. It is a child of the law; it annexes itself to the contract because of the very nature of the transaction. . . . The disclaimer of the implied warranty and exclusion of all obligations except those specifically assumed by the express warranty signify a studied effort to frustrate that protection. True, the Sales Act authorized agreements between buyer and seller qualifying the warranty obligations. But quite obviously the Legislature contemplated lawful stipulations (which are determined by the circumstances of a particular case) arrived at freely by parties of relatively equal bargaining strength. The lawmakers did not authorize the automobile manufacturer to use its grossly disproportionate bargaining power to relieve itself from liability and to impose on the ordinary buyer, who in effect has no real freedom of voice, the grave danger of injury to himself and others that attends the sale of such a dangerous instrumentality as a defectively made automobile. In the framework of this case, illuminated as it is by the facts and the many decisions noted, we are of the opinion that . . . [the] attempted disclaimer of an implied warranty of merchantability and of the obligations arising therefrom is so inimical to the public good as to compel an adjudication of its invalidity.

The Uniform Commercial Code draws some basic guidelines which must be followed in order for provisions which exclude the various types of implied warranties to be effective. *Note* that all exclusionary provisions are also controlled by the provision (previously quoted) declaring unenforceable any terms which the courts find to be "unconscionable."

Exclusion of Implied Warranty of Title.[21]   There is no implied warranty of title if either the seller's words or the circumstances of the transaction lead the buyer to understand that the seller does not claim title in himself, or that the seller is selling only whatever limited title he has the power or authority to transfer.

Exclusion of Implied Warranties of Quality.[22]   An implied warranty which would otherwise arise under the circumstances of a particular transaction can usually be excluded by any of the following:

1. Express exclusion.

a) *Merchantability.*   An effective exclusion of an implied warranty of merchantability may be either oral or in writing; the exclusionary provision however must include the word "merchantability," and if in writing, the exclusionary provision must be conspicuous.

b) *Fitness for Purpose.*   An effective exclusion of an implied warranty of fitness for purpose must be in writing and conspicuous, but need not state directly that it refers to this type of implied warranty.   As the Code states:

> Language to exclude all implied warranties of fitness is sufficient if it states, for example, that "There are no warranties which extend beyond the description on the face hereof."

2. Language that the sale is made "as is," "with all faults," or the like will exclude implied warranties of quality.

3. To the extent that a buyer inspects, he is not relying on any implied assertion or understanding concerning the goods.   Likewise, a seller's demand that the buyer fully inspect the goods, gives the buyer notice that the seller is not undertaking any implied obligation concerning the quality of the goods.   Therefore a buyer's inspection before buying will exclude any implied warranty regarding defects which, under the circumstances, such an inspection ought to reveal, and a buyer's refusal to inspect after the seller demands that the buyer make a full inspection will exclude any implied warranty concerning defects discoverable by such an inspection.

4. A prior course of dealing between the parties or a custom in their type of business can show that the parties do not intend implied warranties.

Under the Uniform Commercial Code, the parol evidence rule does

[21] U.C.C. Sec. 2-312.
[22] U.C.C. Sec. 2-316.

not exclude implied warranties of quality. Suppose that parties enter into a written agreement which shows that it is their complete agreement; suppose further that the agreement contains an express warranty but does not expressly exclude an implied warranty. If the circumstances are such as to give rise to an implied warranty of quality, such a warranty is also a part of the contract—unless inconsistent with the express warranty. If the express and implied warranties would be inconsistent with each other, the Code provides:

> Express warranties displace inconsistent implied warranties other than an implied warranty of fitness for a particular purpose.[23]

In other words, if an express warranty is inconsistent with an implied warranty of merchantability, the implied warranty is considered as excluded. On the other hand, if the circumstances are such that an implied warranty of fitness for particular purpose arises, and such a warranty is not expressly excluded, the implied warranty will remain even in the face of an inconsistent express warranty.

WARRANTIES AND REMOTE PARTIES

Present-day marketing of most any mass-produced goods involves a succession of sales through which goods are transferred from producers or manufacturers to wholesalers, then to retailers, and finally to the ultimate consumers. Since the manufacturer and the ultimate consumer do not deal directly with each other, their relationship in the channels of commerce is classed as remote; to each other they are remote parties. Many marketing practices are designed to speed goods through commercial channels on their way to ultimate consumers. Thus it is quite common for packers, manufacturers, or wholesalers, 1) to package and label goods in such a way that they can be sold and delivered to the ultimate consumers without further packaging or labeling, 2) to advertise in order to induce consumers to buy from independent retailers, and 3) to supply retailers with descriptive circulars for them to distribute in order to promote sales. If the statements which a manufacturer makes in his advertisements or circulars are inaccurate, incomplete, or misleading, or if goods are defective, either or both of two questions will frequently arise:

1. To what extent is an independent retail dealer liable to his customers for the accuracy of a manufacturer's (or wholesaler's) statements?

2. To what extent is a manufacturer or wholesaler liable to a remote consumer for inaccurate statements or for defective goods?

[23] U.C.C. Sec. 2-317.

BUYER'S RIGHTS AGAINST IMMEDIATE SELLER

At the present state of legal evolution, the soundest basis for warranty liability is believed to be the intent of the parties, an intent which is either expressly stated or implied from conduct. In other words, warranty liability rests upon the express or implied assumptions which become a part of the bargain between the seller and buyer in question. Thus not only a dealer's express statements but also statements appearing on the goods or on their containers or labels would seem logically to become a part of a dealer-customer contract. This thought is expressed in the previously quoted Code definitions of express warranties and of merchantability.

A more difficult question is presented when a statement made in a manufacturer's advertisement or descriptive circular is not repeated in a dealer's sales talk or stated on the labels or containers. In appraising the legal effect of advertisements and circulars, a starting point is to note that a buyer's decision to purchase a certain item may be motivated by a wide variety of considerations, even including, for example, advertisements published by manufacturers of competitive products or the location of the selling dealer's showroom and service facilities. Certainly *all* of the factors that may bring about a purchase should not be considered as becoming a part of a dealer-buyer contract. In the absence of an express agreement, no one would contend that a dealer is bound by statements made in advertisements of competitive products, or that a dealer is obligated to continue operating his establishment in a certain locality. But what about statements which are made in advertisements sponsored by the manufacturer of the very items being handled by a dealer? Since the dealer has no control over the manufacturer's advertisements, it would not seem fair, in the absence of the dealer's express agreement, to impose on him a contract obligation as to the accuracy of the advertised statements. The question becomes more debatable when the dealer's own voluntary act brings the manufacturer's statements to the customer's attention, as when the dealer displays and distributes circulars supplied to him by the manufacturer. Certainly a strong argument can be made that the dealer should be held liable for statements contained in a circular which he displays with the products he is selling. The argument against holding the dealer liable is not quite so obvious, but in the eyes of many courts it is an even stronger argument. First, the dealer is not the author of the circular and has no control over what it says. Also, and more important, the dealer in question may not be the source of the particular copy of the circular upon which a customer is relying. Although the dealer has such circulars on display, this particular customer may have obtained his copy of the circular directly from the manufacturer, from another dealer, or even from his next-door neighbor. Or the customer may have obtained the circular several months before the time of his purchase. Can a circular obtained otherwise than directly from the selling dealer, or obtained at a remote time, logically be said to become automatically a part of the selling dealer's *contract?* It would seem not. Therefore if the dealer is to be held liable for circular statements, his liability would seem to depend upon when and where a particular customer obtained his copy of the circular. However, from the standpoint of the customer, what induces him to buy is the circular itself and not when or where he obtained it. Holding the dealer liable therefore would present an anomalous situation: the chief legal basis for the dealer's liability to the customer would be a fact (the dealer's supplying the circular in connection with the sale in question) which to the customer would be unimportant and fortuitous. He would be relying on the circular; where he obtained it would be entirely immaterial to him. The business community and society as a whole are not yet ready to recognize as sound policy a rule which would hold a dealer liable for *all* statements or claims made by manufacturers. Until legal evolution reaches this point, if it ever does, the fairest policy rule would seem to be to limit a seller's contractual obligation to statements or conditions which reasonably appear intended by the parties to be part of their bargain. The courts usually hold therefore that even though a dealer displays a manufacturer's circulars and sells his goods, these two facts alone do not mean that the dealer is adopting the manufacturer's statements and making them a part of the dealer's contract with his customer. Unless the dealer himself in some way actually repeats the circular or advertising statements when he induces a customer to buy, the statements are usually not a part of the dealer-customer contract.

BUYER'S RIGHTS AGAINST REMOTE SELLER

Suppose that after buying goods from a seller, the buyer in turn resells the goods to a second buyer or subpurchaser. As to the first seller, the subpurchaser is a remote party, there being no direct contract relationship between them. If the goods are not discovered to be defective until after the resale to the subpurchaser, the question arises whether the subpurchaser can hold the original seller liable for damages for breach of warranty.

Warranty to Subpurchaser Expressed

In most sales-of-goods contracts, a seller does not express any intent to give a warranty in favor of a subpurchaser. In the infrequent case when a seller wishes to undertake such a warranty liability, he may do so through a third-party beneficiary agreement or (more commonly) through an agency arrangement.

Third-Party Beneficiary Agreement. A third-party beneficiary agreement involves a provision in the buyer-seller contract under which the seller agrees to be liable to a subpurchaser for some specified breach of warranty. Generally such a subpurchaser can enforce a contract provision which is thus made for his benefit, even though he is not a party to the contract. Since third-party beneficiary contracts are not often encountered in connection with warranties, further discussion of such contracts will be deferred until Chapter 10.

Agency Arrangement. Quite often in sales of certain types of goods, such as automobiles and their accessories, a manufacturer intends to undertake an express warranty liability to ultimate consumers. In order to do so the manufacturer supplies the dealer with warranty forms bearing the manufacturer's name; this appoints the dealer as the manufacturer's agent for the limited purpose of making a warranty contract in the manufacturer's name whenever the dealer makes a sale to a consumer. Clearly the consumer can hold the manufacturer liable for breach of such a warranty. However, the scope of such express warranties is frequently limited, for example, to replacement of defective parts only, which would not cover personal injuries or business losses.

Warranty to Subpurchaser Not Expressed

In most sales transactions, sellers do not expressly undertake warranty liability in favor of subpurchasers. In most cases, therefore, a subpurchaser will have no warranty rights against a remote seller unless 1) the intermediate buyer (who does have warranty rights arising from his direct contract with the seller) makes a valid assignment of such rights to the subpurchaser, or 2) a fact situation exists from which the law implies a warranty in favor of a subpurchaser.

Assignment of Warranty Rights. A general discussion concerning the assignment of contract rights is deferred until Chapter 10. In regard to sales-of-goods contracts, the Uniform Commercial Code provides[24] that a buyer may assign all of his contract rights, unless the assignment would materially increase the burden or risk undertaken by the seller. Two points stand out:

1. The buyer must expressly show an intent to assign his warranty rights to his subpurchaser. Usually upon making a resale to a subpurchaser, the buyer will himself be warranting that the goods are merchantable. If the subpurchaser should thereafter recover from the

---

[24] U.C.C. Sec. 2-210.

buyer for breach of this warranty, the buyer would in turn want to be able to recover from his seller. However, if the buyer had assigned his rights he would have thereby relinquished any right to recover from the seller. Certainly in the absence of an express statement the buyer should not be presumed, every time he makes a resale, to intend an assignment and consequent relinquishment of his own rights. Therefore there is an assignment only if it is expressly stated; the buyer's act of reselling goods does not automatically or impliedly assign the buyer's warranty rights.

2. The buyer's warranty right must be capable of assignment. Because of the rarity of such an assignment, relatively few cases have arisen. The cases indicate that warranties of title and of quantity can be assigned, but raise some doubt as to whether a warranty of quality can be validly assigned. Some hold the view that a warranty of quality is, like indemnity insurance, personal to the recipient of the right and not assignable without the consent of the one granting the right.

Implied Warranty to Subpurchaser. When subpurchasers who are injured by defective goods attempt to collect from remote sellers, the theories which are most often attempted are 1) negligence and 2) implied warranty. Negligence liability is well settled. If goods are defective because of a manufacturer's negligence, he is liable for the foreseeable injuries which result to a remote consumer or to anyone else. On the other hand, warranty liability is quite doubtful. In fact, whether or not an implied warranty extends to a subpurchaser is one of the most controversial questions in commercial law.

Under the traditional contract theory of warranties, an implied warranty is thought of as resting upon an assumed consent or understanding of the parties. The existence and scope of this assumed consent is largely a matter of social policy. When parties enter into a transaction (and do not expressly provide otherwise), they are assumed to agree to the usual terms and provisions which society feels will best conform both to common business understanding and to the overall welfare of society. The policy view which most courts take at the present time with respect to implied warranties in sales-of-goods transactions can be summarized as follows:

1. There is no warranty in the absence of a sales contract.

2. Unless the seller expressly assumes a greater liability, the only person to whom the warranty obligation is owed, and who therefore can recover from the seller for breach of warranty, is the one who (either directly or through an agent) buys from the seller. The buyer can of course recover for all of his damages, both personal and property. In addition, the Uniform Commercial Code provides:

A seller's warranty whether express or implied extends to any natural person who is in the family or household of his buyer or who is a guest in his home if it is reasonable to expect that such person may use, consume or be affected by the goods and who is injured in person by breach of the warranty . . .[25]

Some courts believe that the class of persons who are covered by implied warranties should be extended further than this. The law is still developing in connection with warranties to remote parties, and the authors of the Code are careful to point out, in their Comment to the section just quoted, that:

This section expressly includes as beneficiaries within its provisions the family, household, and guests of the purchaser. Beyond this, the section is neutral and is not intended to enlarge or restrict the developing case law on whether the seller's warranties, given to his buyer who resells, extend to other persons in the distributive chain.[26]

When it is considered desirable policy, the law readily agrees that an implied promise or warranty liability can extend beyond the parties to a particular contract. Commercial paper (note, draft, or check) provides one of the most common examples. Compare a typical check case with a sales case.

Check Case: A depositor drew a check for $100 on his account in a New York City bank, naming P as payee. While visiting his uncle in Chicago, P needed money and indorsed and transferred the check to his uncle who paid P $100. Not finding it convenient to go to his bank, the uncle indorsed and transferred the check to his neighbor for $100. The neighbor indorsed and cashed the check at a grocery store. The grocer in turn indorsed and deposited the check in his account in a Chicago bank. After being promptly forwarded to New York City, the check was returned to the Chicago bank with a notation that the balance in the depositor's account was insufficient for payment of the check. The Chicago bank therefore charged the amount of the check back against the grocer.

The grocer could in turn sue and collect from the neighbor for whom the grocer cashed the check, or instead could skip the neighbor and collect from the uncle. As discussed in Chapter 14, when a person indorses a check and does not expressly limit his liability, the indorser *impliedly* promises that if the check is dishonored, he will pay its amount to *any holder* who acts diligently. This implied promise is enforceable not only by the immediate transferee but also by any later transferee of the check.

Sales Case: A California manufacturer sold a shipment of ladders to a Chicago wholesaler. The wholesaler sold some of the ladders to a Chicago

[25] U.C.C. Sec. 2-318
[26] Comment to U.C.C. Sec. 2-318.

retailer who in turn sold one of the ladders to a customer. Unknown to any of the parties (manufacturer, wholesaler, retailer, or customer) there was a hidden defect in the wood, so that on the first time the ladder was used the top broke off, throwing the customer to the ground and injuring him severely. The retailer having become insolvent and the manufacturer being nearly two thousand miles away, the injured customer sued the wholesaler.

Unless the wholesaler-retailer contract provided otherwise, the wholesaler impliedly warranted to the retailer that the ladders were merchantable. However, the wholesaler's liability for breach of this warranty would be limited to the retailer (and to members and guests of his household). Since the customer had no direct contract relationship with the wholesaler, the customer could *not* recover from the wholesaler.

A comparison of the amount of liability and the causal basis of liability in these two types of cases will show the chief policy differences. In a check case:

1. As to the amount of liability: at the time an indorser indorses and transfers a check, the amount of his possible liability is definite and certain—namely, the face amount of the check.

2. As to the causal basis of liability: in general, an indorser becomes liable when the bank upon which a check is drawn dishonors the check by refusing to pay it. In any lawsuit that follows, all parties have equally ready access to impartial evidence which will prove conclusively whether or not the check was actually dishonored.

In a check case therefore, the fact that the plaintiff and defendant are remote parties does not at all affect either the amount of liability or the causal basis of the defendant's liability, nor otherwise complicate reaching a fair adjustment of the rights of the parties. In addition (as discussed in Chapter 14) sound policy reasons exist for recognizing remote party liability on checks and other commercial paper. It is both feasible and desirable therefore for the law to conclude, as it does, that unless expressly agreed otherwise, the promise or warranty of an indorser goes along with the check and can be enforced by any later holder. On the other hand, in a sales case the following considerations apply.

1. As to the amount of liability: the extent of personal and property injuries which may result from defective goods will vary considerably from one owner or user of goods to another. In view of this, it can be strongly argued in the ladder case that it would be unfair to consider the wholesaler liable to any person who happens to buy from the dealer, for damages which might be practically unlimited in amount. This argument is not conclusive since it is often possible for a wholesaler to be indirectly liable for the full amount of the remote customer's damages. If the customer recovers from the retailer for breach of warranty, the retailer can in turn sue the wholesaler on any warranty which was a part

of the retailer-wholesaler contract. Unless limited by that contract, the damages recoverable by the retailer would be measured by the amount of the retailer's legal liability to his customer. However, although not conclusive, the fact that the extent of damages is variable within very wide limits is a significant factor in determining whether it is sound policy to recognize an implied warranty in favor of a subpurchaser.

2. As to the causal basis of liability: liability for breach of a sales-of-goods warranty rests upon proof of the following facts: 1) that the goods were actually defective when they were sold by the defendant, and 2) that such defects caused the injuries suffered by the plaintiff. Compare the simplicity of determining whether or not a check was actually dishonored, with the very complex fact questions of whether goods were actually defective, exactly when the defect arose, and what damages actually and unavoidably resulted. How can a remote seller prove with any certainty what might have happened to goods after they left his hands and passed further along the channels of commerce? The evidence in many goods-warranty cases is quite uncertain, is subject to varying opinions, is not equally available to both plaintiff and defendant, and is frequently impossible to corroborate (or disprove) by impartial evidence. When evidence is uncertain and not equally available, allegations are difficult to disprove and the risk of collusive and faked claims increases. And the more hands the goods have passed through, the more uncertain the evidence and the greater the risk of faked claims. Also juries are often inclined to be quite sympathetic, sometimes even gullible, in a lawsuit involving physical injuries when the defendant is a "big, bad corporation."

Because of these uncertainties in amount and causal basis of liability, the courts (with some exceptions) formerly denied recovery even for negligent (that is, tortious) processing or manufacturing, unless the injured plaintiff had purchased directly from the negligent processor. Over the past fifty years the courts have changed in their view of what is the best policy to follow; now an injured subpurchaser is usually able to recover from a negligent processor without the necessity of a contract relationship between the parties. The important factors responsible for this change of policy include the following:

1. Under modern manufacturing and marketing processes, goods almost invariably pass through a number of hands before reaching the intended user.

2. The intended user is the one primarily jeopardized when goods are defective.

3. Negligence which causes defects in goods is wrongful and blameworthy conduct, and should be discouraged.

The first two of these numbered factors are also present in a breach of warranty lawsuit brought by an ultimate consumer against a remote seller. Generally these two factors are not sufficient to justify recognizing an implied warranty liability in the absence of a direct contract relationship between the plaintiff and defendant. However, if an additional circumstance is also present, as significant as the third numbered factor above, many courts will recognize that an implied warranty runs in favor of a subpurchaser. The two most important of these special fact situations involve:

1) Goods for Human Consumption. If through the fault of a packer or manufacturer, goods intended for human consumption are unwholesome, the packer or manufacturer is held liable to the ultimate consumer. Many such cases are tort actions, in which the injured plaintiff takes advantage of the presumption that the presence of a harmful substance in food is of itself evidence of negligence in preparation. However, even if a packer uses proper care and thereby avoids tort liability, the risk to society is sufficiently great, when products intended for human consumption are unwholesome, that most states also recognize a contract obligation based on an implied warranty running from the packer or manufacturer to the ultimate consumer, to the effect that the goods as packed or processed are merchantable.

2) Misrepresentations in Advertising. If a manufacturer intentionally misstates facts in his advertising, he is liable to the ultimate consumer for the tort of fraudulent misrepresentation. To prove false advertising to be fraudulent, however, requires proof of the advertiser's guilty knowledge, and clear-cut proof of this is frequently quite difficult to obtain. Therefore, some courts say that a manufacturer impliedly warrants to ultimate consumers that his advertising statements are true.

To return now to the hypothetical case of the purchaser of the defective ladder who sued the wholesaler: courts in the majority of states would hold that, at the present state of legal evolution, business understanding does not contemplate a warranty running from the wholesaler to the remote customer, and social policy does not require such a warranty.

In the landmark case of *Henningsen* v. *Bloomfield Motors* (previously referred to on page 198) the New Jersey Supreme Court found little difference between goods intended for human consumption and other potentially dangerous goods, and therefore held that a manufacturer should be considered as impliedly warranting to an ultimate consumer, the safety of a complex and potentially dangerous machine such as an automobile. The court, however, admitted that only a minority of states would reach the same conclusion. In the course of its opinion the court said:

There is no doubt that under early common-law concepts of contractual liability only those persons who were parties to the bargain could sue for breach of it. In more recent times a noticeable disposition has appeared in a number of jurisdictions to break through the narrow barrier of privity[27] when dealing with sales of goods in order to give realistic recognition to a universally accepted fact. . . . The limitations of privity in contracts for the sale of goods developed their place in the law when marketing conditions were simple, when maker and buyer frequently met face to face on an equal bargaining plane and when many of the products were relatively uncomplicated and conducive to inspection by a buyer competent to evaluate their quality. . . . With the advent of mass marketing, the manufacturer became remote from the purchaser, sales were accomplished through intermediaries, and the demand for the product was created by advertising media. In such an economy it became obvious that the consumer was the person being cultivated. . . . Thus where the commodities sold are such that if defectively manufactured they will be dangerous to life or limb, then society's interests can only be protected by eliminating the requirement of privity between the maker and his dealers and the reasonably expected consumer. In that way the burden of losses consequent upon use of defective articles is borne by those who are in a position to either control the danger or make an equitable distribution of the losses when they do occur. . . .

The concept was expressed in a practical way by the Supreme Court of Texas in . . . [a case involving defective food]:

"In fact the manufacturer's interest in the product is not terminated when he has sold it to the wholesaler. He must get it off the wholesaler's shelves before the wholesaler will buy a new supply. The same is not only true of the retailer, but of the housewife, for the housewife will not buy more until the family has consumed that which she has in her pantry. Thus the manufacturer or other vendor intends that this appearance of suitability of the article for human consumption should continue and be effective until some one is induced thereby to consume the goods. It would be but to acknowledge a weakness in the law to say that he could thus create a demand for his products by inducing a belief that they are suitable for human consumption, when, as a matter of fact, they are not, and reap the benefits of the public confidence thus created, and then avoid liability for the injuries caused thereby merely because there was no privity of contract between him and the one whom he induced to consume the food . . ."

Although only a minority of jurisdictions have thus far departed from the requirement of privity, the movement in that direction is most certainly gathering momentum. Liability to the ultimate consumer in the absence of direct contractual connection has been predicated upon a variety of theories. Some courts hold that the warranty runs with the article like a covenant running with land; others recognize a third-party beneficiary thesis; still others rest their decision on

---

[27] The term "privity" is commonly used in the law to signify a *direct* contractual relationship between two persons. Thus if A sells certain goods to B who in turn sells them to C, A, and B are in privity of contract, as also are B and C, but A and C are not in privity of contract.

the ground that public policy requires recognition of a warranty made directly to the consumer. . . .

Most of the cases where lack of privity has not been permitted to interfere with recovery have involved food and drugs. . . . In fact, the rule as to such products has been characterized as an exception to the general doctrine. But more recently courts, sensing the inequity of such limitation, have moved into broader fields: home permanent wave set . . . soap detergent . . . inflammable cowboy suit . . . exploding bottle . . . defective emery wheel . . . defective wire rope . . . defective cinder blocks . . .

Under modern conditions the ordinary layman, on responding to the importuning of colorful advertising, has neither the opportunity nor the capacity to inspect or to determine the fitness of an automobile for use; he must rely on the manufacturer who has control of its construction, and to some degree on the dealer who, to the limited extent called for by the manufacturer's instructions, inspects and services it before delivery. In such a marketing milieu his remedies and those of persons who properly claim through him should not depend "upon the intricacies of the law of sales. The obligation of the manufacturer should not be based alone on privity of contract. It should rest, as was once said, upon 'the demands of social justice.' " . . . "If privity of contract is required," then, under the circumstances of modern merchandising, "privity of contract exists in the consciousness and understanding of all right-thinking persons." . . .

Accordingly we hold that under modern marketing conditions, when a manufacturer puts a new automobile in the stream of trade and promotes its purchase by the public, an implied warranty that it is reasonably suitable for use as such accompanies it into the hands of the ultimate purchaser.

The New Jersey court thus argues that in the case of potentially dangerous goods, the legal concept of implied warranty should be extended to run from manufacturers to subpurchasers. It is interesting to compare the court's argument and conclusion with the following view expressed by Dean Prosser, an eminent legal scholar:

No one doubts that, unless there is privity, liability to the consumer must be in tort and not in contract. There is no need to borrow a concept from the contract law of sales; and it is "only by some violent pounding and twisting" that "warranty" can be made to serve the purpose at all. Why talk of it? If there is to be strict liability in tort, let there be strict liability in tort, declared outright, without an illusory contract mask. Such strict liability is familiar enough in the law of animals, abnormally dangerous activities, nuisance, workmen's compensation, and respondeat superior [that is, a principal's liability for his agent's torts]. There is nothing so shocking about it today that cannot be accepted and stand on its own feet in this new and additional field, provided always that public sentiment, public demand, and "public policy" have reached the point where the change is called for. There are not lacking indications that some of the courts are about ready to throw away the crutch, and to admit what they are really doing, when they say that the warranty is not the one made on the original sale, and does not run with the goods, but is a new and independent one made directly to the consumer; and that it does not arise out of or depend upon any contract, but is imposed by the law, in tort, as a matter of policy.[28]

REMEDIES FOR BREACH OF WARRANTY

If a contract includes an express warranty, frequently there is also included a provision stating what shall be the remedy or remedies for breach of warranty. For example, a buyer's remedy may be limited to return of goods and refund of price, or to repair and replacement of defective goods or parts. If no implied warranty would arise under the circumstances, or if one which would have arisen is properly excluded, the express agreement is the limit of the seller's warranty liability. On the other hand, if parties have not agreed on any limitation of remedies, then when a warranty is breached the buyer usually has the right to select whichever one of two remedies he wishes. He may 1) retain the goods and recover for the damages resulting from the breach of warranty, or 2) rescind the contract and recover anything already paid plus any damages resulting from the breach of warranty. Some of the details of these remedies are discussed in Chapter 16. Two points can be emphasized here:

1. Since a breach of warranty action is a type of action for breach of contract, the contract rule of waiver applies. If performance falls short of what is required under a contract, but the other party nevertheless shows himself to be fully satisfied with the defective performance, this satisfaction constitutes a waiver or excuse of any defect, and usually the satisfied party cannot afterwards change his mind. He thus gives up any right he may have to cancel the contract or even to collect damages.

2. After a buyer has used goods for more than merely testing them, he usually cannot return them (that is, he cannot cancel the contract) even though the goods are defective. Instead, the buyer's only remedy is to recover damages.

The Uniform Commercial Code expresses these two points as follows:

> Where a tender [of goods] has been accepted . . . the buyer must within a reasonable time after he discovers or should have discovered any breach notify the seller of breach *or be barred from any remedy.* . . . [Emphasis added.]
> Revocation of acceptance [which can be accomplished, for example, by the buyer giving notice that he desires to return defective goods] must occur within a reasonable time after the buyer discovers or should have discovered the ground for it *and* before any substantial

[28] "Strict Liability to the Consumer," 69 *Yale L.J.* 1099, p. 1134 (1960).

change in condition of the goods which is not caused by their own defects.[29] [Emphasis added.]

PROBLEMS

1. A construction company was building an Army camp, and in a nearby town, the plaintiff operated a dormitory for workmen. In November the personnel manager of the construction company called the plaintiff to the camp, said that he had more men coming and didn't know where to put them, and asked how many additional men the plaintiff could accommodate. The plaintiff replied that his first floor was about filled but that if he could obtain pipe to extend heat to the second floor of his building, he could take care of about 50 additional men. The personnel manager replied, "I would like to reserve that upstairs for us," to which the plaintiff answered, "O.K." The personnel manager helped the plaintiff to obtain the necessary pipe from the construction company's supplies, and the plaintiff extended heat to his second floor and installed beds. About the middle of December the plaintiff notified the personnel manager that the accommodations were ready. However, the construction company never used or paid for the second-floor accommodations. The following March the plaintiff received from the construction company a bill for the pipe which the plaintiff had used. The plaintiff thereupon sent the construction company a bill for $3,000, as the charge for the second-floor accommodations from the middle of December to March, and when the company failed to pay, the plaintiff sued the company. Explain 1) the reasoning upon which the construction company might attempt to defend, 2) the reasoning upon which the plaintiff might attempt to recover, and 3) which party should be given judgment.

2. B. Brown, a wholesaler, entered into the following written agreement with S. Smith, a miller:

S. Smith hereby agrees to sell and B. Brown to buy the following commodities, f.o.b. car of initial carrier at shipping point, freight allowed to Chicago, Ill.

Time of shipment: December 1 of this year, unless ordered out sooner.

Destination: Track, Chicago, Ill.

Terms of payment: 2/10 net 30 from date of each shipment.

Quantity: 630 barrels

Brand of flour	Price per barrel
Confidence	6.65
Harvester	6.45
De Luxe Pastry	6.40
Sierra Pastry	5.90

Shipping dates: to follow.   (signed) S. Smith
[Date]   (signed) B. Brown

[29] U.C.C. Secs. 2-607, 2-608.

In accordance with the contract and at B's direction, S milled and delivered to B 210 barrels of Confidence brand flour on April 15, for which B paid according to contract. B refused to order any more flour and after December 1, S sued B for damages. Explain 1) the reasoning upon which B might attempt to defend, 2) the reasoning upon which S might attempt to collect, and 3) which party should be given judgment.

3. In writing S agreed to sell and B to buy 10,000 bushels of a specified kind and type of grain, to be delivered in installments of 2,000 bushels by the tenth of each month for five successive months, beginning on a specified month. The only provision as to price read: "The price B is to pay for each installment shall be the Chicago market price on the date of shipment f.o.b. Chicago, payable within ten days after delivery." When S tendered delivery of the first installment according to contract, B refused to accept. S sued B for damages. Explain 1) the reasoning upon which B might attempt to defend, 2) the reasoning upon which S might attempt to collect, and 3) which party should be given judgment.

4. S and B signed a written agreement under which S agreed to sell and deliver to B and B agreed to buy 15,000 pounds of a described type of wool yarn to be delivered in three months, "at a price to be determined between us, subject to market fluctuations, to be not less than $1.27½ in the event of a decline nor more than $1.32½ in the event of advance." Upon S's refusal to agree on a price or to deliver any yarn at the stated time, B sued S for damages for breach of contract. Explain 1) the reasoning upon which S might attempt to defend, 2) the reasoning upon which B might attempt to collect, and 3) which party should be given judgment. (Modified from A.I.C.P.A., May 43-10.)

5. In response to an advertisement in a newspaper, O, the owner of a factory in a small town, met with S to discuss the availability of O's factory for assembling storm windows from materials to be furnished by S. After inspecting O's plant, S said that if O would make certain specified alterations and install certain specified equipment, S would supply O with sufficient material for assembling 1,000 to 3,000 storm windows per day, under an agreement whereby O would pay for the material received at a price to be fixed between the parties and thereafter, upon delivery of the assembled storm windows to S or to a designated customer of S, S would pay O a price sufficient to cover all of O's costs plus a reasonable profit. It was agreed that the final terms, including the duration of the arrangement, would be determined and a formal written contract prepared when O's factory was ready to go into operation. With frequent consultation with S, O promptly made the necessary alterations and purchased and installed the necessary equipment. In the meantime, however, S made other arrangements and refused to have any further dealings with O. The alterations and special equipment cost O $3,000 and were of use only for the specified purpose. O sued S for $3,000. Explain 1) the reasoning upon which S might attempt to defend, 2) the reasoning upon which O might attempt to collect, and 3) which party should be given judgment.

6. A builder entered into a written contract with a landowner under which 1) the builder was to construct 90 dwelling houses on the owner's land, according to stated plans and specifications, 2) the buildings were to be completed within one year, and 3) the owner was to pay $7,000 per house payable in stated installments at specified times as the work progressed. Two months later the builder had 50 houses at the point in their construction when, according to the contract, the owner was to pay the builder the first 30 percent of the contract price for each of the 50 houses. On this date the builder received a notice that the owner wished to modify their contract. When the builder refused, the owner refused to make any payment, saying that he would abandon the entire project unless the builder would agree to amend the original contract, reducing to 50 the total number of houses to be built and reducing the total price per house to $6,000. The builder owed subcontractors and suppliers for work already done and faced financial ruin if he could not obtain the amount of money due from the owner under the contract. In order to obtain the needed money, the builder agreed to a written amendment of the original contract. The owner thereupon paid the installment then due. After completing the construction of the 50 houses and receiving $6,000 per house from the owner, the builder sued the owner for an additional $1,000 for each of the 50 completed houses.

a) Was there consideration for the amendment to the original contract?

b) Explain 1) the reasoning (other than lack of consideration) upon which the builder could attempt to collect an additional $50,000, 2) the reasoning upon which the owner could attempt to defend, and 3) which party should be given judgment in the builder's lawsuit for $50,000.

7. D, who owned and operated a certain business, owed various sums of money to a number of creditors, including a debt of $6,000 owed to a local bank. D went through a bankruptcy proceeding under which the bank was paid $500 on its $6,000 claim. Upon completion of the bankruptcy proceeding D obtained a discharge as to all his unpaid debts. (This meant that after such discharge, none of the creditors including the bank had any legal remedy or right to collect from D for any of the unpaid debts incurred before the bankruptcy proceeding.) Shortly after completion of the bankruptcy proceeding, D started a different kind of business in the same community. An official of the bank called on D and said that unless D would sign a note promising to pay the bank the balance of the unpaid debt ($5,500) the bank would consider D an unsatisfactory credit risk and so report in response to any inquiries concerning D's credit. Needing a favorable credit rating to start his new business, D signed a note promising to pay the bank $5,500 within six months. When the note came due, D refused to pay and the bank sued. D's defenses were: lack of consideration, and duress.

a) Explain whether the first defense was good.

b) Explain whether the second defense was good.

8. In transcribing her notes, an accountant's secretary erroneously wrote to a prospective client that the per diem charge for a senior accountant was $25 (instead of $35 which had been dictated to her), and as the accountant had instructed her to do, she then signed the accountant's name and mailed the letter. The client immediately wrote to the accountant engaging him "at the rates specified in your letter." The accountant satisfactorily performed

the work and billed the client at the rate of $35 per day. As the client was fully aware at all times, $35 per day was the prevailing rate. Could the accountant collect $35 per day from the client? Explain. (Modified from A.I.C.P.A., Nov. 38-4.)

9. On June 6 a New York City importer and seller of souvenir postal cards sent a letter to a Washington, D.C., dealer, enclosing a sample of a new card showing various Washington views. The letter stated that the regular price of the cards was $15 per thousand but that the seller was making a price to jobbers of $1 per thousand. This letter was typed by the seller's stenographer from a circular letter which stated a price of $10 per thousand. She erroneously typed "$1" instead of "$10." The dealer replied by letter: "This is in reply to your letter of the 7th. Your sample card sent us is very good and owing to the price you quote us, the stock must be faulty in some way or your stenographer made a mistake in the price. If the stock is good and the price correct as quoted, we will take several thousand." The seller looked up a copy of the circular letter from which the letter sent to the dealer had been typed (no carbon copy of the letter sent having been retained) and replied by letter that the cards were first class in every respect, that they were being sold at cost, and that the seller would guaranty them in every respect. On receipt of this letter, the dealer wrote ordering "25,000 cards as per sample at price quoted in your letter of the 7th." The seller shipped the ordered cards and mailed a bill to the dealer, billing the cards at $10 per thousand. The dealer received the cards the following day, unpacked them and placed them on his shelves. Later the same day the dealer received the bill and immediately wrote: "We have just received your bill for postal cards and return it for correction. The price of these cards is $1 instead of $10 as you bill them. We refer to your letter of the 7th when you sent us sample and price." The seller replied: "There is evidently an error some place. The price of the cards as quoted you was $10 per thousand and not $1. The import duty alone on these cards costs us $2.25 per thousand, and you can readily understand that it would be impossible for us to sell them at any such price as $1 per thousand. If the price of $10 per thousand is not satisfactory, we request that you send us the cards immediately. Kindly return to us the letter in which you state that you are quoted $1 per thousand." The dealer refused to return the cards and tendered $25 plus shipping charges as payment in full. The seller refused and sued for $250. Explain 1) the reasoning upon which the seller might attempt to collect, 2) the reasoning upon which the dealer might attempt to defend, and 3) which party should be given judgment.

10. On June 13 R. Roger, a retailer in Chicago, telegraphed M. Martin, a manufacturer in New York City, "I can use one hundred children's and juniors' dresses at close-out price." The same day M gave to the telegraph office in New York for transmission to R, the following telegram, "To R. Roger, Chicago. Can ship two hundred junior dresses in linen, silkette, dotted plain and fancy voile at $2.75 net, also six dozen children's dresses, cotton shantungs, voile, poplins, and linens at $16.50 net dozen, advise all close-out prices wonderful opportunity for a big sale. (signed) M. Martin." Because of negligence in transmission, the telegram delivered to R read as to the first

price "twenty seventy-five net" instead of $2.75. R assumed that this meant $20.75 per dozen, and on the same day wired M, "Send entire lot of dresses as per your telegram." On the next day M shipped the described dresses to R and mailed an invoice calculated at $2.75 for each junior dress. Two days later R wired M, "Invoice received does not agree with your telegram of the 13th, will not accept merchandise unless billed as bought wire answer."

a) Explain the legal effect of each telegram.

b) Was there a contract between the parties, and if so what were the terms? Explain.

11. On October 3 S of New York City sent to B. Brown of Chicago a letter which under the circumstances constituted an offer to sell to B certain described goods at a stated price. Receiving the letter on October 5, B immediately dispatched a telegram accepting the offer. The message B gave to the telegraph office in Chicago was addressed to S and read: "Your offer of October 3 accepted. (signed) B. Brown." Through negligence of the telegraph company, the message was garbled in transmission so that the telegram delivered to S in New York on October 5 read: "Your offer of October 3 rejected. (signed) B. Brown." After S sold the goods to another purchaser, the above facts were discovered, and B sued S for damages for breach of contract. Explain 1) the reasoning upon which B might attempt to collect, 2) the reasoning upon which S might attempt to defend, and 3) which party should be given judgment.

12. S sold to B ten shares of stock of the Carter Corporation for $1,360. At the time of the sale, the books of the corporation showed that the shares of stock, which were originally issued at the par value of $100 per share, had a book value of $136 per share. S and B assumed that the true condition of the corporation was accurately described in the books. Unknown to them at that time, some of the corporation's employees had kept the books in such a manner as to conceal defalcations of which they were guilty; actually the assets of the corporation at the time of the sale were so depleted that the stock was worth only $60 per share. Upon discovering these facts a month after the sale, B offered to return the stock to S and demanded return of his purchase price. S refused and B sued to rescind. At the trial S proved that he had made no representations and was not guilty of any fraud. Explain 1) the reasoning upon which B might attempt to recover, 2) the reasoning upon which S might attempt to defend, and 3) which party should be given judgment.

13. The owner of a plot of land contracted with a builder for construction of an office building on the owner's land according to certain stated specifications, at a cost of $190,000. A few days later and before any work had been done under the contract, the builder discovered that he had made a $15,000 error in his calculations. Could the builder have his contract rescinded because of this mistake? Explain. (Modified from A.I.C.P.A., May 51-4.)

14. S owned a stationery business which for a number of years had earned a net profit of $6,000. By falsely stating that the net profit had been $20,000, S induced B to purchase the business. When B discovered the true facts, he sued S to rescind the contract. At the trial, S conclusively proved that if B had made inquiries of other persons or if B had used ordinary diligence, he could have discovered the truth. For whom should judgment be given? Explain. (Modified from A.I.C.P.A., May 31-3.)

15. S was the secretary of a corporation that had been in existence for a number of years, and was duly authorized to solicit subscriptions for unissued capital stock, the par value of which was $100 per share. On July 1, S induced B to subscribe for 100 shares at a total price of $50 per share by telling B 1) that the corporation's gross sales for that July were certain to exceed $40,000, 2) that the certificate of incorporation expressly empowered the corporation to conduct certain activities, and 3) that B would not be liable to the corporation or to any other person or corporation for any amount in excess of the subscription price of $50 per share. B agreed to pay for the stock on the following September 1. On the following August 16, however, B ascertained that the gross sales for the previous July had been slightly less than $10,000, and that the certificate of incorporation did not grant the corporate power stated by S. Also, B was informed by his attorney that according to law, if a corporation should become insolvent, any person to whom par value stock was issued for less than par value can be required to pay to the corporation for the benefit of creditors the difference between what he paid for his stock and its par value. Could B immediately cancel his subscription agreement? Explain. (Modified from A.I.C.P.A., Nov. 37-9.)

16. B, a violin expert, ascertained that S owned an old violin of famous make, worth many thousands of dollars. In talking with S, B found that the violin had been in S's family for many years but that S had no knowledge of its true value. After some persuasion and by offering what to S seemed an excessive price ($350), B succeeded in buying the instrument. Later S learned the true facts and, tendering return of the purchase price, sued B to recover the violin.

a) Was S entitled to judgment against B? Explain.

b) Other facts remaining the same, assume that B was not an expert and was unaware of the actual value of the violin until after buying it. Would this change the answer given in Part (a) of this problem? Explain. (Modified from A.I.C.P.A., May 29-8.)

17. As B was well aware, his business had become insolvent. However, B hoped to earn sufficient profit to restore the business to solvency if he could operate for another month or so. B ordered certain goods from S at a stated price, the terms for payment being 2/10 net 30, and S shipped the goods. At no time did B make any statements to S concerning his financial condition. After a month the business was hopelessly insolvent and a receiver was appointed by the court to take over and liquidate the assets of the business. Included among the assets were the goods S had sold and delivered to B. S realized that if he filed a claim along with all of B's other creditors, he would receive only a fraction of what was due him. Since S had not retained title or an interest in the goods, he had no right to repossess them. However, if he could cancel the contract, he could reclaim the goods. S therefore notified the receiver that he rescinded the sale because of fraud and wished to take back the goods. The receiver refused and S sued. Explain 1) the reasoning upon which S might attempt to cancel and recover possession of the goods, 2) the reasoning upon which the receiver might attempt to defend, and 3) which party should be given judgment.

18. In December, the owner of a nightclub was solicited for advertising by an agent who represented the publisher of a weekly magazine known as *Nightlife*. When the owner expressed reluctance to obligate himself for a year's advertising, the agent said that the contract form permitted an advertiser to cancel at will. Relying upon the agent's statement, and without reading the agent's printed order form, the owner signed a subscription for advertising in 52 weekly issues at $6 per issue. The printed order form stated, "Oral agreements will not be recognized," and contained no provision regarding cancellation. The publisher accepted the subscription and the advertising began in the January 1 issue. In February the owner told the publisher that he wished to cancel the advertising. When the publisher objected, the owner told the publisher of what the agent had said. This was the first that the publisher knew of the agent's statement. The publisher explained that the agent had no authority to say that advertising contracts could be canceled, but offered that if the owner would continue to advertise, the publisher would release him from the written contract if the owner was still dissatisfied, and the owner could then terminate the advertising at will. The owner agreed and continued to pay for advertising until April, when he notified the publisher to cancel his advertising for the remainder of the year. The publisher refused to permit cancellation, and sued the owner for damages. The owner raised two defenses: 1) that he was induced to sign the December contract through the agent's fraud, and 2) that the December contract was superseded by the February agreement under which the publisher had said that the owner could cancel at will. Explain 1) the reasoning upon which the publisher could attempt to answer the first defense, 2) the reasoning upon which the publisher could attempt to answer the second defense, and 3) which party should be given judgment in the lawsuit.

19. S, a manufacturer of certain types of refrigerator equipment, bought a welding unit from its manufacturer, M, for $500. In inducing S to purchase the unit, M orally and also in a descriptive circular which he gave S, asserted to S that the welding unit was well made and would do certain specified welding jobs. Before S made any use of the unit, he changed his manufacturing processes and had no need for such a unit. About six months later S sold and delivered the unit for $300 to B another manufacturer. In inducing B to buy the unit, S said that he had never used the unit and also said and did what is described below. When B attempted to use the unit, he discovered that it was so defective in design that it was unable to do any of the welding jobs specified in M's circular. B demanded that S take back the unit and return B's $300 and when S refused, B sued S. S conclusively proved the he had honestly and reasonably believed that the unit would perform as described in M's circular.

a) In inducing B to buy, S showed B the circular received from M, and said that he himself had had no experience with the unit. Was B entitled to return the welding unit to S and recover $300? Explain.

b) S was unable to find M's circular. However S remembered what the circular had said and so told B: "This unit is well made and will do welding jobs such as [and then S mentioned the jobs]." Was B entitled to return the unit to S and recover $300? Explain.

20. B lived in a small town, a short distance from one large city and a greater distance from another large city. Both cities were in the same direction from B and each city had an FM radio station. Adjacent channels were assigned to the two stations and in B's location, an ordinary FM receiver could not separate the signals from the two stations, could not receive for satisfactory listening the weaker signal from the more distant city. B went to S's radio store to look at a new model of FM receiver. S showed B a descriptive circular from the manufacturer, stating in part: "This receiver can tune with pinpoint sharpness, and because of a newly designed circuit, can separate a weak signal from a stronger signal even on adjacent channels in the same direction." B bought the set, paying $50 down and promising to pay the balance of $250 in one month. In B's location, the set functioned no better (nor worse) than other FM receivers. B still could not separate the weaker signal from the stronger one. B wanted to cancel the contract and made no further use of the receiver. S refused to accept return of the receiver and when the one month expired, sued B for the balance due.

a) Explain 1) the reasoning upon which B could attempt to defend, 2) the reasoning upon which S could attempt to collect, and 3) which party should be given judgment.

b) In addition to the above facts, assume that when S was showing the receiver and circular to B, S said, "This receiver is guaranteed, the company stands behind it." Explain whether your answer would be different than that in Part (a) of this problem.

21. A customer in a small grocery store (not a self-service store) requested a can of food (the customer's request is quoted below), and bought what he requested for 30 cents. The can received by the customer had been sold by the Star Packing Company to a wholesaler and by the wholesaler to the grocer. While eating the food in his home, the customer broke his dental plate on a small stone which had been in the can with the contents. A new plate cost the customer $150. The customer sued the grocer.

a) In stating what he wanted, the customer said, "I want a medium size can of pork and beans. Any brand will do." Explain whether the customer could recover from the grocer and if so how much.

b) In stating what he wanted, the customer said, "I want a can of Star brand pork and beans. I've been looking all over town for that, and I see you handle it." Explain whether the customer could recover from the grocer and if so how much.

c) In stating what he wanted, the customer said, "I want a can of pitted cherries. Any brand will do." The stone on which the customer broke his plate was a cherry pit, still inside one of the cherries. Explain whether the customer could recover from the grocer and if so how much.

d) Other facts being the same, assume that the grocer operated a self-service store. The customer selected a can of peas from the shelf and paid the cashier 30 cents. The small stone on which the customer broke his plate had been in the can with the contents. Explain whether the customer could recover from the grocer and if so how much.

22. A heating dealer sold an oil conversion unit to B, a homeowner, and installed it in B's furnace. Neither the conversation nor the written contract between the dealer and the buyer contained any reference to quality or warranty. When he installed the unit, the dealer took it from the original box as it had come from the manufacturer. One week later a defect in the unit, of which the dealer had been unaware, caused a costly fire in B's house. The defect resulted from faulty manufacture and was such that a dealer using reasonable care would not discover it during his inspection and installation of the unit. The dealer offered to take back the defective unit in exchange for a new one but denied any liability for the fire damages.

a) B sued the dealer for the full amount of the fire damages. What result?

b) Other facts being the same, assume that the written contract between the dealer and B stated: "The dealer warrants the described unit to be free from defects in workmanship and materials for thirty days. Liability under this warranty is limited to replacement of any unit shown to be defective within that period. This is in lieu of all other warranties express or implied." B sued the dealer for the full amount of the fire damages. What result?

23. B, a baker, decided to air-condition his small bakery shop. He measured floor space and ceiling height, calculated volume, and consulted a chart recommending the proper size air-conditioning unit necessary to cool the calculated area to 72 degrees Fahrenheit. B ordered and bought from S, a dealer in heating and ventilating equipment, an air-conditioning unit of the size indicated by the chart, paying a portion of the price down and agreeing to pay the balance in certain monthly installments. S installed the unit in B's shop and, at his request, set the controls for 72 degrees. Although installed and functioning properly, the unit failed to lower the temperature in the shop below 82 degrees. B consulted S who measured and verified B's calculation of area. It then occurred to S that in calculating for the size of unit to buy, B had failed to take into account the output of heat from his baking ovens. The size of unit B had selected was proper for an ordinary shop of that area but was not adequate for the baking shop because of the heat from the ovens. B then proposed to S that either they cancel the contract, or reduce the price so that B could purchase an additional unit. S refused cancellation or reduction. B had the unit disconnected, no longer used it, and told S that he was holding the unit for S. When B failed to make the contract payments, S sued B.

a) Explain 1) the reasoning upon which B could attempt to defend, 2) the reasoning upon which S could attempt to collect, and 3) which party should be given judgment.

b) Other facts being the same, assume the following: B took the shop dimensions to S and told S that he wanted an air-conditioning system that would maintain a temperature of 72 degrees Fahrenheit in his bakery shop. S visited B's shop to verify the measurements, determined from a chart the size of unit to use to maintain the desired temperature for that area, and installed such a unit in B's shop. The contract between the parties contained no express warranty. The unit was the same size as in the preceding part of this problem, with the same result. S had overlooked the heat-producing ovens. When B disconnected the unit, offered to return it, and made no further payments, S sued. Explain whether the changed facts would change any of the answers given for Part (a).

c) Other facts being the same as in Part (b), assume that the written contract between S and B contained the following provision: "S warrants the described equipment to be free from defects of material and workmanship, for the period of six months. This warranty is in lieu of all other warranties express or implied." Would this additional fact change any of the answers given for Part (b)? Explain.

24. Paying $1.99, B, a housewife, purchased from a retail dealer a cotton dress which B had selected from a rack bearing a sign reading as stated below. The dress had been purchased by the dealer from the manufacturer and bore the manufacturer's label. Shortly after the first time B wore the dress she became afflicted with a severe skin irritation. B sued the dealer to recover damages for her injuries. In the lawsuit, it was proved by B's doctor that B had a skin sensitivity or allergy and that the dress dye contained a substance extremely irritating to B. The dealer proved that he had no previous knowledge of the presence of an irritating substance in the dress, that he had sold thousands of this type of dress without any complaint, and that analysis of this type of dress showed it to contain nothing irritating to ordinary persons.

a) The sign on the rack read: "Sale $1.99." Explain whether B was entitled to recover from the dealer.

b) The sign on the rack read: "Sale $1.99. Guaranteed." Explain whether B was entitled to recover from the dealer.

25. a) A thief stole an adding machine from the office of its owner. About a month later the thief sold the adding machine to a dealer who handled both new and used office equipment. The dealer honestly and reasonably thought that the thief owned the machine and paid the thief $140, a fair price. The dealer cleaned and adjusted the machine and put it on display. About a month later the dealer sold and delivered the machine to an accountant for $175, a fair price. Nothing was stated by the dealer or the accountant as to title or ownership; both honestly and reasonably assumed that the dealer owned the machine which he was selling. A year later a part in the machine broke. The accountant returned the machine to the manufacturer for repair. The manufacturer noticed from the serial number that the machine was one reported as having been stolen. The manufacturer notified the owner who proved his ownership and obtained a court order that the machine should be given to him. The accountant then sued the dealer for the value of the machine. Explain whether the accountant could recover.

b) Other facts being the same as above, assume the following: About six months after the accountant bought the machine, he retired from active practice and sold the machine to a lawyer. Nothing was stated by the accountant or the lawyer as to title or ownership, both honestly and reasonably assuming that the accountant owned the machine he was selling. When the machine broke down six months later, the lawyer returned it to the manufacturer. When the court awarded the machine to the owner, the lawyer sued the accountant. Explain whether the lawyer could recover from the accountant.

26. With the baked goods he was handling in his self-service store, a retailer had cakes which had been baked by a certain baker, sold by the baker to a wholesale food distributor, and sold and delivered by the food wholesaler to a retailer. Unknown to any of the parties (baker, wholesaler, or retailer) a pin accidentally fell into the cake batter during its preparation. The cakes on the retailer's shelf were baked from this batter and one of the cakes had the pin baked inside the cake. To stimulate purchases, the retailer had an employee cut one of the cakes into small pieces and walk up and down the aisles offering samples of the cake to customers. One customer who was shopping in the store, took one of the pieces of cake being passed out by the retailer's employee, and started to eat the piece of cake as he pushed his cart up and down the aisles in the store. This piece contained the concealed pin. As the customer, using proper care, bit into the piece of cake, the pin was jammed into his gums, causing a serious infection. The failure of the retailer or any of his employees to discover the pin was not negligence. Explain whether the customer could recover a) from the retailer, b) from the wholesaler, or c) from the baker.

27. A thief stole an auto from its owner, forged the necessary papers, and sold the car to a dealer who bought for value and without knowledge that he was buying from a thief. The dealer sold the car to a buyer for $775 which the buyer paid, without knowledge that it was a stolen car. The buyer used the car continuously for two years before the car was traced and returned to the owner. The car had depreciated and had a value of $400 when taken from the buyer. When informed of the facts, the dealer offered to pay the buyer $400 in full settlement of the buyer's claims against the dealer. The buyer refused the settlement and sued for $775. Explain 1) the reasoning upon which the buyer might attempt to collect $775, 2) the reasoning upon which the dealer might attempt to defend, and 3) how much, if anything, the buyer could recover.

28. On September 16 the owner of a certain house and lot requested a real estate broker to list the property for sale at $19,950. The owner added as a proviso that he would not sign any agreement to sell until he was able to obtain another home for himself. The broker orally agreed to list the property subject to that proviso. On September 19 the broker requested the owner to sign a standard form exclusive real estate agency agreement. The agreement stated the names of the owner and the broker and read: "The owner named above hereby employs the above-named broker for two months as sole and exclusive agent for the sale for not less than $19,950 of the house and lot [describing the location], and agrees to pay said broker 5 percent commission upon production of a purchaser ready, willing, and able to buy at said price." The broker explained that he was requesting the owner to sign the agreement to make sure no other agent would be able to run in and out of the house showing it to prospective buyers. The owner signed and returned the agreement to the broker. At the same time the owner repeated that he would not sell the premises until he secured another home for himself. The broker replied, "I

understand that." One month later the broker secured P, who was ready, willing, and able to buy the owner's house for the listed price. Although searching with reasonable diligence, the owner had not yet found another home and refused to sign a contract with P or to convey the house, and the deal fell through. The broker sued the owner for damages. Explain 1) the reasoning upon which the owner might attempt to defend, 2) the reasoning upon which the broker might attempt to collect, and 3) which party should be given judgment.

chapter *8*

Illegal Agreements

It would be absurd for a court which is supposed to uphold the law to help a person in breaking the law. Certainly a court should not aid a person to collect benefits from his own illegal conduct, or to protect him from a burden or loss resulting from his illegal conduct. Therefore, if a lawsuit between two persons concerns an illegal transaction they have entered into, the court will usually leave the parties in the same position they were in when they came into court. This will often result in a ruling actually favorable to one or the other party. However, the court is not by design preferring one over the other. This is merely the result of the court's refusal to assist *either* party.

An agreement is illegal if either its formation or its performance involves a crime or a tort, or is otherwise opposed to public policy. The principal fact situations which may involve illegal transactions include the following: 1) ordinary kinds of crimes, 2) torts, 3) businesses or professions requiring licenses, 4) excessive interest for loans of money (usury), 5) gambling or wagering, 6) Sunday laws, and 7) other conduct contrary to public policy.

ORDINARY CRIMES

The term "ordinary crimes" includes murder, robbery, assault, buying goods known to be stolen, and the other common crimes. An agreement to suppress evidence of a crime is itself a crime, called *compounding a felony* (if the suppressed crime is serious) or *compounding a misdemeanor* (if the suppressed crime is minor). Obviously the courts should not aid parties in connection with agreements involving any of these crimes.

TORTS

Torts are discussed in Chapter 2. Since a tort is a wrongful act, the courts will refuse to lend their aid to parties in connection with agreements which involve the commission of torts. Since it is usually a tort to intentionally interfere with the contract relations of others, a contract involving such interference is illegal and unenforceable.

Example: A distributor of liquefied petroleum gas contracted to buy all of his requirements from a gas company at stated prices for the next five years. A year later an oil company, knowing of this contract, offered the distributor a better price and thereby induced him to disregard his prior contract and enter into a contract to buy all of his requirements from the oil company. Afterwards the oil company itself defaulted on its contract and the distributor sued the oil company.

Since to the knowledge of both the distributor and the oil company, the second contract involved a breach of the previous contract (between the distributor and the gas company), the general view is that the second contract would be illegal and unenforceable. Under this view, neither party to the second contract could enforce it against the other.

LICENSING STATUTES

Numerous statutes require licenses for persons engaging in various businesses and professions. Some of these are taxing statutes, intended merely to raise revenue, while others are competency statutes, designed to prescribe and enforce qualifications for persons to engage in certain businesses or professions (such as law, medicine, engineering, real estate brokering, and many others).

If the statute requiring a license is a tax measure, the courts in the various states are not agreed as to the result the lack of a license will have on contracts. On the other hand, if the statute is intended to assure the qualifications of persons carrying on specified businesses or professions, any contracts made by an unlicensed person who is illegally engaging in one of these occupations will usually be considered illegal and unenforceable. Although the unlicensed person performs the agreed services completely and competently, he cannot recover any compensation.

USURIOUS INTEREST

The expression "legal rate of interest" has two different connotations. It may be referring to the maximum rate of interest which can lawfully be charged, or instead it may refer to the rate of interest which parties are presumed to intend when they agree that interest will accrue but fail to specify the exact rate of interest. In some states the maximum rate and the presumed rate are not the same. For example, the presumed rate in some states is 6 percent while the maximum rate permitted by law for the same type of obligation is 8 percent. In some other states the two rates are the same. In such states, for obligations which do not come under some special statute, both the presumed rate of interest and the maximum which can lawfully be charged are usually 6 percent per year.

Many states have statutes authorizing higher than the usual maximum rate of interest for certain situations, particularly for loans by licensed small loan companies. Rates of 1, 2, or 3 percent per month are commonly permitted, varying with the amount and duration of the loan. These statutes recognize and meet the social need of persons without property or steady employment to be able to borrow small sums of money. Loans to such persons involve greater risks and thus justify higher than the ordinary rates of interest.

A rate of interest exceeding the maximum which can lawfully be charged is called *usurious interest.* The states differ as a matter of policy on the validity and effect of contracts involving usurious interest. In some states a lender who tries to charge a usurious rate of interest cannot collect even the principal amount of the loan, in some other states he can collect the principal but no interest, while in still other states he has the right to collect the principal amount of the debt together with interest calculated at the lawful rate.

A sale on credit is not treated as a loan of money. Usually the *carrying* or *finance charge* which a seller adds to the amount the buyer is to pay is not considered the same as interest on a loan of money, and therefore is not automatically regulated by the usury statutes. Unless a state also has a statute expressly applying to sales on credit, a seller is unrestricted in the amount he may charge for permitting deferred payments. Some states have no limiting statutes, other states regulate the carrying charges for all credit sales, while still other states prescribe a maximum carrying or finance charge for sales of certain items only.

GAMBLING

In most states gambling is prohibited, and agreements involving gambling are not enforceable. A contest in which a prize is awarded on the basis of merit does not involve gambling, but it is gambling if an award or payment is to be made on the basis of a fortuitous happening. In the case of insurance, the possibility of a loss, called an insurable interest, distinguishes an enforceable insurance contract from an unenforceable gambling contract. For insurance on another's life, the one buying the policy must have an insurable interest at the time he buys the policy; it is immaterial that such interest may cease before the death of the insured person. On the other hand, for fire and similar insurance, the insurable interest must exist not only at the time the policy is taken out but also at the time the insured loss occurs.

SUNDAY AND HOLIDAY LAWS

Sunday Statutes

Practically all states have statutes prohibiting most types of business on Sunday. Such statutes have frequently been challenged as violating the First and Fourteenth Amendments of the United States Constitution; when these two Amendments are read together, the resulting rule pertaining to religion can be paraphrased as follows:

> Neither Congress nor a State shall make a law respecting an establishment of religion, or prohibiting the free exercise thereof.

Sunday statutes have been uniformly upheld as welfare rather than religious laws. In a recent challenge before the United States Supreme Court, Chief Justice Warren, writing for a majority of the court, said:

> Throughout this century and longer both the federal and state governments have oriented their activities very largely toward the improvement of the health, safety, recreation and general well-being of our citizens. . . . Sunday Closing Laws like those before us have become part and parcel of this great governmental concern wholly apart from their original purposes or connotations. The present purpose and effect of most of them is to provide a uniform day of rest for all citizens; the fact that this day is Sunday, a day of particular significance for the dominant Christian sects, does not bar the State from achieving its secular goals. . . .
>
> It is true that if the State's interest were simply to provide for its citizens a periodic respite from work, a regulation demanding that everyone rest one day in seven, leaving the choice of the day to the individual, would suffice.
>
> However, the State's purpose is not merely to provide a one-day-in-seven work stoppage. In addition to this, the States seeks to set one day apart from all others as a day of rest, repose, recreation and tranquility —a day which all members of the family and community have the opportunity to spend and enjoy together, a day on which there exists relative quiet and dissociation from the everyday intensity of commercial activities, a day on which people may visit friends and relatives who are not available during working days.
>
> Obviously, a state is empowered to determine that a rest-one-day-in-seven statute would not accomplish this purpose . . . Furthermore, it seems plain that the problems involved in enforcing such a provision would be exceedingly more difficult than those in enforcing a common-day-of-rest provision.
>
> Moreover, it is common knowledge that the first day of the week has come to have special significance as a rest day in this country. People of all religions and people with no religion regard Sunday as a time for family activity, for visiting friends and relatives, for late sleeping, for passive and active entertainments, for dining out, and the like. . . . Sunday is a day apart from all others. The cause is irrelevant; the fact exists. It would seem unrealistic for enforcement purposes

and perhaps detrimental to the general welfare to require a State to choose a common day of rest other than that which most persons would select of their own accord.[1]

Violations of Sunday statutes are common. The extent of criminal enforcement varies in different communities, depending upon local policy.[2] However, regardless of what may be the enforcement wishes and policy of any particular community, the effect of Sunday statutes on contracts is uniform throughout each state. If a contract involves a violation of the Sunday law, a court will not lend its aid to either party to the contract. The court will leave the parties exactly as they were when they came into court; any acts performed on Sunday will not be disregarded or canceled, but any portion of the agreement not yet performed will not be enforced.

Dating an agreement as of some day other than Sunday does not change the effect of the agreement between the parties, if it can be proved that the parties actually entered into the agreement on a Sunday. If an agreement formed on a weekday expressly requires performance in violation of the Sunday law, the agreement is illegal and unenforceable. However, an agreement formed on a day other than Sunday is not made illegal and unenforceable by the fact that some of the negotiations took place on Sunday. Also, even though an agreement is formed on Sunday, if the parties afterwards, on a weekday, manifest their continued mutual agreement, the courts will usually consider the agreement impliedly remade on the weekday and enforce it as such; what was done and said on Sunday can be used to show the terms of the weekday agreement.

Example: On August 1, a Sunday, a seller and buyer entered into an agreement for the sale and purchase of a home freezer for $200. In entering into the agreement the buyer relied upon the seller's stating, "This freezer is in A-1 condition and will maintain a uniform temperature of 15 degrees."

1. The seller delivered the freezer to the buyer on August 1 (Sunday).

a) The buyer's agreement was to pay $200 within 10 days. When the buyer failed to pay, the seller sued. The seller could not recover, since the court would not enforce the buyer's Sunday promise. Neither could the seller recover possession of the freezer. Title was transferred upon delivery to the buyer and the court would not cancel the transfer merely because it occurred

[1] *McGowan* v.*Maryland*, 366 U.S. 420, 81 S. Ct. 1101, 6 L. Ed. (2d) 393 (1961).

[2] It is poor government and a dangerous practice to enact criminal statutes phrased so broadly that exact, complete enforcement is obviously not intended, and then to leave to enforcement officials the discretion to enforce or not to enforce the statutes as they see fit, or as they feel the community desires. The practice is clearly inconsistent with one of the requirements of good government, as recognized and stated so clearly by the founders of the American system of government, "that this shall be a government of laws and not of men."

on a Sunday. If the court were to undo what had been completed on Sunday, the court would to that extent be helping the seller to avoid a loss incurred through his engaging in illegal conduct. The court would leave the parties in the position they were in when they came into court, with the buyer in possession of both the freezer and his money.

b) The buyer paid $200 on delivery August 1. Upon putting the freezer into use, the buyer found that contrary to the seller's statement, the device would not maintain a temperature lower than 30 degrees. Evidence showed that the seller was fully aware of the freezer's defective condition when he made the above quoted statement. The buyer would have no right to recover damages, either for breach of warranty or for fraud. The buyer's loss resulted from his joining in an illegal agreement, and the court would not help him either to enforce the contract or to avoid the resulting loss.

2. The Sunday agreement provided that the seller deliver the freezer to the buyer on Monday and that the buyer pay $200 within one week. Accordingly the seller delivered and the buyer accepted the freezer on Monday. When the buyer failed to pay as agreed, the seller sued. The seller could recover. Delivery and acceptance of the freezer on Monday was conduct showing continued agreement between the parties, and remade the agreement as an enforceable Monday agreement. The court would look to what was said on Sunday for the terms as to price and time for payment.

HOLIDAYS

If the day an agreement is formed is a legal holiday, this is usually immaterial. Many holiday statutes do not prohibit the transaction of business; unless the holiday statute expressly states otherwise, the observance of holidays is permissive rather than compulsory. Thus under a typical holiday statute, a contract made on July 4, for example, would be fully enforceable.

PUBLIC POLICY

Agreements which are contrary to public policy are illegal and unenforceable. What is considered necessary or desirable for the general public is determined by the legislatures, and for situations not covered by statutes, by the courts. Public policy is involved in a wide variety of situations. The principal ones can be classified as follows:

1. Bribery or undue influence of public officers, business executives, agents, and the like. Most such situations are covered by criminal statutes. Even in the absence of statutes, an agreement will be contrary to public policy if it has the tendency to tempt an agent to disregard his duty to his principal, whether or not the principal is thereby injured. (For a further discussion, see Part 2 of Chapter 12.)

2. Exemption from liability for future acts of negligence in types of

transactions which involve businesses catering to the general public or which involve an unreasonable risk of bodily injury to the general public. Such exemption agreements are frequently considered against public policy and unenforceable. Thus if an agreement otherwise valid contains an invalid exemption from liability provision, the provision will be declared unenforceable while the balance of the agreement remains enforceable. (For a further discussion, see Chapter 15.)

Example: The proprietor of a parking lot who stored cars for the general public used claim checks which provided that the proprietor of the lot would have no liability for loss of cars through fire or theft. A car stored in the lot was stolen as a result of negligence in operation of the lot, and the owner of the car sued the lot proprietor.

The proprietor would be liable. On the grounds of public policy, a business which stores goods for hire for the general public is not permitted to contract away its liability for negligence. Even if actually agreed to by the car owner, the exemption provision in the claim check would be invalid and unenforceable.

3. Unreasonable restraints on property and trade. In the absence of statute, the decision as to when restraints are unreasonable must be made by the courts. In general, it is considered in the public interest that owners be free to use and dispose of their property as they wish and that persons be free to engage in whatever businesses they wish, wherever they wish.

a) Restraint on an owner's use or transfer of his property. In general, an absolute, complete restraint is not valid or enforceable, but a partial restraint, to accomplish a reasonable and proper purpose, is not contrary to public policy and is enforceable.

Example: Five persons organize a corporation to operate a small business. Each person owns 200 shares of stock, a 1/5 interest in the business. They want to keep it a "closed" corporation. However they realize that in years to come, one or some of the original five might become dissatisfied and want to sell stock to an outsider, or might die and the stock of the decedent be inherited by his heirs.

1. They agree and make it a part of the corporation rules that none of the stock will be transferable, except to the corporation or another shareholder. This "absolute" restraint on a person's freedom to sell what he owns is against public policy and not enforceable.

2. They agree and make it a part of the corporation rules that before any stock can be sold or transferred, it must first be offered to the other shareholders at the then book value of the stock. This gives the other shareholders "first option" to buy. Any stock not bought by the shareholders when so offered to them will be transferable to outsiders. This partial restraint, to accomplish a reasonable and proper purpose, is not against public policy and is enforceable.

b) Restraints on trade or competition. Generally such a restraint is not against public policy and therefore is enforceable if the restraint meets all of the following conditions:

1) It does not tend to harmfully affect the general public.
2) It is part of an employment contract or a contract for the sale or leasing of a business or property interest.
3) The restraint is limited to what is appropriate for proper protection of the contracting parties. If the restraint is too broad in scope, the court will try to separate the invalid from the valid part of the restraint. If the restraint is not so divisible, the court will not attempt to rewrite the agreement for the parties but instead will declare the entire restraint invalid.

Example: The owner of an established neighborhood grocery store learned that a newcomer planned to build and operate a grocery store across the street. The established owner paid the newcomer $1,000 for the newcomer's agreement that he would not open a grocery store within a radius of one mile of the established store. The newcomer afterwards decided to follow his original plan and build across the street from the established store, and the established owner sued to enforce the agreement.

Not being a part of an employment or sale of business contract, the restraint was against public policy, and would be unenforceable.

Example: The owner of a grocery store in Collegeville, Illinois, (assume a population of 5,000 people) sold the store, equipment, merchandise, and goodwill to a buyer. As part of the contract, the seller agreed that he would not own, operate, work in, or have an interest in a grocery store anywhere in the area described below. A year later the seller planned to build and operate a grocery store across the street from his previous location. The buyer sued for an injunction to restrain the seller from proceeding with his plan.

1. The area described in the agreement was: "Anywhere in Illinois." The restraint extended much further than the area affected by the store. The injunction would be refused.

2. The area described in the agreement was: "Anywhere in Collegeville, Illinois." The restraint was reasonably related to the area affected by the store. The injunction would be granted.

3. The area described in the agreement was: "Anywhere in Collegeville, Illinois, or elsewhere." The court would usually slice off the invalid "or elsewhere" and grant an injunction restraining the seller from associating himself with a grocery store in Collegeville, Illinois.

PROBLEMS

1. By use of a skeleton key, a college student named Sly wrongfully gained entrance to the college stenciling room where final examinations had been prepared and stole from a shelf two ink-stained but legible copies of the final exam prepared for a certain course. He sold one copy to a student for $25 cash, and the other copy to a student who did not have the immediate cash but who promised to pay $35 within five days. Sly assured each buyer that this was the exam to be used for the coming final exam in that particular course. Sly reasonably believed that this was true.

a) On the sixth day and before the date set for the exam, the student who purchased on credit refused to pay for his copy and Sly sued for the agreed $35. Explain whether Sly could recover.

b) The instructor learned what had been done and used another exam as the final exam. The student who had paid for his copy sued Sly to recover the $25 paid. Explain whether he could recover.

2. In January, R. Roger, owner of the Roger Hotel and holder of a liquor license for the premises, hired E. Edwards as manager at a salary of $500 per month to begin March 1, and to continue from month to month until terminated by either party giving the other one week's notice. E assumed his duties on the agreed date and continued for six months when, after a quarrel with R, E gave the proper notice and quit. Never having received any payment for his services, E sued R for $3,000. The facts in the case showed that from the previous December to June 1, E was also the owner and operator of Edward's Restaurant and held a liquor license issued for the restaurant. Also during this same period (ending June 1) E was manager of the local Sportsmen's Club which also had a liquor license. E's connection with the tavern and the club did not in any way detract from the competency with which E performed his job for R, and R had no grounds to complain concerning E's work. In the latter part of May, E decided to reduce his activities and therefore effective June 1, resigned as manager of the club and also sold his tavern and transferred his liquor license. E continued as manager of the Roger Hotel until September 1. The State Liquor Statute provides: "It shall be unlawful for any hotel, restaurant, or club liquor licensee to be, at the same time, employed directly or indirectly by any other person engaged in the sale of liquor, malt, or brewed beverages or alcohol." Explain 1) the reasoning upon which E might attempt to recover in his lawsuit against R, 2) the reasoning upon which R might attempt to defend, and 3) how much if anything E should recover.

3. The promoter of a championship boxing bout sold to the A television network the exclusive rights for television coverage of the bout. The plaintiff, who designed and made a television camera which was battery-operated and small enough to conceal in a press photographer's camera, approached the D television network with a proposal. The parties agreed that the plaintiff would attend the bout and surreptitiously transmit to D network's mobile pickup unit satisfactory television coverage of the bout, for which D network agreed to pay the plaintiff $5,000. The plaintiff performed his part of the agreement with remarkable success but after the bout the A network filed a lawsuit against the D network. Fearing adverse publicity, D network refused to pay the plaintiff the agreed $5,000 and the plaintiff sued. Explain 1) the reasoning upon which the plaintiff could attempt to recover, 2) the reasoning upon which the D network could attempt to defend, and 3) which party should be given judgment.

4. A homeowner approached a builder to inquire about putting asbestos shingles on the owner's house. When he learned the price, the owner said he did not care to have the job done since he expected to sell his house soon. The builder explained that the new siding would increase the value and resale price of the house. The builder also said that he had considerable contact with people looking for homes and would be willing to assist the owner in selling his house, and, since he was not a licensed real estate broker, he would charge the owner only 2 percent commission if successful in negotiating a sale, rather than the standard 5 percent charged by licensed real estate brokers in the area. The owner had the builder put new siding on the house and completely paid for the job. Three months later the owner notified the builder that he wished to sell for $17,000. The builder said he thought the house could be sold for $20,000 and the owner in writing agreed to pay the builder a 2 percent commission if he negotiated a sale. The builder posted in his office a picture of the owner's house with a notation of its availability for $20,000, and during the next few weeks showed several people through the house. Soon the builder secured and brought around to the owner a buyer to whom the owner sold for $20,000. The owner failed to pay the builder the agreed commission and the builder sued the owner. Explain 1) the reasoning upon which the builder might attempt to recover, 2) the reasoning upon which which the owner might attempt to defend, and 3) which party should be given judgment.

5. While making an audit for a businessman, an accountant found among the accounts payable an indebtedness of $2,500 arising from the businessman's purchase of a light motor truck for business purposes. The record showed that the businessman bought the truck from a certain dealer for $3,000, paying $500 down and agreeing to pay the $2,500 balance in three months. The accountant also learned that the dealer's selling price for that type of vehicle was $2,400 if payment was made in cash. In the state where the credit purchase took place, the maximum contract rate of interest permitted by law was 10 percent per year. The accountant wondered whether the transaction was usurious. Explain whether or not it was. (Modified from A.I.C.P.A., May 59-8.)

6. A builder advertised construction of a certain type of dwelling for $7,625, of which the builder would finance $7,125 to be paid off in monthly payments over a period of ten years. A buyer entered into a contract with the builder for construction of such a dwelling on a lot owned by the owner. Upon completion of the building, the buyer paid the builder $500 in cash and gave the builder a mortgage on the house and lot for $11,400 ($7,125 plus ten years' interest on that amount at the rate of 6 percent per year), payable in 120 monthly installments of $95 each. The maximum interest rate permitted by law was 6 percent per year. The buyer paid monthly installments for eight years and then ceased his payments. The builder brought a lawsuit to collect the balance claimed due or to foreclose the mortgage. Explain 1) the reasoning upon which the buyer might attempt to defend, 2) the reasoning upon which the builder might attempt to collect, and 3) what should be the result of the lawsuit.

7. In a state where gambling was and always had been unlawful, a debtor

owed a creditor a gambling debt. The creditor engaged an agent to collect the debt, agreeing that the agent could retain 25 percent of what he collected as his compensation. The agent collected the entire amount of the debt from the debtor but refused to pay any part of it to the creditor. The creditor sued the agent. Explain whether the creditor could recover. (Modified from A.I.C.P.A., Nov. 34-10.)

8. Each of the large number of participants in a bridge tournament paid an entrance fee of $5, most of which, as was announced in the advance publicity, was used to purchase a costly prize for the top scorer. During the playing the disagreeable personality of the player who accumulated the highest score alienated almost everybody, and the ones in charge of the tournament thereupon refused to turn over to him the first prize award. The winner sued. What result?

9. A manufacturer purchased a quantity of raw material. Under the manufacturer's usual production and marketing schedule, the finished article made from this raw material would be sold six months later. To protect himself from loss in case of a drop in the price of the raw material during that six-month period, the manufacturer, at the time that he purchased the raw material, entered into hedging contract to sell a like quantity of raw material six months later. It was the intent of the manufacturer and the plaintiff with whom he made the hedging contract that no materials would be delivered under the contract; rather, after expiration of the six months, the parties would settle at the then market price. The market price of such raw materials rose and at the end of the six-month period was double the price six months earlier. The manufacturer refused to perform his hedging contract and the plaintiff sued. Explain 1) the reasoning upon which the manufacturer might attempt to defend, 2) the reasoning upon which the plaintiff might attempt to enforce the hedging contract, and 3) which party should be given judgment.

10. On the night of Sunday, March 19, a buyer met a seller at a small hotel in a farming community. Upon learning that the buyer wished to purchase some mules for the government, the seller said that he had 15 mules for sale, and the parties went to the hotel yard where 13 of the seller's mules were corralled and looked at them by the light of a lantern. The seller said that his remaining two mules were just like those in the yard and could be turned over to the buyer the next day. The price of $180 apiece was discussed, with the seller assuming the risk of the mules not passing government inspection, but finally the parties agreed on $160 apiece with the buyer to assume that risk. The parties returned to the hotel and the buyer gave the seller a thirty-day note for $2,400, dating it March 20. The parties then told the hotel keeper that the seller's 13 mules had been sold to the buyer and directed that their keep be charged to the buyer for that night. The next day the seller obtained his two additional mules and added them to the ones in the yard and the buyer thereupon took away the 15 mules purchased from the seller. When the buyer failed to pay the note upon its due date, the seller sued. What result? Explain.

11. Immediately after termination of World War II, as civilian production of automobiles returned to normal, demand greatly exceeded supply. Many used-

car dealers acquired new or almost new cars and sold them at prices considerably in excess of the list prices for new cars. New-car dealers wished to curb the operation of such a "gray market." Smith, a new-car dealer operating under the name Smith Agency, adopted the practice of having a buyer to whom he sold and delivered a new car sign the agreement quoted below. B. Brown purchased a new car from S and signed such an agreement. One week later B resold the car to a used-car dealer for more than the price B had paid for the car. A few days later, when S learned of B's resale, S sued B for $500.

a) The agreement signed by B read as follows: "[Date] In consideration of the sale and delivery to B. Brown of the following described new car [then followed a description of the car by make, model, and serial number] and with an intent to be legally bound, B. Brown hereby agrees with the Smith Agency that B. Brown will not sell the above described car nor any interest in said car during the period of six months from the above date. In case of B. Brown's violation of this agreement B. Brown promises to pay to the Smith Agency the sum of $500 as liquidated damages, which sum the Smith Agency will then pay to the local chapter of the American Red Cross. (signed) B. Brown." In S's lawsuit against B, explain 1) the reasoning upon which B might attempt to defend, 2) the reasoning upon which S might attempt to collect, and 3) which party should be given judgment.

b) The agreement signed by B read as follows: "[Date] In consideration of the sale and delivery to B. Brown of the following described new car [then followed a description of the car by make, model, and serial number] and with an intent to be legally bound, B. Brown hereby agrees with the Smith Agency that for the period of six months from the above date B. Brown will not sell the above described car nor any interest in said car without first offering to sell the said car to the Smith Agency for a price equal to the price B. Brown hereby pays for the car less 3 percent per month depreciation. In case of B. Brown's violation of this agreement, B. Brown promises to pay to the Smith Agency the sum of $500 as liquidated damages, which sum the Smith Agency will then pay to the local chapter of the American Red Cross. (signed) B. Brown." Answer the same questions asked in Part (a) of this problem.

12. For 10 years O owned and operated a restaurant in Centerville, Illinois (assume a population of about 5,000 people). Learning that N intended to open a restaurant in the same town, O entered into a written agreement with N under which O paid N $5,000 and N agreed not to operate a restaurant in the area stated below for the next 5 years. A year later N opened a restaurant in Centerville and O sued to enforce the agreement and restrain N from operating his restaurant.

a) In the written agreement, N agreed not to operate a restaurant any place in Illinois. Explain whether O was entitled to win the lawsuit.

b) In the written agreement, N agreed not to operate a restaurant any place in Centerville, Illinois. Explain whether O was entitled to win the lawsuit. (Modified from A.I.C.P.A., May 52-6.)

13. P. Porter, operating a dancing school in Philadelphia, hired Dora Davis for a period of one year, at a stated compensation, as a dancing instructor, supervisor, and interviewer, and at the start of the contract period gave D

a course of training in dance instructing. The written employment agreement signed by both parties contained the following provision:

> "For a period of two years after termination of Miss Davis' employment, she will not, without the written consent of P. Porter, directly or indirectly engage in teaching dancing to any person within a radius of 25 miles from P. Porter's Philadelphia studio."

To obtain the job, D told P that she was 22 years old, although she was actually only 19 years old. At the expiration of the one-year period, D quit P's employment and the following week, opened and started operating a dancing studio in a small town less than 25 miles from P's studio. P sued D for an injunction to restrain her from operating her dancing studio. D raised the defenses of minority and illegality. Explain 1) the reasoning in support of D's defenses, 2) the reasoning in support of P's lawsuit, and 3) the result of the lawsuit.

14. S, a CPA operating a public accounting office, entered into a contract with M Company to perform certain specified accounting services monthly for M Company for one year, for a stated fee. Six months later S sold his office, his practice, and all outstanding contracts to B, another CPA, and agreed in writing with B that S would not perform any accounting services in that city for the next five years. M Company did not wish B to perform the accounting services specified in the contract with S, and demanded that S perform the specified services. S was willing, but B brought a lawsuit against S for an injunction to prevent S from doing so. Explain 1) the reasoning upon which B might attempt to obtain such an injunction, 2) the reasoning upon which S might attempt to defend and prevent issuance of the injunction, and 3) whether the court should grant the injunction.

chapter *9*

Statutes of Frauds

The term "statutes of frauds" is a generic term for a number of statutes, whose purpose is to help protect persons from being unjustly deprived of their rights through false testimony. The need for protection is great. Just how frequently the testimony of witnesses is inaccurate or even completely wrong comes as a considerable surprise to many people. A brief discussion of the fallibility of witnesses, therefore, will be quite helpful.

Most of the uncertainty regarding the outcome of lawsuits is the result of uncertainty concerning the disputed facts of the cases. If conflicting evidence of equal credibility is presented in a lawsuit, it will often be impossible to predict what the court will decide to be the true fact situation. Actually the expression "true fact situation" is a misnomer. As has been quipped, the true facts are known only to God, and He is reserving judgment until a later time. When facts are disputed, the outcome of a lawsuit depends upon the facts that can be satisfactorily proven, rather than on the abstract, elusive notion of a "true" fact situation. Lawyers frankly admit that a person's case is no stronger than his proofs. As Judge Jerome Frank has written:

> The facts of a case, remember, are not what actually happened but, at best, what the trial courts says it thinks happened.[1]

Evidence consisting of a document or some other tangible item gives relatively little difficulty. Usually, however, most of the evidence in a case will consist of the testimony of persons. Sometimes when there are no impartial witnesses, a litigant's own testimony is all the evidence he has; and the testimony of one litigant may conflict with the testimony of the other. If testimony is conflicting, the court (jury, or judge if trial is without a jury) must make the best guess it can as to what the actual facts are.

Because the outcome of most lawsuits is based largely on oral testimony, the courts and honest litigants are to a great extent at the mercy

---

[1]Jerome Frank, *Courts on Trial* (Princeton, N.J.: Princeton U. P., 1949); Atheneum paperback ed., 1963, p. 326.

of clever, convincing liars. Perjury (testifying falsely under oath) is a serious offense; it is a grave moral wrong, and its punishment is severe. Unfortunately, moral restraints are insufficient for a number of people; if they think they can "get away with it," they will lie without hesitation. Very often they *do* get away with it. Society must necessarily make criminal convictions of perjurers quite difficult to obtain. Otherwise the entire trial system would be fatally throttled, because honest witnesses would be afraid to testify for fear of retaliation in the form of perjury prosecutions, however unjustified. Therefore, merely because in a civil dispute the court decides that the facts are different from the testimony of one party does not mean that the party who was not believed can automatically be found guilty of perjury. To convict a person of perjury requires proof not only that he testified falsely but also that he *knew* his testimony was false. For the further protection of honest witnesses, the law usually requires evidence of two witnesses in order to prove perjury, or the evidence of one witness plus additional circumstances indicating perjury. And since criminal guilt is in issue, the evidence must be sufficient to leave no reasonable doubt of guilt.

Although perjurers have been soundly cursed as serious obstructions to the fair operation of any judicial system, many legal scholars believe that an even greater obstacle to the determination of truth is the honestly mistaken witness, so often present in lawsuits. As Judge Frank has written:

> Sir William Eggleston, a noted lawyer . . . expresses the opinion that "no witness can be expected to be more than 50 percent correct, even if perfectly honest and free from preconception.". . .
>
> The axiom or assumption that, in all or most trials, the truth will out, ignores, then, the several elements of subjectivity and chance. It ignores perjury and bias; ignores the false impression made on the judge or jury by the honest witness who seems untruthful because he is frightened in the courtroom or because he is irascible or over-scrupulous or given to exaggeration. It ignores the mistaken witness who honestly and convincingly testifies that he remembers acts or conversations that happened quite differently than he narrates them in court. It neglects, also, the dead or missing witness without whose testimony a crucial fact cannot be brought out, or an important opposing witness cannot be successfully contradicted. Finally it neglects the missing or destroyed letter, or receipt, or cancelled check.[2]

Another legal scholar has written:

> Once the evidence is received, there is the difficult problem of analyzing it and determining its weight. There are legal rules which act as a check, but the task of sifting truth from falsehood, of in-

[2] *Op. cit.*, pp. 18, 20.

ferring the known from the unknown, is determined mainly by the common sense, experience, and subtlety of the tribunal. . . . The fallibility of human testimony is a well-recognized fact today. Apart altogether from perjury and the unconscious twist to our recollection which bias gives, great inaccuracies exist even in the evidence of dis- interested third parties. . . . Scientific research into the nature of the eye has shown how comparatively easy it is for vision to be mis- taken; lack of observation and faulty memory add to the difficulties. Experiments by criminologists have shown the high percentage of error in the reports of a class of students witnessing an unexpected incident. . . . In the hands of an experienced practitioner, cross- examination is a valuable weapon to sift out the truth, but it cannot always be relied on to defeat either a skillful perjurer, or one who has formed a wrong conclusion as to what he saw and with honest stub- bornness sticks to his story.[3]

Professor Hugo Munsterberg, one-time Harvard psychology professor, was one of the leaders in proposing that the courts seek the help of psychology in evaluating the testimony of witnesses. In his book, *On the Witness Stand*, Professor Munsterberg describes numerous in- stances of mistaken observation and recollection, including a dramatic incident deliberately staged as a complete surprise during a scientific association meeting of about forty jurists, psychologists, and physicians. Not only were there numerous omissions in the forty written reports by the "eye witnesses," but,

> . . . there were only six among the forty which did not contain posi- tively wrong statements; in twenty-four papers up to ten percent of the statements were free inventions, and in ten answers—that is, in one-fourth of the papers,—more than ten percent of the statements were absolutely false, in spite of the fact that they all came from scientifically trained observers. . . . The scientific commission which reported the details of the inquiry came to the general statement that the majority of the observers omitted or falsified about half of the processes which occurred completely in their field of vision.[4]

And Professor Munsterberg himself willingly confessed to the same fal- libility, writing:

> Last summer I had to face a jury as witness in a trial. While I was with my family at the seashore my city house had been burglarised and I was called upon to give an account of my findings against the culprit whom they had caught with a part of the booty. I reported under oath that the burglars had entered through a cellar window, and then described what rooms they had visited. To prove, in answer to a direct question, that they had been there at night, I told

[3] Paton, *A Textbook of Jurisprudence*, 2d ed., (London: Oxford U. P., 1951), pp. 487-488.
[4] Hugo Munsterberg, *On the Witness Stand* (New York: Clark Boardman, Ltd., 1908); reprint, 1933, p. 52.

that I had found drops of candle wax on the second floor. To show that they intended to return, I reported that they had left a large mantel clock, packed in wrapping paper, on the dining-room table. Finally, as to the amount of clothes they had taken, I asserted that the burglars did not get more than a specified list which I had given the police.

Only a few days later I found that every one of these statements was wrong. They had not entered through the window, but had broken the lock of the cellar door; the clock was not packed by them in wrapping paper, but in a tablecloth; the candle droppings were not on the second floor, but in the attic; the list of lost garments was to be increased by seven more pieces; and while my story under oath spoke always of two burglars, I do not know that there was more than one. How did all these mistakes occur? . . .

Of course, I had not made any careful examination of the house. I had rushed in from the seashore as soon as the police notified me, in the fear that valuable contents of the house might have been destroyed or plundered. When I saw that they had treated me mildly, inasmuch as they had started in the wine cellar and had forgotten under its genial influence, on the whole, what they had come for, I had taken only a superficial survey. That a clock was lying on the table, packed ready to be taken away, had impressed itself clearly on my memory; but that it was packed in a tablecloth had made evidently too slight an impression on my consciousness. My imagination gradually substituted the more usual method of packing with wrapping paper, and I was ready to take an oath on it until I went back later, at the end of the summer vacation. In the same way I got a vivid image of the candle droppings on the floor, but as, at the moment of perception, no interest was attached to the peculiar place where I saw them, I slowly substituted in my memory the second floor for the attic, knowing surely from strewn papers and other disorder that they had ransacked both places. As to the clothes, I had simply forgotten that I had put several suits in a remote wardrobe; only later did I find it empty. My other two blunders clearly arose under the influence of suggestion. The police and every one about the house had always taken as a matter of course that the entrance was made by a cellar window, as it would have been much more difficult to use the locked doors. I had thus never examined the other hypothesis, and yet it was found later that they did succeed in removing the lock of a door. And finally, my whole story under oath referred to two burglars, without any doubt at the moment. The fact is, they had caught the gentleman in question when he, a few days later, plundered another house. He then shot a policeman, but was arrested, and in his room they found a jacket with my name written in it by the tailor. That alone gave a hint that my house also had been entered; but from the first moment he insisted that there had been two in this burglary and that the other man had the remainder of the booty. The other has not been found . . . but I never heard any doubt as to his existence, and thus, in mere imitation, I never doubted that there was a companion, in spite of the fact that every part of the performance might just as well have been carried out by one man alone; and, after all, it is not impossible that he should lie as well as shoot and steal.

> *In this way, in spite of my best intentions, in spite of good memory and calm mood, a whole series of confusions, of illusions, of forgetting, of wrong conclusions, and of yielding to suggestions were mingled with what I had to report under oath, and my only consolation is the fact that in a thousand courts at a thousand places all over the world, witnesses every day affirm by oath in exactly the same way much worse mixtures of truth and untruth, combinations of memory and of illusion, of knowledge and of suggestion, of experience and wrong conclusions. . . .* Of course, judge and jury and later, the newspaper reader try their best to weigh the evidence. Not every sworn statement is accepted as absolute reality. Contradictions between witnesses are too familiar. But the instinctive doubt refers primarily to veracity. The public in the main suspects that the witness lies, while taking for granted that if he is normal and conscious of responsibility he may forget a thing, but it would not believe that he could *remember the wrong thing.* The confidence in the reliability of memory is so general that the suspicion of *memory illusions* evidently plays a small role in the mind of the juryman, and even the cross-examining lawyer is mostly dominated by the idea that a false statement is the product of intentional falsehood.

> All this is a popular illusion against which modern psychology must seriously protest. Justice would less often miscarry if all who are to weigh evidence were more conscious of the *treachery of human memory*.[5] [Emphasis added.]

Because of the all-too-frequent presence of deliberate perjurers and of honestly mistaken witnesses, businessmen are constantly warned by their lawyers that all important agreements should be in writing or evidenced by written memoranda.

At a fairly early date (1677) in the development of rules of law, of trial procedure, and of commerce, the English Parliament decided as a matter of policy that perjurers and honestly mistaken witnesses constituted sufficient of a threat to require some remedial action. A statute was passed, entitled "An Act for the Prevention of Frauds and Perjuries" (which is commonly shortened to "Statute of Frauds"). In essence the statute provided that:

> 1. Certain types of agreements [chiefly (1) a lease of real estate for more than three years, (2) a transfer or contract to transfer real estate, (3) a promise to pay the debts of another person, (4) an agreement not to be performed within one year from formation] could not be enforced unless put in writing or evidenced by a written memorandum signed by the party transferring or promising.

> 2. Agreements for the sales of goods for ten pounds sterling or more could not be enforced unless evidenced by a writing signed by the party to be bound by the agreement, or unless the goods or a portion of them were delivered or paid for.

[5] *Op. cit.*, pp. 39-44.

Ever since its adoption and continuing to the present day, the wisdom of statutes of frauds has been the subject of vigorous argument. As one writer has noted:

> The appraisals of the Statute's value in modern society range from Llewellyn's "After two centuries and a half the statute stands in essence better adapted to our need than when first passed," to Ireton's observation that the Statute "has proved to be ambiguous, archaic, arbitrary, uneven, unwieldy, unnecessary and unjust."[6]

The original statute of frauds accomplished its purpose—preventing false testimony from foisting nonexistent contracts upon courts and honest defendants—by requiring (in most cases) written evidence in order for contracts covered by the statute to be enforced. Many lawyers and judges feel that the statute has generated as many frauds as it prevents, since it affords many persons who no longer wish to perform their contracts an easy escape, merely because the evidence of formation of the contract happens not to satisfy the statute of frauds. This objection to the general philosophy of statutes of frauds is quite persuasive. If a person must have written evidence of the principal details of a contract in order to bring a lawsuit to enforce it, it is in a sense almost like requiring the state to prove an accused guilty beyond a reasonable doubt in order to have him held for trial, when the purpose of the trial itself is to determine whether or not he is guilty beyond a reasonable doubt. In criminal procedure an accused person's rights are satisfied and he can be held for trial if the state presents enough evidence at the preliminary hearing to show reasonable grounds for suspecting him. The modern thinking on statutes of frauds tends to the view that a plaintiff's initiation of a breach-of-contract lawsuit certainly should not be more difficult than the state's initiation of a criminal prosecution. "All that is required," write the authors of the Uniform Commercial Code,[7] "is that the writing [to satisfy the statute of frauds] afford a basis for believing that the offered oral evidence rests on a real transaction." The modern view as written into the Code applies to sales-of-goods contracts, while the older, more strict view, applies to other types of contracts covered by statutes of frauds.

The effect of a statute of frauds may be likened to a gate across the courtroom doorway. For certain types of contracts, the gate is locked, and a plaintiff must possess the proper key if he wishes to gain entrance to the courtroom in order to sue on an alleged contract. Under the older type of statute of frauds, a fairly elaborate key is necessary; usually a

[6] 40 *Cornell L.Q.* 531 (1955), the quoted references being taken from Llewellyn, "What Price Contract?—An Essay in Perspective," 40 *Yale L. J.* 704 (1931) and Ireton, "Should We Abolish the Statute of Frauds?" 72 *U. S. L. Rev.* 195 (1938).

[7] Comment to U.C.C. Sec. 2-201.

plaintiff must have written evidence which is sufficient in itself to prove that the specific contract in question was actually formed. Under the modern approach, a much simpler key will suffice. If evidence consisting of something other than unsupported oral testimony tends to show that the parties *probably* formed *some* agreement of the general type alleged by the plaintiff, the gate is unlocked. After gaining entrance to the courtroom, the plaintiff then has the chance (even by unsupported oral testimony, if it is believed) to prove the details of the specific contract upon which he is suing.

It should be emphasized that statutes of frauds have *absolutely no relation whatsover* to any fraudulent misrepresentation which might have been used by one party to induce the other to enter into a contract, as discussed in Chapter 7.

Practically all states have statutes of frauds covering certain types of contracts. Although varying somewhat in coverage and details, most of the states to some extent follow the pattern of the English Statute of Frauds. Thus the principal types of contracts in which the law requires additional evidence to corroborate a plaintiff's oral testimony in order for the contract to be provable and enforceable can be classified as follows: 1) leases of real estate, 2) transfers and contracts for the transfer of real estate, 3) guaranties of debt, 4) contracts not to be performed within one year, 5) sales of goods, and 6) any contract after one party to the contract has died.

Often what is required as corroboration is either a written contract or a written memorandum of a contract, signed sometimes by one party, sometimes by both parties. The term "signed" is not restricted in meaning to a manually handwritten signature at the bottom or end of a paper. A valid and binding signature may be typed, printed, or stamped. A printed name on a letterhead may constitute a signature. In general, a name anyplace on the writing, and in any form, is the signature of the one whose name it is if so intended by that person or his authorized agent. Unless required by statute for particular situations, a typed, printed, or stamped signature needs no further authentication. However, as an aid in proving genuineness or authority if either is later questioned, it is wise for a party entering into a contract to request that whoever applies a stamp or uses a document with a typed or printed signature, add his own handwritten signature or initials to aid in later identifying the one making out the writing. Although desirable, witnesses to a signature are not necessary unless required by some special statute. However, if a person unable to write his name signs by making his mark ("X" is a commonly used mark), usually there must be two witnesses to the making of the mark and they must also sign the paper stating that they were witnesses.

LEASES OF REAL ESTATE

The usual statute provides in substance:

> A lease of real property to extend for not more than three years (the period varies, many statutes saying one year) from the agreement date may be in writing, or may be oral, but a lease to extend for more than the statutory period from the agreement date, to be effective for the full term, must be in writing and signed by the parties or by their agents whose authority must be in writing.

The typical statute also applies to assignments and cancellations of written leases which are for longer than the statutory period.

In many states an oral lease which is to extend for more than the statutory period is considered to be a lease at will during the first year, terminable by either party at any time; after the first year of occupancy, the tenancy usually becomes a year-to-year periodic tenancy. The main features of the latter type of tenancy are:

1. The tenant has the right to occupy for the entire leasehold year. (The leasehold year starts at the time stated in the agreement, and does not necessarily coincide with the calendar year.)

2. The landlord has the right to receive rent for the entire leasehold year.

3. Unless the agreement expressly provides otherwise, the tenancy automatically renews itself for another year and continues to do so, until one party gives the other advance notice that he wishes to terminate the tenancy. The notice must be given a certain time in advance of the end of the current leasehold year; how much in advance is generally regulated by statutes in the different states and usually varies from one month in some states to three months in others. In some states the automatic renewal upon failure to give advance notice is in favor of the tenant only. In these states if the tenant moves out before expiration of his leasehold year, he has no liability after expiration of the year, even though he gives the landlord no previous notice of his intent to move (unless the agreement expressly requires such notice). In most states, however, either party, landlord or tenant, who wishes to stop the automatic renewal of a year-to-year tenancy must give proper notice to the other.

TRANSFERS AND CONTRACTS TO TRANSFER REAL ESTATE

When purchases are quite costly, and especially when real estate is purchased, a transfer is usually made in two steps. First the parties enter into a contract by which they agree that at a stated future date the seller will transfer the described property and the buyer will pay the stated price; then later, at the agreed time, they complete the transaction, transferring title and paying the price. In most states neither a contract to transfer real estate nor an actual transfer of real estate will be effective unless evidenced by a written memorandum which identifies or describes the parties, the price, and the real estate involved. In some states the memorandum must be signed by the party against whom an attempt is being made to enforce the agreement—that is, it must be signed by the buyer if the seller is suing to enforce the alleged agreement against the buyer, or it must be signed by the seller if the buyer is suing the seller. In other states the memorandum only needs to be signed by the seller. In such states a seller can enforce an oral land-purchase contract against a buyer but the buyer cannot enforce the oral agreement against the seller.

In interpreting and applying real estate statutes of frauds, the courts are ever mindful of the reason for the statutes. If a buyer sufficiently relies on a seller's oral transfer or contract to transfer in a way that clearly corroborates the existence of such an agreement, many courts will enforce the agreement against the seller even in the absence of a written memorandum. In defining the limits of this "exception" to the real estate statutes of frauds, the courts weigh principles of fairness and justice on one side against the policy reasons for statutes of frauds on the other side, with some reference to the ancient common law method of transferring real estate—by going on the land and handing the buyer a lump of earth (or some other appropriate symbol) while stating words of transfer. As can be expected in matters of policy, the courts in different states vary somewhat in their opinions as to exactly what conduct will be sufficient to make a seller's oral transfer or contract to transfer enforceable without a writing. In many states, the following conditions must all be present: 1) the terms of the oral contract must be clear and definite, 2) the buyer must take exclusive possession under the agreement, and 3) there must be some additional circumstances making it extremely unfair to the buyer not to enforce the agreement. For example, many courts have held a seller's oral agreement enforceable if (the first two conditions also being present) the buyer has paid the seller the entire purchase price, or the buyer has constructed substantial, permanent improvements on the premises.

Whether a particular case can be brought under the exception will usually be uncertain until litigated. It is, therefore, unwise for a buyer to rely on this exception. He should insist upon having all real estate agreements put in writing and signed by the seller.

GUARANTIES OF DEBT

Most states have guaranty-of-debt statutes of frauds which usually provide something like the following:

No action shall be brought to charge a person upon any promise to answer for the debt or default of another person, unless the agreement upon which such action shall be brought, or some memorandum of it, shall be in writing and signed by the party to be charged or by his duly authorized agent.

The agent's authority is usually not required to be in writing.

A guarantor is a person (or business) who agrees to pay a debt which is not primarily his own debt. The one primarily liable for the debt is usually called the principal debtor. A guarantor promises that he will pay the amount of the debt to the principal debtor's creditor if the debtor himself should fail to pay. If the principal debtor does default so that the guarantor is forced to make good on his promise to pay the creditor, the guarantor will succeed to the creditor's rights and in turn be entitled to recover from the principal debtor.

Sometimes the term "guarantor" is used in a narrower sense, in contradistinction to the term "surety." The distinction is a procedural one. A surety promises to pay if the principal debtor *does not* pay when due, and a guarantor (when the term is used in its narrower sense) promises to pay if the principal *cannot* pay. Therefore, to collect from a guarantor (narrower sense) the creditor usually must first sue the debtor, attempt to collect, and by reason of the debtor's insolvency be unsuccessful. In contrast, a creditor has a right to collect from a surety as soon as the principal debtor defaults, without the necessity of first attempting to collect from the debtor. A number of states declare by statute that a person promising to pay the debt of another is a surety unless the agreement specifies otherwise. The indorser of a check, note, or draft under the Uniform Commercial Code[8] can indicate his intent with respect to this procedural distinction by writing "payment guaranteed," and become a surety, or "collection guaranteed," and become a guarantor in the narrower sense, as distinguished from a surety. In the present discussion, the term guarantor (except when specified otherwise) is used in its broader sense, including both guarantors (in the narrower sense) and sureties.

There must of course be consideration, or a recognized equivalent of consideration (see Chapter 5) in order for a guarantor's promise to be legally enforceable. If a guaranty promise is made either prior to or at the same time the principal debt arises, the act of the creditor in extending credit to the debtor is usually the agreed consideration for the guarantor's promise. On the other hand, if a guaranty promise is made after the principal debt is already in existence, separate consideration is necessary, such as the creditor's giving the debtor more time on the debt, or the guarantor's being paid a sum of money for his guaranty promise.

[8] U.C.C. Sec. 3-416.

The general philosophy of guaranty-of-debt statutes of fraud is quite sound. Suppose that a seller is claiming a right to recover $500 from a guarantor for certain goods which were sold and delivered to a buyer on thirty days' credit. If the seller were suing the buyer, the fact that the seller delivered the goods to the buyer would tend to corroborate the seller's testimony, showing at least that some transaction involving the delivered goods had occurred between the parties. However, the seller's making a delivery to the buyer is not an act which necessarily involves the guarantor at all. An unpaid seller might conceivably pick any name from the telephone book and dishonestly allege that that person had guaranteed the buyer's payment. Since an ordinary guarantor derives no direct benefit from an extension of credit and is not otherwise brought into the picture by the facts, the basic policy of guaranty-of-debt statutes of frauds is to require that a plaintiff have something more than oral testimony and the fact that credit was extended to a debtor, in order to hold a guarantor liable. The statutes uniformly require a signed writing for this purpose. In some guaranty situations, however, special facts are present which afford some corroboration without written evidence. For such special situations, statute-of-frauds protection is unnecessary, and most courts accordingly hold that in such situations the statutes of frauds do not apply. These special situations in which the courts are usually willing to enforce oral promises to pay the debts of other persons include the following:

1) Guarantor Receiving Direct Benefit. If (different from the customary guaranty transaction) the facts in a particular case show that a guarantor himself was directly benefited by the extension of credit to the debtor, this tends to corroborate the creditor's testimony that the guarantor actually did promise to guaranty the debtor's repayment. Under such circumstances oral guaranties have frequently been enforced.

Example: A builder contracted with a landowner to build a house on the latter's lot. A supplier who had previously been extending credit to the builder, refused to make any further deliveries until the builder paid for his prior purchases of materials which he had used in other construction jobs. The landowner who was well known to the supplier, called him on the telephone and said: "If you will let the builder have the materials he needs for use in the house he is building for me, I'll guaranty his payment for such materials."

Many courts would enforce the oral guaranty.

2) Guarantor Undertaking Direct Obligation. Sometimes a promisor enters into a contract with a debtor under which (for a certain consideration) the promisor agrees that he will pay an obligation which the debtor owes to some third party. In making such a promise, the promisor is not really guaranteeing the debtor's obligation but rather is undertaking a direct obligation on his own part. Thus the courts in most states hold that while a guaranty-of-debt statute of frauds will apply to a promise which the promisor makes to a *creditor* (promising to pay the debt which the debtor owes to the creditor), the statute does not apply to a promise which the promisor makes to a *debtor,* to the effect that the promisor will pay the debtor's obligation. The contract between the promisor and the debtor is an independent, third-party-beneficiary contract upon which the creditor can recover (as discussed in Chapter 10), even though the promise is oral.

Similarly, a promisor is considered as undertaking a direct obligation of his own rather than merely guaranteeing another's prior obligation when, at a debtor's request or with his authorization, the promisor makes a promise to a creditor to the effect that the promisor will pay the debtor's obligation out of funds which belong to the debtor and which the promisor has or will acquire for that purpose. For example, suppose a debtor delivers certain goods to a factor with oral instructions to sell the goods and to use the proceeds to pay an obligation which the debtor owes to a certain creditor. If the factor notifies the creditor of the arrangement, and orally assures him that he will pay the debtor's obligation from the proceeds of the sale, the factor is in a sense orally promising the creditor that he will pay the debtor's debt. However, the factor is really promising nothing more than he has already undertaken to do in his agreement with the debtor. The creditor is a third-party beneficiary of the factor-debtor contract and courts in most states hold that the creditor can enforce this contract against the factor.

PROMISES NOT TO BE PERFORMED WITHIN ONE YEAR

The original English Statute of Frauds provided:

> . . . from and after the said fower and twentyeth day of June noe action shall be brought . . . upon any agreement that is not to be performed within the space of one yeare from the makeing thereof unlesse the agreement upon which such action shall be brought or some memorandum or note thereof shall be in writing and signed by the partie to be charged therewith or some other person thereunto by him lawfully authorized.

The results of this provision are sometimes as odd as the seventeenth-century spelling. Suppose an oral contract is formed hiring someone for a year and a day. Even though the employment contract would impliedly be subject to the employee's continuing to live, the terms of the contract express no such qualification. By the terms of the contract it is not to be performed within one year and, therefore, if not in writing, the contract would be unenforceable. On the other hand, an oral contract to hire someone for life would be perfectly valid. By its terms it is possible to perform it within one year from the time it is made, since the employee might die at anytime. Therefore, even though he continues to live for fifty years longer, the contract would continue to be fully enforceable.

It is understandable that this provision of the original Statute of Frauds has provoked considerable criticism. In fact, while preserving in other more modern statutes most of the effect of the original Statute of Frauds, the English Parliament has repealed the original Statute and by doing so has abandoned any attempt to draw a one-year time-line between oral and written contracts. Some states also make no distinction, but the statutes of frauds in many states still draw the one-year line.

SALES OF GOODS[9]

The Uniform Commercial Code contains a statute of frauds section applicable to sales-of-goods contracts, with $500 as the operative amount. A contract for the sale of goods costing less than $500 is enforceable whether proved by written evidence or by uncorroborated oral testimony, but a contract involving a sale of goods for the price of $500 or more requires some sort of corroboration to be enforceable. Under the modern view which the Code follows, any of several different types of corroboration will suffice. The most obvious type of corroboration consists of a written memorandum signed by the alleged promisor (that is, the person against whom an attempt is being made to enforce the alleged contract promise). Under certain conditions a written memorandum signed by the alleged promisee (the party who is attempting to enforce the alleged contract promise) will be sufficient. Other circumstances which show sufficient corroboration in the absence of a written memorandum are: 1) special manufacture, 2) admission in a lawsuit, and 3) payment for or acceptance of goods.

WRITTEN CORROBORATION

Signed by the Promisor

For the usual type of written corroboration to be adequate, the Code requires:

> . . . some writing sufficient to indicate that a contract for sale has been made between the parties and signed by the party against whom enforcement is sought or by his authorized agent or broker. A writing is not insufficient because it omits or incorrectly states a term agreed upon but the contract is not enforceable under this paragraph beyond the quantity of goods shown in such writing.

[9] U.C.C. Sec. 2-201.

As the authors of the Code explain:

> Only three definite and invariable requirements as to the memorandum are made by this subsection. First, it must evidence a contract for the sale of goods; second, it must be "signed," a word which includes any authentication which identifies the party to be charged; and third, it must specify a quantity.[10]

Thus the written memorandum need not state other terms of the alleged contract, such as the amount to be paid, method of payment, time and place of delivery, quality of goods, etc. Oral testimony is adequate to prove these terms.

Signed by the Promisee

Recall the well-known adage that a person cannot pull himself up by his own bootstraps. Likewise a person who writes and signs a memorandum usually cannot expect his own signature to prove anything at all against someone else. However, if the nonsigning person sees the memorandum at a time when he could be expected to object if it were not true, his failure to object tends to corroborate the truth of the writing. Under the Code, if a written memorandum is signed by the party who is attempting to enforce an alleged contract, the memorandum is useable against the other party and is sufficient corroboration to satisfy the statute of frauds if *all* of the following conditions are present:

1. Both parties are businessmen acting in their mercantile capacity.

2. The writing was sent to the other party in confirmation of the alleged contract and would constitute sufficient corroboration to satisfy the statute of frauds if the sender were being sued on the alleged contract.

3. The writing was received by the party to whom sent within a reasonable time after formation of the contract (if a letter correctly addressed and stamped is properly mailed, it is presumed to be received by the addressee in due course of time; if the addressee denies receipt, a jury may nevertheless conclude that the letter was received, especially if the envelope bore a return address and was never returned).

4. Within ten days the recipient did not send written objection to the contents of the writing.

It should be emphasized that failure to object under the above conditions merely indicates that *probably* a contract was formed between the parties. It is sufficient corroboration to open the statute-of-frauds gate and permit the plaintiff (the sender of the written memorandum) to enter the courtroom. As the authors of the Code point out:

> The only effect . . . is to take away from the party who fails to answer the defense of the Statute of Frauds; the burden of persuading the

[10] Comment to U.C.C. Sec. 2-201.

trier of fact [the jury or the judge if the trial is held without a jury] that a contract was in fact made orally prior to the written confirmation is unaffected.[11]

Corroboration Without Written Memorandum

Special Manufacture

Generally a manufacturer will not undertake the expense of producing something which will be of value to only one particular buyer unless the latter has actually contracted to buy it. Admittedly this is not conclusive proof that a contract has been formed, but the special manufacture of unique goods *tends* to indicate that a contract exists. It is sufficient to enable the manufacturer to unlock the statute-of-frauds gate and gain entrance to the court, where he then has the chance to enforce the contract, *if* he can satisfy the court by oral testimony that such a contract was actually formed. The operative facts for this situation are stated by the Code as follows:

> A contract which does not satisfy the requirements of subsection (1) [which pertains to written memoranda] but which is valid in other respects is enforceable . . . if the goods are to be specially manufactured for the buyer and are not suitable for sale to others in the ordinary course of the seller's business and the seller, before notice of repudiation is received and under circumstances which reasonably indicate that the goods are for the buyer, has made either a substantial beginning of their manufacture or commitments for their procurement . . .

Note that the Code (like the prior Uniform Sales Act in this respect)[12] does not prescribe a percentage of unsuitability. All that is required is that the goods be "not suitable for sale to others in the ordinary course of the seller's business," with no express reference concerning how much (or little) it might cost to make the goods suitable for others after the buyer repudiates the contract.

Admisson in Lawsuit

As the authors of the Code explain:

> If the making of a contract is admitted in court, either in a written pleading, by stipulation or by oral statement before the court, no additional writing is necessary for protection against fraud. Under this section it is no longer possible to admit the contract in court and still treat the Statute [statute of frauds] as a defense. However, the contract is not thus conclusively established. The admission so made by

[11] Comment to U.C.C. Sec. 2-201.
[12] Uniform Sales Act, Sec. 4.

a party is itself evidential against him of the truth of the facts so admitted and of nothing more . . .[13]

The plaintiff can go ahead and prove by oral testimony the details of the actual contract between the parties and enforce it, but only for the quantity of goods admitted.

Payment for or Acceptance of Goods

The Code states that a contract is enforceable,

. . . with respect to goods for which payment has been made and accepted or which have been received and accepted. [Goods are "accepted" when they are retained by the buyer in a manner which indicates that he considers them as belonging to him.[14]]

In other words, such conduct of the parties is sufficient indication that a contract exists so that oral testimony can be safely relied upon. Note that the contract is enforceable only as to the portion of goods paid for or accepted. If the subject matter of the contract cannot be apportioned, a part performance is not corroboration and will not make an oral contract enforceable for any quantity.

ORAL MODIFICATION OF WRITTEN CONTRACTS

After a contract has been formed, one of the parties will sometimes assert that the parties entered into a later agreement modifying or canceling the original contract. The mere fact that the original agreement was in writing ordinarily will not prevent a later oral change or cancellation, and the later agreement can be proved by oral testimony without any need for corroboration. However, if the original agreement was one to which a statute of frauds applied, the same statute would have to be satisfied for the alleged later agreement to be enforceable.

Example: A landlord and tenant signed a written agreement, leasing certain described premises to the tenant for six months, at a monthly rental of $100 payable in advance on the first of each month. Four months later, they orally agreed to shorten the total duration of the lease to five months, and at the end of the fifth month the tenant moved out. The landlord thereupon changed his mind about the modification and sued the tenant for the sixth month's rent.

Part 1. Society believes that persons should be fairly free to make whatever contracts they wish, even several contracts which, in succession, cancel or modify their previous contracts. Therefore, if the original six-month lease had been oral, certainly no rule of law would prevent the parties from later

[13] Comment to U.C.C. Sec. 2-201.
[14] U.C.C. Sec. 2-606.

orally changing it to a five-month lease. (Note that the duration of the lease is too short for the ordinary type of statute of frauds to apply and require a written memorandum.) Merely because the original six-month lease was in writing would be no reason to deny to the parties the same freedom of contract. Therefore so long as they actually agreed, the change from a six-month lease to a five-month lease would be effective, whether oral or in writing.

Part 2. Suppose that the original written lease also contained the following provision: "This lease agreement cannot be added to, altered, or rescinded except by written agreement signed by both parties hereto."

As pointed out in Part 1 above, the mere fact that an agreement is put in writing is no reason to prohibit its later oral modification. If therefore parties have both the power and the right to orally modify their previous written agreement, then their oral modification agreement will automatically modify or rescind that portion of their written agreement which states that it cannot be orally modified. For this reason the rule developed at common law that the quoted restrictive provision is ineffective; the parties could still validly change the lease to a five-month lease by their later *oral* agreement.

The reasoning in Part 2 of the preceding example is indisputably sound legal theory. However, businessmen frequently include restrictive provisions in their contracts (to the effect that no changes can be made except by written memoranda), and do so in order to avoid the risk of litigation and possible loss, should one party later dishonestly allege that an oral modification was made. A policy question is thus raised—should the law continue to recognize full freedom of contract, including the freedom to change as well as to make contracts, or instead should the law give legal effect to the assumption of businessmen that a restriction on oral modifications means something? For sales-of-goods contracts the authors of the Code feel that the latter choice is the better policy. In effect, therefore, the Code permits parties to add to the ordinary statute-of-frauds situations by writing their own statute of frauds in regard to any future modification of a written sales-of-goods contract. To accomplish this, the Code states:

> A signed agreement which excludes modification or rescission except by a signed writing cannot be otherwise modified or rescinded, but except as between merchants such a requirement on a form supplied by the merchant must be separately signed by the other party.[15]

Thus for sales-of-goods contracts, if the original agreement is in writing and expressly states that it cannot be amended or canceled except by a signed writing, any later attempt to change the original contract by oral agreement will not be effective, even if the price is less than $500.

[15] U.C.C. Sec. 2-209.

DEATH OF ONE CONTRACTING PARTY

The fact that no statute of frauds applies for many types of contracts reflects the decision of the legislature that, as a matter of policy, the risk of perjured and honestly mistaken testimony is not so great as to justify a general rule declaring such contracts unenforceable unless corroborated. In such situations the only protection a person has against perjured and honestly mistaken testimony is his own testimony in rebuttal. If the person has died, the representative of his estate may often be at a disadvantage; the representative may know nothing about an alleged transaction and the decedent of course is no longer available to deny claims made against him. In almost all states the legislatures feel that even in situations not otherwise coming under a statute of frauds, if one contracting party has died, the risk of false claims is sufficiently great to require relief. In most states the relief consists of a rule barring the surviving party from testifying. The typical statute can be summarized as follows:

> Where any party to a thing or contract is dead (or has been adjudged a lunatic), any surviving or remaining party to such thing or contract, or any other person whose interest shall be adverse to the right of the decedent (or lunatic) party, shall not be a competent witness to any matter occurring before the death of said party (or the adjudication of his lunacy). [Usually such statutes do not apply to litigation involving the rights of partners among themselves.]

The effect of such a statutory provision is that if death has closed the mouth of one party, the law will close the mouth of the other party. If, without using his own testimony or the testimony of any other person with an interest adverse to the decedent's, the surviving party can prove the existence and terms of a contract, he can enforce it against the decedent's estate, otherwise not.

Example: A and B were partners operating a business, A agreeing that all control and management be in B's hands. For the business, B orally contracted for and received labor and materials from S, in the amount of $3,000. B died several months later. A few months after B's death, S presented his claim for $3,000. This was the first that A knew of any contract made with S, and the partnership records did not refer to the contract. S sued A.

S would not be competent to testify to any dealings with B, the decedent. If S could prove his claim by some written memorandum or by the testimony of an impartial witness, S could collect, otherwise not.

PROBLEMS

1. By oral agreement a landlord leased a certain described house and lot to a tenant at an annual rental of $1,200, payable monthly in advance, and the

tenant began occupancy on the effective date of the lease. No mention was
made as to any right to cancel. (Assume that the statute of frauds of the
state involved prescribed a three-year period for real estate leases.

a) The agreement was entered into on February 1 of a certain year, for
three years starting the same day. 1) On June 20 of that year, the landlord
decided he wished to terminate the arrangement. What was the earliest date
the landlord could end the tenant's legal right to occupy? Explain. 2) On
June 20 of the following year, the landlord decided he wished to terminate the
arrangement. What was the earliest date the landlord could end the tenant's
legal right to occupy? Explain.

b) The agreement was entered into on February 1 of a certain year, for
four years starting the same day. 1) Same additional fact as in Part (1)
above. Answer the same question. 2) Same additional fact as in Part (2)
above. Answer the same question.

c) The agreement was entered into on January 21 of a certain year for
three years starting February 1 of that year. 1) Same additional fact as in
Part (1) above. Answer the same question. 2) Same additional fact as in
Part (2) above. Answer the same question.

2. S owned a vacant lot which adjoined his house at 459 West 28th Street.
On the other side of the lot was a house numbered 463 West 28th Street. S
orally agreed to sell the lot to B for the price stated below.

a) At the time of their oral agreement, B signed and gave S a check on
a local bank, made out to S for the full price, and S said that he would give B
possession and a deed in two weeks. On the check B wrote the following:
"In full payment for vacant lot between 459 and 463 West 28th Street, this
city." A few days later S returned the check to B and refused to go ahead
with the sale. S had not yet indorsed the check in any way. B sued S for
specific performance of the contract and offered the check in evidence. 1)
The price upon which S and B orally agreed and for which the check was made
out was $400. Briefly explain (a) the reasoning upon which S might attempt
to defend, (b) the reasoning upon which B might attempt to win, and (c)
whether the court should decree specific performance of the agreement.
2) The price upon which S and B orally agreed and for which the check was
made out was $600. Would your answers be the same as in Part (1) above?
3) Explain whether your answers in Parts (1) or (2) above would be affected
by assuming the following additional fact: W, an impartial person with no
interest in the agreement, was present when S and B reached their oral agreement; W recalls and is available to testify to what S and B said and did.

b) The price upon which S and B orally agreed was $1,000. Upon reach-
ing their agreement B paid S $100 in cash as a down payment and S gave B
the following receipt, after writing the date and name of their city on the
receipt: "Received from B. Brown $100 to apply on purchase of lot between
459 and 463 W. 28 Street, this city. (signed) S Smith." 1) A few days later
B changed his mind about purchasing and so notified S. S insisted that B go
through with the agreement, tendered a deed to B and demanded $900, and
upon B's refusal, S sued B for $900. Explain (a) the reasoning upon which B
might attempt to defend, (b) the reasoning upon which S might attempt to

collect, and (c) which party should be given judgment. 2) A few days later S changed his mind about selling and so notified B, offering to return the $100 to B. B refused to accept return of the money and sued S for specific performance of the contract, offering S's receipt in evidence. Explain (a) the reasoning upon which S might attempt to defend, (b) the reasoning upon which B might attempt to win, and (c) whether the court should decree specific performance of the agreement.

3. B wished to buy goods on credit from S. S refused to sell except for cash, whereupon G who was favorably known to S called S on the telephone and said, "If you sell goods to B on 30 days' credit and B fails to pay, I'll pay up to the amount of $300." S thereupon sold $200 worth of goods to B on 30 days' credit and notified G of the sale. B failed to pay when due and S sued and obtained judgment against B. Because of B's insolvency, S could not collect. S then sued G.

a) G denied liability on the ground that he received nothing for his promise. Explain whether this defense would be good.

b) Explain what other defense G might attempt to raise.

c) Explain whether S could collect from G.

4. B was 20 years old, had a full-time job, and although he still lived with his parents, he was permitted to retain all of his earnings except for an agreed amount which he paid for room and board. B with his father, F, went to S's store where B looked at two new suits priced at $100 apiece. Although the additional suits were not necessary, B said he would like to buy them and requested 30 days' credit. S apologetically refused credit because of B's age. F then made the proposal quoted below. S agreed and delivered the suits to B. When B failed to pay within 30 days, S sued F.

a) In inducing S to deliver the suits to B, F said: "Let my son have the suits on 30 days' credit and if he fails to pay, I'll pay." Explain whether S could recover in his lawsuit against F.

b) In inducing S to deliver the suits to B, F said, "Let my son have the suits and charge them to me." Explain whether S could recover in his lawsuit against F.

5. B. Berg owned and operated a retail clothing store under the name "Berg's Men's Shop." B stocked suits manufactured by several different manufacturers. The labels in the suits read, "Tailored Especially for Berg's Men's Shop, Centertown, Illinois, by [name of manufacturer]." His stock of suits manufactured by S being low, B called S on the phone and placed an order for fifty suits of specified styles, sizes, and colors, as stated in S's catalog, at a stated price totaling over $500. Each suit was to have the label quoted above sewn in the usual place on the inside lining of each suitcoat. S orally accepted the order. Three weeks later S had the suits ready for shipment when B canceled the order. S sued B for damages for breach of contract.

a) Assume that S manufactured the fifty suits after receiving B's order. Explain 1) the reasoning upon which S might attempt to collect, 2) the reasoning upon which B might attempt to defend, and 3) which party should be given judgment.

b) Assume that S had in stock sufficient suits to fill B's order and all that S did to prepare them for shipment was to attach the proper labels. Answer the same three questions asked in Part (a) above.

6. a) B. Brown, a university professor of history, went to the store of S. Smith, a dealer, and orally ordered a television set of a particular make and model for the total price of $600, to be delivered to B's home within two weeks and installed in B's living room. S orally accepted the order and B made a down payment of $100 in cash. S made out and gave to B the following receipt: "[Date] Received from B. Brown $100 to apply on TV set. (signed) S. Smith." 1) When S tendered delivery of the set according to the oral agreement, B refused to accept delivery, saying that he had changed his mind about making the purchase. S sued B for damages for breach of contract. Would S be entitled to obtain judgment? Explain. 2) S refused to deliver at the agreed time and B sued S for damages for breach of contract. Would B be entitled to obtain judgment? Explain.

b) Assume the same facts as in Part (a, 1) except for the following change: When S sued B for damages for breach of contract, B filed a counterclaim in the same lawsuit to recover the $100 he had paid, alleging the facts of his oral order, payment, and refusal to receive delivery. What would be the outcome of the lawsuit? Explain.

c) B. Brown, a university professor of history, orally ordered a television set of a stated make and model from S. Smith, a dealer, for $400, to be delivered to B's home in two weeks and installed in his living room. B made no down payment. S orally accepted the order and later sent to B a signed written confirmation, entitled "Purchase Memorandum No. 1208," containing all of the terms of the order. A duplicate of the purchase memorandum was enclosed with a request that B sign and return it to S. B kept both copies without signing either. When S tendered delivery of the set according to the oral agreement, B refused to accept delivery, saying that he had changed his mind about making the purchase. S sued B for damages for breach of contract. Would S be entitled to obtain judgment? Explain.

d) Assume the same facts as in Part (c) except for the following change: The total price was $600. Answer the same question as is asked in Part (c).

e) Assume the same facts as in Part (c) except for the following changes: The total price was $600. Two days after receiving the "Purchase Memorandum No. 1208," B dated and sent the following note to S: "To S. Smith: Referring to your Purchase Memorandum No. 1208, please be advised that I am canceling this order. (signed) B. Brown." What would be the result of S's lawsuit against B? Explain.

f) Assume the same facts as in Part (c), except for the following changes: The total price was $600. S refused to deliver at the agreed time and B sued S for damages for breach of contract. Would B be entitled to obtain judgment? Explain.

g) B. Brown, owner and operator of a hotel, orally ordered a television set of a stated make and model from S. Smith, a dealer, for $1,000, to be delivered in two weeks, and installed in the hotel lounge. B made no down payment. S orally accepted the order and later sent B a written confirmation, entitled "Purchase Memorandum," containing all of the terms of the order.

A duplicate copy of the purchase memorandum was enclosed with a request that B sign and return it to S. B kept both copies without signing either. When S tendered delivery of the set according to the oral agreement, B refused to accept delivery, saying that he had changed his mind about making the purchase. S sued B for damages for breach of contract. Was S entitled to obtain judgment? Explain. (Modified from A.I.C.P.A., Nov. 50-10.)

7. On May 14 L and T signed a written lease agreement under which L leased to T for one year beginning June 1, of the same year, the business premises known as 17 East 10th Street in a specified city, and T agreed to pay a total rent of $3,600, payable monthly in $300 installments at the beginning of each month. The lease contained the following provision: "This lease agreement cannot be added to, altered, or rescinded except by written agreement signed by both parties hereto." T took possession on June 1 and was making payments as agreed when on September 15, T told L that business conditions were poor and that he would be unable to continue using the premises at the agreed rental. L asked if $200 per month would be satisfactory. When T replied "Yes," L said, "All right, I'll agree that beginning this October 1, and for the balance of the lease period, the total monthly rent will be $200." T agreed to this proposal, thanked L, and paid $200 to L on October 1. T made this payment by his own check which was drawn on a local bank, named L as payee, and contained no notation concerning its purpose. L promptly indorsed the check (by signing his name on the back) and cashed it. On October 27 L phoned T that he had changed his mind, that he wanted another $100 for October, and that T would have to pay $300 on November 1. T objected, and on November 1 tendered to L a check for $200, marked "Payment of rent in full to November 30, this year, for 17 East 10th Street, this city." L refused the check and sued T.

a) What result? Explain.

b) Other facts remaining the same, assume that T marked on his October 1, check, "The October rent in full for 17 East 10th Street, this city." Would this additional fact affect the result in L's lawsuit against T? Explain.

8. B. Brown, shopping for a living-room suite, visited S. Smith's retail store and looked at a display. On the sofa of the display was a tag reading "Smith Furniture Store. Living room suite. Manufactured by Martin Company, Model 220. Price $600." B stated that he wished to buy the suite and S slipped a red "sold" tag on the same string that held the price tag. Printed on the red tag were the words, "Sold. Smith Furniture Store," and written on the tag by S was the name, "B. Brown." B said he would return in about an hour and make a partial payment of $200 and would pay the balance within thirty days. To this S agreed. Before B returned, P, a friend of S's, came into the store and said he would like to buy the living-room suite. S expected another shipment soon and thought B would not mind waiting, and so drew a line through B's name on the red tag and wrote P's name. When B returned he insisted upon receiving this particular living-room suite and when S refused, B sued for damages. Explain 1) the reasoning upon which S might attempt to defend, 2) the reasoning upon which B might attempt to recover, and 3) which party should be given judgment.

9. a) A printer contacted a milk dealer to interest him in ordering calendars to give to his customers. The printer showed the dealer a certain type of calendar with a sample of the advertising statement which could be printed on the calendars along with the dealer's name, and quoted the price for 1,000 calendars as $200, payable thirty days after delivery. The following day the dealer phoned the printer and ordered 1,000 calendars of the type which the printer had showed to the dealer, and with the printing on them that the printer had described. The printer accepted the order during the phone conversation. Within a reasonable time the printer had the calendars ready for delivery, but the dealer died from a sudden heart attack. The dealer's will appointed his son as executor and left all of his property to his son. The dealer's business records contained no reference to the transaction with the printer. The dealer's son assumed operation of the business but refused to accept the calendars. The printer sued the son as executor for damages for breach of contract. Explain 1) the reasoning upon which the printer could attempt to collect, 2) the reasoning upon which the son could attempt to defend, and 3) which party should be given judgment.

b) Other facts being the same, assume the following additional facts: The calendars were delivered to the dealer, but no receipt was given for them. The dealer distributed the calendars among his customers, and had about 100 left over in his office when he suffered the heart attack and died without making any payment for the calendars. When the son as executor refused to pay, the printer sued for the agreed price for the calendars. Explain whether your answers would be different than in Part (a) above.

chapter *10*

Multiple Parties, Co-ownership, and Remote Parties

Part 1 MULTIPLE PARTIES AND CO-OWNERSHIP

While a contract always requires two persons, one on each side of the agreement, nothing prevents more than two persons from joining together in the same contract. For example, in a contract to purchase certain property, two persons (or even more than two) can join together on one side of the contract, both (or all) binding themselves to purchase the property from the seller. When several persons join as buyers, they all acquire rights and obligations under the contract. Whether the co-buyers must be joined together as co-parties when a lawsuit is brought to enforce the contract is a procedural question of concern to lawyers. The important point being emphasized here is that several persons acting in concert can acquire rights as co-owners (and undertake obligations) just as readily as one person can.

When the property in question is real estate, note that a definite distinction exists between co-owners and adjoining owners. If A and B *co-own* a piece of land with two identical buildings, each owns an undivided one-half interest in the total property, comprising the land and both buildings. On the other hand if A and B are adjoining owners of, for example, a two-unit connected or row dwelling building, A owns one of the row homes and B the other. A and B are not co-owners of the entire structure. Each is a separate owner of one of the units, just as if the two units were not physically connected. They are co-owners of nothing more than the common wall which forms one side of each of the two homes.

The several principal types of co-ownership of property are: joint tenancy, tenancy in common, tenancy by entireties, tenancy in partnership, and community property. Tenancy in partnership is the form of co-ownership held by persons who are business partners. It is best considered as a part of partnership law and is briefly discussed in Chapter 13. Community property is a form of co-ownership which developed under the civil law rather than the common law. Community property systems have been adopted by statutes in a few western and south-western states; in all but these few states community property is not a recognized form of property co-ownership in this country.

Co-ownership rights first originated in connection with real estate, and while some states restrict co-ownership to real estate, most states now recognize that some or all of the common-law types of co-ownership can apply both to real estate and to personal property, including in the latter both tangible items of property (like an automobile), quasi-tangible items (like stock in a corporation), and intangible rights to sue and enforce contracts (for example, to collect a money debt).

That persons are married does not mean that they are co-owners of all of their property. Although married, a person can nevertheless be the separate or sole owner of property, and if it is personal property, he or she will have full power to transfer title without his or her spouse joining in the transfer or consenting to it. While real estate can also be solely owned, its transfer is restricted. Since early common-law days it has been considered desirable as a matter of policy to grant to a widow an interest not only in property owned by her husband at the time of his death, but also in any real estate (real estate only, not personal property) owned by him at *any time* during the marriage. Common law also recognized a similar interest in a surviving widower. At common law the interest of a surviving wife was called "dower," that of a surviving husband, "curtesy." In modern times, statutes in many states provide somewhat the same rights to surviving spouses. (Usually the extent of the surviving spouse's statutory interest will vary from a fractional interest to total ownership, depending upon the number and relationship of other heirs left by the deceased spouse.) A purchaser should consult his lawyer before buying land from a married person unless that person's spouse also signs the deed.

Example: The title to certain land was in John Smith, as sole owner. Ten years after acquiring the land, John married Mary. The year following his marriage, John signed a deed transferring this land to A. Adams. Mary did not sign the deed. Twenty-five years after this transfer John died, survived by his widow Mary. When John died the land was owned by D. Davis, having been successively transferred by Adams to Brown, Brown to Carter, and by Carter to Davis.

In many states, an ownership interest in the land would vest in Mary upon John's death. If Davis wished to continue as sole owner of the land he would have to buy Mary's interest at her price. (Whether Davis would have any right to recover for this loss from Carter, Brown, or Adams, or from John's estate, would depend upon the type of contract made in the various deeds.) On the other hand, if Mary along with John had signed the transfer to Adams, Mary would have given up this possible interest.

Example: John signed an enforceable contract to sell certain land to a buyer, the deed to be delivered in two months. One month later John married Mary. A month after the marriage, John signed and tendered a deed to the buyer who refused to pay unless Mary also signed.

Mary would have no interest or possibility of interest (that is no dower interest) and could be enjoined from asserting any interest in the event she should survive John. As soon as a written contract for the sale of land is signed, an interest in the property passes to the buyer (See Chapter 20). Although the seller still has the legal title, not sufficient property interest is left in the seller for dower (or curtesy) to attach in favor of a spouse acquired after the contract date.

A surviving spouse's right in certain property cannot be greater than the interest which the deceased spouse held in that property. If a creditor with a bona fide claim against a husband has the sheriff levy on the husband's real estate, the ensuing sheriff's sale will pass the husband's title free from any dower claim of his wife.

JOINT TENANCY

A feature which the law calls the "right of survivorship" is the chief characteristic of a joint tenancy under the common law. The title of joint tenants is considered as having a singleness or oneness because created and vested in the co-owners by a single transfer. Upon the death of one joint tenant, the title remains as a single entity vested in the surviving co-owner (or co-owners). Because of this singleness-of-title theory, a surviving spouse has no dower or curtesy interest in property owned by the deceased spouse and a third person as joint tenants (unless, under statutes in some states, creation of the joint tenancy involved a transfer of property or money which had previously been solely owned by the deceased spouse during the marriage).

To term this a "right" of survivorship is somewhat of a misnomer. It is a result of this form of co-ownership rather than an irrevocable *right*. The singleness of title can be terminated by the act of one of the joint tenants without the consent of the other (or others). To the extent that the oneness of title is terminated, there is no longer a joint tenancy and, therefore, no longer the survivorship feature. For example, if A and B inherit property as joint tenants and still hold title in that manner when A dies, the entire title will vest in B. However, if A transfers his interest to T, a third person, the oneness of title ends since T's title vests in him at a different time than did B's. T and B are co-owners as tenants in common. Should T die, his interest will pass to his heirs. B will continue to have his original interest but no more (unless he is T's heir).

Any property interest which a person has a right to transfer can be attached by his creditors. Suppose A and B are joint tenants of certain property, and a creditor with a judgment against A has the sheriff levy on A's interest in the co-owned property and sell it at sheriff's sale. The sale will terminate the joint tenancy, and the purchaser at the sheriff's sale will become a co-owner with B, the type of co-ownership being a tenancy in common.

The survivorship feature of a joint tenancy terminates only if the singleness of title is terminated before the death of a co-owner. Suppose that A and B are joint tenants of certain property and A dies, leaving a will stating that his interest in the property is to pass to T. Since a will does not take effect until death, it is not effective to end the singleness of title of A and B *before* A's death. Since the singleness of title exists at the time A dies, B will own the entire interest.

TENANCY IN COMMON

A tenancy in common is the usual type of co-ownership unless the parties are husband and wife. Statutes in many states declare that if two or more persons (other than husband and wife) are co-owners, they are tenants in common unless they expressly manifest an intention to take title as joint tenants. If A and B purchase land and wish to take title as joint tenants (assuming that the law of their state still recognizes joint tenancies), they will usually have the deed read, "to A and B as joint tenants with the right of survivorship and not as tenants in common."

The chief differences between joint tenancies and tenancies in common are:

1. Tenants in common can own unequal interests. Because of the singleness-of-title theory, joint tenants are of necessity equal co-owners so long as they remain joint tenants. While tenants in common are presumed to be equal co-owners unless they indicate otherwise, it is possible for their interests to be unequal, in any ratio that they expressly indicate.

2. There is no right of survivorship in a tenancy in common. If A and B are tenants in common of certain property and A dies, A's interest passes to his heirs; B will continue to own the fractional interest he held before A's death but will have no greater interest—unless he is A's heir.

TENANCY BY ENTIRETIES

In the many states which continue to recognize this common law form of co-ownership, persons can be tenants by entireties only if they are actually husband and wife when they become co-owners. If co-owners are not actually husband and wife when they acquire title to certain property, their later marriage will not of itself convert them into tenants by entireties. If a transfer of title specifies that the transferees are husband and wife (and they actually are), they are usually presumed to own as tenants by entireties unless they expressly indicate their intent to co-own in some other way (for example as tenants in common).

The singleness-of-title theory applies to a tenancy by entireties, with the following results:

1) *Survivorship.* Just as with joint tenancy, upon the death of one tenant by entireties the entire title automatically and immediately vests in the survivor.

2) *Continuance.* At common law, unlike a joint tenancy, a tenancy by entireties cannot be changed or split by the act of either co-owner alone, nor can it be split by claimants who are creditors of only one of the co-owners, so long as the co-owners remain husband and wife. By statute in many states a divorce will change a tenancy by entireties into a tenancy in common. Businessmen frequently use tenancies by entireties to exempt certain of their assets from the claims of business creditors.

Example: A husband and wife own certain property as tenants by entireties. A creditor obtains a judgment against the husband.

In a state which recognizes common-law tenancies by entireties, the creditor has no right at all against the property, while the wife lives and the parties are not divorced. The creditor can proceed only against property owned individually by the husband—if he has any.

However, a debtor is not permitted to transfer his assets in a way that will defraud his creditors. Suppose that a house is titled solely in the name of a husband. Presumably when creditors extend credit to him they know and rely upon the fact that they can attach the real estate. The husband cannot effectively put the property beyond the reach of his creditors unless he retains other assets sufficient to pay all of his obligations. If a husband transfers title from himself to himself and his wife as tenants by entireties and retains insufficient individually owned assets to meet all of his obligations, the transfer is fraudulent as to creditors, and the creditors can have the transfer canceled. (Fraudulent conveyances are further discussed in Chapter 19.) Suppose, however, that the husband is solvent when the entireties title to certain property arises, but is insolvent when he makes payments on the property. In the few states in which such cases have been litigated (chiefly Michigan and Pennsylvania), the courts have reached opposite conclusions. In Pennsylvania the status of the property is determined by the husband's financial condition at the time the entireties title is created. If the husband is solvent then, the property is immune from the claims of his individual creditors even though he is insolvent when he makes payments, while under the Michigan view, any payments which the husband makes after he becomes insolvent are voidable by his creditors.

Example: John Smith purchased a home for himself and his family, paying $1,000 down and financing the balance of $10,000 through a mortgage payable in monthly installments over the next ten years. He was solvent at the time, title to the premises was taken in the names of "John Smith and Mary Smith, his wife," and the mortgage was signed by both husband and wife. Beginning the fourth year thereafter, John began falling behind in payments to the grocer from whom he obtained groceries on credit, but John continued to purchase from that grocer for the next several years. During this time John continued making regular payments on the mortgage so that it was completely paid off by the end of the tenth year. The payments came entirely from John's earnings. In February of the eleventh year Mary became seriously ill and was not expected to live much longer. In an attempt to put the home beyond the reach of John's creditors (especially the grocer) after Mary's death, John and Mary in March signed and recorded a deed transferring the property to their son for $1. Mary died in July, after which John continued in possession of the house, living in it just as though it was still his home. In August the grocer obtained a judgment against John for the unpaid balance of the grocery bill, interests, and costs, a total of $4,000, proved that John had been continuously insolvent since the fourth year of the mortgage, and brought an action to have the transfer to the son canceled.

Under the Pennsylvania view the grocer would not be entitled to the requested decree and would have no right to collect any part of his judgment from the transferred property. John was solvent when the entireties title was acquired. While the marriage continued with both parties alive, the entireties property was not subject to the claims of creditors of one of the parties. The husband's creditors would have rights only if upon the death of the wife, the husband survived, still owning the property. A debtor has no legal obligation to assure that this mere possibility of an interest is preserved for the benefit of his creditors. Since the husband's creditors had no claims against the property before Mary died, they would have no grounds to complain when the husband and wife gave the property away.

On the other hand, under the Michigan view the creditor could attach so much of the value of the house as equaled the amount of mortgage payments which the husband made after he became insolvent.

Part 2   REMOTE PARTIES

When the term "remote party" is used in connection with a contract, it refers to a person who is not a party to the particular contract in question. While a remote party must respect other persons' contracts and is guilty of a tort if he maliciously interferes with the contract rights of another (see Chapter 8), it is obvious that a duty to perform a particular contract cannot be cast upon someone without his consent. And just as he has no obligations, so also a remote party ordinarily has no right to meddle or interfere by attempting to enforce a contract to which he is not a party and in which he has no legally recognized interest. Society maintains the civil court system for the purpose of defining and enforcing individual rights—usually by requiring a defendant who wrongfully violates a plaintiff's rights to compensate the plaintiff for the money loss thereby sustained. Society will not permit this purpose to be perverted or misused by speculators. Suppose, for example, that immediately after a pedestrian has been grazed in an encounter with a car, a spectator dashes up, helps the bruised and shaken pedestrian to his feet, and pays him $100 cash for an assignment of all of his rights against the driver of the car; then the spectator as the assignee of the pedestrian's claim sues the driver for damages. As Sir Frederick Pollack has written:[1]

> It is not thought good for justice, peace, or fair dealing that hostile rights of action, claims for the redress of personal injuries as distinct from claims which are in substance for damage to property, should be marketable. This principle is found, I believe, in all civilized laws; it is at the bottom of the rules of the Common Law against "maintenance" and "champerty," rules which at first sight look technical and even capricious, but which were called forth by real dangers and abuses.[2]

Certainly the right to recover for physical injuries should be considered personal to the injured person (or to his estate if he has died) and not transferable to another. In the early days of the common law, claims for breach of contract were also considered personal. To quote again from Sir Frederick

> . . . most archaic laws, including those of Rome, gave a creditor enormous powers of self-redress, even to imprisoning and practically enslaving the debtor in default of payment. Under such a system the personal character and temper of the creditor might obviously be no less important to the debtor than the debtor's honesty or means of payment to the creditor.[3]

Gradually punishment as a remedy for nonpayment of a debt disappeared from the law, and the law began to recognize that while physical

---

[1] Sir Frederick Pollack, *A First Book of Jurisprudence* (New York: St Martin's Press, paperback ed., 1961), p. 122.
[2] The crimes of "maintenance" and "champerty," offenses against public justice, are committed when a person with no legitimate interest pays for another's lawsuit or bargains to share in his recovery. Blackstone has called such persons "pests of society, who officiously interfere in other men's quarrels." (*Blackstone's Commentaries on The Law*, Washington Law Book Company, 1941, pp. 806-807).
[3] *Op. cit.*, p. 114, fn. 1.

injury claims and some contracts are quite personal, most contracts are fairly impersonal. With physical injuries, the extent of injury caused by a defendant's wrongful act, and the money loss resulting, may vary considerably with the health, strength, economic status, etc., of the injured person, while the extent of damages resulting from a breach of contract is usually impersonally controlled by the scope of the contract itself. Remedies for breach of contract are accorded to the owner of the contract, and it is essential in modern society for the law to recognize that contract rights are also property rights, usually just as marketable as any other items of property. Therefore, while it is a sound and necessary rule that a remote party cannot officiously interfere by suing to enforce a contract to which he is not a party, nevertheless a person who has purchased contract rights or to whom contract rights have otherwise been transferred should usually have a right to sue.

The topic of remote parties also contains another facet. Some contracts are expressly made for the benefit of certain remote parties. Suppose, for example, that A and B enter into a contract under which for a consideration paid by A to B, B agrees to perform in a certain way for another person, C. While C is not a party to the contract, he is the person who is intended to receive a benefit from performance of the contract, and as a matter of fairness should not be ignored when damages for breach of the contract are being calculated. As the New York Court of Appeals has said:

> Contracts for the benefit of third persons have been the prolific source of judicial and academic discussion. . . . The general rule, both in law and equity . . . was that privity between a plaintiff and a defendant is necessary to the maintenance of an action on the contract. . . . On the other hand, the right of the beneficiary to sue on a contract made expressly for his benefit has been fully recognized in many American jurisdictions, either by judicial decision or by legislation, and is said to be "the prevailing rule in this country." . . . It has been said that "the establishment of this doctrine has been gradual, and is a victory of practical utility over theory, of equity over technical subtlety." . . . The reasons for this view are that it is just and practical to permit the person for whose benefit the contract is made to enforce it against one whose duty it is to pay.[4]

To recapitulate, while a remote party cannot officiously intermeddle in someone else's contract, he can (in many but not in all cases) purchase the contract and as the assignee of the assignor's rights sue to enforce the contract; or the remote party can sue if he is a third-party beneficiary.

---

[4] *Seaver* v. *Ransom*, 224 N.Y. 233, 120 N.E. 639 (1918). The expression "privity of contract" is briefly defined and illustrated on page 210, footnote number 27.

ASSIGNMENTS OF CONTRACTS

RIGHTS AND DUTIES IN GENERAL

Because a person who is the complete owner of something of value is usually free to do what he wants with it—either utilizing it himself or transferring it to another—there is no reason to deny such freedom of action to a creditor who owns a contract right to collect money from an obligor. It should make no difference to the obligor to whom he makes his contract payment so long as the payment will adequately discharge his obligations.

Example: A seller sells and delivers certain goods to a buyer in exchange for the buyer's note promising to pay the seller $1,000 in 60 days.
The seller is free either to hold the promissory note until maturity and collect on it himself, or instead to transfer the note to a third person who will then have the right to collect from the buyer when the note matures.

Example: A buyer orders certain goods from a seller for $1,000, the terms for payment being stated as "net 60 days." The seller ships pursuant to the order and records in his accounting books that he is to receive $1,000 from the buyer in 60 days.
Since not evidenced by a promissory note or a similar document, the buyer's obligation is usually referred to as an "open account," "book account," or "account receivable." As with the promissory note in the preceding example, the seller is free to assign or transfer the account receivable to a third person who will thus obtain the right to collect when the obligation matures.

Suppose that a sales contract is bilateral, both parties agreeing to perform at stated future dates; for example, the seller to deliver certain goods 30 days after the date of the contract and the buyer to pay the $1,000 purchase price 60 days after receiving the goods. Under this bilateral contract the seller has not only a right to receive money but also a duty to deliver the described goods. If before the time for delivery the seller wishes to make a complete transfer of the contract, he will not only pass along to the transferee the right to receive money but will also arrange with the transferee for the latter to deliver the described goods to the buyer. The buyer might argue that the contract calls for goods to be delivered by the original seller, not by the transferee. However, as pointed out in Chapter 4, most contracts do not require personal performance. It seems sound policy to say that if goods which conform to the contract are tendered to the buyer, he is obtaining all that he is entitled to under the contract, and he has no ground to object regarding the source of the goods. However, even though the seller has transferred the contract, if the buyer fails to receive satisfactory performance he should still be able to enforce the contract against the seller. The buyer's willingness to enter into a contract with a certain seller is based at least partly on the seller's reputation for good faith and on his financial ability to perform contract obligations which he assumes. Having contracted with a particular seller, the buyer should not without his consent be deprived of his right to enforce the contract against that seller. Therefore, even though the seller arranges for the goods to be delivered by his transferee, the seller remains liable if the transferee should fail to satisfactorily perform the contract. In other words, while the seller can transfer his *right* and thus completely divest himself of the right, he cannot completely divest himself of his *duty* without the consent of the other contracting party.[5] To distinguish between the effects of transferring rights as compared with transferring duties, the law usually speaks of the transfer of a right as an "assignment" and the transfer of a duty as only a "delegation." Of course not every contract right can be assigned nor contract duty delegated. A contract can be transferred (right assigned and/or duty delegated) only if the transfer will not change what the other contracting party is to do or to receive under the contract. If a transfer will make a material change in the performance of the contract, the consent of the other contracting party is necessary for the transfer to be valid.

The general rules which result from the foregoing policy considerations can be summarized as follows:

1. Unless a contract prohibits assignment, a right arising under the contract can be assigned without the consent of the other contracting party, so long as the assignment does not materially change the obligation of the other contracting party.

2. Unless the contract provides otherwise, the performance of a duty can be delegated, without the consent of the other contracting party, so long as performance by the one to whom delegated will conform to the original contract.

3. Delegating performance of a contract duty does not free the original obligor from his contract obligation.

4. A valid assignment gives the assignee or delegate a right to enforce the contract against the other contracting party.

To illustrate the application of these basic principles, assignments of various of the common types of contracts will be briefly considered.

Work and Service Contracts

A person may contract to perform services for another and nevertheless not be an employee. For example, a physician is usually not considered to be an employee of his patient. Only if the one for whom work

[5] A three-party agreement between a seller, buyer, and third person, in which the buyer consents to the substitution of the third person in place of the seller is commonly called a contract of *novation*.

or service is being done has the right to supervise and control the details of performance, does the one who contracts to do the work become an employee. If the one being served has the right to direct only the end result and no right to control the details involved in reaching that result, the one performing the service is called an independent contractor. Suppose that a landowner engages a builder to construct a home according to certain plans and specifications. While the owner can dictate the end result—a building conforming to the agreed plans—he has no right to direct how the builder's business is run, what employees he hires, the amount of their wages, etc. The builder is an independent contractor who contracts to perform services for the landowner.

Employer and Employee. An employer's right to control the details of his employee's performance necessarily makes the contract personal as to both parties. An employee might be willing to dig a certain ditch for his original employer, but not for some third person; the employer might be willing to hire his original employee but not some equally competent third person. Although the general nature of the work would remain the same, the actual performance could vary materially from one employer to another or from one employee to another. Therefore, an employer's contract right to his employee's services cannot be assigned unless the employee consents, and the employee cannot delegate to a substitute the duty of performance unless the employer consents.

Hirer and Independent Contractor. If the service to be rendered by an independent contractor is of such a nature that the quality of performance may vary materially from one person to another, then it is obvious that the hirer engages a certain contractor because of his personal skills and qualifications. Clearly such a contractor cannot delegate the duty of performance to a substitute without the hirer's consent. Likewise, if the performance of services involves a personal relationship between the contractor and the hirer, the latter cannot assign his rights to such services without the contractor's consent. However, if special skills and personal trust and confidence are not involved, a contract right to the services of an independent contractor can be assigned and a contract duty to perform the services can be delegated.

Example: A driller contracted in writing with a landowner to drill a gas well to a specified depth on the owner's property. Under the contract, the driller was to furnish all lumber, tools, cables, and the like, and the landowner was to furnish machinery and water and to pay $3 per foot for drilling. On the same day that he made the contract, the driller orally assigned all of his rights and duties to an assignee for $500. The assignee was also an experienced driller.

Work of this type necessarily requires the labor and attention of a number of men. Therefore, in the absence of circumstances showing reliance on some special knowledge, experience, or pecuniary ability of the driller, there was nothing of a personal nature in the contract. Personal performance by the driller not being required, the driller could validly delegate to the assignee the duty to drill the well. The landowner would be obliged to accept the assignee's tender of performance or become liable for damages for breach of contract. Upon completion of the work the assignee would be entitled to recover the agreed compensation from the landowner.

Real Estate Leases

Even though a rented apartment or building is not subjected to intentional or negligent damage, the ordinary wear and tear on the premises may be much greater with one tenant than with another. For other reasons also, a certain tenant may be either more or less desirable than another tenant. Nevertheless, the law usually considers that a landlord's main interest in a lease contract is his right to receive the specified rent money. Therefore, *unless a lease expressly prohibits assignment*, a tenant's right to occupy for the leasehold period is assignable, and the tenant's assignment is valid and effective without the necessity of the landlord's consent. Because the law takes this view, most standard-form leases expressly provide that a tenant cannot assign or sublet without the written consent of the landlord.

If a tenant is not hindered in his occupancy and enjoyment of rented premises, it is usually immaterial to the tenant who actually owns the property. Therefore, a landlord who sells his property can transfer the lease, thus validly assigning to the buyer the landlord's rights under the lease and delegating performance of any duties the lease imposes on the landlord.

Contracts for Cash Transfers of Real Estate

Assignment and Delegation by the Buyer. Unless the contract prohibits assignment, a buyer who contracts to purchase real estate for cash may assign his right without the consent of the seller. Upon tendering the stated purchase price, the assignee would be entitled to enforce the contract and receive a deed from the seller.

Assignment and Delegation by the Seller. Usually in a contract to transfer real estate, a seller agrees to give a deed in which he will warrant the title to be free and clear of all mortgages or other encumbrances. For several policy reasons, what might be called an "expanded parol-evidence rule" applies to transfers of real estate. If after a buyer enters into a land-purchase contract, he accepts a particular deed as satisfactory performance of the contract, the provisions of the contract are usually considered as merged into or superseded by the deed. In other words, unless clearly stated otherwise by the parties, any provisions of the contract which are not included or repeated in the deed are considered as waived and no longer enforceable. One result of this is that a seller's contract duty to give a warranty deed (a deed in which the seller guarantees title) cannot be delegated to another without the consent of the buyer.

Example: S, owner of a large tract of land, had the land surveyed and divided into numbered building lots. He then contracted in writing to sell Lot Number 1 to B for a stated price. The contract specified one month later as the settlement date—the day on which the buyer was to pay the stated price and the seller was to deliver to the buyer a warranty deed for the property. Two weeks after entering into the S-B contract, S sold and, using a nonwarranty deed, transferred the entire tract to T, subject to the S-B contract which T in writing agreed to perform. On the date specified in the S-B contract for settlement, T signed and tendered to B a warranty deed for Lot Number 1.

If B should accept T's deed, B would obtain title and T's warranty of title, but B would have no warranty which he could enforce against S. Thus, if B should desire to hold S to a warranty of title, B would have a right to refuse T's tender unless accompanied by an enforceable written warranty of title signed by S.

Contracts for Credit Transfers of Real Estate

Often a contract for the transfer of real estate will provide that when the seller transfers a deed to the buyer, the buyer is to make a partial payment and sign a mortgage promising to pay the balance of the price at stated future times. Suppose that the buyer then assigns the contract to a third person. Under the expanded parol evidence rule or rule of merger described in the preceding paragraph, the seller is not required to deliver a deed to the buyer's assignee solely on the assignee's mortgage. Thus the buyer's obligation under a credit real estate contract cannot be delegated to another person without the seller's consent.

Example: By written contract S agreed to sell and B to buy a described tract of land for $15,000, payable as follows: $500 on signing of the contract, $2,500 on the settlement date one month later, and a three-year mortgage for the $12,000 balance with interest at 6 percent per year. A few days after signing the contract and paying the first $500, B in writing assigned the contract to T for $1,200 which T paid to B. T notified S of the assignment, and on the settlement date T tendered $14,500 in cash to S and requested a deed for the property. When S refused, saying that he wanted the agreed mortgage, T sued S for specific performance.

S would not be required to transfer the land to T either on a mortgage signed by T or on tender of the entire price in cash. Payment of the entire price on the settlement date would deprive S of the $2,160 interest (6 percent of $12,000 for three years) to which he had a contract right. Only if T tendered performance exactly in accordance with the contract ($2,500 in cash, a $12,000, three-year, 6 percent mortgage, *plus* an enforceable guaranty of the mortgage debt signed by B) could S be obliged to deliver a deed to T.

Contracts for Sales of Goods[6]

In connection with contracts for sales of goods the Uniform Commercial Code provides:

> Unless otherwise agreed all rights of either seller or buyer can be assigned except where the assignment would materially change the duty of the other party, or increase materially the burden of risk imposed on him by his contract, or impair materially his chance of obtaining return performance.

The Code also provides:

> A party may perform his duty through a delegate unless otherwise agreed or unless the other party has a substantial interest in having his original promisor perform or control the acts required by the contract. No delegation of performance relieves the party delegating of any duty to perform or any liability for breach.

Note that the above-quoted Code provisions merely reiterate the usual common-law rules which apply to all contracts. The last sentence of the latter quotation emphasizes two points:

1. A buyer can assign his right to receive goods and delegate his duty to pay, even though the contract is a credit contract which provides for payment at a specified time after delivery. Some courts have held that a contract for delivery of goods on credit cannot be assigned, saying that a seller cannot be required to accept the credit of the assignee in place of the buyer's credit. Such holdings overlook the fact that while the buyer assigns his right to receive goods, he only delegates to the assignee the duty to pay, and that such a delegation cannot (without the seller's consent) relieve the buyer from his obligation to pay. The rule of merger discussed in connection with land contracts does not apply to sales-of-goods contracts. The seller can deliver to the assignee without worrying about the assignee's credit; if the assignee fails to pay, the seller can collect, either from the assignee or from the buyer.

2. A seller can delegate his duty to deliver even though the contract contains an express warranty. Unlike a land transaction with the rule of merger, the seller remains liable on the express warranty contained in his contract, even after the buyer accepts goods from the seller's delegate.

[6] U.C.C. Sec. 2-210.

Rights to Receive Money

The right to receive money is one of the most impersonal of all contract rights and in almost all cases is fully assignable. When a businessman makes an assignment of a money claim, his purpose is usually to raise funds for the regular operation of his business. Such assignments can be called financing assignments. The method of making a financing assignment and the relative rights of the obligor, the assignor, and the assignee are prescribed by Article 9 of the Uniform Commercial Code which covers financing and secured transactions (see Chapter 18). Assignments which are not associated with the day-to-day conduct of the assignor's business are *nonfinancing assignments,* and are expressly excluded from the Code.[7] The principal nonfinancing assignments include, 1) an assignment made to expedite the collection of an overdue account, 2) a transfer of accounts receivable in connection with the sale of the assignor's business, 3) an isolated assignment involving an insignificant amount, 4) an assignment of wages or salary, and 5) an assignment of an entire unperformed contract, that is (in the language of the Code), "a transfer of a contract right to an assignee who is also to do the performance under the contract."

Assignment of Wages or Salary. Wages to be earned under a contract not yet made or a job not yet obtained (that is, the mere prospect of earning wages from some future job) is a future right which, as discussed in the next paragraph, cannot be assigned. On the other hand, a wage or salary due or to become due under a contract already in existence is at common law, as freely assignable as any other money claim. In some states, however, statutes prohibit or restrict the assignment of wages or salary. Such statutes are based on the public's interest in protecting an employee and his family from an imprudent disposal of their means of livelihood.

Future Rights. If at the time a money obligation is assigned, the obligation is not yet collectible, it is frequently referred to as a future right. Future rights are of two general types, those which are to arise from contracts already in existence, and those which are expected to arise from contracts not yet entered into (as for example future accounts receivable). In the case of nonfinancing assignments (which do not come under the Uniform Commercial Code) the law takes a conservative view. Traditionally, society has considered it unwise and contrary to the general good to permit a person to be able to dispose not only of all that he has but also of everything he hopes to acquire anytime in the future. In general, a line is drawn between a right already created by an existing contract and a right to arise under a possible future con-

---

[7] U.C.C. Secs. 9-104, 9-302.

tract not yet formed. A right created by a contract already in existence can be assigned, even though the right is unmatured and contingent. However, if the contract which is expected to create the right is not yet formed, usually no valid assignment can be made. On the other hand, the less conservative, commercial view is followed for financing assignments. Over the years as business increased in volume and complexity, it gradually appeared desirable from a commercial standpoint that a person sometimes be able to make a binding contract to dispose of interests which he had not yet acquired. The law responded to the needs of business and developed various ways to accomplish this. In consolidating the devices available for raising money, the authors of the Uniform Commercial Code continue this trend. (See chapter 18.) Under the Code therefore, it is possible to make a valid financing assignment of rights to arise under contracts to be entered into in the future. The assignment automatically becomes operative and effective when the assignor later enters into a contract which brings the assigned right into existence.

Example: On June 1 a manufacturer borrowed a substantial sum of money from a bank to finance his manufacturing operations, promising to repay the loan one year later. As collateral security, the manufacturer signed a paper assigning to the bank "all of the accounts receivable now held by the manufacturer or hereafter to be acquired by him." On the following December 1 the manufacturer sold and delivered $1,000 worth of goods to a dealer who had never previously made a purchase from the manufacturer. Because the dealer had a good credit rating, the manufacturer did not hesitate extending 60 days' credit. When the manufacturer delivered the goods on December 1, an account receivable arose, consisting of the right to collect $1,000 from the dealer 60 days later.

Immediately that the account receivable arose on December 1, the prior June 1 assignment served to validly assign the account to the bank.

Partial Assignments. Suppose that after entering into a certain transaction as a result of which an obligor owed his creditor $600, the creditor attempted to assign $200 of this claim to one assignee and $300 to another assignee. If the law were to sanction splitting the assigned claim between two assignees, could the law find a reason to prevent splitting the claim among two hundred assignees? Drawing two hundred separate checks would be a substantial burden which the obligor had not forseen when he incurred the $600 obligation to the single creditor. Similarly, an obligor's burden would be materially increased if he could be subjected to two or more separate lawsuits as a result of the partial assignment of a single obligation. In determining as a matter of policy whether partial assignees should have any rights against an obligor, the starting point is the general rule that the assignment cannot be made if it will materially change what the obligor is to do. In applying this rule, courts in some states flatly deny any validity to partial assignments. Some other states limit the enforcement of partial assignments to equity lawsuits in which all claimants join together in one lawsuit and the obligor can make one payment which the court will distribute among the various claimants. Some states give at least some effect to partial assignments. In view of this diversity of opinion, it is unwise for an obligor to completely ignore a partial assignment and to go ahead and pay the full amount of his obligation to his original creditor. Such an obligor is risking a lawsuit and should consult his lawyer before making any payment.

CONTRACTS EXPRESSLY PROHIBITING ASSIGNMENT

Persons who enter into an impersonal contract and do not specify otherwise are presumed not to care who performs or receives performance under the contract. In such a contract, therefore, the rights can be assigned and the duties delegated. Sometimes, however, parties include in their contract a provision expressly prohibiting any transfer of the contract. Since it is considered socially desirable to accord to parties considerable freedom in making contracts, the law will enforce their restriction—until it clearly appears to be harmful to the overall good of society. When weighed against public policy, the effect of such a restrictive provision can be summarized in the following way:

1) Restriction on Delegation of Duties. Suppose that a contract for the sale and delivery of certain standardized goods contains a provision stating that the duty of delivery cannot be delegated. Without such a restriction, the duty unquestionably could be delegated. However, the restriction is perfectly valid. Because of the restriction the buyer cannot be required to accept goods from any person other than the seller.

2) Restriction on Assignment of Rights. a) *Restriction on Right to Receive Performance Other Than Money.* Usually a contract may validly restrict performance to the contracting parties only. For example, if a real estate lease expressly prohibits assignment, the landlord cannot be required, without his consent, to permit the tenant's assignee to occupy the leased premises.

b) *Restriction on Right to Receive Money.* Courts in the various states disagree as to the effect which should be given to a contract provision expressly prohibiting the assignment of a money claim. While some courts give full effect to the provision, other courts hold that in spite of such a provision, a creditor can nevertheless assign the claim. Under the latter view, as soon as the obligor learns of the assignment, he is bound by it, and when the obligation comes due, the obligor can be required to pay the amount of the obligation to the assignee. The courts holding this view consider that the right to receive money is so impersonal that it is similar to the ownership of tangible property, and apply the rule discussed in Chapter 8, that an absolute restraint on the alienation of property is against public policy and unenforceable. The Uniform Commercial Code adopts this view;[8] for a financing assignment and for an assignment of a right to receive payment for goods delivered by the assignor, any contract provision which prohibits assignment is ineffective and the money claim can be assigned despite the express stipulation otherwise.

Rights of Assignees Against Obligors

Suppose that a seller sold and delivered certain goods to a buyer for $1,000 payable in one month, and then made an assignment of the $1,000 account receivable. As the courts frequently say, an assignee "stands in the shoes" of the assignor, with the same rights the assignor would have had to collect from the obligor. Suppose, however, that the seller was guilty of fraud in inducing the obligor to make his purchase, and that upon discovering the fraud, the obligor gave proper notice of his desire to cancel the contract. If the account had not been assigned, the obligor's defense of fraud would certainly be effective to prevent enforcement of the obligor's promise to pay $1,000. Should the defense also be effective against the assignee who was completely innocent of any fraud?

In answering such questions, courts frequently say that an assignee's rights are like water, which cannot rise higher than its source. At first glance, an assignee's rights appear to be exactly comparable to water in this respect; it would seem to be an impossibility for a person to transfer better rights than he himself owns. And the law so holds in respect to *ordinary* property and contract rights. However, various policy factors compel a different view with certain extraordinary types of property and contract rights. Suppose, for example, that a thief stole a rare book and sold and delivered it to a buyer who paid full value, honestly and reasonably believing that the thief owned the book and had the right to sell it. If the owner succeeded in tracing his book to the buyer's possession, the owner would have the right to recover the book. No matter how innocent the buyer was, he would obtain no better rights than the thief had. Now suppose that the owner had hidden $2,000 in the book, that the thief used the money to purchase a car, and that somehow the owner was able to trace the money and prove that the $2,000 in the innocent car-dealer's possession was the identical currency that had been stolen from the owner. The owner could *not* recover the money. Of course the thief himself

[8] U.C.C. Secs. 2-210, 9-318.

would have no better right to the money than to the book. Nevertheless, while the innocent transferee of the *book* would obtain no better right than was held by his transferor (the thief), the innocent transferee who gave value for the *money* could obtain a better right than his transferor had and would become the absolute owner of the money. In thus distinguishing between such items as books and money, the law calls the former *non-negotiable* and the latter *negotiable*. A book is, of course, transferable—but nevertheless nonnegotiable. Hence it is clear that the word "negotiable" is not synonymous with "transferable." Rather, the term "negotiable" is a tag which the law applies to any of several types of property interests, as to which it is possible for an innocent transferee for value to obtain a better right than was held by his transferor. Money has this attribute, and at an early date, it was recognized as essential in the conduct of business and commerce for certain other property and contract rights to be accorded the same attribute. Thus, while an account receivable not evidenced by a note is not negotiable—although it is assignable—a promissory note will be negotiable, if it complies with certain formal requirements. For example, the following note is negotiable in form:

> Centerville, Ill., [Date]
> One month after date I promise to pay to the order of Sam Smith One Thousand ($1,000) Dollars.
> (signed) Bert Brown

Notice that the quoted note is payable to the "order of" the named payee. For a note to be negotiable it must be payable either to the order of the payee or to the bearer. In addition there are other formal requirements with which a note must comply to be negotiable. Notes which are in common use frequently contain more provisions than the preceding example. Some additional provisions will not interfere with negotiability, whereas some others will render a note nonnegotiable. The requirements for negotiability and its effects are more fully explained and illustrated in Chapter 14. The purpose of the present discussion is to point out that a note payable to "order" or to "bearer" may possibly be a negotiable note, and especially to emphasize that the discussion of assignments in this chapter relates solely to *nonnegotiable* rights.

If a nonnegotiable note or an account receivable is assigned, the assignee will obtain no better rights than his assignor had. Furthermore, until notice of the assignment is given to the obligor, if anything further occurs between the obligor and the assignor which would affect the assignor's right to recover if the account had not been assigned, the assignee's right to recover will likewise be affected. The most obvious example of this is the case of an obligor who, not knowing of the assignment of his account, makes a payment to his original creditor. The assignee will be bound by this payment. On the other hand, after an obligor is notified of an assignment, he is thereafter aware of the assignee's interest in the assigned account and can do nothing from then on to decrease its value. To recapitulate:

1. Until receiving notice of assignment, an obligor is justified in making payment according to his original contract. If the contract does not provide otherwise, the obligor is justified in paying his original creditor (the assignor) and such a payment will discharge the obligor's debt. *After* receiving notice of an assignment, the obligor should pay strictly in accordance with the notice.

2. The right of the assignee to collect from the obligor 1) will be subject to any defenses which the obligor has against the assignor arising from the original contract, and also 2) will not only be subject to the defense of prior payment but also will be subject to any other defenses or claims which the obligor has or acquires against the assignor up to the time the assignee notifies the obligor of the assignment.

On the other hand, if an assigned claim is evidenced by a *negotiable* note, then:

1. The obligor should refuse to pay without seeing the note. Even though the obligor is not notified of a transfer, his contract obligation is to pay the actual owner of the note, whoever that may be. If the obligor pays his original creditor, and the latter dishonestly accepts the payment without disclosing that he no longer holds the note, the obligor can be required to pay again to the proper person. While the obligor will, of course, have the right to recover this mistaken payment from the original creditor, the right is worth no more than the assets which are available for a sheriff's levy.

2. The obligor may be obliged to pay the note even though he has not fully received the item which he was supposed to obtain in exchange for the note. As is explained in Chapter 14, many defenses (including failure of consideration and fraud) are cut off when a negotiable note is properly transferred to an innocent purchaser for value.

Rights of Assignees as to Third Persons

When a debtor defaults and refuses or fails to pay his creditor, the creditor's remedy is the usual collection remedy which applies to any unsecured obligation, namely:

1. The creditor obtains a judgment against the debtor for the amount of the past-due obligation.

2. After obtaining a judgment, the creditor has the sheriff levy on (that is, attach or seize) some property interest belonging to the debtor.

3. The creditor then attempts to realize the amount of his judgment

from the attached property interest, usually through a public-auction, sheriff's sale.

Property interests which belong to the debtor and which the creditor can have attached include not only tangible property in the possession of the debtor (such as the debtor's house or car), but also intangible rights which the debtor owns, including any right which the debtor has to collect money from someone else.

Example: A manufacturer sold and delivered $1,000 worth of goods to a dealer on 60 days' open account. (Each of the following numbered parts is a separate fact situation.)

1. A supplier to whom the manufacturer owed an overdue claim of $2,000 obtained a judgment against the manufacturer, and knowing of the $1,000 account which the dealer owed to the manufacturer, had the sheriff levy on this obligation. The sheriff handed the dealer a formal attachment paper notifying him that the obligation which he owed to the manufacturer was attached by the supplier. Through his attachment the supplier obtained a claim or lien against the $1,000 account owed by the dealer to the manufacturer, and thereby became a lien creditor as to that account.

2. Some of the manufacturer's creditors initiated a proceeding in which the court adjudged the manufacturer to be insolvent and appointed a receiver to take over all of the manufacturer's assets for the benefit of his creditors. Included among the assets which the receiver obtained was the $1,000 account payable by the dealer. The receiver promptly gave the dealer formal notice of the insolvency adjudication together with an instruction that when due, the account should be paid to the receiver. The receiver would thereby become a lien creditor as to the $1,000 account.

In the above example, suppose that immediately after delivering the $1,000 worth of goods to the dealer, the manufacturer had assigned the $1,000 account to a bank, and that after this assignment but without knowledge of it 1) the supplier attached the account, or 2) the receiver was appointed and took over all of the manufacturer's assets. This would raise a question of priority between the assignee (the bank) and the lien creditor (either the supplier or receiver). In other words, as between the lien creditor and the assignee, which party would have a better claim to the assigned account and therefore a better right to collect from the dealer? Another possible claimant could be a second assignee. Suppose that (in the above example) after assigning the $1,000 account to the bank, the manufacturer wrongfully made a second assignment of the same account to a finance company, which had no knowledge of the first assignment. Again a question of priority would arise: as between the first assignee (the bank) and the second assignee (the finance company) which would have a better right to collect the $1,000 account? Questions such as these, concerning relative priorities of equally innocent parties, are policy questions. The overall problem is, what should an assignee be required to do, as a matter of public policy, to protect his interest in an assigned account against subsequent lien creditors or subsequent assignees? Such situations are subdivided according to whether the first assignment is a financing assignment (and thus ruled by the Uniform Commercial Code) or a nonfinancing assignment. If the assignment of an account receivable is a financing assignment, then to protect his interest against a later party (lien creditor or assignee), the first assignee should file in the proper public office a statement which gives notice of the assignment (as is more fully discussed in Chapter 18). The assignee should consult his lawyer to accomplish the necessary filing. If the assignment of an account receivable is a nonfinancing assignment, then in many states the claimant who first gives notice to the obligor who owes the account, will have the better right to collect the account. Thus to protect his interest in a nonfinancing assignment the assignee should usually notify the obligor of the assignment before the obligor learns of the interest of a later lien creditor or second assignee.

THIRD-PARTY BENEFICIARIES

Generally when a person enters into a contract and gives consideration for the promise of the other contracting party, the promisee intends that he himself will be the recipient of the promised performance. However, sometimes the promise for which the promisee contracts is by its terms to be performed for a specified third party. In such a contract, since the one intended to receive the promisor's performance is not a party to the contract, he is commonly referred to as the *third-party beneficiary* of the contract. The following example first reviews the effect of an assignment of rights and delegation of duties, and then fits the third-party beneficiary contract into the picture. The interrelationship of the parties as a result of the two contracts described in the example is illustrated by the diagram on p. 283.

Example: On June 1 Smith and Brown entered into a written contract under which Smith agreed that he would sell and deliver certain described goods to Brown on July 1, for $1,000 payable on delivery. The contract said nothing concerning assignments. On June 5 Brown entered into a written assignment contract with Edwards under which Brown assigned to Edwards all of Brown's rights under the Smith-Brown contract and Edwards agreed that he would accept the described goods on July 1 and pay Smith $1,000 on delivery. Smith was given prompt notice of the Brown-Edwards assignment contract. (Each of the following numbered and lettered parts is a separate fact situation.)

1. Edwards tendered $1,000 to Smith on July 1, demanded the goods

Smith-Brown June 1 Contract

Promise to sell and deliver to B ———(*Right:* To receive goods)

SMITH ⟶ **BROWN**

Promise to buy and pay S $1,000 ———(*Duty:* To pay $1,000)
⟵

Promise to accept goods and pay S $1,000

Assignment of right and delegation of duty

Brown-Edwards June 5 Contract

EDWARDS

described in the Smith-Brown contract, and when Smith refused to deliver, Edwards sued Smith for damages for breach of contract.

Edwards could recover. Under the Smith-Brown contract, Brown had a right to receive the described goods on July 1. By the Brown-Edwards contract, Brown assigned this right to Edwards. Since the Smith-Brown contract did not prohibit assignment, and since such a contract would be classified as an impersonal contract, Brown's right was assignable. As Brown's assignee, Edwards would be entitled to receive the goods and could enforce Smith's contract obligation to deliver.

2. On July 1 Smith tendered delivery of the goods to Edwards, and when Edwards refused to accept or pay for the goods, Smith notified Brown and tendered the goods to Brown, who also refused to accept them or pay for them.

a) Smith sued Brown for damages for breach of contract.

Smith could recover damages from Brown. Under the Smith-Brown contract, Brown had a duty to accept the goods and pay $1,000 for them. Brown's delegation of this duty to Edwards could not, without Smith's consent, free Brown from his contract obligation.

After Smith recovered damages from Brown, Brown could in turn sue Edwards and recover damages. Under the Brown-Edwards contract, in exchange for the assignment of Brown's right under the Smith-Brown contract, Edwards promised that he would take over Brown's duty under that contract, namely that he would accept the goods and pay Smith $1,000. As the promisee of Edwards' promise, Brown would certainly have a right to enforce it.

b) Smith sued Edwards for damages. Although Edwards promised in the Brown-Edwards contract to accept the goods and to pay Smith, Smith was not a party to that contract. However, although Edwards made his promise to Brown, the promise was to accept goods from Smith and to pay Smith for them. Smith was the third-party beneficiary of the Edwards-Brown contract, and in most states could sue Edwards directly and enforce Edwards' promise.

The persons involved in a third-party beneficiary contract are usually referred to as the *promisor* (the one who makes the promise in question—Edwards in the above example), the *promisee* (the one to whom the promisor makes his contract promise—Brown in the above example), and the *beneficiary* (the person intended by the promisor and promisee to receive performance or to be primarily benefited by the performance of the promise—Smith in the above example).

Often the performance of a contract may incidentally or colaterally be beneficial to persons other than the contracting parties. For example, the construction of a beautiful home in a residential area will increase the value of the surrounding land. Suppose a lot owner enters into a contract with a builder for construction of a home on his lot. The purpose of the contract is to benefit the lot owner; he is the intended recipient of the performance of the contract. Any benefit to the neighbors is only incidental. Such *incidental beneficiaries* are not third-party beneficiaries and have no rights to enforce contracts which they have not personally entered into and which have not been assigned to them.

There are two main types of third-party beneficiaries—*creditor beneficiaries* and *donee beneficiaries.* Which type a particular third-party beneficiary is depends upon the relationship existing between the promisee and the beneficiary at the time the third-party beneficiary contract is made. If a debtor-creditor or obligor-obligee relationship exists, that is if the promisee owes an obligation to the beneficiary and contracts for the promisor's promise in order to perform that obligation, the beneficiary is a creditor beneficiary. If the promisee owes no obligation to the beneficiary but instead contracts for the promise as a favor or gift to the beneficiary, the beneficiary, is a donee beneficiary.

Example: A debtor owes a creditor $1,000 payable on a stated date. The debtor enters into a contract with a promisor under which for a consideration moving from the debtor to the promisor, the promisor promises that he will pay $1,000 to the creditor on the stated due date.

The creditor, the third-party beneficiary of the debtor-promisor contract, is a creditor beneficiary. The debtor enters into the contract with the promisor as a way to satisfy the obligation which the debtor owes to his own creditor.

Example: An uncle enters into a contract with a promisor under which for a consideration moving from the uncle to the promisor, the promisor promises that he will pay $1,000 to the uncle's nephew at a stated future date.

The nephew is the third-party beneficiary of the uncle-promisor contract. If the uncle owes no obligation to his nephew, the uncle is entering into the contract as a way of making a gift to his nephew and the nephew is a donee beneficiary.

ENFORCEMENT OF THIRD-PARTY BENEFICIARY CONTRACTS

Obviously, since the promisee is a party to the promisor-promisee contract, he can enforce it. In most states, regardless of whether a third-party beneficiary is a donee beneficiary or a creditor beneficiary, he has a right to enforce the promisor-promisee contract. The Uniform Commercial Code adopts this view for creditor beneficiaries of sales-of-goods contracts, stating:

> An assignment of "the contract" or of "all my rights under the contract" or an assignment in similar general terms is an assignment of rights and unless the language or the circumstances (as in an assignment for security) indicate the contrary, it is a delegation of performance of the duties of the assignor and its acceptance by the assignee constitutes a promise by him to perform those duties. This promise is enforceable by either the assignor *or the other party to the original contract*.[9] [Emphasis added.]

RESCISSION OF THIRD-PARTY BENEFICIARY CONTRACTS

Donee Beneficiary Contracts

Suppose that intending to make an unconditional gift, a donor gives a donee $1,000 in cash. If the donor should happen to change his mind the following day, he cannot recover the money. Once an unconditional gift is made, ownership of the given item passes to and vests in the donee, and the donor no longer has any right to that item or control over it—unless he expressly reserved some control at the time he transferred it. For the same reason the right of a donee beneficiary to enforce a third-party beneficiary contract is considered irrevocable. After a right to enforce the promisor's promise vests in the donee beneficiary, the

[9] U.C.C. Sec. 2-210.

promisor and promisee cannot change or cancel their contract without the donee beneficiary's consent, unless they have reserved such a power when first forming their contract. As to when a right vests in a donee beneficiary, the various courts follow one of two theories. Courts in some states say that no right vests until the beneficiary is given notice of or learns of the promisor-promisee contract. On the other hand, courts in some other states assume that the beneficiary will be agreeable to the third-party beneficiary contract and willing to accept its benefits, therefore consider obtaining his actual consent a needless formality, and hold that an irrevocable right vests in the donee beneficiary as soon as the promisor-promisee contract is made.

Creditor Beneficiary Contracts

If a third-party beneficiary is a creditor beneficiary, there is no intent to make a gift to him and therefore in theory no irrevocable right immediately vests in him. Unless injustice would result, the promisor and promisee can amend or cancel their contract without the consent of the beneficiary, and thus change or cancel the beneficiary's right to collect under the contract. Usually such a change or cancellation is not unfair to the beneficiary. He still has his right as a creditor to collect from his debtor (the promisee of the third-party beneficiary contract). However, if the beneficiary has materially changed his position in reliance on the contract (for example, by starting a lawsuit against the promisor) it would be unfair and unjust for the contract afterwards to be changed or canceled; the creditor beneficiary's material action under the contract would therefore make his right to collect from the promisor irrevocable.

PROBLEMS

1. Andrew Adams' rich uncle died owning a number of pieces of real estate. In the uncle's will, three of these properties were properly and fully described and left as follows:

First property: "to Andrew Adams and Bernard Brown, equally as tenants in common."

Second property: "to Andrew Adams and Mary Adams, his wife, as tenants by entireties."

Third property: "to Andrew Adams and Charles Carter, equally, as joint tenants with the right of survivorship and not as tenants in common."

Neither Brown nor Carter was related to Adams.

a) Assume that Adams became insolvent before his uncle's death, and remained insolvent thereafter. Two years later, one of Adams' creditors obtained a judgment against Adams and wished to collect his claim from the above properties. 1) As to the first property, would the creditor have the right to proceed against (a) the entire title; (b) a one-half interest; (c) some other fractional interest; (d) no interest? 2) As to the second property, select one of the four choices listed above. 3) As to the third property, select one of the four choices listed above.

b) Assume that Adams remained fully solvent at all times and, when he died two years after his uncle's death, he left enough money to pay all debts and taxes, and in his will left the three properties to his two sons, Robert and William Adams. 1) As to the first property, after Andrew Adams' death, would Bernard Brown own (a) the entire title; (b) a one-half interest; (c) some other fractional interest; (d) no interest? 2) As to the second property, would Mary Adams own (a), (b), (c) or (d) (select one of the four choices listed above)? 3) As to the third property, would Charles Carter own (a), (b), (c) or (d) (select one of the four choices listed above)?

2. A manufacturing company from another state planned erection of a plant in a small town. The company enlisted the aid of a lawyer to assist in procuring land desired by the company, without inflating land values. On March 20 the lawyer entered into a contract with the owner of a 9-acre tract of land, under which the owner agreed to sell and the lawyer to buy the described land for $14,000, payment and transfer of the deed to be made the following July 1. At the time the agreement was signed, the lawyer knew that the new manufacturing plant was to be located in close proximity to the owner's land, knew that the owner was ignorant of that fact, and during negotiations refrained from mentioning anything as to the purpose for which the lawyer wanted the land. On April 2 the plans for the company were made public and within 60 days, the value of owner's land increased 100 percent. The lawyer assigned the contract to the company and the owner was notified. On July 1, when the company tendered $14,000, the owner refused to transfer the land. The Company sued the owner for specific performance. The owner's defense was a) that he had not agreed to sell to the company and b) that he had been defrauded. What result?

3. A lumber-mill operator who also was a logging contractor entered into an agreement with a lumber dealer in which the lumberman agreed to sell and the dealer to buy the quantity of lumber described below, cut in specified sizes, the dealer to pay specified prices thirty days after delivery f.o.b. the mill. One month later the lumberman sold his logging and mill business to a buyer and assigned to the buyer the lumberman's contract with the dealer. The dealer refused to accept lumber from the assignee and the assignee sued the dealer for damages for breach of contract.

a) The contract was for all of the merchantable lumber from certain specified tracts of land, to be delivered six months after the formation of the contract. Explain whether the assignee could recover from the dealer.

b) The contract was for the entire output from the lumberman's mill for the period of one year after the formation of the contract. Explain whether the assignee could recover from the dealer.

4. Under a written contract S agreed to sell and B to buy 200 drums of a stated kind of acid, meeting stated specifications as to purity. Delivery was to be at the rate of two drums per day, title to pass upon delivery. After each delivery, the acid was to be sampled and tested, and if found satisfactory to B, was to be paid for within one week after delivery, the amount paid to be the market price prevailing in New York City on the delivery date. One week after formation of the contract B sold his business, including the contract with S, to E. S refused to make deliveries to E, who thereupon sued S for damages. Explain 1) the reasoning upon which S could attempt to defend, 2) the reasoning upon which E could attempt to recover, and 3) which party should be given judgment. (Modified from A.I.C.P.A., 27-6.)

5. S entered into a contract with B for sale and delivery to B of certain described, standardized goods at a stated price, to be delivered at a stated time.

a) Before the time for delivery or payment under the contract, B assigned to E the entire contract, E agreed with B to perform the contract, and S was notified of the assignment. 1) The contract between S and B contained no provision pertaining to assignment; under the contract, payment was to be made upon delivery. When the time came for delivery, E tendered to S the proper price but S refused to deliver to E. E sued S for damages. Explain whether E was entitled to recover. 2) Other facts remaining the same, suppose that the contract provided for payment 30 days after delivery. Explain whether this would change your answer to Part (1) above. 3) The contract between S and B contained a provision stating that neither party could assign his rights or delegate his duties under the contract, and that payment was to be made upon delivery. When the time came for delivery, E tendered to S the proper price but S refused to deliver to E. E sued S for damages. Explain whether E was entitled to recover.

b) Under the contract, payment was to be made 30 days after delivery. S made delivery to B according to contract, and then assigned to F the right to receive payment. F notified B of the assignment. The contract contained a provision stating that neither party could assign his rights or delegate his duties under the contract. B refused to pay F but instead made payment to S. Before F could obtain the money from S, S became insolvent and a receiver was appointed who took over all of S's assets. F sued B for the purchase price of the goods. Explain whether F could recover.

6. A manufacturer sold and delivered certain machinery to an oil refiner on open account for $2,000, payable in 60 days. A few days later the manufacturer sold and assigned this account to a bank which paid the manufacturer full value less the usual discount fee. A month later the refiner sold and delivered to the manufacturer a quantity of oil on open account for $800, payable in 30 days. The manufacturer defaulted on the $800 obligation owed to the refiner, whereupon the refiner refused to pay the maufacturer anything on the past-due $2,000 obligation. At this point the bank claimed $2,000 from the refiner. This was the first that the refiner knew of the manufacturer's assigning the account. When the refiner refused to pay, the bank sued the refiner. What result?

7. Smith and Brown entered into a written contract under which Smith agreed to sell and deliver to Brown 500 units of certain described, standardized goods, in monthly installments of 100 units on the first of the next month and 100 units on the first of each month thereafter, for which Brown agreed to pay $5 per unit, payable 10 days after each delivery. The day after formation of the contract, Smith and Edwards entered into a written agreement under which Smith sold and assigned the Smith-Brown contract to Edwards and Edwards agreed to make the contract deliveries to Brown. When Brown was notified of Smith's transfer of the contract, Brown did not express any objection. Thereafter Brown received from Edwards the first two installments, which conformed with the Smith-Brown contract in every respect (except for being delivered by Edwards instead of Smith), and Brown paid Edwards for the goods. At the time for delivery of the third installment, the market price for such goods had advanced and Edwards refused to deliver any more goods to Brown. Brown promptly notified Smith who refused to take any action. Brown sued Smith for damages for breach of contract.

a) Smith argued that Brown could recover damages from Edwards, and that therefore Smith was no longer liable on the contract. Could Brown recover damages from Edwards? If so, would this be a good defense in Brown's lawsuit against Smith? Explain.

b) Smith argued that since Brown had accepted two shipments from Edwards, Smith was no longer liable on the contract. Would this be a good defense? Explain.

8. Effective January 1, a manufacturer and a labor union entered into a contract upon which the manufacturer agreed that thereafter he would pay wages at a specified rate to employees who were members of the union. E, a member of the union, had been employed by the manufacturer for many years at a lesser rate. E continued working at the old rate for six months after the date of the union contract before he learned of the terms of the union contract. E sued the manufacturer for the difference between the wages he received and the wages specified in the union contract, for the six-month period. The manufacturer denied liability on the ground that E was not a party to the January 1 contract. What result? (Modified from A.I.C.P.A. May 49-3.)

9. At a time when D owed C $100 due in one month, R sought to borrow $100 from D. D lent $100 to R upon R's oral promise to D to pay to C in one month the $100 which D owed to C. When R failed to pay, C sued R.

a) R claimed the statute of frauds as a defense. Explain whether this would be a good defense.

b) What other defense might R attempt to raise? Would it be a valid defense? (Modified from A.I.C.P.A., Nov. 41-8.)

10. The owner of a business employed a general manager under a three-year contract at a salary of $800 per month. The manager's duties required skill and sound judgment. The owner also employed a file clerk under a one-year contract at a salary of $200 a month. The assigned duties of the file clerk were such as could be done by any mediocre clerk. Six months after making the above mentioned employment contracts, the owner entered into a written agreement with a buyer under which the owner sold his business to the buyer and assigned to the buyer all outstanding customer and employ-

ment contracts, and the buyer agreed to perform satisfactorily all of the owner's outstanding contracts.

a) When the buyer took over the business, the manager and the clerk both decided to quit. In separate lawsuits the buyer sued the manager and the clerk for damages for breach of contract. What result?

b) When the buyer took over the business, he decided to dispense with the services of the manager and the file clerk and fired them. In separate lawsuits the manager and the clerk sued the buyer for damages for breach of contract. What result?

11. An owner of certain land planned the construction and leasing of a number of store buildings to form a shopping center. The owner entered into contracts with various persons for various phases of construction and outfitting of the stores. The owner made one such written contract with a dealer who handled General Electric products only. Under the contract the owner agreed to buy from the dealer and the dealer agreed to sell at stated prices all the refrigeration equipment required by the plans and specifications referred to in the contract. The dealer in turn informed the General Electric Company of the contract and sent a copy of the specifications. The dealer made the contract in his own name, not in the name of the General Electric Company. The dealer was not an employee or agent of the General Electric Company; he was an independent retail dealer with a contract arrangement to handle GE refrigeration products for the area. Later the owner obtained a better price on some Westinghouse refrigeration equipment and had this equipment installed in various of the store buildings, instead of GE equipment. The General Electric Company sued the owner for damages. Explain 1) the reasoning upon which the General Electric Company might attempt to recover, 2) the reasoning upon which the owner might attempt to defend, and 3) which party should be given judgment.

12. An elderly woman who was being cared for by her niece wished to reward the latter but at the same time did not want to ignore her nephew. On February 1 the aunt signed and delivered to the niece a deed transferring a certain house and lot to the niece, in exchange for which the niece dated, signed, and gave to her aunt the following writing: "In consideration of the transfer to me of the house and lot at [describing the property], I hereby agree with the grantor of the premises that I will pay the sum of $8,000 to the grantor's nephew [naming him] within six months after the grantor's death." A few months later the aunt changed her mind about providing for her nephew and on April 15 dated and signed with her niece the following writing: "In consideration of the promise herein made by my niece [naming her] to care for me for the remainder of my life, I hereby release my niece from her obligation to pay $8,000 to my nephew [naming him] as previously provided in the agreement signed by my niece on February 1 of this year." The niece properly cared for her aunt until the latter died in December. When the nephew demanded $8,000 six months later, the niece refused to pay, and the nephew sued the niece.

a) Assume that the aunt told her nephew of the February 1 agreement immediately after it was signed. In the lawsuit of the nephew against the niece, explain 1) the reasoning upon which the nephew might attempt to collect, 2) the reasoning upon which the niece might attempt to defend, and 3) which party should be given judgment.

b) Assume that the nephew first learned of the February agreement shortly after his aunt's death. Answer the same questions asked in Part (a).

13. In connection with extensive remodeling of an owner's house, a builder agreed with the owner not only that the builder would do a certain described portion of the work for $5,000, but also that the builder would loan the owner a total of $7,000 to finance the remodeling. The owner signed and gave to the builder a written promise to repay the $7,000 loan within five years with interest at 6 percent, and as security gave the builder a mortgage on the premises. The parties orally agreed that the builder would disburse the $7,000 as follows: 1) the builder would retain $5,000 as payment in full for labor and materials in connection with his part of the remodeling, 2) the builder would pay a plumber selected by the owner the amount of the plumber's charges (but not exceeding the balance of the loan fund) for plumbing work in connection with the remodeling, and 3) the builder would then pay to the owner any balance that remained. The owner engaged a certain plumber who agreed to do the described work for $1,000, if this amount was agreeable to the builder. When the owner told the builder of the plumber's proposition, the builder agreed and said to the owner that he would pay $1,000 to the plumber. Upon learning of this, the plumber began work. When the remodeling including the plumbing was finished, the owner requested that the builder pay the entire $2,000 balance of the loan ($7,000 minus the builder's $5,000) to the owner. The builder did so. When the owner thereafter failed to pay the plumber, the plumber sued the builder who argued in defense that his promise was oral and that it was changed by the later arrangement between the builder and the owner. Explain 1) the reasoning upon which the plumber might attempt to collect from the builder, 2) the reasoning upon which the builder might attempt to defend, and 3) which party should be given judgment.

chapter 11

Excuses for Nonperformance

Just as it is essential in modern society that most contracts be legally enforced, so also is it considered necessary social policy that, if certain unexpected events occur, persons should be excused from their contractual obligations—sometimes completely excused, sometimes partially. The discussion of Mistakes Concerning Extrinsic Facts in Chapter 7 concerns fact situations in which, unknown to the parties, certain circumstances were in existence at the time they entered into their contract. Excuse in the present chapter will concentrate on circumstances or events occurring *after* the parties enter into their contract. The two types of fact situations are closely related and sometimes overlap, so that the applicable policy factors will often be the same.

Example: On June 1, S and B entered into a contract for the sale and purchase of a certain quantity of cotton owned by S and stored in an independent warehouse in another city, the parties agreeing on a stated price and specifying June 10 as the delivery date. The cotton was destroyed in a fire and a question arose concerning what effect the destruction of the cotton should have on the contract between S and B.

If the fire occurred on May 31, the question would be whether the casualty was sufficient to prevent an enforceable contract from being formed on June 1. This type of question is discussed in Chapter 7.

If the fire occurred on June 2, it would of course not affect the *formation* on June 1 of a valid and enforceable contract between the parties. The question instead would be whether the casualty should cancel or excuse performance of the contract already formed.

Example: A builder entered into a contract with a landowner in which, for a stated price, the builder agreed to excavate for a cellar of certain stated dimensions on the landowner's land. Unexpectedly the builder soon encountered solid rock which would increase his costs far beyond the original contract price for the job.

Some would classify this case as involving a mutual mistake concerning a condition in existence at the time the contract was formed, some others would classify the case as concerning a circumstance (discovery of the rock condition) arising after formation of the contract. Clearly whichever way the case is classified, the same policy factors will apply in determining whether the builder should be bound by his contract or excused from it.

292

Two types of excuse from contract obligations are widely accepted as being wise and desirable public policy—namely 1) excuse resulting from the expiration of the period of a statute of limitations, and 2) excuse resulting from a discharge in bankruptcy. Other situations in which questions of excuse frequently arise are much less clear cut. The most important of these situations involve 1) performance more burdensome or impossible—new circumstances (or newly discovered circumstances) adversely affect the expense of performance or the ability of the party claiming excuse to perform at all, and 2) disappointment in exchange performance—new circumstances (or newly discovered circumstances) adversely affect the item which the party claiming excuse is to receive in exchange for his agreed performance.

STATUTES OF LIMITATIONS

Various statutes fix periods of time within which any type of lawsuit, tort as well as contract, must be brought. A defendant may have a good defense to a plaintiff's claim, but after a time his evidence may be lost and his witnesses may forget or die. The purpose of the various statutes of limitations is to prevent the unfair enforcement of stale claims after the expiration of such a period of time as could adversely affect the proof of a defense. The period of time is designated by the legislature of the state concerned, and, being a policy determination, can be expected to vary in different states and with different types of lawsuits. The Uniform Commercial Code prescribes a limitation period for contracts involving the sales of goods, stating:

> (1) An action for breach of any contract for sale must be commenced within four years after the cause of action has accrued. By the original agreement the parties may reduce the period of limitation to not less than one year but may not extend it.
> (2) A cause of action accrues when the breach occurs, regardless of the aggrieved party's lack of knowledge of the breach. A breach of warranty occurs when tender of delivery is made, except that where a warranty explicitly extends to future performance of the goods and discovery of the breach must await the time of such performance the cause of action accrues when the breach is or should have been discovered.[1]

The limitation periods for other types of contracts (involving services, loans, and sales of land) vary among the different states. Some states prescribe a shorter period for unwritten contracts than for written contracts, other states make no such distinction. For other than sales-of-goods contracts, most of the statutory periods in the various states fall between two and six years for unwritten contracts and between three and twenty

[1] U.C.C. Sec. 2-725.

years for written contracts. Some statutes distinguish between sealed and unsealed promises, some allowing a longer time for a sealed promise, and a few not providing any statute of limitations at all for a sealed promise. In the latter type of state, usually the expiration of a substantial period of time (for example, twenty years) gives rise to a presumption that a sealed obligation has been paid. The presumption is not conclusive and if evidence affirmatively shows that a sealed promise has not been performed, it can be enforced even after expiration of the twenty-year period. Statutes in most states make no distinction in regard to sealed promises. The Uniform Commercial Code follows this view by providing in regard to sales-of-goods contracts:

> The affixing of a seal to a writing evidencing a contract for sale or an offer to buy or sell goods does not constitute the writing a sealed instrument and the law with respect to sealed instruments does not apply to such a contract or offer.[2]

After expiration of the prescribed limitation period, an obligation is considered stale and cannot be enforced without the obligor's consent. The statutory period usually begins to run on a particular promise from the time a lawsuit could be brought to enforce the promise. Starting at that time, the claim begins to grow stale. Should the obligor later admit that there is an enforceable obligation, he is admitting, as of that date, that he has no defense and that there is no longer any reason for the time which has already passed to prevent enforcement of his obligation. The claim becomes as fresh and enforceable as it was when originally contracted. With the further passage of time after such an admission, the claim again begins to grow stale. Such an admission, therefore, whether made before or after the expiration of the limitation period, has the effect of starting the limitation period running again.

An admission which is sufficient to renew the running of the limitation period can be made in various ways, including: 1) a clear, unequivocal promise to pay, or an acknowledgment of the obligation in such a manner as to imply a promise to pay, or 2) a part payment of the particular obligation in question.

If a debtor owes his creditor two separate obligations arising from two separate and distinct extensions of credit, and the debtor makes a payment smaller than the amount of either debt, and fails to specify the debt upon which he is making a payment, the creditor is usually permitted to apply the payment to the oldest debt—even though the collection of that debt is barred by the statute of limitations. Such an application by the *creditor*, however, certainly cannot be construed as an admission by the *debtor* as to the continued validity and enforce-

[2] U.C.C. Sec. 2-203.

ability of any particular debt, and, therefore, would not start the limitations period running anew on the older debt. On the other hand, if a debtor opens a charge account and makes a series of purchases, even though each purchase is a separate contract, the charge account obligation is a running account, a single extension of credit, which is understood by the parties to be a single obligation. Any payment by the debtor, therefore, would be an admission as to the entire account.

If when a debtor is sued on an obligation he fails to promptly claim the defense of the statute of limitations, it seems fair to construe his conduct as an admission that the obligation is enforceable, just as if he had expressly acknowledged the existence and enforceability of the obligation, and with the same effect.

Occasionally a contract includes an express provision that the contract promise will remain enforceable no matter how much time passes. In most states in which the question has arisen, such a provision is considered against public policy and not effective at all. Cases in some states consider such a waiver effective for a limited time. In one case, for example,[3] the court accorded limited effect to an unlimited waiver. In this case an obligor stated in his promissory note, "I also disclaim all limitations of whatever kind." The court said that this provision extended the obligation for an additional statute of limitations period, and that after the expiration of double the statutory period, the obligation could not be enforced.

BANKRUPTCY

The affairs of a person or business in financial difficulty may be settled in one of two ways: 1) through a liquidation of assets, which of course terminates the business enterprise, or 2) through financial rehabilitation, which enables the business to continue. Either of these two can be accomplished without court action (by agreement between the insolvent debtor and his creditors), or by court action, either through a state court insolvency proceeding or through a Federal court bankruptcy proceeding. Whichever is the objective—liquidation or rehabilitation—all debts will very rarely be paid in full. Participants in such a proceeding are well aware of this and therefore usually expect that any obligations remaining after available assets are exhausted will be canceled. Such a cancellation can be accomplished in one of two ways: 1) by each creditor voluntarily entering into an agreement discharging all unpaid claims, or 2) through a discharge decreed upon completion of a bankruptcy proceeding. After a bankruptcy discharge, the unpaid portion of most (but not all) debts cannot be collected. The debtor is

---

[3] *Hoffman* v. *Fisher*, 2 W.N.C. (Pa.) 17 (1875).

in effect excused from the balance of such obligations. A state court insolvency proceeding cannot discharge the claim of any creditor who refuses to agree to a discharge, the United States Constitution and Congress having reserved that power exclusively for Federal bankruptcy proceedings.

A bankruptcy proceeding has two important objectives: 1) to assure a fair distribution of the insolvent debtor's available assets among all his creditors, and 2) to free the debtor from his debts. The first objective is obviously fair, the second may be challenged. Some will argue that if a person incurs a just debt, he ought to be held to his obligation until it is paid. More persuasive, however (as evidenced by the fact that since an early date Congress has been so persuaded), is the argument 1) that a debtor's insolvency is not necessarily the result of his poor judgment but may instead be the result of economic conditions against which he is powerless, and 2) regardless of who is at fault in a debtor's becoming insolvent, if he remains saddled with an overwhelming burden of debt, his incentive and ability are stifled and he ceases to be a producing member of society. A method by which an honest debtor may be freed from oppressive indebtedness and restored as a contributing party in the economy is sound policy from which all of society benefits.

PERFORMANCE MORE BURDENSOME OR IMPOSSIBLE

Many contracts include "excuse" or "escape" provisions which state that the occurrence of certain specified events will excuse the parties from their contractual commitments. For example, sales-of-goods contracts frequently contain strike-escape provisions. Suppose, however, that some event not covered by an express escape provision unexpectedly occurs and renders a promisor's performance considerably more burdensome or even impossible. If the strict letter of the contract is all that matters, the promisor must nevertheless perform in spite of the unexpected occurrence—or pay damages for nonperformance. Before the present century the courts were inclined to hold persons rigidly to their contracts. The chief mission of the courts in contract disputes was limited to defining the terms of agreements, interpreting their meaning, and enforcing them. Present-day society, on the other hand, has broadened the role of the courts. In the words of Professor Morris Cohen,

> The roots of the law of contract are many rather than one. . . . The law must also go beyond the original intention of the parties, to settle controversies as to the distribution of gains and losses that the parties did not anticipate in the same way. . . .[4]

[4] Morris Cohen, *Law and the Social Order* (New York: Harcourt, 1933), p. 110.

In other words, it is considered sound, overall policy to permit persons *sometimes* to escape from burdensome contracts. Explaining in greater detail, Professor Cohen writes:

> Now the human power to foresee all the consequences of an agreement is limited, even if we suppose that the two parties understand each other's meaning to begin with. Disputes or disagreements are therefore bound to come up; and the law of contract may thus be viewed as an attempt to determine the rights and duties of the two parties under circumstances that were not anticipated exactly in the same way by the two contracting parties, or at any rate were not expressly provided for in an unambiguous way. One can therefore say that the court's adjudication *supplements* the original contract as a *method of distributing gains and losses.*
>
> From this point of view we may look upon the law of contract as a number of rules according to which courts distribute gains and losses according to the equities of such cases; and the pretense that the result follows exclusively from the agreement of the two parties is fictional. Just as the process of interpreting a statute is really a process of subsidiary legislation, so is the interpretation of a contract really a method of supplementing the original agreement by such provisions as are necessary to determine the point at issue.
>
> If we view the law of contract as directed to strengthening the security of transactions by enabling men to rely more fully on promises, we see only one phase of its actual workings. The other phase is the determination of the rights of the contracting parties as to contingencies that they have not foreseen, and for which they have not provided. In this latter respect the law of contract is a way of enforcing some kind of *distributive justice* within the legal system. And technical doctrines of contract may thus be viewed as a set of rules that will systematize decisions in this field and thus give lawyers and their clients some guidance in the problem of anticipating future decisions. . . . In any case, the essential problem of the law of contract is the problem of distribution of risks. The other phase, namely, the assurance that what the parties have actually agreed on will be fulfilled, is a limiting principle.[5]   [Emphasis added.]

Some theorists suggest that when a court is determining the circumstances under which a contract duty should be considered excused, the court is merely interpreting what the parties would have intended if they had thought of the unexpected event. In the passage just quoted, Professor Cohen rejects this view. So also does Professor Roscoe Pound, who has written:

> Often the words finally written in a contract after a long negotiation are the result of hard-fought compromises. They are not ideal provisions from the standpoint of either side, but are what each is willing to concede in order to reach agreement. After some frustrating event has happened and a party who has suffered damage from nonper-

[5] *Op. cit.,* pp. 101–102.

formance is suing for it, to say that he intended and would have consented to insert a condition which the court conjures up to relieve the promisor is to make a new contract under the fiction of interpretation. This sort of interpretation, which has much vogue in the service state, is said by a judge of one of our courts to be a process of distillation. We are told that the meaning is distilled from the words. It might be suggested that distilling is often illicit and the product moonshine.[6]

To avoid "distilling moonshine" and to achieve Professor Cohen's "distributive justice," the courts recognize that society is a necessary third party in every contract. The courts represent the interests of society in determining and allocating risks in a socially desirable way. This function imposes a difficult task on the courts. Weighing heavily on one side is the strong economic and social necessity for contractual commitments to be stable and not easily avoided. Woven into this is the fact that the obligation from which a promisor is seeking to be excused is one which he voluntarily assumed without any express agreement for an escape provision covering the event in question. Against this the courts must weigh the nature and degree of the unexpected burden resulting from the particular event which has occurred. One very helpful guide in thus balancing stability against flexibility is to classify events according to whether they render performance 1) more burdensome but not impossible, 2) personally impossible, or 3) completely impossible.

1) *Increased Burden.* When used in distinction to the term "impossibility," the term "increased burden" means that although performance has become more difficult or expensive, the burden is not so extreme or unreasonable as to make performance prohibitive.

2) *Personal Impossibility.* Sometimes also called "subjective impossibility," the term "personal impossibility" refers to a situation in which, while it is impossible (or extremely unreasonable) for the promisor himself to perform his contractual commitment, performance exactly according to the contract is possible by someone else.

Example: A sales contract involves standardized goods. Before the seller can make delivery, the goods which he intends to deliver are destroyed through no fault of his.

Since the goods are standardized, other persons have goods which exactly meet the description in the contract. However, if the seller has insufficient funds or credit to procure additional goods, performance will be impossible for the seller personally, although the contract is capable of being performed exactly according to its terms by some other person.

3) *Complete Impossibility.* Sometimes also called "objective impossibility," the term "complete impossibility" is used to describe a situation

[6] Roscoe Pound, *An Introduction to the Philosophy of Law* (New Haven: Yale U. P., 1954); Yale paperback ed., 1959, p. 167.

in which it has become impossible (or extremely unreasonable) for the promisor or anyone else to perform the commitment according to the contract.

Example: A sales contract involves a rare, original painting which, through no fault of the seller, is destroyed before the seller can deliver it to the buyer.

Inasmuch as the contract involves unique goods, the casualty renders performance of the contract completely impossible. Nobody can perform it, neither the seller nor anyone else.

The general tendency of the courts is frequently (but not always) to favor excusing a promisor in the case of complete impossibility, but usually not in cases of personal impossibility or increased burden. This general tendency can be further discussed and illustrated by briefly examining work and service contracts and contracts for sales of goods— two types of contracts in which questions involving the effect of impossibility or increased burden frequently arise.

CONTRACTS FOR WORK OR SERVICES

If a promisor's contractual commitment is to perform work or services of the type which cannot be delegated to another (as discussed in Chapter 10), and the promisor becomes incapable of performing, performance can be classified as completely impossible. The duty of the promisor to perform such a personal contract is excused if the promisor dies or is prevented by illness from performing (unless the evidence clearly shows that the promisor's incapacity is self-induced to avoid the contract). On the other hand, if the contracted work or services are such that performance could be delegated to some other person, the promisor's death or other incapacity would render his performance personally impossible rather than completely impossible. Although the dead or incapacitated promisor cannot personally perform, another person can render performance exactly in accordance with the contract. Generally the duty of a promisor to perform an impersonal contract is not excused and the promisor (or if he is dead, his estate) will be held liable if the contractual commitment is not performed.

CONTRACTS FOR SALES OF GOODS

When a question of possible excuse arises in a contract for the future sale and delivery of goods, one important factor to consider is the status of the goods at the time the contract is formed, whether the goods are 1) identified, or 2) merely described but not yet identified. Goods are identified when certain particular goods are segregated or designated for delivery under the contract. On the other hand, a contract for de-

livery of described but unidentified goods states the quantity and kind
of goods involved, but the particular item, lot, or batch which fits the
description and is to be delivered under the contract is not yet segregated or designated.

Example (involving identified goods): A seller, a college student, owner
of a new copy of a book entitled *Introduction to Basic Legal Principles* showed
the book to a buyer, after which the seller entered into a contract with the
buyer, the seller agreeing to sell and deliver "this book" to the buyer one
week later and the buyer to pay $5 upon delivery. That night the seller's
book was destroyed through no fault of the seller.

It seems a fair interpretation of the intent of the parties that their contract
presupposed the continued existence of the very book which both had in mind
when they reached their agreement. While other copies of the same title
might be readily available, the seller's contract was to deliver the specified
or identified book, not just any copy of the book.

Example (involving unidentified goods): A buyer phoned a book dealer
and ordered one copy of a book entitled *Introduction to Basic Legal Principles*,
for $5 to be delivered one week later and paid for on delivery. The dealer
accepted the order. That night through no fault of the dealer, his one remaining copy of the book was destroyed.

Since the parties were not dealing with one particular copy of the book
but rather with any copy of the described book, the continued existence of
the dealer's copy would not seem to be an implied term of the contract nor
important for enforcement of the contract.

Goods Identified When Contract Formed

The Uniform Commercial Code provides:

> Where the contract requires for its performance goods identified
> when the contract is made, and the goods suffer casualty without fault
> of either party before the risk of loss passes to the buyer . . . then
>
> (a) if the loss is total the contract is avoided; and
>
> (b) if the loss is partial or the goods have so deteriorated as no
> longer to conform to the contract the buyer may nevertheless demand
> inspection and at his option either treat the contract as avoided or
> accept the goods with due allowance from the contract price for the
> deterioration or the deficiency in quantity but without further right
> against the seller.[7]

The "risk of loss" referred to in the above quotation usually (but not
always) remains with the seller until he ships the goods, or if transportation of the goods is not contemplated, until he turns the goods over to
the buyer (see Chapter 16). Notice that the casualty referred to in the
above-quoted rule is treated as rendering performance completely impossible, thus fully excusing both parties from their contract.

[7] U.C.C. Sec. 2-613.

Goods Not Identified When Contract Formed

The Uniform Commercial Code provides:

> Except so far as a seller may have assumed a greater obligation . . . :
>
> (a) Delay in delivery or nondelivery in whole or in part by a seller who complies with paragraphs (b) and (c) is not a breach of his duty under a contract for sale *if performance as agreed has been made impracticable by the occurrence of a contingency the non-occurrence of which was a basic assumption on which the contract was made* or by compliance in good faith with any applicable foreign or domestic governmental regulation or order. . . .
>
> (b) Where the causes mentioned in paragraph (a) affect only a part of the seller's capacity to perform, he must allocate production and deliveries among his customers but may at his option include regular customers not then under contract as well as his own requirements for further manufacture. He may so allocate in any manner which is fair and reasonable.
>
> (c) The seller must notify the buyer seasonably that there will be delay or non-delivery and, when allocation is required under paragraph (b), of the estimated quota thus made available for the buyer.[8] [Emphasis added.]

In other words, excuse depends upon the risks which parties assume, or which as a matter of policy they should be considered to assume when entering into contracts. If the event which renders performance unreasonably burdensome or impossible concerns a matter totally unexpected, a matter assumed by the parties to be stable and not subject to variation, it is a matter concerning which they are not assuming the risk of some casualty or change. In such a case it seems fair, reasonable, and practical to hold that the occurrence of the unexpected event excuses performance. Notice that the key factor—risk—is the same as applied to Mistakes Concerning Extrinsic Facts, discussed in Chapter 7. Notice also that any attempt to formulate a statement of this principle is so inexact that it leaves considerable latitude to courts to differ in particular situations concerning the risks which contracting parties should be considered to assume, and concerning the policy conclusions which should be reached in balancing (on the one side) fairness, reasonableness, and practicality against (on the other side) the need for stability of contracts. In view of this vagueness and indefiniteness, a careful businessman should attempt to look ahead to unexpected but possible occurrences, and consult his lawyer in regard to escape provisions which it would be wise for him to include in his future business contracts.

The most common casualities which may occur in connection with described but unidentified goods concern either 1) the seller's possession

[8] U.C.C. Sec. 2-615.

(that is, his procuring and preparing the goods for shipment) or 2) the seller's ability to make shipment.

1) *Occurrences Affecting Seller's Possession.* Such occurrences may be further subdivided according to whether or not the seller is the producer of the goods which he has contracted to sell.

a) Seller is to produce the contract goods. If a seller agrees to manufacture the contract goods at his factory or to grow them on his farm, accidental destruction of the seller's factory or failure of his crop causes, to some extent at least, complete impossibility. Even though the described goods are standardized, similar goods procured elsewhere do not exactly fit the contract description, since the contract specifies the particular source. Although from the standpoint of assignment and delegation discussed in Chapter 10, the contract may be nonpersonal, so that the seller could validly delegate performance and the buyer be required to accept goods from another source, still in allocating losses resulting from a destruction of the seller's production facilities, many courts feel that since the seller has lost the facilities specified in the contract, the buyer should bear the loss of his bargain under the contract— with the result that the buyer cannot enforce the contract against the seller. Although the cases tend in this direction, court decisions in the various states are not uniform.

If a contract makes no reference to the seller's factory or farm, it is arguable that such a reference is implied if the parties contemplate that the seller is to produce what he has agreed to sell.

If a seller is unable to manufacture and deliver because his factory is closed by strike, the seller is usually not excused. A labor dispute is considered as a moderate, foreseeable increase of burden. When the seller's factory is destroyed, his loss is great (even though the physical plant is insured), and there is a strong urge to allocate losses between the parties by excusing the seller from his contract. There is not nearly as great a loss or the same urge when a labor dispute prevents the seller from performing.

b) Seller is not to produce the contract goods. If the seller is not expected to produce the goods he has contracted to sell, any casualty to his expected source or to his inventory usually will not excuse the seller.

2) *Occurrences Affecting Seller's Ability to Ship.* Sometimes (as for example when a general railroad strike occurs) a seller's contemplated means of transportation suddenly becomes unavailable to him. An old Pennsylvania case[9] excused a seller when a flood destroyed the navigation facilities which the seller had intended to use, and it is arguable that this would also be the correct view under the Uniform Commercial Code.

[9] *Lovering v. Buck Mt. Coal Co.,* 54 Pa. 291 (1867).

However, most court decisions have, in the past, taken the opposite view, holding that if a disruption of transportation is not highly extraordinary, it is a risk which a seller assumes and, therefore, is not an excuse.

DISAPPOINTMENT IN OTHER PARTY'S PERFORMANCE

Suppose that A and B enter into a contract under which A agrees to pay a specified sum, or to perform in some other way, in exchange for certain performance by B. Suppose further that after formation of the contract, an event occurs which depreciates the value of what B does or is to do, or otherwise disappoints A in what he is to receive in exchange for his own performance. A might thereupon argue that he should no longer be obliged to pay or otherwise perform his own part of the contract. The principal events which might thus cause A to be disappointed in B's performance and consequently claim to be excused, can be classified as follows:

1. Solvency reasonably doubtful: A learns that B is insolvent and therefore A fears that he will not be paid for his performance.

2. Defective performance: B fails to perform fully or properly according to the agreement, and A is unwilling to pay anything at all for B's partial or defective performance.

3. Frustration of purpose: Although B performs in full accordance with the agreement, B's performance is of less value to A than when the contract was formed and for this reason A is unwilling to pay.

Solvency Reasonably Doubtful

Suppose that a builder contracts with a landowner for construction of a certain building for $50,000 payable at stated times as the work progresses, and suppose further that after formation of the contract, the landowner becomes insolvent. Even though the time for payment may not yet have arrived so that technically the landowner cannot be said to have breached his contract, there is a strong likelihood that he will breach the contract. Under such circumstances it would be quite unreasonable to require the builder to continue his performance. Therefore when one party to a contract is insolvent, the other party is excused from performing unless and until he receives adequate assurance that he will be fully paid.

Actual proof of insolvency may be difficult. Therefore (as discussed in Chapter 16) in phrasing this rule for sales-of-goods contracts, the Uniform Commercial Code[10] extends the excuse to cases in which the

---

[10] U.C.C. Sec. 2-609.

seller has reasonable grounds to be worried about the buyer's solvency, even though evidence subsequently produced shows that the buyer was not actually insolvent.

DEFECTIVE PERFORMANCE

If the performance of a contract obligation is somewhat defective in certain respects, a question frequently arises as to whether the party who performed is entitled to partial payment for the portion of his performance which does conform to the contract. The party who performs defectively, the recipient of the performance, and society in general all have interests in such a question. If the performing party is unable to recover for the portion of his performance which is properly done, to that extent he is penalized or punished for what may be an inadvertent and unimportant breach of contract. On the other hand, if the recipient of the performance is required to make a partial payment for defective performance, to that extent he is forced to pay for something which he did not agree to buy. Society, of course, has an interest in encouraging proper and complete performance of contract obligations and in not unduly weakening the stability of contracts. Upon weighing the various conflicting interests, the courts have decided that *in some cases* it is sound policy (fair, reasonable, and practical) to permit partial recovery for slightly defective performance. In formulating and applying this principle, the courts weigh the following interrelated factors:

1. The amount of deviation or defect (extent and value) in proportion to the entire contract.

2. The reason for the deviation—that is, whether it results from a deliberate and intentional disregard of the contract or only from an inadvertent and careless oversight.

3. The benefits received by the party for whom the performance is rendered.

4. The forfeiture threatened to the performer if recovery is denied.

5. The adequacy of money damages to fully protect or compensate the party for whom the performance is rendered.

6. The time when the deviation is discovered in relation to the time for performance of the entire contract.

7. The feasibility of the performer correcting the defects so that his performance will exactly comply with the contract.

The question of whether or not recovery should be allowed for substantial but incomplete performance most often arises in connection with land contracts (either sale or construction contracts); recovery for defective performance is seldom permitted in sales-of-goods contracts.

Construction and Sale-of-Land Contracts

Partial recovery for incomplete performance is most often permitted in connection with the construction of a building on land already owned by the other party to the contract, the party for whom the building is being constructed. While the landowner has a right to receive a building constructed according to the contract and completed on time, if the owner is permitted to completely reject a building because of minor defects or a minor delay the builder will lose much of his labor and material. Taking back a building as a unit is a limited remedy; taking back the materials usually leaves the builder with a pile of rubble. It seems fair, therefore, to say that if the owner can be fully compensated by money damages, the builder should recover for his substantial performance less any damages the owner sustains.

No exact definition or formula can be stated for determining when a certain building will be considered as substantially complying with a construction contract. The degree of correct compliance is a major factor. Thus, defective performance is not substantial unless the defects can be corrected for a cost which is low in comparison with the entire contract price. Also, for performance to be substantial, the defects must concern unimportant details which do not affect the general plan and purpose of the building. However, while the percentage of compliance is quite important, the other factors which have been previously listed are also important.

If a builder's performance is not substantial, he is not entitled to be paid the contracted compensation. However, if a landowner derives a benefit from accepting and using what the builder has done, some courts argue that since the purpose of the civil law (as distinguished from the criminal law) is not to punish or to penalize the builder, he should be able to recover for the value of the benefit which the owner actually receives. Other courts however argue that since an owner cannot be expected to give up the use of his land, he really has no opportunity to reject a building or work done to a building on his land. These courts have held, therefore, that the benefit to the owner does not entitle the builder to collect anything at all unless his performance is sufficient to be classed as substantial.

A building construction contract will often contain a provision specifying the amount of damages which the builder must pay to the owner for each day of delay after a certain date. Such a provision is called an agreed or liquidated damage provision. If reasonably related to actual loss, the liquidated damage provision is enforceable. If, on the other hand, no reasonable relationship appears between the agreed damage provision and the actual losses which might possibly result, the provision really amounts to a penalty which the civil courts will not enforce.

In a contract for the sale and purchase of land, it is common for the parties to agree on a certain settlement time, a date when the seller is to deliver the deed for the property and the buyer is to pay the agreed price. Many such contracts expressly state, "Time is of the essence of this contract." Such a provision will be enforced; for even a slight delay by one party, the other may cancel the entire contract. On the other hand, if time is not made vitally important (or of the essence) either expressly or by circumstances, a delay will justify cancellation only if it is a material delay. A "time is of the essence" provision is uncommon in building construction contracts. However, if such a provision is included, it will be enforced; the builder cannot collect under the contract even though his delay is slight. Even so, if the work which the builder has done is on the owner's land and the owner makes use of it, some will argue that the owner should be obliged to pay for the value of the benefit which he receives.

Example: A builder and a landowner entered into a contract under which the builder agreed to construct a building on the owner's land according to certain plans and specifications, and the owner agreed to pay $77,000, payable in installments at stated times as the work progressed, with the final payment of $3,500 to be made after completion of construction. The specifications provided that the pipe used for plumbing should be "wrought-iron pipe, galvanized, lap welded, standard grade, manufactured by the Reading Company." The pipe used met these specifications exactly except that inadvertently about one-half of the pipe used was made by manufacturers other than the Reading Company. The deviation was not discovered until the architect was going over the invoices, which was after all of the plastering was completed. The owner refused to make the final payment until the pipe manufactured by others was replaced by Reading Company pipe. The builder refused to tear out the walls in order to change the pipe, and sued the owner for the amount of the final payment.

Admittedly, there was nothing in the circumstances sufficient to excuse the builder from performing his commitment. He, therefore, would be liable for any damages which might result from his defective performance.

However, in the case upon which this example is based, the court (the New York Court of Appeals[11]) decided that under the circumstances (substantial performance, inadvertent deviation, penalty to builder and gratuitous gift to owner if recovery denied) the builder was entitled to recover under the contract, less damages for the deviation. Since under the particular circumstances the owner could prove no actual damages, the builder recovered the entire final payment for which he had sued.

[11] *Jacob & Young, Inc.* v. *Kent,* 230 N.Y. 239, 129 N.E. 889, 23 A.L.R. 1429 (1921).

The decision was a close one, four to three. The three minority judges felt that the builder should not recover because, through his neglect, he failed to give the owner the pipe for which the owner had contracted, regardless of the reason why the owner wanted pipe from a certain company and even though designating that certain company might have been only a whim of the owner's.

Example: A builder contracted to build a certain type of roof on an owner's building for $325. Upon completion of the work, the owner wrote to the builder that the roof was not satisfactory, that it was leaking in several places, was not smooth, not saturated between layers, and not adequately covered, and that the owner would not pay unless the builder would take off the unsatisfactory roof and put on one that conformed to the contract. The builder denied that the roof was defective. Although the owner used the building without having the new roof fixed, he persisted in his refusal to pay. The builder sued the owner for the agreed price. From the evidence the jury concluded 1) that the roof was defective and would cost $80 to repair in order to conform to the contract, and 2) that because of leakage through the defective roof, the walls of the owner's building were damaged to the extent of $75. The trial court entered a judgment for the builder for $170, the contract price ($325) less the cost of remedying the defects ($80) and less the amount of damages caused by the defects ($75).

In the case upon which this example is based, the Wisconsin Supreme Court[12] reversed the judgment and directed the trial court to enter judgment against the builder for the owner's $75 damages. The court said that the builder could recover nothing under the contract because his performance was not substantial, and that since the owner had no reasonable alternative but to continue to use his building, his use of the roof which the builder had constructed would not give rise to any obligation to pay anything for the roof.

Some courts would be in complete agreement with this conclusion, while other courts would agree only partially. The latter courts would agree that since the builder's performance was not substantial, he would not be entitled to any recovery measured by the contract price. However, these courts nevertheless would say that since the owner derived a benefit from the builder's work, he should be required to pay the builder whatever was determined to be the money value of that benefit.

Sales-of-Goods Contracts

Society's permitting a building contractor to recover a partial payment when his performance is slightly defective, is based mainly on the builder's inability to remove an already completed building from the owner's land, and the consequent severe loss or penalty the builder would sustain. A seller of goods on the other hand can take the rejected goods back. Generally, therefore, in sales-of-goods contracts (unless delivery

---

[12] *Nees* v. *Weaver*, 222 Wis. 492, 269 N.W. 266, 107 A.L.R. 1405 (1936).

in installments is involved, as discussed later) a buyer is permitted to reject for any deviation at all.

Some earlier court decisions excepted from this general rule cases in which goods had been specially manufactured for the particular buyer in question and were not suitable for others (for example, a machine specially designed for the buyer and useless to anyone else except as scrap metal). Permitting the buyer to reject for minor defects would penalize the seller, forfeiting much of his labor. However, such a case still differs from the case of a building erected on an owner's land, because when the buyer rejects the machine, he does not retain or enjoy any benefit from the seller's work. Other early court cases, therefore, declared as a matter of policy that there should be no distinction between specially manufactured goods and standardized goods. The Uniform Sales Act (which was formerly in effect in about two-thirds of the states) and the Uniform Commercial Code[13] which supersedes the Sales Act, both follow this latter view. Even goods specially manufactured for a buyer and not reasonably useful to others, can be rejected if they do not *exactly* conform to the contract in all respects—quality, quantity, time and place of delivery, etc. (except in installment delivery contracts). Note, however, that it is possible for a particular shipment to actually conform to a contract even though it is somewhat defective. This is so when a certain percentage of defects are considered as commercially acceptable, by virtue of a usage or custom of the particular trade involved. For example, in one case involving a contract for a quantity of goat skins, the evidence showed that dealers of such goods could expect from 1½ to 3 percent of the skins in a sizable shipment to be defective. If the quantity of defective skins in a shipment did not exceed this percentage, the shipment would be considered as fully conforming to the contract. The Uniform Commercial Code states this rule as follows:

> A course of dealing between parties and any usage of trade in the vocation or trade in which they are engaged or of which they are or should be aware give particular meaning to and supplement or qualify terms of an agreement.[14]

Contract for Installment Deliveries.[15] Goods are supposed to be delivered in a single lot unless installment delivery is agreed upon or understood. In a contract for delivery in installments, any one installment is only a fraction of the entire contract, even though it may be a sizable fraction. If a defect in a shipment is minor and the shipment is only a portion of the total contract, the defect, already minor, shrinks to insignificance from the standpoint of the entire contract. The authors

[13] U.C.C. Sec. 2-601.
[14] U.C.C. Sec. 1-205.
[15] U.C.C. Secs. 2-307, 2-612.

of the Uniform Commercial Code therefore feel (following a similar view in the Uniform Sales Act) that it is sound policy to deny to a buyer a right to reject for such an insignificant defect. The Code provides:

> The buyer may reject any installment which is non-conforming *if* the non-conformity substantially impairs the value of that installment and cannot be cured. . . . [Emphasis added.]

However, the authors of the Code further suggest[16] that if, for a commercially sound reason, a contract expressly requires exact compliance, then even under the Code a court could decide that *any* noncompliance in an installment would amount to a substantial breach and justify rejection.

FRUSTRATION OF PURPOSE

Several English cases, generically referred to as the "Coronation Cases"[17] are probably the most famous lawsuits involving the question of excuse on the ground of frustration of purpose. When Edward VII ascended to the English throne after the death of Queen Victoria, an elaborate coronation ceremony was planned for a certain date, to include a parade over a specified route and a naval review. Numerous contracts were entered into by persons seeking to obtain facilities for viewing the pageantry. One defendant contracted to pay a certain sum for use, on the stated date, of the window space in the plaintiff's apartment which overlooked the line of the parade. Another defendant, intending to take paying passengers to watch the naval review, contracted to hire a ship for the stated date. When the King became ill the coronation plans were indefinitely postponed and the defendants sought to avoid their contract obligations, while the plaintiffs tendered the contracted window space and ship and sued to collect the agreed payments. Notice the similarity of such cases to mistake in value cases discussed in Chapter 7, where disappointment arises from some extrinsic fact in existence but unknown at the time a contract is formed. The only difference is that in the Coronation Cases the event occurred *after* the formation of the contracts. The plaintiffs were able to tender the exact physical items they had contracted to give, a seat by a certain window on the contract date, the use of a certain ship on the contract date. The postponement of the coronation made no change at all in the window or the ship, it merely changed their expected use and value to the defendants. Since value is constantly fluctuating as innumerable conditions constantly change, the

---

[16] Comment to Sec. 2-612.

[17] Chiefly the following: *Herne Bay S.S. Co.* v. *Hutton,* 2 K.B. 683 (1903); *Krell* v. *Henry,* 2 K.B. 740 (1903); *Civil Serv. Co-op. Soc.* v. *Gen. Steam Nav. Co.,* 2 K.B. 756 (1903); *Chandler* v. *Webster,* 1 K.B. 493 (1904).

law feels that it is usually not sound policy to excuse a person from his contract to buy a described item merely because later events have decreased its value. Sometimes, however, the courts soften this rule by attempting to spread losses which result from totally unexpected occurrences. In the Coronation Cases the court somewhat arbitrarily (as the court admitted) ruled that the defendants would be required to pay all that became due and payable under their contracts up to the time the coronation plans were changed—even if this was the entire contract price—but that any amounts due and payable after the change was announced could not be collected. Some legal scholars argue that a party should be discharged from a promise on the theory of frustration of purpose if the following conditions are *all* present:[18]

1. A later event completely changes or eliminates a certain fact situation which both parties, at the time of contracting, assumed would exist in the future.

2. The assumed fact situation was the motive for both parties entering into the contract.

3. The assumed fact situation concerned a matter reasonably believed by both parties to be stable and not subject to variation, and a matter as to which persons entering into such contracts could not reasonably be expected to assume the risk of change.

Under this suggested theory it is arguable that the defendants in the Coronation Cases would be considered excused from paying for the contracted window space or ship.

The field of real estate leasing has provided many frustration-of-purpose cases, with the general tendency being that a tenant who obtains the interest contemplated by the lease is not excused from paying rent when a later occurrence lessens the value of his leasehold interest or renders it entirely worthless. If the use specified in the lease has become totally illegal (as in liquor prohibition cases), some courts have recognized an exception and considered a tenant excused.

Example: A landlord leased to a tenant a described piece of land and the building erected thereon for a period of five years, beginning on June 1 of a certain year, for an annual rental of $1,200, payable in monthly installments in advance. The tenant enjoyed occupancy and use of the building until August 25 of the first year, when a fire completely destroyed the building. When the tenant abandoned the premises after the fire and refused to pay any further rent, the landlord sued the tenant. Nothing in the lease covered such an eventuality.

At common law and in many states the tenant would remain obligated to pay rent for the entire leasehold period. In any discussion of the rights

[18] See Restatement, Contracts, Sec. 288.

and duties of landlords and tenants, two legal principles predominate: 1) for a person to become a tenant of certain premises, he must have an agreement or contract with the landlord, and 2) such an agreement grants to the tenant a real estate interest in the rented premises. Since a tenant has a real estate interest, he is actually a limited owner of the rented premises for the duration of the lease. If an entire building is leased to a tenant, his interest includes not only the building but also the land upon which it stands. As a limited owner of a property interest, the tenant enjoys the advantages and bears the burdens of ownership—he gains if the property increases in value, he loses if value declines or the property becomes worthless. If the tenant is conducting a business on the premises and is only half as successful as he had hoped, his disappointment does not mitigate his obligation to pay rent. If he is not excused when he is 50 percent disappointed, it is arguable that he should not be excused when he is 100 percent disappointed. He is still the limited owner of the property interest for which he agreed to pay a stated rent.

Other factors are also involved in the case of total destruction of a rented building, including the following:

1. *Sharing of Losses.* Since the landlord loses the total value of his building, losses are somewhat shared if the tenant loses the value of his leasehold use. In other words, if the tenant has paid the full amount of the rent in advance, he should not recover it; if he still owes rent, his obligation continues. (Of course if the landlord has fire insurance, that fact and the amount of insurance becloud but do not necessarily negate this factor.)

2. *Inducing Carefulness.* In cases involving the destruction of a leased building, the facts often state that the tenant was not at fault. Frequently, however, this is a conclusion resulting from the absence of evidence to prove otherwise. Since the tenant is in exclusive occupancy, a valid argument can be made that if the law requires the tenant to bear the risk of loss as a limited property owner, he will be induced to use greater care.

Therefore it is considered sound policy under the common law of many states to hold that a casualty to the premises will usually not excuse a tenant from his obligation to pay rent. That the landlord is reimbursed under his fire insurance policy and refuses to repair or rebuild is usually immaterial; usually it is also immaterial that the casualty may have resulted from a concealed defect in the building (for example, defective wiring), unless the defect was actually known to the landlord at the time of leasing.

On the other hand, if only a portion of a building (an apartment or an office) is leased to a tenant, the tenant has a real estate interest in that portion of the building but no interest in the land. It would be impractical to consider that occupants of different portions of a building have interests in sections or slices of the land upon which the building stands, or interests in portions of the air space over the surface of the land. Therefore it seems fair, reasonable, and practical to say that a casualty sufficient to prevent the tenant's beneficial use of the portion leased to him destroys the *entire* interest of the tenant and frees him from further payment of rent.

PROBLEMS

1. On his sixteenth birthday, B purchased a bicycle from S, an adult, for $95, payable $10 down and the balance to be paid at the rate of $5 per month. After making two monthly payments, B made no further payments. S did nothing concerning the bicycle until three months after B came of age. Two months after B came of age he sold the bicycle to P. One month thereafter S sued B to recover the unpaid balance of the purchase price of the bicycle.

a) Explain 1) the reasoning upon which B might attempt to defend, 2) the reasoning upon which S might attempt to collect, and 3) which party should be given judgment.

b) Other facts remaining the same, assume that B never sold the bicycle, but that two months after coming of age, he orally promised S that within one month he would pay the full amount of the balance due on the bicycle. When B defaulted on this promise, S sued. Answer the same questions asked in Part (a). (Modifed from A.I.C.P.A., Nov. 51-6.)

2. On February 1, C loaned his good friend D $500 to be repaid within six months. By the middle of the year D was in financial difficulty and C did not press for repayment. Although D and C saw each other frequently, nothing further was said about the loan until March, ten years later, when D, during a conversation with C, said that in going over some old records he had been reminded of the $500 loan. D added, "I can't pay right now but don't worry, I'll pay you as soon as I can." C replied, "Oh, forget it—I have." However, the following June, when D unexpectedly inherited a large sum of money, C reminded D of the $500 obligation. When D failed to pay by September 1, C sued.

a) Assume that the statute of limitations on such debts was five years. Explain 1) the reasoning upon which D might attempt to defend, 2) the reasoning upon which C might attempt to collect, and 3) which party should be given judgment.

b) Assume that the statute of limitations on such debts was ten years. Answer the same questions as are asked in Part (a).

3. On thirty different occasions between January 1 and November 1, a supplier sold and delivered to a contractor, on open account, various building materials in the aggregate amount of $4,550. Assume that open-account purchases were payable by the tenth of the month following the month of purchase. Most of the supplies were purchased before June 1. From June 2 until November 1 the total sales aggregated only $500, after which the contractor made no further purchases from the supplier. From time to time the contractor made nine payments on the account, in varying amounts totaling altogether $2,500. The last two payments were of $100 each and were made on June 20 and July 10 respectively. On July 6, four years later, the supplier started a lawsuit against the contractor for the $2,050 balance due. Explain 1) the reasoning upon which the contractor might attempt a complete or partial defense, 2) the reasoning upon which the supplier might attempt to collect the entire amount claimed, and 3) how much if anything the supplier was entitled to recover in his lawsuit.

4. R who owned and operated a small manufacturing business employed E as purchasing agent on a five-year contract at a salary of $8,000 per year. Three years later, business reversals not at all the fault of R rendered R's business hopelessly insolvent. In an action initiated by R's creditors and vigorously opposed by R, the state court appointed a receiver for R's assets and ordered the sale of all assets, thus forcing the termination of R's business. E filed a claim with the receiver for 1) $1,000 wages due and unpaid at the time of the court adjudication, and 2) $500 damages sustained by E as a result of the termination of R's business and consequently of E's job. Should E's claims be allowed?

5. For some years T had successfully operated various dance pavilions. Knowing this, O, the owner of a newly constructed dance hall leased the hall to T for two years at a stated rental. One year later T died. T's executor considered the lease terminated and so notified O. No provision in the lease covered this eventuality. O refused to agree to termination of the lease and when the executor refused to pay any rent accruing after T's death, O sued T's estate. Explain 1) the reasoning upon which T's executor might attempt to defend, 2) the reasoning upon which O might attempt to collect, and 3) which party should be given judgment.

6. An engineering company employed E as a beginning draftsman for a six-month period, at $250 per month, $175 of which was to be paid to E at the end of each month, with the balance payable to E upon the satisfactory completion of his six-month's service. During the next four months E's work was satisfactory. At the end of the fourth month, E, while driving carefully on a weekend fishing trip, was killed in an auto accident by a car carelessly driven by D. The company sustained $400 damages through being suddenly deprived of E's services.

a) E's administrator requested payment of the withheld portion of E's salary and when the company refused to pay, the administrator sued the company. What result? Explain.

b) The company sued D for damages sustained through being deprived of E's services. What result? Explain.

7. E was a bookkeeper for the R Mills, receiving his salary monthly under a contract which provided that if E left without giving a two-week notice, he would receive nothing for wages accrued during the current month. On May 31 E was arrested for manslaughter following an auto accident. Unable to pay bail, E was kept in the county jail until trial. Upon trial E was convicted and sentenced to state prison. R Mills refused to pay E any salary for the month of May. The damages which R Mills sustained through being deprived of E's services without two-week's advance notice, exceeded the amount of E's May Salary.

a) Would E be entitled to any salary for May? Explain.

b) Other facts being the same, assume that E's trial was held early in

June, and that E was acquitted of the crime charged and released. Would E be entitled to any salary for May? Explain. (Modified from A.I.C.P.A., Nov. 30-9.)

8. The owner of a plot of land entered into a written contract with a contractor under which the contractor agreed to excavate for a cellar of stated size at a certain location on the owner's land, for which the owner agreed to pay a stated amount upon completion of the work. Soon after the contractor commenced work he encountered considerable solid rock. Neither the contractor nor the owner had suspected the presence of the rock. The contractor met with the owner and they orally agreed that the contractor would complete the excavation described in the written contract, and that the owner would thereupon pay a specified unit price for all rock excavated. The agreed price for excavating rock was about nine times greater than the price for excavating earth; the parties had used the latter figure in calculating the original contract price for the entire job. After the parties reached their second agreement, the contractor completed the excavation. Rock constituted about two-thirds of the entire material excavated. Upon completion of the job, the owner paid the contractor only the original contract price, and the contractor sued for the additional compensation promised. Explain 1) the reasoning upon which the owner might attempt to defend, 2) the reasoning upon which the contractor might attempt to collect, and 3) which party should be given judgment.

9. A landlord and a tenant entered into a ten-year lease agreement for a warehouse building at a described location in a certain city. The warehouse was constructed of wood and the lease included a provision, that if during the leasehold term the building should be damaged or destroyed by a fire not the fault of the tenant, the landlord would with all possible diligence repair or rebuild the building for the tenant's continued use. After about three years the building was completely destroyed by fire through no fault of the tenant. Meanwhile the city had amended its earlier zoning laws. Under the amended ordinance, new erection of wooden commercial buildings in that area was prohibited. When the landlord refused to rebuild the destroyed building, the tenant sued the landlord for damages. Explain 1) the reasoning upon which the landlord might attempt to defend, 2) the reasoning upon which the tenant might attempt to win, and 3) which party should be given judgment. (Modified from A.I.C.P.A., Nov. 22-5.)

10. S, owner of a large apple orchard, entered into a written contract under which S was to sell and deliver to B by a certain date 1,000 bushels of apples to be picked from S's orchard, and B was to pay $2 per bushel upon delivery.

a) Before the apples were ripe enough to be picked, a windstorm destroyed the entire crop. When S failed to deliver any apples to B, B sued for damages. What result?

b) Assume that the windstorm destroyed half of the crop. On the agreed delivery date, S tendered to B 500 bushels. What were the rights of the parties? (Modified from A.I.C.P.A., May 59-10.)

11. In January, S Company entered into a contract with B Company under which S Company agreed to sell and deliver to B Company and B Company to buy at 4¾ cents per gallon, 1,500,000 wine gallons of refined blackstrap molasses of the usual run, from the M Company refinery, to test about 60 percent sugars, delivery to be in stated installments over most of the year. In February, because of rising sugar prices, the operators of M Company refinery decided to decrease output, a decision over which S Company had no control. During that year, the refinery's output totaled only 485,000 gallons, of which 344,083 gallons were allotted by M Company to S Company and by S Company to B Company. The market price for such molasses went up and in June was 7½ cents per gallon and by October 8¼ cents per gallon. The above-mentioned 344,083 gallons was all the molasses S Company shipped to B Company during the contract period. Upon expiration of the contract period, B Company sued S Company for damages for failure to deliver the contracted quantity of molasses.

a) Assume that at the time of the January contract, S Company had a contract with M Company to buy during the year a quantity of molasses greater than that specified in the S Company-B Company contract. When B Company sued S Company, explain 1) the reasoning upon which S Company could attempt to defend, 2) the reasoning upon which B Company could attempt to win, and 3) which party should be given judgment.

b) Assume that over the prior several years, without any advance contract with M Company, S Company had regularly ordered and received from M Company a greater quantity of molasses than was specified in the S Company-B Company contract, and that therefore S Company, reasonably believing it to be unnecessary, had no advance contract with M Company for deliveries during the year of the S Company-B Company contract. Answer the same questions asked in Part (a).

12. S entered into a written contract with B agreeing to manufacture and deliver to B, at a stated price, 5,000 ladies' sweaters of specified types, deliveries to be made in equal quantities over a five-month period. Before any deliveries could be made, S's employees went on strike which remained unsettled for three months beyond the last delivery date.

a) B sued S for damages for breach of contract. What result? Explain.

b) If you were S, and were negotiating the above contract with B, what would you have done and why, in order to avoid such a dispute as described above. (Modified from A.I.C.P.A., May 29-3.)

13. On June 1 a seller, desiring to sell a certain house and lot, listed the property with a real estate broker. On June 15 the broker negotiated a written contract between the seller and a buyer for the sale and purchase of the premises for $10,000, conditioned upon the buyer being able to obtain a first mortgage loan in the amount of $15,000. The contract specified that closing was to be on or before July 15. On June 15 the buyer applied to a building and loan association for a loan which was approved on June 24. The mortgage loan funds were made available on July 20, and the broker notified the seller to appear in the office of the loan association attorney on that date or at any time thereafter to close the transaction. The seller refused, saying that there had been too long a delay, whereupon the buyer sued the seller for breach of contract, the damages claimed being $100 for expenses and $1,000 for loss of the bargain. Explain 1) the reasoning upon which the seller might attempt to defend, 2) the reasoning upon which the buyer might attempt to win, and 3) which party should be given judgment.

14. The owner of a real estate lot entered into a contract with a builder for the construction of a small house on the owner's lot, according to certain plans and specifications, for $12,000, payable $8,000 at stated intervals during construction, and $4,000 upon completion of the house. The agreed plans and specifications called for building paper to be placed between the inner siding and outer sheeting boards of the house. About half of the outer sheeting boards had been attached when the owner noticed that the builder's workmen, through oversight, had not tacked building paper over the siding boards before nailing on the sheeting boards. When the owner called this to the attention of the builder, the builder had building paper tacked over the remainder of the exposed siding but refused to remove the sheeting boards already in place in order to insert building paper. By this time the owner had paid the builder $7,000. When the building was completed, the owner moved in but refused to make any further payments until the builder installed the omitted building paper. The builder sued for the remaining $5,000. Evidence in the lawsuit showed that removal of the portion of sheeting boards involved, attaching the omitted building paper, and replacing the sheeting boards would cost about $1,500. The evidence also showed that the fair value of the building at the time of the lawsuit was $10,000.

a) Did the builder substantially perform the contract?

b) Assume that the court would decide that the builder's performance was substantial, explain 1) the reasoning upon which the owner could attempt to defend in the builder's lawsuit for $5,000, 2) the reasoning upon which the builder could attempt to recover, and 3) which party should be given judgment.

c) Assume that the court would decide that the builder's performance was not substantial. Answer the same questions asked in Part (b).

15. Near a small town with a total population of about 300 people, a large manufacturing company decided to construct extensive research and fabrication facilities, which, after completion, would employ about 5,000 people. Large numbers of homes were built by various contractors, and when the company's buildings were completed and in full operation, the population in and near the town grew to over 3,000 families. For a number of years, T had owned and operated the largest retail store in the town, using a building rented from the owner, O. When manufacturing began, T's lease, providing for a monthly rental of $75, had one year yet to run. During this year T's store operations and profits multiplied tremendously. Upon expiration of the lease, O and T entered into a new five year lease for the store building at a rental of $300 per month. One year later, the management of the company was changed and the new board of directors unexpectedly decided to com-

pletely abandon the new plant. A year and a half after the start of T's five-year lease, the plant was closed down and the population of the area shrank to less than 1,000 people. With the drastic decrease in the volume of his business, T could no longer profitably pay $300 per month rent. O refused to renegotiate the lease and a few months after the plant closed, T moved his store to another location, still owing rent for the past three months. O thereupon sued T for all unpaid rent to date. Explain 1) the reasoning upon which T might attempt to defend, 2) the reasoning upon which O might attempt to claim, and 3) which party should be given judgment.

16. The owner of a plot of land entered into a contract with a builder for the construction of a summer resort hotel building on the owner's land, according to certain plans and specifications. The agreed price was $80,000, of which $75,000 was to be paid at stated intervals during the construction and the remaining $5,000 upon final completion, which was to be three months after the date the parties formed the contract. The contract provided that for each day's delay in final completion beyond the contracted completion date, the builder would be liable to the owner for damages in the amount of $50 per day. Each of the following is a separate fact situation; for each, assume that the contract contained no provision expressly referring to such a situation.

a) One month after formation of the owner-builder contract, when the work was about one-third completed, the builder, through no fault of his own, was seriously injured in an auto accident. He was in a coma for two weeks, unable to conduct any business for another two weeks, and confined in his hospital bed for six weeks longer. Explain the effect of this on the builder's contract obligation.

b) Two months after formation of the owner-builder contract, when the work was about two-thirds completed, a hurricane occurred of unprecedented ferocity for that part of the country. 1) The resulting flooding conditions made it impossible for any work to be done on the job for the next three weeks. Explain the effect of this on the builder's contract obligation. 2) The force of the wind and flooding totally destroyed the two-month's construction work. Explain the effect of this on the builder's contract obligation.

c) One week after formation of the owner-builder contract, and before any steel had been delivered to the job, there was a steel strike coupled with a tense international situation, as a result of which the government issued an order freezing all steel supplies except for certain essential purposes —which did not include summer resort hotels. The freeze order continued in effect for the next six months. Explain the effect of this on the builder's contract obligation.

d) One week after formation of the owner-builder contract, the owner was adjudged bankrupt in a Federal court bankruptcy proceeding. Explain the effect of this on the builder's contract.

e) One week after formation of the owner-builder contract, when the builder began to excavate, he discovered quicksand at various points. The condition had been unknown to either party, had not been disclosed by the test borings, and would increase the cost of construction several thousand dollars. When the owner refused to agree to any increase in the contract price, the builder refused to proceed with construction. Explain the effect of this on the builder's contract obligation. (Modified from A.I.C.P.A., Nov. 52-7.)

book *III*

The Basic Law of Business Organization

chapter *12*

Agency

In modern society all people, businessmen and nonbusinessmen alike, are affected by the rules of law which have developed in connection with agency relationships. In the broadest sense, an *agent* is a person who has agreed 1) to act on behalf of someone else (called the principal), and 2) either to be under the close supervision of the principal or at least to have an obligation to advance the principal's best interests.

When the term "agent" is used in this broad sense, two types of persons are included, servants and independent contractors. The relationship between an employer and his employee is commonly termed by the law a master-servant relationship. In general, if a principal has the right to control the physical conduct of his agent, the latter is classified as a servant. On the other hand, if the principal has only a right of general control—for example, a right to give directions as to the desired result to be accomplished or the general method of performance but no right to control the detailed physical acts of the agent—the agent is classified as an independent contractor.

Part I CREATING PRINCIPAL-AGENCY RELATIONSHIPS

Usually an agency is created by a contract in which the principal hires the agent and agrees to pay him for his services. An employment contract, however, is not essential. For example, if a buyer who has a charge account at a department store requests as a favor that his neighbor purchase a specified item and charge it to the buyer, the neighbor has no expectation of being compensated; nevertheless the neighbor is the buyer's authorized agent.

An agency relationship can arise from an express authorization or it may arise by implication, either 1) from prior conduct of the parties, 2) from one person having a right to control the physical acts of another, or 3) to some extent from the parties being married. A person can also obtain the rights and liabilities of a principal through approving or ratifying a contract which has been made for him, but without his prior authorization.

AGENCY IMPLIED FROM PRIOR CONDUCT

Just as contract rights and obligations can arise from the conduct of parties without any expressly stated agreement, so also an agency relationship can arise or be found to exist through the conduct of the parties.

Example: A buyer purchased and received a car from a dealer, paying part of the price in cash and giving a one-month negotiable promissory note for the $500 balance. On the following day the dealer sold, indorsed, and transferred the note to a finance company. When the note matured, the buyer, not knowing of the transfer of the note, paid $500 to the dealer. Before the dealer turned the money over to the finance company, he was adjudged insolvent and a court-appointed receiver took over the dealer's assets (including this $500) for the benefit of all of the dealer's creditors. When the finance company was unable to collect the $500 from the dealer, the company sued the buyer for $500.

According to the law concerning negotiable notes (discussed in Chapter 14), even though an obligor is given no notice of the transfer of a note, he is obligated to pay the actual owner of the note, whoever that may be; if the obligor pays his original creditor, the obligor will have to pay again to the proper person, if the recipient of the first payment fails to give the money to the owner of the note. Therefore in this example the buyer's payment to the dealer would be binding on the finance company only if the dealer was an agent with authority to collect for the finance company.

Although the finance company had never expressly appointed the dealer as its collecting agent, the evidence showed that during the three-year period before this dispute arose, the dealer transferred a large number of similar notes to the finance company, and that on an average of ten or fifteen times a week the dealer received payments on the transferred notes, periodically remitting to the finance company the money so collected. Each time the dealer received a payment he made out a receipt in triplicate. One copy of the receipt was given to the party making payment. Then when next remitting to the finance company, the dealer presented with the money the other two copies of each receipt. The finance company retained one copy of each receipt so as to know to whose account each payment should be credited, and initialed and returned to the dealer the third copy of each receipt as evidence that the dealer had turned over to the finance company the money described in the receipt.

The conduct of the parties over the three-year period showed that the dealer was actually an agent to collect for the finance company. The buyer's payment to an authorized agent of the finance company was a sufficient payment, and therefore the finance company was unable to require the buyer to pay a second time.

AGENCY IMPLIED FROM RIGHT TO CONTROL
ANOTHER'S ACTS

Sometimes even though no agency relationship is expressly undertaken, one person will have a legal right to control the physical conduct of another person while the latter is performing certain acts. To that extent, the one with the right of control is the master, and the other person, when performing those certain acts, assumes the status of a servant. One of the most common instances in which this implied master-servant relationship arises is when the owner of a car permits another to drive while the owner rides as a passenger. Generally, by virtue of his presence and ownership, the owner has the right to control the manner in which his car is being driven, and thus the owner is the master and the driver is his servant. The owner's *right* to control makes him the master; whether he is exercising control or is asleep in the back seat is immaterial. It is, likewise, immaterial whether the particular journey is benefiting the owner or the driver. If the owner-passenger has no legal right to control the driver, as for example when the driver is the husband of the owner (in the eyes of the law the husband being the head of the family and not subject to his wife's control), a master-servant relationship does not arise.

AGENCY IMPLIED FROM MARITAL RELATIONSHIP

Ordinarily no agency relationship arises solely from the fact that persons are married; husbands and wives are not automatically agents in the conduct of their spouses' business affairs. However, unless a different arrangement is shown to exist, a wife usually serves as the manager of her husband's household, and as such is impliedly an agent to purchase in her husband's name items for the ordinary day-to-day care and maintenance of the household.

RATIFICATION

Suppose that an agent purporting to act for a certain principal enters into a contract with a third person, that in doing so the agent exceeds his authority so that the principal is not bound by the contract, and that when the principal later learns of what the agent has done, the principal expresses (either to the agent or to the third person) his approval and willingness to be bound by the contract. Since the contract was originally made in the principal's name, the third person certainly intends that the principal be bound by the contract and have rights under it. It is usually considered sound policy, therefore, to permit the principal, by his postcontract ratification, to obtain rights under the contract and to assume its obligations. On the other hand, if an agent does not purport to be acting for a principal when he enters into a contract with a third person, then the latter does not manifest any intent to form a contract with anyone other than the agent. If the contract is assignable, the principal can obtain rights through receiving an assignment from the agent, but the theory of ratification will not apply. An undisclosed principal who attempts to ratify the unauthorized contract of an agent obtains nothing through his attempted ratification.

Any conduct that evidences the fact that a purported principal approves of a contract and is willing to be bound by it is sufficient to constitute a ratification. A person's accepting or retaining benefits under a contract, with full knowledge of the facts, generally shows such approval. A purported principal's failure to repudiate a contract upon learning of it may show approval if, under the circumstances, a reasonable person would be expected to express objection if he disapproved of the contract. If the one making an unauthorized contract is actually the principal's agent and merely exceeds his authority (as contrasted with a person who is not an agent and has no authority whatsoever to act for the purported principal), the principal is usually expected to promptly notify the third person of his disapproval of the unauthorized contract. In such a case the principal's failure to repudiate the unauthorized contract would indicate approval and constitute ratification.

CAPACITY TO ACT AS AGENT

If pursuant to his principal's instructions, an agent enters into a contract with a third person in the principal's name, the parties who are legally bound by the contract are the principal and the third person. The agent's legal capacity to bind himself by contracts is immaterial. Therefore, a minor can be as effective an agent as an adult can be.

Part 2　RIGHTS AND OBLIGATIONS BETWEEN PRINCIPALS AND AGENTS

DUTIES OF AGENTS TO PRINCIPALS

When an agent is entrusted with his principal's affairs, the agent has the power to cause considerable loss to his principal. It is sound policy, therefore, for the law to hold agents to a high standard of conduct—to require them to obey their principals' instructions, to use proper care in performing services or transacting business for their principals, and to be loyal to their principals' best interests. If an agent fails to meet these standards, he is liable for any loss which the principal thereby sustains, and, of course, an agent is not entitled to any compensation for services which are defectively or improperly performed.

DUTY OF OBEDIENCE

In performing services for his principal, an agent is obliged to comply with his principal's instructions; if the agent disobeys his instructions without justification, he is liable to the principal for any damages which result. Usually the agent is liable even though his deviation from instructions is in good faith and reasonable. However, in the rare case in which all of the following three conditions are present, the agent will be considered as justified in deviating from his instructions to the extent that seems reasonably necessary to prevent loss to the principal; the three conditions are: 1) After creation of the agency an unforeseen event occurs; 2) This event threatens a substantial loss to the principal if the agent acts as instructed; and 3) It is impracticable for the agent to communicate with his principal in time to prevent the loss.

Example: P authorized A to make certain purchases in foreign countries and to ship the purchased goods to P by certain specified carrier systems. After making one such purchase, which according to instructions was to be shipped by a carrier passing through Country X, A was reliably informed that a revolution in Country X was imminent. Since a revolution would jeopardize the shipment, A attempted to communicate with P. Unable to contact P before the time for shipment, A made a reasonable decision to have the goods shipped by a different carrier through Country Y. Although no revolution occurred in Country X, an unexpected revolutionary uprising in Country Y resulted in destruction of the entire shipment. P sued A for the value of the destroyed goods.

The three conditions under which an agent is permitted to reasonably deviate from his instructions having been present, the agent would not be liable to his principal for loss of the shipment.

Duty of Care

An agent is obliged to use the care of a reasonable person having the skill which the agent professes. For failure to use such care the agent is guilty of negligence and is liable to his principal for any loss that results.

Duty of Loyalty

An agent with power over another's property interests is always subject to temptations to misuse his power for his own benefit. The law attempts to reduce temptation to a minimum by prohibiting any exercise of the agency powers for the agent's own personal benefit, unless the principal consents. In attempting to assure that an agent will act solely for the benefit of his principal, the law prohibits all acts for the agent's personal benefit, even though a particular act does not actually harm the principal. The chief situations to which this prohibition applies include the following:

1. An agent has a personal interest in a contract negotiated for his principal.

2. An agent derives a gain from business transacted for his principal.

3. An agent acts for both sides in a contract negotiation.

4. An agent misuses confidential information.

Personal Interest

Unless the principal consents, an agent is not permitted to have a personal interest in any business he transacts for his principal.

Example: P engaged A, a stockbroker, to act as P's agent in purchasing for P fifty shares of the stock of the Carter Corporation at not over $60 per share. A was unable to locate on the market a block of fifty shares which he could purchase. However, A himself owned one hundred shares in that corporation and arranged a transfer of fifty of these shares to P for $50 per share. After P paid for the transfer, the corporation was adjudged insolvent, to the complete surprise of many people, including A who had honestly and reasonably believed that the stock was worth $50 per share. After the collapse of the corporation, P for the first time learned that A had previously owned the stock for which P had paid. P sued A to recover the $2,500 P paid for the stock.

P would recover. In a similar case, the Pennsylvania Supreme Court said that the rule "forbids that anyone intrusted with the interests of others shall in any manner make the business an object of personal interest to himself, because, from a frailty of nature, one who has the power will be too readily seized with the inclination to use the opportunity for serving his own interests at the expense of his principal. . . . It matters not that no fraud was meditated, and no injury done. The rule is not intended to be remedial of actual wrong, but preventive of the possibility of it."[1]

Usually an agent will be considered as violating his duty to his principal if he so mingles his principal's money or property with his own that all separate identity is lost. Such conduct is improper because not only does the agent appear to acquire a personal interest in his principal's funds, but also he improperly subjects his principal's funds to the claims of the agent's creditors.

Outside Benefit

An agent's compensation is supposed to be limited to the amount agreed upon by his principal. Thus unless the principal consents an agent is not permitted to obtain any additional gain or benefit for performing services or transacting business for his principal, and anything an agent receives in violation of this duty must be surrendered to the principal. Some states have implemented this rule by statute. For example, one such statute provides, in effect:

[1] *Haines v. Biddle*, 325 Pa. 441, 188 A. 843 (1937).

Whoever offers or gives to any agent, to a member of his family, or to anyone for his use or benefit, directly or indirectly, any commission, money, property, or other valuable thing, without the knowledge and consent of the principal, and in relation to the affairs or business of the principal, or whoever accepts or takes the same, is guilty of a misdemeanor, and subject to a fine not exceeding $500 or imprisonment not exceeding one year, or both. That the making of such gifts is customary in any business shall not be a defense in any prosecution under this section. This section does not apply to the practice commonly known as "tipping."

Double Agency

An agent who is negotiating a contract between two parties is not permitted to act as agent for both parties unless, before the contract is negotiated, both parties consent to the double agency. If a contract is negotiated by a double agent without the consent of both parties, it can be canceled by either party, and the agent is not entitled to compensation from either party for his services.

Example: The co-owners of certain land listed the property with A, a real estate broker, for $60,000, and agreed to pay A $1,200 for negotiating a sale at that price. A buyer desiring to purchase the property engaged A to negotiate a purchase, agreeing to pay A a 2 percent commission for his services. Neither the owners nor the buyer knew of A's commission arrangement with the other until after A had negotiated the transfer of the property for $60,000. When the owners learned of A's arrangement with the buyer, they refused to pay A the agreed $1,200, and A sued the owners.

A's argument: He was engaged merely as a middleman or intermediary to bring the owners and buyer together, and held a neutral position between them. Because no discretionary authority was vested in A and he had no obligation or opportunity to exercise his judgment, there was no possibility that he could injure either side by preferring one over the other. Therefore, he was not subject to any temptation to show preference and could properly represent both sides.

In a similar case, the Pennsylvania Superior Court held that A could not recover, saying: "He placed himself in the doubtful position of being active for each and claims that he was the immediate and efficient cause in effecting the sale or at least in bringing the two parties together. . . . The defendants had a right to repose special trust and confidence in him as their agent, and . . . he owed to them the utmost good faith, which required him to keep them fully apprised of every fact and circumstance relating to the business or to their interest. No broker, agent or middleman can recover for services which uncover double dealing and a secret agreement with one of the persons."[2]

---

[2] *Linderman v. McKenna*, 20 Pa. Super. 409 (1902).

Confidential Information

During Continuation of Agency. If through his agency an agent acquires information concerning his principal's business affairs, he owes to the principal a duty not to use the information in a way that will benefit the agent at the expense of the principal.

After Termination of Agency. Many employment contracts provide that for a stated period after termination of the employment the employee will not engage in a business which competes with his former employer. Even in the absence of such a restrictive provision, a former agent owes to his former principal a duty not to make use of or to disclose confidential information or trade secrets. What information should be classed as confidential or secret is a matter of public policy. Any definition of these terms must be both fair and realistic or practical, taking into account the exact nature of the information and the expressed or assumed intent of the principal. For example, if a deliveryman quits his job with the Old Bakery and goes to work for the New Bakery, it would be neither fair nor realistic to say that the deliveryman should forget the names of the customers with whom he became acquainted while working for the Old Bakery. Therefore, in the absence of a restrictive provision in his employment contract, the deliveryman has a right to contact his old customers and to urge them to switch their patronage to the New Bakery. However, it would not be fair for the deliveryman while working for the Old Bakery to copy from the office records a list of customers served by the other drivers, and then after starting for New Bakery to contact all of these customers. The court would restrain the deliveryman from using his "stolen" list. Determining when information concerning trade and production techniques should be treated as confidential is especially difficult. Through associating with a certain business a man gains general experience and knowledge which is properly valuable to himself and to some new employer, and which it is neither fair nor possible to completely erase. Thus a man can continue to use the general skill and knowledge which he acquired while working for a former employer, but at the same time he should refrain from using or disclosing unique production processes which his former employer was keeping secret.

DUTIES OF PRINCIPALS TO AGENTS

The chief obligations of a principal to his agent are to reimburse the agent for any personal expense he incurs at the principal's request and to pay the agent the compensation agreed upon in the agency contract. Sometimes a principal and an agent disagree as to whether the agent's performance is sufficient to entitle him to the compensation specified in the contract. Useful examples can be found in disputes between property owners and real estate brokers engaged to negotiate sales of properties. The rules that apply to such cases may be classified as follows:

1. The parties may expressly agree that the broker will be entitled to a commission only when a transfer at the listed price is consummated.

2. The parties may expressly agree that the broker will be entitled to a commission if a transfer is consummated during the contract period even though the transfer is not brought about by anything the broker does. In many states such agreements are further classified into two types:

a) *Exclusive Agency Agreement.* The owner expressly agrees that during the contract period he will not sell through another broker. If the owner violates this agreement, the broker is entitled to recover as damages the amount of the agreed commission, but a sale of property solely through the owner's own efforts does not violate an exclusive agency arrangement.

b) *Exclusive Sale.* The owner expressly agrees that if the listed property is sold during the contract period, no matter who brings about the sale, the broker will be entitled to the stated commission.

3. In the absence of any special agreement to the contrary, a broker is entitled to an agreed commission if any *one* of the following three events occurs:

a) The broker procures a buyer with whom the owner makes a contract.

b) The broker procures a buyer ready, willing, and able to buy at the listed price.

c) The broker is an effective or procuring cause of a sale which is actually completed.

Example: P, the owner of certain real estate, engaged A, a real estate broker, to negotiate a sale of the property within the next three months for $20,000 and agreed to pay A a 5 percent commission in the event of sale.

1. As a result of A's efforts, B decided to purchase the property. A obtained B's signature on a written contract form which A then took to P who also signed. The written contract stated that P agreed to sell and B to buy the described property for $20,000, title to be transferred and purchase price to be paid one month later. Upon expiration of the month, B said that he had changed his mind and refused to accept a deed or to pay any money for the property. A nevertheless demanded a commission from P.

The expression "in the event of sale" is usually interpreted as pertaining to the rate of commission and not as stating a condition or time for payment. Therefore, the quoted words do not require consummation of the transfer as a condition for payment of the commission. Such expressions as "at settlement" or "for bringing about a sale" have been similarly interpreted. Thus, since B committed himself to a contract which P ███ ██████ against B, and since A's commission was not expressly made depend██ ██ █████summation of the transfer, A earned his commission by negotiating the contract.

2. As a result of A's efforts, B, a responsible person, decided to purchase the property for the listed price and signed a written contract form to that effect. However, P refused to sign the contract. A sued P for the agreed commission.

When A produced B ready, willing, and able to buy at the listed price, A earned his commission.

3. B, attracted by the "For Sale" sign A erected on the property, contacted P directly. After some negotiation directly between B and P, P transferred the property to B for $19,500 which B paid to P. A sued P for a 5 percent commission on $19,500.

A was an effective cause of the sale in that something he did was material in bringing about the sale. Therefore, A would be entitled to collect the claimed commission.

4. Two months after the listing, B, a resident of another town, learned directly from P of the latter's desire to sell his property. B bought the property from P for $20,000 which B paid directly to P. Nothing A did was an effective or procuring cause of the sale. A sued P for his commission.

Just as in Part 1 of this Example, the expression "in the event of sale" would not be construed as a statement of a condition or of a time for payment. P did not agree to pay A a commission regardless of who effected a sale. Since the sale was not procured by A, A would not be entitled to any commission on the sale.

Example: P. Porter, the owner of certain real estate, entered into the following written contract with A. Adams, a real estate broker: "[Date] I hereby list exclusively with you for the nonwithdrawal period of three months from date the following real estate [describing the property] for $20,000, and in the event of a sale, agree to pay you a commission of 5 percent of the purchase price. (signed) P. Porter. Accepted, I hereby agree to use my best efforts to negotiate a sale of the above described premises. (signed) A. Adams." Two months later P sold and transferred the property to B for $20,000 which B paid directly to P, and P promptly notified A of the sale. The transfer was made entirely through P's efforts, and not brought about by anything done by A or by any other broker. Up to the time P notified A of the sale, A had not found a buyer for the property. A sued P for the amount of commission he would have earned if he had negotiated the sale.

P did not expressly agree to pay A a commission regardless of who effected the sale. Therefore in many states the agreement would be construed as creating an exclusive-agency rather than an exclusive-sale relationship. If P had sold the property through the efforts of another broker, P would have breached his exclusive-agency agreement with A; for breach of the agreement, A would have been entitled to damages in the amount of the agreed commission. In making a sale not procured thro~~~h any broker, P did not breach the exclusive part of the agreement. H· w ~~~ ~~~lling during the three-month period, P breached his agreement to ~ ~~~ ~ property with A for three months. For breach of this agreement, A would be entitled to recover the costs and expenses he incurred in attempting to sell the property up to the time P notified A of the sale.

Part 3 RIGHTS AND OBLIGATIONS OF PRINCIPALS AND THIRD PERSONS

Sometimes a person who enters into a contract may, unknown to the other contracting party, actually be acting as an agent for another person. If a party is unaware that he is dealing with an agent, the principal for whom the agent is actually acting is said to be "undisclosed." If a party is aware that he is dealing with an agent but does not know whom the agent represents, the principal is said to be "partially disclosed." A principal is classified as "fully disclosed" if, at the time his agent enters into a contract, the other contracting party 1) knows that he is dealing with an agent, and 2) knows the identity of the person for whom the agent is acting.

CONTRACT LIABILITY OF FULLY DISCLOSED PRINCIPALS

The courts frequently reiterate that a person deals with an agent at his own risk. This means that if a principal denies liability for a contract made in his name by a particular agent, the other party to the contract has the burden of proving the agent's authority. The principal is not bound unless the agent acts either within his actual or his apparent authority.

ACTUAL AUTHORITY

Actual authority may be express or implied:

1. Express authority is that authority which the principal has expressly granted to his agent.

2. Implied authority is that authority which, although not expressly mentioned by the principal, is implied or understood, either from what the principal has expressly authorized the agent to do or from some other conduct of the principal and agent. Suppose that the general manager of a retail food store is expressly authorized to make sales to customers and to collect the purchase prices, to hire and fire employees and fix their wages, to purchase a stated quantity and kind of produce locally, and to maintain a checking account in the name of the store. Even though he may not be expressly authorized to purchase fuel for

heating the store building, it is fair to conclude that the manager has the implied (and therefore actual) authority to do so if no other arrangement has been made by the principal. The finance company example on page 322 is a situation in which actual authority was implied from the conduct of the parties.

What is sometimes called an agency or authority "by necessity" is one type of implied authority. While the conductor on a freight train ordinarily has no authority to make contracts in the name of the employer railroad, if a crewman is injured in the middle of the night at some remote location and needs immediate medical attention, the conductor as the highest person in authority present is authorized to engage a physician in the name of the railroad.

APPARENT AUTHORITY

Although the act of an agent in a principal's name is outside any actual authority (either express or implied) granted to the agent, the principal will nevertheless be bound by the agent's act if the following three conditions are all present: 1) A certain situation or appearance exists, 2) for which the principal is responsible, and 3) from which the third person is justified in assuming that the agent has the authority he presumes to exercise. If these conditions are all present, the agent is said to have the appearance of authority to bind his principal. When a principal denies liability for an agent's act and a third person is unable to prove that the agent actually had the authority he was presuming to exercise, the third person will usually attempt to prove that the agent was acting within his apparent authority, thereby obligating the principal. In such a case the chief issue usually is the third condition listed above —namely, justification for assuming that the agent had the authority in question. In business transactions this issue arises most often in cases involving agents having actual authority to sell or negotiate sales of goods, and with agents having actual authority to manage any of their principals' business affairs.

Apparent Authority, Salesmen of Goods

Salesmen of goods can be classified into two types, 1) those who have actual authority to make contracts in their principals' names, and 2) those whose authority is merely to solicit orders for goods. The latter type of salesman, the order taker, has no authority to make a contract binding on his principal; he merely solicits orders (offers to buy) which he forwards to his principal. The principal then decides whether or not to sell the ordered goods, and no contract arises until the principal accepts the offer. If a principal authorizes his salesmen to make binding contracts, he runs the risk of being overcontracted. Several of his salesmen might unexpectedly have phenomenal success and contract to sell more goods than the principal can deliver. For this reason the most common type of salesman is merely an order taker.

A salesman, whether a contracting salesman or merely an order taker, has the apparent authority to do what is usual or customary for the type of transaction which he is actually authorized to negotiate. A salesman authorized to sell and deliver goods or to make a contract for sale has the apparent authority to sell at the usual price and to make such warranties as are usual in such transactions. Generally his apparent authority is limited to contracting for cash payable on delivery rather than for sales on credit. Therefore a salesman (contract maker or order taker) generally has the apparent authority to collect a portion or all of the purchase price only if and when he delivers goods to the buyer. If the principal delivers to the buyer directly and not through the salesman, the latter usually has no apparent authority to collect for the goods.

Whether knowledge acquired by a salesman but not reported to his principal is nevertheless binding on the principal depends on several factors, including the type of information and the time it is acquired by the salesman. Generally a salesman has the apparent authority to receive notices 1) at the time he is dealing with a third person, *and* 2) which come under the actual authority of the agent in regard to the contract he is making or the order he is soliciting.

Time of Notice. An agent's having authority to enter into a contract does not of itself give him the appearance of authority *at a later date* to modify the contract or to receive a notice affecting rights under the contract. For example (as discussed in Chapter 7), if a warranty accompanies the sale of goods, a buyer may lose his right to collect for breach of warranty unless he gives prompt notice to the seller that the goods are defective. It may seem quite reasonable for the buyer to give such a notice to the salesman through whom he ordered the goods, but to adequately protect his rights the buyer should also give a notice directly to the seller.

Relationship of Notice to Agent's Actual Authority. Partnership dissolution cases provide an excellent illustration. It is a rule of partnership law (as discussed in Chapter 13) that if a business is continued after the withdrawal of one partner, a creditor who had previously extended credit to the partnership can hold the withdrawing partner liable for obligations incurred by the business after that partner withdrew, unless the creditor had personal knowledge of the partner's withdrawal. A number of courts have held that if a salesman's only authority is to take orders, he has no apparent authority to receive partnership withdrawal notices. On the other hand, if in addition to taking orders the duties of a salesman include reporting on the credit standing of customers or making collections, the salesman has apparent authority to receive notices pertaining to credit matters. In such a case, if notice that a partner has withdrawn is given to the salesman along with an order, it will be binding on the salesman's principal even though the salesman neglects to pass the information along.

Example: On March 9 a salesman employed by a Chicago meatpacker visited a wholesaler in a distant community and solicited an order for 50 cases of pigs' feet packed in cans of a specified size, at $2.30 per case, payable on delivery. The order blank signed by the wholesaler stated: "All orders are subject to approval by the packer at the Chicago office. All merchandise is guaranteed first quality. No claims for defective merchandise shall be entertained unless made within 30 days after receipt of merchandise." After the salesman sent the order to Chicago, the packer shipped the ordered goods to the wholesaler who received and paid for the shipment on March 21. On April 1 the wholesaler received a complaint from a retailer to whom two cases had been sold that the contents of some of the cans were spoiled. The wholesaler immediately discontinued making any further sales from the shipment. The following day, when the packer's salesman again called on the wholesaler, the latter told the salesman of the complaint and together they opened several cans, finding the contents of most of them spoiled. Admittedly the cans were not first quality. The salesman said he would notify the packer and ask for instructions as to return or other adjustment. When the wholesaler heard nothing further by May 15, he wrote to the packer offering to return the merchandise. The packer refused to make any adjustment and the wholesaler sued the packer for damages. The salesman testified that he had forgotten to report the defective cans to the packer.

Under somewhat similar facts, the Pennsylvania Superior Court held[3] that the wholesaler failed to give proper notice to the packer and could not recover. Generally a salesman who solicits orders has no apparent authority to receive a notice that the goods shipped in response to the order are defective. The April 2 notice to the salesman, therefore, was not notice to the packer, and the May 15 notice to the packer was not within the thirty-day period specified in the contract.

Apparent Authority, Buying Agents

An agent with authority to buy is usually expected to make cash purchases; usually he has no appearance of authority to buy on his principal's credit. An implied authority (as distinguished from apparent authority) to buy on credit can arise from the prior conduct of the parties or from the fact that the principal neglects to give the agent funds with which to make the authorized purchases.

[3] *Foell Packing Co.* v. *Harris*, 127 Pa. Super. 494, 193 A. 152 (1937).

Apparent Authority, Loaning Agents

In many cases the courts have pointed out that an agent authorized to negotiate a loan of his principal's money is not necessarily the proper party to whom the debt should be repaid when it matures. Suppose than an agent 1) negotiates a loan, 2) has actual authority to collect interest on the loan as it periodically comes due, and 3) is in possession of the document which evidences the loan. These three facts taken together do not necessarily clothe the agent with the appearance of authority to collect a payment on the principal amount of the loan when it comes due, especially if the agent's possession of the loan document is appropriate or convenient for his collecting and noting the periodic interest payments.

If a debtor is making a loan repayment to an agent, the debtor should verify the agent's actual authority to collect—or as is frequently simpler, should pay by check made out to the principal himself and thereby avoid any question of the agent's authority to collect money. The debtor thus shifts to his bank the question of the agent's authority if the agent should indorse his principal's name and attempt to cash the check. The bank will usually ask to see the agent's written, express authorization to indorse his principal's checks, because an agent generally has no authority to indorse his principal's name to commercial paper (notes, checks, and drafts) unless the principal *expressly* authorizes the agent to do so. Only very rarely is an agent considered as having implied or apparent authority to indorse.

Apparent Authority, Subagents

An agent of the type classified as a servant generally has no apparent authority to delegate performance of his duties to an assistant or subagent. An independent contractor may also be likewise limited. However, with many types of independent contractors, it may clearly appear that the principal expects the agent to engage one or more assistants to help. An example is a broker or factor who receives from a number of different owners goods to sell on commission. Such an agent will usually be expected to work through a staff of employees and the act of one of the agent's authorized subagents may therefore be binding on the principal.

Apparent Authority, Managing Agents

A servant with authority to manage his principal's business affairs over a period of time, or to manage a continuing segment of his principal's affairs has fairly broad implied and apparent authority to do what is usual in such cases. A retail store manager commonly has the authority to hire necessary employees, as well as the authority of a selling and buying agent as previously discussed.

Although a managing agent will frequently have implied or apparent authority to purchase on his principal's credit, he generally will have no authority to borrow money in his principal's name unless such authority is *expressly* granted to him. Only very rarely is an agent considered as having implied or apparent authority to borrow money.

RATIFICATION

If a principal receives an actual benefit from the performance of a contract made by someone acting as the principal's purported agent, it is not fair for the principal to retain the benefit and at the same time repudiate the contract as being outside the agent's actual and apparent authority. When fully apprised of the facts, the principal must return or account for such actual benefit, or be assumed to ratify and thus become bound by his agent's contract.

Example: Pauline Porter, an elderly widow residing in a southern state, appointed Albert Adams as her agent to manage her extensive real estate holdings and investments in a distant community, signing and giving to A a form power of attorney, authorizing A as follows:

> To take charge of, care for, manage, control, and sell any and all real estate now or hereafter owned by me; to sign and deliver any and all deeds or other instruments in writing which may be at any time necessary or advisable to convey the title thereof; to collect the interest and principal of any mortgage now or hereafter held by me and in case of default to foreclose the same by sale or otherwise; to effect any insurance necessary or proper to protect any property belonging to me; to pay all taxes and other assessments; and in general to do every act and thing concerning the premises, which I might myself do if personally present. It is understood the foregoing enumeration of specific powers does not in any way limit or cut down the general powers herein granted, or which should have been granted in order to carry out the purposes hereinbefore expressed. Hereby granting unto my said agent full power and authority to act in and concerning the premises as fully and effectually as I might do if personally present. This authority is to continue until expressly revoked by me.

1. A year later, A decided to redecorate some of the properties. The funds on hand being insufficient to pay for the redecoration, A went to a local bank, showed his written power of attorney to the bank, explained the purpose of the loan, and borrowed $1,500, signing a three-month note, "Pauline Porter by Albert Adams, her agent." A used the $1,500 for the stated purpose. Upon maturity of the note and demand for payment, P learned for the first time of the loan and the redecorations. Claiming, as was true, that the properties did not need redecorating and that she had never authorized A to undertake any redecorating, P refused to pay and the bank sued P.

Since P did not expressly grant A authority to borrow money, he had no such authority, actual or apparent. However, whether P would have desired the redecorating or not, her property obtained an actual net benefit or gain from the borrowed money. To disaffirm the loan, P would therefore have to return to the bank the borrowed $1,500. If P failed to repay the borrowed money to the bank, P would in effect be ratifying the loan and would be bound by the note signed by A.

2. Soon A began speculating in his own name with funds collected through his management. Within a year, A had lost through speculations about $7,000 of P's money. The funds were so depleted that there was not sufficient to pay some of the current taxes on the various properties. Believing that some of his speculations would permit recoupment of past losses, A applied to a local bank for a three-month loan of $1,500. A showed his written power of attorney to the bank, explained that the money was to pay real estate taxes on the various properties, and falsely said that the temporary shortage of funds was due to expenses of redecorating various of the properties. The bank made the loan and A signed a three-month note, "Pauline Porter by Albert Adams, her agent." A used the $1,500 to pay the taxes. Thereafter A's investments further depreciated and A disappeared. Upon maturity of the note and demand for payment P learned for the first time of A's dishonesty. P refused to pay and the bank sued P.

As stated in the answer to Part 1 of this Example, A had no authority to borrow. Furthermore although the loan was used to pay taxes on P's property, P received no *net* benefit from the loan, the money merely making up for sums A had previously embezzled. The bank could not recover from P.

UNDISCLOSED AND PARTIALLY DISCLOSED PRINCIPALS

Suppose that pursuant to instructions from P, A enters into a contract with T for P's benefit, but that either by design or inadvertance, A fails to disclose that he is acting for P. Since P directs A to make the contract and intends the contract for his own benefit, it is only fair that P should be bound by the contract. For these reasons it seems equally fair that P should have rights under the contract. When P claims contract rights, T might protest that he had no intention of making a contract with P; T might further object that he would have refused to enter into the contract had he known it was being made for P. T's protest is fully met, however, by the same reasoning that supports assignments of contracts (discussed in Chapter 10). If an assignment does not materially change the obligation of the other contracting party, then unless the contract prohibits assignment, a right arising under the contract can be assigned without the consent of the other party. If an assignment by A to P would not be unfair to T, it is not unfair to accord to P a contract right by virtue of his responsibility for the contract. If the identity of the person who may obtain contract rights is so important to a contracting party, he can specify in the contract that it is not assignable and that no undisclosed principal will have any rights under it. If an agent lies about the existence or identity of a principal, the agent would be guilty of fraud, which would enable the third person to cancel the contract. However if the third person neglects to ask whether the other party is acting as an agent, the latter's failure to volunteer the information is not fraud.

TORT LIABILITY OF PRINCIPALS

Suppose that an employer hires an employee to drive a delivery truck, uses proper care in selecting a competent driver, and instructs the driver to operate the truck carefully and never in excess of 35 miles per hour; later while driving his route the employee drives carelessly, at 50 miles per hour, and runs into a third person's carefully driven car, injuring the third person. While the driver would, of course, be liable for his own tort, employee drivers are frequently financially unable to pay for damages they cause. Usually therefore injured third persons will seek to collect from employers. It seems fair that as between the two equally innocent parties—the third person and the employer—the employer should bear the expense or burden resulting from the accident if 1) as the employment relationship implies, the employer has the right to control the physical conduct of the employee, *and* 2) at the time of the accident the employee is advancing the employer's general interests, or, in other words, is acting within the general scope of his authorized services. If either of these two numbered elements is missing, it is usually not considered fair to hold a principal liable for his agent's tort. As previously discussed, a principal has no right to control the physical conduct of an agent who is an independent contractor as distinguished from a servant. Lacking the right of control, the principal is usually not liable for the torts of such an agent—with the possible exception of misrepresentations, discussed later. If the agent is a servant, but the tort which he commits occurs while he is acting outside the general scope of his authorized services, the principal is not liable.

Example: An owner listed his house with a real estate broker to negotiate a sale for $20,000. As the owner knew, the broker had in his employ a salesman who assisted the broker in negotiating sales. While a prospective buyer was being taken by auto to examine the owner's house, the driver of the auto was negligent and injured the buyer.

1. The driver was the broker and the injured buyer sued the owner. Since the owner had no right to control the physical conduct of the broker, the broker was an independent contractor type of agent, and the owner would not be liable for the broker's tort.

2. The driver was the broker's salesman and the injured buyer sued the broker. Since the broker had the right to control the physical conduct of his salesman, the latter was a servant of the broker, and the broker would be liable for the salesman's negligence.

Example: A father, needing medicine for his sick child and not wishing to leave the child for the time required to go to the drugstore ten miles away, requested his neighbor to drive to the drugstore and procure the medicine. While performing the errand, the neighbor drove negligently and injured a third person. The third person sued the father.

1. At the father's request, the neighbor used the father's car for the errand. When ownership of the instrumentality being used and sole benefit from its use are combined in the same person, the owner usually has the right to control the physical conduct of the user. Under these circumstances, therefore, the neighbor could be considered the servant of the father, thus rendering the father liable for the neighbor's negligence.

2. The neighbor used his own car on the errand. The fact that the errand was for the sole benefit of the father's family, would not, standing alone, give the father any right to control the manner in which the neighbor drove his own car. Therefore, a master-servant relationship would not exist and the father would not be liable for the neighbor's negligence.

Even though a servant is disobeying certain specific instructions of his master, the servant's conduct can nevertheless be within the *general* scope of his service. Usually a servant is acting within the general scope of his authorized services if his conduct, 1) is of the same general nature as the service he is authorized to perform, or 2) is incidental to such authorized conduct, or 3) is not a highly unusual or totally unexpected way to perform the authorized services. For example, if a short-order cook at a lunch counter, although instructed to be considerate of the welfare of customers, is carelessly wielding his spatula in exaggerated flourishes while he is cooking, and strikes and injures a customer, the cook is acting within the general scope of his services; but if the cook becomes irritated at a remark made by one of the customers and strikes out with the spatula, hitting and injuring the customer, the cook's conduct would be outside the general scope of his service.

Example: An ice-cream manufacturer employed a truck driver and helper to deliver ice cream to various stores. The driver was instructed to collect the purchase price on delivery but to use no force in making collections, and in case of dispute to call the manufacturer's office. On one occasion when the driver tendered boxes of ice cream to a retailer, the latter refused to accept delivery, claiming that the ice cream had been permitted to thaw and had become too soft. When the driver insisted on leaving the ice cream, the retailer refused to pay and locked his cash register to prevent the driver from taking the payment. The driver and his helper then attempted to carry the cash register away. This resulted in a struggle for possession of the cash register, during the course of which the retailer was kicked and severely beaten by the driver and his helper. The retailer sued the manufacturer for the damages sustained.

In a similar case, the Connecticut Supreme Court held that the manufacturer was liable because the driver was acting within the general scope of his services. In the course of its opinion, the court said, "When the servant is doing or attempting to do the very thing which he was directed to do, the master is liable, though the servant's method of doing it be wholly unauthorized or forbidden."[4]

The quoted statement should be limited to the facts of the case. If the driver had pulled a gun, shot and wounded the retailer, and then stepping over the unconscious retailer, had taken the ice-cream money from the cash register, the court would probably have held that although the servant's act was a means of accomplishing the authorized result, it was done in so outrageous a manner and with force so totally out-of-line with performance of the authorized acts that the servant would be acting outside the general scope of his services— with the result that the manufacturer would not be liable for the driver's violence.

A servant's wrongful act may be done while he is performing authorized services and nevertheless be outside the *scope* of his services. An employee carelessly smoking on the job provides a good illustration of this. The employer is liable only if the employee's smoking is done at such a time and under such circumstances that his carelessness in smoking makes him careless in the manner in which he performs authorized services.

Example: An oil refiner employed a driver to deliver gasoline in the refiner's tank truck. While delivering gasoline to a manufacturer's plant, the driver unavoidably spilled some gasoline. While still in the process of delivering the gasoline, the driver lighted a cigarette and carelessly tossed the match into some of the spilled gasoline. The resulting conflagration destroyed part of the manufacturing plant and the manufacturer sued the refiner.

The driver's careless smoking would make him a careless deliveryman; for negligence within the scope of the driver's authorized services, the employer would be liable.

Suppose that while driving the gasoline tank truck toward the manufacturing plant, the driver lighted a cigarette and carelessly tossed the lighted match out the window, starting a costly grass fire. The driver's careless smoking would not make him a careless truck driver, and therefore the employer would not be liable for the grass-fire damages.

Liability for Agent's Fraudulent Misrepresentation

If an agent is guilty of making a fraudulent misrepresentation in negotiating a contract between his principal and a third person, the

[4] *Son v. Hartford Ice Cream Co.*, 102 Conn. 696, 129 A.778 (1925).

agent is of course liable to the third person for damages. Also, unless the contract limits the agent's power concerning making statements, the third person has a right to cancel the contract dishonestly negotiated by the agent and to recover from the principal anything paid under the contract. However, whether the defrauded third person can hold the principal liable for damages is a point upon which the courts do not entirely agree. In most states, the question of a principal's liability for his agent's fraudulent misrepresentation is decided on the basis of the actual or apparent authority of the agent to make representations. If a representation involves a matter concerning which an agent might be expected to make statements in dealing with third persons, the agent has the apparent authority to make such a statement. If the agent makes a misstatement in regard to such a matter, his principal has a contract obligation to the third person for the misstatement, and (in most states) likewise a tort liability for a misstatement fraudulently made. A few states, however, do not impose tort liability on a principal unless he actually participates in his agent's fraud.

Example: In a small community in which all houses were not yet connected with the recently expanded sewer system, an owner listed his house with a real estate broker to negotiate a sale for $15,000, the broker to receive a 3 percent commission. The owner instructed the broker to tell prospective buyers that the house still used a septic tank, not yet having been connected to the new sewer line. Falsely saying that he had investigated and found that the house was connected with the sewer line, the broker interested a buyer in buying the premises. The buyer signed a contract form and paid $500 down. The broker then took the contract form to the owner who also signed it. By the contract the owner agreed to sell and the buyer to buy the described house and lot for $15,000, $500 of which was stated as having been paid, with the balance to be paid upon delivery of the deed thirty days later. No reference to any sewer connection was made in the contract. Of the $500 paid by the buyer, the broker turned over to the owner $50, retaining $450 as his commission. At the time for settlement the buyer learned the truth concerning the sewerage system of the house and the owner for the first time learned of the broker's fraudulent misrepresentation. To excavate through underground rock and connect the house with the new sewer line would cost $1,500.

1. The buyer subtracted the sewer connection cost from the balance due under his contract, tendered $13,000 to the owner, and demanded a deed for the property. When the owner refused to give a deed for less than $14,500 the buyer sued for a decree of specific performance to require the owner to deliver the deed for $13,000.

In many states the buyer could recover. In a few states, the buyer would not be entitled to a deed unless he would pay the owner the full $14,500, inasmuch as the owner did not authorize or participate in the broker's fraud.

2. The buyer demanded that the $1,500 cost of connecting to the sewer

line be deducted from the purchase price. When the owner refused, the buyer thereupon said that the deal was off and demanded return of his $500 down payment. When the owner refused this, the buyer sued the owner for $500. The owner in turn tendered a deed to the buyer and filed a counterclaim against the buyer for the $14,500 purchase price due under the contract.

The owner would not be permitted to retain the benefit (the contract) obtained through his agent's fraud. This would be true even in the few states which would refuse to hold the owner liable for tort damages. Therefore, the owner would recover nothing from the buyer on the counterclaim, while the buyer would have a right to recover from the owner the amount of the $500 down payment.

Part 4   RIGHTS AND OBLIGATIONS OF AGENTS AND THIRD PERSONS

CONTRACT OBLIGATIONS OF AGENTS TO THIRD PERSONS

AGENTS WITH AUTHORITY

An agent who enters into a contract for his principal usually has no contract liability himself, even though the principal breaches the contract, if the agent 1) identifies the principal for whom he is acting, 2) has authority (either actual or apparent) to bind the principal by the particular contract, and 3) does not expressly guarantee the principal's performance or otherwise make himself a party to the contract.

Principal Fully Disclosed

Even though a principal is fully disclosed and a contract is authorized, if the contract is in writing the agent may sometimes be held liable as a co-party or a guarantor because of the manner in which he signs. The most common forms in which agent's signatures have been made are as follows (assume P. Porter is the principal and A. Adams, the agent):

Form 1.   "P. Porter
                by A. Adams, his agent."
Form 2.   "P. Porter hereby agrees as follows . . .
                                (signed) A. Adams, his agent."
Form 3.   "P. Porter
                A. Adams"
Form 4.   "P. Porter Corporation
                A. Adams, President"
Form 5.   "A. Adams, President
                P. Porter Corporation"

Form 6.   "A. Adams, agent for P. Porter" or "A. Adams, agent for
          P. Porter Corporation."
Form 7.   "A. Adams, agent."

The first form, of course, is the best for an agent to use. In Form
1, and (under the better-reasoned decisions) in Form 2, the agent
clearly shows that he is making the contract for his principal and in
his principal's name, and that he does not intend to obligate himself
personally. The other numbered forms leave the agent's intended status
open to some argument. The better view is that if the intention of the
parties (of both the agent and the other contracting party) is not made
clear by the writing or is ambiguous from the manner in which the
agent signs, oral evidence may be heard to prove what the parties
intended. In the absence of such oral evidence, the agent would be liable
if he signs as in Forms 3 and 7, and some courts would hold him
liable if he signs as in Forms 4, 5, and 6.

Example: On a printed order form supplied by a sign manufacturer, two
signs were ordered to be constructed and erected for $795. The signs were to
advertise a soft-drink product called "Osce-Y-Ola." The order form read as
follows (the portions printed on the form are italicized):

Enter our order for two signs [stating specifications and price] *at*
Osce-Y-Ola Co., Steeplechase Pier, Atlantic City, N. J. (signed) Arthur
Adams *by* Sec. & Treas. Osce-Y-Ola.

When the price was not paid, the sign manufacturer sued Arthur Adams who
denied personal liability and asserted that he was contracting as an agent for the
Osce-Y-Ola Sales Company. Since no oral evidence was offered by either
party, the case turned entirely on the meaning and effect of the written order.

The Pennsylvania Superior Court held that, in the absence of further
evidence, Adams was personally liable on the contract. The court pointed out
that Adams had not disclosed the full name of the corporation for which he
claimed to be acting, and also said,

> . . . the individual signature imports a personal liability. . . . The addi-
> tion of a corporate name *in connection with other evidence* might tend
> to contradict this import of personal liability; but here no other evi-
> dence was offered. We must conclude that the mere addition of the
> words "Sec. & Treas. Osce-Y-Ola" were insufficient, standing alone, to
> indicate that the defendant did not sign in his individual capacity.[5]
> [Emphasis added.]

Principal Undisclosed or Partially Disclosed

If at the time a contract is entered into by A and T, T is unaware
that A is acting as an agent, clearly A is a party to the contract and is
bound by it. If T is aware that A is an agent, but does not know who

---

[5] *Flexume Corp.* v. *Norris*, 98 Pa. Super. 530 (1929).

A represents, then usually T is to some extent relying on A's good faith and solvency, and unless the parties clearly state otherwise, A is a party to the contract and is bound by it.

AGENTS WITHOUT AUTHORITY

Through his conduct of entering into a contract in the name of another person, a purported agent is asserting as a fact that he has the authority he is presuming to exercise. If he lacks such authority, either actual or apparent, the other contracting party can hold the purported agent liable for damages for breach of this implied assertion or warranty of authority.

TORT LIABILITY OF AGENTS TO THIRD PERSONS

Whether a person who commits a tort is acting for himself or as an agent for another, he is personally liable for the damages resulting from his tort. If a principal instructs an agent to do an act which constitutes a tort, the agent is not relieved from liability by the fact that he was merely carrying out his principal's instructions. If an agent is unaware that carrying out his principal's instructions will constitute a tort, the agent is nevertheless liable for any tort for which guilty knowledge is not a requisite—such as a tort involving an unjustified interference with another's person or property.

As discussed in Chapter 2, liability for negligence is not unlimited. If the plaintiff who is suing for damages sustained as a result of the defendant's carelessness is not of the class unduly jeopardized by the defendant's act, the plaintiff cannot recover. In other words, as to this particular plaintiff, the defendant's careless act is not considered a tort. One of the common applications of this policy rule in agency situations arises when an agent carelessly gives his principal erroneous information upon which some third person relies to his detriment. As is more fully discussed in Chapter 7, unless bodily injury and not merely property damage is threatened by a negligent misrepresentation, the courts are reluctant to extend liability beyond the parties to the information-supplying contract. Thus an agent who makes a negligent misrepresentation to his principal is usually not committing a tort to a third person—unless bodily injury to such a person is a foreseeable result of the erroneous information.

RIGHT OF AGENTS AGAINST THIRD PERSONS

Generally, unless an agent is a party to a contract, he has no right to enforce the contract.

Example: The owner of a plot of land engaged a real estate broker to negotiate a sale of the land for not less than $20,000. The broker was to receive as compensation a commission of 3 percent but only if and when an actual transfer of the property and full payment of the price were completed. The broker interested a buyer in buying the property and obtained the buyer's signature on a contract form. The broker then took the contract form to the owner who also signed it. In the contract the owner agreed to sell and the buyer to buy the described real estate for $20,000; performance (payment of the price and delivery of the deed) was to take place one month later. On the settlement date the buyer announced that he had changed his mind and refused to go through with the contract. When the owner decided not to undertake the expense and inconvenience of attempting to enforce the contract against the buyer, the broker himself sued the buyer for damages for breach of contract, claiming a right to recover the amount of the commission the broker would have earned if the buyer had not defaulted on the contract.

Not being a party to the contract, the broker would have no right to enforce the contract and could not collect damages from the buyer for breach of the contract. (Whether the owner would be liable to the broker for not attempting to enforce the contract against the buyer, is a point upon which court decisions conflict.)

Part 5 TERMINATION OF AGENCY POWERS

Usually a principal appoints an agent and grants him power to act in order to obtain for himself the benefit of the agent's performance. However, sometimes a person will grant an agency power over certain of his property in order to assure that an obligation owed to the recipient of the power will be paid, or perhaps as a way of paying or performing the obligation. A common example is a pledge transaction in which an obligor who owns corporate stock borrows a sum of money from a bank, signs a note promising to repay the loan at a stated time, and, as collateral security, delivers to the bank his stock certificate together with an authorization to sell the stock should the obligor default in repaying the loan. This power—to sell the stock in the obligor's name—is an agency power which is held and exercised for the primary benefit of the holder of the power (the obligee bank) rather than for the grantor of the power (the obligor). Such an agency power is frequently termed an agency given as security, or a power coupled with a creditor's or obligee's interest. It would be contrary to the parties' intent and quite unfair to the obligee to permit this agency power to be revoked or terminated before the obligation is satisfied. Therefore, the rules for termination of ordinary agency powers do not apply in situations involving agency powers coupled with an obligee's interest.

ORDINARY AGENCY POWERS

An agency relationship or power can end in any of a variety of ways. Since an agency relationship involves the consent of both the principal and the agent, the relationship can be terminated as they provide in their original agreement or in any later agreement. Other ways in which the relationship can end or be suspended include, 1) revocation or renunciation, 2) occurrence of an event reasonably leading the agent to doubt that he should proceed, and 3) death of the principal.

REVOCATION OR RENUNCIATION

Since an agency relationship involves personal trust and confidence, the law will not compel parties to continue such a relationship if either wishes to repudiate it. If a repudiation breaks a contract between the principal and agent, the repudiating party is liable to the other for damages for breach of contract—but the agency is terminated. Thus it is frequently said that either party has the *power* even though he may not have the *right* to terminate the agency.

CHANGE OF CIRCUMSTANCES

The purpose of an ordinary agency is the performance of services for the principal. Since the agent is obliged to act for the best interests of his principal, it is reasonable to assume that an agent's authority will be terminated, or at least suspended, if the agent learns facts which should reasonably lead him to doubt that the principal still wishes the agency carried out.

Example: P, a resident of New York City, inherited a tract of land in Colorado. The tract consisted partly of pasture land and partly of rocky wasteland. After receiving from A, a Colorado real estate broker, an appraisal of the land, P in writing authorized A to sell the land for $5,000, the appraised price. Shortly afterwards A learned that uranium had been discovered on adjoining land.

Obviously A's authority to sell for $5,000 would be terminated or at least suspended until A could tell P of the new development.

DEATH OF PRINCIPAL

Since an agent is to act for the benefit of his principal and subject to the principal's direction and control—and also subject to the principal's power to terminate the agency at any time—it is reasonable to say that the death of the principal will terminate the agent's authority or power.

Notice of Principal's Death

The common-law rule which is followed in most states holds that the principal's death will immediately terminate the agent's authority, even though neither the agent nor a third party with whom the agent is dealing knows of the principal's death. However, the courts in some states feel that what is sometimes called the civil-law rule is more fair and more closely attuned to business practices. These courts hold that although the death of the principal revokes the agency, the revocation becomes effective only when the agent learns of the principal's death. The legislatures in some states, convinced of the fairness of the civil-law rule, have adopted it by statute, some statutes covering all agencies and some being limited to certain special agents, such as agents representing men in the armed services or agents authorized to sell land.

APPARENT AUTHORITY AFTER TERMINATION

As previously discussed, a principal may be bound not only by what his agent is actually authorized to do but also by an act within the agent's apparent authority. An agent authorized to enter into only a single, isolated transaction has no apparent authority outside that transaction; on the other hand, a continuing or general agent, engaged to enter into a series of transactions, has a much broader apparent authority. If a continuing agency is terminated, a third person who is unaware of the termination is justified in assuming that the agency still exists until the principal takes reasonable steps to give notice of its termination. What the principal should do to give notice to a particular third person depends on the prior experience of that third person with the agent. If the third person previously extended credit to the principal through the agent, or if to the knowledge of the principal the agent has commenced negotiating with the third person for a particular contract, the agent's authority will reasonably appear to continue until the principal gives the third person personal notice of termination. On the other hand, the principal's inserting a classified advertisement in a newspaper published in the town where the agency is carried on is sufficient notice to third persons who have not so completely relied on the agency.

Example: P of Chicago owned a store in Harrisburg, Pennsylvania, known as the Elite Clothing Store, and employed M as the local manager. As authorized by P, store funds were handled through a checking account in a Harrisburg bank, the account being in the name of "Elite Clothing Store, by M. Martin." P authorized M to purchase merchandise in the name of the store from various manufacturers, including S Shirt Company of New York City and T Tie Company of Boston. All such orders were signed, "Elite Clothing Store by

M. Martin." Both S Company and T Company knew that P owned the store. Purchases from T Company were c.o.d., paid by M out of store funds; purchases from S Company were on thirty days' credit, paid by M with checks drawn on the Harrisburg account. Every month M sent P a report of all income and disbursements, and remitted the net profits by check drawn on the Harrisburg account. After operating in this way for several years, P sold the store to M and inserted in a Harrisburg newspaper a classified advertisement telling of the transfer, and consequent termination of M's authority to act as P's agent. Later, by orders signed in the same way previous orders had been signed, M ordered shirts from S Company and ties from T Company. Both conformed to quantities previously ordered and both orders were for thirty days' credit. The goods were delivered to the store, and when payment was not made when due, both companies investigated and learned for the first time of the transfer of the business. Both companies sued P for the unpaid goods sold after transfer of the store to M.

The usual credit-reporting services watch for and file termination of authority notices. Since a seller who is asked to extend credit for the first time is expected to make a credit investigation, P's advertisement was all that should be expected of him in order to give notice to the public generally (including businesses like T Company), and P would have no liability to T Company.

A seller who has already been extending credit will not make a new credit investigation every time a new order is received. Therefore, P should have given S Company a personal notice of the sale of the store and the consequent termination of M's authority. A personal notice not having been given, M had the apparent authority to bind P, and S Company could recover from P.

AGENCY COUPLED WITH OBLIGEE'S INTEREST

An agency power given to an obligee as security for an obligation or as a way to collect the obligation cannot be revoked without the obligee's consent and is not terminated by the obligor's death.

Some courts distinguish between two types of agencies coupled with obligees' interests:

1. An agency in which the obligee has an actual property interest in, or possession of, the item concerning which he holds the agency interest—for example an obligee bank in possession of a stock certificate pledged by the obligor as collateral security for his obligation. The bank's agency cannot be withdrawn by the obligor and is not terminated by the obligor's death.

2. An agency in which the grant of agency power to the obligee does not give him an actual property interest in or possession of the item over which the power is to be exercised. The status of this type of agency is summarized in the following example.

Example: T owes D $1,000, payable $100 per month over the next ten months. D borrows $500 from C and gives C a written authorization to collect

T's payment of $100 per month until D's $500 debt to C is fully paid. Since D's $500 debt is smaller than T's $1,000 debt, D does not assign to C all of D's claim against T but merely authorizes C to collect for the next five months. C therefore acquires no property interest in T's obligation.

Some courts would hold that although D cannot withdraw the authorization he has given to C, D's death will terminate C's authorization.

Other courts would hold (and this appears to be the modern trend) that even though C acquires no property interest in D's claim against T, an agency power such as this is not revocable either by D's act or death, since the power is given at the time D's obligation to C arises, and also is given either to secure D's debt or as a method for paying the debt.

PROBLEMS

1. A traveling salesman, authorized to contract to sell certain securities at par, reported to his principal that he had contracted in the principal's name to sell a large quantity at 1 percent below par. The principal withheld action upon the report for one month and then notified the buyer that the contract was repudiated. Was the principal bound by the contract? (Modified from A.I.C.P.A., Nov. 47-8g.)

2. O. Osborn, the owner of a building and the land on which erected, listed the premises with A. Adams, a real estate broker, to find a purchaser at not less than $50,000, for which O agreed to pay A a 3 percent commission in case he effected a sale. Shortly afterwards, A told O that three parties were dickering for the property. A had O sign a contract form in which O agreed to sell the described premises for $50,000. The name of the purchaser was to be filled in by A. The agreement also stated: "O. Osborn is to pay A. Adams a 3 percent commission on the amount of this sale. Deed is to be delivered to purchaser and price paid one month from date hereof." A few weeks later, A filled in his wife's name as the buyer and notified O. O replied that he would not pay the commission. On the closing date specified in the signed agreement, O transferred the property to A's wife, receiving her check for $50,000, but O still refused to pay any commission. A sued O for $1,500. Explain whether A was entitled to recover.

3. M Company, a manufacturer of farm machinery, employed A at a fixed monthly salary as factory representative for a territory covering the western half of North Dakota. A's duties included making sales, writing contracts, helping local dealers, and making collections. D who held the dealer-franchise to sell M Company's products in three specified counties in the western half of North Dakota, proposed to A an arrangement under which if A would help D to establish subdealers in D's territory, the subdealers to receive one half of the commissions on their sales, D and A would split the remaining one-half. A agreed to the arrangement and established subdealers, made sales, took second-hand machinery in trade, accepted payments, and made collections on behalf of D. D failed to pay, and A sued for $4,500, his share of the commissions earned through the subdealers' sales. Was A entitled to judgment against D? Explain.

4. Most of the real estate brokers in a certain community formed an association, one of the chief features of which was an arrangement for sharing listings. Under the arrangement, whenever a member of the association received an exclusive listing and failed to sell the listed property within one month, he would report the property to the association office which would then send a description of the property to all members. If a sale of the property were later negotiated by a broker other than the one with whom it was originally listed, the commission earned on the transfer would be equally split between the two brokers. Each included in his advertising a statement that he was a member of the association and that a listing with him would be a listing with all the association brokers.

A and B were both members of the association. O, the owner of certain property, signed an exclusive sale agreement with A, listing the property with A for $80,000 and agreeing to pay A a 5 percent commission in the event of sale within the next six months, no matter by whom the sale was negotiated. After one month, descriptions of the property were sent to all association members. A few weeks later P consulted B and inquired concerning a certain type of property. B showed P a list containing descriptions of various properties, including that belonging to O. P expressed an interest in O's property and engaged B to negotiate a purchase, agreeing to pay B a 4 percent commission. B agreed to use his best efforts to negotiate a purchase agreeable to P. B then called A who notified O that B had a prospective buyer. After B and P inspected O's property, B negotiated a transfer from O to P for $70,000. O paid A a 5 percent commission on the transfer, but B returned to A the check for 2½ percent which A sent to B. However, P then refused to pay B the agreed 4 percent and B sued P. What result? Explain.

5. R owned several retail shops selling women's clothing. At one of the shops, which was operated on rented premises, he employed his sister and brother as salesclerks. About six months before expiration of the lease, R commenced negotiations with the landlord for a five-year renewal. The negotiations were still pending when R left the city for two weeks on a business trip. Unknown to R, his sister and brother were planning to form a partnership to operate a women's clothing store. During R's absence from the city his sister and brother told the landlord of their business plans and successfully negotiated a five-year lease of the store premises to themselves, the lease period to begin upon expiration of R's lease two months later. When R returned to the city his sister and brother gave him a one-month notice that they were leaving his employment. When R learned of the new lease, R sued his sister and brother and requested the court to decree that they assign the new lease to him. What result? Explain.

6. a) A was a salesman employed by P to travel a certain territory and to solicit orders from hardware dealers. A received an order for 10 garden plows from T, a hardware dealer. A sent the order to P who then shipped the plows to T. At the end of the month A collected the purchase price of the plows from T, but failed to turn the money over to P. P had given A no express authority to collect. Could P require T to pay again? Explain.

b) Assume that A promised to have the plows shipped promptly to T and that in gratitude and without ulterior motive or agreement T gave A a radio as a gift. Assume further that there was no custom or agreement between P and A permitting the latter to accept a gift in such circumstances. P learned of the gift and demanded the radio. Would A be required to give the radio to P. Explain. (Modified from A.I.C.P.A., May 54-4a,c.)

7. P engaged A as a traveling salesman to sell certain goods and instructed A not to deliver to any buyer unless payment was made by certified check naming P as the payee. On his first trip A sold and delivered certain of these goods to T. T paid the price to A in cash, without knowledge of A's instructions and without any investigation of A's authority to collect. A disappeared with the money, and P sued T to recover either the purchase price or the goods. Was P entitled to recover? Explain.

8. Wishing to acquire a site for his factory without provoking a rise in the price of land, P, in writing, engaged A, a real estate broker, to secure certain specified pieces of land without disclosing that he was acting for P. Following this plan, A entered into a written contract in his own name with S to buy S's lot for a stated price, transfer to be made on the following June 1. Believing that B, another real estate broker, would succeed better with T for T's lot, A engaged B for that purpose, and B signed a contract with T to buy T's lot for a stated price, transfer to be made on the following June 1. Actually T's lot was not contiguous with the other lots P was acquiring and, therefore, not within the actual authority given by P to A. However, when P learned of the contract, he decided that he wished to acquire T's lot also. One week prior to the time for transfer of title under the two contracts, P notified S and T to have deeds made out to P. P's plans having by that time been publicized, the value of all real estate in the area advanced sharply. On the contract settlement date, S and T refused to transfer to P. In separate lawsuits P sued S and T to enforce the contracts made by A and B.

a) Could P enforce the contract entered into by A and S? Explain.

b) Could P enforce the contract entered into by B and T? Explain.

c) Other facts remaining the same, assume that after P gave the above-described notices to S and T, P gave them each a second notice stating that he had changed his mind, and on the settlement day, P refused to accept deeds from either S or T or to pay anything for their lands. 1) Could S enforce against P the contract entered into by A and S? Explain. 2) Could T enforce against P the contract entered into by B and T? Explain. (Modified from A.I.C.P.A., Nov. 48-12.)

9. A plaintiff began a lawsuit against a defendant who was an elderly widow. The widow thereupon made an appointment with her lawyer. The widow's sister who lived about a mile from the widow's house owned a car. Having no car herself, the widow asked her sister to take her to the lawyer's office to keep the appointment. On the way to the office, the widow was busy looking over various documents she was going to give the lawyer and was paying no attention to her sister's driving. The sister negligently failed to stop at a stop sign and collided with a car being carelessly driven by X.

The widow suffered severe personal injuries as a result of the accident. In agreeing to drive the widow to the lawyer's office, the sister was doing a favor with no expectation or right of compensation.

a) Assume that the widow sued her sister for damages. Could the widow recover? Explain.

b) Assume that the widow sued X for damages. Could the widow recover? Explain.

10. P, a dealer in household furnishings sold a piano to B on a title-retaining installment contract. B fell behind in his payments and P sent A to B's house. A was employed by P to collect unpaid installments and to repossess from defaulting buyers. P instructed A to repossess the piano but only if he could take it without trouble. P particularly instructed A not to commit assault and battery or otherwise break the law. With two other of P's employees, A went to B's house and when B refused to permit removal of the piano, A and his men threatened B, pushed him around, and removed the piano. B sued P for damages for assault and battery. Was B entitled to judgment against P. Explain.

11. T Convoy Company was in the business of trucking new automobiles, and had interstate and state carrier permits for that purpose. Forty trucks were used in the business, fifteen owned by T Company and twenty-five owned by the individual drivers. The drivers of the company-owned trucks received a specified fixed compensation, the amount depending on the haul made and the number of autos delivered. For each haul made by an owner-driver, T Company paid him 77 percent of the freight rate charged for the haul; this payment was compensation for use of the truck and compensation to the driver. Except for the method of calculating pay, both classes of drivers were treated alike. The practice was for both classes of drivers, after completion of a run, to report to the company terminal and receive: 1) a load of autos and the freight bill which stated the name and address of the consignee, the description of the cargo, and the trucking charges; 2) instructions as to the route to be taken; and 3) oil, gas, and necessary cash for traveling expenses. All drivers were instructed to drive carefully. For some consignees T Company instructed the drivers to collect the trucking charges upon delivery; for others T Company extended credit and billed the consignees after delivery.

While returning to the terminal over the route prescribed by T Company after delivering a load of autos, D was driving negligently and collided with P, causing considerable injury to P's person and property. D's carelessness was the sole cause of the accident. P sued T Company.

a) T Company owned the truck which D was driving. Explain 1) the reasoning upon which P might attempt to base his claim, 2) the reasoning upon which T Company might attempt to base its defense, and 3) which party should be given judgment.

b) D owned the truck which he was driving. Explain whether this would change any of the answers given in Part (a).

12. A map of the Eastwood Acres Subdivision was on file in the county courthouse, showing the location of the subdivision and the location and size of numbered lots in the subdivision. S, owner of Lot No. 40, engaged a surveyor to survey the property and place stakes showing the boundaries. Through the negligence of one of the surveyor's linemen, the stakes that were placed included one-half of Lot 39 and omitted half of Lot 40. B, considering purchasing S's lot, went with S to view the lot. B inquired as to the location of the boundaries. S indicated the stakes that his surveyor had placed and said, "These stakes are on the boundary lines." Satisfied with the property, B purchased the lot, paying S $2,000 and receiving from S a deed for "Lot Number 40 of the Eastwood Acres Subdivision, as shown on a plat recorded in the Recorder of Deeds office in this county in Map Book, Volume 4 at Page 300." B engaged a contractor to fill and grade his new lot, pointing out the stakes to the contractor as the boundaries of the lot. Later when B engaged an architect to draw plans for a building, the erroneous placement of the stakes was discovered. Of the $1,000 B paid for filling and grading, one-half was spent on Lot 39. Would B have a right to recover $500 a) from N, the owner of Lot 39, b) from the surveyor, c) from S? Explain.

13. A wholesaler employed an agent to sell and deliver certain goods, and instructed him not to sell below $1.50 for 25-pound sacks, and not to give any warranties of quality. The agent sold some of the goods in the wholesaler's name at $1 for 25-pound sacks, the then market price, and with a warranty of quality similar to that given by other sellers of such goods. The agent honestly believed that the goods were of the quality warranted. The goods were delivered to the buyer by the agent, and the buyer paid the agent the agreed $1 per sack.

a) Assume that the goods were of the proper quality. 1) Briefly explain if the wholesaler would have a right against the buyer either to recover the goods or to collect an additional 50¢ per sack. 2) Briefly explain the wholesaler's rights, if any, against the agent.

b) Assume that the goods were not of the quality warranted. Briefly explain if the buyer would have a right to collect 1) from the wholesaler for breach of warranty; 2) from the agent for breach of warranty. (Modified from A.I.C.P.A., May 42-2.)

14. P, a 20-year old orphan, gave A, an adult stock and bond broker, a sum of money and instructed A to purchase certain bonds for P. A purchased the bonds from T and paid for them with P's money. When A purchased the bonds, he disclosed that he was buying for P. Although A knew P's age and knew that P was a stranger to T, it did not occur to A to say anything to T about P's age. By the time P reached 21 years of age, the bonds had depreciated in value. On his twenty-first birthday, P returned the bonds to T, who under protest repaid P the amount A had paid for the bonds. T then sued A. On what theory and with what result? Explain. (Modified from A.I.C.P.A., Nov. 36-7.)

15. On June 20, an agent, in the name of his principal, mailed to a merchant an order for certain goods. As authorized by his principal, the agent had an arrangement with the merchant for goods to be shipped to the principal's place of business on the agent's periodic orders. The principal

died June 21, and the agent sent a notice of this to the merchant. Before he received the notice, the merchant shipped the goods to the principal's place of business. The principal's executor refused to accept or pay for the goods. From whom, if anyone, could the merchant recover damages? Explain. (Modified from A.I.C.P.A., Nov. 47-8f.)

16. For a number of years F. Martin, as sole proprietor, owned and operated a business engaged in quarrying and burning limestone under the name "Martin Lime Company." F employed his two sons, A and B, in the production part of the business; F himself did all the buying for the business. From time to time, S, a coal dealer, attempted to sell coal to F, but F never made any purchases from him. F then sold his entire business and plant to the two sons, A and B, for a substantial sum, payable to F in stated installments. A and B thereafter conducted the business under the same name and F withdrew from any participation in it. A and B purchased quantities of coal from S, the purchases being made on credit in the name of "Martin Lime Company." After several months S for the first time learned of the transfer of the business, S as well as the general public having had no prior knowledge of the sale, although there had been no attempt to keep the transfer secret and F, A, and B had all talked of it to their friends and acquaintances. When the company failed to pay S for $3,000 worth of coal, S sued F. Upon what grounds and with what result? Explain.

17. In addition to the facts in Problem 16, assume the following: All of the purchases A and B made from S were on orders obtained by S's salesman. The first time A and B gave the salesman an order, they told him of the change of the ownership, but the salesman neglected to pass the information on to S. How, if at all, would this additional fact affect the lawsuit of S against F? Explain.

18. D borrowed money from C and gave C as security a power of attorney to collect future rents from D's tenants.

a) Would this power of attorney be canceled by D's death prior to the repayment of the loan? Explain.

b) Could a tenant knowing of D's death discharge his obligation for rent accrued prior to D's death by paying C? Explain. (Modified from A.I.C.P.A., Nov. 34-5.)

chapter *13*

Partnerships and Corporations

Part 1 INTRODUCTION

Most business organizations are either sole proprietorships, partnerships, or corporations. In a *sole proprietorship*, the business is owned and operated by one individual. He may employ hundreds of assistants and delegate to certain of them most of the decision making in the business, but the ultimate control and the right to change or countermand any employee's decision rests exclusively in the sole proprietor.

A *partnership* can be termed a co-owned proprietorship as distinguished from a sole proprietorship. Instead of having a single owner, a partnership is owned and operated by two or more co-owners.

In legal theory a *corporation* can be termed a sole proprietorship in which the business is owned and operated by an artificial person created by the law rather than by a natural person. In others words, a corporation is considered as having a legal personality separate and distinct from the persons who own and operate the business. This concept is frequently referred to as the "separate entity theory." A similar theory is associated with the legal and philosophical concept of a sovereign state. Suppose that the United States entered into a treaty with England in 1830, and that since then the treaty has never been expressly nor impliedly canceled. Although none of the actual persons who negotiated the 1830 treaty is still alive, although in fact no person who was a citizen of either country at that time is alive today, the treaty would still be considered as a binding undertaking between the nations. It is a binding undertaking today because the United States and England, today, are the same legal entities which entered into the treaty in 1830. People come and go, but the nation as an entity exists and continues to exist separate and distinct from the individual citizens who are its inhabitants at any particular time. Each individual nation also finds it highly convenient, essential in fact, to treat the political subdivisions within the nation as separate legal entities. Thus if New York City entered into an obligation in 1830, the obligation is just as binding today, because the city today is the same legal personality that existed and assumed the obligation in 1830.

Although a nation or a city is a separate legal personality, it is an artificial rather than a natural legal person; it cannot act for itself but must necessarily act through natural persons as its agents. A tiny baby is in a somewhat analagous position. In the eyes of the law the baby is a separate legal personality with legally protected rights. A premeditated, unjustified killing of the baby would be murder, a wrongful injury of the baby would be a tort, even though the baby cannot act for himself but is entirely dependent on his parents to provide for him.

The separate-entity theory was recognized as a needful legal tool and adapted to business operations in the early days of business growth and expansion. A New York judge has written in a frequently quoted opinion:

> The vast growth of corporate organizations in this country and the extension of the rights and powers granted to them by the legislatures of the several states during the past three-quarters of a century are facts familiar to every student of the law. The corporate conception, however, long antedated this period. The reason for its vastly extended use in this later period lay in the need for greater aggregations of capital to develop the tremendous potential resources of the country than were reasonably available to any single individual or small group of individuals. Furthermore, many of the projects confronting the pioneers of business, whereas offering great probabilities of profit presented corresponding possibilities of loss, and whereas the inherent natural willingness of the pioneering spirit furnished an incentive to gamble for the rich reward which would crown success in the enterprise, the substratum of caution interposed an inhibition to the act of placing the total resources of the individual at the hazard of the event. Finally, many of the most promising projects of construction and development were of such considerable magnitude that their completion might well postdate the lives of the individuals who initiated them. The need for a method of organization which would eliminate these three difficulties was met by the conception of the modern business corporation, and it is the presence of these three characteristics which furnishes the essential points distinguishing a corporation from every other variety of business organization.
>
> To meet this need, the several Legislatures provided from time to time that one or more individuals might devote specified portions of their capital to the promotion of a clearly stated business object without personal financial liability for any sums beyond those voluntarily dedicated thereto, and that the sums thus contributed should remain dedicated to the object, irrespective of the deaths of the contributors unless or until a specified percentage of their number should signify the desire to terminate the enterprise. . . .[1]

Example: An owner of real estate in Virginia had his property divided into building lots which he began selling to various persons including S. Every deed by which the subdivider transferred title included the following restrictive provision: "Title to this land is never to vest in a person or persons

[1] *In re Steinberg's Estate*, 153 Misc. 339, 274 N.Y.S. 914 (1934).

of African descent." Shortly after buying one lot, S contracted to sell the property to a corporation known as "People's Pleasure Park Company, Inc." This corporation was formed, owned, and operated by Negroes who intended to establish and operate on this lot an amusement park for Negroes. The subdivider sued S and the corporation to have the contract canceled and to have S restrained from selling the property in violation of the restrictive provision.

The Supreme Court of Appeals of Virginia decided that the transfer did not violate the restrictive provision and refused to restrain the transfer. In the course of its opinion the court said:

> Such a conveyance, by no rule of construction, vests title to the property conveyed in " a person or persons of African descent." . . .
>
> "A corporation is an artificial person, like the state. It is a distinct existence—an existence separate from that of its stockholders and directors." . . .
>
> Prof. Rudolph Sohm, in his Institutes of Roman Law, pp. 104-106, says: "In Roman law the property of the corporation is the sole property of the collective whole; and the debts of a corporation are the sole debts of the collective whole. . . . It represents a kind of ideal private person, an independent subject capable of holding property, totally distinct from all previously existing persons, including its own members. It possesses, as such, rights and liabilities of its own. It leads its own life, as it were, quite unaffected by any change of members. It stands apart as a separate subject or proprietary capacity, and, in contemplation of law, as a stranger to its own members. The collective whole, as such, can hold property. Its property, therefore, is, as far as its members are concerned, another's property, its debts another's debts. . . . Roman law contrived to accomplish a veritable masterpiece of juristic ingenuity in discovering the notion of a collective person; in clearly grasping and distinguishing from its members the collective whole as the ideal unity of the members bound together by the corporate constitution; in raising this whole to the rank of a person (a juristic person, namely); and in securing it a place in private law as an independent subject of proprietary capacity standing on the same footing as other private persons."[2]

The basic legal distinction between a partnership and a corporation is that a partnership is not considered to be a separate legal entity while the corporation is a legal entity separate and distinct from the person or persons who form, own, and operate the corporation. From this distinction in legal theory flow the following chief differences between partnerships and corporations.

[2] *People's Pleasure Park Co., Inc.* v. *Rohleder,* 109 Va. 439, 61 S.E. 794 (1908). This case is used here as a corporate theory case, on which point the decision of the court is as true today as it was when it was decided in 1908. In the field of constitutional rights, as interpreted in more recent decisions of the United States Supreme Court, a restrictive provision such as the one in this case would be unenforceable even if S were selling to a Negro individual rather than to a corporation.

1. Manner of creating the business unit. A partnership is formed by the agreement of the parties while a corporation cannot exist unless the state creates it or breathes legal life into it.

2. Activities in which the business unit is permitted to engage. Persons combined as partners are permitted to engage in any activity which they could engage in as individuals. On the other hand, since the corporation is a separate legal personality, it has only the powers granted to it by the state which has created it.

3. Authority to act for the business. Since there is really no separation between the partnership and the partners, each partner is necessarily a representative of the partnership; a corporation with a legal personality separate from its shareholders is not necessarily represented by any one of its shareholders nor bound by his act.

4. Liability for business debts. The debts of a partnership business are the debts of the individual partners, while, if a creditor extends credit to a corporation, the debt is owed by the corporation rather than by the ones who own stock in the corporation.

5. Transfer by an owner or death of an owner. Since a partnership is an aggregate of co-owners, any change in the identity of the co-owners is a change in the partnership itself. In a corporation, a shareholder's transfer of his stock, or the shareholder's death, has no effect on the separate legal life being enjoyed by the corporation.

6. Citizenship. Since a partnership is not a separate legal entity, the partnership firm is not considered as having citizenship separate from the citizenship of its members, while a corporation is a citizen of the state in which it is created or incorporated, regardless of the citizenship of its shareholders. Thus a corporation incorporated in Delaware is a citizen of that state, even though all of its shareholders may be citizens of California.

The law applicable to partnerships and corporations is largely statutory. Most states have adopted the Uniform Partnership Act, and all states have statutes pertaining to the formation and operation of corporations.

Part 2 PARTNERSHIPS

FORMATION OF PARTNERSHIPS

The Uniform Partnership Act definition of a partnership may be summarized as follows:

> A partnership is an unincorporated association of two or more persons to carry on as co-owners a business for profit.[3]

---

[3] Uniform Partnership Act (U.P.A.), Sec. 6.

A partnership is formed by a contract. Any person who has the capacity to enter into a contract may become a partner. Since a minor is not prohibited from making contracts, he can become a partner; however, he can disaffirm his partnership contract and thus avoid future liability.

Usually when persons form a partnership they enter into an express contract to that effect—preferably in writing. However, since contracts may be made by implication, it is possible for persons to actually form a partnership even though they do not expressly state an intent to do so. It is possible that even though persons expressly state that they are not partners, their conduct may amount to forming a partnership agreement. In determining whether or not a partnership exists, the principal question is whether the parties have undertaken an association which, as a matter of policy, the courts feel should carry with it the rights and obligations of a partnership. This question most often arises when a creditor, unable to collect from his business debtor, seeks to hold liable a person who was associated with the debtor in the business operation.

Partners are co-owners of a business, but all co-owners of property are not necessarily partners. The Partnership Act states:

> Joint tenancy, tenancy in common, tenancy by the entireties, joint property, common property, or part ownership does not of itself establish a partnership, whether such co-owners do or do not share any profits made by the use of the property.[4]

If co-ownership of property is an isolated or temporary arrangement, the co-owners' working together to handle their property usually does not show an implied agreement to become partners. But if their co-ownership and co-management are to extend over a substantial period of time and to involve a major part of their attention, the parties would seem to be actually carrying on a business and to be partners.

A partnership almost invariably involves a sharing of profits, but the fact that persons are sharing profits from a business operation does not of itself necessarily make them partners. The Partnership Act states:

> The sharing of gross returns does not of itself establish a partnership, whether or not the persons sharing them have a joint or common right or interest in any property from which the returns are derived. . . .
> The receipt by a person of a share of the profits of a business is prima facie evidence [sufficient without any other proof] that he is a partner in the business, but no such inference shall be drawn if such profits were received in payment:
> (a) As a debt by installments or otherwise,

[4] U.P.A. Sec. 7.

(b) As wages of an employee or rent to a landlord,

(c) As an annuity to a widow or representative of a deceased partner,

(d) As interest on a loan, though the amount of payment vary with the profits of the business,

(e) As the consideration for the sale of a good-will of a business or other property by installments or otherwise.[5]

If parties share profits *and* management in a substantial undertaking, they are usually considered partners.

Example: A food distributor entered into an agreement with X and Y who were partners in the ownership and operation of a cannery business. The agreement provided that, for the one-year duration of the contract:

1. The distributor would, if requested, supply all cans, cases, and labels, and provide sufficient money to pay employees and purchase produce.

2. The distributor would have the exclusive right to sell the entire output of the cannery. For his services as sole distributor, the distributor would receive 5 percent of gross sales.

3. At the expiration of the contract year the distributor would be repaid for all money and supplies advanced for operation of the cannery. As interest for such advances, the distributor would be entitled to 50 percent of the net profits of the year's operations.

4. X and Y would retain full ownership and control of the cannery and would be liable for all losses. The distributor would have no liability for any losses.

5. The distributor would have the right to determine salaries and wages paid by the cannery during the contract year.

During the contract year, a supplier sold certain goods to X and Y for operation of the cannery. When X and Y failed to pay for these goods, the supplier sued the distributor.

Under similar facts, the Maryland Court of Appeals decided[6] that in addition to sharing in profits, the distributor held substantial power to participate in management of the cannery, and therefore had actually become a partner in the business and was liable for its debts.

Apparent Partnerships

Sometimes although a person is not actually a partner with the owner of a particular business, he will indicate that he is a partner in order to help the owner borrow money or purchase on credit. Calling such a person a "partner by estoppel," the Partnership Act, as a matter of fairness, provides that if by words or conduct a defendant represents himself as a partner in a business, or consents to being represented as a partner, a creditor who extends credit to the business relying

[5] *Ibid.*
[6] *Southern Can Co.* v. *Sayler*, 152 Md. 303, 136 A. 624 (1927).

on the representation can hold the defendant liable as if he were actually a partner. If such a representation is made to the general public, it is presumed that subsequent creditors rely on the representation, and proof of actual reliance by a particular creditor is unnecessary.

RIGHTS AND OBLIGATIONS OF PARTNERS AMONG THEMSELVES

The proprietary interest of a partner in a partnership business usually includes the following rights: 1) A right to participate in management, 2) A monetary interest in the partnership, and 3) An ownership interest in specific partnership property.

PARTNERS' RIGHTS AS TO MANAGEMENT

Unless a partnership agreement expressly provides otherwise, the partners' rights as to management are as follows:

1. Each partner has an equal voice in the management and conduct of the partnership business, regardless of the ratio in which the partners contribute to the partnership capital or the ratio in which they agree to distribute profits and losses.

2. If partners cannot agree, the decision of a majority controls in matters involving the ordinary day-to-day operation of the business; when there is no majority, no action can be taken. On the other hand, unanimous consent of all partners is required in matters which go further than the ordinary conduct of the partnership business (for example a decision involving a change in the nature or location of the business or a change in the partnership agreement).

3. A partner can, if he wishes, agree with his co-partners to relinquish some or all of his right to participate in management. Thus, a partnership agreement can validly specify that all management decisions shall be made by certain designated members of the partners, or even by one specified partner—who would then be called the managing partner.

PARTNERS' MONETARY INTERESTS

Unless the partnership agreement provides otherwise, the partners' monetary interests are as follows:

1. Each partner is entitled to an equal share in profits, and must contribute toward losses in the same ratio in which he is to share profits.

2. Upon liquidation of the partnership business, each partner is entitled to share equally in the surplus remaining after payment of all

debts and repayment to each partner of the amount of the contribution, advances, and loans which he made to the partnership.

3. No partner is entitled to remuneration for acting in the partnership business—except for a surviving partner who is winding up the partnership business.

4. The partnership must indemnify each partner for payments made and liabilities incurred by him in the ordinary and proper conduct of the partnership business.

PARTNERS' OWNERSHIP INTERESTS IN PARTNERSHIP PROPERTY

Whether property used in a partnership is partnership property or is individual property owned personally by one or more of the partners is determined by the intent of the parties. If, upon formation of a partnership, property was brought into the partnership by one of the partners, a question may arise whether the ownership or merely the use of the property was contributed to the partnership. It is wise for the parties to settle this question in their partnership agreement. If after formation of a partnership the parties purchase property with partnership funds, they are presumed to intend that the property become partnership property unless they express a different intent.

The three chief types of property co-ownership which developed under the common law are tenancy in common, joint tenancy, and tenancy by entireties. None of these being entirely suited to the co-ownership of partnership property, the Partnership Act creates a fourth type of co-ownership, called "tenancy in partnership." The chief characteristics of this form of co-ownership are:

1. Unless agreed otherwise, the partners have co-equal rights to possess partnership property for partnership purposes. A partner has no right of possession for any other purpose without the consent of his co-partners.

2. A partner cannot make an assignment or transfer his co-ownership interest separate from the interests of the other partners.

3. A partner's individual creditors cannot levy on partnership property.

4. Upon the death of a partner, his heirs will not inherit any ownership interest in specific partnership property.

TRANSFERS OF PARTNERS' INTERESTS

Since a partnership can arise only from the agreement of all parties, a right to participate (or to interfere) in the management of a partnership cannot vest in outsiders without the consent of all the partners. Therefore a partner's monetary interest is the only interest, 1) which a partner can assign without the consent of his co-partners, 2) which a partner's individual creditors can levy on, or 3) which a deceased partner's heirs can inherit.

The individual creditor of a partner can obtain what is called a "charging order"—an order of court requiring that when profits (and upon liquidation, advances and surplus) are being distributed, the share due the debtor partner shall be paid to his attaching creditor up to the amount of the creditor's claim.

A partner who assigns to an outsider his interest in a partnership may intend merely to pledge his interest as collateral security for a personal obligation, and have no intent to separate himself from the partnership business. Therefore, the Partnership Act expressly provides that a partnership is not automatically dissolved either when a partner assigns his interest or when an individual creditor of a partner levies on his interest.

OBLIGATIONS OF PARTNERS TO EACH OTHER

The chief obligations of a partner to his co-partners include the following:

1. Each partner must contribute toward losses in the same ratio in which he is to share profits, unless the partnership agreement provides a different loss-sharing ratio.

2. A partner must on demand give his co-partners true and full information concerning all things affecting the partnership.

3. Each partner must account to the partnership for any benefit derived without his co-partners' consent from any transaction connected with the conduct of the partnership or the use of its property. As the United States Supreme Court has said, it is well settled:

> . . . that one partner cannot, directly or indirectly, use partnership assets for his own benefit; that he cannot, in conducting the business of a partnership, take any profit clandestinely for himself; that he cannot carry on another business in competition or rivalry with that of the firm, thereby depriving it of the benefit of his time, skill, and fidelity, without being accountable to his copartners for any profit that may accrue to him therefrom; that he cannot be permitted to secure for himself that which it is his duty to obtain, if at all, for the firm of which he is a member; nor can he avail himself of knowledge or information which may be properly regarded as the property of the partnership, in the sense that it is available or useful to the firm for any purpose within the scope of the partnership business.[7]

4. If any loss results from a partner's wrongful conduct, he is obliged to indemnify the partnership or his co-partners.

[7] *Latta* v. *Kilbourn*, 150 U.S. 524, 14 S. Ct. 201, 37 L. Ed. 1169 (1893).

OBLIGATIONS OF PARTNERS TO THIRD PERSONS

Each partner is personally liable for all of the debts and liabilities of the partnership business. In determining whether an obligation is a partnership liability, the law recognizes that each partner has the apparent authority of a general agent in the conduct of the partnership business. Although partners usually cooperate in the day-to-day operation of their business, they can agree among themselves that certain functions (for example the buying of goods for the business) shall be handled exclusively by a certain partner; they can even agree that all management powers shall be vested in one partner. However, third persons who are not advised otherwise are justified in assuming that the partnership business is being operated in the customary way— through the equal cooperation of all partners. The Partnership Act states:

(1) Every partner is an agent of the partnership for the purpose of its business, and the act of every partner, including the execution in the partnership name of any instrument, for apparently carrying on in the usual way the business of the partnership of which he is a member binds the partnership, unless the partner so acting has in fact no authority to act for the partnership in the particular matter, and the person with whom he is dealing has knowledge of the fact that he has no such authority.

(2) An act of a partner which is not apparently for the carrying on of the business of the partnership in the usual way does not bind the partnership unless authorized by the other partners.

(3) Unless authorized by the other partners or unless they have abandoned the business, one or more but less than all the partners have no authority to:

(a) Assign the partnership property in trust for creditors or on the assignee's promise to pay the debts of the partnership,

(b) Dispose of the goodwill of the business,

(c) Do any other act which would make it impossible to carry on the ordinary business of a partnership,

(d) Confess a judgment,

(e) Submit a partnership claim or liability to arbitration or reference.

(4) No act of a partner in contravention of a restriction on authority shall bind the partnership to persons having knowledge of the restriction.[8]

Since each partner is an agent of the partnership, the liability of the partnership (and of every partner) for torts committed by a partner is the same as the liability of a principal for his agent's torts. Accordingly the Partnership Act states:

[8] U.P.A. Sec. 9.

Where, by any wrongful act or omission of any partner acting in the ordinary course of the business of the partnership or with the authority of his copartners, loss or injury is caused to any person, not being a partner in the partnership, or any penalty is incurred, the partnership is liable therefor to the same extent as the partner so acting or omitting to act.[9]

LIMITED PARTNERSHIPS

Many states believe that sanctioning what might be called an investment partner accomplishes a useful economic purpose, and have adopted statutes accordingly. The chief statute in effect in a number of states is the Uniform Limited Partnership Act. Under this act:

1. A limited partnership may be formed but must include at least one general partner who is individually liable for all partnership obligations.

2. The name of the business must not include the name of any limited partner.

3. A signed statement identifying the co-partners and designating them as general and limited (and also giving some other details) must be filed in a specified public office.

4. If the business becomes insolvent, the limited partner will lose his investment but will have no personal liability for obligations of the partnership.

5. A limited partner must not work for or contribute his services to the partnership; a limited partner becomes liable as a general partner if he takes part in the control of the business.

SILENT AND SECRET PARTNERSHIPS

Sometimes a person's connection with a partnership business is not publicly known, perhaps not known by anyone outside of the business itself. Such a person is frequently called a secret partner. Some partners have no duties or obligations in regard to management or conduct of the partnership business, and are commonly called silent or dormant partners. A partner may achieve limited liability only as provided by a statute, such as the Limited Partnership Act. Therefore (assuming a limited partnership has not been properly formed) a secret partner, once his membership in a firm is discovered, or a silent partner, or one who is both secret and silent, is a general partner with full liability for partnership obligations.

[9] U.P.A. Sec. 13.

PARTNERSHIPS PROVIDING FOR IMMUNITY FROM DEBT

Suppose that when A, B, and C form a partnership, they expressly agree that A shall have no liability for debts. If A is not a limited partner in a limited partnership formed according to statute, then he is a general partner with full liability to third persons for partnership obligations. The immunity agreement is merely an arrangement among the partners, and means that whatever A is forced to pay to creditors, he can recover from B and C. Since this is merely an arrangement among the partners for sharing losses, a creditor who extends credit to the partnership with knowledge of the immunity agreement is not thereby agreeing to release A from personal liability.

OBLIGATIONS AFTER CHANGE OF MEMBERSHIP

Suppose that a business is owned and operated by a partnership consisting of A, B, and C; A retires and sells his interest to D who, with the consent of B and C, takes A's place in the firm. As a matter of law, the partnership of A, B, and C is dissolved and a new partnership is formed consisting of D, B, and C. Since such a change in membership is not unusual, the law attempts to give effect to the intent and understanding of businessmen (without, however, actually changing the law as to the dissolution of the old partnership and the formation of a new one) by speaking in terms of an incoming or new partner, a withdrawing partner, and the continuation of a partnership business after a change in membership. Thus the Partnership Act provides, in effect:

1. If a change occurs in the membership of a partnership and the business is continued without liquidation of the partnership affairs, the creditors of the first or dissolved partnership are also creditors of the new partnership (or of the sole proprietor or corporation) so continuing the business.

2. A person admitted as a partner into an existing partnership is not personally liable to creditors for debts incurred before he joined the partnership—unless the incoming partner expressly assumes such a liability. An incoming partner, however, is obliged to contribute towards losses of the partnership of which he is a member. In view of Item 1 above, therefore, the contribution of an incoming partner can be used to pay old debts (that is, debts incurred before the incoming partner joined the partnership), and the incoming partner is liable to his co-partners for all losses—including the portion of losses resulting from the old debts.

3. If a partner withdraws from a partnership and terminates his association with the business, he (or his estate in the case of a deceased partner) remains liable for debts incurred before his withdrawal—ex-

cept, of course, there would be no liability to any creditor who enters into an enforceable agreement releasing the withdrawing partner.

4. If a partner withdraws from a partnership, he (or his estate in the case of a deceased partner) is liable for a debt incurred by the business *after* he ceases to be a partner, if the creditor with whom the debt is incurred 1) knew of the former partner's membership in the firm, 2) is unaware of the dissolution of the former partnership, and 3) did not receive proper notice of the dissolution. For a creditor who extended credit to the firm before the withdrawal or dissolution, personal notice is required; for a creditor who had not so extended credit, public notice is sufficient. A public notice is properly given if notice of the withdrawal is published in a newspaper of general circulation in the place where the dissolved partnership business was operating at the time of its dissolution.

TERMINATION OF PARTNERSHIPS

CAUSES OF TERMINATION

Since a partnership is formed by the agreement of all partners, it can be terminated as they provide in their original agreement or in any later agreement. Other ways in which a partnership can be ended include 1) renunciation, 2) death or bankruptcy of any partner, and 3) decree of court.

Renunciation

Since a partnership involves mutual confidence in the personal competence, goodwill, and loyalty of the partners, the law will not compel a party to remain a partner against his will. However, if a partner who repudiates and thus terminates a partnership breaks a contract with his co-partners, the repudiating partner is liable to the others for damages resulting from the breach of contract. Thus, as with agency, a partner has the *power* even though he may not have the *right* to terminate a partnership.

Death or Bankruptcy of a Partner

Under the Partnership Act a partnership is automatically dissolved by the death or bankruptcy of any partner. The surviving or solvent partner or partners may if they wish continue to operate the business, but unless agreed otherwise, the survivors must pay to the estate of the deceased partner (or of the bankrupt partner) the net value of his interest at the time of the partnership dissolution. As a practical matter paying off the deceased or bankrupt partner's interest may be impossible without liquidation of the business. A well-planned partnership agreement therefore, will often attempt to avoid such a forced liquidation of the business, by providing that each partner's life be insured for the benefit of the partnership in an amount equal to each partner's interest in the business; the agreement should also provide a formula for calculating each partner's interest at any particular time. A partnership agreement may also provide that upon dissolution of the partnership by death or bankruptcy of any partner, his investment shall remain in the partnership business for a stated period of time. Such a contract provision is binding upon the heirs of a deceased partner, and upon the creditors or receiver of an insolvent partner.

Decree of Court

Upon petition by any partner, a court is empowered to decree dissolution of a partnership for various reasons, including the following:

1. A partner is adjudged mentally incompetent.

2. A partner persistently breaches the partnership agreement or otherwise so conducts himself in matters relating to the partnership business that it is not reasonably practical to carry on the business in association with him.

3. The business of the partnership can only be carried on at a loss.

Note that bickering or disagreement among partners, even bitter animosity between partners, is not grounds for a court to decree dissolution unless the disagreement prevents successful operation of the business.

DISTRIBUTION UPON LIQUIDATION

The Partnership Act provides:

In settling accounts between the partners after dissolution, the following rules shall be observed, subject to any agreement to the contrary:
  (a) The assets of the partnership are:
    (I)   The partnership property,
    (II) The contributions of the partners necessary for the payment of all the liabilities specified in clause (b) of this paragraph.
  (b) The liabilities of the partnership shall rank in order of payment, as follows:
    (I)   Those owing to creditors other than partners,
    (II) Those owing to partners other than for capital and profits,
    (III) Those owing to partners in respect of capital,
    (IV)   Those owing to partners in respect of profits.

(c) The assets shall be applied in the order of their declaration in clause (a) of this paragraph to the satisfaction of the liabilities.

(d) The partners shall contribute . . . the amount necessary to satisfy the liabilities; but if any, but not all, of the partners are insolvent, or, not being subject to process, refuse to contribute, the other partners shall contribute their share of the liabilities, and, in the relative proportions in which they share the profits, the additional amount necessary to pay the liabilities.

* * * * *

(f) Any partner or his legal representative shall have the right to enforce the contributions specified in clauses (d) of this paragraph.

* * * * *

(h) When partnership property and the individual properties of partners are in possession of a court for distribution, partnership creditors shall have priority on partnership property and separate creditors on individual property, saving the rights of lien or secured creditors as heretofore.[10]

The Partnership Act provision pertaining to a partner's obligation to contribute toward losses (see page 363 of this Chapter) must be kept in mind in connection with the above rules for distribution. If a partner's share of losses exceeds his capital contribution, any loan he made to the partnership should not be repaid to him unless his obligation to contribute toward losses is fully satisfied.

Part 3 CORPORATIONS

LIMITATIONS ON CORPORATE SEPARATE-ENTITY THEORY

As discussed in Part 1 of this chapter, the chief characteristic of a corporation arises from the separate entity theory; a corporation is considered as having a legal personality separate and distinct from its members. However, the law does not permit this entity theory to be perverted and misused to the detriment of the public welfare. As an outstanding Federal judge has written:

> If any general rule can be laid down, in the present state of authority, it is that a corporation will be looked upon as a legal entity as a general rule, and until sufficient reason to the contrary appears; but, when the notion of legal entity is used to defeat public convenience, justify wrong, protect fraud, or defend crime, the law will regard the corporation as an association of persons. This much may be expressed without approving the theory that the legal entity is a fiction, or a mere mental creation; or that the idea of invisibility or intangibility is a sophism. A corporation, as expressive of legal rights and powers, is no more fictitious or intangible than a man's rights to his own home or his own liberty.[11]

[10] U.P.A. Sec. 40.
[11] *U.S. v. Milwaukee Refrigerator Transit Co.*, 142 F. 247 (1905).

It is not fraudulent or improper for a businessman to use the corporate device for the primary purpose or even for the sole purpose of avoiding personal liability for the debts of his business; limited liability is one of the chief incidents and advantages of the corporate form of business. But if a businessman attempts to hide behind the corporate's separate entity to accomplish a dishonest or illegal purpose, the courts will disregard the separate entity. The fact that one corporation owns all the stock of another (such corporations commonly being called parent and subsidiary corporations), and the fact that the parent corporation carries on part of its functions through the subsidiary are not reasons for legal theory to merge the two corporations. Unless the separate entity theory is being misused, it will be observed even though the same persons serve as officers and directors of both the parent and the subsidiary corporations.

Example: O owned and operated a small manufacturing business. The business premises included two buildings, one smaller and older than the other and usable only as a warehouse. Both buildings were insured for their fair replacement value. O was in financial difficulty and having no further need for the small building, secretly set fire to the building and destroyed it. The insurance investigator, however, found evidence sufficient to prove O's wrongful act.

1. Assume that the business and its assets were owned and operated by O as a sole proprietor. O sued the insurance company to collect for the destroyed building.

O would not be permitted to recover. The law will not permit a person to profit from his own wrongful act.

2. Assume that the business and its assets were owned and operated by a corporation in which O held all of the stock. The corporation sued the insurance company to collect for the destroyed building.

Ordinarily the corporation would be considered as a separate legal entity distinct from O. However, to permit the corporation to recover would be permitting O to accomplish indirectly the illegal purpose which he clearly could not accomplish directly. Therefore, in such a case the court would disregard the separate entity and consider the corporation as identical with the sole shareholder.

Example: If a railroad could carry on a wholesale or retail business and transport its goods to market on its own lines, the railroad would be hauling at cost and have a rate preference over non-carriers in the same line of business. To prevent such rate preference, a Federal statute provides in effect that it is unlawful for any railroad to transport in interstate commerce any article or commodity owned by the railroad, except such articles as are necessary and intended for use in the conduct of its business as a common carrier.

A railroad corporation which owned a coal mine organized a subsidiary corporation to own and operate the coal mine and to engage in the wholesale and retail selling of the coal. The railroad then entered into a contract with the mining corporation to haul the coal to market, and claimed that since the coal was not owned by the railroad but instead by the mining corporation, the railroad was not violating the above statute.

Since the separate entity of the mining corporation was being used to accomplish an illegal purpose, the railroad doing indirectly what it was prohibited from doing directly, the court would disregard the separate entity of the mining corporation and rule that the railroad was violating the above statute.

If the owner and operator of a corporate business completely ignores the separate legal personality of the corporation, the courts will also be inclined to ignore the separate legal entity. A person (or group of persons or parent corporation) who wishes to use the corporate device to secure immunity from the debts of a business, must not only have the business organized as a corporation, but should also use proper corporate formalities in the operation of the business.

FORMATION OF CORPORATIONS

Corporations are usually formed under the authority of the general corporation statute of some state. The Pennsylvania Business Corporation Law, which is typical of many such statutes, says:

> Three or more natural persons of full age and either sex, married or single, at least two-thirds of whom are citizens of the United States or of its territories or possessions, may form a business corporation, under the provisions of this act, for any lawful purpose or purposes.

The usual procedure involves the organizers (or incorporators as they are usually called) applying to the proper state government office for a charter. Statutes usually term this application the "articles of incorporation." Various facts concerning the proposed corporation are stated in the application or articles, such as the type of business the corporation is to operate, the name it will use, its principal place of business, the amount of capital stock it will be authorized to issue, and the rights which stockholders are to have. Then, as the Pennsylvania statute provides:

> If the [Pennsylvania] Department of State [office to which the articles are submitted] finds that the articles conform to law, it shall forthwith endorse its approval thereon, and when all . . . charges have been paid, as required by law, shall issue to the incorporators . . . a certificate of incorporation, to which shall be attached the approved articles. . . . The articles, upon being approved by the Department of State, shall constitute the charter of the corporation. . . .
>
> Upon the approval of the articles of incorporation by the Department of State, the corporate existence shall begin . . .

Some statutes require each incorporator to subscribe for at least one share of stock. However he is not required to retain the stock. He can transfer his stock as he wishes, and even before the corporation is formed, can validly contract that he will transfer his stock when it is later issued to him. Therefore, under the statutes in most states, it is both possible and proper to have a corporation in which all the stock is held by one person or by one corporation.

DEFECTIVE INCORPORATION

If in forming a corporation the incorporators inadvertently overlook some formal requirement specified by the state corporation statute, it cannot be said that the corporation has come into existence strictly in accordance with law. Third persons who deal with the purported corporation may later discover the oversight, claim that no corporation was ever formed, and assert therefore that those who are associated together in carrying on the business are partners and are personally liable as such. However, if the third person believed he was dealing with a corporation and was not injured by the oversight of the incorporators, there is no reason as between the parties to consider the business unit as anything other than a corporation in fact. This reasoning is known as the "corporation de facto" theory. In most jurisdictions, a corporation de facto will be declared to exist if:

1. There is a statute under which such a corporation could have been organized.

2. The incorporators in good faith attempted to organize a corporation under such statute.

3. The business unit has been operated as a corporation.

Statutes frequently adopt and simplify the corporation de facto theory and at the same time reserve a right to the state to insist upon exact compliance with the statute in material matters. For example, one typical statute provides:

> The certificate of incorporation shall be conclusive evidence of the fact that the corporation has been incorporated, but proceedings may be instituted by the state to dissolve, wind up and terminate a corporation which should not have been formed under this act, or which has been formed without a substantial compliance with the conditions prescribed by this act as precedent to incorporation.

OPERATING A CORPORATE BUSINESS

The rules for operating a corporate business are found in statutes, in the corporate charter, and in the corporate bylaws. For example, a typical statute provides:

The by-laws may contain any provisions for the regulation and management of the affairs of the corporation not inconsistent with law or the articles. . . .

The shareholders shall have the power to make, alter, amend, and repeal the by-laws of a business corporation, but the authority . . . may be vested by the articles or the by-laws in the board of directors, subject always to the power of the shareholders to change such action.

SHAREHOLDERS, DIRECTORS, AND OFFICERS

The corporate method of operation is quite similar to the operation of representative government in a state or nation. The shareholders as contractual owners of the business enterprise elect representatives—the directors. The directors determine business policy which is then carried out by the executive officers and other employees who are usually chosen by the directors.

Shareholders

The role of shareholders in corporate management under a typical corporation statute may be summarized as follows:

1. At least one meeting of the shareholders is held each year for the election of directors, at such time and place as provided in the bylaws.

2. At a shareholders' meeting, each shareholder has the right of one vote for every share of voting stock standing in his name on the books of the corporation.

3. A shareholder may vote either in person or by proxy, but he cannot sell his vote or proxy. Unless coupled with a creditor's interest, a proxy is revocable at will. Even if unrevoked, a proxy is not valid for longer than eleven months unless a longer time is expressly stated. If a longer time is expressly stated, a proxy (unless coupled with a creditor's interest) may still be revoked at will, and if not revoked, will not be valid for longer than three years.

4. In electing directors, cumulative voting is permitted. In cumulative voting, a shareholder multiplies the number of shares which he is entitled to vote by the number of directors to be elected. The shareholder can then cast this total number of votes for one candidate or distribute his votes among any two or more candidates. For example, if three directors are to be elected, a shareholder owning 100 shares of stock has a total of 300 votes; he can cast all 300 votes for one candidate or distribute his votes as he wishes among two or three candidates.

5. A shareholder who pledges his shares (for example by delivering his share certificate to a bank as collateral security for a loan) can vote the pledged shares unless and until a transfer to the pledgee is noted on

the books of the corporation. After a pledge is noted on the corporate stock records, the pledgee will vote the stock.

6. Unless a record date is fixed by the bylaws or by the board of directors, shares transferred on the books of the corporation within the ten-day period preceding a shareholders' meeting are not entitled to vote. The bylaws may specify a record date; if they do not, the board of directors may specify a record date not more than fifty days prior to the date of the shareholders' meeting. If a record date is thus specified, only persons who are on the corporate records as shareholders on that date are entitled to vote.

7. Being a part owner of the corporate business, a shareholder is entitled to information concerning the affairs of the business, and has the right to inspect corporate records for this purpose. In addition, an annual report must be rendered to each shareholder.

8. As to minority shareholders: a person who invests money in a corporation should realize that he is entrusting his investment to the will of the majority. So long as the majority act lawfully and in good faith, a minority shareholder has no legal right to "take his marbles and go home." However, if the majority makes a major change in the corporation, a minority shareholder who dissents is entitled to withdraw his capital from the business enterprise. Changes which would be classed as major and therefore not binding on a dissenting shareholder include 1) a merger or consolidation, 2) a disposal of substantially all of the corporate assets other than in the ordinary course of the operation or relocation of the corporate business, and 3) a major change in the corporate purpose or in the stock rights of shareholders.

Directors

The chief provisions of a typical corporation statute, may be summarized as follows:

1. The affairs of a business corporation are managed by a board of at least three directors.

2. A director must be a natural person (that is, not another corporation) and of full age. A director need not be a resident of the state nor a shareholder in the corporation, unless the articles or bylaws so require. A director may be a salaried officer of the corporation.

3. Unless the bylaws provide otherwise, a majority of the directors is necessary to constitute a quorum for the transaction of business; if a quorum is present at a directors' meeting, the action of a majority of the directors present at that meeting is binding on the corporation.

4. Each director must be loyal to the best interests of the corporation and use the same care which an ordinarily prudent man would use in

his personal business affairs. If a director acting in his personal capacity contracts with the corporation of which he is a director, the contract is not valid unless 1) it is fair and reasonable to the corporation, *and* 2) it is approved by an impartial, disinterested majority of the board of directors.

5. Directors will not be compensated unless compensation in a stated amount is authorized by the articles or by a majority vote of the shareholders.

Officers

A typical corporation statute will usually provide as follows:

1. Every business corporation must have at least a president, a secretary, and a treasurer, and may have additional officers. The treasurer may be another corporation (for example, a bank or trust company) or may be a natural person of full age. The president and secretary must be natural persons of full age. If the bylaws so provide, any two of the required offices may be held by the same person except that the same person cannot be both president and secretary.

2. Officers may (but do not have to be) directors.

3. The officers owe to the corporation the same duties of loyalty and care that a director owes to the corporation.

4. Compensation for any particular officer must be authorized by an impartial majority of the board of directors.

Promoters' Contracts

While the incorporators are the persons who apply to the state for a charter, one person, called a promoter (or a couple of such persons), may be doing the work of organizing the corporation and laying the groundwork for it to begin operations. Sometimes such a promoter believes it advisable to enter into contracts for goods, lands, or buildings, even before the corporation is formed. If the promoter enters into such a contract in the name of the proposed corporation, an unusual agency question arises, because the promoter is purporting to act in the name of a principal (the corporation) which does not yet exist. For this reason the promoter is personally liable on such a contract and remains liable unless expressly released by the other contracting party. Such a release, either written into the original contract or agreed to later, is rare. After the corporation comes into existence, it is liable on the contract only if it adopts or approves the contract, either expressly (for example, by a resolution of the board of directors) or impliedly (for example, by accepting benefits under the contract).

A promoter owes to the corporation he is organizing, and to the persons who will become its shareholders, the same duties of loyalty and care which directors owe to a corporation.

Corporate Powers

A typical corporation statute provides:

> A business corporation shall have the capacity of natural persons to act, but shall have authority to perform only such acts as are necessary or proper to accomplish the purpose or purposes for which it is organized, and which are not repugnant to law.

If a corporation engages in activities which are beyond its power, such activities are commonly referred to by the Latin term *ultra vires.* At common law, until an *ultra vires* contract is performed either by the corporation or by the other contracting party, the contract is completely unenforceable, but after either party performs his part of the contract, he is entitled to collect for his performance. Recognizing that if a corporation exceeds its powers, the only ones really concerned with that fact are the shareholders and the state, a number of the more modern corporation statutes have liberalized the common-law rule. For example, one such statute provides, in effect:

> No limitation upon the business, purpose, or powers of a corporation shall be asserted in order to defend any action between the corporation and a third person involving any contract to which the corporation is a party.
>
> A shareholder may sue a corporation to enjoin its performance of an unauthorized contract. If the court deems such action equitable, it may set aside and enjoin the performance of the contract. In doing so, the court shall allow to the corporation or to the other contracting party, as the case may be, compensation for the loss or damage sustained by either of them, as a result of the court's setting aside the contract—but anticipated profits shall not be a factor in calculating the amount of recoverable damages.
>
> The state may sue a corporation to enjoin the transaction of unauthorized or unlawful business.

Foreign Corporations

The term "foreign corporation" applies to a corporation outside the state of its incorporation. Thus a business incorporated in Kansas is a foreign corporation in Ohio.

The status of out-of-state businesses under the American constitutional system is a synthesis of two concepts, 1) interstate commerce, and 2) interstate citizenship.

1) Interstate Commerce. Under the American constitutional system, no state can unreasonably interfere with interstate commerce.

2) *Interstate Citizenship.* In assuring the formation of a unified nation rather than a loose federation of independent states, the drafters of the United States Constitution included what is frequently referred to as the "privileges and immunities" or "interstate citizenship" provision, which reads as follows:

> The citizens of each State shall be entitled to all privileges and immunities of citizens in the several States.

As used in this provision, the term "citizen" is limited to a natural person— a political citizen—and does *not* extend to a corporate citizen.

Under these two concepts therefore, a corporation does not have the right of mobility possessed by a natural person. While a state cannot interfere with a foreign corporation carrying on interstate commerce, a state can completely exclude foreign corporations from carrying on local business, and therefore can admit them subject to conditions and regulations. For example, a typical statute provides as follows:

> A foreign business corporation, before doing any business in this state, shall procure a certificate of authority to do so from the Department of State, in the manner hereinafter provided in this statute, unless the entire business operations of the corporation within this state are within the protection of the Commerce Clause of the Federal Constitution, in which event the corporation may engage in such business operations without procuring a certificate of authority.

To obtain a certificate for carrying on a local business or (in the language of the statutes of some states) to register for carrying on a local business, a foreign corporation must file an application which (among other things) must state the corporate name and business and describe its share structure.

What constitutes carrying on a local business is not always clear. The Model Business Corporation Act prepared under the auspices of the Commissioners on Uniform State Laws contains the following definition, which is a useful summary of the majority of the court decisions:

> Without excluding other activities which may not constitute transacting business in this state, a foreign corporation shall not be considered to be transacting business in this state, for the purpose of this Act, by reason of carrying on in this state any one or more of the following activities:
>
> (a) Maintaining or defending any action or suit or any administrative or arbitration proceeding, or effecting the settlement thereof or the settlement of claims or disputes.
>
> (b) Holding meetings of its directors or shareholders or carrying on other activities concerning its internal affairs.
>
> (c) Maintaining bank accounts.
>
> (d) Maintaining offices or agencies for the transfer, exchange,

and registration of its securities, or appointing and maintaining trustees or depositaries with relation to its securities.

(e) Effecting sales through independent contractors.

(f) Soliciting or procuring orders, whether by mail or through employees or agents or otherwise, where such orders require acceptance without this state before becoming binding contracts.

(g) Creating evidences of debt, mortgages, or liens on real or personal property.

(h) Securing or collecting debts or enforcing any rights in property securing the same.

(i) Transacting any business in interstate commerce.

(j) Conducting an isolated transaction completed within a period of thirty days and not in the course of a number of repeated transactions of like nature.[12]

If an interstate sale of goods involves local installation by the seller, the usual view is that a highly technical installation of intricate mechanism, which is to be completed in a fairly short time, is considered a part of the interstate sale, and the seller is not required to register in the buyer's state. Any other installation, whether done by workmen brought in from outside the state or by local workmen, is considered local business.

Penalties

The penalty imposed upon a foreign corporation for transacting local business without registering varies in different states. Most statutes include some variation of the following penalties:

1. *Criminal punishment.* The following is a typical statutory provision:

> Any foreign business corporation which is required by the provisions of this act to procure a certificate of authority, but has not done so, or any person, agent, officer or employee who shall transact any business within this state for any foreign business corporation, which has failed to procure a certificate of authority . . . shall be guilty of a misdemeanor, and, upon conviction thereof, shall be punished by imprisonment not exceeding thirty days, or by a fine not exceeding one thousand dollars ($1000), or both . . .

2. *Limitation on contract enforcement.* In most states if a foreign corporation has not registered to carry on a local business in that particular state, it is not permitted to sue on any contracts made while transacting such business. In some states if the corporation registers later and pays a fine, it can then enforce contracts made before the corporation registered. In some other states, the corporation's registra-

---

[12] Model Business Corporation Act, Sec. 99.

tion enables it to enforce subsequent contracts only; local contracts made prior to the late registration remain unenforceable by the corporation.

CORPORATE STOCK

Two of the principal results from a corporation being a separate legal entity are 1) that the ownership interest can be divided among a large number of people (called shareholders or stockholders), and 2) that such owners have no liability, or only a limited liability, for the debts of the corporate business.

SHARES OF STOCK

An ownership interest in a corporation is referred to as a "share" or sometimes as a "share of stock."

The rights of a shareholder, as an owner of a business enterprise, usually include at least some of the following:

1. A right to share in management, through voting at shareholders' meetings (unless the stock is expressly stated to have limited or no voting rights).

2. A right to share in distribution of profits, through dividends, and in the distribution of surplus upon liquidation of the corporation.

3. A first option to buy a certain percentage of newly issued stock, usually called a preemptive right.

Frequently it is advantageous for the organizers of a corporation to provide for various classes of stock with differing rights. The following is a typical statutory provision which makes this possible:

> Every business corporation shall have power to create and issue one or more classes or kinds of shares, any or all of which classes or kinds may consist of shares with par value or shares without par value, with full, limited, or no voting rights, and with such designations, preferences, qualifications, privileges, limitations, options, conversion rights, and other special rights as shall be stated or authorized in the articles.

If two classes of shares are issued with different rights, usually one will have some preferences or priorities over the other and therefore will be termed "preferred."

If the certificate which the corporation issues to evidence share ownership (share or stock certificate) states on its face the amount of consideration received by the corporation in exchange for the certificate, the stock is called "par value stock." If the certificate merely evidences a stated ownership interest in the corporation without stating the consideration received upon issuance of the certificate, the stock is called "no par value stock."

Example: The articles of a particular corporation describe the share structure as follows: "The corporation shall be authorized to issue 1,000 shares of $100 par value, 6 percent, cumulative, participating preferred stock, and 2,000 shares of $100 par value common stock." All of the authorized stock is issued and outstanding. After paying no dividends last year, the directors decide at the end of the present year to pay out $30,000 in dividends.

The division of the money is calculated as follows:

	Preferred Stock	Common Stock
For last year	$ 6,000	Nothing
For the present year	6,000	$12,000
Additional profit-sharing	2,000	4,000
Totals	$14,000	$16,000

Each preferred shareholder receives $14 per share and each common shareholder $8 per share. The reasons can be summarized as follows:

1. The preferred stock is 6 percent preferred. This means that each preferred shareholder is entitled to a dividend of 6 percent of the $100 par value of the stock (that is, $6 per share) before any dividend is paid to a common shareholder.

2. The preferred stock is cumulative. This means that for any year in which a 6 percent dividend is not paid, the right to receive that amount accumulates and must be paid before any other distribution of profits is made. In many states preferred stock is presumed to be cumulative unless the articles expressly state otherwise. On the other hand since common stock is not assured any particular dividend at all, it would not have any cumulative rights.

3. The preferred stock is participating. This means that after there is allocated to the common shareholders a dividend at the same rate paid to the preferred shareholders for the current year, the preferred shareholders have the right to share proportionately with the common shareholders in any further distribution of profits. In many states preferred stock is presumed to be fully participating unless the articles expressly state otherwise. Common stock is always fully participating.

IMMUNITY FROM BUSINESS DEBTS

Obligation to Pay for Stock

After a share of stock is issued and paid for, the owner can sell it for any price he wishes; he can even give it away. However, when a share is first issued by a corporation, the laws of most states require that 1) if the share has a par value, at least that amount must be paid to the corporation, in money or other property, and 2) if the share has no par value, the board of directors determines the amount of consideration which must be paid to the corporation. Unless this amount (par value, or the consideration fixed by the directors for no par stock) is paid to the corporation, the stock cannot be considered fully paid for. If stock is not fully paid for, either the corporation or, in case of insolvency, its creditors, can require the person to whom the stock was issued to make up the shortage in payment. In most states, innocent transferees of such stock are not liable, but the person to whom the stock was first issued remains liable even after he has disposed of the stock.

Stock Subscriptions. A subscriber may be defined as a person who agrees, either before or after formation of a corporation, to buy from the corporation a stated number of previously unissued shares. The agreement may provide either for a lump-sum payment or for payment by installments. When payments are deferred, a question sometimes arises whether a subscriber is a shareholder, or instead is a contract buyer intended to become a shareholder at some future time, usually upon his making certain payments. If a subscriber is a shareholder, he has a right to vote and to receive dividends. Also, if the corporation should become insolvent, the subscriber-shareholder can be required, for the benefit of creditors, to pay the balance due on his subscription. On the other hand if a subscriber is a contract buyer and not yet a shareholder, he has no stock rights, and cannot be required to pay the balance due on his subscription unless the corporation tenders to him the stock and stock rights for which he agreed to pay. A corporation which is adjudged insolvent is for all practical purposes dead and its stock lifeless. After a corporation is adjudged insolvent, the stock rights for which the buyer agreed to pay can no longer be tendered to him, and therefore he cannot be required to pay anything more on his subscription agreement. The chief rules for determining the status of a subscriber may be summarized as follows:

1. Preincorporation subscriptions.

a) A person who subscribes for stock in a corporation not yet organized can cancel his agreement at any time before the corporation comes into existence. If he so notifies the organizers, he never becomes a shareholder and has no further liability. However, as a matter of fairness, some courts have held that he cannot recover any payments he made before his cancellation.

b) Under some corporation statutes, all subscribers who have not previously given notice canceling their subscriptions, immediately and automatically become shareholders when a charter is issued to the corporation. (Notice that such statutes recognize that a person can be a shareholder before he pays anything for his stock and before a stock certificate is issued to him.)

2. Postincorporation subscriptions. If a person makes an offer to an existing corporation to buy a certain number of shares of previously unissued stock, and the corporation accepts the offer, a contract is formed. The status of a subscriber before completing his agreed payment is deter-

mined by the manifested intent of both parties. When not expressly stated, the intent of the parties is implied from their conduct. Thus if a corporation extends to a subscriber a right usually exercised only by shareholders, and the subscriber exercises the right, he is a shareholder; otherwise he is only a contract buyer and not yet a shareholder.

Liability of Holders of Fully Paid Shares

If stock is classed as assessable, this means that the holder has agreed that the directors can assess him and require him to pay some specified additional amount to the corporation. Assessable stock is fairly rare.

In most states, if stock is fully paid for and nonassessable, the shareholder has no liability for any debts of the business. However, a few states feel that it is sound policy to impose a limited liability upon shareholders. For example the Pennsylvania statute provides, in effect:

> A shareholder of fully paid, nonassessable stock shall not be personally liable for any debt or liability of the corporation, except for salaries and wages due and owing to its employees. To this extent, every shareholder shall be personally liable in an amount equal to the value of his shares, but no shareholder shall be so liable unless suit for the collection of such salaries and wages shall be brought against him within six months after the same shall become due. The term value, as used here, means the aggregate par value of the shares or in the case of shares without par value, the consideration received by the corporation on the original issuance of such shares.
>
> In any lawsuit brought to enforce this liability, the plaintiff employee may sue the corporation and any one or more shareholders as defendants. If the plaintiff wins his lawsuit, judgment shall be entered against the corporation and the defendant shareholder or shareholders. Execution upon such judgment shall be first levied on property of the corporation located within Pennsylvania; if sufficient property cannot be found, then execution shall be levied on the property of the defendant shareholder or shareholders for the amount of his or their liability. The defendant shareholder or shareholders shall, for the amount so collected, have a right to collect from the corporation, and if contribution from the corporation is unobtainable, then the defendant shareholder or shareholders shall have a right to collect pro rata from other solvent shareholders to the extent of their original liability for the claims on which the plaintiff obtained judgment.

Transfer of Stock

Stock certificates are usually transferred by delivery of the certificate to the transferee, together with any one of the following: 1) the registered owner's indorsement on the stock certificate, 2) an assignment of the stock certificate, signed by the registered owner, or 3) a power of attorney authorizing assignment of the stock certificate, signed by the registered owner. To facilitate transfer, stock certificate forms are frequently prepared with assignment or power of attorney forms printed on the reverse side.

The transferee becomes the owner of the certificate and the rights it evidences as soon as it is transferred to him by the transferor with the latter's appropriate signature. Usually the transferee then has the certificate sent to the issuing corporation which notes the transfer on its records and issues a new certificate to the transferee. Until the transfer is noted on the corporation records, the corporation is permitted to treat the registered owner as the person entitled to vote and to receive notices and dividends.

Stock certificates are negotiable, just like negotiable commercial paper, order bills of lading, and order warehouse receipts. Thus a bona fide purchaser who receives a stock certificate together with a transfer signed by the registered owner, acquires not only the rights of his transferor but also acquires the certificate free from the adverse claims of any other person. The legal concept of negotiability is discussed in Part 1 of Chapter 14.

Example: To evidence O's stock ownership in a particular corporation, the corporation issued to O a stock certificate for 100 shares, made out to O. O sold the stock to B, indorsed the certificate by merely signing his name on the reverse side, and delivered the certificate to B. B who was purchasing other shares in the same corporation wished to wait and submit all of his purchased shares together for transfer on the corporation records, and therefore locked in his safe the certificate obtained from O. That night a thief broke into B's safe, stealing various items including this stock certificate. The thief sold and delivered the certificate to P who purchased for value, in good faith, and with no knowledge that the certificate had been stolen. When P had the certificate submitted to the corporation for transfer, the corporation notified B who had previously advised the corporation of the theft. B sued P and requested the court to order return of the certificate to B.

The thief never became the owner of the certificate. However, since the certificate was negotiable, P, the innocent purchaser for value, took the certificate free from all adverse claims; he obtained better rights than the thief had and became the owner of the certificate and the share interest which it evidenced. Therefore, the court would refuse B's request.

PREEMPTIVE RIGHTS

Suppose that in a corporation which has 1,000 shares authorized and issued, O owns 100 shares. O therefore owns a 100/1,000 or a 1/10 interest in the corporation. His voting strength and his right to share in dividends is 1/10. Suppose further that in order to raise additional capital, a majority of the directors and shareholders approve increasing the authorized stock to 1,500 shares, and that the charter of the corporation is amended accordingly. If when the 500 additional shares are issued, O is given no opportunity to purchase any, then while O still retains his 100 shares, his interest in the corporation will shrink from 1/10 to 100/1,500 or 1/15.

If, on the other hand, O is given a right (called a "preemptive right") to purchase 1/10 of the newly authorized shares, and does so, O will then own 150 shares or a 150/1,500 interest, and will thus maintain intact his 1/10 interest in the corporation. When presented in this simple situation, it seems only fair that O should be accorded a preemptive right. However, the stock structure of most corporations is not this simple and various complex questions can arise, including:

1. Should the holder of common stock have a preemptive right to purchase a new authorization of preferred stock—and vice versa?

2. If the corporation previously issued only a specified portion of its originally authorized stock, should a shareholder have a preemptive right when the directors decide to issue the remainder of the stock?

3. If the corporation share structure already consists of common stock Class A and common stock Class B, each with voting powers but having slightly different stock rights, and the new authorization is also voting stock but with still different stock rights in respect to dividends or liquidation, so that it is called common stock Class C, should a shareholder of A or B stock have a preemptive right to purchase C stock?

4. If because of the corporation's favorable prospects a new issuance of stock can be marketed at more than par value, should a shareholder's preemptive right be to purchase at par or at the higher price the corporation can obtain elsewhere?

Instead of attempting to write a rule which could fit these and other complex situations, the drafters of some of the modern corporation statutes have decided that whatever preemptive right a shareholder is to have should be written by the corporate managers for their particular situation. Thus, for example, the Pennsylvania statute provides in effect:

> Unless otherwise provided in its articles, a corporation may issue shares, option rights, or other securities without first offering them to shareholders of any class.

DIVIDENDS

In most states, a corporation cannot lawfully pay a money dividend which will exceed the amount of the corporation's earned surplus. If there is sufficient earned surplus so that this basic requirement is met, then the decision as to whether or not to declare a dividend, or as to the amount of the dividend, is pretty much left to the discretion of the board of directors. Thus if the directors decide to retain profits for some valid business purpose, a court will not attempt to substitute its judgment for that of the directors. Only in the rare case when the directors' refusal to declare a dividend (or to declare a higher dividend) is for a dishonest or otherwise improper motive will the courts interfere.

If a money dividend which unlawfully exceeds a corporation's earned surplus is declared and paid, the corporation will sometimes attempt at a later date to obtain reimbursement from the directors or shareholders. Any director who approves of an unlawful dividend is personally liable to the corporation for the amount paid out. Some states relieve a director from this liability if he relied in good faith on a misleading financial statement which had been certified as correct by the corporate officers or an independent accountant. In most states a shareholder need not return an illegal dividend if at the time he received it 1) he was unaware that it was an illegal dividend, and 2) the corporation was a solvent, going concern.

As soon as the directors declare a lawful dividend, a contract right to receive the amount of the dividend attaches to and becomes a part of the stock ownership. For the amount of the declared dividend, the shareholders are creditors of the corporation, with the same rights as any other corporate creditors. More specifically:

1. Neither a resolution of the directors canceling a dividend nor a vote of the majority of shareholders to that effect will cancel the debt.

2. Should the corporation become insolvent and be liquidated before paying the dividend (assuming, of course, that there was sufficient surplus when the dividend was declared), then:

a) For the amount of the dividend debt, shareholders are entitled to share equally (that is proportionately) with outside creditors in the distribution of available assets.

b) If while still solvent, the corporation set aside a fund for the purpose of paying the dividend (for example by opening a dividend checking account), this fund must be applied exclusively to the dividend debt and cannot be reached by other creditors of the corporation.

3. If the resolution declaring a dividend does not specify a record date, the actual owner of stock on the resolution date is the owner of the dividend claim. If the resolution specifies a record date (for example, a resolution of June 1, declaring a dividend payable December 1 to all shareholders of record on July 1), the actual owner of shares on the record date is the owner of the dividend claim. In either case the corporation is permitted to send the dividend to the person registered on its books as the shareholder. If another person was the actual owner of the stock on the resolution date (or the record date, if specified), the

registered owner holds the dividend money for the benefit of that person, unless the parties have agreed otherwise.

4. If a stockholder, as a debtor, pledges and delivers his stock to a creditor who holds it as collateral security for an obligation, the corporation may nevertheless send to the debtor any dividend that is declared unless a transfer to the pledgee is noted on the books of the corporation. However, any stock dividend which the debtor receives he should turn over to the pledgee to be held as additional collateral; any money dividend the debtor receives he should turn over to the pledgee if the latter wishes to apply the money immediately to the debtor's obligation.[13]

PROBLEMS

1. O was the sole proprietor of a picture frame manufacturing business which he operated in a building rented from L. Deciding to sell the business, O entered into a written agreement with a business broker, engaging the services of the broker to negotiate a sale of the business for a stated price. One paragraph of the agreement stated: "If the described business shall be sold or exchanged during the term of this contract, whether the sale or exchange shall be effected by the above-named broker, by the owner, or by any other person, the owner shall pay the broker a commission of 5 percent of the selling price." Within the term of the contract, O's lease expired and L refused to renew it. O so informed the broker and moved his materials and equipment into another building where P was already conducting a similar business. O and P pooled their respective assets and formed a partnership to trade under the name, "Artistic Products Company," the name O had previously used. Neither partner put any cash into the business, but O was credited on the books with a capital contribution of $9,400, the fair value of the assets of his sole proprietorship business. When the broker learned of the formation of the partnership, he sued O for a 5 percent commission on $9,400. What result? Explain.

2. A, B, and C, partners engaged in the real estate and stock and bond brokerage business, were in financial difficulty and being pressed by their creditors. Much of their capital was tied up in investments which, if held for a longer time, might be profitable, but if disposed of quickly, would result in considerable loss. They entered into an agreement with X which provided: 1) X loaned to the firm two million dollars, to be repaid in five years; as collateral security various stocks and bonds owned by the firm were pledged with X; 2) As compensation for the loan X was to receive 40 percent of the net profits of the firm, but not over $500,000 nor less than $100,000 per year, payable at stated times; 3) During the term of the agreement, management of the firm was to be in A's hands; 4) X was to have the right to inspect the firm's books at any time; 5) X was to have the right to veto any business transaction X deemed inadvisable. During the next three years, the firm of A, B, and C incurred certain obligations to T. T, not having been paid, sued X. What result? Explain.

[13] U.C.C. Sec. 9-207.

3. O owned a completely equipped summer resort hotel. On March 1, O entered into an agreement with M the main provisions of which can be summarized as follows: 1) O leased to M the described premises together with all equipment, for a term of 3 months from June 15, to be used exclusively as a summer hotel; 2) M would give his undivided attention and best efforts to promotion and operation of the business; 3) O or his authorized representative would have the right of unlimited access to the premises to make inspections at any time; 4) As rent, M would pay O a total of $20,000 in four equal installments at times specified in the agreement; 5) Upon termination of the lease, in addition to the $20,000, O would receive 80 percent of the net profits; 6) A person to be designated by O would keep the books, act as cashier, receive all money coming into the business, deposit the money in his own name, and make all payments for expenses incurred by M in operation of the business; 7) Upon termination of the lease, M would receive 20 percent of the net profits; 8) O could terminate the lease upon twenty-four hour's notice to M and at once resume possession of the premises; 9) Upon expiration of the lease or its prior termination by O, M would receive $1,000 from O; 10) M would have absolute control and management of the business during the continuance of the lease and O would not be liable for any debts or obligations incurred by M in the operation of the business.

During the summer, a supplier sold a large quantity of goods to the hotel on which $1,800 remained unpaid. The supplier sued O for payment. Explain 1) the reasoning upon which the supplier might attempt to collect, 2) the reasoning upon which O might attempt to defend, and 3) which party should be given judgment.

4. Frank and Sam Andrew, father and son, were engaged in business under the name "Andrew Paper Works." Becoming insolvent, they entered into a written agreement with B Brown and C Carter, two of their many creditors. The agreement was in the nature of a deed of trust, by which the Andrews transferred the business to B and C as trustees; B and C were to carry on the business under the name "Andrew Paper Company," were to divide the profits among the creditors pro rata, and when all were paid, were to retransfer the business to the original proprietors. During the subsequent operation of the business, B and C borrowed $1,000 from P, signed a note "Andrew Paper Company by B. Brown and C. Carter, Trustees," and used the money in the business. The note was not paid when due, and P sued B, C, and also D who was another of the original creditors of the Paper Works. What should be the decision? Explain. (Modified from A.I.C.P.A., Nov. 29-2.)

5. After managing the grain and hay business of Carter Corporation for a number of years, A. Adams retired and was replaced by B. Brown. After several years, B resigned from Carter Corporation to start his own business. Shortly after B's resignation, the following news item appeared in a newspaper published in that community: "B. Brown, who managed the grain and hay business of Carter Corporation since the retirement of A. Adams, has concluded to embark in the same business on his own account, having formed a co-partnership with A. Adams for that purpose. Mr. Brown is a gentleman of experience and ability and will undoubtedly meet with the full measure of success."

Actually A and B had not formed a partnership, and A did not authorize or see the article. When A was informed of the news item, he asked B to have the statement denied. There was no further publication in the paper but B distributed a circular to the trade announcing that he was embarking on the grain and hay business under the name of B. Brown & Company. S, a grain dealer who had seen the newspaper item, sold a carload of rye to B. Brown & Co. and when it was not paid for, S sued A and B. What result? Explain.

6. On May 1 the three partners in the firm of A, B, and C signed a dissolution agreement whereby the firm's affairs were to be liquidated as of the following June 30. On May 15 B, without the knowledge of A or C, procured for himself a five-year lease on the premises occupied by the firm, to run from the following July 1, and on July 1, B sold the lease at a profit. Did A and C have a legal right to share in B's profit? (Modified from A.I.C.P.A., Nov. 41-6b.)

7. A, B, and C, as equal partners, operated a small luggage manufacturing plant under the trade name "C & Company." In August after several years successful operation the partners discussed expanding to include the manufacture of table model TV receivers. C opposed any such expansion. During September, while C was away on a one-month vacation, A and B began laying plans for manufacture of TV receivers, sure that C would agree when he learned the details of their plan. On September 21 in the firm name and with concurrence of B, A ordered from a manufacturer for thirty-day delivery, a quantity of speakers suitable for the type of receiver A and B were planning. On September 25 the manufacturer in writing accepted the order and agreed to ship. Upon delivery according to order, C for the first time learned of the order. C's opposition continued and to avoid further dispute A and B moved the speakers to different premises, started a TV manufacturing business, and notified the manufacturer that they had taken over the speakers from C & Company. The manufacturer replied that he was not agreeable to releasing C & Company and the partners from liability. The speakers not being paid for, the manufacturer sued A, B, and C. How much could the manufacturer recover from C? Explain.

8. Adams and Brown were partners in a refrigerator manufacturing business, operating under the name "Brown & Company." A borrowed $500 from a bank, made out a note to the bank promising repayment in one month, and signed the note "Brown & Company by A. Adams, Partner." The note was not paid when due and the bank sued A and B as partners for recovery of the $500. B proved in defense that he had never authorized or received any benefit from the loan, and had no knowledge of it until the bank demanded payment, the money, unknown to the bank, having been used by A for personal purposes. Was the bank entitled to judgment against B as well as against A? Explain.

9. A, B, and C were partners operating a saw mill. C had contributed three-fourths of the firm capital, A and B together one-fourth. By the terms of the partnership agreement, C was to receive one-half of the profits and A and B were to share the balance equally. From time to time the firm had purchased supplies from S. C thought it inadvisable to deal further with S, but when he expressed this view to his partners, they did not agree. C then

notified S that he, C, would not be liable for goods furnished the mill. Following this, A and B ordered and received from S further supplies necessary for carrying on the mill, giving S a note signed in the name of the partnership by A. Subsequently the mill and A and B became insolvent, and S sued C on the unpaid note. Was S entitled to judgment against C? Explain.

10. A, B, and C as partners carried on a business as real estate brokers. A and B, older and more experienced than C, instructed C to be scrupulously honest and truthful in all dealings. O, owner of a lot in a suburban section, listed his lot with the realty firm to negotiate a sale. While showing the lot to P, fully aware that he was ignorant of true conditions, C fraudulently said to P that there was a water supply in the street on which the lot fronted. Relying on this, P purchased the lot, paying his money to and receiving a deed from O. O had no knowledge of the statement made by C to P, and the deed said nothing about the water main. According to the agreement, the real estate firm received from O a commission of $50 for negotiating the sale. About a year later P began construction of a house and discovered that there was no water supply in the street. To connect with the nearest water main cost P $600. P demanded this sum from the real estate firm of A, B, and C, and A and B for the first time learned of the statement C had made concerning the water line. A and B offered to pay P the $50 the firm had received as real estate commission, but P refused to settle for $50 and sued A for $600 damages. What result? Explain.

11. The partnership articles of A and B stipulated that A should furnish all the capital and that B should manage the business but without any liability on B for firm debts. S, knowing of these provisions, sold goods on credit to the firm.

a) If the firm failed to pay for the goods, from whom could S recover? Explain.

b) Other facts remaining the same, assume further that the partnership articles also stipulated that B was a limited partner, and assume further that the proper certificate of limited partnership was duly filed. If the firm failed to pay for the goods, from whom could S recover? Explain. (Modified from A.I.C.P.A., May 45-8d.)

12. F. Smith and S. Smith, father and son, as partners, operated a hardware store in a small town in Georgia, under the name "Smith Hardware Store." They purchased from various sources including a Chicago manufacturer. An agent, as the sole Georgia salesman for the manufacturer, solicited orders subject to acceptance by the manufacturer, reported to the manufacturer references given by new credit customers, and in a general way reported on the business conditions of the manufacturer's customers. For almost a year, about every thirty days, this agent visited the Smith store soliciting and receiving orders for items of hardware which were shipped and paid for on delivery. On September 1 the partnership was dissolved, the father withdrawing from the business and selling his interest to the son who took over entire ownership and management and retained the same name for the store. Notice of the partnership dissolution was published in a local paper but no written notices were sent to any businesses. On September 17 the agent again visited the store and took

an order for a quantity of hardware, to be shipped on thirty days' credit. The order was signed "Smith Hardware Store by S. Smith," and was forwarded by the agent to the manufacturer.

a) The father instructed his son to inform the agent of the father's withdrawal. However, the son forgot to do this. On September 27 the manufacturer shipped the ordered goods. When payment was not made when due, the agent and the manufacturer learned for the first time of dissolution of the partnership. The manufacturer sued both father and son. Could the manufacturer collect from the father? Explain.

b) When signing the order, the son told the agent his father had withdrawn from the business. This information was not written on the order and the agent neglected to tell the manufacturer of the change. On September 27 the manufacturer shipped the ordered goods. When payment was not made when due, the manufacturer learned for the first time of dissolution of the partnership. The manufacturer sued both father and son. Could the manufacturer collect from the father? Explain.

13. A, B, C, and D were general partners. According to their agreement, A contributed $5,000 to the firm capital, B $10,000, C nothing, and D $25,000. A devoted one-half of his time to the business, B one-third, C all of his time, and D no time. The agreement said nothing as to the ratio of sharing profits or losses or as to salaries. After commencement of the business, A made a loan of $5,000 to the firm without interest. Several years later the partners decided to liquidate the business.

a) $55,000 was realized on liquidation of assets, liabilities to outside creditors totaled $20,000. How much would each party receive or be required to pay? Explain.

b) $80,000 was realized on liquidation of assets, liabilities to outside creditors totaled $20,000. How much would each party receive or be required to pay? Explain.

14. A and B formed a partnership, each contributing $20,000. Several years later C joined the firm and paid $20,000 as his capital contribution. When C joined the business, he did not expressly assume liability for existing debts. A few years later the partnership business became insolvent and was dissolved. The partnership agreement did not specify the ratio for sharing profits or losses. Upon liquidation, the partnership assets realized $25,000. Debts owed by the business to outside creditors totaled $40,000. Of this total obligation, $15,000 was incurred before C joined the firm, $25,000 after C joined the firm. On final settlement and distribution, how much would each partner receive or be required to pay,

a) If A, B, and C were fully solvent? Explain.

b) If A and B were insolvent and unable to contribute anything but C was fully solvent? Explain.

15. A, B, and C formed a partnership, A contributing $10,000, B, $4,000, and C, $1,000. The agreement did not specify any ratio for sharing of profits or losses. A year after the partnership was formed, C, at the request of A and B, loaned $5,000 to the partnership, without interest, and A and B signed a note promising in the partnership name to repay the loan to C in one year. A year

later the partnership was insolvent and dissolved. Upon liquidation, the partnership assets realized $30,000, debts owed to outside creditors totaled $19,000. C was personally insolvent. One of C's creditors with a judgment against C for $8,000 had the sheriff serve attachment papers on all the partners, attaching the $5,000 which the partnership owed to C. On final settlement and distribution, who would get how much? Explain.

16. To separate their mercantile operations from realty holdings, the operators of the Roger Mercantile Corporation had another corporation formed, entitled the Roger Realty Corporation. The entire stock of the Realty Corporation was owned by the Mercantile Corporation, and although separate books and records were kept, the officers and directors of the two corporations were the same. The owner of certain property leased it to the Realty Corporation for a term of ninety years, at a rental of $300,000 per year, plus taxes and assessments, and with a provision binding the Realty Corporation to erect, within one year, a building costing $1,500,000. The Realty Corporation in turn leased the premises to the Mercantile Corporation for a term of ten years. Within the time stipulated, a building costing the specified amount was erected. Before expiration of the ten-year lease, the Mercantile Corporation moved to a new location but continued to pay rent until the expiration of the ten-year term. When that term expired, the Realty Corporation was unable to procure a new tenant and, having no assets but this lease, defaulted in its payment of rent to L. L sued the Mercantile Corporation to recover the unpaid rent. What result? Explain.

17. A. Adams was the sole proprietor of a business operating under the the name, "Adams Manufacturing Company." Through sound business policies, A increased both his individual and business wealth; whereupon A decided to form a corporation to operate the business so that he would no longer be risking all of his personal assets in the business. With A and two of his employees acting as incorporators, a charter was obtained, forming a business corporation under the name, "Adams Manufacturing Company," with a capitalization of 1,000 shares of $100 par value common stock. The two employees as incorporators each subscribed for one share of stock. After formation of the corporation each transferred to A the right to receive the one share of stock. A transferred to the corporation all of the assets of the business, reasonably worth $100,000, and made out to himself a certificate for 1,000 shares of stock. A signed the certificate as president and had his chief bookkeeper sign as secretary and treasurer. A gave proper advertised and personal notice of the formation of the corporation. For the next two years, A continued operating the business in the same manner and following the same policies as he had before formation of the corporation. However, because of a depression of business conditions and not at all the fault of A, the business became insolvent. C who had extended considerable credit to the business with knowledge that it was a corporation, sued to hold A individually liable for the debt. At the trial, A produced the corporation share register and minute book, showed the charter of the corporation, and showed in the minute book the description of the transfer of the business assets to the corporation in exchange for its stock. This was the only notation in the minute

book. C proved that A's purpose in forming the corporation was to avoid personal liability for its debts. In C's lawsuit against A individually, explain 1) the reasoning upon which A might attempt to defend, 2) the reasoning upon which C might attempt to recover, and 3) which party should be given judgment.

18. A, B, and C obtained a charter for a business corporation to conduct a small manufacturing business. They were the sole shareholders, directors, and officers, and their stock was fully paid and nonassessable. Admittedly the only reason they formed the corporation was to avoid personal liability for business debts. A few years later, after the corporate business sustained net losses and was close to insolvency, C, driving the corporate truck on corporate business, failed to see a stop sign and collided with a car being carefully driven by T. T sustained serious personal and property injuries in the amount of $25,000. It was then discovered that B, treasurer of the corporation, had overlooked renewing the corporate liability insurance on the truck, and the insurance had expired. T sued A, B, and C personally for tort damages, arguing that the corporate device could properly be used to shield the owners and operators from liability for contracts of their business, but that it is improper to use the corporate separate entity to shield persons from tort liability. What result? Explain.

19. A, B, and C were the incorporators, shareholders, directors, and officers of the Adams Corporation, a small manufacturing concern. The total authorized stock (300 shares of $20 par value stock) was issued equally to A, B, and C, in exchange for which each paid the corporation $2,000. In addition each party loaned $5,000 to the corporation, without interest, for which each received a note signed in the corporate name by themselves as officers. After the parties operated the business for several years, using proper corporate formalities, the corporation was adjudged insolvent, and a receiver was appointed by court to liquidate the corporate assets. The receiver realized $15,000, the fair value of the assets, and outside creditors filed claims against the corporate business totaling $30,000. In addition A, B, and C filed claims on their notes.

a) The outside creditors argued that A, B, and C had no right to collect on their notes until after outside debts were paid in full. Was this contention correct? Explain.

b) The outside creditors argued that A, B, and C were personally liable for the unpaid debts of the corporation. On what theory and with what result? Explain.

20. After operating a retail hardware store for a number of years under the name, "Economy Hardware," S, the sole proprietor, sold the store premises, equipment, stock in trade, and goodwill to B. The written transfer agreement contained the following provision: "S. Smith agrees that he will not operate a retail hardware store within a radius of one mile of [describing the location of the Economy Hardware], for the period of five years from date hereof."

a) One year later S entered into a partnership with P and the partnership began operating a retail hardware store within the proscribed area, under the name "Thrifty Hardware." B sued for an injunction. What result? Explain.

b) One year later S and P formed a corporation which began operating a retail hardware store within the proscribed area, under the name "Thrifty Hardware Company." B sued for an injunction. What would be the result 1) if S and P each owned 50 percent of the corporate stock; 2) if S owned 75 percent of the corporate stock and P 25 percent? Explain.

21. A and M owned all the stock of a business corporation, each owning the number of shares stated below. At a shareholders' meeting held for the election of five directors, M cast all his votes equally for five candidates, namely, M, N, O, P, and Q. A voted as stated below.

A) Assume that there was no provision in corporation charter or bylaws specifically covering the matter in dispute.

 1) A owned 400 shares, M 600 shares.
  a) A cast all the votes he lawfully could for A. Was A elected as a director? Explain.
  b) A cast all the votes he lawfully could, equally, for A and B. Were A and B elected as directors? Explain.
  c) A cast all the votes he lawfully could, equally, for A, B, and C. Were A, B, and C elected as directors? Explain.
 2) A owned 200 shares, M 800 shares.
  a), b), c). Assume the same additional facts and answer the same questions as in (1) above.
 3) A owned 150 shares, M 850 shares.
  a), b), c). Assume the same additional facts and answer the same questions as in (1) above.

B) Assume that a bylaw adopted when the corporation was organized, provided: "Every shareholder shall have the right to one vote for each share held by him for as many persons as there are directors to be elected. No cumulative voting for directors shall be permitted." A knew of this bylaw at the time he acquired his stock.

 1) a), b), c). Assume the same additional facts and answer the same questions as in (1) above.
 2) a), b), c). Assume the same additional facts and answer the same questions as in (2) above.

22. The directors of a corporation passed a resolution directing that $5,000 worth of the corporate stock be issued to each director after the directors successfully procured subscriptions for $1,000,000 of unissued corporate stock, the money being necessary for success of the corporation. The directors procured such subscriptions but a shareholder filed a bill in equity to restrain the directors from issuing any stock to themselves. What result? Explain. (Modified from A.I.C.P.A., Nov. 47-9e.)

23. A business corporation needed an additional plot of land for its business operations. The board of directors was comprised of five members, A, B, C, D, and E. A owned a plot of land and offered to sell it to the corporation for $5,000. The directors adopted a resolution accepting the offer, the vote being as stated below. Several months later before any use had been made of the land, the membership of the board changed. The new directors, D, E, M, N, and O decided to build elsewhere, offered to return the land to A, and upon his refusal, brought an action in the name of the corporation to cancel the prior transaction. In the lawsuit it was proved that at all times the reasonable value of the land to the corporation was $5,000.

a) The vote on the resolution approving the purchase was A, B, and C in favor, D and E against. Should the court decree cancellation of the land purchase transaction? Explain.

b) The vote on the resolution approving the purchase was A, B, C, and D in favor, E against. Should the court decree cancellation of the land purchase transaction? Explain.

c) Other facts remaining the same, suppose that in the lawsuit it was proved that at all times the reasonable value of the land to the corporation was $2,500. The evidence also showed that without doubt A and the other directors who had approved the purchase had acted honestly, in good faith believing the land was reasonably worth $5,000. Would this additional fact change the answers in Parts (a) or (b) above? Explain.

24. A and B were the only shareholders and respectively president and secretary of the Adams Building Supply Corporation, a successful corporation, organized for the purpose, as stated in its charter, "to sell at wholesale and retail lumber and other building supplies." Together with C and D, A and B formed another corporation under the name "Brown Construction Corporation," to acquire land and construct and sell a large number of homes. The Construction Corporation wished to engage a certain contractor to excavate for a row of homes and lay water and sewer lines, payment to be made upon completion of the entire work. The contractor was unwilling to accept the job on the credit of the Construction Corporation alone. Thereupon A and B, as officers acting in the name of the Supply Corporation, gave the contractor a written guaranty that the Construction Corporation would pay for the contractor's work. Several month later the Construction Corporation project was abandoned, hopelessly insolvent, and the Supply Corporation went into bankruptcy. The contractor filed a claim against the Supply Corporation for the value of the work done. Other creditors of the Supply Corporation objected to allowance of the claim. On what ground and with what result? Explain.

25. S Company, a Delaware corporation, was registered to carry on local business in Illinois and had its principal place of business in Chicago. S Company entered into a written contract with B who was building a hotel building in a town in South Dakota. Under the contract, S Company agreed to furnish and install specified furnishings and equipment for the hotel (including kitchen equipment, all bedroom, lounge, and dining room furniture, wall and floor coverings, dishes, silverware, glassware, etc.) for the agreed price of $36,000, payable $5,000 when the contract was signed, $7,000 when installation was completed, and the balance in stated installments. When construction of the building was completed, shipments of the equipment and furnishings began to arrive, some from S Company's Chicago warehouse but most directly from various manufacturers outside South Dakota, from whom S Company was purchasing, and S Company sent a crew of its employees to install the equipment and furnishings. S Company completely performed its contract within two months, which was a reasonable time, but B who had made the initial $5,000 payment, failed to make any further payments under the contract. Explaining that it was only an extra precautionary measure, S Company's lawyer had S Company thereupon register with South Dakota as a foreign corporation to carry on a local business in South Dakota, and sued B in the Federal District Court for South Dakota for the unpaid price. South Dakota statute required foreign corporations carrying on local business in South Dakota, as distinguished from interstate commerce, to register with the state. The statute further provided, in effect: "Every contract made by a foreign corporation before it shall have complied with the provisions of this statute shall be wholly void on its behalf but shall be enforceable against it." What would be the result of S Company's lawsuit against B? Explain.

26. M Company, a Michigan corporation, manufactured articles and merchandise used all over the United States. Its business in Massachusetts was handled by S who operated a large jobbing house, purchasing from various manufacturers, including M Company, and reselling to retailers in Massachusetts. M Company did not own or control S's business nor have any voice in S's management. M Company maintained no office in Massachusetts, was never licensed to do business in Massachusetts, and paid no taxes to that state. Four times a year salesmen from the home office of M Company canvassed the retail trade in Massachusetts, instructing customers in the most efficient use of M Company's products, and taking orders. Such orders were immediately turned over to S by the salesmen, and S filled the orders from his own warehouse with merchandise previously purchased by S from M Company. The state of Massachusetts levied taxes against M Company on the business thus done and added heavy penalties on the ground that M Company was doing business in Massachusetts without having obtained the necessary license. Was the state correct? Explain. (Modified from A.I.C.P.A., May 24-11.)

27. Together with a number of other persons, some signing the same paper before and some after B, B signed a paper agreeing to subscribe and pay for 15 shares of $50 par value common stock to be issued by a proposed business corporation, the money payable on call of the promoters, balance payable upon formation of the corporation. The paper stated that the subscription was irrevocable. At various times thereafter, meetings of the subscribers were held, with B attending, for arrangement of some of the preliminary details. Expenses incurred were paid out of a fund raised through each subscriber paying a proportionate amount on his subscription. In this way B paid in $187.50. Some time thereafter, B notified the promoters of withdrawal of his subscription and of his determination to go no further in the enterprise. The promoters replied that they refused to release him and would hold him liable on his original agreement. The remaining parties proceeded with their preparations, procured a charter, and organized the corporation. The corporation sued B for the balance due on his subscrip-

tion.   B counterclaimed for return of the $187.50 he had paid.   What result?
Explain.

28. An accountant rendered services connected with the reorganization
of a corporation.   His services were fairly and reasonably worth $5,000 and
the accountant rendered a bill to the reorganized corporation for that amount.
Instead of paying the accountant in cash, the directors authorized the issuance
to him of 100 shares of fully paid, nonassessable, $100 par stock of the
corporation.   The accountant accepted the stock as payment in full for his
services.   Later the corporation was adjudged insolvent.   Could the accountant
be held liable for the benefit of outside creditors?   Explain.   (Modified from
A.I.C.P.A., Nov. 21-10.)

29. A business corporation had issued and outstanding 1,500 shares.   One
hundred shares were issued to D, and were pledged by him with the corporation as collateral security for an obligation of $9,000 owned by him to the
corporation.   Fifteen years later, this obligation together with a considerable
accumulation of unpaid interest had been in default for several years, whereupon the five directors unanimously voted to foreclose the pledged stock and
transfer it to the corporation, as permitted by the terms of the pledge.   At the
same meeting, the five directors unanimously authorized the sale of the one
hundred shares to P at $80 per share.   P was the president of the corporation,
one of the directors, and owned 656 shares.   No prior notice of the sale was
given and the company had no need for additional capital.   M, an owner of
160 shares, had at various times expressed dissatisfaction with the volume of
business done by the corporation and the profits it was making, but had never
previously objected to any particular decision of the directors.   However, after
the August meeting M brought an equity action against the corporation and the
directors to have the sale to P declared void.   The evidence indicated that the
small block of shares could not have been sold for more than $80 per share.
What should be the result of M's lawsuit?   Explain.

30. A business corporation was organized for the purpose of constructing
and operating a radio broadcasting station.   The incorporators, A, B, and C
subscribed equally for the entire stock, fully paid for their shares in cash and
other property, and as sole shareholders, elected themselves as directors and
officers.   Fifteen years later, the corporation engaged an appraisal firm which
appraised all assets at their current valuation, and reported to the directors
that the assets were worth $20,000 more than the value shown on the books
of the corporation.   The directors, therefore, had the book value increased by
$20,000 and balanced that with a like increase in the surplus account.   The
balance sheet of the corporation five years after this, showed a surplus of
$5,000.   At the end of the following year, net profits totaled $12,000 whereupon the directors declared and paid out a dividend totaling $6,000.   Two
months later, the three shareholders sold their stock to other persons, who,
as the new shareholders, directors, and officers, instituted an action in the
name of the corporation against A and B to recover the dividend payment of
$6,000.   What result?   Explain.

31. From 1903 to 1916 the Ford Motor Company was phenomenally
profitable.   Starting in 1911, a regular dividend of 5 percent per month was

paid, and in addition special dividends were declared and paid from time to time. In 1916, the board of directors decided to continue the regular dividend (5 percent per month) but to discontinue declaring and paying special dividends. Dodge, a minority shareholder, sued for a court decree to force the Ford Company to pay a larger dividend. Admitted facts included the following: 1) The corporation had a surplus of $112 million and yearly net profits of $60 million; 2) After completion of expansion plans approved by the board of directors and payment of the regular 5 percent dividend, there would remain a surplus of $30 million; 3) It had been the policy of the company for a considerable time to annually reduce the selling price while keeping up or improving its quality; 4) The 1916 plans called for a reduction in price of $80 per car, although the total plant output could have been sold at the previous price; 5) Henry Ford stated: "My ambition is to employ still more men, to spread the benefits of this industrial system to the greatest possible number, to help them build up their lives and their homes. To do this we are putting the greatest share of our profits back in the business." What should be the result of Dodge's lawsuit? Explain.

32. The stock structure of a corporation consisted of both preferred stock and common stock, both having a par value of $100. The charter of the corporation provided:

> The holders of the preferred stock shall be entitled to receive when and as declared and the corporation shall be bound to pay a yearly cumulative dividend of 6 percent before any dividend shall be set apart on the common stock.

No dividend was declared on either preferred or common stock until, at the end of the fourth year, a dividend of $24 per share was declared on the preferred stock, covering the current year and all arrearages, and at the same time a dividend of $12 per share was declared on the common stock. There was sufficient surplus for payment of the declared dividends.

a) Would a common shareholder be able to restrain payment of the declared dividend to the preferred shareholders? Explain.

b) Would a preferred shareholder be able to restrain payment of the declared dividend to the common shareholders? Explain.

33. On December 2 the board of directors of a business corporation passed a resolution declaring a lawful 12 percent dividend. By the terms of the resolution the dividend was divided into four equal installments of 3 percent each, payable on February 15, May 15, August 15, and November 15 of the following year. The first installment was duly paid. On May 6, however the directors decided to purchase additional property and equipment for expansion of the business of the corporation, and also decided to increase reserves for losses. Both decisions were reasonable. To carry them out, the directors unanimously adopted a resolution amending the December 2 resolution to read that the total rate of the dividend be 3 percent payable February 15. The resolution, as amended, conformed to what had been done up to May 5, inasmuch as 3 percent had already been paid on February 15. On May 15 X, who had been a registered shareholder of the corporation for over 2 years, protested the action of the directors in amending the

December 2 resolution and demanded that he be paid a 3 percent dividend for the May installment. X made similar demands on August 15 and November 15. The directors disregarded each demand and refused to pay anything further. On November 21 X sued the corporation to recover the amount of a 9 percent dividend on his shares. What result? Explain.

34. On February 1 D, a registered shareholder in a business corporation, indorsed his share certificate for 50 shares ($100 par value), by merely signing his name, and delivered it to C as security for an eight-month loan of $1,000 from C to D. No attempt was made to transfer the shares on the books of the corporation at any time, by any person, although the corporation had knowledge of the pledge.

a) At the annual shareholders meeting held May 15, who was entitled to vote the 50 shares?

b) On June 1, the board of directors declared a legally valid dividend of $6 per share, payable on July 1. 1) Immediately after declaration of the dividend, C requested that the corporation treasurer send the dividend check to C to apply on D's debt. The corporation treasurer refused and on July 1, before any checks had been sent out, C sued the corporation to recover the amount of the dividend due on D's stock. Was C entitled to recover? Explain. 2) On July 1, C not having demanded from the corporation that it send the dividend check to him, the corporation sent the dividend check to D who immediately cashed it. C demanded from D the money so received to apply on the debt, and upon D's refusal to pay, C sued D on July 3. D proved that no part of the debt was due until October 1. Was C entitled to recover from D in the July 3 lawsuit? Explain.

c) On September 5, without permission from D, C sold, indorsed and delivered to B the certificate for 50 shares. On October 1, when D came to repay the loan to C, D learned for the first time of C's wrongful sale of the stock. B was able to prove that he bought the stock honestly, thinking C was the owner, paid C $5,000, its fair value, and knew nothing of the transaction between D and C. B still had the certificate he had obtained from C, B not having registered the transfer. Stock in the corporation being closely held, D was unable to purchase any of the stock anywhere. 1) D offered B $1,000, the amount of the loan for which the stock had been pledged, and demanded return of the certificate. When B refused, D sued B to recover the certificate. Was D entitled to recover from B upon paying $1,000 into court for B? Explain. 2) D offered B what the latter had paid for the stock and demanded return of the certificate. When B refused, D sued B to recover the certificate. Was D entitled to recover from B upon paying $5,000 into court for B? Explain.

book *IV*

Commercial Transactions

The term "commercial transactions" is commonly used to designate business dealings in personal property interests. The concept of property is of vital importance for a free society. The rights of life, liberty, and the pursuit of happiness, proclaimed as essential by the Declaration of Independence, find legal protection in various constitutional provisions, chiefly in the provisions which prohibit unreasonable governmental interference with life, liberty, and property. Of these three protected rights, property (although, of course, not more important than life or liberty) is by far the broadest and most frequently asserted right. The man in the street uses the term "property" to designate something of value which a person can own or use. The legal concept of property is broader. Any legally enforceable right which a person can acquire in something of value is a property right. Thus if a vehicle rental company leases a delivery truck to a retailer, the retailer's contract right to use the truck and the rental company's contract right to receive the agreed rent are both *property* rights, as well as contract rights.

The law has found it quite useful to classify property as either real estate or personal property. Real estate consists of the land and things fairly firmly attached to the land (such as buildings, growing trees, etc.); personal property consists of everything else.

The personal property interests to which the generic term "commercial transactions" is commonly applied include interests evidenced by commercial paper and interests involved in the storage, shipment, sale, and financing of goods.

chapter *14*

Commercial Paper

Part 1 INTRODUCTION

Article 3 of the Uniform Commercial Code, entitled "Commercial Paper," is concerned with notes, drafts, checks, and certificates of deposit. Most such instruments are negotiable in form. Other types of negotiable property interests which are not considered commercial paper (e.g., stock and bond certificates, order or bearer bills of lading and warehouse receipts) are covered by other portions of the Code.

During the early growth of trade in Europe the rules of law pertaining to commercial paper originated among the traders and merchants themselves, starting as customs and practices which they believed contributed to the fair and efficient conduct of business. As these customs and practices multiplied, a body of rules gradually evolved which came to be referred to as the law of the merchants (or as it is frequently termed, the law merchant). Gradually with the expansion of the regular common-law courts and of formal legal systems, disputes involving merchants began with more and more frequency to appear in the regular courts. In settling the increasing number of such disputes the courts gradually adopted and declared as rules of law much of the law merchant. Later, because of the very great importance of commercial paper in the smooth conduct of business, the rules of law concerning commercial paper were systematized and codified by legislation. The Uniform Negotiable Instruments Law (frequently abbreviated NIL) was the first of the uniform business statutes drafted under the auspices of the Commissioners on Uniform State Laws. The NIL was adopted by the legislatures of all the states and provided the basic pattern for Article 3 of the Uniform Commercial Code, which supersedes the NIL in states which have adopted the Code.

The term "negotiable" is not synonymous with "transferable." "Negotiable" is a tag applied to any of several types of property interests, as to which it is possible for an innocent purchaser or transferee for value to obtain a better right than was held by his transferor. Money has this characteristic, and at an early date, as business and commerce began to develop, it was recognized as essential that certain written instruments calling for the payment of money (commercial paper) should have the same characteristic. Negotiable checks, notes, and drafts evidence a large part of the wealth of the country and are essential tools for the efficient conduct of the greater part of the commerce and business of the nation.

Example: A thief stole a satchel of money which a businessman intended to use to meet his payroll. The thief used $1,500 of the money to buy a used car from a dealer. At the time of the sale, the dealer had no knowledge that the money was stolen. The businessman's bank had a list of the serial numbers of the stolen currency, and copies of the list were sent to all banks in the area. When the dealer deposited the $1,500 in his bank, it was quickly identified as some of the stolen payroll money.

Although the thief, of course, did not own the $1,500, the dealer, who received the money innocently and for value, became the owner of it.

Example: In selling a used TV set, the dealer, D. Davis, warranted that the buyer, B. Brown, would have six-months' trouble-free reception. The buyer's promise to pay the purchase price within two months was evidenced by the note quoted below. After the sale, the dealer sold and assigned the note to a bank which paid to the dealer the face amount of the note, less the discount fee. About two weeks after the purchase, the set became totally inoperative through no fault of the buyer, and the buyer promptly notified the dealer. However, the dealer made no attempt to repair or replace the set, and a few weeks later the dealer's business was adjudged insolvent and liquidated. Upon the buyer's refusal to pay his note when it came due, the bank sued the buyer.

1. Assume that the buyer's note read as follows:

> Chicago, Illinois, [Date]
> Two months after date I promise to pay D. Davis $500.
> (signed) B. Brown

This note is nonnegotiable in form. The bank as the assignee of a nonnegotiable claim would have only the rights of the dealer. If the dealer still owned the note, he could not recover because of his breach of warranty. Therefore, although the bank purchased the note for value and before the dealer breached his warranty, the bank likewise could not collect from the buyer.

2. Assume that the buyer's note read as follows:

> Chicago, Illinois, [Date]
> Two months after date I promise to pay to D. Davis or order $500.
> (signed) B. Brown

The meaning and effect are exactly the same whether the note reads, "to D. Davis or order," or instead, "to the order of D. Davis." This is a negotiable note. Although the dealer would have no right to recover on the note (because of his breach of warranty), the bank, as the innocent purchaser for value, received the note free from this defense and could collect from the buyer.

Therefore, the bank would be willing to take the note without investigating the transaction from which the note arose, and the bank would be willing to pay more for the note than it would otherwise. Thus easy transfer of the note is made possible by the fact that it is a negotiable note. The buyer shows that he intends his note to be readily transferable, when he makes it payable to the dealer's order (meaning that the note is to be paid according to the way the dealer, by indorsement, directs or orders payment to be made).

A simple form of note is shown in the above example. The parties to a note are usually referred to as the *maker* (the one making the promise) and the *payee*. A *judgment note* is a note containing an agency authorization which, under common-law rules, makes it possible for the holder to obtain a judgment without a full-scale lawsuit. The theory and use of such notes is referred to briefly in Chapter 1. A typical form of a judgment note appears on the following page.

A *certificate of deposit* is essentially a type of note inasmuch as it evidences a promise to pay. The following is an example of a certificate of deposit:

Central National Bank of Centerville, Illinois   [Date]
    This is to certify that P. Porter has deposited in this bank Five Hundred Dollars ($500), payable to his order six months from date with interest at the rate of 2 percent per year, upon return of this certificate properly indorsed. No payment before, and no interest after, maturity.

(signed) C. Carter, Cashier

A draft is entirely different from a note. In a *note* the signer promises that he himself will pay a certain sum of money; in a *draft* the signer orders or directs some other person or institution to pay the stated sum.

If the one ordered to pay is a bank and the payment is to be made on demand, the draft is a *check*. The parties are usually referred to as the *drawer* (the one signing the check or draft), the *drawee* or drawee bank (the one upon whom the instrument is drawn, that is, the one who is being ordered or directed to make payment), and the *payee*. Forms of checks and their various uses are well known. Drafts other than checks also serve a variety of purposes. Drafts are often used in connection with the sale of goods, they are sometimes used to collect accounts, and drafts as well as checks are common devices for making payments or remittances.

Example: B. Brown, a buyer in Philadelphia, whose credit rating is not high enough to enable him to buy on credit, or who does not wish to buy on credit, orders certain goods from S. Smith, a seller of Chicago, to be shipped, "sight draft, bill of lading attached, cash against documents." In his order, B names the Philadelphia National Bank as convenient for him. S ships the ordered goods to Philadelphia, obtaining from the railroad an order bill of

$ _____

_____, PA., _____, 19__

_____ AFTER DATE _____ PROMISE TO PAY TO THE ORDER

OF _____

_____ DOLLARS

at the PENNSYLVANIA NATIONAL BANK AND TRUST COMPANY, _____ Pa. WITHOUT DEFALCATION,
FOR VALUE RECEIVED, WITH INTEREST.

And further I/we do each hereby authorize and empower any attorney of any Court of record of Pennsylvania, or elsewhere, to appear for me/us, or any of us, and to enter judgment in favor of said payee or holder of this Note, against me/us, or any of us, for the full amount of this note, with or without declaration, with costs of suit, release of errors, without stay of execution, and with ten per cent added as Attorney's commission for collection; and I/we each also waive the right of inquisition on any real estate, that may be levied upon to collect this sum, and do hereby voluntarily condemn the same, and authorize the Prothonotary to enter upon the Fi. Fa., my/our, or any of our said voluntary condemnation; and I/we each further agree that said estate may be sold on a Fi. Fa. and I/we each hereby waive and release all relief from any and all appraisement, stay or exemption laws of any State or Nation, now in force or hereafter to be passed. The makers of this Note, when more than one, shall be jointly and severally liable thereon.

Witness:

_____ [SEAL]

_____ [SEAL]

_____ [SEAL]

77 – 19 (Rev. 2/60)

FOR VALUE RECEIVED, each undersigned endorser does hereby endorse and transfer the within Note to the Pennsylvania National Bank and Trust Company, or bearer, and does jointly and severally guarantee the payment of the same at maturity, hereby waiving demand, presentment for payment, notice of non-payment, protest, and notice of protest or dishonor; and each said endorser does hereby jointly and severally authorize and empower any attorney of any Court of record of Pennsylvania, or elsewhere, to appear for said endorser, and enter judgment against such endorser, jointly or severally, or against any two or more endorsers, in favor of the Pennsylvania National Bank and Trust Company, or bearer, for the amount of said Note, with interest, with or without declaration, and with costs of suit, said judgment to be with waivers and releases of all rights of each endorser as to inquisition on any real estate levied upon, which real estate is hereby voluntarily condemned, and with waiver of stay of execution, waiver of errors, waiver of right of appeal, and waiver of all appraisement and exemption laws of any State or Nation now in force or hereafter passed.

_____ (SEAL)

_____ (SEAL)

_____ (SEAL)

77 – 19 (Rev. 2-60)

(front)   *(back)*

Typical Judgment Note

lading which names S as the consignee. S then writes the following draft (or as is more usual, fills in a form which he obtains from his bank):

Chicago, Illinois, [Date]
On demand pay to the order of S. Smith Five Hundred Dollars ($500).
To B. Brown   (signed) S. Smith
Philadelphia, Pa.

S indorses the draft, "Pay to the Philadelphia National Bank, for collection, (signed) S. Smith," indorses the bill of lading, "Deliver to B. Brown, (signed) S. Smith," clips the two documents together, and mails them to the Philadelphia bank. Upon receiving the documents the bank notifies B that it has a draft drawn on him. B pays the bank the amount of the draft and receives the bill of lading, with which, upon arrival of the goods, he can obtain delivery from the carrier. The bank remits to S the collected sum of money, less its collection fee (unless the seller and buyer had agreed that the buyer should pay for the bank's services). The draft, as the commercial paper part of the transaction, provides a convenient method for stating exactly what B and the bank are to do.

Example: Suppose a sale of goods as in the above example, except that B is purchasing on sixty-days' credit. S, however, wanting to obtain his money before expiration of the sixty days, specifies as one of his terms that the goods will be sold on a sixty-day draft (or trade acceptance as illustrated on page 512), and makes proper arrangements with his own Chicago bank. S ships as in the above example and prepares the following draft:

Chicago, Illinois, [Date]
Sixty days after date pay to the order of S. Smith Five Hundred Dollars ($500).
To B. Brown   (signed) S. Smith
Philadelphia, Pa.

S indorses the draft, "Pay to the Chicago Bank and Trust Company (signed) S. Smith," indorses the bill of lading, and sells both documents to the Chicago bank. The Chicago bank sends the documents to a Philadelphia bank. Upon receiving the documents, the bank notifies B; B comes to the bank, writes across the face of the draft (or signs the appropriate portion of a printed form on the face of the draft), "Accepted [Date]. (signed) B. Brown," and obtains the bill of lading. The accepted draft is returned to the Chicago bank. When it comes due, the draft is again forwarded to Philadelphia for collection. Here the draft is a convenient form upon which S can raise money and a convenient device to evidence B's obligation to pay.

Example: D, a debtor in Philadelphia, owes C, a creditor of Chicago, $500. C draws a sight draft on D and sends it to a Philadelphia bank for collection. Not only is C using the banking system as a convenient way to collect, but also he is exerting some pressure to induce D to pay. D, who wishes to keep his local credit rating good, will be reluctant to arouse the bank's suspicion by refusing to pay the draft when it is presented to him.

Example: A buyer of Chicago who owes $500 to a seller in Philadelphia mails to the seller a check drawn on a Chicago bank. A debtor in Philadelphia who owes a creditor in Chicago $600 mails to the creditor a check drawn on a Philadelphia bank.

This simplified example suggests how through the use of checks (and other drafts) considerable shipment of money back and forth is avoided. While from time to time money must be shipped from one place to another, this is done only after balances are struck at key banking centers.

Part 2   REQUISITES FOR NEGOTIABILITY

Whether or not commercial paper is classed as negotiable paper depends entirely upon the form and contents of the paper. To be negotiable, commercial paper must comply with the following four requirements:[1]

1. It must be in writing and signed by the maker or drawer.

2. It must contain an unconditional promise or order to pay a certain sum in money and no other promise, order, obligation, or power except such as is authorized by Article 3 (the commercial paper article) of the Code.

3. It must be payable on demand, or at a definite time.

4. It must be payable either to order or to bearer.

The policy factors which give rise to any rule of law must be kept in mind to provide a guide in interpreting and applying the law. Since the needs of businessmen themselves gave rise to the rules of law pertaining to commercial paper, these rules must be interpreted in the light of commercial customs and practices. When, in stating the requirements for negotiability, the law speaks of an "unconditional" promise or order, a "certain" sum, a "definite" time, etc., these terms are not used as absolutes. It is not necessary that a promise be absolutely unconditional but only unconditional in the usual, commercial sense; the amount to be paid need not be absolutely certain but rather commercially certain, etc.

FIRST REQUIREMENT

To be negotiable, commercial paper must be in writing and signed by the maker or drawer.

WRITING

There is no express requirement concerning the materials with which or on which a negotiable instrument should be written. The Code merely states:

[1] U.C.C. Sec. 3-104.

"Written" or "writing" includes printing, typewriting or any other intentional reduction to tangible form.[2]

Even though there is no such thing as *oral* commercial paper, it is nevertheless possible, after an obligation has been put in writing, to prove the existence of the obligation and to collect on it entirely through oral testimony. In this connection, the Code states:

> The owner of an instrument which is lost, whether by destruction, theft or otherwise, may maintain an action in his own name and recover from any party liable thereon upon due proof of his ownership, the facts which prevent his production of the instrument and its terms. The court may require security indemnifying the defendant against loss by reason of further claims on the instrument.[3]

SIGNED

The Code states:

> "Signed" includes any symbol executed or adopted by a party with present intention to authenticate a writing.[4]

A valid signature may be manually handwritten, printed, typed, or stamped. If not manually written, it is wise (but not essential) for the recipient of the instrument to request that whoever applies the stamp or makes out the document with the typed or printed signature also add his own personal, handwritten signature or initials as an aid in proving genuineness or authority if either is later questioned.

Obligations under seal are referred to in Chapter 5. With respect to commercial paper, the Code provides that neither the presence nor the absence of a seal will have any effect on negotiability;[5] in addition, the Code limits the common-law value of seals. Only a few states still accord to a seal its common-law effect as an equivalent of consideration. Most states have eliminated this effect by statute, and the Code does likewise. Under the Code, a seal is not the equivalent of consideration either, 1) in negotiable commercial paper, or 2) in nonnegotiable commercial paper if the paper is nonnegotiable for the sole reason that it is not payable to order or bearer.[6] Although with such instruments the seal is no longer an equivalent of consideration, the instrument is still a sealed instrument so far as any statute of limitations is concerned. (In some states the statutory period is longer for a sealed instrument than for an unsealed instrument, while in some other states the statutes of limitations do not apply to sealed instruments at all.)

[2] U.C.C. Sec. 1-201.
[3] U.C.C. Sec. 3-804.
[4] U.C.C. Sec. 1-201.
[5] U.C.C. Sec. 3-113.
[6] U.C.C. Secs. 3-408, 3-805.

SECOND REQUIREMENT

To be negotiable, commercial paper must contain an unconditional promise or order to pay a certain sum in money, and no other promise, order, obligation, or power except such as are authorized by Article 3 (the commercial paper article) of the Code.

PROMISE OR ORDER

As to a promise, the Code states:

A "promise" is an undertaking to pay and must be more than an acknowledgment of an obligation.[7]

As is demonstrated in the negotiable certificate of deposit example in Part 1 of this chapter, the word "promise" need not be used. However, an I.O.U. which merely acknowledges an obligation is not a negotiable instrument.

As to an order, the Code states:

An "order" is a direction to pay and must be more than an authorization or request.[8]

A draft reading, "Please pay . . ." or which otherwise uses words of politeness or courtesy is still an order or direction to pay, so long as the drawer does not expressly leave payment to the discretion or option of the drawee.

Example: A draft reads: "To E. Edwards. At sight please pay to the order of P. Porter $500. (signed) R. Roger."
This is a negotiable draft.

Example: A draft reads: "To E. Edwards. At sight I wish you would pay to the order of P. Porter $500. (signed) R. Roger."
While this is a valid authorization for E to make payment from funds being held for R, it is a nonnegotiable draft, since it is not an unequivocal order or direction to make payment.[9]

UNCONDITIONAL PROMISE OR ORDER

Fact situations in which, as a matter of policy, an order or promise is deemed to be either conditional or unconditional in the commercial sense may be summarized as follows:

[7] U.C.C. Sec. 3-102.
[8] U.C.C. Sec. 3-102.
[9] Comment to U.C.C. Sec. 3-102.

Unconditional. A promise or order to make a payment is unconditional in the commercial sense:[10]

1. Even though it contains a statement of the reason for which the instrument is signed and delivered. Such a statement may be:

a) A statement of the consideration for the instrument, whether performed or unperformed.

b) A statement of the transaction which gives rise to the instrument.

c) A statement that the promise or order is made, or the instrument matures, in accordance with or "as per" a designated transaction.

d) A statement that it arises out of a separate agreement.

2. Even though it states that it is secured by a mortgage, reservation of title, or any other security, or refers to a separate agreement for rights as to prepayment or acceleration.

3. Even though it indicates a particular account to be debited with the payment, or any other fund or source from which the drawee may expect reimbursement.

4. Even though it states a place for payment. A statement of a place for payment is no more conditional than is a statement of the time for payment.

Example: A note reads, "[Date]. One year after date I promise to pay to the order of P. Porter $1,000, at the First National Bank, Chicago, Illinois. (signed) M. Martin."

As is explained in Part 6 of this chapter, presentment at a specified date and place is necessary for the holder to be able to collect from an indorser, but the maker is not relieved from liability by the holder's failure to make due presentment (unless, as is also explained in Part 6, failure of the named bank, during the delay, deprives the maker of ready access to funds he was maintaining to cover the note). The maker may be held liable anywhere that the holder finds him and anytime after maturity of the note—until the statute of limitations expires on the obligation. It would not be reasonable to interpret the above quoted note as meaning that the maker is obligated only if the note is presented to him exactly one year from date and no later, or only if it is presented at the stated place. The parties could make such a contract, but it is so unusual that they would have to state the condition expressly—then, of course, the note would be nonnegotiable.

5. Even though it contains a provision expressly requiring return of the instrument to the one making payment, as for example in the certificate of deposit form previously quoted. This is merely stating a right which the party making payment has anyway. The Code expressly

[10] U.C.C. Sec. 3-105.

states[11] that upon making full payment, the payor is entitled to a signed receipt on the instrument and to surrender of the instrument (unless, as has been previously discussed, the instrument is lost).

Conditional. A promise or order is conditional (and therefore non-negotiable):[12]

1. If it states that it is subject to or governed by any other agreement; or

2. If (with some exceptions)[13] it states that it is to be paid only out of a particular fund or source.

Example: A dealer and a customer entered into a contract for the purchase of a TV set, to be delivered in two weeks. As part of the transaction the customer signed and gave to the dealer the note described below, promising to pay the agreed purchase price in one month. The following day the dealer discounted the note at his bank, receiving the face amount less the usual discount fee. Thereafter the dealer failed to deliver the TV set. Accordingly the customer refused to pay the note when it came due, and the bank sued the customer. If the note was negotiable the bank could recover.

Assume that the note, otherwise properly negotiable in form, stated:

1. "This note is given for an RCA TV set Model 123." The note would be negotiable.

2. In addition to (1) above, assume that the note also stated: "to be delivered two weeks from date." The note would still be negotiable.

3. In addition to (2) above, assume that the note also stated: "in accordance with contract this date between payee and maker." This is still negotiable.

4. In addition to (3) above, assume that the note also stated: "and subject to said contract." Now the note would be nonnegotiable.

Example: R. Roger followed the practice of shipping certain produce to E. Edwards, a broker or factor, for sale. According to their arrangement R could draw sixty-day drafts on E up to $1,000. R drew the following draft: "[Date]. To E. Edwards: Sixty days after date, pay to the order of P. Porter $500, out of the proceeds of the sale of New York Central freight car number 12345. (signed) R. Roger."

An order to pay *out of* a certain fund is conditional on there being that much in the fund, and would therefore be a conditional order.

Suppose that the draft drawn by R read: "[Date]. To E. Edwards: Sixty days after date pay to the order of P. Porter $500, and charge to the proceeds of the sale of New York Central freight car number 12345. (signed) R. Roger." If the market price dropped sharply, so that E would fail to realize $500 from the sale of the produce, he would probably refuse to pay the draft,

---

[11] U.C.C. Sec. 3-505.

[12] U.C.C. Sec. 3-105.

[13] There are two exceptions. A promise or order is unconditional even though 1) limited to payment out of a particular fund, if the instrument is issued by a governmental agency; or 2) limited to payment out of the entire assets of a partnership, trust, or the like.

whichever way it was drawn. Nevertheless, the "out of" draft contains a condition, modifying the order to pay, while the "and charge to" draft contains no such condition. The latter, therefore, is an unconditional order to pay and would be negotiable.

CERTAIN SUM

For commercial paper to be negotiable, the sum which is to be paid must be commercially certain. In general, this requirement is met if, entirely from data on the face of the note, a definite sum can be calculated, which either a) is the exact amount which the payor is to pay to the holder, or b) is the net amount assured to the holder after deduction of expenses which are closely associated with the holder's obtaining payment.[14]

Under a) above, the sum is commercially certain:

1. Even though it is to be paid with stated interest or by stated installments. If the instrument fails to specify a rate of interest, the amount is nevertheless certain; the rate of interest is presumed to be the same as would accrue on unpaid judgments at the place of payment.

2. Even though it is to be paid with different rates of interest before and after default or before and after some other specified date.

3. Even though it is to be paid with a stated discount or addition if paid before or after the due date.

Under b) above, the sum is commercially certain:

1. Even though the payor is to pay the stated amount plus (or less) the cost of exchange to a certain place.

2. Even though, should the payor default, he is to pay the stated sum plus the holder's costs of collection or plus the holder's attorney's fee, or with both costs of collection and attorney's fee added.

Example: A note reads, "Chicago, Illinois, [Date]. One year after date I promise to pay to the order of P. Porter $2,000, with exchange on New York City. (signed) M. Martin."

This is negotiable. What M is to pay in Chicago is $2,000 plus what it will cost to transport $2,000 to New York City, that is, the cost in Chicago of a bank draft for payment of $2,000 in New York City. Although what M is to pay is slightly uncertain, what the holder is to receive is quite certain, namely an amount equal to $2,000 in New York City.

Example: A note reads, "Chicago, Illinois, [Date]. One year after date I promise to pay to the order of P. Porter $1,000 with interest at the rate of 4 percent per year, together with the amount of any taxes assessed and paid upon this note by the payee or any holder hereof. (signed) M. Martin."

This is nonnegotiable. The additional sum that M is to pay is not certain

[14] U.C.C. Sec. 3-106.

from the face of the note, and is not a cost or expense incidental to M's act of paying or otherwise associated with the holder's obtaining payment.

In Money

An instrument is payable in money if it is payable in something which, at the time the instrument is made out, is the medium of exchange adopted by any government as part of its currency.[15]

No Other Promise, Order, Obligation, or Power

Sometimes, in addition to providing for the payment of money, commercial paper will also include other obligations or provide for other matters. Emphasizing the fact that the chief reason for making commercial paper negotiable is to facilitate its easy transfer, some courts have allegorically termed negotiable commercial paper as "a courier without luggage whose face is his passport." Burdening the courier with too much luggage will hamper his mobility. In other words, including in commercial paper any provision which is not customary in instruments that pass freely in the channels of commerce, will prevent the paper from being negotiable. The paper may still evidence an enforceable contract, but it will be a nonnegotiable contract.

In stating what provisions may be included without affecting negotiability, the Code is careful to state that the listing will not change the law of any particular state where any such provision may be invalid or illegal. For example, the statutes of many states declare that confession of judgment provisions are invalid; the Code makes no attempt to change such statutes.

The additional provisions which are authorized by the Code pertain to or are closely associated with the payment or collection of the money obligation evidenced by the instrument. The following are authorized provisions, and will not interfere with negotiability:[16]

1. A statement that collateral has been given for the instrument, and that in case of default the collateral may be sold. (Some notes say that the described collateral is security not only for the obligation evidenced by the note but also for any other obligations that may be owed by the obligor to the holder, and that in case of default on any of these obligations, the collateral can be sold. This broader type of provision is also authorized.)

2. A promise or power to maintain or protect collateral or to give additional collateral if requested.

3. A term authorizing a confession of judgment on the instrument

[15] U.C.C. Sec. 3-107.
[16] U.C.C. Sec. 3-112.

if it is not paid when due. (Notice that a provision under which it is possible to obtain judgment by confession *before* maturity, renders the instrument nonnegotiable, whether or not such a judgment is actually obtained.)

4. A term waiving the benefit of any law intended for the advantage or protection of the obligor. (Examples include waivers of a debtor's exemptions, of a stay of execution, and the like; see Chapter 19.)

5. A term in a draft providing that the payee by indorsing or cashing it acknowledges full satisfaction of a particular obligation.

Example: A note reads, "[Date]. Two months after date I promise to pay to the order of P. Porter $500. This note is given for the purchase price of an RCA TV set Model 123, title to which is to remain in the holder hereof until this note is paid. Until this note is paid, the maker agrees to keep the described TV set insured for at least the amount of this note. (signed) M. Martin."

Up to the last sentence the note is clearly negotiable in form. It is arguable (but not certain) that the last sentence is a promise to protect collateral, is therefore authorized, and would not prevent the note from being negotiable.

THIRD REQUIREMENT

To be negotiable, commercial paper must be payable on demand or at a definite time.

DEMAND

The Code states:

Instruments payable on demand include those payable at sight or on presentation and those in which no time for payment is stated.[17]

DEFINITE TIME

An instrument is payable at a definite time if payable:[18]

1. At a stated date or at a fixed period after a stated date; for example, "One year after date . . ."

2. At a fixed period after sight or demand; for example, "Thirty days after sight . . ."

3. At a definite time, with an additional provision that it can be extended;

a) At the option of the holder; or

b) To a further time stated in the original instrument, at the option of the maker; or

c) to a further time stated in the original instrument, upon the occurrence of a specified event.

[17] U.C.C. Sec. 3-108.
[18] U.C.C. Sec. 3-109.

4. At a definite time, subject to any acceleration. The acceleration might be:

a) Entirely at the maker's option; or

b) Entirely at the holder's option; or

c) Upon the occurrence of some event, whether the occurrence is certain or conditional.

Example: A note reads, "On or before [Date], I promise to pay to P. Porter on order $500. (signed) M. Martin."

This is negotiable. While somewhat ambiguous, the usual interpretation of "on or before" is that the holder has no right to payment before the stated date, but that the maker can pay earlier if he chooses. Any acceleration would be entirely at the maker's option.

Example: A note reads, "[Date]. One year after date I promise to pay to the order of P. Porter $500. Should the holder deem himself insecure, he can demand payment at any time and this note shall thereupon become immediately due and payable. (signed) M. Martin."

This is negotiable.

Example: A note reads, "On [Date], or before if I sell my house for more than $10,000, I promise to pay to the order of P. Porter $500. (signed) M. Martin."

This is negotiable. The note is not conditional because there is a fixed date when it will become absolutely due. The fact that maturity may be accelerated by an event which may or may not occur does not affect negotiability.

An instrument is not payable at a definite time (and therefore is non-negotiable) if by its terms it is made payable upon the happening of a stated event, which is uncertain as to the time of occurrence, even though the event is such as will inevitably happen sometime (like the death of the maker). Furthermore, the occurrence of the stated event will not cure the defect.

Example: A note reads, "[Date]. Upon sale of my house, I promise to pay P. Porter on order $500. (signed) M. Martin."

This is not payable at a definite time and also is conditional; if M should sell his house one month later, the condition for M's contract to pay would be met, and there would be an enforceable contract, but the note would still be nonnegotiable.

The negotiability of a demand instrument is not affected by the fact that it is undated.[19] However, if the date is omitted from a time instrument which states that it is payable a stated period after date, the instrument is incomplete and not enforceable. When completed by someone

---

[19] U.C.C. Sec. 3-114.

inserting the date, the instrument would then be negotiable.[20]   Should a wrong date be inserted, the relative rights of the parties are as discussed in connection with defenses in Part 5 of this chapter.

FOURTH REQUIREMENT

To be negotiable, commercial paper must be payable either to order or to bearer.

Commercial paper is not negotiable unless the maker or drawer intends the instrument to be easily transferable, and manifests this intent either by making the instrument payable to the bearer, or by making it payable according to the order or direction of the person named as the payee.   Although usually either the word "bearer" or the word "order" is used in designating the payee, these specific words do not have to be used; other terms having the same legal effect will satisfy this requirement.   An instrument which is payable to the order or direction of a named payee is frequently referred to as *order paper*, one payable to the bearer as *bearer paper*.

Under the Code, an instrument has the legal effect of being payable to order:[21]

1. If it is expressly made payable to a named person or to his "order." It is immaterial whether the word "order" precedes or follows the name of the payee.   Thus ". . . pay to P. Porter or order . . ." and ". . . pay to the order of P. Porter . . ." mean exactly the same.

2. If it is expressly made payable to a named person or to his assignees or transferees.

3. If the instrument names a payee and clearly states that the maker or drawer intends the instrument to have the effect of negotiable commercial paper.

Example: A note reads, "[Date].   One year after date I promise to pay to P. Porter $500.   This note is negotiable.   (signed) M. Martin."

The note satisfies the requisites for negotiability.   The clear expression of intent that the instrument be negotiable has the effect of making it payable to the order of P. Porter.

An instrument payable to "P. Porter or his indorsees" is an order instrument, but a general reference to indorsement will not make an instrument payable to order.   As the Code states:

> An instrument not payable to order is not made so payable by such words as "payable upon return of this instrument properly indorsed."[22]

[20] U.C.C. Sec. 3-115.
[21] U.C.C. Sec. 3-110.
[22] U.C.C. Sec. 3-110.

Under the Code, an instrument has the legal effect of being payable to bearer:[23]

1. If it is expressly made payable to bearer. An instrument designating the payee in any of the following ways is a bearer instrument: ". . . pay to bearer . . ."; ". . . pay to the order of bearer . . ."; ". . . pay to P. Porter or bearer . . ."

2. If the term used to identify the payee does not purport to designate a specific person. For example, instruments payable to "cash," "sundries," or "bills payable" are bearer instruments.

A hybrid form reading ". . . pay to the order of P. Porter or bearer . . ." sometimes appears, usually when inappropriate printed forms are used. This is order paper unless the bearer words are handwritten or typewritten.[24]

Part 3 NEGOTIATION OF COMMERCIAL PAPER

The Code states:

Negotiation is the transfer of an instrument in such form that the transferee becomes a holder.[25] [A "holder" is almost the same as an "owner"; the term is further explained in Part 4 of this chapter.]

Order paper is negotiated by the transferor's indorsing the paper and delivering it to the new holder. Although it is possible to negotiate bearer paper by delivery without an indorsement, a transferee will frequently request an indorsement anyway, in order to obtain the advantage of the broader contract liability which a transferor undertakes by an indorsement.

TYPES OF INDORSEMENTS

BLANK INDORSEMENT[26]

An indorsement in blank names no particular indorsee; it usually consists of the indorser's signature and nothing more. Even though an instrument is payable to order, when it is indorsed in blank it becomes payable to bearer and may be further negotiated by delivery alone.

SPECIAL INDORSEMENT

The Code states:

A special indorsement specifies the person to whom or to whose order it makes the instrument payable. Any instrument specially

[23] U.C.C. Sec. 3-111.
[24] U.C.C. Sec. 3-110.
[25] U.C.C. Sec. 3-202.
[26] U.C.C. Sec. 3-204.

indorsed becomes payable to the order of the special indorsee and may be further negotiated only by his indorsement.[27]

Although to be negotiable an instrument must on its face be made payable to order or to bearer, this requirement does not apply to an indorsement. There is no difference between an indorsement reading, "Pay to the order of A. Adams. (signed) P. Porter," and one reading, "Pay to A. Adams. (signed) P. Porter."

Under the Code provision quoted above, if an instrument is specially indorsed, it becomes an order instrument even though the maker or drawer expressly made it payable to bearer. Likewise, an order instrument, changed into a bearer instrument by a blank indorsement, becomes an order instrument upon being further specially indorsed.

Continuing a common practice, the Code expressly authorizes a holder to convert a blank indorsement into a special indorsement by writing, above the signature of the blank indorser, "Pay to . . . " and inserting his own name (or the name of any other person).

The transfer of a nonnegotiable, written contract is frequently accomplished by the transferor writing on the contract something like the following: "I hereby assign to A. Adams all my right, title, and interest to the within contract. (signed) P. Porter." If this is written on a negotiable instrument, it is in legal effect a special indorsement, because, as the Code states:

> Words of assignment, condition, waiver, guaranty, limitation or disclaimer of liability and the like accompanying an indorsement do not affect its character as an indorsement.[28]

Qualified Indorsement[29]

An indorser not only transfers his title but also, as is discussed in Part 6 of this chapter, makes a promise that he will pay if certain conditions are met. If the one intended to make payment (the maker of a note or the drawee of a draft) fails to pay and the holder fulfills the specified conditions, the holder has recourse back to the indorser. An indorser can transfer without making such a promise by expressly stating in his indorsement that there is to be no recourse back to him. The common expression is "without recourse." Such an indorser does not completely avoid liability on the instrument, but he considerably qualifies his liability. This is frequently referred to as a qualified indorsement. Either a blank or a special indorsement can be qualified. For example: "Pay to A. Adams without recourse, (signed) P. Porter," or "Without recourse, (signed) P. Porter."

[27] U.C.C. Sec. 3-204.
[28] U.C.C. Sec. 3-202.
[29] U.C.C. Sec. 3-414.

Restrictive Indorsement

An indorsement expressly made for a specified limited purpose is called a "restrictive indorsement."

The Code states:

An indorsement is restrictive which either
(a) is conditional; or
(b) purports to prohibit further transfer of the instrument; or
(c) includes the words "for collection," "for deposit," "pay any bank," or like terms signifying a purpose of deposit or collection; or
(d) otherwise states that it is for the benefit or use of the indorser or of another person.[30]

The exact effect of a restrictive indorsement depends upon several factors, including the particular type of restrictive indorsement, the type of instrument, and whether the instrument passes through banking channels.

The Code divides banks into two main classes, those which buy instruments and thus become owners, and those which serve merely as conduits or reservoirs for instruments. For many purposes, the latter may be considered as having no greater connection with the transfer of commercial paper than does a pipe line and storage tank on the quality of oil being pumped and stored. The Code defines these "conduit" and "storage" banks as follows:

"Depositary bank" means the first bank to which an item is transferred for collection . . .
"Payor bank" means a bank by which an item is payable as drawn or accepted. [The chief type of payor bank is a drawee bank, the bank in which the drawer has an account and upon which he draws checks.]
"Intermediary bank" means any bank to which an item is transferred in course of collection except the depositary or payor bank . . .[31]

Example: The payee of a negotiable check, drawn on a Cleveland, Ohio, bank, deposits the check in his account in a Pittsburgh, Pennsylvania, bank. In collecting (or receiving credit) on the check, the Pittsburgh bank sends the check to the Federal Reserve bank for that area. From there the check is sent to the Cleveland drawee bank. The Pittsburgh bank is the depositary bank, the drawee bank in Cleveland is the payor bank, and the Federal Reserve bank, the intermediary bank.

The types of restrictive indorsements most commonly used are collection and deposit indorsements. In general, if the holder of an instrument indorses it for collection or for deposit, any transferee (except an intermediary or payor bank) will take with notice of the limited purpose

[30] U.C.C. Sec. 3-205. See also U.C.C. Secs. 3-206 and 3-603.
[31] U.C.C. Sec. 4-105.

of the transfer and is obligated to see that the one indorsing restrictively receives what he should for the instrument.

Example: M signed and delivered to P a six-months negotiable note for $500, naming P as payee. P indorsed and delivered the note to A with the following indorsement: "Pay to A. Adams for collection, (signed) P. Porter." A indorsed in blank and sold and delivered the note to B receiving $500. A failed to pay over to P the money received from B. Upon maturity, M paid B.

A possible interpretation of the Code is that P would have a choice of actions:

1. P could probably recover the amount of the note from B. B in turn would have a right to recover from A.

2. Suppose that P sued M. The Code states in effect that if a note is restrictively indorsed, a maker who pays the holder "in a manner not consistent with the terms of such indorsement" is not discharged from the liability which the note evidences.

Example: R drew a check on a Cleveland bank for $500, naming P as payee. P indorsed the check "For deposit, (signed) P. Porter," and gave it to his office boy, together with a number of other checks, to deposit in the bank in which P had an account. On the way to the bank the boy lost the check. The person who found it dishonestly indorsed it in blank and cashed it at a store in Pittsburgh. The storekeeper indorsed the check in blank and deposited it in a Pittsburgh (depositary) bank in which the storekeeper had an account. The check was forwarded through the Federal Reserve (intermediary) bank and paid by the Cleveland (payor) bank.

P would, of course, have a right to collect from the finder. As alternatives P would have a right to collect the amount of the check from the storekeeper, or (probably) from the Pittsburgh bank; P could not collect from the Federal Reserve bank or from the Cleveland bank.

Accommodation Indorsement

A person who signs commercial paper to help out or accommodate someone else is called an accommodation party. As the Code states:

> An accommodation party is one who signs the instrument in any capacity for the purpose of lending his name to another party to it . . .[32]

An indorsement which shows that it is not in the chain of title gives notice of its accommodation character. Depending upon where and how an accommodation party signs, such a person may be an accommodation maker, comaker, or indorser.

Example: M wishes to borrow $1,000 from P, to be repaid in six months. P, unwilling to trust M's credit alone, says that he will make the requested loan only if A also will join in the transaction. When A agrees, M makes out a six-month negotiable note for $1,000, naming P as payee. M signs the note

[32] U.C.C. Sec. 3-415.

as maker, A indorses it, and M then delivers the note to P and receives from P the requested loan.

A is an accommodation indorser. Although he is not transferring the instrument, he is making an indorser's promise (discussed in Part 6 of this chapter), which is quite similar to a guaranty of payment.

Part 4   HOLDERS IN DUE COURSE

Refer back to the second example in Part 1 of this chapter. Because the dealer's fraudulent misrepresentation induced the buyer to purchase the TV set and sign the quoted negotiable note, the buyer would have a good defense if the dealer were to sue for the amount of the note. However, the note became fully enforceable upon transfer to the bank. The type of transferee who can thus obtain superior rights to negotiable commercial paper is called a "holder in due course." To be a holder in due course, a person (or business) must be:[33]

1. A holder,
2. For value,
3. In good faith, and
4. Without reason to know of the possible existence of any defense concerning the instrument. More specifically he must take the instrument:

a) Before it is overdue, or at least without notice that it is overdue;

b) Before it has been dishonored, or at least without notice that it has been dishonored; and

c) Without other notice of any defenses or claims to it on the part of any person.

HOLDER

The term "holder" as defined in the Code[34] is almost but not exactly synonymous with "owner." A person is the holder of bearer paper if he is in possession of the paper. For a person to be the holder of order paper, he must not only be in possession of the paper, but he must also be either the payee or an indorsee. In relation to any prior party, a person can be an indorsee of order paper only if the paper bears the genuine or authorized indorsement of that prior party. Suppose that a thief steals an unindorsed, order note from the payee, forges the payee's indorsement, and sells and delivers the note to A; A indorses, sells, and delivers the note to B who in turn indorses, sells, and delivers the note to C. C would be a holder as to A and B; but since the payee had never indorsed, C would not be an indorsee as to the payee and, therefore, would not be a holder as to either the payee or the maker.

[33] U.C.C. Sec. 3-302.
[34] U.C.C. Sec. 1-201.

Forged or Unauthorized Indorsement

Any forged or unauthorized signature is wholly inoperative as the signature of the person (or business) whose name is signed, unless one of the following three situations is present:[35]

1. *Ratification.* A forged or unauthorized signature can be approved or ratified by the one whose name is signed, and thereby become an effective signature.

2. *Negligence.* If the making of the unauthorized signature has been substantially aided by the negligence of the person whose name is signed, then as a matter of fairness he cannot deny the validity of the signature as to any later taker who otherwise fulfills the requirements of a holder in due course. Although possible, it is rare that a holder's negligence will substantially help someone to forge the holder's indorsement. Much more common, of course, is negligence which substantially aids the forging of the careless person's signature as a drawer or maker —for example, through inadequate security for the safekeeping of a signature stamp.

3. *Imposter or Fictitious Payee.* Suppose that a drawer writes a check payable to "cash." Undoubtedly someplace in the world someone can be found who is named "Cash." Naturally it is not the drawer's intent that such a person receive the money for the check so drawn or otherwise have an interest in the check. Although the check is in the form of an order instrument payable to cash (reading, "Pay to the order of cash"), it, of course, does not need an indorsement by some Mr. Cash to negotiate it. This situation is covered by the rule mentioned in Part 2 of this chapter which declares such a check to be a bearer instrument; clearly, the word used to designate the payee is not intended to mean an actual person. Suppose, however, that although an actual name is used to designate the payee of a check, the drawer does not intend that person, or any person of that actual name, to have an interest in the check. Although there may be an actual person of that name, the name is assumed or fictitious from the standpoint of the instrument and the one making it out. Therefore, as a matter of fairness to later takers or to the drawee, the indorsement of the named person should not be required. Because the check is in the form of order paper naming an apparently real person as payee, it is quite artificial to call it bearer paper (as does the old Negotiable Instruments Law). However, it should have the same effect as bearer paper, and the Code provides that if the drawer does not intend indorsement by the actual person named, then *anyone* can validly indorse it in that name.

The Code states:

[35] U.C.C. Secs. 3-404, 3-405, 3-406.

An indorsement by any person in the name of a named payee is effective if

(a) an imposter by use of the mails or otherwise has induced the maker or drawer to issue the instrument to him or his confederate in the name of the payee; or

(b) a person signing as or on behalf of a maker or drawer intends the payee to have no interest in the instrument; or

(c) an agent or employee of the maker or drawer has supplied him with the name of the payee intending the latter to have no such interest.[36]

Example: P. Porter rented a certain house and lot to a tenant, T. Thomas. While still occupying the premises, T conceived of a scheme to obtain money fraudulently from R who was in the business of loaning money on mortgages. First, T signed a contract with Porter, agreeing to purchase the property. Ostensibly to facilitate searching the title records, T borrowed the deed which Porter had received some years before when he had purchased the property. (This is a common practice in real estate transactions; since it is recorded, the deed is not irreplaceable, and it aids a title searcher if he has easy access to the old deed with its exact description of the property and references to the prior chain of title.) With the deed and some forged club membership cards, T went to the office of R, introduced himself as P. Porter, applied for a $3,000 mortgage on Porter's property, and left Porter's deed with R to facilitate R's title search. Upon searching the title records, R found that Porter had good title to the property, approved the loan, and prepared the mortgage papers for Porter to sign. On the day fixed for completion of the transaction, T again came to R's office, and, still pretending to be Porter, forged Porter's signature to the mortgage papers, and received R's negotiable check for $3,000 drawn on E Bank, naming Porter as payee. T indorsed the check with Porter's name, then with his own name, cashed the check at the H Bank where he was known by his actual name (T. Thomas), and absconded. Upon presentment, E Bank paid H Bank the amount of the check. Discovering the fraud, R demanded that E Bank restore the $3,000 to his account, and upon E Bank's refusal, R sued E Bank. Assume that R exercised the care usual for mortgage lenders.

R's Argument: Since the check read, "Pay to the order of P. Porter," R intended that Porter, the one who owned the mortgaged property, should receive the money, or direct its payment. The bank did not make payment to Porter. Since Porter never indorsed the check, Porter never ordered payment to be made to someone else. Therefore, since the drawee bank did not pay to Porter or to his order, the payment was not made according to the depositor's direction, and the bank could not charge the depositor's account.

E Bank's Argument: Regardless of the name, the *person* whom R intended should receive the money actually did receive it. For the purpose of this transaction and of R's check, Thomas, the person with whom R was dealing was Porter. The bank actually paid that person according to R's direction, and therefore could charge the payment to R's account.

Notice the strong arguments that can be made on each side of the dispute.

[36] U.C.C. Sec. 3-405.

The drawer's argument would be even stronger if he had dealt with the imposter through the mail rather than face to face.

To the question of whether R was dealing with the *person* or with the *name*, the correct answer seems to be that he was dealing with both. The authors of the Code feel that the above quoted imposter rule is the most fair, reasonable, and practical. Under the Code the above lawsuit would be decided in favor of E Bank.

Example: T. Thomas was head of the purchasing division of R. Roger's business, which operated under the name, "R. Rogers Company." For goods purchased and received from P. Porter, R owed $100. T prepared a negotiable check drawn on the E Bank, for $350, naming Porter as payee, and altered the invoice to read $350. The check was signed as stated below. After it was signed, T indorsed the check with Porter's name, then with his own name, and cashed the check at H Bank where T was known. T sent the correct amount to Porter by another method. When R discovered T's fraudulent scheme, T absconded; R demanded that E Bank restore the amount of the check to his account. Upon the bank's refusal, R sued E Bank. Assume that R was not negligent in failing to discover T's dishonesty sooner.

1. Assume that T had authority to sign checks on R's account, and signed the check, "R. Roger Company by T. Thomas, Agent."

2. Assume instead that T brought this check and invoice to R, together with a number of other checks and invoices; R signed the checks and returned them to T for mailing to the various payees.

R could not recover from E Bank under either of these fact assumptions. If T signed the check for R, it is fair to say that T's intent should control. If R signed the check prepared by T, then as between the innocent drawer and the innocent drawee (or other innocent party such as a holder in due course), the authors of the Code think that it is fair to place the loss on the drawer within whose business the loss originated.

A valid and effective indorsement may be made by an agent, provided the agent has authority to indorse his principal's name.

The Code states:

> A signature may be made by an agent or other representative, and his authority to make it may be established as in other cases of representation. No particular form of appointment is necessary to establish such authority.[37]

Usually an agent will not be deemed to have authority to indorse unless the authority has been expressly granted to him; therefore when such authority exists, it is usually evidenced by a writing signed by the principal. A person asked to take commercial paper on the faith of an agent's indorsement should usually hesitate unless the agent shows written authorization, expressly stating that it includes the authority to indorse commercial paper.

[37] U.C.C. Sec. 3-403.

Payee's Name Incorrectly Stated

The Code states:

> Where an instrument is made payable to a person under a mis-spelled name or one other than his own he may indorse in that name or his own or both; but signature in both names may be required by a person paying or giving value for the instrument.[38]

Of course, the term "person" used in the Code includes not only an individual but also any organization, corporation, etc.

Another Person with Same Name[39]

For almost any name, many people can be found with the same legal name. Suppose that a check made out to "John Smith" comes into the possession of a person so named, who, however, is not the payee intended by the drawer. An indorsement by the wrong "John Smith" would not be valid or effective. Unless the maker or drawer had been negligent (for example, by mailing the instrument to the wrong address), an innocent transferee of the instrument who relies on the indorsement of the wrong "John Smith" would not become a holder, and a drawee bank making payment could not charge the payment to the drawer's account.

Multiple Payees[40]

If an instrument is made out to more than one payee, the indorsement of only one will be sufficient for transfer if the payees are named disjunctively (A. Adams *or* B. Brown), while the indorsements of both or all will be necessary if the payees are named conjunctively (A. Adams *and* B. Brown).

Partial Indorsement

The Code states:

> An indorsement is effective for negotiation only when it conveys the entire instrument or any unpaid residue. If it purports to be of less it operates only as a partial assignment.[41]

Example: M signed and delivered to P a six-month negotiable note for $500, naming P as payee. P sold and delivered the note to A and B with the indorsement quoted below. M refused to pay upon maturity, proved that the note was intended as a gift to P, and stated that he had changed his mind about making the gift. This defense (namely, lack of consideration) would be

---

[38] U.C.C. Sec. 3-203.
[39] Am. Jur. 2d., Bills and Notes, Sec. 706.
[40] U.C.C. Sec. 3-116.
[41] U.C.C. Sec. 3-202.

cut off if A and B were holders in due course. Assume that they otherwise met the requirements of holders in due course, except that the note was indorsed as follows:

1. "Pay to A. Adams and B. Brown, (signed) P. Porter." A and B would be co-owners of a joint right against M, would be joint holders in due course, and could collect from M.

2. "Pay to A. Adams, $300, and to B. Brown, $200. (signed) P. Porter." The partial indorsement, attempting to split the instrument into two parts, is not appropriate for negotiable commercial paper and would not pass negotiable rights. A and B would be partial assignees subject to the same defense that M could raise if he were being sued by P.

VOIDABLE CONTRACT[42]

The most common type of voidable contract is that made by a minor. If a holder in due course is in possession of a negotiable note which has been indorsed and transferred by a minor, the minor will usually be able to avoid the liability which would otherwise arise from the indorsement (as discussed in Parts 5 and 6 of this chapter), but his transfer of title is irrevocable; in other words while he usually can avoid his personal liability, he cannot require return of the note from a holder in due course.

VALUE

The Code states:

A holder takes the instrument for value
(a) to the extent that the agreed consideration has been performed . . . or
(b) when he takes the instrument in payment of or as security for an antecedent claim against any person whether or not the claim is due; or
(c) when he gives a negotiable instrument for it or makes an irrevocable commitment to a third person.[43]

Note that the Code distinguishes between consideration and value. When a note is transferred, the transferee's nonnegotiable promise to pay the transferor a stated amount at a future date is consideration—but it is not value. Value is given only when (and to the extent that) the transferee's promise is performed. If at the time a transferee learns of some defense to the instrument, he has not yet paid any of the agreed consideration, he can justifiably refuse to pay and thus save himself any monetary loss. He stands to suffer a loss and therefore needs the superior rights of a holder in due course only for the amount of consideration

---

[42] U.C.C. Sec. 3-207.
[43] U.C.C. Sec. 3-303.

which he has already paid. A common example arises when a note is transferred to a bank for an agreed amount which the bank credits to the transferor's checking account. If a transferor's checking account is active with a number of deposits and withdrawals being made, then in determining whether a particular credit has been paid:[44]

1. The Code adopts the "first-in, first-out" rule (that is, payment is presumed to be made from the oldest money or credit in the acount); and,

2. The Code provides that if several instruments are deposited at the same time, they should be added together and treated as a single item.

Example: On April 1 M signed and delivered to P a negotiable, one-month note for $700, as payment for certain goods which P agreed to deliver to M within one week. On April 3 P discounted the note at H Bank for $600, receiving a credit of that amount in his checking acount. This credit brought the balance in P's account to $900. On April 6 P made an additional deposit of $200. Thereafter P never delivered the agreed goods to M; therefore M refused to pay when the note came due. The bank sued M. Assume that the bank otherwise met the requirements for a holder in due course, except that, at the times stated below, the bank learned of M's defense—failure of consideration—which arose from P's nondelivery.

1. The bank learned of M's defense on April 15, by which time the bank had honored P's checks totaling $250. This amount would be presumed to have been paid out of the $300 in the account before the note was discounted. The bank therefore had not yet paid any value for the note and could not recover anything from M. (Of course, the bank could charge P's account with the amount of the note.)

2. The bank learned of M's defense on April 22, by which time the bank had honored P's checks totaling $500. The bank had paid $200 from the $600 credit given, would in effect be a partial holder in due course in the amount of $200, and could recover that amount from M (with a right to recover the balance from P or to charge that amount against his account).

3. The bank learned of M's defense on April 25, by which time the bank had honored P's checks totaling $899.99. The bank had paid $599.99 of the $600 credit and would be a partial holder in due course with the right to collect $599.99 from M.

4. The bank learned of M's defense on April 26, by which time the bank had honored P's checks totaling $900. The bank had paid the full $600 of the credit given and would be a full holder in due course with the right to collect $700 (the face of the note) from M.

5. Other facts remaining the same, assume that upon transfer of the note, instead of giving P credit in his checking account, the bank gave P a negotiable certificate of deposit in the amount of $600. The bank would be considered as giving value from that moment, and (assuming the other requirements were met) would be a full holder in due course with the right to collect $700 from M.

[44] U.C.C. Sec. 4-208.

GOOD FAITH

In discussing good faith, an Illinois appellate court once said:

> Mere lack of notice [of a defense] is not sufficient; good faith implies honest intent. It is consistent with negligence, even gross negligence. A blundering fool may therefore be found to have acted in good faith, though under like circumstances a shrewd businessman might be deemed to have acted in bad faith.[45]

Similarly, the Code defines good faith as "honesty in fact in the conduct or transaction concerned."[46] Thus a transferee may deal with a stranger and nevertheless qualify as a holder in due course. Furthermore, a transferee is not expected to investigate the antecedents of every instrument being transferred to him. In fact, the law of negotiable instruments developed in order to free transferees from the need to make such investigations. The picture changes, however, if, while having no actual knowledge of a defense, a transferee knows such facts that his failure to make inquiry indicates a deliberate desire on his part to avoid knowledge, for fear that investigation will disclose some flaw in the transaction. Under such circumstances he cannot be deemed to be taking in due or proper course of business or in good faith, and, therefore, he is not entitled to the superior protection of being classed as a holder in due course.

NOTICE OF DEFENSES

INSTRUMENT OVERDUE

The fact that an instrument is past due immediately raises the question, "Why was it not presented and paid upon its due date?" A transferee who receives an overdue instrument, therefore, has reason to know that there may be some defense, and cannot be a holder in due course.

Time Instrument

The transferee of a time instrument can readily determine from the face of the instrument whether it is overdue. Time is computed in the usual method, namely:

1. If the time is stated in months or years, the instrument comes due on the corresponding date of the indicated month or year (or as near as possible to that date), regardless of variations in the number of days in the various months. For example, a note dated December 31,

a) If due in one year, would be due on December 31 of the following year;

[45] *Schintz* v. *Amer. Trust & Sec. Bank*, 152 Ill. App. 76 (1909).
[46] U.C.C. Sec. 1-201.

b) If due in nine months, would be due on September 30 (that being the last day of the month);

c) If due in two months, would be due on February 28 (or February 29 in a leap year).

2. If the time is stated in days, actual days are counted, with the first day after the date of the instrument being number one, and so on. For example:

a) A note dated April 1, due in thirty days, would be due on May 1.

b) A note dated July 1, due in thirty days, would be due on July 31.

Demand Instrument[47]

A demand instrument is overdue after the expiration of more than a reasonable length of time from the date of its issuance. What is a reasonable time will vary, depending upon the nature of the instrument, its purpose, and the circumstances surrounding its issuance. For example, a check or sight draft is used as a device for making a present payment, while a demand note is used to delay payment at least for a while. The time for a demand note will therefore be longer than for a check or sight draft. Usually the time before a demand note becomes overdue will be longer for an interest-bearing note than for one not bearing interest. Sometimes other material factors will also be present, so that no definite period can be stated as the time when a demand note becomes overdue. A prominent legal writer[48] has suggested that two or three months is the usual permissible time. A transferee should hesitate and consult his attorney before taking a demand note much older than that. Likewise, no definite time is expressly stated for a sight draft, but it should probably be no longer than the time for a check. Because of the large volume of checks in use, the authors of the Code believe that it is desirable to fix a definite time for checks. The Code therefore states:

> A reasonable time for a check drawn and payable within the states and territories of the United States and the District of Columbia is presumed to be thirty days.[49]

A transferee receiving a check more than thirty days after the date of its issuance will not be a holder in due course.

Accelerated Instrument[50]

Suppose that a holder accelerates an instrument which by its terms permits acceleration at his option, and then upon failure of the maker

---

[47] U.C.C. Sec. 3-304, 1-204.
[48] Williston, Contracts, Sec. 1176A (1936).
[49] U.C.C. Sec. 3-304.
[50] *Ibid.*

to pay, transfers the instrument before its stated (unaccelerated) due date, and does not tell the transferee of the prior acceleration and dishonor. Although the instrument is actually overdue and has been dishonored, if the transferee has no reason to know of this, he may rely on the stated due date and qualify as a holder in due course.

OTHER DEFENSES

Even though an instrument is not overdue so that there is no delay in payment to raise a suspicion, certain other circumstances concerning the instrument or its transfer may be so irregular as to warn a transferor of some possible defense or claim, and thereby prevent him from becoming a holder in due course. The basic policy which the law follows in regard to holders in due course might be termed a policy of "general status" rather than "specific innocence." This general status theory may be illustrated by a fanciful example. Suppose that King Arthur's sorcerer, Merlin, conjured up a supply of magic cloaks that would protect the knights from almost any adversity. A knight who was pure of heart and adequately armored was entitled to such a cloak. Sir Adam met these requirements and went forth wearing a cloak. Sir Bart, however, although equally pure of heart, was wearing ill-fitting armor which left a gap at the neck, and therefore was not entitled to a cloak. Both knights riding together stumbled into a well-camouflaged pitfall. Sir Bart fell into the pit while Sir Adam was sustained and saved by his cloak. While the danger of the pit was entirely remote from any danger arising from the gap in Sir Bart's armor, Sir Bart would be subject to the danger because he had failed to qualify for a magic cloak. Thus with commercial paper, if a transferee has notice of a certain irregularity, he cannot himself achieve the general status of a holder in due course, and without the rights of a holder in due course, he is subject to *any* defense, even one of which he was entirely ignorant and which was totally remote from the irregularity about which he knew.

Some legal scholars point out that the early common law followed the "specific innocence" rather than the "general status" approach in recognizing holder-in-due-course rights, and argue that the "specific innocence" approach should be reinstated in the law as the better policy. Both the Negotiable Instruments Law and the modern Uniform Commercial Code, however, follow the "the general status" approach, the policy apparently being that just as only certain instruments (namely negotiable instruments) are entitled to swim freely in the channels of commerce, so also only certain persons (persons whose taking of the instruments is *entirely* in "due course" and without *any* blemish) should be entitled to catch such instruments and obtain the superior rights of holders in due course.

The Code classifies in detail the most common fact situations which may arise, and states as to each whether or not the situation should be considered as giving notice to a transferee of a possible defense—and thus prevent him from achieving the status of a holder in due course.

Notice of Defense Given[51]

Obviously, as the Code states, "A person has 'notice' of a fact when . . . he has actual knowledge of it . . ." Clearly the transferee of a negotiable instrument cannot be a holder in due course if, at the time of transfer to him, he has actual knowledge of any defense or adverse claim.

Sometimes the appearance of an instrument may be sufficient of itself to give notice of a defense or adverse claim. As the Code says:

> The purchaser has notice of a claim or defense if . . . the instrument is so incomplete, bears such visible evidence of forgery or alteration, or is otherwise so irregular as to call into question its validity, terms or ownership or to create an ambiguity as to the party to pay. . . .

Sometimes the transferor of a negotiable instrument is a fiduciary (such as an agent, trustee, or corporate officer) who is making a wrongful transfer of fiduciary funds. Ordinarily a transferee may assume that a fiduciary's transfer is proper. Therefore, the transferee's knowledge that fiduciary funds are involved does not make him liable to the one for whom the fiduciary was holding the funds, should the transfer be actually wrongful.

However, as the Code says:

> The purchaser has notice of a claim against the instrument when he has knowledge that a fiduciary has negotiated the instrument in payment of or as security for his own debt or in any transaction for his own benefit or otherwise in breach of duty.

Example: To cover his personal losses incurred through speculating on the stock market, P. Porter, president of the Carter Corporation, gave his stock broker three negotiable checks, all drawn on the Edwards Bank, and the bank paid the broker the amounts for which the checks were drawn. The first check was drawn by R. Roger, a depositor, named Carter Corporation as payee, and was indorsed, "Carter Corporation by P. Porter, President." The second check named the broker as the payee and the drawer's signature read, "Carter Corporation, by P. Porter, President." The third check named P. Porter as payee, the drawer's signature read, "Carter Corporation, by P. Porter, President," and the check was indorsed "P. Porter." P had general authority to draw and indorse checks in the name of the corporation, but with each of these three checks, P was actually embezzling money from the corpora-

[51] U.C.C. Secs. 3-206, 3-304, 1-201.

tion. When the embezzlements were discovered, Carter Corporation sued the broker for the amounts of the checks. The broker proved that he had no actual knowledge of P's embezzlement.

Under the Code the corporation could collect for the first two checks and probably also for the third check.

Collection and deposit indorsements, discussed in Part 3 of this chapter, have a limited effect on holders in due course. While such an indorsement does not prevent a transferee from achieving the general status of a holder in due course, the indorsement gives notice to any transferee (except an intermediary or payor bank) of the limited purpose of the indorsement and requires the transferee to "pay or apply any value given by him for . . . the instrument consistently with the indorsement. . . ."

Notice of Defense Not Given[52]

A transferee's knowledge of any of the following facts will not of itself give the transferee notice of any defense or claim:

1. That the instrument is antedated or postdated.

2. That it was issued or negotiated in return for a promise not yet performed, or that it was accompanied by a separate agreement, unless the transferee also has notice that the promise is in default or that any other defense or claim has arisen under the separate agreement.

Example: M gave a six-month negotiable note to P for the purchase price of goods which were to be delivered by P to M in two weeks. The note so stated. P discounted the note at a bank and then failed to make the agreed delivery of goods.

The statement in the note, that it was given for goods to be delivered in the future, would not interfere with negotiability, and would not give the bank any notice that P intended to or would default in making the future delivery.

3. That an incomplete instrument has been completed, unless the transferee also has notice that it has been completed in excess of authority.

4. That there has been a default in the payment of interest on the instrument.

5. That any party has signed for the accommodation of another.

6. That the transfer of the instrument is by a qualified ("without recourse") indorsement.

7. That a transferee pays somewhat less than the face amount for transfer of the instrument. If what the transferee pays is considerably less than the face amount, he may have to explain the circumstances of

[52] U.C.C. Sec. 3-304.

the transfer. However, if the circumstances show no bad faith or notice of defenses, he can still qualify as a holder in due course.

Example: An agent for P Company of New York obtained from M, a feed retailer in Arkansas, an order for a specified number of sacks of feed, for a total price of $750, payable as provided in four notes which M signed. The written order dated March 21, was sent to P Company together with the four negotiable notes for the purchase price. The notes, all signed by M, named P Company as payee; each note was for $187.50, payable the first of the following July, August, September, and October, respectively. On March 28 P Company shipped the feed. On March 29, as was P Company's frequent practice in order to obtain funds for current expenses, P Company indorsed and transferred all of the notes to H bank of New York, receiving a $300 credit which P Company thereafter used in the ordinary course of its business. When the goods arrived several days later, M discovered that the shipment did not comply with his order and refused to accept delivery. When P Company refused to permit return of the feed, it was sold by the railroad which held the money for whoever claimed it. M refused to pay the notes, and in October the bank sued on all four of the notes. M's defense was that the goods did not conform to the contract, and that H Bank, paying only $300 for notes totaling $750, was not a holder in due course. Officials of the bank testified that the bank discounted a number of notes for P Company in the ordinary course of business, that the amount paid was governed largely by financial reports on the makers, and that M's notes were the only ones to be dishonored out of all of the notes which the bank had previously discounted for P Company.

The bank was entitled to judgment against M for $750 plus interest.

Part 5   DEFENSES

Whether or not an instrument is negotiable is primarily of importance only if 1) some defense is raised, and 2) the claimant is a holder in due course or a person with such rights. If the payee is attempting to collect, and is not himself a holder in due course (possible but not common), he has no better right to collect on a negotiable instrument than on one that is nonnegotiable.[53]

By definition, a holder in due course must receive an instrument without notice of any defense which may exist. If a defense actually exists, therefore, the holder in due course must necessarily be a remote rather than an immediate party to the transaction which gave rise to the defense. Persons who deal directly with each other are termed immediate parties, while those not dealing directly with each other are remote parties. Suppose that M signs and gives P a note naming P as payee;

[53] U.C.C. Sec. 3-302.

P indorses and delivers the note to A who in turn indorses and delivers it to B. This series of transactions can be diagrammed as follows:

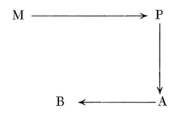

P is an immediate party to M, as likewise is A to P, and B to A; both A and B are remote parties as to M, and B is a remote party as to P.

Most of the contract defenses which may be asserted against an immediate party or against a remote party who does not have the rights of a holder in due course, are cut off when a negotiable instrument is transferred to a holder in due course. Such defenses are commonly referred to as "personal." Some defenses, however, remain and are effective even against a holder in due course. These are often called "real" or "absolute" defenses. Real defenses are of two general types, 1) those involving a lack of contractual intent, and 2) those involving certain aspects of public policy.

LACK OF CONTRACTUAL INTENT

It should be emphasized at the outset that not all situations involving a lack of contractual intent operate as real defenses. In general, when a holder in due course is suing the maker or drawer of a negotiable instrument, the defendant has a real defense if two conditions are both present: 1) the contract evidenced by the writing upon which the holder is suing was not—at least in that form—entered into by the defendant, and also 2) the contract is not the result of any negligence of the defendant or of any other conduct on his part which as a matter of policy is deemed sufficient to make him liable to an innocent holder. The most common fact situations in which a defendant can show that he did not intend to make the contract upon which he is being sued can be classified in the following way:

1. The signature of the defendant from whom the holder is claiming is neither genuine nor authorized. Such situations can be further subdivided as follows:[54]

a) *Forgery.* Clearly a defendant who never signed an instrument should have no liability on the instrument even to a holder in due course—unless the defendant's negligence substantially contributed

[54] U.C.C. Secs. 3-403, 3-404, 3-406.

to the successful making of his forged signature. In that case, it is only fair that the holder in due course should prevail over the negligent defendant. The most obvious example of such negligence is a failure to exercise proper precautions for the safekeeping of a signature stamp or plate.

b) *Lack of Agency Authority.* Suppose that a holder in due course is suing M on a note which is signed, "M. Martin, by A. Adams, his agent." M would not be liable unless A had authority to sign the instrument, and the holder would have the burden of proving A's authority. A person asked to buy such commercial paper should usually hesitate until he is shown a power of attorney expressly authorizing the agent to sign commercial paper.

2. Although the defendant's signature is genuine, he did not intend to make the contract upon which the holder is suing. This general situation can be further subdivided into several fact situations, of which the most common are the following:

a) *Nondelivery.*[55] Suppose that after writing and signing a promissory note, the maker put the note in his own pocket. Usually the maker does not manifest an intent to make the contract stated in the note until he delivers the note for the purpose of giving effect to it. If the payee named in the note should steal it from the maker, the payee would certainly have no right to collect on the note. However, should the note be transferred to a holder in due course, the law feels as a matter of policy that as between the innocent holder and the innocent maker who voluntarily signed the note, the holder in due course should have the better right. Nondelivery of an instrument therefore is a personal defense, cut off when the instrument gets into the hands of a holder in due course.

b) *Mistake as to Contents.*[56] Sometimes a defendant will assert that at the time he signed and delivered an instrument, he was ignorant of its true contents and had no intent to make the contract actually stated in the instrument. However, the innocent holder of an instrument is certainly justified in assuming that the signer knew and intended what he was signing. As between the signer and a holder in due course, therefore, it is clearly better policy to prefer the holder— except in the unusual case when the signer had no reasonable opportunity to know the character or terms of the instrument. Thus the fact that the signer was mistaken as to the contents of the instrument is usually a personal defense. The signer has a real defense only if he was completely free from negligence, as for example: 1) if unable to read, the signer took due precautions to have the paper read to him and

[55] U.C.C. Sec. 3-305.
[56] *Ibid.*

it was misread; or 2) if through sleight of hand sufficiently skillful to deceive a reasonable person, another paper was substituted for the paper the signer had examined and intended to sign.

c) *Alteration.*[57] In some cases, after an instrument has been completed and delivered, it is fraudulently changed in some way so that it reads differently from what the signer intended. If the signer was not negligent, he is not liable for the instrument as changed; the only right a holder in due course has is to enforce the instrument as it was originally written. On the other hand, if the signer's negligence materially aided in making the alteration possible, he is liable to a holder in due course for the instrument in its changed form. Possible situations include the following:

1) *Change in nature or contents by cutting or tearing off a portion of paper.* In a few cases, nonnegotiable forms have been dishonestly designed so that if a portion is cut off, the remainder will be a signed negotiable instrument. Only if the signer, through the exercise of reasonable care, could foresee that such a separation would be possible, would he be negligent in signing—and consequently liable to a holder in due course for the instrument in its changed form.

Example: P, a "city-slicker," entered into an agreement with M, a farmer, appointing M as an agent to sell certain goods in his rural community, and agreeing to ship a stated quantity of the goods to M for him to sell. The arrangement was that anytime after a six-month period, when the receipts from M's sales totaled $250, M was to pay $125 to P and retain the remainder of the $250 as his profit. To evidence the agreement, P filled in a printed negotiable note form for $125, making it due in six months and naming himself as payee, and asked M to sign. M refused until the agreed condition was added. P thereupon wrote along the left margin, "Only payable after profits amount to $250," and M then signed. Later P cut off the portion of the left margin upon which the condition was written and negotiated the note to a holder in due course. P disappeared, never having shipped any goods to M. After expiration of the six-month period, M refused to pay and the holder in due course sued M.

The court held that the holder in due course could collect because M was careless. The court pointed out[58] that M was obliged, ". . . to guard not only himself but the public against frauds and alterations, by refusing to sign negotiable paper made in such a form as to admit of fraudulent practices upon them, with ease and without ready detection."

2) *Alteration of certain words or figures.* It is certainly unwise, and possibly negligent for a person to write a check on other than safety paper when check forms printed on safety paper are readily

[57] U.C.C. Sec. 3-407.
[58] *Zimmerman* v. *Rote,* 75 Pa. 188 (1872).

available, or to write any type of commercial paper with an ordinary pencil.

d) *Unauthorized Completion.* This fact situation arises when a maker or drawer signs an incomplete instrument which, afterwards, someone else completes in a manner different from the signer's intent and then negotiates to a holder in due course. Such situations can be further subdivided as follows:

1) *Instrument voluntarily delivered.* Sometimes a maker or drawer will deliver a signed instrument to a payee with obvious blanks, either because the signer negligently overlooks the blanks or because he trusts the payee to fill in the blanks properly. In either case, when the blanks are filled in differently from the signer's intent, it seems fair to prefer a holder in due course (or innocent drawee bank) over the signer.

Example: Using a printed form, P prepared for M's signature a one-year negotiable note for $100, naming P as payee. When M signed the note, the amount was stated in the following way:
"_____ One Hundred _____ Dollars"
Later P added "and fifty" in the space between the written word "hundred" and the printed word, "Dollars," and transferred the note to a holder in due course.

Upon maturity of the note the holder in due course sued and recovered the full $150 from M. Although P filled in the note form, M by signing became the obligor of the note and responsible for leaving the blank which made the alteration possible. M should have drawn a line both before and after the words "One hundred."

Example: M signed and delivered to P a negotiable note for $8, naming P as payee. Later P raised the amount to $80 by adding a "0" after the numeral "8" and a "y" at the end of the word "Eight."

A court held under similar circumstances that M had used sufficient care, noting that few people write words and figures so closely together for it to be impossible to add a single figure or letter. Therefore since M was free from negligence, the holder in due course could collect no more than $8 from M.

Example: On June 1 M signed and delivered to P a six-month negotiable note naming P as payee. M inadvertently neglected to date the note. (This impliedly authorized P or any holder to fill in the correct date.) P fraudulently filled in the previous February 1 as the date of the note and on June 15 negotiated the note to a holder in due course.

The holder in due course could collect from M on August 1.

2) *Instrument not delivered.*[59] Sometimes a maker or drawer will sign a blank note or check intending that his agent will complete and use the instrument in a certain way at some future time, and then

[59] U.C.C. Sec. 3-115.

before completion, the instrument is stolen, filled in, and negotiated to a holder in due course or paid by an innocent drawee bank. The defense of lack of delivery is a personal defense; so also is the defense of unauthorized completion. Accordingly the authors of the Code feel that a defense consisting of both of these together should also be classified as a personal defense. In support of this conclusion the authors of the Code argue that since an innocent party relies on the genuine signature of the maker or drawer, any loss should fall on such a signer, whose conduct in signing blank paper made the loss possible.

PUBLIC POLICY

In the interest of overall public policy, the legislatures and courts have concluded that certain instruments should not be enforceable even by holders in due course. The chief situations which can be classified in this way are, in the language of the Code,

> (a) infancy, to the extent that it is a defense to a simple contract; and
> (b) such other incapacity, or duress, or illegality of the transtion, as renders the obligation of the party a nullity . . .[60]

Lack of Contractual Capacity

Whatever defense the law of a particular state accords to a minor in a nonnegotiable contract, the Code gives him for negotiable commercial paper, even as against a holder in due course. Most states permit a minor to disaffirm his contracts. In such states the fact that the maker of a negotiable instrument is a minor is therefore a real defense. As discussed in Chapter 6, some states restrict the protection given to a minor. For example, some states limit to some extent a minor's right to disaffirm if he is unable to fully restore what he received under the contract, or if he has fraudulently misrepresented his age. In such states the minor's defense to commercial paper would likewise be limited.

Illegality

The defense of illegality of contract is a real defense when the law of the particular state involved classifies the illegal transaction as wholly void or a nullity. Otherwise, illegality of contract will usually be only a personal defense, cut off by transfer to a holder in due course. Certain of the more common types of illegality are the following:

[60] U.C.C. Sec. 3-305.

Sunday Contract

If an instrument is dated, a holder receives the instrument with notice of what a calendar will show as to that date, even though he does not consult a calendar at the time the instrument is transferred to him. If the date is a Sunday and the contract therefore is illegal under the law of the particular state involved, the holder takes with notice that it is a Sunday contract, and thus will not be a holder in due course. If a signer actually signed and delivered an instrument on a Sunday but inserted a weekday date on the instrument, the signer's defense that his contract was actually an illegal Sunday contract is a personal defense, good against an immediate party but cut off as to a holder in due course.

Gambling

Many statutes which prohibit gambling expressly declare that any instrument given to pay a gambling debt is wholly void. Under such a statute, therefore, the fact that an instrument was given in payment of a gambling debt is a real defense.

Usury

If a usurious rate of interest appears on the face of an instrument, a transferee takes with notice of the usury and is not a holder in due course. For example, suppose that a state statute prescribes 6 percent a year as the maximum rate of interest that can legally be charged and collected (with some exceptions, such as loans by licensed money lenders). If a note, signed and payable in such a state, does not come under one of the exceptions and expressly provides for interest at the rate of 10 percent a year, any holder takes with notice of the usurious rate. On the other hand, if the usurious interest is merged into the principal amount payable and cannot be detected from the face of the instrument, a transferee has no notice of the usury.

Example: P (not a licensed money lender) loans M $1,000 and M signs and delivers to P the following instrument: "[Date]. One year after date I promise to pay P. Porter or order $1,200. (signed) M. Martin."

Assuming that the maximum interest rate in the state in question is 6 percent a year, $200 is usurious interest. However, the usury is concealed; it is not apparent from the face of the note.

The statutes of each state determine what effect usury will have on the enforceability of a contract. The principal types of statutes may be classified as follows:

1. Some statutes declare that the instrument is void. Under such

a statute even a holder in due course can collect nothing from the obligor.

2. Some statutes declare that the usurious portion of the instrument is void. This is a *partial* real defense. The holder in due course can collect the principal of the debt and interest at the lawful rate.

3. Some statutes do not specify whether usurious instruments are void, or otherwise refer to holders in due course. Courts in such states conflict as to the effect of concealed usury.

4. Some statutes declare usury not collectible but expressly provide that usury is no defense against a holder in due course. If the preceding example (involving a $1,200 one-year note for a $1,000 loan) occurred under such a statute, P would have a right to collect $1,060, the principal of the obligation plus lawful interest; a holder in due course could collect the full $1,200 from M.

Compounding a Crime

A payment or a promise to pay someone so that he will conceal evidence or keep quiet about the commission of a crime is called "compounding" the crime—compounding a misdemeanor if the suppressed crime is a misdemeanor, compounding a felony if the suppressed crime is a felony. Unless a state statute expressly makes instruments connected with compounding a crime void, this is a personal defense.

Duress

The degree of force used or threatened will vary in different cases. Forcing a person to sign at gunpoint would render a negotiable instrument a nullity or wholly void, and be a real defense, while threatening criminal prosecution of the signer or his near relative would be only a personal defense.

PERSONAL DEFENSES

Lack of consideration and failure of consideration are two of the most common personal defenses. As to these defenses, the Code provides:

> Want or failure of consideration is a defense as against any person not having the rights of a holder in due course . . . except that no consideration is necessary for an instrument or obligation thereon given in payment of or as security for an antecedent obligation of any kind.[61]

Some states have statutes declaring certain promises enforceable without consideration. An example is the Uniform Written Obligations

[61] U.C.C. Sec. 3-408.

Act (discussed in Chapter 5) under which a signed promise is enforceable without consideration, if it contains (in any form of language) an additional express statement that the signer intends to be legally bound. In regard to such statutes, the section of the Code just quoted, adds:

> Nothing in this section shall be taken to displace any statute outside this Act under which a promise is enforceable notwithstanding lack or failure of consideration.

Even under common-law rules certain promises are enforceable without consideration. A common example is a promise to a charity, generally enforceable without consideration after the charity acts in reliance on the promise (see Chapter 5). Although the Code does not expressly refer to such common-law rules, the authors of the Code explain that any equivalent or substitute for consideration is to be recognized just as in other contract cases.

Certain personal defenses have been previously referred to, including nondelivery and unauthorized completion of a genuinely signed instrument. Other important personal defenses include: set-off or counterclaim, misrepresentation inducing a person to enter into a contract, prior payment without notation on the instrument, and payment to the wrong party (illustrated in the example which follows).

Example: M signed and delivered to P a one-year negotiable note for $1,000, naming P as payee. P negotiated the note to a holder in due course who failed until after maturity to give M notice of the transfer. Upon the due date M paid P the amount of the note. P wrongfully accepted M's payment without disclosing the prior transfer of the note. Later the holder presented the note to M.

The holder could collect from M. M would in turn have a right to recover his erroneous payment from P, *if* P were still around with sufficient assets from which M could collect. As a matter of caution, a maker of a negotiable note should refuse to pay unless he sees the note. When a claimant maintains that he has lost the note, a careful maker should consider the desirability of insisting on obtaining a bond to protect himself if the note should turn up in the hands of a holder in due course. A maker paying a portion of an installment note should verify that the fact and amount of his payment are written on the note, and should insist on obtaining possession of the note when he pays it in full.

PERSON TAKING THROUGH A HOLDER IN DUE COURSE

Generally, once a defense is cut off by transfer to a holder in due course, the defense is not revived or reinstated when the instrument is later transferred to a person who is not a holder in due course. The Code states:

Transfer of an instrument vests in the transferee such rights as the transferor has therein, except that a transferee who has himself been a party to any fraud or illegality affecting the instrument or who as a prior holder had notice of a defense or claim against it cannot improve his position by taking from a later holder in due course.[62]

Example: Through fraudulent misrepresentation, P induced M to purchase certain goods. M's promise to pay for the goods was evidenced by a negotiable ten-day note for $500; the note was dated April 1 and named P as payee. On April 6, P negotiated the note to A who took as a holder in due course. On April 10, M discovered that he had been defrauded, offered to return the goods to P, and demanded return of his note. When P refused, M set the goods aside for the benefit of whoever claimed a right to them. On the due date, A requested payment from M. M refused and told A of the fraud. On April 15, A sold and transferred the note to B and on April 17, B sold and transferred the note to C.

1. Assume that C sued M on the note. Since C took the note when it was overdue, he was not a holder in due course; therefore he would have only the rights of B, the person from whom he obtained the note. B also (for the same reason) was not a holder in due course and so would have only the rights of A. As to A, who was a holder in due course, M's defense was cut off, so that A could have collected the full amount of the note from M. A could and did transfer to B his right to collect from M, and in turn C obtained A's rights. C therefore could collect the full amount of the note from M. An individual who takes through a holder in due course has all the rights of a holder in due course, except for the two cases of reacquisition referred to in the Code section just quoted.

2. Assume that C transferred the note back to P, and that P sued M. If P had never transferred the note at all, and upon M's refusal to pay, if P had sued M, M would have had a good defense—P's fraud would have prevented P from recovering. Being dishonestly guilty of fraud, P should not be able to improve his position by having the note pass through a holder in due course. Therefore if P received the note from C and sued M, P could not recover.

Example: Intending to make a gift, M signed and delivered to P a one-month negotiable note for $500; the note was dated April 1 and named P as payee. On April 3 P indorsed and made a gift of the note to A. On April 10 A learned that the note had been a gift to P. On April 15 A negotiated the note to B, a holder in due course. M changed his mind about the gift and refused to pay when B presented the note on its due date. Rather than go to the inconvenience of suing M, B sold the note back to A.

Since M's defense (lack of consideration) was cut off as to B, a holder in due course, B could have collected if he had sued M. However, A would come under the second restriction in the previously quoted Code provision, and thus could have no better right than was vested in him before he transferred the note to B. Because the transfer from P to A was a gift, A was not himself a holder

[62] U.C.C. Sec. 3-201.

in due course. Since A could not claim B's rights, A, therefore, could not recover from M.

Part 6 LIABILITY OF PARTIES

Numerous customs have gradually evolved among merchants over centuries of trading. These customs are of greater importance in the field of commercial paper than in any other branch of contract law. Probably the best illustration of the importance of customs in the formulation of commercial paper rules of law is found with respect to the liabilities of parties. Most persons who assume some liability on commercial paper do so by implication, as a matter of custom, rather than expressly in words. Of all the persons who commonly assume obligations on the millions of notes, drafts, and checks which are in constant circulation, only the makers of promissory notes expressly state the obligations they are undertaking. For example, suppose that a maker dates, signs, and delivers to a payee a negotiable one-year note for $1,000, which the payee indorses and sells to A who in turn indorses and sells the note to H. When the note matures, H as the holder clearly has a contract right against the maker—the note expressly states the terms of the maker's obligation. The holder also has contract rights against both the payee and A as indorsers, but the note itself says little or nothing about the indorsers' obligations. To learn the details of these obligations, the parties will have to look to the rules of law pertaining to commercial paper. In codifying the customs of merchants, the law "fills in" the terms of the indorsers' contracts. In a sense a person who uses commercial paper is making contracts by shorthand symbols. The details of the contracts are stated in the rules of law pertaining to commercial paper; these rules, therefore, can be likened to a shorthand dictionary which translates the symbols into meaningful language.

Parties who may be involved with commercial paper include the following:

1. *On a Note.* The usual parties are the maker, possibly one or more transferors, and the holder. The normal procedure is for the holder to present the note to the maker for payment. Should the maker fail or refuse to pay, the holder will usually have certain rights against prior transferors.

2. *On a Draft.* The usual parties are the drawer, the drawee on whom the draft is drawn (a drawee bank for a check), possibly one or more transferors, and the holder. Depending on the type of draft and also on the needs or wishes of the holder, some drafts are presented to the drawee only once—for payment—while some drafts are presented

at two different times—once for the drawee's written agreement to pay (called the drawee's acceptance), and later for the drawee's payment. In accepting a draft, the drawee will usually write across the face of the draft "Accepted [Date]" and sign it. A drawee bank usually indicates its acceptance and agreement to pay a check by writing "Certified" on the face of the check and signing it. A typical fact situation involving the acceptance of a draft is described in the example of the sixty-day draft on page 405.

The obligations undertaken by most parties to commercial paper can be classified into two principal types, promise liability and warranty liability, the chief details of which can be outlined in the following manner:

1. A promise liability arises from a promise to pay the amount of the instrument.

   a) The promise to pay may be unconditional, that is, not dependent on the occurrence of anything else. In the law of commercial paper, a person who makes such a promise is frequently referred to as a *primary* party. The Negotiable Instruments Law (the uniform statute which the Code supersedes) stated:

> The person "primarily" liable on an instrument is the person who by the terms of the instrument is absolutely required to pay the same. All other parties are "secondarily" liable.[63]

Although the Code continues the same classification of parties into primary and secondary parties, the authors of the Code feel that it is unnecessary to say any more by way of definition than that:

> "Secondary party" means a drawer or indorser.[64]

   b) The promise to pay may be conditioned on the occurrence of some event. Such a promisor is a *secondary* party. The three common types of conditional promises are:

1) A promise to pay if the payor does not pay when due. (A *payor* is the person who by the terms of the instrument is supposed or intended to pay the instrument—the maker in the case of a note, the drawee for a draft.)
2) A promise to pay if, after the payor fails to pay when due, the holder is unable to collect from the payor.
3) A promise to pay if:
   a) On due presentment to the payor,
   b) The payor dishonors by failing to pay or arrange to pay, and
   c) Notice is promptly given to the promisor.

[63] NIL Sec. 192.
[64] U.C.C. Sec. 3-102.

2. A warranty liability arises when an assertion as to certain facts is coupled with and obligation to pay damages which are sustained if the facts are not as asserted.

a) The warranty may be an absolute assertion that certain facts exist; or

b) The warranty may be an assertion merely that so far as the warrantor knows certain facts exist.

MAKER OF A NOTE[65]

The maker of a note expressly promises to pay the instrument. Observe that the maker's promise is not conditioned on anything else; in fact if the maker's promise were conditional, the instrument would be nonnegotiable. Thus it is not a condition for the maker's liability that the note be presented at some particular time or place.

GUARANTOR[66]

Guarantors of commercial paper are of two types, unconditional and conditional.

1. An unconditional guarantor promises to pay if the payor fails to pay when the instrument comes due. As soon as the instrument is due and the payor fails to pay, the holder can require the guarantor to pay, without first attempting to enforce the instrument against the payor. Usually a guarantor undertakes such an obligation by writing on the instrument "Payment guaranteed," or the like—and then, of course, signing the instrument.

2. The liability of a conditional guarantor depends on the existence and proof of certain facts stated or implied by the condition. The usual condition is that the holder be unable to collect from the payor when the instrument comes due. Usually this type of conditional guaranty promise is made by the signer writing "Collection guaranteed," or the like on the instrument. The condition is met or satisfied when any of the following occurs:

a) The holder obtains a judgment against the payor, has the sheriff go out to levy on property to satisfy the judgment, and the sheriff returns stating that he is unable to find any property upon which he can levy.

b) The payor becomes insolvent.

c) It otherwise appears to be fruitless for the holder to initiate a legal action to collect from the payor—as for example when the payor has absconded.

[65] U.C.C. Sec. 3-413.
[66] U.C.C. Sec. 3-416.

TRANSFEROR

Since the days of the early merchants (whose customs form the basis of the law of commercial paper) the ready transferability of commercial paper has been considered essential for the efficient conduct of business. Paper money is readily transferable because the government stands behind it, guaranteeing its value. There likewise must be some trustworthy guaranty of value if commercial paper is to be readily and repeatedly transferable. The credit of each transferor provides this necessary stability. Therefore, under the law of commercial paper, not only is the maker or drawer who initiates the paper liable, but also each transferor undertakes an obligation when he transfers the paper. This obligation can be subdivided into two basic types of liability, 1) a liability to a later transferee or holder, and 2) a liability to the payor of the instrument.

Liability to a Holder

A desirable flexibility for various types of business transactions is achieved through the recognition of different types of transferors, the three main types being, 1) an indorser who does not qualify his liability, 2) an indorser who qualifies his liability, and 3) a transferor without indorsement.

The nature and extent of the obligation which a transferor should be assumed to undertake when he transfers commercial paper is entirely a matter of policy, based primarily upon the following factors:

1. Ownership. As is discussed in Chapter 7, a seller of goods, through the act of selling, impliedly asserts that he owns the goods and has the right to sell them. Even if the goods had been stolen from their true owner and were purchased by the present seller from a reputable party, the seller's innocence would not reduce or change in any way his liability for this implied warranty of title. Likewise with commercial paper, a transferor is assumed to assert as a part of his transfer contract that he owns the paper and has the right to transfer it.

2. Genuineness. If a buyer however innocently pays for a purchase with counterfeit money, it is fair to require him to pay the seller a like amount in good money when the falsity of the counterfeit bill is later discovered. Certainly the transfer of commercial paper should carry no less an obligation. Therefore, as a matter of policy, an innocent transferee of commercial paper is assumed to warrant that the paper he transfers is in all respects what it seems to be—that is, neither forged nor altered.

3. Enforceability. When it comes to further liability after the basic requirements of ownership and genuineness are met, merchants have found it convenient, since early in the days of the transfer of commercial paper, to recognize both a standard (unqualified) and a substandard (qualified) level of responsibility.

a) *Unqualified.* If a transferor of commercial paper does not specify otherwise, he is assumed to intend to add his own credit to the paper in order to facilitate its transfer. Specifically he is assumed to warrant that the paper is legally enforceable against prior parties, and also he is assumed to agree that if with due diligence the transferee is unable to collect from the payor, the transferor will himself be liable for the face amount of the paper. This latter obligation is frequently referred to as the "indorser's promise."

b) *Qualified.* If they wish, the parties can specifically agree that, aside from the basic requirements of ownership and genuineness, the transferor will not be liable for the paper. This is usually accomplished through the use of a "without recourse" indorsement. Such a transferor must still act honestly. It is dishonest to transfer paper if the transferor knows that he himself could not legally enforce it. Therefore a qualified transferor is assumed to warrant that he knows of no fact which would prevent him from enforcing the contract of any prior party. If the qualified transferor knows of such a fact, his warranty is breached, even though he may be ignorant of the law and thus not actually aware that the fact would prevent him from enforcing the contract of a prior party.

4. Beneficiaries of a Transferor's Obligation. If a transferor indorses commercial paper, his credit presumably facilitates further transfer of the instrument to later transferees. A signing transferor is therefore liable to any later transferee of the paper. On the other hand, a person who transfers without signing is not adding as much of his credit to the transfer and is not in any way influencing later transfers. A nonsigning transferor therefore is liable to his immediate transferee only.

With respect to the order of liability of successive indorsers, the Code states:

> Unless they otherwise agree indorsers are liable to one another in the order in which they indorse, which is presumed to be the order in which their signatures appear on the instrument.[67]

Thus if the holder of an instrument has a right to collect from indorsers, and the instrument has been successively indorsed by A, B, and C, the holder can recover from any one of the three. If the holder recovers from B, B in turn can recover from A but not from C.

The rules of law which give effect to the foregoing policy factors can be summarized as 1) warranties to holders and 2) promises to holders.

---

[67] U.C.C. Sec. 3-414.

Warranties to Holders[68]

Unqualified Indorser	Qualified Indorser	Transferor Without Indorsement
An unqualified indorser, who receives consideration, warrants to his transferee and to any subsequent holder who receives the instrument in good faith:	A qualified indorser, who receives consideration, warrants to his transferee and to any subsequent holder who receives the instrument in good faith.	A transferor without indorsement, who receives consideration, warrants to his *transferee only* (and not to any subsequent holder) who receives the instrument in good faith:
1. That he has good title to the instrument, or represents a person with title, and that his transfer is otherwise rightful.	1. Same.	1. Same.
2. That all signatures are genuine or authorized.	2. Same.	2. Same.
3. That the instrument has not been materially altered.	3. Same.	3. Same.
4. That no defense of any prior party is good against him (i.e., against the person making the transfer).	4. That he has no knowledge of any facts which would prevent him from recovering from any prior party.	4. Same wording as the fourth warranty in the first (unqualified indorser) column.
5. That he has no knowledge of any insolvency proceeding involving the payor.	5. Same.	5. Same.

Example: On April 1, as a result of a session of poker involving M, P, and several other persons, it was determined that M owed P $500. To evidence this obligation, M dated and gave P the following note: "One month after date I promise to pay P. Porter or order $500. (signed) M. Martin." P indorsed the note "without recourse," and sold and delivered it to X. X in turn sold the note to Y, who sold and delivered it to H. X, Y, and H were successively holders in due course. On May 15, when H presented the note to M and requested payment, M refused to pay, correctly asserting that the note was an illegal gambling note. Neither H, X, nor Y had previously known of the illegality.

[68] U.C.C. Sec. 3-417.

1. Assume that both X and Y indorsed without qualification.

a) H sued Y. The fact that the note was given for gambling would be a real defense, good even against a holder in due course. Y warranted among other things that no defense of any prior party was good against him. If Y still had the note and sued M, Y could not have recovered. Since M had a defense good against Y, Y's warranty was breached and H could recover from Y. Y could in turn recover from X for the same reason.

b) H sued X. H could recover from X for the same reason as in Part 1(a) above.

2. Assume that neither X nor Y indorsed the note.

a) H sued Y. H could recover for the same reason as in Part 1 (a) above. Y could in turn recover from X.

b) H sued X. H could *not* recover. As a transferor without indorsement, X warranted to his immediate transferee, Y, that there were no defenses. X would be liable to Y for breach of this warranty but would not be liable to H.

3. Assume that both X and Y indorsed in the same way as P, that is, "Without recourse."

a) H sued Y. At the time of the transfer Y was unaware of the facts giving rise to M's defense. Therefore, the fourth warranty made by Y as a qualified indorser was not breached; none of the other warrants being breached, H could not recover from Y.

b) H sued X. H could not recover, for the same reason as in Part 3 (a) above.

c) H sued P. Since P was one of the participants in the poker game, P obviously knew of the facts which gave rise to M's defense. For breach of his warranty that he had no knowledge of any defense, P would be liable to H.

Promises to Holders[69]

While all three types of transferors (unqualified indorser, qualified indorser, and transferor without indorsement) are assumed to warrant certain facts and to be liable if the facts warranted are not true, only an unqualified indorser is assumed to undertake the additional obligation which is frequently called the "indorser's promise." By indorsing commercial paper, an unqualified indorser impliedly promises that he will pay the amount of the instrument to the holder, or to any subsequent indorser who takes it up, if three conditions are all met, namely: 1) due presentment, 2) dishonor, and 3) prompt notice of dishonor (and, if required, protest).

These conditions will be explained only briefly here; they are discussed more fully in Part 7 of this chapter, where also are mentioned some of the circumstances under which the conditions are waived

---

[69] U.C.C. Secs. 3-414, 3-501, 3-502.

or excused. With a time note, for example, "due presentment" means a request for payment made to the maker on the due date of the note. If the maker refuses or fails to pay, the note is considered as "dishonored." The holder must then give "prompt notice" to any prior indorser, telling him that the maker has dishonored the note. Notice is required to enable the notified person to preserve and enforce his rights against persons liable to him. For example, if the maker's financial condition is worsening, an indorser may wish to take the instrument up immediately (that is, to pay the holder to whom he is liable) and attempt to collect from the maker or start a lawsuit against him before the maker's finances become hopeless. Under the Code, protest is required as a condition for an indorser's liability only in the case of drafts drawn or payable outside the United States. If these three conditions are neither met, excused, nor waived, an indorser is not liable on his promise.

Example: M signed and delivered to P a negotiable note for $500, naming P as payee, due April 8 of a specified year. P sold, unqualifiedly indorsed, and delivered the note to A who sold, unqualifiedly indorsed, and delivered the note to H. Assume that the due date of the note was a Monday, a full business day for both H and M.

1. H made due presentment to M on April 8, and when M failed to pay, H promptly notified A and P. He could recover the face amount of the note from either A or P, since the conditions for each of the indorser's promises were met. If H recovered from A, A could in turn recover from P.

2. H presented the note to M on April 9, M failed to pay and H immediately notified A and P. Assuming that presentment on April 8 was neither excused nor waived, H could not recover from either A or P, because he failed to make due presentment.

LIABILITY TO A PAYOR

The person who by the terms of an instrument is intended to pay it—the maker of a note, the drawee of a draft—is frequently referred to as the payor. If a payor should unwittingly pay the wrong person or the wrong amount, and the recipient of the payment is himself innocent of any conscious wrongdoing, a very perplexing question arises as to whether the payor should have a right to recover the amount of his erroneous payment. The warranties which a transferor makes to a transferee or holder are no help in answering this question. After the maker (of a note) or the drawee (of a draft) pays an instrument, it is considered canceled or dead. Therefore, although the payor obtains possession of the instrument when he pays it, the payor is not treated as the holder of active commercial paper and cannot claim under any of the warranties which a transferor is assumed to make to a transferee or holder. Of course, if it were desirable for a payor to have the same rights as a transferee or holder, the warranty rules could be so written. However, as a matter of policy, there are sound reasons for treating the relationship between a payor and the party presenting an instrument for payment as quite different from the relationship between a transferee and a prior transferor. Different warranty rules have therefore been formulated stating just when a payor should be able to recover for an erroneous payment. The chief policy factors which have shaped these rules can be summarized in the following way:

1. Usually a person who innocently receives an erroneous payment will spend the money or otherwise change his position before the error is discovered; to require him to return the money would subject him to considerable inconvenience, and frequently would result in an actual loss for him—through forced liquidation of assets or through the expense of borrowing. Therefore, if no other factor is present to tip the scales in favor of the payor, it seems fair to hold that once a payor has paid an instrument he should have no right to require the recipient of the erroneous payment, or any prior transferor, to return the amount of the payment.

2. Suppose that after paying an instrument, the payor learns that one of the indorsements on the instrument is a forgery. As previously discussed in defining holders (Part 4 of this chapter), if an essential indorsement is forged, a later possessor of the instrument has no title to it. However innocent he may be, a person with no title to an instrument should have no right to retain any money received in exchange for the instrument. Therefore, if in reliance on a forged indorsement, a payor erroneously pays the wrong party, the payor should be able to recover the erroneous payment.

3. Suppose that after paying an instrument, the payor learns that the instrument has been cleverly altered (for example, the amount being raised) in such a manner that the alteration cannot be detected on ordinary examination. If the instrument is a note which the payor signed as maker, the payor is certainly in a better position than any other innocent person to know the terms of the obligation which he signed. Therefore, if the payor pays the note according to its altered terms, it is not fair to permit him to recover his excess payment from any other innocent party. On the other hand, if the instrument is a draft the drawee never previously saw the instrument, and is no more able than any other innocent party to detect the alteration. If the drawer used proper care in writing the instrument, the drawee cannot charge the excessive payment against the drawer. Therefore in the case of an altered draft it is fair to permit the drawee to recover the excess amount which he has unwittingly paid.

4. Suppose that after making payment, the payor learns that the

entire instrument is a forgery. If the instrument is a note, the alleged maker is certainly in a better position than any other innocent party to know what obligations he has undertaken and to determine whether the signature on the note is his own. With drafts (including checks), the important fact should be borne in mind that drawees will not pay drafts unless they have made suitable prior arrangements with the drawers. In making such an arrangement a drawee will either procure a sample of the drawer's signature or otherwise be familiar with his handwriting. Thus as between a drawee and other innocent parties, the drawee is in a better position to detect a forged draft (including a check). Therefore, it seems fair to hold that a payor who pays a forged instrument cannot recover his erroneous payment from any innocent party.

5. Even though a person is innocent and becomes a holder in due course at the time an instrument is transferred to him, if he later learns of a forgery or alteration, it will be dishonest for him to further transfer the instrument or to present it for payment without disclosing what he knows. For example, if a holder in due course, after learning that the note he is holding has been fraudulently altered from $100 to $500, nevertheless presents the note to the maker and demands and receives $500, the holder's dishonesty should enable the payor to recover the erroneous payment. Likewise, if a holder in due course learns that the check he holds is a complete forgery and nevertheless presents it to the drawee bank and receives payment before the bank detects the forgery; upon proving the holder's guilty knowledge, the bank can require him to return the money which the bank erroneously paid to him. Suppose, however, that the drawee bank had certified the check without detecting the forgery and the holder in due course thereafter acquired the check. As is more fully discussed later (in connection with the liability of a drawee), a drawee who accepts or certifies a check or other draft assumes a status exactly like that of the maker of a note. He undertakes a new, personal obligation, unconditionally promising to pay the instrument as it reads when he accepts it. The fact that the original draft is a forgery, or that it was fraudulently altered before the acceptance or certification, does not relieve the acceptor from this personal obligation to pay the amount of the instrument to any person who thereafter innocently acquires the instrument. Thus if a check had been fraudulently raised from $100 to $500, then certified by the drawee bank for $500, and then transferred to a holder in due course, the latter would have an absolute right to collect $500 from the drawee bank. Should the holder learn of the alteration before presenting the check, it might be dishonest for him to hurry to the bank and present the check without mentioning his knowledge. However, since he would already have an absolute right

to collect the full $500 from the bank, his dishonesty would be no reason for the bank to recover any of the excess payment from him.

The conclusions drawn from these various factors are expressed in the Code[70] as warranties made to or for the benefit of a payor. These warranties are assumed to be made 1) by any transferor (unqualified indorser, qualified indorser, or transferor without indorsement), 2) by the person who obtains the drawee's acceptance, if any, and 3) by the person who receives payment from the payor. The chief features of these warranties are summarized on p. 453.

Example: The payee of a negotiable $200 check sold, indorsed, and transferred the check to A who sold, indorsed, and transferred it to H. H received $200 for the check from the drawee bank. Both A and H were holders in due course and knew nothing about the fact stated below until after the bank paid. After making payment, the bank learned, for the reason stated below, that it could not charge the $200 payment against the drawer's account.

1. The bank learned that the drawer's signature was a forgery. The bank could not recover anything from either A or H.

2. The bank learned that the drawer had originally made the check out for $2, that the drawer was not careless in the way the check was made out, and that the payee had skillfully raised the check to $200. The bank could charge only $2 against the drawer's account and could recover from either A or H the $198 balance.

Example: R signed and delivered a negotiable check to P, naming P as payee. The check was stolen from P by a thief who forged a blank indorsement in P's name and transferred the check to A. A in turn sold and transferred the check to B who sold and transferred it to H. H received payment for the check from the drawee bank. H, A, and B were innocent takers for value, and had no notice of the forged indorsement until after the bank paid. Because of the forged payee's indorsement the bank could not charge the payment against R's account. The bank sued B.

Whether B was an unqualified indorser or a qualified indorser, or instead transferred with no indorsement at all, he warranted in favor of the payor that he had good title. B could not have title because the payee's indorsement was forged; therefore, the bank could collect from B. Instead of collecting from B, the bank could collect for the same reason from either H or A.

DRAWER

Different from a note in which the maker expressly promises that he will pay a stated sum of money, all that a draft expressly states is the drawer's order that someone else—the drawee—is to pay. Although a drawer does not expressly state any obligation on his own part, it has

[70] U.C.C. Sec. 3-417.

Notes	Drafts (Including Checks)	
	Not accepted (or certified) before acquired by warrantor	*Accepted (or certified) before acquired by warrantor*

1. Title (absolute warranty). At the time a person transfers an instrument or receives payment (or obtains acceptance if the instrument is a draft) he warrants to the payor or acceptor that he has good title or represents a person with good title.

2. Alteration (limited warranty). At the time a person transfers a note or receives payment, he warrants to the payor that he has no knowledge that the instrument has been materially altered.	2. Alteration (absolute warranty). At the time a person transfers a draft, obtains acceptance, or receives payment, he warrants to the acceptor or payor that the instrument has not been materially altered.	2. Alteration (limited warranty). At the time a person transfers an accepted draft or receives payment, he warrants to the payor that he has no knowledge that the instrument has been materially altered *after* acceptance. He assumes no obligation as to alteration *before* acceptance.

3. Forgery (limited warranty). At the time the warrantor transfers the instrument or receives payment (or obtains acceptance if the instrument is a draft) he warrants to the payor (or acceptor) that he has no knowledge that the signature of the maker or drawer is unauthorized.	3. Forgery (limited warranty). At the time a person transfers an accepted draft or receives payment, he warrants to the payor that he has no knowledge that the signature of the *acceptor* is forged. He assumes no obligation respecting either the genuiness of the drawer's signature, or his knowledge concerning its genuineness.

been considered sound policy, since the days of the early merchants, to hold that by issuing a draft and not expressly stating otherwise, a drawer impliedly promises that if the drawee fails to pay when the draft is diligently presented, the drawer will himself pay the amount for which the draft is made out. At an early date this policy view as to a drawer's implied promise became a rule of law, which is continued in the modern law of the Code as follows:

> The drawer engages that upon dishonor of the draft and any necessary notice of dishonor or protest he will pay the amount of the draft to the holder or to any indorser who takes it up. The drawer may disclaim this liability by drawing without recourse. . . .[71]

As to the conditions of due presentment and prompt notice of dishonor, the Code further states:

> Where without excuse any necessary presentment or notice of dishonor is delayed beyond the time when it is due . . . any drawer . . . the acceptor of a draft payable at a bank, or the maker of a note payable at a bank, who, because the drawee or payor bank becomes insolvent during the delay, is deprived of funds maintained with the drawee or payor bank to cover the instrument, may discharge his liability by written assignment to the holder of his rights against the drawee or payor bank in respect of such funds, but such drawer, acceptor or maker is not otherwise discharged. . . .[72] [Punctuation added.]

In the provision just quoted, the Code is saying that while a drawer will be assumed to make the same promise as an unqualified indorser— to pay if the conditions of due presentment, dishonor, and prompt notice of dishonor (and protest if necessary) are met—a drawer, unlike an indorser, is relieved from liability by a holder's failure to meet all of these conditions only to the extent that the drawer is injured by the holder's delay. To understand the policy reason for this distinction between the liability of a drawer and the liability of an unqualified indorser, it will be helpful to consider briefly the commercial environment of notes and drafts, comparing the respective objectives of 1) makers (of notes), 2) unqualified indorsers, and 3) drawers (of drafts).

1) *Makers.* The typical maker of a note obtains something of value in exchange for his note. The parties intend that the maker shall pay for what he has received and the instrument so states. To relieve the maker from liability if the holder should fail to make due presentment would result in gratuitously giving the maker what he received upon issuing the note, with no obligation to pay for it. This would be quite unfair. Therefore, it is sound policy (and is the law) that the maker is *not* discharged from liability by lack of due presentment. Instead, the maker's liability continues for the full period of the statute of limitations.

2) *Unqualified Indorsers.* Although a typical unqualified indorser receives something of value when he indorses and transfers an instrument, what he receives is not clear profit because usually he paid something

[71] U.C.C. Sec. 3-413.
[72] U.C.C. Sec. 3-502.

when he obtained the instrument. The difference between what the indorser has paid and what he receives, frequently quite small, is all that the indorser would gain if he were relieved from his indorser's promise. Furthermore, the debt which the instrument evidences is usually not the indorser's own debt. By his indorser's promise, the indorser is guaranteeing that the debt of another person will be paid upon maturity. This is a conditional rather than a general guaranty. If an indorser were undertaking the greater risk of a general guarantor, he would usually want to be paid something additional for the risk. Consequently, it would not be fair to consider an unqualified indorser as a general guarantor, liable without notice for the full period of the statute of limitations. It is sound policy, therefore (and is the law), that an indorser *is* discharged from liability on his indorser's promise if the holder fails to make due presentment and to give prompt notice of dishonor.

3) *Drawers.* A typical drawer bears a much closer resemblance to the maker of a note than he does to an unqualified indorser. Usually the drawer is buying something with his draft or check. The payment ordered by the draft involves the drawer's money, not paid directly as in the note, but indirectly through the drawee who is to pay out of funds which he is holding for the drawer. If the drawer is still able to obtain these funds from the drawee, and nevertheless is relieved from liability when the holder fails to make due presentment, then the drawer would be gratuitously receiving what he bought with his draft, with no obligation to pay for it. On the other hand, to hold that the drawer's liability for the drawee's failure to pay should continue over the entire period of the statute of limitations, would unfairly require him to assume too extensive a risk as to the drawee's financial status. Therefore, it is sound policy (and is the law) that the drawer's liability on his draft is keyed both to the holder's diligence and to the drawee's financial condition. Upon the same reasoning, the acceptor of a draft which is expressly made payable at a bank, and the maker of a note expressly payable at a bank, will be relieved from absolute liability by the combination of the holder's lack of diligence and the insolvency of the bank.

As shaped by the foregoing policy factors, the promise which the drawer of a draft is assumed to make can be summarized as follows: The drawer promises that if the drawee fails to pay the draft, the drawer owes some sort of obligation, either to the holder or to any indorser who himself pays the draft. If the holder makes due presentment to the drawee and gives prompt notice of the drawee's dishonor, the drawer's obligation is to pay the amount of the draft. However, if the holder misses on either due presentment or prompt notice of dishonor, then:

1. If the drawer *is* prejudiced by the delay, the drawer's only obligation is to assign to the holder (or indorser who takes the instrument up)

the contract rights, in the amount of the draft, which the drawer has against the insolvent drawee. A drawer would be prejudiced by a delay if 1) the drawee became insolvent during the delay, and 2) thus deprived the drawer of ready access to the funds which he was maintaining with the drawee to cover the draft.

2. If the drawer is *not* prejudiced by the delay, the drawer remains fully obligated to pay the amount of the draft.

DRAWER'S CRIMINAL LIABILITY

All states have criminal statutes which forbid and prescribe punishments for the dishonest passing of bad checks. These statutes (which have been more fully discussed in Chapter 3) afford a powerful weapon to assist in recovering from a drawer when the drawee bank "bounces" the drawer's check back to a holder, with a notation that the drawer has insufficient funds for payment of the check.

DRAWEE

ACCEPTED DRAFT

With the concept of acceptance or acquiescence in another's proposal being so basic to the law of contracts, it is confusing to nonlawyers that the word "acceptance" is applied to acquiescence in three different types of situations—to the acceptance of an offer in the general field of contracts (see Chapter 4), to the acceptance of goods in connection with the sales of goods (see Chapter 16), and in the present chapter to the acceptance of a draft. In regard to the later type of acceptance, the Code states:

> Acceptance is the drawee's signed engagement to honor the draft as presented. It must be written on the draft, and may consist of his signature alone. . . .[73]

To be effective, the acceptance must be 1) in writing, *and* 2) on the draft itself. Although a drawee is deemed to accept a draft when he writes nothing more than his name on the face of the draft, a drawee will frequently write across the face of the draft, "Accepted [Date]," and then sign his name. In accepting a check, the drawee bank usually uses the term "certified";[74] this constitutes an acceptance of the check when signed by an authorized agent of the bank.

Example: R. Roger, an auto dealer in a small town in Ohio, had a checking account in the Edwards Bank of that town. On August 31, while on a trip to Michigan, R purchased a car from the manufacturer, P. Porter, and offered to pay by means of his personal check, which named P as payee and

[73] U.C.C. Sec. 3-410.
[74] U.C.C. Sec. 3-411.

was drawn for $1,500 on the E Bank. P telephoned the E Bank and, talking to the vice president, asked if R had sufficient funds on hand to cover the $1,500 check. After verifying from the records, the vice president replied that R had plenty of funds to take care of the check and said that the bank would hold that amount for P and mark the records accordingly. P asked if the conversation should be confirmed by a telegram. The vice president replied "No, send the check through in the regular way and we will take care of it." The vice president then wrote on a slip of paper, which he placed with the records of R's account "Check of R. Roger to P. Porter for $1,500. Hold this amount until check comes in." On September 4 R was adjudged insolvent and the court appointed a receiver for his business. On September 5, E Bank telegraphed P, "Roger check will not be paid. Receiver appointed." However, the check was in banking channels on the way for collection and on September 6 was presented to E Bank. The bank refused payment, having applied the entire balance in R's account, $2,159, to payment of R's note, held by the bank. P sued E Bank.

1. The Ohio Appellate Court held that P could not recover.[75] The bank's promise was not enforceable because it was not in writing.

2. Other facts being the same, suppose that the phone call had been confirmed by the bank sending to P the following telegram: "We will pay R. Roger's check for $1,500, naming P. Porter as payee. (signed) Edwards Bank." Under the Code this would still not constitute a certification of the check, since an acceptance or certification must not only be in writing, but also must be on the instrument itself. The authors of the Code point out that a drawee may still be held liable on general contract principles or for tort if deliberate misrepresentation is involved. However, if P sued E Bank on its telegraphed promise to pay, E Bank would of course raise the defense of lack of consideration. Enforceability of the promise would then depend upon whether, under the law of contracts, P's reliance would be sufficient as an equivalent of consideration.

Certified Checks

Unless otherwise agreed, a bank owes no duty either to its depositor or to any other person to certify the depositor's check.[76] Usually, however, a bank will comply with a depositor's request and certify his check as a service to him. If it wishes, a bank may certify at the request of the payee or of some other holder. Though not of common occurrence, the following are typical situations in which a holder might desire to procure certification:

1. The holder does not himself have a bank account and wishes to retain the check as a safe way to carry the money it represents, but is not content to rely on the drawer's liability alone.

[75] *Reo Motor Car Co.* v. *Western Bank & Trust Co.*, 48 Ohio App. 387, 194 N.E. 392 (1934).
[76] U.C.C. Sec. 3-411.

2. The holder is a stranger. The drawee bank refuses to cash the check until the holder obtains proper identification. While obtaining the identification, the holder wants in effect to freeze the money in the account and requests the bank to certify the check.

3. The payee inadvertently neglected to indorse the check when he sold and transferred it to the person who is presenting it. When the absence of the indorsement is noticed, the person presenting the check requests the bank to certify it so that the amount will be frozen in the drawer's account while the necessary indorsement is being obtained.

If a bank certifies a check at the request of the drawer, the drawer's liability continues. On the other hand, for a bank to certify a check at the request of a holder is almost the same as the holder obtaining the cash and redepositing it. It is a new arrangement between the holder and the bank, not contemplated by the drawer or prior indorsers, and the drawer and any prior indorsers are relieved from liability—except as to a later holder in due course who takes without notice of who procured the certification.[77]

Stopping Payment. A drawer has no right to stop payment on a certified check, regardless of whether the certification was procured by the drawer or by a holder. However, although not obligated by a drawer's stop payment request, a bank may be willing to cooperate with the drawer and refuse payment upon presentment of the check. There seems to be nothing in the Code requiring a change from the view taken by many courts prior to the Code, namely that:

1. If the certification was procured by someone other than the drawer, the bank is absolutely liable to the holder who is presenting the check.

2. If the certification was procured by the drawer, the bank has against the person who presents the check the same defenses the drawer would have if that person were suing the drawer. Thus if a certified check is given in payment for goods which the payee defrauds the drawer into buying, the payee could not recover from the drawer and he likewise cannot recover from the bank on its certification. On the other hand, if the check passes to a holder in due course, the drawer's defense is cut off, and, therefore, the bank would be absolutely liable to the holder in due course. A bank's refusal to pay a certified check will frequently lead to a lawsuit against the bank, with its resulting expenses and costs. The bank may require a drawer to promise to idemnify the bank for all such expenses and costs, before the bank will comply with the drawer's stop payment request.

[77] U.C.C. Sec. 3-411. The Code protects holders in due course from any discharge of liability not apparent on the instrument, by providing: "No discharge of any party provided by this Article is effective against a subsequent holder in due course unless he has notice thereof when he takes the instrument." (Sec. 3-602.)

Unaccepted Draft

Since checks are by far the most numerous type of draft, much of the following discussion will apply particularly to checks. A check or other draft is an order to the drawee to make a certain payment. Usually before writing checks or other drafts, a drawer will make a suitable arrangement with the drawee for the latter to honor the drafts. If the drawee breaches this agreement by refusing to honor a particular draft, the drawee will be liable to the drawer for damages. In respect to a bank's liability, the Code provides:

> A payor bank is liable to its customer for damages proximately caused by the wrongful dishonor of an item. When the dishonor occurs through mistake liability is limited to actual damages proved. If so proximately caused and proved damages may include damages for an arrest or prosecution of the customer or other consequential damages.[78]

Even though a drawee may owe an obligation to the *drawer* to pay a certain draft, a drawee who has not accepted the draft has no obligation on the draft itself to any *holder*. As the Code states:

> A check or other draft does not of itself operate as an assignment of any funds in the hands of the drawee available for its payment, and the drawee is not liable on the instrument until he accepts it.[79]

When a drawee pays a draft, he can charge the payment to the drawer only if the payment is made strictly in accordance with the drawer's order or with an order for which the drawer is responsible.

Rescinding a Draft

Sometimes after issuing a draft, a drawer later decides to countermand the order contained in the draft and notifies the drawee not to pay. Particularly in regard to checks, the Code provides:

> A customer may by order to his bank stop payment of any item payable for his account but the order must be received at such time and in such manner as to afford the bank a reasonable opportunity to act on it prior to any action by the bank with respect to the item [such as paying or certifying] . . .
> An oral order is binding upon the bank only for fourteen calendar days unless confirmed in writing within that period. A written order is effective for only six months unless renewed in writing.[80]

A bank usually provides an appropriate "stop-payment" form to be filled in and signed by a drawer when he desires to stop payment on a

[78] U.C.C. Sec. 4-402.
[79] U.C.C. Sec. 3-409.
[80] U.C.C. Sec. 4-403.

check. Frequently such a form will contain a provision shortening the effective duration of the order to some reasonable period less than the statutory six months. Such a provision is effective if agreed to and signed by the drawer.

Some stop-payment forms also include a provision attempting to relieve the bank from liability if it carelessly overlooks the drawer's stop-payment order and pays the check anyway. In many states the courts have declared such a provision invalid, and the Code does likewise.[81] However, the Code gives a drawee bank certain rights to recover if it pays a check upon which payment had been stopped. The Code provides:

> If a payor bank has paid an item over the stop payment order of the drawer . . . to prevent unjust enrichment and only to the extent necessary to prevent loss to the bank by reason of its payment of the item, the payor bank shall be subrogated to the rights
> (a) of any holder in due course on the item against the drawer . . . ; and
> (b) of the payee or any other holder of the item against the drawer . . . either on the item or under the transaction out of which the item arose; and
> (c) of the drawer . . . against the payee or any other holder of the item with respect to the transaction out of which the item arose.[82]

Example: Through fraudulent misrepresentations P induced R to purchase certain goods for which R gave P a check for $200, the amount of the purchase price. Discovering that he had been defrauded, R stopped payment on his check, notified P that the transaction was canceled, and offered to return the goods to P. When P refused the tender of the goods, R put them aside and notified P that they were being held for him. In disregard of R's stop-payment order the drawee bank paid the amount of the check when it was presented. (The bank's disregard of the stop-payment order might be either inadvertent or deliberate.)

1. The person to whom the drawee bank paid the $200 was a holder in due course. If the bank had refused to pay, the holder in due course could have recovered the $200 from R. Having paid the holder in due course, the bank would succeed to his rights against R. Therefore, the bank could charge the payment against R's account. (In dissatisfaction with the bank's service, R might close his account, but that, of course, would not affect the bank's previously acquired rights against R.)

2. The person to whom the drawee bank paid the $200 was P. If R had paid P the $200 in cash, R could have recovered the payment upon canceling the contract and returning or offering to return the goods. Having paid the $200 to P, the bank would succeed to R's rights. The bank could take over the goods and upon tendering them to P, recover the $200 paid to P.

[81] U.C.C. Sec. 4-103.
[82] U.C.C. Sec. 4-407.

Overdraft[83]

If a drawee pays a draft in accordance with the drawer's direction, the drawee has the right to charge the payment to the drawer. Particularly with checks, a drawee bank will sometimes, either inadvertently or deliberately, pay a check drawn for a larger amount than the drawer has in his account. The account is then said to be overdrawn. The drawer might argue that the bank should not pay a check for more than the balance in his account. The bank has a decisive answer: the check states no condition, it does not say to pay only out of the drawer's account; therefore in paying the check the bank is doing only what the drawer in his check directs the bank to do. An overdraft is in the nature of an irregular loan made by the drawee bank at the request of the drawer; therefore, the bank clearly should have the right to recover the amount of the overdraft from the drawer.

Suppose that (as is usual) a drawee bank refuses to pay an overdrawn check. As previously pointed out, unless a drawee bank has certified a check, the bank has no liability to the holder even if the drawer's account exceeds the amount of the check. Certainly, therefore, the bank owes no duty to the holder of an uncertified check if the payment would overdraw the account. The holder will, of course, have a right to collect from the drawer. To expedite collection of a portion of the obligation, especially if the drawer is "slippery" or in financial difficulty, the holder may ask the bank to pay him whatever is in the account. Since the bank owes no duty at all to the holder of an uncertified check, it need not cooperate. However, the bank may, *if it wishes*, help the holder by making a partial payment and marking the check accordingly. Or the parties may accomplish the same result in a needlessly roundabout way, the holder making a sufficient deposit to bring the drawer's account up to the amount of the check and then presenting the check for payment.

Death or Incompetence of Drawer

Sometimes a drawer dies or is adjudged incompetent while checks which he has drawn are still outstanding. The Code states:

> Neither death nor incompetence of a customer revokes . . . [a payor bank's] authority to accept [or] pay . . . until the bank knows of the fact of death or of an adjudication of incompetence and has reasonable opportunity to act on it. . . . Even with knowledge a bank may for ten days after the date of death pay or certify checks drawn on or prior to that date unless ordered to stop payment by a person claiming an interest in the account.[84]

[83] U.C.C. Sec. 4-401.
[84] U.C.C. Sec. 4-405.

Even before the Code many states had similar statutory provisions, based on the policy that checks are usually given for payment of the drawer's debts, and to force court administration of an estate just to make these payments would be needlessly burdensome.

Stale Check

If a check is not presented to the drawee bank until a considerable period after its issuance, a suspicion is raised that possibly the debt for which the drawer gave the check has already been paid in some other manner, or that possibly for some other reason the drawer has ceased to be liable on the check. Some older court decisions indicated that if the drawee bank paid a stale check without first contacting the drawer, the bank could not charge the payment against the drawer's account. On the other hand if a check is not sufficiently old to be considered stale, the drawee bank's refusal to pay might be considered a wrongful dishonor for which the bank would be liable to the drawer for injuring his credit. Many states have stale check statutes which take drawee banks out of this dilemma, and a similar provision is included in the Code, stating:

> A bank is under no obligation to a customer having a checking account to pay a check, other than a certified check, which is presented more than six months after its date, but it may charge its customer's account for a payment made thereafter in good faith.[85]

Notice of Improper Payment[86]

If a drawee bank honestly and reasonably charges to a drawer's account a payment made on a forged or altered check, the bank is not required to restore the amount of the charge if the drawer fails to promptly notify the bank of the improper payment. A drawer should carefully examine his bank statement and canceled checks, and notify the bank of any forged or altered item within the time agreed upon by the parties; if no time has been agreed upon, the notice must be given within a reasonable time.

Drawee's Obligation to Act Promptly

Drafts Other than Checks.[87] If a drawee decides not to accept or pay a draft, he should promptly return it to the person who presented it. The draft evidences various contracts, that of the drawer and possibly one or more indorsers' contracts. Since it is quite difficult (although not impossible) to sue on such contracts without having possession of the

[85] U.C.C. Sec. 4-404.
[86] U.C.C. Sec. 4-406.
[87] U.C.C. Sec. 3-419.

paper, the paper is valuable to the holder. If the drawee fails to return it upon demand, he is guilty of the tort of conversion and is liable for damages in an amount equal to the face amount of the draft.

Checks.[88] An individual Federal Reserve Bank may process over a million items a day, a large metropolitan bank as many as 300,000 a day, and even a small bank may process more than 2,000 items per day.[89] Therefore special rules for items passing in banking channels and especially for checks are essential.

A very small percentage of checks come to drawee banks by being presented across the counter for payment in cash. If a check is presented in this way, the bank either will pay the holder upon proper identification, or will return the check with an explanation of why it refuses to pay— for example, that the drawer has insufficient funds or has stopped payment, or that the check does not seem to be genuine. Some items come to a drawee bank when the holders who also have accounts in that bank deposit the checks for credit to their accounts. However, most checks come to drawee banks in sizeable bundles from other banks, coming by mail or express, by messenger delivery, or through a clearing house. In determining whether or not to pay an item, the drawee bank must decide 1) that the drawer has an account in the bank with sufficient funds for payment of the check, 2) that the check appears to be genuine and valid (properly signed, not altered, properly indorsed), and 3) that the drawer has not stopped payment on the check. Because more than 99 percent of the checks which a drawee bank receives meet these conditions, and also because of the tremendous volume of checks handled each day, a number of states have by statute authorized a banking practice known as "deferred posting." The Code also authorizes this practice. Very briefly the procedure is as follows: except for a check paid in cash across the counter, the drawee bank provisionally settles for a check, usually either by giving its depositor credit in his account, by a remittance draft sent to the presenting bank, or by adjusting balances through a clearing house, through a Federal Reserve Bank, or directly between the drawee bank and the presenting bank. This the drawee bank must do before midnight of the banking day upon which it receives the item involved. (An item received after banking hours is considered as received the next banking day.) Then the day following the banking day of receipt, when it is determined that the above three conditions are met (sufficient funds, genuineness, and no stop-payment order), the item is posted to the drawer's account. The very few checks that fail to meet these conditions can then be returned with notice that the provisional credit given is canceled. If a drawee bank fails to act within these times,

[88] U.C.C. Secs. 4-101, 4-109, 4-212, 4-213, 4-301, 4-302.
[89] See Comment to U.C.C. Sec. 4-101.

it is liable on the item unless it has a valid defense (such as breach of a warranty).

COSIGNERS

In regard to multiple signers, the Code states:

> Unless the instrument otherwise specifies two or more persons who sign as maker, acceptor or drawer or indorser and as a part of the same transaction are jointly and severally liable even though the instrument contains such words as "I promise to pay."[90]

ACCOMMODATION PARTY

As stated in Part 3 of this chapter, the Code defines an accommodation party as "one who signs the instrument in any capacity for the purpose of lending his name to another party to it." In regard to such a party, the Code states:

> When the instrument has been taken for value before it is due the accommodation party is liable in the capacity in which he has signed even though the taker knows of the accommodation.[91]

Note that while an accommodation indorser who signs without qualification makes the ordinary indorser's promise, he does not make any warranties—since these are made only by a transferor who receives consideration. An accommodation indorser is usually not a transferor and by definition does not receive consideration.

DISCHARGE OF LIABILITY[92]

As already discussed, an unqualified indorser is released from liability on his indorser's promise if the holder, without excuse, fails to make due presentment to the payor or to give the indorser prompt notice of the payor's dishonor. Other ways in which the liability of a person on commercial paper may be lost, canceled, or otherwise discharged, include the following:

1. Discharge of liability by cancellation or renunciation. The Code states:

> The holder of an instrument may even without consideration discharge any party
> (a) in any manner apparent on the face of the instrument or the indorsement, as by intentionally cancelling the instrument or the party's signature by destruction or mutilation, or by striking out the party's signature; or

[90] U.C.C. Sec. 3-118.
[91] U.C.C. Sec. 3-415.
[92] U.C.C. Secs. 3-601, 3-605, 3-606.

(b) by renouncing his rights by a writing signed and delivered or by surrender of the instrument to the party to be discharged. . . .

2. Discharge of secondary liability by changing primary contract. Note that when a guarantor (or indorser) promises that the obligation of the principal debtor will be paid at the stated maturity date, the guarantor is 1) underwriting the debt of another person, 2) for a stated period of time only. From these two points, two results follow as a matter of fairness: 1) if the guarantor has to pay on his guaranty, since it is actually the debt of another which the guarantor is paying, he in turn should have a right to collect from the principal debtor—therefore, he succeeds to the creditor's rights against the principal debtor; 2) the guarantor should not be required, without his consent, to take a chance on the debtor's credit for longer than the agreed period. Since the creditor is not permitted to extend the duration of the guarantor's obligation without the latter's consent, the creditor releases the guarantor from his obligation if any act of the creditor effectively blocks the guarantor from himself paying the debt at its original maturity date. One result of the foregoing is a rule which can be summarized as follows: If the holder of a note enters into an enforceable extension agreement with the maker, giving the latter more time to pay, any indorser or guarantor of the note will be discharged from liability, unless the holder expressly reserves rights against the indorser or guarantor.

Example: On February 1 C. Carter loaned D. Davis $1,000 (without interest) for three months, and G. Gordon guaranteed D's payment. The obligation was evidenced by a three-month negotiable note which D signed as maker and on which G indorsed "Payment guaranteed." When the note matured on May 1, D asked C for a three-month extension.

1. Without obtaining G's permission, C orally agreed to extend D's obligation until August 1.

There being no consideration or effective equivalent of consideration for C's extension promise, C would not have to wait until August 1 to collect from D. Likewise if G did not want to continue taking a chance on D's credit, G could pay the debt anytime on or after May 1, the original maturity date, and immediately collect from D. Therefore, G would not be released or discharged by C's oral extension.

2. Without obtaining G's permission, C dated, signed, and gave D the following writing: "To D. Davis: This is in reference to your $1,000 note held by me and due today. I hereby agree to give you until August 1 of this year to pay this note. (signed) C. Carter."

Under the Code this would (probably) be a legally enforceable extension.[93] Thus C could not collect before August 1, and if G paid C, G likewise

---

[93] U.C.C. Sec. 1-107 provides: "Any claim or right arising out of an alleged breach can be discharged in whole or in part without consideration by a written waiver or renunciation signed and delivered by the aggrieved party."

could not collect from D before August 1. Because C thus changed G's rights without his consent, C's agreement would discharge G from liability.

3. Assume that the last sentence of C's written agreement quoted in Part 2 of this problem read: "I hereby agree to give you until August 1 of this year to pay this note, hereby reserving however all rights against G. Gordon."

If C's right against G were to continue, then likewise G's right to pay the debt at its original maturity and immediately collect from D must also continue. Therefore, in effect the extension agreement was a limited rather than a general one. Although binding on C, it would not be binding on G. While C could not collect from D until August 1, G could pay C anytime on or after the original maturity date (May 1) and immediately collect from D. Since the extension agreement did not change G's original contract, G would not be discharged.

Part 7 PRESENTMENT, DISHONOR, NOTICE OF DISHONOR, PROTEST

If a holder of commercial paper wishes to preserve his right to recover from secondary parties (unqualified indorsers and drawers), he must exercise proper diligence in attempting to collect from the payor (the maker of a note or the drawee of a draft). To show proper diligence a holder must make due presentment, and upon the payor's dishonor, the holder must give prompt notice of dishonor, and sometimes also must undertake the formality of having the instrument protested.

PRESENTMENT

Presentment is a request or demand made by the holder that the payor either accept the instrument if it is not yet due or pay the amount of the instrument if it is due.

If a time draft is presented to the drawee before its due date, the drawee is not asked to pay since payment is not yet due, but rather he is asked to accept—to sign the draft and thus agree to pay it when it comes due. For the requirement of due presentment to be satisfied, some drafts *must* be presented for acceptance. These are:[94]

1. Drafts which expressly require presentment for acceptance;

2. Drafts expressly made payable elsewhere than at the residence or place of business of the drawee;

3. Drafts in which the time for payment depends upon presentment. An example would be a draft which reads, "Thirty days after sight, pay to the order of . . ."

With any time draft other than those listed above, a holder will not be

[94] U.C.C. Sec. 3-501.

guilty of a lack of diligence if he fails to present the instrument for acceptance; he may present it for acceptance or not as he wishes.

To satisfy the requirement of due presentment, the holder of *any* instrument *must* present it for payment, whether the instrument is a note, an unaccepted draft, or a draft which has been previously accepted by the drawee.

PLACE AND MANNER OF PRESENTMENT[95]

If a draft is accepted as payable at a bank, or a note is made payable at a bank, the instrument *must* be presented at the named bank during banking hours, to comply with the requirement of due presentment. Except for this restriction, a choice is open to the holder as to the manner and place of presentment. Actually exhibiting the instrument to the payor is a common way to make presentment; however, showing the instrument is not required unless specifically requested by the payor. Whatever the manner selected, the presentment must be at a reasonable hour. The ways in which a presentment may be made include:

1. Sending the payor a notice describing the instrument, identifying the holder, and requesting either acceptance or payment, whichever is appropriate. Such a notice is not a presentment until it is received.

2. Requesting acceptance or payment at the place specified in the instrument, or if there be none specified, at the place of business or residence of the payor.

3. If the instrument is a check, sending it to the drawee bank either directly or through a clearing house.

If the instrument names more than one payor, presentment may be made to any one of those named.

Because of this wide choice of methods, the payor is protected by a provision in the Code[96] permitting him to request any of the following without being considered as having refused to acknowledge the instrument:

1. Tender of the instrument at the place specified in it, or if there is no place specified, at any place reasonable under the circumstances;

2. Reasonable identification of the person making presentment, and evidence of his authority if he is acting as an agent;

3. A signed receipt on the instrument for any partial or full payment, and surrender of the instrument upon full payment.

It is definitely an advantage for all parties if an instrument states a place for payment. The advantage to the holder is obvious. If the holder is unacquainted with the payor, he may encounter some difficulty, espe-

[95] U.C.C. Secs. 3-504, 3-505.
[96] U.C.C. Sec. 3-505.

cially in a large city, in locating the payor in order to present the instrument. If the instrument states a place for presentment, merely presenting it at that place is sufficient. As the Code states:

> If neither the party to accept or pay nor anyone authorized to act for him is present or accessible at such place presentment is excused.[97]

The definite advantage to a maker of having his note state a place for payment springs from the basic rule of contract law that a debt will draw interest according to its terms, or if not provided for, then from its due date, and that such interest will continue to accrue until the debt is paid or until the debtor makes a tender of payment. A "tender of payment" consists of the debtor's doing all that he can to pay his debt up to the point of the creditor accepting the payment. If the creditor refuses to receive the tendered payment, the debt remains collectible but interest stops running. In other words, the creditor cannot require the debtor to continue to pay interest merely by refusing to accept payment of the debt when due. Repeating this common-law rule the Code states:

> Any party making tender of full payment to a holder when or after it is due is discharged to the extent of all subsequent liability for interest, costs and attorney's fees.[98]

Usually for a debtor to make an effective tender of payment, he must offer to pay the proper party the proper amount at the proper time and place. Because a negotiable note is easily transferable, the maker may encounter some difficulty in learning who holds his note on its due date. If a prior transferor has forgotten to whom he transferred the note, it will be impossible for the maker to learn the identity of the holder until the holder makes presentment. If the holder delays and the maker is therefore unable to tender payment, interest will continue to run. The interest period could thus be extended for any time less than the full period of the statute of limitations on the note. On the other hand, if the maker specifies in the note a place for payment (the maker's bank is a convenient place) and can prove (from the bank records) that he had the proper amount of money at that place on the due date, and has kept that amount available, he can stop interest from running on the obligation; as the Code states:

> Where the maker or acceptor of an instrument payable otherwise than on demand is able and ready to pay at every place of payment specified in the instrument when it is due, it is equivalent to tender.[99]

Commercial practices differ concerning what a bank may do, or should do, upon presentment of a depositor's note which expressly states that

[97] U.C.C. Sec. 3-504.
[98] U.C.C. Sec. 3-604.
[99] U.C.C. Sec. 3-604.

it is payable at that bank. In the northeastern part of the United States, commercial practice treats such a note as equivalent to a check; upon presentment the bank is authorized to pay and to charge the maker's account, even though the maker has given no special instructions concerning the note. In some western and southern states, a contrary commercial practice is followed. Only if the maker specially so instructs, is the bank authorized to pay the note when presented. The Code recognizes[100] that both practices are well established and presents alternative provisions either of which can be selected by a state upon adoption of the Code.

TIME OF PRESENTMENT[101]

Presentment for Acceptance

With a draft payable at a stated future date, any presentment for acceptance should of course be made before the indicated due date, while an instrument payable a stated period after sight must be presented for acceptance within a reasonable time.

Presentment for Payment—Time Instrument

If an instrument indicates the date on which it is payable, presentment for payment is due on that date. If that date is not a full business day for both the holder and the payor, presentment is due on the next day which is a full business day for both parties.

Presentment for Payment—Demand Instrument

As to the drawer of a demand draft or the indorser of a demand note or draft, due presentment means presentment for payment within a reasonable time after such party signs the instrument.

The Code states:

> A reasonable time for presentment is determined by the nature of the instrument, any usage of banking or trade and the facts of the particular case.

Demand Note. The discussion in Part 4 of this chapter concerning when a demand note is overdue also applies to the question of when a demand note should be presented.

Sight Draft and Check. The Code states:

> In the case of an uncertified check which is drawn and payable within the United States and which is not a draft drawn by a bank the following are presumed to be reasonable periods within which to present for payment or to initiate bank collection:

[100] U.C.C. Sec. 3-121.
[101] U.C.C. Sec. 3-503.

(a) with respect to the liability of the drawer, thirty days after date or issue whichever is later; and

(b) with respect to the liability of an indorser, seven days after his indorsement.

It is arguable that the time for presentment of a sight draft would be the same as for a check.

Example: In Philadelphia, on April 1, R drew and delivered to P a negotiable check drawn on a Philadelphia bank, naming P as payee. The check was thereafter sold, unqualifiedly indorsed, and transferred as follows: On April 3, P to A; on April 8, A to B; on April 10, B to H. On April 16, H deposited the check in his account in a Chicago bank. The check was forwarded, presented to the drawee Philadelphia bank for payment, and payment was refused because of insufficient funds in R's account. The Chicago bank notified H who promptly notified R, P, A, and B.

As to the indorser's contract made by P on April 3, due presentment would be by April 10; as to A's contract made April 8, due presentment would be by April 15; as to B's contract made April 10, due presentment would be by April 17. H initiated bank collection on April 16. H made due presentment as to B and of course R, but not as to A or P. H could recover from B or R but not from A or P. If H recovered from B, B could in turn recover from R but not from A or P.

DISHONOR

The Code defines "dishonor" of an instrument in the following language:

> An instrument is dishonored when . . . a necessary or optional presentment is duly made and due acceptance or payment is refused or cannot be obtained within the prescribed time.[102]

For a draft which is presented for *acceptance*, the "prescribed time" referred to in the foregoing quotation is defined by the Code as follows:

> Acceptance may be deferred without dishonor until the close of the next business day following presentment. The holder may also in a good faith effort to obtain acceptance and without either dishonor of the instrument or discharge of secondary parties allow postponement of acceptance for an additional business day.[103]

Also, the Code states:

> Where the drawee's proffered acceptance in any manner varies from the draft as presented, the holder may refuse the acceptance and treat the draft as dishonored. . . .[104]

[102] U.C.C. Sec. 3-507.
[103] U.C.C. Sec. 3-506.
[104] U.C.C. Sec. 3-412.

A draft which is not unconditionally accepted within the statutory time is considered as dishonored, and the holder should give prompt notice to any indorser and to the drawer. The holder will then have an *immediate* right to recover from any unqualified indorser or from the drawer[105] even though (with a time draft) the payment which the instrument directed the drawee to make is not yet due. This latter point is sound policy. If a holder pays value for a sixty-day draft, he shows that he is willing to wait sixty days for payment by the drawee. However, if, before the sixty days has expired, the drawee says that he will not pay (by refusing to accept the draft), the expectations of the parties are changed and there is no reason to require the holder to wait.

Example: On April 1 R dated, signed, and delivered to P the following draft:

[Date]

Six months after date pay to the order of P. Porter $500.
To E. Edwards   (signed) R. Roger

P unqualifiedly indorsed and delivered the draft to H. One month later, H presented the draft to E for acceptance. (This was optional with H, the draft not being the type *requiring* presentment for acceptance.) E refused to accept, and H gave prompt notice to P and to R.

H would have an immediate right to recover from either P or R.

NOTICE OF DISHONOR[106]

Manner and Effect of Notice

The Code states:

Notice may be given in any reasonable manner. It may be oral or written and in any terms which identify the instrument and state that it has been dishonored. . . .

When any party is dead or incompetent notice may be sent to his last known address or given to his personal representative. . . .

Notice operates for the benefit of all parties who have rights on the instrument against the party notified.

Time of Notice

In giving notice of dishonor, banks, as professionals in the handling of commercial paper, are required to show more efficiency and promptness than other persons and institutions. When a bank presents an instrument and it is dishonored, the bank must give notice of dishonor before midnight of the next banking day. If the bank did not itself present the

[105] U.C.C. Sec. 3-507.
[106] U.C.C. Sec. 3-508.

instrument but rather learned of the dishonor by receiving notice from the one who did present it, the bank must pass the notice of dishonor along before midnight of the next banking day following the day on which the bank received the notice. Other persons and businesses have more time to act. They must give notice of dishonor before midnight of the third business day after the dishonor, or after receiving notice of the dishonor.

A written notice is considered "given" when it is properly sent—more specifically, when:[107]

1. Deposited in the mail or delivered for transmission by any other usual means of communication,

2. With postage or cost of transmission provided for, and

3. Properly addressed,

a) To the address specified in the instrument, or

b) If no address is specified, to any address reasonable under the circumstances.

Example: Assume the calendar for the month involved in this example is as follows:

S	M	T	W	T	F	S
1	2	3	4	5	6	7
8	9	10	11	12	13	14
15	16	17	18	19	20	21
22	23	24	25	26	27	28

H was the holder of a negotiable note which had been signed by M, naming P as payee, and which had been sold, unqualifiedly indorsed, and transferred successively by P, A, and B. None of these parties was a bank. When H made due presentment on the 2nd, M failed to pay.

1. Notices were mailed and received as follows: H to B, mailed the 5th, received the 6th; B to A, mailed the 10th, received the 11th; A to P, mailed the 14th, received the 16th. H sued P.

H could recover. Although it would be unwise for H to rely on the others to give notice, and unwise for each to wait until the last permissible day as was done in the example, proper notices were given to P, A, and B; therefore, H could recover from any of them.

2. Assume other facts as above except that B delayed and did not mail a notice to A until the 11th. A received this on the 12th and, acting faster than required, mailed a notice to P on the 14th, which was received by P on the 16th. H sued P.

P obtained the notice at exactly the same time as in Part 1 of this example. However, B's delay interrupted the chain so that not only was notice not probably given to A but also proper notice, as the term is defined, was not given to P. In other words, an intermediate party's greater diligence does not weld together the chain once it has been broken. Therefore, H could not recover from P.

[107] U.C.C. Sec. 1-201.

Installment Note

A note payable in successive installments is like a series of separate notes. If the note is not paid, a series of dishonors occurs and following each, the holder must be diligent in giving notice of dishonor to an indorser. Otherwise the indorser will not be liable on his indorser's promise as to any installment for which notice of dishonor has not been given.

Frequently an installment note contains an acceleration provision. The provision may be one of two types: 1) at the option of the holder or 2) automatic.

1) Acceleration Provision at Holder's Option. Until the holder demands the entire balance, this is like a note without an acceleration provision. The holder must give a series of notices as dishonors occur.

2) Automatic Acceleration Provision. If the holder fails to give notice of dishonor upon the first default, the indorser is relieved from liability for the entire balance.

Example: M signed and delivered to P (the payee) a negotiable note made out for the principal sum of $500, payable $100 starting the next August 1, and $100 on the first of each month thereafter. P sold, unqualifiedly indorsed, and transferred the note to H who notified M of the transfer. M fell behind in his payments and by December 1 had paid a total of only $200. On that date H for the first time demanded from M payment of the entire unpaid balance and upon M's refusal to pay, immediately notified P. This was the first that P knew anything of M's default. On December 20 H sued P.

1. Assume that the note contained the following provision: "In the event of my failure to pay any of such installments at the time specified herein, all of the remaining principal shall become immediately due and payable." This is an automatic acceleration provision. M defaulted on October 1 if not before. The entire unpaid balance then came due. Notice to P on December 1, of a dishonor occurring on October 1, was of course not prompt notice. H could recover nothing from P.

2. Assume that the note contained the following provision: "In the event of my failure to pay any of such installments at the time specified herein, all of the remaining principal shall at the option of the holder, become immediately due and payable." Default occurred on October 1, but since H did not demand the entire amount until December 1, acceleration never occurred. P received prompt notice of the December 1 default but not of any previous default. H could recover $100 from P but no more.

PROTEST[108]

Sometimes when an instrument is dishonored the holder will have it protested—that is, have a notary public (or other appropriate official) pre-

[108] U.C.C. Secs. 3-509, 3-510.

pare, sign, and apply his official seal to a certificate stating the details of the dishonor. Usually the protest certificate describes the instrument and states when, where, and to whom the instrument was presented, whether payment or acceptance was requested, and the result—that is dishonor either by nonpayment or nonacceptance. Sometimes the holder will also request the notary to give notices of dishonor and report in his certificate to whom and in what manner notices were given. If the holder later sues an indorser, the protest certificate creates (as the Code states) ". . . a presumption of dishonor and of any notice of dishonor therein shown . . ." In explaining the effect of presumptive evidence, the Code says:

> "Presumption" or "presumed" means that the trier of fact must find the existence of the fact presumed unless and until evidence is introduced which would support a finding of its nonexistence.[109]

In other words, the burden of presenting further evidence is shifted to the defendant. If the indorser-defendant challenges a protest certificate by denying that the instrument was presented as stated, or by denying that the stated notice was given, the burden is on him to present evidence to support his denial.

Under the Code, protest is not *required* as a condition for the liability of an indorser or drawer except for drafts drawn or payable outside the United States. Even though usually not necessary, however, instruments are frequently protested because of the convenience the certificate affords in proving due presentment, dishonor, and notice of dishonor.

WAIVER OF PRESENTMENT, NOTICE, PROTEST[110]

Due presentment and the giving of prompt notice (and protest when required) can be waived by the party for whose benefit they would otherwise be required. An effective waiver can be oral or written, express or implied, and can be made either before or after the presentment and notice should have been accomplished. Usually the waiver is written on the instrument. Sometimes it is written on the face of the instrument, in which case it is binding upon all persons who later sign the instrument, whether they sign on the face or the back. If a waiver is written on the back of an instrument as a part of a particular indorsement, it is binding upon that indorser only.

The most commonly used forms of waivers are the following:

1. "Due presentment waived." This form does not waive the giving of notice of dishonor or protest.

2. "Due presentment and notice of dishonor waived."

---

[109] U.C.C. Sec. 1-201.
[110] U.C.C. Sec. 3-511.

3. "Protest waived." Explaining the scope of this waiver, the Code says:

> A waiver of protest is also a waiver of presentment and of notice of dishonor even though protest is not required.

EXCUSE FROM PRESENTMENT, NOTICE, PROTEST[111]

As previously discussed in connection with liability of parties, a holder does not have a right to recover on an unqualified indorser's promise until after the holder has diligently attempted to obtain payment from the payor. To show proper diligence, a holder must usually make due presentment to the payor and give prompt notice of the payor's dishonor. Sometimes however, it is either useless or not reasonably possible for a holder to meet either one, or both, of these conditions; to that extent the holder is considered excused. Thus:

1. When the payor is dead or has been adjudged insolvent, due presentment is excused (except in the case of a documentary draft—that is a draft with a bill of lading attached or a similarly secured draft).[112] If presentment is thus excused, the holder should give due notice of that fact to prior secondary parties.

2. After a draft has been presented to the drawee for acceptance and dishonored by his refusal to accept—and prompt notice of the dishonor has been given—it would be useless, later when the unaccepted draft matures, to require the holder to present it again for payment and to give another notice of dishonor; the useless formalities are therefore excused.

3. After the drawer has notified the drawee not to pay the draft, making presentment and giving the drawer notice of dishonor would be useless formalities and both are excused.

4. When a holder exercises reasonable diligence but is unable through no fault of his own to make due presentment, the holder is excused from making presentment for so long as his inability continues. In such a case the holder should promptly notify the prior secondary parties of his inability to make due presentment. Certain policy guidelines exist for determining just when the holder's efforts to make due presentment show sufficient diligence. Thus, for example:[113]

a) If at a reasonable hour the holder attempts presentment at the address specified in the instrument and neither the payor nor anyone

---

[111] U.C.C. Sec. 3-511.

[112] In the case of a documentary draft, the holder should duly present it to the person in charge of the drawee's estate, so that the latter will have the opportunity to pay the draft and obtain the goods represented by the bill of lading, in order to apply any profit obtainable therefrom for the benefit of the drawee's creditors.

[113] U.C.C. Sec. 3-504.

authorized to act for him is present or available at that address, present-ment is excused.

b) If no address is specified in the instrument and, at a reasonable hour, the holder attempts presentment at the payor's place of business or at his residence if he has no place of business, and no one is there to act for the payor, presentment is excused.

c) If the holder does not know the payor's address and is unable to find it in either the city directory or the telephone directory, the holder is *not* exercising reasonable diligence if he makes no further effort to locate the payor. For example, the holder should also attempt to contact other persons whose names are on the instrument, and ask them where the payor can be found.

5. When a holder exercises reasonable diligence but is unable through no fault of his own to give notice of dishonor to prior parties, the holder is excused for so long as his inability continues. However, the death of an indorser does not excuse a holder from giving notice; he should send the notice to the last known address of the indorser or give it to the per-sonal representative of his estate.[114] If the holder cannot find an indorser's address either in the city directory or telephone book, the holder should attempt to inquire from other prior parties.

PROBLEMS

1. Determine whether or not each of the following quoted or described instruments is negotiable.

a) "I.O.U. or bearer due on demand $500. (signed) M. Martin."

b) "Philadelphia, Pa., [Date]. Three months after date, we promise to pay P. Porter or order $300 for the privilege of one framed advertising sign, size ____×____, in one end of each of 159 street-cars of the North Philadelphia City Railway Company, for a term of six months from date hereof. (signed) M. Martin Company."

c) "Philadelphia, Pa., [Date.] I hereby certify that P. Porter has deposited with me $500 which I promise to pay to his order on demand with interest from date, on the return to me of this instrument and of my guarantee for the note for $500 dated this date made by said P. Porter to A. Adams. (signed) M. Martin." (Modified from A.I.C.P.A., Nov. 22-1.)

d)

Mr. C. Carter   [Date]
Cashier of the First National Bank, Centerville, Illinois.

    Pay to the order of P. Porter the sum of $500 and charge the same against the $1,000 insurance draft issued by the Hartford Insurance Company in my favor, the same being the balance of my account with him.

Respectfully,
(signed) R. Roger

[114] U.C.C. Sec. 3-508.

e)

First National Bank of Centerville, Illinois   [Date]
   Pay to the Order of P. Porter $500.00
   Five hundred and 00/100_____ __ __ __ __ __ __ __ __ __Dollars
   Preferred Stock Dividend Account
                (signed) R. Roger Corp.
                by T. Thomas, Treas.

f)

                New York, N.Y. [Date]
   Sixty days after date pay to the order of ourselves $500. The obligation of the acceptor hereof arises out of the purchase of goods from the drawer, maturity being in accordance with the original terms of purchase.
To E. Edward
   Chicago, Ill.   (signed) R. Roger Co.

g)

First National Bank of Centerville, Ill.   [Date]
   Pay to the order of Porter Realty Co. $500.00
   Five hundred and 00/100_____ __ __ __ __ __ __ __ __ __Dollars
   For earnest money on 123 Main St., Centerville,
   check to be returned if deal not consummated
               (signed) R. Roger

   h) "Philadelphia, Pa., [Date]. Five years after date I promise to pay to P. Porter or order $3,000 with interest at the rate of 4 percent per year, payable annually from date until paid: Provided however that if any of the principal or interest due on this note is not paid on or before maturity, it shall bear interest at 6 percent (signed) M. Martin."

   i) "London, England, [Date]. One month after date I promise to pay to the order of P. Porter One thousand Pounds. Payable at the First National Bank of Centerville, Ill., USA. (signed) M. Martin."

   j) "Chicago, Ill., [Date]. One year after date, for value received, we promise to pay to the order of P. Porter $3,000 with interest at the office of the Martin Corp., Chicago, Ill., or at the option of the holder hereof upon the surrender of this note, to issue to the holder hereof in lieu thereof thirty shares of the preferred stock of the Martin Corp. and to pay to the holder hereof in cash the interest then due upon said sum. (signed) Martin Corp. By M. Martin, President." (Modified from A.I.C.P.A. Nov. 20-1.)

   k) "Centerville, Ill., [Date]. One year from date, for value received, I promise to pay to the order of the First National Bank of Centerville, the sum of $216, there having been deposited herewith as collateral security Pass Book No. 15043 issued by your savings department in my name, and I agree to deposit in said savings account the sum of $18 on the fifteenth of every month hereafter until a total of the face amount of this note shall have been deposited. (signed) M. Martin." (Modified from A.I.C.P.A., Nov. 38-7.)

   l) On April 1, induced by P's fraudulent misrepresentations M bought and received certain goods from P for $500. M signed and gave P a one-month note for that amount, made out on the standard judgment note form of the Pennsylvania National Bank and Trust Company (as reproduced on page 404). On April 2 P sold, indorsed, and transferred the note to H who received it for value, without knowledge of the fraud. On April 3 M discovered that he had been defrauded. M offered to return the goods to P and demanded back his note. Upon P's refusal, M set the goods aside and made no further use of them. When the note came due, M refused to pay, and H sued M. M contended that the note was nonnegotiable. If M's contention was correct, H could not recover from M. Was M's contention correct?

m) In the preceding problem, suppose that there was no fraud but that M signed the described note intending a gift to P. Would M have a good defense against H?

n) "Chicago, Ill., [Date]. One year after date I promise to pay to the order of P. Porter $1,000. As security for this note, I have this day executed and delivered to the payee a chattel mortgage on the chattels described therein, and agree that upon default in the performance of any of the covenants in said chattel mortgage, the balance then owing on this note, as enlarged by the amount of all advances and expenses that may have been paid by the mortgagee for taxes, levies, assessments, and other impositions levied upon the goods and chattels, as well as for insurance premiums and the cost of repairs to or maintenance of the said goods and chattels, shall, at the option of the holder, at once become due and payable. (signed) M. Martin."

o) "I promise to pay bearer $500. (signed) M. Martin."

p) "Chicago, Ill., [Date]. One year after date or on demand, I promise to pay to the order of P. Porter $500. (signed) M. Martin."

q)

Centerville, Ill. [Date]

Six months after date for value received I promise to pay to the order of the First National Bank of Centerville Ill., $4,500 with interest from maturity until paid at the rate of 6 percent per year. To secure the payment of this note and of any and all other indebtedness which I owe to the holder hereof, or may owe him at any time before the payment of this note I have hereto attached as collateral security the following:

Stock certificate No. 137 of the Porter Refrigerating Company of Centerville for 50 shares of the stock of said company, par value $5,000.

The above collateral has a present market value of $6,250. If in the judgment of the holder of this note, said collateral depreciates in value, the undersigned agrees to deliver when demanded additional security to the satisfaction of said holder; otherwise this note shall mature at once. And I hereby authorize the holder hereof on default of this note, or any part thereof, according to the terms hereof to sell said collateral or any part thereof, at public or private sale and with or without notice.

(signed) M. Martin

r) Desiring to make a gift to P, M signed and gave P the following instrument: "Centerville, Ill., [Date]. One month after date I promise to pay

P. Porter $1,000 at the First National Bank of Centerville, Ill. (signed) M. Martin." Two weeks later P sold, indorsed, and transferred the note to H who paid fair value without knowledge of the purpose for which the note was given. On maturity, M refused to pay and H sued M. H could recover if the note was negotiable. Was it negotiable?

s)

First National Bank of Centerville, Ill.   [Date]

    This is to certify that P. Porter has deposited in this bank $500, payable six months from date with interest at the rate of 2 percent per year, upon return of this certificate properly indorsed. No payment before, and no interest after, maturity.

                        (signed) C. Carter, Cashier

t)

First National Bank of Centerville, Ill.   [Date]

    Pay to the order of Bills Payable $50.00

    Fifty and 00/100————————————————————Dollars

                        (signed) Roger Corp.

                        by T. Thomas, Treas.

2. R drew and delivered to P. Porter a check for $500, naming P. Porter as payee. The check was negotiable. P. Porter indorsed the check in blank and delivered it to H. Howard in payment of a debt. H wanted to keep the check for a few weeks but did not want to restrict himself to eventually depositing it in a bank. What risk, if any, would H be assuming if he merely put the check in his billfold? What should H do?

3. H. Howard, owner and operator of a grocery store, regularly takes in a number of checks drawn on various banks. H's regular practice is to send one of his clerks, each morning, to deposit the previous day's checks in H's account in the Centerville, Ill., First National Bank. H wishes to assure maximum protection to himself from loss of the money represented by the checks, should the checks be lost or stolen while his clerk is on the way to the bank. What should H do?

4. M signed and delivered to P. Porter a six-month negotiable promissory note for $500, naming Porter as payee. T stole the note from Porter, without authority indorsed the note "(signed) P. Porter," and sold and transferred the note for value to A. A sold, indorsed, and transferred the note to B who paid value and had no knowledge of the prior circumstances. Upon maturity, B presented the note to M for payment. M having been advised of theft of the note, refused to pay. B asserted that he was a holder in due course. Was he?

5. A. Adams falsely stated that he represented P. Porter, head of the Porter Health Center, a charitable tuberculosis camp, and that he was soliciting funds for the camp. R signed and gave A a negotiable check for $100, naming P. Porter as payee, as a contribution to the camp fund. A indorsed the check with P's name and transferred it for cash to B who indorsed and transferred the check to H. Both B and H received the check for value, in good faith, and with no knowledge of the prior circumstances. A few days later R learned that there was no such person as P. Porter and no such camp as the Porter Health Center, and notified his bank not to pay the check. The bank accordingly refused payment when H made prompt presentment. H asserted that he was a holder in due course. Was he?

6. On August 1 S sold goods to B, to be delivered the following day, and B agreed to pay $200 in 30 days, signing and giving S a negotiable promissory note to that effect. On August 3 S sold and indorsed the note to H, an innocent party, for $190 of which $50 was paid immediately and the balance was to be paid on August 15. By August 10 S still had not delivered the goods and B so informed H. On August 15 H paid S the agreed balance, and upon maturity of the note, demanded payment from B. The goods were still undelivered and B refused to pay. H asserted that he was a holder in due course. Was he? (Modified from A.I.C.P.A., May 48-1a.)

7. In Chicago, Ill., on December 16, for goods to be delivered by P to R, R drew and delivered to P a check for $700, drawn on a Philadelphia bank, naming P as payee. P had an account in a Chicago bank. On December 17 P deposited the check in his account in the Chicago bank; the balance of P's account at the close of that day was $982.49, including the $700 check. The goods R received being defective, R stopped payment on the check, and when the check was duly presented to the Philadelphia bank, payment was refused. Notice was immediately given to the Chicago bank, which between December 17 and receipt of the notice had paid out on checks drawn by P a total of $381.71. Was the Chicago bank a holder in due course?

8. On January 10 S and B entered into a written contract under which: 1) S sold to B a certain air-conditioning unit for $350; 2) B paid $50 down and agreed to pay $30 a month for ten months, as evidenced by B's note; 3) title was to remain in S until completion of the payments; 4) S guaranteed satisfactory operation of the machine for one year. On the contract form, underneath the signatures of the parties was a row of perforations across the paper, below which was printed a promissory note form. This was filled in for $300 payable in monthly installments of $30, S was named as payee, B was the signer, and the note, otherwise negotiable in form, stated: "This note is given to cover deferred installments under a contract of this date. Upon default in payment of any installments, the entire balance shall immediately become due and payable at the election of the holder." On January 12 S assigned the contract and indorsed the note (the two still being fastened together) to H Bank for $270 paid to S, and B was notified to make payments to the bank. After paying two monthly installments, B notified S and the bank that the machine was not operating satisfactorily, which was true. Upon their refusal to repair or replace the machine, B requested either or both of them to remove the machine and return his $110. They refused and B made no further payments and no further use of the machine. On April 15, the bank sued B for $240. What result?

9. Intending to make a gift, M gave his son, P, an unsealed, negotiable promissory note for $1,000, payable in two months, signed by M and naming P as payee. By the time the note came due, M had died and his administrator refused to pay the note, still held by P. P sued M's estate. Was P entitled to judgment?

10. Other facts remaining the same, assume that the note in the previous problem was under seal. How would this affect the answer to the previous problem?

11. R who had a checking account in a Philadelphia bank frequently signed checks with a rubber-stamp facsimile of his handwritten signature. R always kept the stamp in a compartment inside his safe. This compartment was locked and the key was kept in a drawer in the safe, behind some papers. This drawer was locked and the key was kept in another, unlocked drawer in the safe. The safe had a key lock rather than a combination lock. The safe key was kept in a small wooden box which was kept in a larger wooden box, on top of another safe. The signature stamp was removed, apparently by an employee whom R had no previous reason to distrust, and applied to several check forms. The drawee bank paid these checks. When the bank refused to comply with R's demand that the bank restore to R's account the amount paid on the forged checks, R sued the bank. What result?

12. Smith Company of Chicago, Illl., carried on a mail-order business and distributed with its catalog the following printed order form:

SMITH COMPANY ORDER FORM

To Smith Company
Chicago, Ill.

Please enter the following order for the described goods at the prices stated, f.o.b. Chicago, Ill.:
[A space was left here on the order form for a buyer to insert a description of the goods he was ordering and the prices.]

SMITH COMPANY WARRANTY: Any buyer who is not perfectly satisfied with any item purchased from Smith Company may, within ten days after receipt, return the item at Smith Company's expense; Smith Company will thereupon refund any payment made for such item and cancel any unpaid charges.

TERMS FOR PAYMENT: In payment for the above described goods and subject to the Smith Company warranty stated above, I hereby promise to pay to Smith Company or order the sum of ————————————————————Dollars, within two months after date, less 2 percent discount if payment is made within ten days after date.
Date:——————————————— Buyer's signature————————————
                                Buyer's address ————————————

On February 1 B completely filled in such an order form for goods totaling $500. Not having in stock the items ordered by B, S Company sent substitute goods together with a letter explaining the circumstances and assuring that if the substitute goods were not satisfactory, B could return them. Finding the substitute goods unsatisfactory for his purposes, B returned them and thought nothing more about the transaction until April 1, when a local bank presented a note to B and demanded payment. The note consisted of the lower portion of the above form, cut between the second and third lines in the "Terms for Payment" paragraph. Without knowledge or notice of the note's being cut from an order form, or of the transaction between S Company and B, a Chicago bank had, on February 11, discounted the note for S company, paying S Company the face amount less its usual discount fee. On March 25, S Company was adjudged bankrupt. On March 30, the Chicago bank indorsed and mailed the note to B's local bank for collection. When B refused to pay, the Chicago bank sued B. What result?

13. R, owner and operator of a business, maintained a checking account in his own name. While away on business trips, it was R's practice to leave some signed blank checks in the safe for use by his trusted employees. One night while R was away on a business trip the safe was broken open and among other things some signed checks were stolen. The thief completed one of the checks, inserting $250 as the amount, and naming P. Porter, an assumed name, as payee, and in that name cashed the check at the drawee bank. Upon being advised of the facts, the bank refused to restore to R's account the amount paid. R sued the bank. What result?

14. R was about to leave his office for a luncheon engagement, to be followed by an afternoon conference which would keep him away from the office for the remainder of the day. The bookkeeper stopped R at the office door and explained that they needed $50 for petty cash that afternoon. R had the bookkeeper fill in a standard check form, making it payable to "cash" and inserting the amount of $50 in figures. R signed the check and gave it to the bookkeeper, instructing him to run the check through the check writing machine (which would impress the amount in words) and then obtain the needed petty cash from the bank. After R left the office, the bookkeeper added another zero to the "$50" and impressed "Five Hundred Dollars" on the check with the check writing machine. The bookkeeper cashed the check and absconded. R had no previous reason to doubt the bookkeeper's honesty. Discovering what had happened, R demanded that the bank restore $450 to his account and upon the bank's refusal, R sued the bank. What result? (Modified from A.I.C.P.A., May 22-4.)

15. M. Martin purchased some securities from P. Porter. In exchange for the securities M executed and delivered the following instrument to P: "Chicago, Ill., [Date]. For value received I promise to pay to the order of P. Porter six months after date $900. If at any time the holder of this note shall so desire he may declare the note due immediately. (signed) M. Martin." M's signature was placed by him at the bottom of the instrument with a rubber stamp. With a blank indorsement P negotiated the instrument to A for value. A had no knowledge of the securities transaction, and on the due date presented the instrument to the maker for payment. M refused to pay the note alleging a failure of consideration, and claimed that the securities were absolutely worthless. A sued M.

a) What was the effect of the signature having been made by rubber stamp?

b) What was the effect of the holder having a right to declare the note due immediately?

c) If the securities were worthless, would M be justified in refusing to pay the note?
(Modified from A.I.C.P.A., Nov. 56-8.)

16. Desiring to make a gift to P, M dated, signed, and gave P a negotiable demand note, naming P as payee, and made out for $1,000 with interest at the rate of 6 percent per year. Ten days later P sold, indorsed, and transferred the note to A for $1,000 which A paid to P, without knowledge of the prior circumstances. Two years later A sold, indorsed, and transferred the note to H for $1,000, which H paid to A without knowledge of the prior circumstances. Two weeks after purchasing the note, H demanded payment from M and upon M's refusal to pay, H sued M. Was H entitled to recover from M and if so, how much?

17. H was the holder of the following note:

[Date]
Seven months after date I promise to pay to the order of P. Porter $500.

(signed) M. Martin

On the reverse side, reading downward from the top were written: "Without recourse (signed) P. Porter"; "(signed) A. Adams"; "Without recourse (signed) B. Brown"; "Payment guaranteed (signed) C. Carter." These were four separate indorsements, each signed at a different time. C sold and delivered the instrument to D. Davis who in turn sold and delivered it to E. Edwards. On the fourth month after the date on the note, E told H of obtaining the instrument from D and delivered it to H. A, B, C, D, E, and H were each in turn holders in due course of the note. Neither D nor E indorsed the note.

a) Through sudden business reverses, M became insolvent during the fifth month after the date on the note, and remained insolvent thereafter. When H presented the instrument to M and demanded payment, on the date stated below, M was unable to pay because of his insolvency, and H immediately gave notice of the dishonor to P, A, B, C, D, and E and made no further attempt to collect from M. 1) H presented the note, demanded payment, and gave the notices mentioned above, all on the day the note came due, which was a full business day for all parties. Could H collect from P? From A? From B? From C? From D? From E? 2) With one month after the due date as the date of presentment, dishonor, and notice of dishonor, answer the same questions as in (1) above.

b) The note was given for M's losses in an all-night poker game with P and others. When H presented the note to M and demanded payment, M refused to pay on the ground that it was a gambling note. H immediately gave notice of the dishonor to P, A, B, C, D, and E. 1) Same additional facts as in Part (a1) above. Could H collect from M? From any of the other parties named above? 2) Same additional facts as in Part (a2) above. Could H collect from M? From any of the other parties named above?

18. The payee of a negotiable note wrote on the back of it, "I hereby assign to Albert Adams all my right, title, and interest in this note, (signed) Paul Porter," and sold and transferred the note to A. He in turn indorsed the

note "Pay to Harry Howard without recourse, (signed) Albert Adams," and sold and transferred the note to H. The maker was financially unable to pay the note when H duly presented it at maturity. H immediately notified P and A. This was the first they knew of the maker's insolvency. H sued to collect the amount of the note. Could H collect from P? From A? (Modified from A.I.C.P.A., May 33-2.)

19. In payment for goods purchased from P. Porter, R signed and gave P a negotiable check for $1,000 drawn on the E bank, naming P as payee. The next day P indorsed the check "(signed) P. Porter" and transferred it to A. Adams who, the same day, transferred the check to H. Both A and H were holders in due course. Upon H's due presentment of the check, E Bank refused to pay and H promptly notified R, A, and P of the nonpayment. The evidence showed that: 1) the balance in R's account was $1,500; 2) R was in financial difficulty; 3) a prominent businessman in the community had requested the bank to hold the balance in R's account pending a lawsuit the businessman was going to initiate against R; 4) it was for the latter reason that the bank refused to pay H. H sued for the amount of the check.

a) If H sued E Bank, could H recover?

b) If H sued R, could H recover?

c) If H sued P, could H recover?

d) If H sued A, could H recover, assuming that A had: 1) Indorsed "(signed) A. Adams"? 2) Indorsed "Without recourse (signed) A. Adams"? 3) Not indorsed at all?

20. Through fraudulent misrepresentations P induced R to purchase certain goods. In payment for the goods R signed and gave P a negotiable check, drawn on the E Bank, in the amount of $400, naming P as payee. The next day, P indorsed "Without recourse (signed) P. Porter" and transferred the check to A who, the next day, transferred to check to H. Both A and H were holders in due course. Discovering the fraud, R stopped payment on his check, and E Bank accordingly refused to pay when H made due presentment. H promptly notified R, P, and A, and sued for $400.

a), b), c), d) Answer the same questions as are asked in Problem 19.

21. For this problem, assume that April 1 was a Monday. On April 7, R signed and delivered to P a check so dated, naming P as payee and drawn for $150. On the date stated below, H cashed the check for P, giving P $145. When the check was returned to H marked "Payment stopped," H immediately notified R. R refused to pay H, and proved that he originally gave the check to P as a gift, a fact previously unknown to H. H sued R. How much could H recover from R, if H cashed the check for P a) on May 9, b) on April 29?

22. On September 21 a thief stole a car belonging to P. Porter, and also stole the certificate of title for the car, and various identifying papers belonging to P. On September 23 the thief took the car to R, a reputable car dealer, introduced himself as P, and showed P's identifying papers. R agreed to buy the car for $1,200 and signed and gave to the thief a negotiable check for that amount. The check named P as the payee and was dated September 25. The entire check, including the date, was written in broad, rounded words and figures. R dated the check ahead to give himself time to verify the title to the car. On September 24 R learned of the theft and immediately stopped payment on his check. On September 29 the thief bought a car from H, another car dealer. The thief offered to pay the price of $764 with R's $1,200 check, the thief indorsing the check with the payee's name and using P's identifying papers again to deceive H into thinking that the thief was P. H in good faith believed he was dealing with P and took the check, paying the thief the difference of $436 in cash. Shortly after H deposited the check in his own bank, the check was returned marked, "payment stopped." H sued R.

(a) Was H entitled to recover from R?

(b) In addition to the above facts, assume that when H received the check, it was dated September 28 instead of September 25, the "5," unknown to H, having been changed to an "8" by a straight narrow, diagonal line in a type of ink different from that used in making the "5." Would H be entitled to recover from R?

23. In payment of an obligation, R, without negligence, signed and gave P a negotiable check drawn on E Bank in the amount of $9, naming P as payee. The next day P transferred the check to A. Adams with an unqualified indorsement. The same day A dishonestly raised the check to $190, so skillfully that the alteration was not noticeable on ordinary inspection, indorsed the check "Without recourse (signed) A. Adams," and transferred it to B. Brown, who, the following day, transferred the check to H. Both H and B were holders in due course.

(a) Upon presentment of the check, E bank paid H $190. Upon receiving his statement and canceled checks, R promptly notified E Bank of the alteration. (1) Could E Bank properly charge the $190 payment against R's account? (2) Could E Bank recover from P? (3) Could E Bank recover from A? (4) Could E Bank recover from B, assuming that he had: (a) Indorsed "(signed) B. Brown"? (b) Indorsed "Without recourse (signed) B. Brown"? (c) Not indorsed at all? (5) Could E Bank recover from H?

(b) Pursuant to R's stop payment order, E Bank refused to pay the check when H duly presented it and H promptly notified all prior parties. (1) Could H recover from R? (2) Could H recover from P? (3) Could H recover from A? (4) Could H recover from B, assuming the additional facts stated in (a), (b), and (c) in Part (a4) of this problem?

24. On May 1 P. Porter made out a negotiable check on the E Bank, in the amount of $500, naming himself as payee, and without authority signed R's name as drawer. On May 2 P indorsed the check "Without recourse (signed) P. Porter," and transferred the check to A. Adams, who transferred it to H. Both A and H were holders in due course. On May 5, unaware of the forgery, E Bank paid H $500 on the check. Upon receiving his statement and canceled checks, R promptly notified E Bank of the forgery.

a) Could E Bank charge the $500 payment against R's account?

b) Could E Bank recover from H?

c) Could E Bank recover from A, assuming that he had 1) Indorsed

"(signed) A. Adams"? 2) Indorsed "Without recourse (signed) A. Adams"?
3) Not indorsed at all?

d) Could E Bank recover from P?

25. Other facts remaining the same as in the preceding problem, assume
that the bank refused to pay the check. H sued A. Assume the same facts as
in (1), (2), and (3) of Part (c) above. Could H recover from A?

26. R signed and gave P. Porter a negotiable check drawn on the E Bank
in the amount of $500, dated May 1 and naming P as payee. A thief stole the
check from P, without authority indorsed the check, "(signed) P. Porter," and
on May 2 transferred the check to A. Adams, who transferred the check to H
on May 4. Both A and H gave value for the check, without knowledge of the
prior circumstances. In good faith and without carelessness, E Bank paid H
$500 on the check on May 5. Upon receiving his statement and canceled
checks, R promptly notified E Bank of the forged indorsement.

a) Answer the same questions asked in Parts (a), (b), (c), and (d) in
Problem 24.

b) Other facts remaining the same, assume that R, advised of theft of the
check, stopped payment. Accordingly E Bank refused payment when H
presented the check on May 5. H promptly notified all prior parties. 1) H
sued A. Assume the same facts as in (1), (2), and (3) of Part (c) of Problem
24. Could H recover from A? 2) Could H recover from P?

27. P, an appliance dealer, made a practice of discounting with H Bank
the security agreements with notes attached that arose from his sale of appliances. The procedure was that when a sale was in prospect, P would report to
H Bank the name of the prospective customer. If the bank found the credit
rating of the prospective customer satisfactory, P would make the sale and have
the customer sign a contract form and a negotiable note form. Both forms
were on the same sheet of paper, with the paper perforated between them. P
would then take the paper to the bank where, after the proper amounts were
inserted, P would transfer the paper to the bank. On May 1 M bought and
received a TV set from P and signed both a contract and a note form. The
following day P took the paper to the bank, where the paper was correctly
filled in for a total of $291.92, payable in stated monthly installments. For
value received from the bank, P then assigned the contract and indorsed the
note to H Bank "without recourse."

a) Thereafter M discovered that he had been defrauded by P into
making the purchase, returned the TV set to P, and repudiated the agreement.
Upon maturity of the note, the bank sued. Could the bank recover 1) from
M? 2) from P?

b) Thereafter the TV set was destroyed through M's carelessness. M
proved that he was a minor, which fact neither P nor the bank had previously
known, and stated that he was disaffirming his contract. Upon maturity of the
note, the bank made due presentment, gave prompt notice to P of nonpayment,
and sued. Could the bank recover 1) from M? 2) from P?

28. In payment for goods purchased, R drew a negotiable check on the

E Bank naming P as payee. P indorsed, sold, and delivered the check to H, a holder in due course, who held the check more than three months before presenting it for payment. During that time E Bank failed. R had withdrawn all of his money and closed his account before the failure. H sued R for the amount of the check. What result? (Modified from A.I.C.P.A. May 23-2.)

29. R was a seller of goods with whom E. Edwards had frequent dealings. Knowing of this, P. Porter forged an order bill of lading purporting to evidence goods shipped by R to E, and drew a sixty-day negotiable draft on E, naming P as payee. P signed R's name to the draft as drawer, attached the forged draft to the forged bill of lading and sent them to a bank in E's town. Believing that the draft covered goods which R was shipping to E, E accepted the draft by writing "Accepted (signed) E. Edwards" across the face of the instrument. The bank delivered the bill of lading to E and returned the draft to P. P transferred the draft to H. Howard by indorsing "Pay to H. Howard (signed) P. Porter." H was a holder in due course. When the draft came due, H presented it to E for payment. E had learned of the forgery and refused to pay. H sued E. What result?

30. Induced by P's fraudulent misrepresentations, R purchased and received certain goods from P, paying for them by negotiable check drawn by R on the E Bank, in the amount of $500, naming P as payee. Discovering the fraud through due diligence, R stopped payment on the check and returned the goods to P. Accordingly the bank refused to pay when the holder, identified below, duly presented the check. The holder sued for the amount of the check.

a) At the request of R, E Bank had certified the check before it was delivered to P. 1) P was the holder suing. Could P collect (a) from R? (b) from E Bank? 2) H, a holder in due course, was suing. Could H collect (a) from R? (b) from E Bank?

b) At the request of P, E Bank certified the check after it was delivered to P but before R stopped payment. 1), 2) same additional facts and questions as above.

31. a) On May 1, in payment of an obligation, R, without negligence, signed and gave P a negotiable check drawn on E Bank in the amount of $9, naming P as payee. On May 2 P transferred the check to A with an unqualified indorsement. The same day, A dishonestly raised the check to $190, so skillfully that the alteration was not noticeable on ordinary inspection. On May 4 E Bank certified the check at the request of A. Adams who then indorsed "Without recourse (signed) A. Adams" and transferred the check to B. Brown who the following day transferred the check to H. Both H and B were holders in due course. H did not immediately cash the check and still had it in his possession when, on June 3, in a conversation with R, H learned that the check had been raised. Before R could notify the bank, H presented the check and received $190 from E Bank. With due diligence R notified E Bank of the alteration. Could E Bank recover from H?

b) Other facts remaining the same, assume that E Bank refused to pay the check when H presented it. Could H recover from B, assuming that B had: 1) Indorsed "(signed) B. Brown?" 2) Indorsed "Without recourse (signed) B. Brown?" 3) Not indorsed at all?

32. On April 1, P. Porter induced R. Roger by fraudulent misrepresentations to purchase certain goods for which R paid with his negotiable check drawn on the E Bank of Philadelphia in the amount of $500, naming P as payee. On April 2 R discovered that he had been defrauded, returned the goods to P, and in the manner described below, requested E Bank not to pay the check. On April 4, through an oversight of one of the bank's employees, E Bank inadvertently paid the check to P.

a) On April 2 R went to E Bank and told the cashier he wished to stop payment on a check. The cashier gave R a printed card, which, when filled in, signed, and returned to the cashier, read as follows:

STOP-PAYMENT REQUEST

To E Bank
Philadelphia, Pa.

I hereby request that, as a favor to me, you do not pay my check number 1234, dated April 1 of this year, drawn in favor of P. Porter in the amount of $500.

I expressly agree, with an intent to be legally bound hereby, that should you unintentionally pay the above-described check in the ordinary course of your business, you will not be in any way liable for the payment. This request will expire 30 days from date unless renewed in writing.
[Date]

(signed) R. Roger

Could E Bank charge the payment against R's account?

b) On April 2 R phoned E Bank and told the cashier he wished to stop payment on his check, describing the check as above. The cashier asked R to stop in the bank at his earliest convenience and sign a written stop payment request. R went to the bank on April 5 to sign such a request. 1) Could E Bank charge the payment against R's account (a) if the payment was made to P? (b) if the payment was made to H, a holder in due course? 2) Could E Bank recover from the person to whom it inadvertently paid the check, (a) if that person was P? (b) if that person was H, a holder in due course?

33. a) Without receiving any consideration, and to enable P to borrow $500, M signed a negotiable promissory note in that amount, naming P as payee. P indorsed and transferred the note to H for value. When H took the note, he knew that M had received no consideration for it. When the note matured, P was in financial difficulty and H sued M. Could H recover from M? (Modified from A.I.C.P.A., Nov. 45-3a.)

b) Other facts being the same, assume that to avoid a lawsuit M paid H. Could M obtain a judgment against P?

34. M signed a ninety-day note in the amount of $1,000, naming P as payee. The note contained a power of attorney to confess a judgment at any time. Before M delivered the note to P, A indorsed it in blank for the accommodation of M. When P demanded payment upon the due date, M had become insolvent and was unable to pay. P promptly notified A. When A refused to pay, P sued A. What result?

35. M wished to purchase goods from P on two-months' credit. P was unwilling to extend credit unless M obtained an acceptable guarantor. P agreed that A, a friend of M's would be acceptable. On May 1 P delivered the goods to M, receiving in exchange the following: "[Date]. Two months after date I promise to pay to the order of P. Porter $500 with interest. (signed) M. Martin." When received by P, the note was indorsed, "Payment guaranteed (signed) A. Adams." On July 3, M called upon P in his office and requested an additional thirty days on the note. Since M's business was showing signs of becoming successful, P agreed and said that he would wait until August 1. However, M failed to pay by August 1, and P demanded payment from A. This was the first that A had heard of the note since he had indorsed it on May 1. Upon A's refusal to pay, P sued A. What result?

36. M signed and gave to P a negotiable one-year note in the amount of $5,000 with interest at the rate of 6 percent. When the note which named P as payee was delivered to P, it bore the unqualified indorsement of A. One month later P permitted M to cross out the words "six percent" on the note and write in "four percent." When M failed to pay upon P's due presentment, P promptly notified A. This was the first that A knew of the change in the interest rate. A refused to pay anything and P sued A. What result? (Modified from A.I.C.P.A., Nov. 30-7.)

37. On February 1 M dated, signed, and delivered to P. Porter the following: "[Date] For value received I promise to pay to the order of P. Porter the principal sum of $600, said principal sum to be payable as follows: $100 on the first of next month, and $100 on the same day of each and every month thereafter until the entire amount has been paid. In the event of my failure to pay any of such installments at the time specified herein, all of the remaining principal shall at the option of the holder become immediately due and payable. (signed) M. Martin." On February 9 P indorsed the note, "(signed) P. Porter" and sold it to H for value. H immediately notified M of the transfer, but made no presentment until July 2. M paid H $100 on March 1, $50 on April 1, $25 on April 15, $25 on May 2, $50 on June 1, and nothing further. On July 2, H presented the note to M and demanded payment of the entire unpaid balance. Upon M's failure to pay, H promptly notified P, who had previously been unaware of any default. H sued P. How much if anything was H entitled to recover?

38. For fair consideration, M dated, signed, and gave P the following note: "[Date] On demand I promise to pay to the order of P. Porter $1,000. Protest waived. (signed) M. Martin." Five days later P sold, unqualifiedly indorsed, and transferred the note to A. Two years later, A sold, unqualifiedly indorsed, and transferred the note to H. One month after receiving the note, H for the first time requested payment from M and upon M's failure to pay, promptly notified A and P. H sued for the face amount of the note. Could H recover 1) from P? 2) from A?

39. On February 1, for fair consideration, M dated, signed, and gave P. Porter the following: "Centerville, Ill. [Date]. Six months after date I promise to pay to P. Porter or bearer $1,000. (signed) M. Martin." M made the note in this manner to avoid the risk of forged indorsements. P sold and transferred the note to A. Adams, who sold and transferred it to B. Brown of New York City. On July 25 a thief stole the note from B's locked desk, forged B's indorsement, and on July 27 sold and transferred the note to C. Carter, who, on July 29, sold and transferred it to D. Davis of New York City. On July 31 D forwarded the note to the Centerville National Bank, which, on August 1, collected $1,000 from M, delivered the note to M, and remitted to D less the bank's collection fee. Indorsements on the note read as follows: "(signed) P. Porter"; "Pay to B. Brown (signed) A. Adams"; "(Signed—by the thief) B. Brown"; "Pay to D. Davis (signed) C. Carter"; "Pay to the Centerville National Bank for collection (signed) D. Davis"; "Payment received (signed) Centerville National Bank."

With due diligence, B discovered the theft on August 2, and wrote to the Centerville National Bank describing the note and its theft, and requesting that the bank contact M and tell him of the theft, offer M a bond in the usual form to indemnify him against later appearance of the note, collect $1,000, and remit to B after deducting the bank's service charge and bond expense. The bank's reply told B of presentment and payment of the note on August 1. B demanded payment from M and upon M's failure to pay, sued M. What result?

40. R drew a negotiable sight draft on E. Edwards, naming P as payee. P promptly presented the draft to E who wrote on it, "Accepted, payable in 10 days (signed) E. Edwards." At the expiration of the ten-day period, P demanded payment from E and upon E's failure to pay, promptly notified R. This was the first R knew of any difficulty concerning the draft. P sued R. What result? (Modified from A.I.C.P.A., Nov. 53-4b.)

41. Arthur Adams, together with several other members of an incorporated club, indorsed the club's negotiable note which named P as payee. The club defaulted on the note, and P procured from the president of the club a typed list stating the names and addresses of the indorsers. When P attempted to verify the addresses by comparing with the current telephone directory, he found an Arthur Adams listed at an address different from the one on the typed list. Within proper time, P sent a notice of dishonor of the note, by certified mail, addressed to Arthur Adams at the address stated on the typed list. Four days later the post office returned the letter to P with a notation, "Moved, left no address." P then promptly contacted Arthur Adams at the telephone directory address, found that it was the same Arthur Adams who had indorsed the note, and gave him notice of dishonor. This was the first that Arthur Adams knew of nonpayment of the note. Could P hold Arthur Adams liable as an indorser? (Modified from A.I.C.P.A., May 35-6.)

chapter 15

Bailments and Shipments of Goods

The term "bailment" describes the commonly recurring relationship of persons and goods in which one person is in rightful possession of certain goods belonging to someone else. The party in possession is commonly called the *bailee;* the person who owns the goods which are in the bailee's possession is the *bailor.*

Bailment relationships usually arise from contracts between bailors and bailees. For example, the owner of an automobile may contract with a garageman for certain repairs and leave his car with the garageman; this is a bailment for services. Or the owner of an automobile may contract to rent his car to a businessman temporarily in town, and deliver the car to the businessman for his use; this is a bailment for use. However, a contract prescribing certain compensation (e.g. for repairs or rental) is not essential for the creation of a bailment relationship. For example, a friend may borrow his neighbor's book or agree to keep his neighbor's household plants while the neighbor is away; such persons usually do not expect that compensation will be paid for use of the book or care of the plants. Also, a bailment relationship can arise even though the parties have never formed an agreement and may never even have seen each other. For example, suppose that a pedestrian finds a wallet lying on the sidewalk, learns from a driver's license in the wallet the identity of the owner, and pockets the wallet in order to return it to its owner. Being in rightful possession of goods which belong to someone else, the finder is a bailee, although no actual contract has been formed between the parties. Whatever the type of bailment, whether created by an actual contract or not, a bailment relationship does not arise without the consent or intent of the bailee. In essence therefore, a bailment involves not only a property relationship but also a contractual or consensual relationship, which gives rise to certain rights and obligations between the bailor and the bailee.

OBLIGATIONS OF BAILEES OTHER THAN CARRIERS

Since the bailed goods in the bailee's possession belong to someone else, it is proper and fair to expect the bailee to exercise certain care in their safekeeping. Some bailment contracts expressly prescribe the care the bailee will be obliged to exercise. In the absence of any special contract obligations, the law imposes certain standards, which can be referred to as a bailee's ordinary obligations.

BAILEES' ORDINARY OBLIGATIONS

In the absence of an express agreement otherwise, a bailee is obliged to comply with the ordinary terms and conditions of a bailment agreement and to exercise proper care for the safety of the bailed goods.

Breach of Bailment Agreement

Misdelivery. A bailee expressly or impliedly agrees to return the bailed goods to the bailor at the expiration of the bailment period. No matter how much care the bailee exercises, if he delivers the bailed goods to a person not authorized by the bailor to receive them, the bailee is liable to the bailor, unless the bailee's delivery is by order of court or unless the person to whom the bailee delivers is the owner of the goods and entitled to immediate possession.

Misuse. Regardless of the care exercised, a bailee is liable to the bailor for any damages arising in connection with the bailee's use of the bailed goods in a manner not authorized (expressly or impliedly) by the bailor.

Sometimes a bailee's employee steals and disposes of bailed goods or without authority misuses and damages them. Whether or not the bailee should be held liable for the unauthorized act of his employee is a question of policy upon which courts in the various states do not agree. The courts in some states feel it to be better policy (more fair, reasonable, and practical) to view this as an agency question, whereas the courts in other states view it as a question of contractual or consensual obligation. The latter appears to be the modern trend.

The Agency Approach. An employer is not liable for his employee's tort unless the tort falls within the general scope of the employee's authorized services. Since the employee's theft or unauthorized use of bailed goods is clearly outside the scope of his services, his employer, the bailee, is not liable to the bailor.

The Obligation Approach. A person who chooses to perform a contract through an agent does not adequately perform the contract if the agent fails to perform properly, whatever the reason for the agent's failure. Suppose that a builder contracts with a property owner to erect a frame garage adjacent to the owner's house; the builder hires carpenters reasonably believed to be competent and honest, but during the construction a disgruntled employee secretly weakens several of the ceiling joists so that the garage collapses in the first strong wind.

Although the builder has used reasonable care, he certainly has not adequately performed his contract obligation.

Example: O stored his car in G's garage. One night, G's attendant, who had previously been a satisfactory employee, took O's car and drove about a mile to the nearest beer distributor. On the way back to the garage with a quart bottle of beer, the attendant was driving carelessly and collided with a car owned and operated by T, damaging both cars. T was not guilty of contributory negligence. In separate lawsuits, T and O sued G for damages to their respective cars.

As to T's car: G would not be liable to T, because the attendant's tort was outside the general scope of his employment.

As to O's car: Under the agency approach, G would not be liable to O; under the obligation approach, G would be liable to O for the damages to O's car.

Negligence

A bailee is obliged to use proper care for the safekeeping of bailed goods. If the goods are stolen or damaged as a result of the negligence of the bailee, he is liable; if the bailee and his agents are not negligent or otherwise at fault, the bailee is not liable.

The degree of care which must be exercised depends upon all of the circumstances, including 1) the value of the bailed item, 2) its susceptibility to theft or damage, 3) the known facilities of the bailee for safekeeping, 4) the customs and prior course of dealing of the parties, and 5) whether possession of the bailed goods is an advantage or a burden to the bailee. In regard to the fifth factor, if the bailee is deriving no benefit, the law imposes upon him less of an obligation as to care; in the usual situation when both parties are being benefited, the law imposes the ordinary standard of care; if the bailor is doing a favor for the bailee and the bailee is deriving the sole benefit, the law imposes upon him an obligation to use greater care.

Burden of Proof

The ambiguous expression "burden of proof" refers to either of two related but different legal concepts, 1) the burden of first presenting evidence concerning a certain point; 2) the additional burden of ultimately persuading or convincing the trier of fact (the jury, or the judge if the trial is held without a jury) that certain facts exist. In most lawsuits both of these burdens rest on the plaintiff. Thus in order to recover from the defendant, the plaintiff must not only lead off with evidence tending to show that the defendant acted in some wrongful manner (by committing a tort or breaching a contract), but also, after the defendant in turn presents evidence tending to refute that of the plaintiff, the total effect of all the evidence must favor the plaintiff. In some types of cases, however, evidence of the defendant's conduct is particularly within the defendant's knowledge and not available to the plaintiff. In such cases it is considered fair to shift to the defendant the burden of first presenting evidence. Since a bailee is in exclusive possession of the bailed goods, this theory of shifting the burden of presenting evidence applies to a lawsuit brought by a bailor against a bailee for a casualty to bailed goods.

However, while there is general agreement that a bailee should bear the burden of presenting evidence, the courts in the various states do not agree on whether the burden of persuading the jury should also be shifted from the plaintiff (the bailor) to the defendant (the bailee). Many courts say that after the bailee presents evidence tending to show that he was free from negligence, the burden of persuasion remains on the plaintiff-bailor; that for the bailor to win, the jury must feel, from all the evidence, that it is more likely than not that the bailee was negligent. In other words, unless the jury feels by the preponderance of the evidence that the bailee was negligent, the decision will be in favor of the bailee. On the other hand, other courts say that the burden of persuasion is on the bailee, that the bailor will win unless the jury feels from all the evidence that it is more likely than not that the bailee was free from negligence. In other words, unless the jury feels by the preponderance of the evidence that the bailee was free from negligence, the decision will be in favor of the bailor. If the mind of the jury is in equilibrum—not persuaded one way or the other—then 1) if the burden of persuasion is on the plaintiff-bailor, judgment will be given to the defendant-bailee, but 2) if the burden of persuasion is on the defendant-bailee, judgment will be given to the plaintiff-bailor. Professor Ray A. Brown has described and illustrated the effect which the burden of persuasion has on the outcome of a bailment lawsuit:

> The testimony is, of course, often conflicting and contradictory, so that it cannot be said with certainty what the true fact situation is. In such a situation, the jury must be instructed which of the two parties has the burden of persuading the jury by a preponderance of evidence concerning the truth of the disputed facts in issue. The determination of this question is often decisive of the case. Suppose, for example, that the palintiff has deposited valuables with the defendant for safekeeping and that the same have been destroyed by fire of an unknown origin. If the bailor has the burden of proving that the bailee was negligent the bailor cannot recover; for, not knowing the cause of the fire, he cannot show that the bailee failed in his duty of due care. If, on the other hand, the bailee must convince the jury that he was

careful he will likely be defeated, for he also cannot show that the fire may not have been due to some carelessness on his part.[1]

In restating the rules of law concerning bills of lading and warehouse receipts, the authors of the Uniform Commercial Code have recognized this difference of view concerning the burden of persuasion. Feeling that the policy difference does not substantially interfere with the uniformity of law which the Code is designed to achieve, the authors have written alternative provisions for this portion of the Code, stating:

> (1) The bailee must deliver the goods to a person entitled under the document [bill of lading or warehouse receipt] . . . unless and to the extent that the bailee establishes any of the following: . . .
> (b) damage to or delay, loss or destruction of the goods for which the bailee is not liable; [In some states, subsection (1) (b) stops here; in other states, the following clause is added] but the burden of establishing negligence in such cases is on the person entitled under the document [meaning the bailor] . . .[2]

BAILEES' SPECIAL CONTRACT OBLIGATIONS

Special contract provisions sometimes attempt to either increase or decrease a bailee's obligation.

Extension of Liability

Some extension of liability provisions pertain only to certain particular occurrences; some others extend liability generally, making the bailee in effect an insurer of the bailed goods and liable for any casualty no matter how it is caused. For liability as an insurer to arise, it must be clearly and definitely stated in the bailment agreement.

In this connection, the effect of the following, very common provision has been frequently litigated:

> At the expiration of the bailment period, the bailee shall return the bailed goods to the bailor in the same condition the goods were in at the inception of the bailment.

Since such a provision does not clearly and definitely express an intent that the bailee be absolutely liable, it is usually interpreted as stating nothing more than the bailee's ordinary obligation.

Limitation of Liability

Sum for Which Liable. Bailment contracts sometimes provide that even if a bailee is negligent, his liability shall be limited to a certain

---

[1] Ray A. Brown, *The Law of Personal Property*, 2d ed. (Chicago: Callaghan & Company, 1955), Sec. 87.

[2] U.C.C. Sec. 7-403.

stated amount; some contracts go further and state that the bailee will not be liable at all. If a bailee is in the business of storing goods for hire for the general public, a contract provision which either exempts liability or unreasonably limits liability is considered against public policy and not enforceable. Such a bailee would be held fully liable for casualty to goods caused by the bailee's conduct or by conduct for which the bailee is responsible. For other types of bailees, many states do not consider an exemption or limitation provision as necessarily contrary to the public interest and therefore frequently will enforce the provision.

Time Limit on Liability. In some types of bailment transactions the parties agree on a time limit for the bailment. For example, a dry cleaner posts a sign reading "Not liable for goods left after thirty days." If a customer has no knowledge of the time limit, it does not become a part of the bailment contract. However, if a customer with actual knowledge of the sign leaves garments to be cleaned, he agrees to the time limit.

When a time limit has been agreed upon and has expired, if the bailee is still in physical possession of the bailed goods, the bailment does not end—the bailee is not free to throw the goods away or to arbitrarily dispose of them. However, after expiration of the time limit, he is an unwilling bailee. Very few cases have litigated the point, but it seems fair to say that such an unwilling bailee should not be obliged to exercise as much care as an ordinary bailee. Some courts have suggested that if the bailor delays in claiming his goods until after expiration of the agreed time limit, and the goods are then discovered to be missing or damaged, the burden of proof does not shift to the bailee but remains with the bailor to discover and present evidence of the bailee's negligence—which in many cases is quite difficult or impossible for the bailor to do. Also, a time limit agreement can frequently be construed as exempting the bailee from liability for any casualty to the bailed goods occurring after expiration of the time limit, even if the casualty is caused by the bailee's negligence. It would seem, therefore, that if parties actually agree on a time limit in a bailment contract, the bailee will have little if any liability for unintentional casualty to the goods should the bailor fail to claim his goods within the agreed time.

OBLIGATIONS OF COMMON CARRIERS

Bailees in the business of transporting the goods of others are classed as either common carriers or private carriers (the latter also frequently being called contract carriers). In distinguishing between common and private carriers, the Pennsylvania Superior Court has said:

Despite variations in language, the definitions found in the cases stress the all-important factor that a common carrier is one that holds itself out and undertakes to carry the goods of all persons indifferently, or of all who choose to employ it, and one that invites the custom of the public indiscriminately.[3]

And the Kentucky Court of Appeals has said:

When a person has assumed the character of a common carrier, either by expressly offering his services to all who will hire him, or by so conducting his business as to justify the belief on the part of the public that he means to become the servant of the public, and to carry for all, he may be safely presumed to have intended to assume the liabilities of a common carrier. . . .

But in order to impress upon him the character, and impose upon him the liabilities of a common carrier, his conduct must amount to a public offer to carry for all who tender him such goods as he is accustomed to carry.[4]

Common carriers have a greater liability than do ordinary bailees. When goods shipped by a common carrier (railroad, truckline, airline, etc.) suffer some casualty (damage, destruction, loss, theft, or delay), the carrier is absolutely liable to the owner or shipper unless the casualty is caused by one of the following: 1) an act of God; 2) an act of a public enemy; 3) an act of the state; 4) an act of the shipper; or 5) the inherent nature of the goods. The standard form of bill of lading used with freight shipments repeats these common-law exceptions and also adds a few others—including casualties resulting from riots or strikes, provided the carrier is free from negligence.

The rule that a carrier is absolutely liable is a policy rule associated in its origin and present-day continuation with the following interrelated factors:

1. The hazards of transportation in the early days of commerce: When commerce began to expand in England, thieves and outlaws roamed the countryside. Travel and transportation were hazardous and carriers were sometimes tempted to work in collusion with outlaw bands. While such a temptation still exists, it is much reduced.

2. The fact that common carriers are public utilities: Because of the public's vital concern with the proper and successful operation of common carriers, the public imposes certain burdens and obligations upon them which are not imposed upon private carriers or on other ordinary businesses; and commensurate with the burdens, the public grants common carriers certain special rights. Thus in addition to ab-

---

[3] *Merchants Parcel Del. Inc. v. Pa. PUC*, 150 Pa. Super. 120, 28 A. (2d) 340 (1942).

[4] *Varble v. Bigley*, 14 Bush. (Ky.) 698, 29 Am. Rep. 435 (1879).

solute liability for goods, a common carrier has an obligation to accept all goods which are properly offered and which come within the scope of its facilities, and the carrier must submit to public regulation of its rates. A common carrier's special advantages include public subsidies and statutory protection from unlimited competition.

3. The risk of casualty to goods during handling and transportation: Obviously, goods which are being transported are exposed to much greater risks than are stationary goods.

4. The exclusive control which a carrier exercises over transported goods and over information pertaining to such goods: Although any bailor will encounter great difficulty in ascertaining the cause of a casualty to his goods (hence the special burden-of-proof rule in bailment law), a bailor's difficulty is compounded with transported goods; a casualty can occur a great distance from the starting point and is usually exclusively within the knowledge and control of the carrier.

Exceptions to Carrier's Absolute Liability

The policy factors which support the rule of the carrier's absolute liability also explain the exceptions to this liability.

Acts of God

At the time the term "act of God" was coined, scientific knowledge concerning unusual, natural occurrences was limited. It was believed that the Creator had set in motion the ordinary forces of nature, including the tides and the seasons (summer heat, winter cold, sunshine, rain, snow, etc.), and that the natural cycle once begun continued to operate without further Divine impetus. When an unexpected and unusually violent act of nature occurred, the only explanation that could be formulated was that for some reason known only to Himself, the Creator occasionally intervened and interrupted the natural order of things, sending an unusually violent wind storm, an earthquake, a tidal wave, a bolt of lightning, or the like. Although greater scientific knowledge now provides explanations for these violent upheavals of nature, there is a modern-day reason to continue the act-of-God exception. If a violent upheaval of nature occurs, it usually becomes common knowledge. As a result, there is less chance for collusion or deception by a carrier, and also evidence of such an unusual occurrence is usually readily available to a shipper. Therefore, just as it is considered sound policy to continue the rule of absolute carrier liability, it is also considered sound policy to free the carrier from liability for a so-called act of God.

There is not entire agreement among the courts of the various states as to the incidents which should be classified as acts of God. In general, an act of God involves 1) an act of natural forces, 2) which is unusual or unexpected, and therefore 3) which cannot reasonably be foreseen or prevented. While lightning is not an unusual phenomenon, exactly where it will strike is unpredictable and unexpected; therefore a bolt of lightning is classed as an act of God. Ordinary winter snowfalls and spring flooding are usual and can be expected, but an unusually heavy fall of snow or an unexpectedly extensive flood would be classed as an act of God.

Acts of the Public Enemy

This exception to a carrier's absolute liability arises from the same policy reasons as the act-of-God exception; namely, that if such an incident causes a casualty to goods, it is highly unusual and its occurrence is likely to be a matter of common knowledge. As with acts of God, the policy reasons for the exception indicate its scope. Theft of freight shipments is not highly unusual, nor is the fact that a box car has been rifled likely to become common knowledge. Thieves, outlaws, and even mobs are therefore not "public enemies" in this sense. The term is reserved for the organized military forces of a government claiming sovereignty—usually an invading army. Since the Confederate States claimed sovereignty, the term applied to the acts of the Confederate forces during the American Civil War.

Acts of the State

This exception includes judicial attachment and executive seizure (such as a seizure of contraband or of harmful foods).

Acts of the Shipper

This exception covers casualty to goods caused by the shipper's improper packing, provided that the defective packing is not reasonably noticeable to the carrier. A carrier is liable for a casualty resulting from improper packing of which the carrier should reasonably have been aware.

Inherent Nature of the Goods

If a casualty to goods results solely from the nature of the goods and could not reasonably have been prevented by the carrier, the carrier is not liable.

Duration of Carrier's Absolute Liability

Many carriers have warehouse facilities, and in addition to transporting goods also operate public warehouse businesses, storing goods for agreed prices. Even if a carrier does not operate a public warehouse, the carrier is permitted to charge for storage if goods are left in the carrier's hands longer than contemplated by the shipment. The policy reasons for a carrier's absolute liability apply only to casualties sustained in close connection with the transportation of goods. Therefore, a carrier in possession of goods may either be acting as a warehouseman and be liable for casualty to the goods only if negligent or otherwise at fault, or may instead be acting as a carrier with the carrier's absolute liability.

Commencement of Absolute Liability

A common carrier's absolute liability begins when the carrier is in possession of goods under an agreement for their immediate transportation.

Termination of Absolute Liability

After goods arrive at their destination, the consignee to whom delivery is intended sometimes fails or refuses to take the goods from the carrier, thus extending the carrier's possession beyond the time originally contemplated by the transportation contract. The policy reasons which support the theory of absolute liability do not require that such liability continue over this additional period. Therefore, the law states that after completion of transportation—that is, after a carrier does all that is required under the transportation contract—the carrier holds goods only as a warehouseman. Three of the most common types of transportation contracts involve 1) baggage, 2) goods to be delivered to a certain street address, and 3) freight.

Baggage. This term includes goods of the type which a traveler commonly delivers into a carrier's possession for transportation in connection with the carrier's transportation of the traveler. Usually the baggage which a traveler checks through on his ticket is carried in the baggage facilities of the same conveyance in which the traveler is riding; at the destination the traveler is expected to wait a few minutes until his baggage is unloaded and brought into the terminal. Therefore, the transportation of such baggage is considered as completed a reasonable time after arrival at destination. If the traveler delays en route or for some other reason fails to call for his baggage promptly after its expected time of arrival, the carrier's liability is reduced to that of a warehouseman.

Shipments Deliverable to a Certain Address. An express shipment is the most common example of this type. The transportation is considered as completed when the carrier reasonably attempts to deliver at the stated address. If the carrier is unable to deliver through no fault of its own, its liability thereafter is that of a warehouseman.

Freight Shipments. Unlike shipments which a carrier contracts to deliver to a certain address, ordinary freight shipments are transported to the freight station or freight facilities at the destination; the consignee then comes and takes the goods away. Under the law covering most freight shipments, the transportation is considered as completed. (and the carrier is thereafter liable only as a warehouseman) after the consignee has had a reasonable opportunity to call for the goods—more specifically 1) after proper notice of arrival has been sent or given, and 2) following such notice, after expiration of the time specified in the approved rate scale on file with the public regulatory commission (or if no time is specified in the filed tariffs, after expiration of the time agreed upon in the transportation contract, or if no time is agreed upon, after the expiration of a reasonable time).

Contracts Limiting Liability

Some carriers have attempted by special contract with shippers to relieve themselves from the carrier's absolute liability. Since the rule of absolute liability is based upon what courts and legislatures believe to be sound public policy, a contract provision exempting a common carrier from its absolute liability is considered to be against public policy and not enforceable. However, although a common carrier cannot exempt itself from absolute liability, it can under many state statutes[5] and under Federal statutes limit its liability to stated amounts, unless higher values are declared, for which the statutes prescribe proportionately higher transportation charges.

DETERMINING EXISTENCE OF BAILMENTS

By definition, a bailment involves the possession of goods by someone other than the owner. The concept of possession is important in many different fields of the law. The word "possession" is a tag or symbol that the law applies to a certain relationship which exists between a person and a particular item of property, a relationship which involves 1) the person having manual or physical contact with or control over the item, or the right and ability to take immediate physical control over it, and 2) the person having an obvious or manifested intent to

[5] U.C.C. Sec. 7-309.

exclude others from taking or exercising control over the particular item.

The chief features of the concept of possession include the following:

1. A person may have a manual grip on an item and thus have it entirely within his physical control and nevertheless not be in possession of it. For example, a jeweler hands a watch to a shopper to enable him to examine the watch more closely. Although the shopper holds the watch in his hand, the jeweler does not intend that the shopper leave with the watch until making some arrangement for payment, and the shopper manifests no intent to exercise exclusive control over the watch. Therefore, the law feels that it is not sound policy to accord to the shopper the rights ordinarily associated with possession. The shopper has temporary custody of the watch but is not legally in possession of it.

2. A person may be in possession of an item even though he does not have hold of or other physical contact with the item. For example, an owner parks his car along the curb outside a store, puts a coin in the appropriate parking meter, and enters the store. The law feels it reasonable to consider that once an owner has possession of an item of property, his possession continues until he abandons the item or until another person takes possession of it. Since the car owner does not surrender possession to some other person, the car owner, although in the store and separated from his car, is still in possession of the car. By using the parking meter, the owner pays the city for the privilege of parking at that spot. However, it is neither reasonable nor practical to consider that the owner thus surrenders his car into the possession of the city.

3. Although all courts do not agree, the better-reasoned cases recognize that a person can be in possession of an item even though he is unaware of its nature or of its existence. The numerous items contained in a small boy's pockets or a woman's purse have long been the subject of jokes and cartoons. Although the boy or the woman might not be able to remember and accurately inventory all of the items being carried, certainly the boy and the woman are in possession of all such items. If A surreptitiously drops a wallet into the pocket of the suit coat B is wearing, B may be unaware of the presence of the wallet in his pocket, but nevertheless, through his control and intent to exclude others, B is in possession of the wallet.

Example: A customer enters a restaurant, hangs his hat and coat on a convenient hook, and takes a place at one of the tables. After finishing his meal, the customer does not have to identify himself or obtain permission to remove his hat and coat from the hook upon which they are hanging. Clearly when he uses the hook, the customer does not surrender possession of his hat and coat to the restaurant owner or to anyone else. Therefore, there is no bailment of the hat and coat; should the hat and coat be stolen, the restaurant owner would not be liable.

Many restaurants display signs disclaiming responsibility for hats and coats. The presence or absence of such a sign has no effect on whether or not there is a bailment of a hat and coat; the sign merely serves to remind customers of the rule of law which would prevail even in the absence of the sign.

Example: A customer in a restaurant hands his hat and coat to a clerk on duty in the checkroom and receives a ticket bearing a certain number. Should the customer lose the ticket, he would have to otherwise identify himself as the owner of that particular hat and coat in order to reobtain them from the checkroom clerk. Therefore, it is apparent that when the customer checks his hat and coat, he transfers possession to the restaurant, and a bailment arises.

Example: A customer entered a clothing store to purchase a pair of slacks. After a clerk showed the customer a number of slacks, the customer expressed an interest in a certain pair. The clerk directed the customer to a dressing booth so that he could try on the new slacks. The customer left his own trousers in the dressing booth while he rejoined the clerk who had been waiting on him and together they discussed the appearance of the new slacks while standing in front of a mirror. The customer decided not to purchase the slacks and returned to the dressing booth. After waiting a few minutes until another person finished using the dressing booth, the customer entered the booth and changed into his own trousers. The customer immediately noticed that his wallet was missing. The wallet had been in the back pocket of the trousers when left in the booth and had contained $90. The customer reported the loss to the clerk. They searched and found the empty wallet in a scrap can near the dressing booth, but the person who had been in the booth when the customer returned to it had disappeared. The customer sued the clothing store for $90.

The courts of a number of states would hold that when the trousers were left in the booth, there was a bailment of the customer's trousers, together with the usual contents of trouser pockets. For example, the Pennsylvania Supreme Court has said:

> When the defendants opened a retail clothing store, they thereby invited the public to come into their place of business and purchase clothing in the usual manner. And when they extended this invitation, they assumed some duty to the people who should respond to it. . . . Whatever thus necessarily, or, in common with people generally, he habitually carries with him, and must necessarily lay aside in the store while making or examining his purchases, he is invited to lay aside by the invitation to come and purchase, and, having laid it aside upon such invitation and with the knowledge of the dealer, he has committed it to his custody. And this being a necessary incident of the business

upon which the customer was invited to come to the store, the care of the property would be within the authority of the salesman assigned to wait upon him; it would be part of the transaction in which he is authorized to represent his employer.[6]

The clothing stores cases are about as far as the courts have gone in finding an implied surrender of possession by an owner and an implied acceptance of possession by an alleged bailee. No implied transfer of possession is found in other somewhat similar situations, such as the restaurant cases. In comparing a typical clothing-store case (which involves an implied transfer of possession and therefore a bailment) with a typical restaurant case (in which no implied transfer of possession takes place), the following differences appear:

1. In a clothing store the contact between the clerk and customer is usually continuous while the customer is in the store. In a restaurant, after the waiter serves the meal, he usually does not remain in continuous contact with the customer all the while the meal is being eaten.

2. In a clothing store, the customer's taking off certain of his own clothing is directly associated with the business of the store and the purpose of the customer in coming into the store, and is at the direction of the clerk. In a restaurant, a customer usually removes his outer street clothing before he has any contact with a waiter; furthermore, removing such clothing is a matter of convenience and good manners and is not essential for the consumption of food.

When a transfer of possession is only implied (as in clothing-store cases) rather than actual, a notice of unwillingness to accept implied custody can frequently prevent a bailment from arising. For example, when a sign prominently displayed in a dressing booth read, "Not responsible for customer's garments or other property unless left at credit desk on this floor," it has been held that the clothing store was not liable for a wallet stolen from trousers which a customer had hung in the dressing booth.

Parking Lots

Parking lots are of two distinct types, bailment type parking lots and the nonbailment type. The distinction turns upon whether or not possession is transferred to the parking lot owner. If a person must in some way identify himself as the one entitled to a particular car before being allowed to remove that car, this indicates that the parking-lot proprietor is in possession of the car, and therefore that a bailment exists. On the other hand, if a person may drive his car away without the necessity of

---

[6] *Woodruff* v. *Painter*, 150 Pa. 91, 24 A. 621, 16 L.R.A. 451, 30 Am. St. Rep. 786 (1892).

being identified or recognized, this indicates that the owner has remained in possession of the car while it is parked, and therefore that no bailment exists. Usually in a bailment type of parking lot, the ignition key is left in the car or with the proprietor of the lot, while in a nonbailment type of lot the owner takes the key with him. The location of the key is an important factor but is not conclusive. While unusual, it is possible to have a bailment even though the owner retains the key and no bailment even though the owner is requested to leave the key.

VALUABLES CONCEALED IN BAILED PROPERTY

Suppose that when an owner checks his overcoat at the check stand in a restaurant, the bailee is unaware that the owner has left a $500 watch in one of the coat pockets, and that when the coat is returned to the bailor the watch is missing. In most such cases the courts agree that the bailee should not be liable. However, the courts disagree as to the applicable theory. Some courts would say that there is no bailment of the watch because the alleged bailee is unaware of its presence. This view seems unrealistic. Certainly the bailee is in possession of the coat, having both physical control over it and a manifested intent to exclude unauthorized persons from taking the coat. It seems unreasonable to say that although the bailee is in possession of the coat, he is not in possession of an item contained within the coat. The more reasonable view is to consider that there is a bailment of both the coat and the watch, but at the same time to recognize that it is not fair to hold the bailee liable for casualty to an item if the bailee is reasonably unaware of the presence or value of that item. If the bailee were advised of the presence of the watch in the overcoat, he might want to handle the watch in a special manner or he might refuse to receive and undertake responsibility for it. Therefore, the bailee's knowledge of the presence or value of an item is an important factor in defining both the standard of care required of a bailee and the scope of his liability for negligence. A bailee is required to use the care considered proper for items which he knows, or reasonably should know, are in his custody. Even when a bailee is negligent, he is not liable for damages which are highly unlikely to result from his lack of care.

Thus in the case of the overcoat containing the concealed $500 watch, if the bailee returns the coat together with any items which were in the pockets and which are usually associated with overcoats (such as gloves or a scarf), the fact that the watch is missing would not evidence any carelessness on the part of the bailee. If the coat itself is missing together with the watch, the bailee would be liable for the value of the coat and its expected contents but not for the unexpected watch.

BAILEES' LIENS

The common law has long recognized that if a bailee in the ordinary course of his business contracts to perform work on certain bailed goods, or otherwise to provide services relating to the goods, the bailee has the

---

UNIFORM ORDER BILL OF LADING
THE ROGER RAILROAD COMPANY

Received, subject to the classifications and tariffs in effect on the date of issue of this Bill of Lading, the property described below, in apparent good order, except as noted (contents and condition of contents of packages unknown), marked, consigned, and destined as indicated below, which the carrier agrees to carry to its usual place of delivery at said destination, if on its own road or water line, otherwise to deliver to another carrier on the route to said destination. It is mutually agreed that every service to be performed hereunder shall be subject to all the conditions herein contained, including the conditions on back hereof, which are hereby agreed to by the shipper.

The surrender of this original ORDER Bill of Lading properly indorsed shall be required before the delivery of the property. Inspection of property covered by this bill of lading will not be permitted unless provided by law or unless permission is indorsed on this original bill of lading or given in writing by the shipper.

Date [date] At _____ Philadelphia, Pa. _____ From _____ S. Smith _____

Consigned to the ORDER of _____ S. Smith _____

Destination _____ Centerville, _____ State of _____ Illinois _____

Notify _____ B. Brown _____ At _____ Centerville _____ State of _____ Illinois _____

No. Pkgs.	Description of Articles	Weight
5	Television Sets	240 lbs

The carrier shall not make delivery of this shipment without payment of freight and all other lawful charges.

The agreed or declared value of the property is hereby specifically stated by the shipper to be _____ $1,000 _____

Shipper (signed) S. Smith   Freight Agent (signed) A. Adams

---

right to retain possession of the goods which have had the benefit of his services until the bailor pays the contract price—unless the bailee had also agreed that payment could be deferred until sometime after return of the goods to the bailor. Statutes in most states enlarge upon this common-law lien, giving a bailee a right (after waiting a stated time and by following a specified procedure) to sell the bailed goods in order to collect the contract price for his services and materials.

DOCUMENTS OF TITLE

Either the storage of goods or their shipment is usually accompanied by an appropriate written contract called a *document of title*—so called because the document represents or evidences the title of, or ownership

---

UNIFORM STRAIGHT BILL OF LADING—NOT NEGOTIABLE
THE ROGER RAILROAD COMPANY

Received, subject to the classifications and tariffs in effect on the date of issue of this Bill of Lading, the property described below, in apparent good order, except as noted (contents and conditions of contents of packages unknown), marked, consigned, and destined as indicated below, which the carrier agrees to carry to its usual place of delivery at said destination, if on its own road or water line, otherwise to deliver to another carrier on the route to said destination. It is mutually agreed that every service to be performed hereunder shall be subject to all the conditions herein contained, including the conditions on back hereof, which are hereby agreed to by the shipper.

Date [date] At Philadelphia, Pa. From S. Smith

Consigned to B. Brown

Destination Centerville State of Illinois

No. Pkgs.	Description of Articles	Weight
5	Television Sets	240 lbs

The carrier shall not make delivery of this shipment without payment of freight and all other lawful charges.

The agreed or declared value of the property is hereby specifically stated by the shipper to be $1,000

Shipper (signed) S. Smith Freight Agent (signed) A. Adams

---

interest in, the particular goods it describes. The most common documents of title are warehouse receipts for goods stored in a warehouse, and bills of lading for goods shipped by freight.

There are two main types of warehouse receipts and bills of lading: 1) negotiable (also sometimes called *order*) and 2) nonnegotiable (also sometimes called *straight*).

Example: B. Brown of Centerville, Illinois, orders five television sets of a specified make and model from S. Smith of Philadelphia for $1,000, to be shipped by railway freight, f.o.b. Philadelphia.

1. Assume that when S ships the goods, he requests from the carrier an

order bill of lading. Omitting some of the details appearing on the standard forms, a *simplified version* showing the chief provisions contained on the front page of the bill of lading would read as shown on page 506.

2. Assume that when S ships the goods, he requests that the carrier use a straight bill rather than an order bill. A *simplified version* of the front page of this bill of lading would read as shown on page 507.

Note that in addition to the different headings, the two types of bills differ in the followings ways: 1) the second paragraph of the order bill requiring surrender of the bill before delivery of the goods is omitted from the straight bill; 2) in the space for the consignee's name, the word ORDER used in the order bill is omitted from the straight bill; 3) the order bill contains a "notify" space for insertion of the name of the person to be notified upon arrival of the goods at destination; this space is omitted from the straight bill. Note also that in the order bill used in this example, the seller is named as the consignee (in addition to being named as the consignor) with the stated destination being the buyer's town, while in the straight bill the goods are consigned directly to the buyer. When an order bill is used, a seller will usually have himself named as the consignee. The reason for this common practice will be explained later.

The expression "to the order of" used in an order bill of lading is common in other types of commercial documents. For example, the standard form for a check states, "Pay to the order of . . ." A provision in a document that goods are deliverable (or that money is payable) to the order of a named person (or to the bearer of the document) is essential for the document to be classed as negotiable. The term "negotiable" is a tag applied to any of several types of property interests as to which it is possible for an innocent purchaser or transferee for value to obtain a better right than was held by his transferor.

The effect of an instrument being negotiable is further explained and illustrated in the discussion of commercial paper in Part 1 of Chapter 14.

Note the example on page 440 which emphasizes that the obligor of a negotiable note should not pay the original payee of the note or anyone else, until the note is produced and the obligor verifies that the one presenting the note is the proper party to receive payment. The same is true of a negotiable warehouse receipt or bill of lading. The warehouseman or carrier will refuse to deliver until the document is produced and the bailee verifies that the one presenting the document is entitled to receive the goods. This refusal of the bailee to deliver until the properly indorsed document is produced, in effect, gives the holder of a negotiable document a hold over the goods. Upon this is based the chief use of negotiable documents of title (especially bills of lading) in sales transactions, both in cash transactions and in credit transactions.

USE OF BILLS OF LADING IN SALES TRANSACTIONS

Cash Sales

Suppose that a buyer, B. Brown of Centerville, Illinois, orders five television sets of a specified make and model from a seller, S. Smith of Philadelphia, for $1,000, to be shipped by railroad freight, f.o.b. Philadelphia, and that neither party is willing to extend credit to the other—the buyer does not want to pay in advance of obtaining the goods and the seller does not want to deliver in advance of payment. A c.o.d. (cash or collect on delivery) shipment would accomplish this purpose of neither extending credit to the other. However, the c.o.d. device is not entirely suitable for such a costly shipment. The freight agent at the destination may hesitate to take the buyer's check, and the buyer may not have $1,000 in cash on hand or may not want to entrust the handling of $1,000 in currency to the employee who is sent to the freight station. Through using the proper type of bill of lading, the parties can more conveniently accomplish their purpose of neither extending credit to the other.

If the sale and purchase are to be accomplished through the use of a bill of lading, usually the buyer will so indicate in his order by stating that the goods are to be shipped, "sight draft, bill of lading attached, cash against documents." In such a transaction, when the seller ships the goods, he requests and obtains from the carrier an order bill of lading. (Usually a seller who is making numerous shipments has a pad of bill of lading forms; he fills in one of the forms—original and carbon copies—and takes it with the goods to the freight agent. The agent checks in the goods and signs the bill of lading, thus issuing the bill in the name of the carrier.) Since the carrier will not deliver until the bill of lading is surrendered to the carrier, the seller knows that as long as he withholds the bill of lading, the buyer cannot obtain the goods. The seller then offers the bill of lading to the buyer in exchange for his payment of the price. Usually the seller offers the bill of lading and collects the price through a bank in the buyer's town. The seller engages the bank to act as his collecting agent by mailing the bill of lading to the bank with proper instructions. The instructions are usually given in a draft which the seller writes (or fills in on a printed form). A draft for the $1,000 sale from Smith to Brown could read:

Philadelphia, Pennsylvania. [Date]

At sight pay to the order of S. Smith One Thousand Dollars ($1,000).

(signed) S. Smith

To B. Brown
Centerville, Illinois.

On the reverse side of the draft the seller writes the following indorsement:

Pay to the Centerville, Illinois National Bank
for collection
(signed) S. Smith

The seller then clips the bill of lading and draft together and mails them to the indicated bank. Upon receiving the documents, the bank notifies the buyer that it has a draft drawn on him (that is, addressed to him) with the bill of lading attached. When the buyer pays $1,000 to the bank (or makes the necessary arrangements for a loan from the bank), the bank gives the bill of lading to the buyer and mails to the seller the bank's own check for $1,000 (less the bank's collection fee, unless the seller and buyer had agreed that the buyer pay for the bank's services). Since the carrier will not deliver the goods without receiving back the bill of lading, the buyer is willing to pay when the bank tenders the bill of lading. The buyer knows that if the bill of lading is still outstanding, the goods must still be in the hands of the carrier, and that with the bill of lading the buyer can obtain the goods upon their arrival.

Frequently for the buyer's greater convenience the seller will use as his collecting agent the bank in which the buyer does his banking. Then when the buyer comes to the bank to pay the $1,000 and receive the bill of lading, there will be no question about the buyer's bank balance if the buyer pays by check, and if the buyer intends to borrow in order to finance the purchase, he can arrange for the loan and obtain the bill of lading at the same bank.

The order bill of lading which the carrier issues for the shipment can name either the buyer or the seller as the consignee of the goods. If the buyer is named as the consignee and the buyer defaults and refuses to pay, the seller still has his hold on the goods by means of the bill of lading and can request the carrier to return the goods or to ship them elsewhere. However, when the buyer is named as the consignee, the carrier thereby contracts to deliver "to the order of" the buyer. For its own protection, the carrier may require the seller to prove that the buyer has defaulted and forfeited his interest in the goods before the carrier will comply with the seller's request to retransport the goods. The seller can avoid this additional obstacle by having the bill of lading name the seller as the consignee, with the destination stated as the buyer's town. Then when the seller writes and indorses the draft, he will also indorse the bill of lading. The best practice is for the seller to use a special indorsement, which, for the Smith-Brown transaction, would read:

Deliver to B. Brown,
(signed) S. Smith

When the buyer pays the draft and receives the bill of lading, the buyer can, by means of the seller's indorsement on the bill of lading, obtain the goods just as readily as he could if the bill named the buyer as the consignee. If the buyer defaults, then since the seller is still in possession of the bill of lading (through his agent, the bank) *and also* is the consignee named in the bill, the seller has the immediate right to have the carrier return the goods or ship them elsewhere. Therefore, the standard practice in a "bill of lading, draft attached" sale is for the seller to ship the goods by an order bill, which names the seller as the consignee and the buyer's town as the destination. So that the carrier can give proper notice of arrival, the buyer's name is inserted in the "notify" space on the order bill. Designating a specific buyer in this manner, however, in no way restricts the complete negotiability of the order bill.

Note that when a seller wishes to retain a hold on goods, he has the carrier issue an order bill of lading. If goods are shipped under a straight bill of lading, they will be delivered to the consignee without his surrender of the bill of lading, or even showing that he is in possession of it. Suppose that a seller ships goods on a straight bill of lading, naming the buyer as the consignee, and then withholds the bill of lading waiting for the buyer to pay the agreed price. When the goods arrive, the carrier will deliver them to the buyer even though the buyer does not yet have possession of the bill of lading. Accordingly, a straight bill which names the buyer as the consignee gives no protection to the seller. Suppose, therefore, that the seller ships the goods on a straight bill which names himself, the seller, as the consignee. The seller can then write an assignment of the goods together with a direction that the carier should deliver the goods to the buyer, writing either on a separate document or on the back of the bill of lading. The seller can then withhold the assignment and delivery instruction until the buyer pays the agreed price. However, since the carrier will deliver without surrender of the bill, the buyer has no assurance that merely because the straight bill of lading is outstanding, the goods must still be in the hands of the carrier. The seller could have dishonestly accepted delivery from the carrier or given a similar delivery order to another purchaser who could have already obtained the goods from the carrier. Therefore, while the straight bill of lading which names the seller as the consignee gives the seller control over the goods, it affords no protection to the buyer. When the parties intend the bill of lading to represent the goods, a straight bill of lading will not serve their purpose. Contrariwise, if the parties do not intend the bill of lading to represent the goods, they should use a straight rather than an order bill. When a seller ships goods to a buyer on an open or charge account, the seller has no intention of withholding the goods until the buyer pays. If in such a case the seller ships on an *order* bill of lading, he will have to send the bill of lading to the buyer in order for the buyer to obtain the goods. Should the buyer mislay the bill of lading while awaiting arrival of the goods, he is put to needless inconvenience and expense.

Credit Sales

Suppose that in order to induce B. Brown of Centerville to purchase $1,000 worth of television sets, the seller has to extend sixty-days' credit, but that nevertheless the seller needs or wants his money before the expiration of the sixty-day period. The seller can accomplish this by delivering the goods to the buyer and then selling or assigning to a bank the right to receive the $1,000 payment from the buyer. If the seller makes an ordinary charge or open account sale, the seller can assign his account receivable to the bank. Or instead, the seller can obtain the buyer's signed promise to pay $1,000 in sixty days and assign and raise money on the buyer's written promise. In using the latter sales device, the seller would want to retain a hold on the goods until the buyer signed the appropriate written promise. This the seller could do through the use of an order bill of lading. If a sale is to be accomplished in this way, usually the buyer will so indicate in his order for goods, by stating that the goods are to be shipped "on sixty-day trade acceptance." In such a transaction, the seller ships the goods on an order bill of lading naming the seller as the consignee. The seller then draws a sixty-day draft or trade acceptance on the buyer. A typical draft would read:

Philadelphia, Pennsylvania. [Date]
Sixty days after date pay to the order of S. Smith One Thousand Dollars ($1,000).

The obligation of the acceptor hereof arises out of the purchase of goods from the drawer, maturity being in accordance with the original terms of purchase.

To B. Brown
Centerville, Illinois.

(signed) S. Smith

S then clips the draft and bill of lading together and mails them to a bank in the buyer's town. Upon receiving the documents the bank so notifies the buyer. The buyer comes to the bank and signs the draft; by signing the draft, the buyer promises to pay the stated amount at the stated time. The best form is for the buyer to write across the face of the draft (or sign the appropriate portion of a printed form on the face of the draft), "Accepted [Date], (signed) B. Brown." The bank then gives the bill of lading to the buyer and mails the accepted draft back to the seller. The accepted draft is a convenient document which the seller can sell or discount before the expiration of the sixty days, thus promptly obtaining the $1,000 (less the bank's discount fee). Frequently in such transactions, the seller will go to his own bank immediately after making shipment, and discount the draft with the bill of lading attached. The seller's bank then forwards the draft to a bank in the buyer's town for the buyer's signature on the draft, after which it is returned to the seller's bank to be held until maturity or to be further transferred by the seller's bank—for example, transferred to a Federal Reserve Bank. In this way the buyer buys on credit, while the seller obtains the purchase price (less the discount fee) before expiration of the credit period, with the mechanics of the transaction being accomplished through the use of two standard commercial documents, the order bill of lading and the time draft or trade acceptance.

Transfer of Documents of Title

A document of title is usually transferred from one person to another by an assignment (with a nonnegotiable document) or an indorsement (with a negotiable document) written on the document, after which the document is delivered to the transferee. Just as with an instrument calling for the payment of money (a check, note, or draft), so also with a document of title which calls for delivery of goods to a certain named person—an indorsement or assignment by that person (or by his authorized agent) is essential for anyone else to obtain an interest in the document.

The transferor of a negotiable document of title will usually use either a special indorsement or a blank indorsement. A special indorsement specifically names the transferee and is signed by the transferor, while a blank indorsement consists of the transferor's signature only and does not name a specific transferee.

A blank indorsement written on a negotiable bill of lading makes the goods deliverable to bearer. It is just as though the transferor were to write on the back of the document, "Deliver to bearer, (signed) S. Smith." A document of title under which goods are deliverable to bearer can be further transferred by delivery alone without the necessity of any further indorsement.

Example: B. Brown ordered certain goods from S. Smith and agreed to pay on a sight draft with the bill of lading attached. S shipped the goods on an order bill of lading which named S as consignee, drew a draft on B, indorsed the bill of lading as shown below, clipped the bill of lading and draft together, and mailed the documents to a bank in B's town. A thief somehow obtained possession of the documents, threw the draft away, further indorsed the bill of lading by signing (without authority) "B. Brown," and sold and transferred the bill of lading to P, a purchaser, who paid value in the regular course of business, without knowing of the theft and forged indorsement. Both S and P claimed the goods from the carrier.

1. Assume that S used a special indorsement by writing on the back of the bill of lading, "Deliver to B. Brown, (signed) S. Smith." Indorsement by B would be necessary to further negotiate the document. Since the indorsement purporting to be B's was neither genuine nor authorized, P obtained no rights under it. P would have no better rights than the thief had, and in the dispute between S and P, S would be entitled to the goods.

2. Assume that S used a blank indorsement by writing on the back of the bill of lading, "(signed) S. Smith." Since the document was indorsed in blank, it could be further transferred without the necessity of a further indorsement by any particular person. Although B's indorsement was forged, it was not a necessary indorsement for P's title. Although the thief had no title to the bill of lading or to the goods it evidenced, P obtained full rights by virtue of the fact that the document was negotiable and was effectively transferred. In the dispute between S and P, P would be entitled to the goods.

Risks Undertaken by Purchasers of Bills of Lading

Accommodation Bill of Lading[7]

An accommodation bill of lading is one which a carrier issues as an accommodation to the shipper, *before* the goods are delivered to the carrier.

Example: B of Erie, Pennsylvania, ordered certain goods from S of Philadelphia, for $1,000, payable on presentment of a sight draft with the bill of lading attached, cash against documents. S accepted the order agreeing to ship, but did not have the requested goods on hand nor the capital with which to procure them. S described to the railroad's Philadelphia freight agent the goods which S had contracted to ship to B. Since S's credit had previously been satisfactory and since the freight agent desired S's shipping business, the freight agent issued to S a bill of lading for the goods which were to be shipped. S drew a sight draft on B, clipped the draft to the bill, and discounted both documents at S's Philadelphia bank, receiving $1,000, less the bank's discount fee. With the money S purchased the goods described in the S-B contract. However, before S took the goods to the freight station, S was adjudged insolvent and a court-appointed receiver took over all of S's assets, including the goods intended for the S-B contract. In the meantime, the Philadelphia bank had forwarded the documents to an Erie bank which presented them to B. B paid $1,000 to the Erie bank and received the bill of lading. A week later B learned that the goods described in the bill of lading had never been received by the carrier. B sued the carrier for the value of the goods described in the bill of lading.

1. Assume that the bill of lading was an order bill of lading. B could recover from the carrier.

2. Assume that the bill of lading was a straight bill of lading. For an

[7] U.C.C. Sec. 7-301.

intrastate shipment (under either the Uniform Commercial Code or the older Uniform Bills of Lading Act) the carrier would be liable to the consignee (or to the consignee's transferee) who gave value relying in good faith on the bill of lading. If the railroad's line between Philadelphia and Erie remained entirely within Pennsylvania, the intrastate rule would apply, and B could recover from the carrier. However, if this had been an interstate shipment to which the slightly different provisions of the Federal Bills of Lading Act would apply, B could not collect from the carrier.

A buyer who pays on a straight bill of lading in advance of receiving the described goods should realize that he is trusting his seller and should refuse to pay unless he is willing to take a chance on the seller's good faith and solvency.

Diversion of Shipment[8]

Under the Uniform Commercial Code, if an intrastate shipment is made by a straight bill of lading, the seller as the consignor has power to divert the shipment by requesting the carrier to return the shipment, or to deliver to a person other than as stated in the bill of lading. The seller has this power even though the straight bill names the buyer as the consignee. If a seller wrongfully diverts goods and causes them to be delivered to another person who takes them as a purchaser in ordinary course of the seller's business, the rights of the first buyer as to the shipped goods are cut off and a good title passes to the purchaser. The first buyer has no recourse against the carrier or against the innocent purchaser; his only remedy is to recover damages from the seller who wrongfully diverted the goods. This emphasizes the caution given in the preceding example: a buyer who pays on a *straight* bill prior to receipt of goods should realize that he is trusting the good faith and solvency of his seller.

With a shipment by an order bill of lading, only the holder of the bill of lading has power to divert the goods.

Misdescription of Goods[9]

Frequently, bills of lading are made out by shippers and then brought to the carrier's agent along with the goods being shipped. Before signing a bill of lading, the freight agent is expected to do all that he reasonably can to verify the accuracy of the description of goods which the shipper has written on the bill of lading form.

Kind of Goods. A freight agent is not expected to open packages and analyze their contents. Therefore, a carrier is not liable to the holder

[8] U.C.C. Secs. 7-303, 7-504.
[9] U.C.C. Sec. 7-301.

of a bill of lading if, unknown to the carrier, the shipper has mislabeled the packages. Note that the carrier calls attention to this point by stating it in the standard form of bill of lading, "contents and condition of contents of packages unknown."

Quantity of Goods. When he reasonably can, a freight agent is expected to count packages and to weigh bulk freight, and in such a case the carrier is liable if the quantity of goods actually shipped is less than that described in the bill of lading. On the other hand if the freight agent cannot reasonably verify the quantity of goods shipped and marks the bill of lading to that effect, the carrier is not liable. For example, in many full-car rail shipments the railroad will shunt an empty car onto the shipper's railroad siding, so that the shipper's employees can load the car. The shipper then turns the car over to the freight agent together with a bill of lading form already filled in and ready for the freight agent's signature. If the freight agent cannot verify the count of packages or the weight of bulk goods without unloading the car, the agent will so indicate by marking the bill of lading, "Shipper's weight, load and count." This warns any purchaser of the bill of lading that the carrier will not be liable for any error in weight or count which the carrier actually could not verify.

Shipper's Lack of Title[10]

Although it is possible for an innocent purchaser of a negotiable document of title to obtain better rights to the document than were held by his transferor, nobody can obtain better rights to the bailed goods than the original bailor had or could transfer.

Example: B ordered certain goods from S to be shipped on a sight draft with the bill of lading attached, B to pay cash against the documents. S stole such goods from their owner, O, shipped them by order bill of lading to B, and forwarded the bill of lading and a draft to a bank in B's town. B paid the draft and received the bill of lading. However, by the time the goods arrived in B's town, O had successfully traced the goods and both B and O claimed the goods from the carrier.

O would be entitled to receive possession of the goods. B would have no better right to the goods than S had or could transfer.

Forgery of a Necessary Indorsement

As previously discussed and illustrated in connection with "Transfer of Documents of Title," forgery of an essential indorsement passes no rights.

[10] U.C.C. Sec. 7-503.

Forged or Altered Bill of Lading[11]

Checks are usually written on safety paper and either in ink or with a check-writer device which perforates the paper. Drafts and notes are ordinarily written in ink, usually on a fairly good grade of paper. However, the bill of lading forms in common use are printed on a very cheap grade of paper and frequently are hastily scribbled in pencil. Also printed bill of lading forms are readily available to anyone. It is not surprising therefore that, as some scholars in the field of documents of title point out, the risk that a bill of lading has been forged or altered is probably the greatest risk assumed by a purchaser of the bill. If a bill of lading is fraudulently altered, the issuing carrier is only liable for the bill as originally made out. If a carrier never issued a particular bill of lading, the innocent holder of the forged bill has no rights at all against the carrier. The only recourse the innocent holder has is to proceed against his transferor. However, this may be an empty remedy; if the transferor is the one who forged or altered the bill, he usually disappears before his fraud is discovered.

PROBLEMS

1. As a favor and without consideration, O loaned his car to D of St. Louis, Missouri, for the avowed purpose of driving from St. Louis to Memphis and return in order to make an audit in Memphis. Without O's knowledge or consent, D also drove this car to Kansas City and return, and on the return trip, although D was driving with proper care, the car was damaged as a result of a highway defect. This trip to Kansas City was occasioned by an unexpected request that D make an audit there. O was not in any way associated with D and had no interest in or connection with either of these audits. Could O hold D financially responsible for the damage to the car? Explain. (Modified from A.I.C.P.A., Nov. 40-5.)

2. D hired an automobile from the Drive-Yur-Self Auto Company at $1 an hour. Through no fault of D's the car was damaged in a collision with a truck carelessly driven by T.

a) The renting corporation sued D to recover for the damages to the car. What result? Explain.

b) The renting corporation sued T to recover for the damages to the car. What result? Explain. (Modified from A.I.C.P.A., Nov. 27-5.)

3. P, making an automobile trip from New York City to Boston, agreed to take a valuable parcel belonging to his friend O and to deliver it to O's son in Providence. When P stopped in Bridgeport for dinner, he took his own property out of the car but left O's parcel in the car. The parcel was stolen from the car while P was eating dinner. What are the principles involved? (Modified from A.I.C.P.A., Nov. 29-6.)

[11] U.C.C. Sec. 7-306.

4. O took his best suit to a dry-cleaning company to have the suit altered, cleaned, and pressed. He delivered the suit to the manager and received a receipt in which the suit was described, the work to be performed indicated, and the charge shown. A week later, O returned to the store, presented his receipt and asked for his suit. The manager searched the racks but was unable to find the suit. He asked O to return in a few days as he thought the suit had not yet been returned or had been misplaced. The manager then contacted the cleaning plant; the suit could not be located there, and the records indicated that the suit had been returned to the store with other garments. The manager diligently searched through all the clothing in the store and questioned all of his employees, but to no avail. O returned five days later, presented the receipt, tendered the amount due, and demanded the suit. The manager explained that the suit had just disappeared, that neither he nor any of his employees had taken it or knew what had happened to it. O sued the company for the value of his suit.

a) Explain who would prevail in the lawsuit if both parties proved only the facts stated.

b) Suppose that the suit had been destroyed by an accidental fire in the store, and the company could prove that the fire had started through no fault of its own. Explain who would prevail in O's lawsuit against the company. (Modified from A.I.C.P.A., May 61-6.)

5. When the owner of a valuable fur coat delivered the coat to a fur dealer for storage over the summer months, the parties signed the following written agreement: "[Date]. Fur storage agreement for the following described coat: [then followed a brief description of the coat]. In consideration of $25 charges to be paid upon return of the above-described fur coat to the undersigned owner on October 1 of this year, the undersigned dealer agrees to keep the said coat free from damage by moths and to return the said coat to the owner on October 1, in the same condition as when received by the dealer." On October 1 the coat could not be found. Investigation disclosed that, without fault or negligence on the part of the dealer, the coat had been stolen and disposed of by one of the dealer's employees who previously had been wholly trustworthy. The owned sued the dealer for the value of the stolen coat. What result? Explain.

6. When O delivered 20 shirts to a launderer, O was given a duplicate laundry slip upon which was printed, "The liability of the laundry for loss or damage regardless of nature or cause, shall be limited to an amount not exceeding ten times the charge for laundering the items described hereon." Through the launderer's carelessness, all 20 shirts were lost. The total value of the shirts was $125, the charge for laundering 20 shirts was $3. How much if anything would O have a right to collect from the launderer? Explain.

7. A common carrier accepted a shipment of goods at Chicago for delivery to a buyer in Boston, Massachusetts. The goods were in transit between the two cities when they were destroyed by the incident described below. For each of the following, explain what would be the carrier's liability:

a) The goods were destroyed by a fire caused by a bolt of lightning.

b) The goods were destroyed by a riot of 100 people.

c) A discharged employee, holding a grudge against the carrier, caused a wreck which destroyed the goods.

d) The goods were destroyed in a fire caused by the negligence of a third party.

e) The goods were destroyed because of improper packing by the shipper of the goods.

f) The goods were destroyed in a fire resulting from train robbers derailing the train in order to steal a shipment of gold bullion carried on the train. (Modified from A.I.C.P.A., Nov. 49-7.)

8. O of New York City planned to move to Chicago and delivered his office furniture to the Porter Warehouse and Transit Company. The company was to transport the furniture as soon as it had available van space. Before the company had shipped the furniture, O telephoned that he had decided not to move to Chicago and that therefore he desired the company to hold the furniture for further instructions. The day after this phone call, the company's warehouse and contents, including O's furniture, were destroyed by fire, through no fault of the company. One week later O, ignorant of the fire, wrote instructing the company to ship the furniture to St. Louis. In what capacity and to what extent, if at all, was the company liable for the loss of O's furniture? Explain. (Modified from A.I.C.P.A., May 53-10.)

9. Declaring a value of $500, O shipped a trunk by Railway Express from New York City to be delivered to O at 123 Main Street, Centerville, Ill. When the trunk arrived in Centerville, it was loaded on an Express Company truck which at 2 o'clock, Wednesday afternoon, started for the Main Street address. While driving with proper care, the express driver was involved in a collision with a carelessly driven auto. The collision started a fire and the express driver was unable to save the trunk from being destroyed. Since the driver of the auto was insolvent, O sued the Express Company for $500.

a) The collision and fire occurred while the truck was on the way to the Main Street address. What would be the result of O's lawsuit against the Express Company? Explain.

b) The collision and fire occurred while the truck was on the way from the Main Street address back to the Express Company office. The trunk was still on the truck because nobody had answered when the driver had rung the doorbell at the Main Street address. Could O recover from the carrier? Explain.

10. A railroad company transported goods to their destination and notified the consignee that the goods were ready for delivery. The consignee did not call for the goods until a week later. The day before he called for the goods they were destroyed by fire without negligence on the part of the carrier. Was the railroad company liable for the loss of the goods? Explain. (Modified from A.I.C.P.A., Nov. 45-9.)

11. P owned a panel truck which he used to operate a parcel delivery service for several women's and children's low-price specialty shops. One day

while he was making a delivery to an apartment house in the suburbs, a number of packages were stolen from the truck.

a) P had left the truck unlocked. Would P bear the loss? Explain.

b) P had carefully placed a strong padlock on the truck, which the thief had been obliged to break in order to steal the packages. Would P bear the loss? Explain.

c) Would the answer to Part (b) be different if, other facts remaining the same, P had been engaged by a few exclusive jewelry stores rather than by a group of specialty shops? Explain. (Modified from A.I.C.P.A., May 60-7b.)

12. R was a retailer who occasionally purchased goods from M, a local manufacturer. A thief phoned M, pretended to be speaking for R, and ordered certain small goods worth $500 to be delivered to R's store on thirty-days' credit. Immediately after the goods had been delivered to R's receiving room, the thief phoned R, pretended to be speaking for M, and said some goods had been delivered to R by mistake and would be called for by M's office assistant. The thief then went to R's store, introduced himself as M's office assistant, received the goods which had been delivered by M, and disappeared. When the parties discovered the fraudulent trick, M sued R for $500. What result? Explain.

13. One evening O and two other young women attended a session at a dancing school operated by P. The fee for the class was 90 cents with an additional charge of 10 cents for checking wraps. O paid $1 at the ticket booth and received a ticket to be presented at the checking window with the items checked. O was wearing a topcoat worth $50, and a separate fur neckpiece worth $300. Knowing that checked items were placed in bins rather than hung on hangers, O folded her topcoat with the neckpiece inside and gave the bundle to the checkroom attendant together with the checking ticket. The attendant put the bundle in a numbered bin and gave O a claim check bearing the same number. When the class was finished, O presented the claim check at the check window and received back her topcoat folded in the same manner as O had folded it. However, the fur neckpiece was not inside the bundle and could not be found anyplace. O sued P for $300. What result? Explain.

14. P planned to attend a dance at a dancing pavilion known as the Lakeside Park. P borrowed $50 from O, promising to repay the money within one week, and also borrowed O's car for the dance, promising to return the car the following day. When P drove into the parking lot at the Lakeside Park, he paid 10 cents to an attendant at the entrance, and parked in the space indicated by another attendant. When P paid the 10 cents he received a cardboard tag upon which was printed:

> In consideration of the charge made upon issuing this tag, the Lakeside Park leases to the holder hereof, space on its premises sufficient for the purpose of parking his auto. It is expressly stipulated that the lessee of such space assumes all risk of fire, theft, or other damages while on the premises, and that Lakeside Park at no time

assumes the custody of said auto or any of its contents. No attendant has any authority to vary, modify, alter, or enlarge any of the foregoing conditions.

P read the tag and then pocketed it together with the car key, after locking the car. About an hour later, P returned to the parking lot to get his girl's purse which she had left in the car. As P was unlocking the car door, someone came from behind an adjoining car and struck P on the head, knocking him unconscious. The assailant took P's wallet which contained the $50 P had borrowed from O, took the car key, and drove away in O's car. In rifling P's pockets, the thief missed the Lakeside Park parking tag in P's coat pocket. At the time of the theft, an attendant was still on duty at the entrance to the parking lot, but he did not see or hear the assault, and he made no attempt to stop the car as the thief was driving away.

a) Would P be liable to O 1) for the stolen money? 2) for the stolen car? Explain.

b) Would the Lakeside Park be liable 1) for the money? 2) for the car? Explain.

15. The proprietor of a parking lot in the theater district of a city displayed a large sign reading, "Evening Parking 50¢. Lot closes at 1 A.M.," and operated the lot in the following manner: A driver would stop his car at the entrance to the lot, get out, and pay 50 cents to the proprietor. The proprietor would give the driver a ticket stub with an identifying number, place the remainder of the ticket bearing the same number under the windshield wiper of the car, and drive the car into the lot and park it. All keys were left in the cars. If a person returned before 1 A.M., he would surrender his ticket stub to the proprietor who would secure the car from the lot and bring it to the exit, for the owner to drive away. At 1 A.M. the proprietor would make sure that no car remaining in the lot was blocked in by another car and would then depart. Any person returning to the lot after 1 A.M. would locate his car in the lot and drive it away.

O used the lot a number of times and knew the manner in which it was operated. One evening O returned to the lot about 2 A.M., later than his usual time. A few cars were still in the lot, but O's car was missing. It had been stolen, and O sued the parking lot proprietor for the value of his car. What result? Explain.

16. A man and his wife stopped for dinner at a restaurant in Philadelphia. The headwaiter escorted them to a table and summoned a waiter. The waiter assisted the woman in removing her fur coat and, after holding her chair while she sat down at the table, hung the coat on the nearest empty hook, about 25 feet from the table. The man removed his overcoat and hung it on the empty hook beside his wife's coat. Finishing the meal, the man paid the waiter, received his change, and gave the usual tip to the waiter. The waiter drew back the woman's chair while she arose from the table, and then the waiter and the man went to the hooks where the coats had been hung. Both coats were missing and diligent search and investigation by the restaurant staff and by the police failed to disclose the whereabouts of the coats.

Both the man and the woman sued the restaurant owner for the value of their respective coats, $300 for the man's coat and $700 for the woman's. What result? Explain.

17. For some years, a manufacturing jeweler made periodic business trips to various towns in Illinois. While in Centerville, the jeweler always stopped at the Howard Hotel. A woman, a resident of Centerville, had a ring (a large sapphire surround by diamonds, in a platinum setting) which had been made by this jeweler. Losing one of the diamonds, she wrote to the jeweler concerning its replacement. In his answering letter, the jeweler told the woman that he would be in Centerville the week of October 21, staying at the Howard Hotel, and that she could give her ring to him then. On October 23 the woman taped her ring between two pieces of cardboard, writing her name and address on one of the cardboards, put it in an envelope, sealed the envelope, and wrote the jeweler's name on the front of the envelope. She took the envelope to the Howard Hotel and asked the desk clerk if the jeweler was in. The desk clerk replied that the jeweler was registered at the hotel but was out at the time. The woman asked the clerk if he would give the envelope to the jeweler when he came in, and the clerk replied that he would. The woman gave the envelope to the clerk and left the hotel. At that moment several other persons came into the hotel to register and the clerk laid the envelope down on the counter while he was waiting on the newcomers. When he looked for the envelope, it was gone. Diligent search and investigation by the hotel staff and by the police failed to disclose the whereabouts of the ring. The woman sued the hotel for $2,000, the reasonable value of the ring. What result? Explain.

18. O, a retail jeweler from Newark, bought various items of jewelry in New York City for a total of $2,800, put the jewelry in a briefcase, and returned to the railroad station. Learning that the next train to Newark would leave in forty-five minutes, O put his briefcase in a coin-operated locker, inserted 10 cents, and removed the key, locking the locker. After finishing lunch, O returned for his briefcase, unlocked the locker, and found it empty. When O reported the loss, an agent from the locker company came with a master key and opened and looked in vain in all of the lockers in that particular area. Under the rules of the locker company (as printed on a tag on each locker) the company would remove the contents of a locker after twenty-four hours. However, O's briefcase had been in the locker for only a half an hour. The locker company denied having removed the briefcase or having any knowledge at all concerning its whereabouts. O sued the locker company for $2,800. What result? Explain.

19. M operated a factory in which he manufactured sport shirts. His usual method of business was to have customers furnish the cloth and patterns, while M would furnish buttons, thread, linings, and other minor materials, in addition to performing all of the labor and machine work to make the completed garments. O delivered a quantity of cloth, described below, to M to be made into shirts. While the shirts were in process, a fire occurred in the building adjoining M's factory. The material was severely damaged by smoke and

water, and there was no practical means of recovering damages from the persons at fault in causing the fire.

a) The cloth O delivered to M was sufficient rare imported wool gabardine material to make up 1,000 dozen shirts for an exclusive trade. Would M or O bear the burden of damage done to the material? Explain.

b) The cloth O delivered to M was sufficient standard broadcloth material for 10,000 dozen shirts. At the time of the fire M was using part of this material to complete a rush order for another customer, knowing that there would be no difficulty in replacing the broadcloth in time to complete the order for O. Would M or O bear the burden of the damage done to the material? Explain. (Modified from A.I.C.P.A., May 60-7a.)

20. S owed $1,000 to a common carrier of goods for the carrier's transportation of S's automobile. Subsequently S delivered a truck to the carrier for transportation, receiving from the carrier a negotiable bill of lading naming S as consignee. S indorsed, sold, and delivered the bill of lading to B who paid S $5,000 for it. The transportation charges on the truck were $200.

a) For how much would the carrier have a lien on the truck? Explain.

b) If B tendered the bill of lading and $200 to the carrier, which the carrier refused to accept, could B compel the carrier to deliver the truck to him? Explain.

c) If the bill of lading were nonnegotiable and the carrier, ignorant of S's transfer of the bill of lading to B, delivered the truck to S without obtaining the bill of lading, would B have any rights against the carrier? Explain. (Modified from A.I.C.P.A., Nov. 52-2.)

21. By letter, B, a dealer in Erie, Pennsylvania, ordered from S, a wholesaler in Philadelphia, 100 units of certain described goods at a stated price, f.o.b. Philadelphia. Terms were sight draft, bill of lading attached, cash against documents. S promptly accepted the order by return mail and shipped goods to Erie via the Pennsylvania Railroad Company, receiving from the carrier a bill of lading stating that it covered, "ten boxes marked as each containing ten units of [the described goods]." S drew a sight draft on B and sent it, together with the bill of lading, to a bank in Erie. B promptly paid the draft and received the bill of lading. However, for the reason stated below, the carrier refused to deliver to B the ten boxes described in the bill of lading. Three weeks after B's payment, S became insolvent and all of his assets were taken over by a court-appointed receiver.

a) The goods S delivered to the carrier for shipment to Erie conformed to B's order and to the description on the bill of lading. While the goods were in transit toward Erie, S received from P, a customer in Buffalo, a rush order for the same kind and quantity of goods. The shipment to Erie had exhausted S's supply, but S expected within a week to obtain a new supply from the manufacturer. Accordingly, S requested the carrier to divert the Erie shipment and deliver the goods to P in Buffalo. The carrier did so. Neither S nor his receiver made any additional shipment to B. B, not receiving any of the boxes described in the bill of lading, sued the carrier for the value of the goods. 1) The bill of lading was an order bill of lading, naming

S as consignee, indorsed in blank by S. Was B entitled to judgment in his lawsuit against the carrier? Explain. 2) The bill of lading was a straight bill of lading, naming B as consignee. Was B entitled to judgment in his lawsuit against the carrier? Explain.

b) Although the carrier gave S a bill of lading for ten boxes marked as each containing ten units of the described goods, S delivered to the carrier only nine boxes, assuring the freight agent that he would bring in the tenth box the following day. S failed to bring in the tenth box and his receiver refused to do so. The carrier delivered the nine boxes to B, and B sued the carrier for the value of the tenth box. 1) Same additional fact and question as in 1) above. 2) Same additional fact and question as in 2) above. 3) If the railroad had stamped on the bill of lading, "Shipper's weight, load, and count," would this additional fact change any of your answers? Explain.

c) The goods S delivered to the carrier for shipment to Erie conformed to B's order and to the description on the bill of lading. However, S had stolen the goods from their owner, O. O located the goods when they arrived in Erie, and both O and B claimed them from the carrier. 1) The bill of lading was an order bill of lading, naming S as consignee, indorsed in blank by S. As between O and B, who had the better title to the goods? Explain. 2) The bill of lading was a straight bill of lading, naming B as consignee. As between O and B, who had the better title to the goods? Explain.

22. By letter, B, a dealer in Chicago, ordered from S, a manufacturer in Philadelphia, certain described goods for $500, f.o.b. Chicago, terms sixty-day trade acceptance, bill of lading attached. S shipped the goods by Pennsylvania Railroad Company, freight, requesting and receiving from the carrier an order bill of lading naming S as consignee. S indorsed the bill of lading in blank, drew a sixty-day draft on B, and mailed the documents to a bank in Chicago. T, a dealer in such goods, stole the documents from the mail, threw away the draft, and sold and indorsed the bill of lading to P who paid fair value to T in the regular course of business, without knowledge of the preceding details involving the bill of lading. T then disappeared. The parties learned of the theft, and when the goods arrived in Chicago, B and P both claimed them.

a) Assume that S will be paid whatever is legally owed to him. As between P and B, who would have the better right to obtain the goods from the carrier? Explain.

b) Would the winner in Part (a) above have an obligation to S, and if so, what obligation? Explain.

c) Would the loser in Part (a) have an obligation to S, and if so, what obligation? Explain.

23. B of Louisville, Kentucky, ordered ten tractors of a specified make and model from S in Philadelphia, Pennsylvania, making a cash deposit of 25 percent, of the purchase price at the time the order was placed and agreeing to pay the balance on a sight draft with the bill of lading attached. At S's request, the railroad placed an empty car on S's siding. Shortly afterwards S notified the freight agent that the shipment was being loaded and would be completely loaded before the end of the day, and requested and received a straight bill of lading for 10 tractors. S drew a sight draft on B, attached the bill of lading, and sent the documents to a Louisville bank. B paid the draft and received the bill of lading. Shortly afterwards S was adjudged bankrupt, without ever having loaded and shipped the ten tractors. B sued the railroad company for the price paid. What result? Explain.

chapter 16

Sales of Goods

The common-law rules pertaining to sales of goods were patterned somewhat after the rules which developed in an earlier period in connection with real estate transactions. The early English law gave considerably more attention to land than to goods. Under the feudal system the entire structure of society—social, political, and economic—was built upon land ownership and rights in land. Even after the breakdown of the feudal system, land continued for some time to be the most important asset which a person could own. It is understandable, therefore, that the development of legal rights and remedies was more rapid in respect to land than in other fields. In fact, as early as the thirteenth century a detailed and organized body of land law had developed, while the law of commercial transactions had its principal development several centuries later.

The most important concept in real estate law is ownership or title. The exact nature of this concept is difficult to define; the terms "ownership" and "title" are really collective terms—tags for a legal conclusion. If a person's factual relationship to a certain item of property is fairly complete, exclusive, and uncontested, he is considered as having the legally protected rights of possession, use, and disposition of that item. He has about all of the rights which can exist in respect to that item of property, and a person who has this bundle of rights is referred to as having ownership or title. The terms "ownership" and "title" therefore are convenient ways of expressing 1) that a certain fact relationship exists, and 2) that a certain legal status results from those facts. With the facts and legal rights which these terms imply, the terms themselves become useful symbols for expressing other legal consequences. Thus if an item of property should depreciate in value or sustain some casualty not caused by the wrongful act of some other person, it is fair in most cases to consider the loss as falling on the person who has all of the rights regarding that property. This process of analysis and reasoning is then shortened into a rule of law that risk of loss usually follows title.

During the evolution of ideas concerning ownership or title, the English courts gradually found it highly convenient to expand the concept of ownership, and recognize that several different types of interests can exist simultaneously in the same plot of land. For example, suppose that a house upon which a creditor holds a mortgage is leased by the owner to a tenant for one year, and that a few months later the owner contracts to sell the house and lot to a buyer, the transfer to be made at a stated future date (subject, of course, to the mortgage and lease). Several interests coexist: 1) the creditor's mortgage or security interest, 2) the tenant's leasehold interest giving him possession and use, 3) the contract buyer's interest (frequently termed an equitable title), and 4) the owner's legal title consisting of all the remaining rights in the land.

When commerce began to develop and grow, it was natural to classify commercial transactions involving goods in terms of the legal pattern which was already fully developed and working fairly well with land transactions. Just as the most vital step in a land dispute was to identify the title holder and the nature of his title, rules of law pertaining to goods gradually developed around the same core—title. As society shifted from real estate orientation to personal property orientation, disputes arising from dealings with goods multiplied enormously. From simple transfers in small quantities by craftsmen, farmers, or other producers, directly and personally to consumers, today's tremendous complex of mass transactions developed—mass production, mass wholesale and retail distribution, mass consumer buying, and mass financing. This expansion has demanded in the field of goods transactions more than in any other field of human activity a legal system which is able to operate simply, smoothly, and efficiently. To meet this need, various attempts were made to consolidate the rules of law pertaining to the sales of goods. Finally in 1893 the English Parliament adopted a statute entitled the "Sale of Goods Act." Soon afterwards in the United States, the Commissioners on Uniform State Laws promulgated the "Uniform Sales Act," which was closely patterned after the English statute and was eventually adopted by most of the states. Both of these statutes were codifications of the common law and were designed around the same foundation—title. Thus in answering the questions which most frequently arise in sales-of-goods transactions—risk of loss at the time a casualty to goods occurs, remedies of one party in case of default by the other party—both of these statutes begin by determining where title to the goods rests at the particular time in question; then, according to this determination, the statutes define the relative rights of the parties.

The title approach has worked fairly well in real estate law for centuries and continues to be serviceable. This is because, starting at a very early date, title to land has been evidenced by written charters, grants, or deeds; in fact, under modern recording statutes, real estate titles are matters of public record. Also, the formal written documents which accompany most real estate transactions will usually, to some extent, expressly define the ownership interests of the parties. On the other hand, goods transactions are much less formal, and rarely or only imperfectly is any attempt made to define title. The title approach has proven to be too complex and elusory to be retained as a satisfactory framework for the present-day law of sales. In the introduction to Article 2 of the Uniform Commercial Code, the Article which deals with sales of goods, the authors explain:

> This Article is a complete revision and modernization of the Uniform Sales Act. . . .
>
> The coverage of the present Article is much more extensive than that of the old Sales Act and extends to the various bodies of case law which have been developed both outside of and under the latter.
>
> The arrangement of the present Article is in terms of contract for sale and the various steps of its performance. The legal consequences are stated as following directly from the contract and action taken under it without resorting to the idea of when property or title passed or was to pass as being the determining factor. *The purpose is to avoid making practical issues between practical men turn upon the location of an intangible something, the passing of which no man can prove by evidence and to substitute for such abstractions proof of words and actions of a tangible character.*[1] [Emphasis added.]

While the change from the "title approach" of the Uniform Sales Act to the "performance approach" of the Code makes very little change in the final outcome of most sales-of-goods disputes, the Code approach offers much simpler and more effective theories for resolving the conflicting claims of buyers and sellers.

Most sales-of-goods disputes can be classified into two main types:

1. Disputes concerning the relative rights of buyers and sellers—the subject of the present chapter. Usually these disputes involve either the obligations of the parties as to delivery and payment (including risk of loss), or the remedies of one party in case of default by the other party.

2. Disputes involving the rights of either a buyer or seller in relation to some remote third party who acquires an interest in or possession of the goods in question. The basic principles involved in these disputes will be discussed in the following chapter.

Part 1   CONTRACT OBLIGATIONS OF THE PARTIES

As the starting point for defining the obligations of the parties, the Code states:

> The obligation of the seller is to transfer and deliver and that of the buyer is to accept and pay in accordance with the contract.[2]

[1] Comment to U.C.C. Sec. 2-101.
[2] U.C.C. Sec. 2-301.

Some sales contracts state in minute detail everything that the parties agree to do. Most agreements, however, are not so detailed; they leave some terms either to be implied from prior dealings between the parties, or more often, to be implied from general business customs. Disputes as to just what term should be presumed or implied have given rise to much litigation. The Code attempts to reduce the number of disputes by prescribing in considerable detail the terms that are to be considered as customary and controlling unless the parties expressly agree otherwise. (The obligations which a seller customarily assumes in regard to the quality of goods—that is, the seller's warranties—have been previously discussed in Chapter 7.)

PRESUMED DELIVERY TERMS[3]

Unless otherwise expressly or impliedly agreed, a seller is supposed to deliver or ship in a single lot and within a reasonable time. In respect to what time is reasonable, the Code states:

> What is a reasonable time for taking any action depends on the nature, purpose and circumstances of such action.

Because the circumstances of cases may vary widely, it is not practicable for the Code to attempt a more exact, less flexible definition, but at the same time a person should not be permitted to misuse this flexibility. For example, a buyer wishing to escape from a burdensome contract might refuse to accept goods when the seller tenders them and try to claim that he is excused from the contract because the seller's tender came too late, even though the buyer had never previously complained about the delay. To prevent such unfairness and introduce some degree of certainty in particular cases, the Code provides that if a contract fails to specify a delivery date, neither party can accuse the other party of undue delay without first giving the other party advance notice and an opportunity to perform. Thus before a buyer can cancel because of the seller's alleged delay in delivering, the buyer must first demand delivery by a certain specified date. If the proposed time is unreasonably early, the seller can object. However, if the seller fails to object, he is admitting that the buyer's demand is reasonable. Then if (after failing to object to the buyer's demand) the seller does not deliver by the specified time, the buyer is justified in considering that the seller has breached the contract.

The seller's obligation as to place and manner of delivery depends upon the type of contract involved. For this purpose, most sales-of-goods contracts can be classified into one of the following types:

[3] U.C.C. Secs. 1-204; 2-307, 2-309, 2-319, 2-320, 2-503, 2-504.

1) Shipment Contract. The seller is obligated or authorized to initiate shipment of the goods to a particular place.

2) Destination Contract. Not only must the seller initiate transportation of the goods to a particular place, but the seller is responsible for the arrival of the goods at that place.

3) Contract for Delivery Without Transportation. The seller is not required to do anything involving transportation of the goods.

4) Contract Permitting Return. The buyer has a contract right to return the goods to the seller, even though the goods properly conform to the contract.

If goods are to be transported in connection with their sale, the term stating the price usually indicates whether the contract is a shipment or a destination contract. Suppose that a seller is located in St. Louis and a buyer in Boston, and that the price is stated as "$500, f.o.b. St. Louis, Mo." The term "f.o.b." (free on board) means that the price to the buyer is the indicated price at the place stated; if the buyer wants the goods in Boston or anywhere else, transporting or further transporting them will be at the buyer's expense. If the price is stated as $500, f.o.b. cars, St. Louis, Mo.," the seller is obliged to load the goods on cars and then turn the loaded cars over to the carrier. Such a statement of price (that is, f.o.b. point of shipment) identifies the contract as a shipment contract; the seller is required to ship, but he has no obligation as to arrival. On the other hand if the price is stated as f.o.b. destination (e.g., "$500, f.o.b. Boston, Mass."), the contract is a destination contract. Sometimes the price is stated in a hybrid form, such as, "$500, f.o.b. St. Louis, Mo., freight allowed to Boston, Mass." This is a shipment contract; the authors of the Code explain that (as a change from the prior statute) a contract is a shipment contract if that intent clearly appears even though the seller contracts to pay transportation to a particular place.

If goods are to be transported in connection with their sale but the price statement contains no f.o.b. term and says nothing about who pays freight, it is presumed that the buyer is to pay the shipping charges and that the contract is a shipment contract.

Sometimes the statement of price includes the letters "c.i.f." or "c. & f.," for example, for a St. Louis to Boston shipment, "$500, c. & f. Boston, Mass." The "c" means costs of the goods; "i" means insurance to the stated destination; and "f" means freight to the stated destination. The total expression means that the seller prepays freight (and insurance in the c.i.f. contract) at a stated figure which he then collects from the buyer, in addition to the cost or purchase price of the goods. The chief purpose of a c.i.f. or c. & f. contract is to relieve the buyer from the risk of fluctuations in freight and insurance rates. The seller calculates the rates and adds them to the cost, thus assuming the risk (or benefit) of any change in rates between the time the contract is formed and the time of shipment. From the standpoint of how much the buyer is to pay, the contract closely resembles an f.o.b. shipping point contract, and is a shipment contract rather than a destination contract. Since freight and insurance rates are less stable with foreign shipments than with domestic shipments, the terms are more commonly (although not exclusively) used in foreign trade.

SHIPMENT CONTRACT

Seller's Obligation[4]

In a shipment contract, the seller is supposed to 1) deliver the goods to a carrier and make a reasonable contract for their transportation, 2) deliver or tender to the buyer any document of title necessary for the buyer to obtain possession, and 3) notify the buyer that the goods have been shipped. Often a seller gives notice by sending the invoice to the buyer (in an open credit sale) or by sending the documents to a collecting bank in the buyer's town (in a sight draft, bill of lading attached sale).

If the seller fails to make a reasonable contract for transportation, or to give the buyer notice of shipment, but does not thereby cause material loss, the failure is entirely immaterial and cannot be seized upon by the buyer as a way to escape from the contract. As the Code says:

> Failure to notify the buyer . . . or to make a proper contract . . .
> is a ground for rejection only if material delay or loss ensues.

Risk of Loss[5]

In a shipment contract, the risk of casualty to the goods (damage, destruction, theft, etc.) passes to the buyer when the seller makes a proper delivery of the goods to a carrier. It is immaterial whether payment is deferred or instead is to be made on delivery (c.o.d.), whether the shipment is by straight or order bill of lading, or whether the goods are consigned to the seller or to the buyer. If the agreed terms are stated as, "sight draft, bill of lading attached, cash against documents," the seller will usually have the goods shipped by an order bill of lading which names the seller as the consignee. This is done to facilitate collection and has no effect on risk of loss (or on title).

Example: B in Allenhurst, New Jersey, ordered from S in New York City, certain described auto tires to be shipped by express from New York to

[4] U.C.C. Sec. 2-504.
[5] U.C.C. Sec. 2-509.

Allenhurst. B paid the full price of $95.43 with the order and was to pay the express charges upon arrival of the goods. S shipped the ordered tires without declaring their value. According to the contract (standard form) between S and the Express Company, the liability of the Express Company was automatically limited to $50 unless a higher value was declared at the time of shipment. Had S declared the actual value, the shipping charge would have been about ten cents more. The shipment was lost in transit. At B's request, S sent a duplicate shipment which was duly received by B. S collected $50 from the Express Company for the lost shipment and demanded from B the remaining $45.43. B refused to pay and S sued. (For $45.43 the case upon which this example is based was taken to the New York Court of Appeals, the highest appellate court of that state.)[6]

The contract was a shipment contract. If S had made proper shipment, risk of loss in transit would have been on B, and S could have required B to pay for the lost shipment, thus forcing B to collect from the carrier (assuming that the loss did not occur under circumstances which would have relieved the carrier from liability). However, because S did not declare the actual value, he did not make a reasonable contract for shipment, and therefore risk of loss did not pass to B. S could not recover in his lawsuit against B.

DESTINATION CONTRACT

Seller's Obligation[7]

In the case of a destination contract, the seller is supposed to deliver or tender delivery to the buyer at the agreed place. In a sight draft, bill of lading attached sale, the seller usually makes his tender by having the order bill of lading presented to the buyer by a collecting bank.

Risk of Loss[8]

Under a destination contract, if transportation is by common carrier, the risk of loss passes to the buyer when the goods are duly tendered to the buyer at the agreed place. If transportation is in the seller's trucks and the goods arrive at the agreed destination but are still in the seller's possession, the rules as to when risk of loss passes are the same as for a contract not involving transportation, discussed next.

CONTRACT FOR DELIVERY WITHOUT TRANSPORTATION[9]

Under such a contract, the goods may be in the possession either of the seller or of an independent bailee.

[6] *Miller* v. *Harvey*, 221 N.Y. 54, 116 N.E. 781 (1917).
[7] U.C.C. Sec. 2-503.
[8] U.C.C. Sec. 2-509.
[9] U.C.C. Secs. 2-503, 2-509, 2-510.

Goods in Seller's Possession

The seller must 1) have the goods available for the buyer according to the agreement, and 2) so notify the buyer. After the seller does this, then:

1. If the seller is not a merchant, the risk of loss passes to the buyer after he has had a reasonable time to take the goods.

2. If the seller is a merchant, the risk of loss remains with the seller

    a) until the buyer receives the goods, or

    b) until the buyer fails to take the goods according to the contract or gives notice that he will not take them—in which case, the risk of any loss which is not covered by the seller's insurance will fall on the buyer.

Goods in Bailee's Possession

Since in the type of contract being discussed here, the seller's performance does not involve transportation of the goods, the bailee will be someone other than a common carrier in the process of transporting the goods. The seller may properly perform his obligation by doing any one of the following:

1. The seller may give (or tender) to the buyer a negotiable document of title covering the goods. If the seller performs in this way, the risk of loss passes to the buyer upon his receipt of the document.

2. The seller may procure from the bailee an acknowledgment that he is holding the goods for the buyer. If the seller performs in this way, the risk of loss passes to the buyer when the bailee makes such an acknowledgment.

3. The seller may, if the buyer does not object, give the buyer a nonnegotiable document of title or a written direction that the bailee turn the goods over to the buyer. If the seller performs in this way (with concurrence of the buyer), the risk of loss passes to the buyer after he has had a reasonable time to present the document or writing to the bailee.

Contract Permitting Return[10]

There are two types of sales contract which permit a buyer to return goods even though they conform to the contract, namely 1) a sale on approval, and 2) a sale or return. The Code states:

> Unless otherwise agreed, if delivered goods may be returned by the buyer even though they conform to the contract, the transaction is

[10] U.C.C. Sec. 2-326.

(a) a "sale on approval" if the goods are delivered primarily for use, and

(b) a "sale or return" if the goods are delivered primarily for re-sale.

Sale on Approval

Unless otherwise agreed, the risk of loss (and title) remain with the seller until:

1. The buyer approves or otherwise indicates that he considers himself the owner of the goods, or

2. The time within which the buyer should give notice of disapproval passes without the buyer giving such notice.

If the buyer gives a proper notice of his desire to return the goods, the risk remains on the seller and the return is at the seller's risk and expense.

Sale or Return

Risk of loss is on the buyer from the time he would have had the risk in an ordinary contract without the return feature; any return under the contract is at the buyer's risk and expense.

RISK OF LOSS WHEN CONTRACT BREACHED[11]

In a shipment contract, if a seller makes a shipment which does not conform to the contract in every respect, the shipment will not have the effect of passing the risk of loss to the buyer. Instead, the risk will remain on the seller, unless and until the buyer chooses to accept the goods with knowledge of the defects.

Similarly, a breach of contract by a buyer will change the ordinary risk-of-loss rules. As the Code states:

> Where the buyer as to conforming goods already identified to the contract for sale repudiates or is otherwise in breach before risk of their loss has passed to him, the seller may to the extent of any deficiency in his effective insurance coverage treat the risk of loss as resting on the buyer for a commercially reasonable time.

PRESUMED PAYMENT TERMS

MANNER OF PAYMENT[12]

The Codes states:

> Tender of payment is sufficient when made by any means or in any manner current in the ordinary course of business unless the seller

[11] U.C.C. Sec. 2-510.
[12] U.C.C. Sec. 2-511.

demands payment in legal tender and gives any extension of time reasonably necessary to procure it.

Very often a buyer will tender payment by his own, uncertified check. The quoted rule is especially designed as a guide for this situation.

TIME OF PAYMENT[13]

Sales contracts are presumed to be cash transactions unless the seller actually agrees to deliver on credit. If a credit transaction states that payment is to be made within a certain period of time, the credit period is presumed to run from the time when the seller ships the goods (or delivers them if no shipment is involved) and sends (or gives) the invoice to the buyer. If no credit is extended, it is presumed that the buyer is to pay at the time and place he receives the goods. When credit is not extended and the shipment is sizable or consists of packaged or crated goods, the question sometimes arises as to whether the buyer is permitted to inspect the goods before being obliged to pay for them. The Code writes into law the usual business practices; the main provisions can be summarized as follows:

1. As the Code states:

> Unless otherwise agreed . . . where goods are tendered or delivered . . ., the buyer has a right before payment or acceptance to inspect them at any reasonable place and time and in any reasonable manner. . . . Expenses of inspection must be borne by the buyer but may be recovered from the seller if the goods do not conform and are rejected.

This provision does not reverse any of the risk-of-loss rules; the buyer's obligation to pay is not necessarily conditioned on his actually having a chance to inspect the goods. If risk of loss is on the buyer while the goods are in transit and the goods are destroyed before they arrive so that the buyer never has a chance to see them, the buyer's payment is due when the goods would ordinarily have arrived and been inspected.

2. A transaction may expressly provide that the buyer must pay before having any chance to inspect the goods. Such a provision is usually expressed by one of the following terms:

a) "C.o.d."

b) "Sight draft, bill of lading attached, cash against documents." The expression, "Sight draft, bill of lading attached," without more, does not expressly require the buyer to pay in advance of the time when the goods are expected to arrive. The statement is incomplete; for completeness there should be added either 1) "cash against documents" or its equivalent, requiring the buyer to pay upon presentment of the docu-

[13] U.C.C. Sec. 2-310, 2-513, 2-709.

ments, or 2) "inspection allowed" or its equivalent, permitting the buyer to wait until the time when the goods arrive—or would have arrived, if the goods are lost in transit after the risk of loss passed to the buyer.

c) "C.i.f." or "c. & f." Unless expressly agreed otherwise, these terms imply "cash against documents;" therefore the buyer must pay upon tender of the proper document of title.

PASSING OF TITLE OR OTHER PROPERTY INTEREST

As discussed in the introduction to the present chapter, the law has found it highly convenient to recognize that two or more persons may simultaneously hold varying title or ownership interests in the same item of real estate. Various interests may also coexist in personal property. The Code defines three such interests, 1) title, 2) security interest, and 3) buyer's contract interest, termed by the Code a "special property" in the goods.

SECURITY INTEREST[14]

A security interest in goods is an interest which an obligor gives to secure or assure that he will pay a certain amount of money or that he will perform in some other agreed manner.

Example: A buyer orders certain goods to be shipped, the terms being stated as "order bill of lading, sight draft attached, cash against documents." The seller ships the goods to the buyer and (as is the common commercial practice) uses an order bill of lading in which the seller is named as the consignee.

Upon shipment, the seller has a security interest in the goods. As the Code states:

> The retention or reservation of title by a seller of goods notwithstanding shipment or delivery to the buyer . . . is limited in effect to a reservation of a "security interest."

Example: A dealer sells and delivers certain goods to a buyer who signs a written agreement promising to pay the agreed price in stated installments and acknowledging that title is to remain in the dealer until the full price is paid.

The dealer's interest is a security interest.

Any security interest arising in connection with the sale of goods is governed chiefly by the Sales Article of the Code until the buyer obtains lawful possession of the goods, after which the rights of the parties are determined by the Secured Transactions Article of the Code (discussed in Chapter 18).

[14] U.C.C. Sec. 1-201.

SPECIAL PROPERTY[15]

Even though goods are still in the seller's possession, a special property interest in them passes to the buyer when they are designated or set aside for the contract. This special property gives the buyer some protection from the seller's lien creditors, some rights in case of the seller's insolvency, and a limited right to sue for possession of the goods if the seller wrongfully refuses to deliver.

TITLE[16]

Title may be said to consist of all the rights which remain after deduction of any other outstanding interests such as security interest, leasehold interest, special property, etc.

Under the Code, the location of title is for most purposes unimportant in determining the relative rights of the seller and buyer. Location of title becomes important if the rights of third persons are involved, as discussed in the next chapter.

In general, as the Code states:

> Unless otherwise explicitly agreed title passes to the buyer at the time and place at which the seller completes his performance with reference to the physical delivery [that is, transportation] of the goods. . . .

Thus in a shipment contract, title passes upon shipment. In a destination contract, title passes when the goods are tendered to the buyer at the destination. In a contract for delivery without transportation, the Code provides:

> (a) if the seller is to deliver a document of title, title passes at the time when and the place where he delivers such documents; or
> (b) if the goods are at the time of contracting already identified [segregated or designated for the buyer] and no documents are to be delivered, title passes at the time and place of contracting.

The Code also provides:

> A rejection or other refusal by the buyer to receive or retain the goods, whether or not justified, or a justified revocation of acceptance revests title to the goods in the seller. Such a revesting occurs by operation of law and is not a "sale."

Part 2   REMEDIES OF SELLERS

If a buyer who has agreed to purchase certain goods breaches his agreement by refusing to receive or pay for the goods, the seller is

[15] U.C.C. Sec. 2-501.
[16] U.C.C. Sec. 2-401.

certainly entitled to a legal remedy—a remedy which will give him, as nearly as is reasonably possible, what he would have obtained had the buyer not defaulted. Suppose, however, that the buyer is not actually breaching his contract but rather is merely threatening to do so. For example, suppose that a buyer has agreed to purchase goods to be shipped on June 1 and paid for on delivery, and that one month *before* the shipment date the buyer notifies the seller to cancel the contract. It would not be reasonable to require the seller to wait until June 1 and to fruitlessly ship the goods before allowing him a legal remedy. Or suppose that a buyer who agrees to pay for goods thirty days after shipment, becomes insolvent *before* the goods are shipped. It would not be reasonable to require the seller to ship and then wait until the buyer's inevitable default before allowing him a legal remedy. In order to cope with these and a wide variety of other situations which may arise, the law has worked out a scheme or pattern of remedies, classifying possible fact situations according to two variables, 1) the circumstance or event which makes awarding a legal remedy to the seller necessary or desirable, and 2) the location of the goods at the time this event occurs.

1) First Variable. A seller is considered as sufficiently threatened with a loss so as to be entitled to a legal remedy:

1. When the buyer repudiates in advance of the time for performance of the contract (sometimes called "anticipatory repudiation").

2. When the buyer breaches the contract, either by failing to make an agreed payment or by refusing to receive the goods when tendered.

3. When the seller discovers that the buyer is insolvent, or at least when the seller has reason to doubt the buyer's solvency.

2) Second Variable. At the time when one of the above events occurs, the goods may be located 1) in the seller's possession, 2) in the possession of a carrier or other bailee, or 3) in the buyer's possession.

Before outlining the pattern of the law as to particular remedies, it will be helpful to list the usual remedies:[17]

1. Withholding delivery.

2. Reobtaining control over goods, by stopping them in transit or by reclaiming them from the buyer's possession.

3. Reselling the goods elsewhere and recovering damages.

4. Retaining the goods and recovering damages.

5. Recovering the purchase price.

6. Canceling the contract. The buyer's breach will usually excuse the seller from performing his part of the contract, in which case the seller can declare the contract canceled. The seller's canceling the contract, however, does not automatically cancel his rights against the buyer. As the Code states:

[17] U.C.C. Sec. 2-703.

Unless the contrary intention clearly appears, expressions of "cancellation" or "rescission" of the contract or the like shall not be construed as a renunciation or discharge of any claim in damages for an antecedent breach.[18]

GOODS IN SELLER'S POSSESSION

BUYER REPUDIATES[19]

If by words or other conduct prior to the time for delivery a buyer reasonably leads a seller to believe that the contracted goods will not be accepted, the seller 1) may consider the repudiation as a breach and act accordingly, even though no actual breach has yet occurred, or instead 2) may wait for not exceeding a commercially reasonable time (which usually could extend up to the time for actual performance of the contract) before considering the contract breached. Until the seller does take some affirmative action on the repudiation (by giving notice of cancellation or by materially changing his position—for example, by reprograming his purchasing or manufacturing operations), the buyer is permitted to retract his repudiation. Such a retraction will restore the buyer's right to receive delivery under the contract, but the buyer must give adequate assurance that he will not again repudiate and must compensate the seller for any delay caused by the repudiation.

If a buyer repudiates at a time when the seller has not yet completed his own preparations to deliver under the contract, the seller is permitted to minimize his possible loss by stopping or suspending his own preparations. A question of considerable importance to a seller is whether he *must* stop or suspend his own preparations, upon receiving the buyer's repudiation.

In the law of damages and compensation, as with all law, "reasonableness" or "reasonable conduct" is the standard or measure. An injured person is entitled to be compensated for his loss, but he is expected to act reasonably. Once a wrongful act has been committed—whether a tort or a breach of contract—the innocent, injured party must do what he reasonably can to keep his loss at a minimum. The amount he can collect as damages, therefore, is limited to the amount of loss he would have suffered had he acted reasonably to minimize his loss, regardless of the amount of loss he actually does sustain.

Example: A seller wrongfully refused to deliver at the contract price of $1 per unit. At the time for delivery, goods of the same kind and grade were available on the market at $1.25 per unit. The buyer unreasonably waited four weeks and then bought the same type of goods elsewhere, paying the then market price of $1.50 per unit.

[18] U.C.C. Sec. 2-720.
[19] U.C.C. Secs. 2-510, 2-610, 2-611, 2-704, 2-709.

The buyer would be entitled to collect as damages only 25 cents per unit rather than his actual loss which he unreasonably aggravated to 50 cents per unit.

Example: S contracted to sell certain goods for $3,500, and agreed to take B's sixty-day negotiable note for that amount. S thereafter wrongfully refused to deliver unless B would sign a thirty-day note for the price. B bought elsewhere on sixty-days' credit, paying $4,500.

Usually it would not be reasonable for B to pay a higher price when he could obtain the goods from S at a lower price, even though taking advantage of the lower price would require B to deal with the defaulting seller. As damages B could recover no more than the interest on $3,500 for thirty days; he could not recover his actual loss which he unreasonably aggravated to $1,000.[20]

Example: Two weeks before time for delivery, B told the seller, S, that he would refuse to receive the goods when tendered. At the time of B's repudiation, the goods could be sold on the market for the contract price of $1 per unit. S waited and when B refused to receive delivery upon tender according to contract, S promptly resold at the market price, which on the day of resale was 75 cents per unit.

Had S resold immediately upon B's repudiation, he would have sustained no loss except for the expenses of resale. Nevertheless, under the Code provision discussed above, S was probably justified in waiting and could therefore collect 25 cents per unit as damages.

This concept of "reasonable conduct" requires that upon *actual* breach, the seller do what he reasonably can to minimize his loss. Anticipatory repudiation is not actual or present breach. What a seller should do upon the buyer's anticipatory repudiation will depend upon how far the seller has proceeded in his preparations to perform the contract. The principal fact situations can be classified as follows:

1. At the time when the buyer repudiates, the seller has not yet completed procuring or manufacturing the goods.

a) The seller has not yet begun procuring or manufacturing goods for the contract: He clearly should not begin, once he has learned of the repudiation.

b) The seller is in the process of procuring or manufacturing goods for the contract: The seller must assume for the moment that the buyer will not retract the repudiation, and must estimate, as well as he reasonably can, the amount of loss which he would sustain if he completed

---

[20] Recalling that an agreement modifying a sales-of-goods contract needs no consideration to be enforceable, how should B phrase his reply to S in order to obtain the goods on a thirty-day note, without at the same time surrendering his rights and in effect agreeing to an enforceable modification from a sixty-day to a thirty-day contract? This is one of the many occasions when a businessman should call his lawyer—and be quite grateful that there are lawyers.

the process, as compared with the loss which would result from stopping and salvaging what he could from the incomplete goods. If the estimated loss through completion is substantially greater than with stopping, the seller must stop the process. Otherwise, he may, if he wishes, continue and complete the process.

2. At the time when the buyer repudiates, the seller has the goods ready for shipment. At common law there is respectable authority for the view that it is not reasonable for a seller to ship goods after a buyer has unequivocally repudiated his agreement to buy, and that if a seller does so, he cannot recover the unnecessary shipping expenses from the defaulting buyer. The same view would probably prevail under the Code.

BUYER BREACHES[21]

The most common types of breaches of contract by buyers are 1) failures to make contracted payments when due, and 2) refusals to receive delivery of contracted goods.

Failure to Pay

If a buyer fails to pay according to his agreement, the seller has the right to retain any undelivered goods until the buyer makes up the delinquent payment. Also, if any further payments are to come due under the contract, the seller can continue to withhold delivery until the buyer gives adequate assurance that he will make the future payments on time.

Failure to Accept

If a buyer wrongfully refuses to accept or retain goods, the seller's possible remedies include the following:

1. In certain cases the seller can tender the goods to the buyer and sue for the purchase price. This is an extraordinary remedy and is available only if the goods are so unique that the seller cannot reasonably resell them elsewhere.

2. Usually a seller will give reasonable advance notice to the buyer, and if the buyer persists in his default, the seller will resell the goods elsewhere and sue the buyer for any damages that result. If the seller should happen to make a profit on the resale, he may keep the profit on the theory that the defaulting buyer's interest in the goods was not sufficient to entitle him to the profit.

3. Although a seller will usually attempt to resell as soon as he is able to find another buyer, he has no obligation to do so. He may

[21] U.C.C. Secs. 2-302, 2-609, 2-703, 2-706, 2-708, 2-709, 2-718.

instead retain the goods or make any other disposition he wishes, and recover from the buyer for the damages sustained.

Measure of Damages

The basic rules for measuring the amount of damages which a seller is entitled to recover can be summarized in the following way.

Standard Measure of Damages. If a seller makes a reasonable resale, he will usually have the right to recover from the buyer the amount of loss resulting from the resale. This is calculated by subtracting the amount received by means of the resale, from the amount which the seller would have received if the buyer had not defaulted. If on the other hand the seller does not resell at all (as is his privilege), or if the seller makes a resale which is not reasonable, the amount (if any) by which the goods declined in value is the measure of the seller's damages. This is calculated by subtracting the market price of the contracted goods (as of the time and place for delivery), from the contract price which the seller would have received if the buyer had not defaulted. If the buyer made a partial payment before defaulting, the seller has an alternative to suing for damages. He can do whatever he wishes with the contracted goods and, as his total damages, retain so much of the down payment as does not exceed 20 percent or $500, whichever is smaller. In the absence of an express agreement otherwise, any payment in excess of this maximum should be returned to the buyer.

Special Measure of Damages. Sometimes the standard measure of damages (the difference between reasonable resale price and contract price, or the difference between market value and contract price) does not adequately compensate a seller. The most common example is the case of a dealer who sells standard-priced goods, and who can always obtain more goods than he can sell. In such a case the measure of recoverable damages is the amount of net profit which the seller would have made on the buyer's purchase.

Example: A TV dealer entered into a contract with a buyer for the sale and delivery of a TV set for the list price of $395. The buyer thereafter refused to accept delivery of the set, and the dealer sold the set to another purchaser for $395.

If the first buyer had not breached the contract, the dealer would have obtained another TV set from his supplier so that when the second purchaser came in, the dealer would still have made the second sale. The buyer's breach deprived the dealer of the net profit which he would have made on the first sale and the dealer could recover this amount as damages from the buyer.

Agreed Measure of Damages. In some contracts the parties expressly agree on what their remedies and the measure of damages are to be in case of a future breach by either party. In order to be enforceable, the agreed measure must be reasonable in amount. A very common type of provision expressly states that the seller may retain the buyer's down payment as agreed or liquidated damages. Under the Code, such a provision is presumed to be valid and enforceable for so much of the buyer's down payment as does not exceed 20 percent or $500, whichever is smaller. An agreement authorizing the retention of more than this maximum will be valid only if reasonable under the circumstances.

Buyer's Solvency Reasonably Doubtful[22]

Included under this heading are situations in which the seller can prove that the buyer is actually insolvent, and also situations in which, although lacking proof of actual insolvency, the seller has reasonable grounds to suspect that the buyer may be insolvent.

If either of these situations occurs before a seller makes delivery under a credit agreement, the seller can refuse to deliver unless he receives cash or some adequate assurance of payment. However, the seller cannot treat the contract as breached and resell the goods immediately. He must give the buyer a reasonable time to respond. If within a reasonable time —not exceeding thirty days—the buyer fails to pay or give adequate assurance of payment, the seller is then permitted to consider the contract as repudiated and to proceed accordingly.

What kind of assurance should be considered "adequate" depends entirely upon what has made the seller doubtful of the buyer's solvency. Sometimes a favorable credit report from the buyer's bank will be sufficient assurance, sometimes a bond guaranteeing the buyer's payment will be required. Vague as it is, about the best general guide is that stated in the Code:

> Between merchants the reasonableness of grounds for insecurity and the adequacy of any assurance offered shall be determined according to commercial standards.

GOODS IN POSSESSION OF CARRIER OR OTHER BAILEE[23]

During transportation of goods to a buyer, a seller may want to have the goods stopped and returned. The Code provides:

> (1) The seller may stop delivery of goods in the possession of a carrier or other bailee when he discovers the buyer to be insolvent . . . and may stop delivery of carload, truckload, planeload or larger shipments of express or freight when the buyer repudiates or fails to make

[22] U.C.C. Secs. 2-609, 2-702.
[23] U.C.C. Secs. 2-705, 2-710.

a payment due before delivery or if for any other reason the seller has a right to withhold or reclaim the goods.

    (2) As against such buyer the seller may stop delivery until

        (a) receipt of the goods by the buyer; or

        (b) acknowledgment to the buyer by any bailee of the goods except a carrier that the bailee holds the goods for the buyer; or

        (c) such acknowledgment to the buyer by a carrier by reshipment or as warehouseman; or

        (d) negotiation to the buyer of any negotiable document of title covering the goods.

    (3) (a) To stop delivery the seller must so notify as to enable the bailee by reasonable diligence to prevent delivery of the goods.

        (b) After such notification the bailee must hold and deliver the goods according to the directions of the seller but the seller is liable to the bailee for any ensuing charges or damages. [These charges then become part of the damages which the seller can recover from the defaulting buyer.]

        (c) If a negotiable document of title has been issued for goods the bailee is not obliged to obey a notification to stop until surrender of the document. . . .

GOODS IN BUYER'S POSSESSION

BUYER INSOLVENT[24]

Obviously a seller should not sell on credit unless he is willing to take a chance on his buyer's future ability to pay. A seller may protect himself somewhat by making the sale a secured transaction (as discussed in Chapter 18), and thus reserve a right to repossess the goods should the buyer fail to pay. If instead of making a secured sale, the seller sells and delivers on what is frequently called "open account," without reserving the title or a security interest in the goods, the seller has only a very limited right to repossess. For such a seller to repossess from an insolvent buyer 1) he must prove that the buyer acted fraudulently (by misrepresenting his solvency), or at least somewhat unfairly (by failing to disclose his insolvency), and also 2) the seller must demand return of the goods promptly, before some third person has acquired an interest in the goods.

Third Persons. Possible third persons include 1) a person purchasing from the buyer, in good faith and for value; 2) an attaching creditor who has obtained a judgment against the buyer and has had the sheriff levy on the goods in the buyer's possession; 3) a receiver or other representative of creditors appointed by a court in an insolvency proceeding against the buyer. A receiver takes possession of the buyer's assets and obtains the same rights as an attaching creditor. Both an attaching creditor and a

---

[24] U.C.C. Sec. 2-702.

court-appointed representative of creditors come under the Code's definition of "lien creditors."

Prompt Demand. The seller's demand must be made within ten days after the insolvent buyer's receipt of the goods, unless the buyer recently (within three months before delivery) made a written misrepresentation of solvency to the seller.

BUYER REFUSES TO RETAIN GOODS[25]

In the law of sales, the term "acceptance of goods" involves more than receiving delivery. A buyer may be in possession of goods and still not have accepted them. A buyer is considered to have accepted goods if he indicates that he will keep or retain the goods as their owner. Such an indication may be expressed in words, or it may be implied from acts, such as the buyer's using the goods or failing to reject them after having a reasonable opportunity to inspect. Suppose for example that after receiving delivery, a buyer looks the goods over, decides that he does not want them, and so notifies the seller. If the goods conform to the contract, the buyer is guilty of breaching the contract when he refuses to accept and pay for the goods. Nevertheless he *is* refusing to accept, and if the goods are such that the seller can with reasonable effort resell them elsewhere for a reasonable price, the only course open to the seller is to take the goods back and sue the buyer for damages. Only if the goods are not reasonably resalable can the seller leave them in the buyer's possession and recover the purchase price from the buyer. On the other hand, if a buyer actually accepts goods and then changes his mind and wrongfully refuses to pay for them, the seller has the right to sue and recover the purchase price from the buyer.

INSTALLMENT CONTRACTS[26]

Discussion of remedies up to this point has concerned contracts for single lot deliveries rather than installment deliveries. In a contract for a single lot delivery, the buyer's failure to make a payment when due excuses the seller from his obligation to deliver; the seller is entitled to resell the goods elsewhere, or to avail himself of any of the other remedies which have been discussed. However, if a contract calls for successive deliveries in installments, a failure to make one payment may not be considered sufficiently serious to excuse the seller from the remainder of the contract. In the language of the Code, only when "default with respect to one or more installments substantially impairs the value of the whole contract," is there a breach of the whole contract.

[25] U.C.C. Secs. 2-606, 2-709.
[26] U.C.C. Secs. 2-612, 2-703.

Example: On April 1 S and B entered into a contract for delivery on June 1 of 1,000 units of certain described goods, at a price of $1 per unit, payable $200 on May 15, the balance on June 30. B failed to make the May 15 payment. S immediately notified B that if he did not make the overdue payment by May 22, S would resell the goods and hold B liable for any deficiency. Assume that under the circumstances this was a reasonable advance notice. B protested, requesting more time, and was still in default on May 22, when S resold the goods elsewhere.

S was justified in what he did. B's breach completely excused S from his obligation to deliver under the contract.

Example: On April 1 S and B entered into a contract for delivery of 1,000 units of certain described goods at a price of $1 per unit, the goods to be delivered as follows: 200 units on May 1, and 200 units on the first of each month thereafter, the price for each installment to be paid within two weeks after delivery. S properly made the May 1 delivery, but B failed to pay within two weeks. S immediately notified B that unless payment was made by May 22, S would cancel the entire contract, resell the contracted goods elsewhere, and hold B liable for any deficiency. B protested, requesting more time, and was still in default on May 22.

In the absence of special circumstances, B's default would not excuse S from the entire balance of the contract. S would be justified in withholding the June 1 shipment, but if B belatedly (say on June 6) made or tendered the May payment plus interest, and gave adequate assurance that succeeding payments would be made on time, then, in the absence of special circumstances, B would be entitled to have deliveries resumed. S would be liable for damages if he refused to resume deliveries.

Part 3 REMEDIES OF BUYERS

In providing remedies for buyers, the Code closely parallels the pattern followed for sellers' remedies. The usual remedies which, under varying circumstances, may be available to a buyer include the following:[27]

1. Recovering the agreed goods from the seller.

2. Rejecting nonconforming goods which the seller delivers or tenders.

3. Accepting some or all of the goods delivered by the seller even though they do not conform to the contract, with a price reduction or damages for the nonconformity.

4. Buying similar goods elsewhere and recovering damages.

5. Recovering damages without attempting to purchase elsewhere.

6. Canceling the contract. When the seller's breach excuses the buyer from taking goods under the contract, the buyer may so declare,

[27] U.C.C. Sec. 2-711.

thus canceling the contract but nevertheless preserving his right to recover damages from the seller.[28]

Which remedy is available or appropriate depends upon what the seller has done. A buyer is considered sufficiently threatened with a loss so as to be entitled to a legal remedy:

1. When the seller repudiates in advance of time for performance.
2. When the seller actually breaches the contract
   a) By failing to make delivery according to the contract, or
   b) By making or tendering a delivery which does not conform to the contract, either as to time of delivery, or as to kind, quantity, or quality of goods.
3. When the buyer discovers that the seller is insolvent.

SELLER REPUDIATES[29]

The effect of a seller's anticipatory repudiation is exactly the same (with the parties reversed of course) as previously discussed for a buyer's repudiation. Thus the buyer may consider the repudiation as a breach and act accordingly, even though no actual breach has yet occurred, or instead may wait for a commercially reasonable time before considering the contract breached. Until the buyer does take some affirmative action on the repudiation (by giving notice of cancellation or materially changing his position), the seller is permitted to retract his repudiation. Although the retraction will restore the seller's rights under the contract, the seller must also give adequate assurance that he will not again repudiate, and must compensate the buyer for damages resulting from the repudiation.

SELLER FAILS TO DELIVER[30]

When a seller refuses to deliver according to contract, the first question to settle is whether the buyer should be permitted to recover the actual goods from the seller or instead only money damages. This is quite similar to the previously discussed situation of a buyer refusing to accept goods according to contract, and the question which there arose—whether the seller could recover the purchase price or only damages. As a matter of policy, the recovery of damages is considered the standard or usual remedy; recovery of the purchase price by the seller or recovery of actual goods by the buyer is an extraordinary remedy, available only when the standard or usual remedy of money damages is not adequate. Thus when the seller fails to deliver (or repudiates in advance), the

[28] U.C.C. Sec. 2-720.
[29] U.C.C. Secs. 2-610, 2-611.
[30] U.C.C. Secs. 2-712, 2-713, 2-716.

buyer may cover his needs by purchasing elsewhere. If he has to pay a higher price than the contract price, the new (cover) price is the chief factor in determining the amount of his damages; the buyer can recover from the seller the amount of this extra payment. The buyer is not obliged to purchase elsewhere in order to recover damages. If he does not cover (or if his purchase is not reasonable), the chief factor in measuring the buyer's damages is the market value at the time and place of delivery. If the goods which the buyer should have obtained under the contract would have been worth more than the contract price, the buyer can recover this difference as the damages resulting from the seller's breach. The limited remedy of suing for specific goods is available in only two situations, 1) if the goods are unique, or 2) if the goods have already been shipped.

1) *Unique Goods.* If the buyer is unable through reasonable effort to obtain similar goods elsewhere, he can sue to obtain the goods from the seller. Note that the buyer's right does not depend upon who has title to the goods.

2) *Shipped Goods.* After a seller begins performance by shipping goods according to the contract, it is reasonable to require the seller to continue his performance. Thus if the seller wrongfully refuses to permit the shipped goods to be delivered (for example by refusing to surrender an order bill of lading when the buyer properly tenders payment), the buyer may offer to pay as agreed, and sue the seller to obtain possession or control of the goods.

Example: A builder entered into a contract with a lumber dealer for the purchase of all the lumber in two specified piles in the dealer's yard. The piles were identified by stakes driven into the ground in front of each pile. The letter "A" was painted on one stake, "B" on the other. Under the agreement the builder was to load the lumber and haul it away within the next three months, using his own trucks and labor, and was to pay the agreed price for each load within one week after taking it away. One month later, at a time when the builder had removed and paid for approximately one-third of pile A and none of pile B, the market price of lumber suddenly advanced about 20 percent. The dealer notified the builder that the balance of the contract was canceled and refused to permit the builder to remove any more lumber. Assume that the original contract gave the dealer no right to cancel. After the price increase, lumber of the same kind and grade was available on the market, but the price was 20 percent higher than the contract price. The builder sued the dealer to obtain possession of the remaining lumber in pile A and all of the lumber in pile B.

As discussed in Part 1 of this chapter, title to the lumber in both designated piles had passed to the builder, inasmuch as the dealer had nothing further to do with regard to physical delivery. However, since through reasonable effort the builder could obtain lumber of the same quality on the market, the builder would have no right to sue the dealer and obtain possession of the specified lumber. The builder's only recourse would be to buy on the market and sue the dealer for the additional cost as damages.

Other facts being the same, suppose that the contract required the builder to pay when the contract was signed and that, accordingly, the builder had fully paid for the lumber. Nevertheless the builder would have no right to recover possession of the lumber from the dealer.

SELLER MAKES IMPROPER DELIVERY

If goods are shipped on credit or paid for in advance, they are frequently delivered to a buyer and left with him before he has an opportunity to inspect them. This is especially true if goods are cased or crated, or if a buyer receives a large volume of goods from a number of different sellers. If the buyer's subsequent inspection discloses that the goods are defective or in some other way do not conform to contract, the buyer must then promptly decide whether he wishes to retain the goods or reject them.

Sometimes a buyer who does not act diligently will lose his right to reject nonconforming goods; he may even lose his right to recover damages. Whether a buyer has a right to reject or to recover damages depends upon a combination of three factors: 1) whether the buyer has already indicated acceptance of the goods, 2) the time when the buyer discovers or should discover the nonconformity, and 3) the time when the buyer notifies the seller of the nonconformity and what such notice states.

As previously discussed, a buyer is considered to have accepted goods when he indicates that he will keep or retain them as their owner.[31] A buyer's indication of acceptance may be expressed in words or implied from acts such as using the goods or failing to reject them after having a reasonable opportunity to inspect. A buyer cannot indefinitely refrain from expressing acceptance and thereby attempt to retain full rejection rights a long time after delivery; the expiration of more than a reasonable length of time without the buyer taking any action at all would itself amount to an indication of acceptance.

Goods Not Yet Accepted[32]

Rejection

If a buyer has not yet accepted a shipment of goods, he may reject any which do not conform to the contract. His rejection, however, will

---

[31] U.C.C. Sec. 2-606.
[32] U.C.C. Secs. 2-105, 2-601–605, 2-607, 2-711, 2-714, 2-717.

not always terminate the seller's rights under the contract. The fact that a seller's delivery fails to conform to his contract does not necessarily show either bad faith on the part of the seller or an intent to repudiate the contract. It is possible for a seller to be quite unaware that his shipment is defective, as for example when a distributor who is not a manufacturer ships goods which are still in the manufacturer's original packages. If sufficient time remains so that the seller can correct the nonconformity within contract time (for example, by repairing a defect or making a supplementary shipment), the seller should be given an opportunity to do so. However, if time is quite short or if no time at all remains, the buyer may have to make other arrangements immediately after rejecting in order to assure against loss from not having the desired goods on the contract date. Whether the seller is able to correct the nonconformity within contract time, therefore, is an important factor in determining what the buyer must do to accomplish rejection and his rights after rejection.

Requirements for Rejection. To accomplish an effective rejection, a buyer should give the seller a reasonably prompt notice to that effect. While the notice of rejection need not follow any particular form, the buyer should usually inform the seller of why the goods are being rejected, especially if the seller can correct the nonconformity within contract time.

Disposition of Rejected Goods. If a buyer notices a defect when goods are tendered to him, he can refuse to receive delivery. Usually, however, a buyer does not discover any grounds for rejection until after delivery. If defective goods in the buyer's possession are not perishable or speedily declining in value, the buyer's only obligation, upon giving a proper notice of rejection, is to hold the goods with reasonable care, awaiting the seller's disposition. If the seller gives no instructions within a reasonable time, the buyer may take whatever reasonable action is most convenient for him. He may 1) store the goods at the seller's expense, 2) return them at the latter's expense, or 3) resell them and pay the net proceeds to the seller. If, on the other hand, the goods are perishable or speedily declining in value, a merchant-buyer must try to sell the goods for the benefit of the seller. Because a merchant has procedures and contacts for the sale of goods, it is only fair that he promptly use his facilities to dispose of rejected goods that are perishable or rapidly declining in value—with, of course, reasonable compensation for his expenses and services.

Remedies in Addition to Rejection. As stated previously, if there is sufficient time for the seller to correct a nonconformity the buyer's notice of rejection must say what is wrong with the goods. Then if the seller intends to correct the nonconformity, he must promptly notify the buyer accordingly. If 1) the seller's notice reaches the buyer before the latter would be reasonably justified in making other arrangements, and also 2) if following such notice the seller tenders a correction of the defective delivery within contract time, the buyer must accept the correction. A late correction need not be accepted unless the buyer has led the seller reasonably to believe that the delay would be unimportant.

If insufficient time remains or if the seller does not attempt to correct the shipment, then the buyer, in addition to rejection, has as possible remedies those previously discussed for the seller's failure to make any delivery at all.

Retention

Upon discovering that goods are defective, a buyer may nevertheless decide that the goods can be of some use to him and retain them. For goods which the buyer retains, he is obliged to pay the contract price, less the damages he sustains as a result of the goods not conforming to contract. However, in order to have a right to deduct from the price or to collect for the damages sustained, the buyer must notify the seller that the goods are defective. This notice *must* be given within a reasonable time after the buyer discovers or should have discovered that the goods are defective; if a buyer fails to give proper notice, he will lose *all* rights to recover damages from the seller. This is in accord with the general law of contracts; if a contracting party fails to object to defective performance by the time when he could be expected to raise an objection, he is assumed, as a matter of fairness to the other party, to have waived or excused the defect, and to have shown himself to be fully satisfied with the performance, although defective. He cannot afterwards change his mind or change the impression he has given the other party, and thus he will lose any right he previously had to cancel the contract or even to collect damages.

Partial Rejection and Partial Retention

Upon discovering that goods do not conform to contract, a buyer may if he wishes retain any portion of the goods and reject the remainder. To do this, the buyer must promptly notify the seller of what is wrong, and state what he is retaining and what he is rejecting. The only restriction on his choice as to what he keeps and what he rejects is that his division must be commercially reasonable. The buyer should not split a commercial unit, since this would materially impair the character or value of the remainder. For example, the buyer cannot choose to accept a sofa and reject the remainder of a suite of furniture.

Example: S and B entered into a contract for shipment of 500 units of certain described goods, trade-named "reds," and 400 units of other described goods, trade-named "blues," for which B agreed to pay $1 per unit, payable thirty days after delivery. S, however, made a nonconforming shipment, shipping 900 units of reds.

1. B could reject the entire shipment. B would not be required to assume the burden of separating the conforming from the nonconforming goods.

2. B could accept the entire shipment. He would then be obliged to pay the contract price for all that he accepted, less damages (if any) for the nonconformity.

3. Although B ordered 500 reds, he could accept 200 reds (or any other quantity) and reject the remainder. Since the shipment did not conform, B could divide the shipment in any way that he wished, so long as he did not split a commercial unit.

Goods Accepted[33]

With Knowledge of Defect

Suppose that when a buyer receives a defective shipment, he assumes that the defect will be corrected, and therefore keeps the goods. If the defect substantially impairs the value of the goods to the buyer and is not corrected within a reasonable time, the buyer is permitted to revoke his acceptance and reject all of the goods or any number of commercial units which he has not yet used. On the other hand, if a buyer accepts a shipment with knowledge of its nonconformity and with no valid reason to expect that the nonconformity will be remedied or corrected, he cannot afterwards change his mind and reject the goods. If he has given the seller proper notice of the nonconformity, the buyer may recover for any damages sustained, but he cannot revoke his acceptance.

Example: B, a manufacturer of refrigerator cases, ordered from S 500 door latches of a certain type, trade-named "roll-lock," at $4 per latch. S had no roll-lock latches on hand, but had a type of latch, trade-named "spring-lock," which usually sold for $4.25 per latch, and which many manufacturers had found superior to the roll-lock latches. Desiring to obtain B's future patronage, S shipped to B 500 spring-lock latches invoiced at $4 per latch. The carrier delivered the boxed latches to B's receiving room. Upon B's inspection within a reasonable time after receipt, B at once noticed the substitution.

1. B promptly notified S that he rejected the latches because they were spring-lock rather than roll-lock and asked for instructions as to what to do with the rejected goods. This was an effective rejection. B also demanded that S ship the ordered latches. If S did not explain, with or in advance of the shipment, that he was sending the other type of latches as an accommodation, S's shipping spring-lock latches in response to B's order would probably

[33] U.C.C. Secs. 2-607, 2-608, 2-714.

constitute an acceptance of the original order and form an enforceable contract for roll-lock latches.   (See page 95 and problem 8, page 111.)

2. B notified S that although the latches did not conform to his order, he would retain and use them.   After two weeks (assume that this was a reasonable time) B discovered that because of the unique design of the cases upon which the latches were to be installed, the spring-lock latches would not work satisfactorily without a costly alteration of the cases.   B promptly notified S of this and said that he rejected the latches.   Having accepted with knowledge of the nonconformity (and, of course, with no expectation that the nonconformity would be corrected), B could not reject.   He could recover damages if any were reasonably sustained (but, of course, it would be unreasonable to include as damages the cost of altering the cases).

Without Knowledge of Defect

If at the time a buyer accepts a defective shipment, he is excusably ignorant of its nonconformity, and then within a reasonable time he discovers a nonconformity which substantially impairs the value of the goods to him, he may, if he wishes, revoke his acceptance and reject all of the goods or any number of commercial units that he has not yet used. The buyer will then have the same rights and duties as if he had initially rejected the goods.

A buyer's ignorance of a nonconformity would be excused if he could not reasonably have been expected to discover the defect sooner, either because of the difficulty of discovery, or because of an assurance from the seller (for example, an express warranty) which led the buyer to assume that the goods were satisfactory and therefore to delay his inspection.

Notice that only *unused* goods can be rejected.   Whatever the reason that would otherwise give the buyer a right to reject, a buyer *cannot reject* after any substantial change in the condition of the goods (except such as is caused by their own defects).

Example: A thief stole an auto from its owner, forged the necessary papers, and sold the car to a dealer who bought it for value and without notice that he was buying from a thief.   Still in justifiable ignorance of the theft, the dealer sold the car to B for $775, which B paid, without knowledge of the theft.   B used the car continuously for two years before the owner's insurance company was successful in tracing the car.   The insurance company, succeeding to the owner's rights, repossessed the car from B.   By that time the car had depreciated and had a fair value of $400.   When informed of the facts, the dealer offered to pay B $400 in full settlement of B's claim against the dealer.   B refused the settlement and sued for $775.

B's theory was that because of the breach of the dealer's implied warranty of title, B could cancel the contract by revoking his acceptance and giving notice of rejection; and that he could reject even though no longer in possession of the car and thus unable to return it, because his inability to return the car was the result of the very defect in title which formed the basis of his claim against the dealer. However, under the Code (as well as under the Uniform Sales Act), a buyer cannot cancel, rescind, or reject goods after "any substantial change in the goods which is not caused by their own defects." The depreciation of the car from $775 to $400 was certainly a substantial change and was not at all associated with the defect in title. B therefore could not use the theory of cancellation. He could only recover for the damages resulting to him from the dealer's breach of warranty, namely the loss B sustained when the insurance company repossessed the car—$400.

If a buyer accepts goods in ignorance of a defect which, however, he should reasonably have discovered before his acceptance, he is bound by his acceptance and has no other remedy against the seller, not even a claim for damages.

Reasonable Time[34]

The time within which notice of nonconformity should be given is the time stated in the agreement (if not clearly unreasonable). If no time is stated in the agreement, then whether notice is given within a reasonable time is a question of fact, depending upon the purpose of the notice and the circumstances of each case. For example, a buyer will usually have a shorter period to give notice of a defect and claim damages than to give notice that he revokes his acceptance and wants to reject and return the goods, after being disappointed in his expectation that a defect will be corrected; in the latter case the parties usually will already have been in communication concerning the defect.

Example: S sold to B twelve cases of rayon yarn, expressly warranted to be of first quality. To be such, rayon must dye evenly and uniformly. S knew that B was a manufacturer of rayon cloth linings which B sold undyed. The fact that the rayon was not first quality was not ascertainable by ordinary inspection; it could be discovered only by dyeing cloth made from the rayon. B first learned of the defective quality from his purchasers who had dyed the cloth for their own trade. Three of the twelve cases had already been used. Thereafter B promptly notified S, rejecting the unused cases. S refused to permit return and sued for the full price of all the cases.

Verdict and judgment were given[35] in favor of B, both as to rejection of the unused cases and damages for the used cases. If an ordinary inspection would have disclosed the defect, B would have been obliged to give notice sooner. But when the test required a manufacturing step not a part of B's process, B could rely on the warranty, and was not obliged to go to the expense of having some cloth dyed to ascertain its quality. B's notice to S was given within a proper time.

[34] U.C.C. Secs. 1-204, 2-608.
[35] *Industrial Rayon Corp.* v. *Caplan,* 125 Pa. Super. 414, 190 A. 185 (1937).

Example: B, a manufacturer of women's clothing, bought a 64-yard piece of red broadcloth from S. S expressly warranted fast color. Three weeks previously B had purchased from S five yards of similar cloth to make samples. The 64-yard piece was delivered to B on January 8. B had the cloth cut and sewn as piping on white blouses, and on February 4, had the blouses laundered. The color of the red piping ran and spoiled the blouses. B immediately notified S and sued for damages. Evidence showed that although there were two simple tests to determine whether the color was fast—dampen and iron or merely dip in water—B did not so test the 64-yard piece, because the five-yard piece previously purchased had been satisfactory.

B recovered a verdict and judgment for $406.88. On appeal this was reversed and judgment was given[36] in favor of S. Not having promptly made the simple test or inspection which would have been sufficient to determine if color was fast, B was disqualified from recovering the consequential damages he claimed.

BUYER DISCOVERS SELLER TO BE INSOLVENT

It is primarily when a seller delivers in advance of payment that a buyer's insolvency threatens a loss to the seller. This situation has previously been discussed in connection with sellers' remedies. Likewise it is only when a buyer pays in advance of delivery that the buyer is seriously threatened with a loss by the seller's insolvency. Similar as these two types of situations may at first appear, there are policy reasons for treating them differently. When a seller delivers on credit, he quite often will retain title or a security interest and thereby protect himself against any third person who may acquire an interest in the goods. The seller's use of a security agreement is so common that it is not considered unreasonably obstructive to the smooth flow of business; it seems sound policy, therefore, to conclude that if an unpaid seller does not require a security agreement, he is not entitled to protection against third persons. On the other hand when a buyer pays in advance of delivery, a security agreement is not so common, especially if a shipment in the near future is expected. To require a security agreement in every such case would tend to unreasonably hamper the smooth flow of business. Therefore, it seems sound policy to extend to a prepaying buyer some protection against third persons, even though comparable protection is denied a predelivering seller. The general scope of the buyer's protection is discussed in the next chapter.

CONTRACT FOR INSTALLMENT DELIVERIES[37]

Even though a seller's delivery is defective, the buyer's right to reject the shipment and to cancel his own obligation is somewhat restricted in an installment contract. As defined by the Code:

[36] *Bomze v. Schwartz Textile Corp.,* 100 Pa. Super. 588 (1930).
[37] U.C.C. Secs. 2-601, 2-612.

An "installment contract" is one which requires or authorizes the delivery of goods in separate lots to be separately accepted, even though the contract contains a clause "each delivery is a separate contract" or its equivalent.

In a noninstallment contract, a buyer may reject goods even for a slight defect in the shipment. However, the same defect in only one of several installments may not be considered sufficiently grave to justify rejection. Thus in a contract for delivery by successive installments, a buyer may not reject an installment that fails to conform to the contract unless the nonconformity substantially impairs the value of the entire installment. If a reduction in price would adequately compensate the buyer, the nonconformity would usually not be considered substantial.

PROBLEMS

1. B in Buffalo contracted to buy 20 cases of a specified brand and size of canned corn from S of Chicago, for a contract price of $600 payable in thirty days. Pursuant to the contract, S selected and set aside 20 cases meeting the contract description and tagged them with B's name. The contract required S to ship the corn to B via the New York Central Railroad Company, f.o.b. Chicago. Before S delivered the corn to the railroad, the 20 cases were stolen from S's warehouse.

a) As between S and B, who would stand the loss of the corn? Explain.

b) Suppose S had delivered the corn to the railroad. After the corn had been loaded on a freight car, but before the train left the yard, the car was broken open and its contents, including the corn, stolen. As between S and B, who would stand the loss? Explain.

c) Other facts remaining the same, would the answer in Part (b) be the same if: 1) The terms were $600 c. o. d.? 2) The terms were $600 sight draft, bill of lading attached, cash against documents? 3) The terms were $600, sight draft, bill of lading attached, inspection allowed? 4) The terms were $600, c.i.f., Buffalo, New York? (Modified from A.I.C.P.A., Nov. 50-8.)

2. S, the owner of a retail furniture store, entered into an agreement with B under which S delivered a chair to B's home. B was to use the chair for one week, and then either return it to the store or pay S the purchase price of $75. Before B communicated with S or did anything further in regard to the chair, B's home and its contents (including the chair) were destroyed by fire, through no fault of B.

a) Assume that the fire occurred five days after B received the chair. As between S and B, upon whom would the loss of the chair fall? Explain.

b) Assume that the fire occurred ten days after B received the chair. As between S and B, upon whom would the loss of the chair fall? Explain. (Modified from A.I.C.P.A., Nov. 52-8b.)

3. B, a retail appliance dealer in Chicago, ordered from S of Philadelphia 25 refrigerators of a specified make, model, and price. The terms were as stated below. Although B used proper care, the refrigerators were destroyed in an accidental fire one week after they were delivered to B.

a) The agreed terms between S and B were f.o.b. Chicago, price payable within sixty days, but B was to have the right to return at his own expense within the sixty-day period any one or more of the refrigerators (if still unused) and thereby cancel his obligation to pay for the returned refrigerators. Nothing was stated between S and B as to ownership or risk, and there were no further communications between them from the time B received the goods until after their destruction. Had risk of loss passed to B, and if so, when? Explain.

b) The agreed terms between S and B were: goods on consignment to B, B to place them in stock in his store and sell at the list price of $195.50 apiece; after sixty days B was to remit $125 to S for each refrigerator sold, and return at S's expense the unsold refrigerators; ownership was to remain in S until sale by B. Nothing was stated as to risk, and there were no further communications between S and B from the time B received the goods until after their destruction. Had risk of loss passed to B, and if so, when? Explain.

4. On April 3 S entered into a written contract with a railway, under which S agreed to sell and the railway to buy, within thirty days, 40 white oak poles of a specified size, at a stated price, f.o.b. cars at a designated station along the railway's line. By April 28, S accumulated poles of the required size and number at the designated station and notified the railway to send cars. In spite of S's repeated requests, the railway failed to bring the necessary cars to that station, and two weeks later, although S had piled the poles properly, an unusually heavy rainstorm washed the poles into the river, and they were lost. S sued the railway for the value of the poles. Was S entitled to recover? Explain.

5. On April 1 B. Brown, a grocery wholesaler in Pittsburgh, gave the following order to A. Adams, a salesman for S. Smith, a sign manufacturer:

Chicago, Illinois

Order No. 1321
[Date]

Sold to: B. Brown, Pittsburgh, Pennsylvania

Ship: via express. When: At once. Terms: 2/10 net 30 f.o.b. Chicago

As it is impossible to make the exact quantity, it is agreed that an overage or shortage, not to exceed 10 percent shall be accepted as filling this contract. All contracts are taken contingent upon strikes and accidents beyond S. Smith's control. Not subject to countermand.

Quantity	Price
75 window signs reading "Teas & Coffees" as per sketch enclosed.	$1.35 per sign

(signed) A. Adams, Salesman   (signed) B. Brown

On April 3 S wrote to B accepting the order. On April 20 S delivered to the Chicago office of the express company for transportation to B 117 window signs reading "Teas & Coffees," made according to the sketch which had accompanied B's order. The signs were lost in transit by the express company. S demanded that B pay. B refused but did not claim that there had been an undue delay in filling the order. S sued B. Was S entitled to judgment against B, and if so, for how much? Explain.

6. By letter addressed to S's place of business (stated below) B, a dealer in Boston, Massachusetts, ordered certain goods at a specified price. The terms for payment were stated as "2/10 net 30." On February 1, S properly shipped the goods to B in accordance with the contract, and on the same day, dated and mailed the invoice.

a) B received the goods within the usual transportation time. 1) S's place of business was in New York City. B received the invoice on February 3 and the goods on February 5. By what date would B have to pay in order to obtain the 2 percent discount? Explain. 2) S's place of business was in Los Angeles, California. B received the invoice on February 4 and the goods on February 16. By what date would B have to pay in order to obtain the contracted 2 percent discount? Explain.

b) S's place of business was in New York City. B received the invoice on February 3 and should have received the goods on February 5, but did not actually receive them until February 10, the delay in transit being solely the fault of the carrier. By what date would B have to pay in order to obtain the 2 percent discount. Explain.

7. B agreed to purchase from S, a clothing retailer, a fur coat priced at $295. B paid a deposit of $25 and received a purchase slip upon which S had written the total price of the coat, the payment of $25, and the balance due. The coat was marked with a "Will Call" ticket bearing B's name, and placed by S in S's storage room, to be delivered to B upon payment of the balance of the price. Late in the fall when B completed payments, S attempted to deliver to B a coat of a different size and style, claiming that it was the coat B had purchased. Investigation showed that S had been removing "Will Call" tickets from coats, and displaying the coats to new customers and taking deposits from them, making final delivery of each such coat to the person who first completed payments on it. The coat B had originally agreed to purchase could not be located, and S was charged with larceny of that coat under the following statute: "Any person, having in his possession as bailee any property of another, who, with intent to deprive the true owner of his property, appropriates it to his own use or to that of any person other than the true owner, steals such property and is guilty of larceny." Could S be held guilty of the crime of larceny as defined? Explain.

8. On June 1 B of Cleveland sent an order to S of New York City for a specified standardized machine for $1,000, f.o.b. New York City, to be shipped on August 1 and paid for by October 1. S promptly sent B a written acceptance. On July 26 B telegraphed S canceling the order. Since the contract gave B no right to cancel, S replied by telegraph that he intended to hold B to the contract, and shipped the machine. When the machine arrived in Cleveland, B refused to receive delivery. There being no market for the machine in Cleveland or any place closer than New York City, S had the

machine returned to New York. The freight charges for the round trip to Cleveland and back to New York totaled $600, which S had to pay to the carrier before the carrier would redeliver the machine to S. S then resold the machine to another purchaser for $800, the best price that S, through reasonable effort, could obtain. S thereupon sued B for damages. How much, if anything, could S recover from B? Explain.

9. B looked at and expressed satisfaction with a particular commercial refrigerator in S's showroom. The parties then entered into a written contract under which S unconditionally sold the refrigerator to B, and B signed a thirty-day promissory note for the purchase price. B's store, in which the refrigerator was to be installed, was under construction and scheduled to be finished in about two weeks, and S agreed to keep the refrigerator for B, without any charge for storage, until it was wanted and picked up by B. Thereafter completion of the store was delayed, and S agreed to store the refrigerator for a longer time. Upon maturity of the note, B did not pay it and has not since paid it. Now about six weeks after the sale B has run into some unexpected, temporary financial difficulty. C, one of B's creditors, has obtained a judgment against B and has had the sheriff levy on the refrigerator still in S's stock room. Although B is temporarily financially embarrassed, he is fully solvent and has been so at all times.

a) 1) In whom is legal title to the refrigerator? Explain. 2) Must S turn the refrigerator over to the sheriff? Explain.

b) Other facts remaining the same, assume that C obtained his judgment and had the levy made two weeks after the date of the S-B contract. Would this change in fact affect either of the answers given in Part (a)? Explain.

10. B sent S a written order for 100 scales of a certain type at $45 apiece, to be shipped in three weeks, f.o.b shipping point. The stated terms for payment were $1,500 down, the balance payable in two equal installments, one installment three months after shipment, the other six months. B accompanied the order with his check for $1,500. S promptly wrote to B acknowledging receipt of the order and agreeing to ship as ordered. However, a few days later S's bank returned B's check to S marked, "payment refused because of insufficient funds." When S notified B that his check had bounced, B explained that he had inadvertently overdrawn his account and was depositing further funds, and requested that S redeposit the check. S did so and was paid the $1,500. S then had a credit investigation made and learned that over the past three years ten judgments had been entered against B, totaling $700, all still unsatisfied. S wrote to B refusing to ship the scales unless B would pay the balance on delivery. B refused and bought the same type of scale from another supplier on the same credit terms, paying $65 per scale, the lowest price B could reasonably find. B then sued S for damages for breach of contract. The evidence showed that although slow in paying some of his accounts, B was solvent at all times.

a) What would be the result of B's lawsuit against S? Explain.

b) Other facts remaining the same, assume that S had already shipped the goods and they were still in transit when B's check bounced and S's investigation gave S reasonable grounds to doubt B's solvency. What could S do? Explain.

11. On April 16, B of Chicago sent a letter to S of New York City, ordering 15 refrigerators of a specified standard make and model, at a stated price, terms 2/10 net 30, f.o.b. New York City. B had never made any specific statement as to solvency, but he had made frequent prior credit purchases. Therefore, without further investigation of B's credit, S, on April 18 shipped the goods by railway freight on a straight bill of lading naming B as consignee, and mailed the bill of lading to B, together with an invoice for the goods. Nothing was stated as to title, security interest, or risk of loss. On April 19 B suffered financial reverses and became insolvent, and thereafter remained insolvent. On April 23 S learned of B's insolvency, immediately investigated as to the location of the 15 refrigerators, and discovered the facts stated below.

a) On April 23 the goods had left New York City and not yet arrived in Chicago. Assuming S would pay any railroad charges due, would S have the legal right to obtain possession of the goods from the railroad, 1) If the 15 refrigerators constituted a full carload shipment? 2) If the refrigerators constituted about one-half of a carload? Explain.

b) Assume that the goods constituted a full carload shipment. On April 23 the goods were in the Chicago railroad freight station, and B had been notified of arrival. Because of B's failure to pay or tender freight charges, the goods had not been delivered to B. The free time provided in the bill of lading had expired so that the railroad's liability had become that of a warehouseman and storage charges were accruing. Assuming that S would pay any freight and storage charges due, would S have the legal right to obtain possession of the goods from the railroad? Explain.

c) B had entered into a contract in the ordinary course of his business to sell to T, of St. Louis, 15 refrigerators of this same make and model, f.o.b. St. Louis, at a specified price, payable in ten days. Upon receiving notice from the railroad of the arrival of the shipment in Chicago, B directed the railroad to ship the goods to T in St. Louis. The railroad issued to B a straight bill of lading naming T as consignee, and B forwarded the bill of lading to T. Assume that the goods constituted a full carload shipment. On April 23 the goods were in the Chicago freight station, not yet having been loaded for shipment to St. Louis. Assuming that S would pay any railroad charges due, would S have the legal right to obtain possession of the goods from the railroad? Explain.

12. On January 3 B, an appliance retailer, sent to S, a manufacturer, a written order for 10 TV sets of a specified model at a stated price to be paid 3 months later. The order stated nothing as to title, security interest, or risk. B had never made to S any specific statement of solvency but had made frequent prior purchases on the same credit terms. On January 6 S shipped the ordered goods consigned to B. The sets were of contract quality and current models for which S had a ready market for sale.

a) On January 12, when the sets arrived at their destination, B wrote S that he had changed his mind and did not wish to purchase the sets. When

B refused delivery, the carrier returned the goods to S. Upon receiving the sets, S notified B that the goods would be held for B and on April 25 S, still holding the goods for B, sued B for the purchase price. What result? Explain.

b) On January 12, when the sets were delivered, B wrote S that he had changed his mind, did not wish to purchase the sets, and was holding the sets for S. S replied refusing to accept return of the goods. Nothing further was done as to the goods and on April 25 S sued B for the purchase price. What result? Explain.

c) On January 12, when the sets were delivered, B put them in his stockroom. There were no further communications between the parties until April 15 when S wrote requesting payment. 1) B offered to return the sets. S refused and on April 25 sued B for the purchase price. What result? Explain. 2) When B failed to reply or pay, S on April 25 sent an agent to B's store to reclaim the sets. B refused to surrender possession but still failed to make any payment. Did S have a right to obtain possession of the sets? Explain.

13. On March 15 a wholesaler of greeting cards sent to a manufacturer a written order for 500,000 Christmas cards of a certain style number as listed in the manufacturer's catalog. The order specified that the cards were to be shipped by August 1 and that the price of $3,000 was to be paid by December 1. The manufacturer accepted the order in writing. On July 16 the wholesaler wrote to the manufacturer canceling the order. The manufacturer's method of operating was to produce cards when ordered rather than to maintain large quantities in stock. Since production of the cards ordered by the wholesaler was already completed by July 16, the manufacturer refused to accept the cancellation and notified the wholesaler that the cards would be held for him. The wholesaler persisted in his refusal to receive the cards, and on August 2, the manufacturer sued the wholesaler for $3,000. The evidence in the case showed that wholesalers usually placed orders for Christmas cards by April 1, that after July 1 no wholesale market existed for Christmas cards, and that retail orders were placed with wholesalers in the fall. What would be the result of the lawsuit of the manufacturer against the wholesaler? Explain.

14. On March 5 B, a metal products manufacturer, ordered by telegram from S, a copper producer, a stated quantity of copper of specified purity and size, at 35 cents per pound, f.o.b. shipping point, the copper to be shipped April 1 and paid for by May 2. S accepted by telegram the same day. On March 21 S had copper conforming to the contract ready for shipment and marked with B's name. However on March 21, without any legal justification, S telegraphed B canceling the contract. S did not thereafter reply to the answering telegram received the same day from B demanding that S retract his concellation. The market prices for this type of copper were as follows: from March 21 through March 27, 40 cents; March 28 through April 4, 37 cents; April 5 through April 12, 40 cents; April 13 through April 20, 42 cents; from April 21 to the time of trial of the lawsuit described below, 45 cents. From March 21 on, B had ample opportunity to purchase from other sellers at current market prices the quantity of copper described in the S-B contract.

a) On the date specified below, B purchased copper conforming to the contract from another supplier. The purchase price was the market price current on the date of purchase, and B paid that amount on May 2. On May 5 B sued S for damages. Ignoring costs and interest, how much per pound (if anything) could B recover if the date of B's repurchase was: 1) March 25; 2) April 1, 3) May 2? Explain.

b) Making no attempt to purchase copper elsewhere, B, on April 1, demanded that S ship according to the contract. S refused. 1) The copper S had set aside for the contract and marked with B's name was still so set aside and marked when, on April 2, B sued S to obtain possession of the copper. Was B entitled to win the lawsuit? Explain. 2) S had sold elsewhere the copper that had been set aside for shipment to B but was in possession of copper of the same type and quantity. On April 2 B sued S to obtain possession of copper sufficient to fill the contract. Was B entitled to win the lawsuit? Explain. 3) After S's April 1 refusal to ship, B made no attempt to obtain copper from S or to purchase elsewhere. On May 5 B sued S for damages. Ignoring interest and costs, how much per pound (if anything) was B entitled to recover? Explain.

15. In writing, B ordered from S 1,000 units of certain described first quality goods for $5 apiece, f.o.b. destination, terms 2/10 net 30. "First," "second," and "third" quality were recognized commercial standards for the kind of goods involved. The goods were not perishable, and the market price was stable. S in writing accepted the order, but then S shipped to B 1,000 units of the described kind of goods which were actually of "third" quality and reasonably worth to B only $3 apiece. Three weeks later B had not yet paid for the goods.

a) B inspected with proper promptness and thoroughness, but the defect in quality being difficult to discover, B did not detect it. After three weeks B discovered the lower quality. Assume that this was proper diligence. B immediately notified S of the nonconformity and of what B wished to do. The goods were still in the same condition as when received by B. Would B have a legal right to: 1) reject the goods; 2) keep the goods with an obligation to pay S only $3 apiece; 3) keep half the goods, paying the proper price for them and reject the remainder of the goods? Explain.

b) On reasonably prompt inspection B discovered the defect in quality and immediately notified S that although the goods did not conform, B was accepting and would use the goods, but would expect an adjustment in the price. After a reasonable attempt to use the goods for three weeks, which was a reasonable time, B found that because of the lower quality the goods were wholly unuseable by him and immediately notified S to that effect and of what B then wished to do. The goods were still in the same condition as when received by B. Would B have a legal right to 1) reject the goods; 2) keep the goods with an obligation to pay S only $3 apiece; 3) keep half the goods, paying the proper price for them and reject the remainder of the goods? Explain.

chapter *17*

Interests of Remote Parties

As discussed in the preceding chapter, title and ownership are policy concepts and are necessarily flexible as policy factors change. A decision as to who has title as between a seller and a buyer does not necessarily determine who should have title or ownership when the interests of a third party enter the picture.

Assume the following fact situation: On June 1 a seller sold a small TV set to a buyer for $200, the buyer paying $150 down and agreeing to call for the set on June 4 and to pay the balance of the price at that time; on June 2 the seller dishonestly sold and delivered the same set to a second buyer who, having no knowledge of the previous transaction with the first buyer, paid the full price of $200 to the seller and took the set with him; on June 3 the seller absconded, leaving his business hopelessly insolvent; on June 4, learning of what the seller had done, the first buyer tendered $50 to the second buyer and demanded possession of the TV set, or as an alternative, demanded that the second buyer pay him $150. Because each buyer dealt separately with the seller, the buyers would be classed as remote parties to each other. Since each buyer would seem to have acquired some sort of an interest in the TV set, the policy question would arise as to which interest should be considered superior. Inasmuch as the contract with the first buyer did not require the seller to transport the set, title passed to the first buyer when the agreement was made—according to the rule stated in the preceding chapter. Thus when the seller sold and delivered the TV set to the second buyer, the set already belonged to the first buyer. However, the concept of title or ownership is itself a product of various policy considerations. To apply it automatically and indiscriminately would be a prime example of unsound, "mechanical" jurisprudence. The location of title is a good place to begin a debate between remote parties, but the argument will not necessarily end there—other factors may urge that the title or ownership interest of a prior claimant should be considered cut off or unenforceable against a certain later claimant. In other words, while a buyer will ordinarily be considered as acquiring only the rights of the possessor from whom he buys, and a lien creditor (for example, an attaching creditor or a court-appointed receiver) as attach-

563

ing only the rights of the person against whom he has his claim, sometimes, as a matter of policy, the claim of someone who previously dealt
with the possessor will be considered cut off or unenforceable against a
later innocent buyer or later lien creditor.

The policy factors which are most important in resolving the relative
rights of prior and later claimants are the following:

1) Appearance of Ownership. Is the person with whom a later
claimant deals, in such possession of goods that he appears to be the
absolute owner of the goods or an agent for the owner? Although important, this factor cannot be considered conclusive. To a later buyer
or lien creditor, there may be no difference in appearance between the
possession of a thief and that of an agent.

2) Responsibility for First Factor. To what extent is the person who
claims a prior interest responsible for the possession and appearance of
ownership which has misled the later claimant?

3) Social Values Involved in Second Factor. Suppose that an owner
is asked if he will loan certain goods to another person. If the law were
to say that the owner could lose his title if the borrower's possession
should happen to mislead someone into thinking that the borrower was
the owner and dealing with him as such, then to that extent the law
would be discouraging people from loaning goods. Thus an important
policy factor is whether the type of transaction which gives rise to the
misleading possession, should be 1) encouraged, 2) hindered somewhat
(for example, by requiring the owner to file a public notice of his interest), or 3) altogether discouraged.

The various fact situations in which conflicts between the interests
of remote parties often arise can be classified according to the status
of the possessor or person in control of the goods in question; classified
in this way, the most common situations are the following:

1. The possessor is a thief or buyer through a thief.

2. The possessor has voidable title.

3. The possessor is a rightful possessor. This can be further subdivided as follows:

a) The goods in the possessor's hands are subject to a security
interest.

b) The possessor has some additional indication of ownership.

c) The possessor is an agent with authority to sell.

d) The possessor is a merchant.

e) The possessor retains possession of goods after selling them.

f) The possessor is a merchant selling in bulk.

4. Although not a possessor, a shipper has control through having the power to divert goods in transit.

THIEF OR BUYER THROUGH A THIEF[1]

Goods stolen from their rightful owner may be in the possession of the thief, in the possession of an innocent buyer who has purchased from the thief, or in the possession of a subsequent innocent buyer who has purchased from a prior innocent possessor. The interest of the owner from whom the goods were stolen is superior to the interest of any good-faith buyer or lien creditor, regardless of how many prior innocent buyers may have purchased and sold the goods since the original theft.

Even if the owner's negligence made the theft possible or easier, this usually will not prevent the owner from successfully asserting his interest. The expiration of a substantial period of time, however, may cut off the owner's interest. All states have statutes of limitations which fix a period of time within which an owner must sue to recover his goods from the possession of a person who claims to own them. After the expiration of the statutory period, the owner is barred from suing; in other words, the owner's title is unenforceable and in effect terminated. Court decisions in various states conflict as to when the statutory period will begin to run. Some courts say that the statutory period does not begin until the owner learns who has his goods, while other courts hold that the period begins as soon as the goods are acquired and openly possessed by an innocent buyer.

VOIDABLE TITLE[2]

A voidable title is one that can be canceled or rescinded. Suppose that when a buyer purchases and receives certain goods he dishonestly pays for them with a check which he knows is bad. If (as is usual in noncredit sales transactions) the seller does not expressly reserve to himself an ownership or security interest, a complete title passes to the buyer when the sale is made. However, because of the buyer's fraud, the seller has the right to rescind the transaction and reobtain title. Therefore the title which is vested in the buyer until the seller does rescind is a voidable title. A remote party question will arise if the buyer resells the goods or if the buyer's creditor attaches the goods before the seller discovers that he has been defrauded and gives notice to the buyer that he is rescinding the transaction.

[1] U.C.C. Sec. 2-403.
[2] U.C.C. Sec. 2-401.

Rights of a Purchaser[3]

The Uniform Commercial Code states:

A purchaser of goods acquires all title which his transferor had or had power to transfer. . . . A person with voidable title has power to transfer a good title to a good faith purchaser for value. When goods have been delivered under a transaction of purchase the purchaser has such power even though

(a) the transferor was deceived as to the identity of the purchaser, or

(b) the delivery was in exchange for a check which is later dishonored, or

(c) it was agreed that the transaction was to be a "cash sale," or

(d) the delivery was procured through fraud punishable as larcenous under the criminal law.

Rights of a Lien Creditor

If at a time when the possessor of goods holds only a voidable title his creditor attaches the goods, the attaching creditor (or other lien creditor) will obtain no better right to the goods than the possessor has. The one who can avoid or cancel the possessor's title can still avoid it after the attachment, and thereby free the goods from the attachment.

POSSESSOR IS RIGHTFUL POSSESSOR

The term "rightful possessor" is used here in contradistinction to persons whose possession is based on theft or on fraudulent purchase. A rightful possessor is a person to whom the owner gives possession of certain goods, voluntarily and without being induced by fraud; the owner's purpose may range all the way from temporary loan to sale. Although an innocent buyer or lien creditor may be misled into thinking that the possessor is the absolute owner and deal with him accordingly, the mere fact that the owner has voluntarily delivered his goods to the possessor is not *of itself* sufficient to justify cutting off any interest which the owner may continue to have.

Goods Subject to a Security Interest

Suppose that a seller sells and delivers a TV set to a buyer for a certain agreed price, payable in stated future installments. To be protected in case the buyer dishonestly sells the TV set before paying for it, or in case a creditor attaches the set (or in case the buyer is adjudged insolvent and a court-appointed receiver takes possession of the set for the benefit of all creditors), the seller may expressly reserve an owner-

[3] U.C.C. Sec. 2-403.

ship or security interest in the set until the full price is paid. Installment sales should of course not be discouraged. At the same time care should be taken so that subsequent buyers or creditors are not misled into thinking that the installment buyer is the absolute owner of the merchandise before he has fully paid for it. Chapter 18 discusses this type of transaction and outlines what a seller who reserves a security interest must do to avoid misleading later parties.

POSSESSOR WITH ADDITIONAL INDICATION OF OWNERSHIP

If, together with the goods in question, the possessor has from the owner or with his permission some additional evidence seeming to indicate that the possessor himself is the owner, the actual owner may be cut off by the possessor's wrongful sale to a good-faith purchaser who buys from the possessor in reliance on such evidence.

Example: In the days when hauling was done by wagons, P. Porter for a time operated a small hauling business. P discontinued his business and was employed by O, owner and operator of a larger hauling business. O was having a new wagon built and with P's consent, had the builder paint on the side of the wagon, "P. Porter, Piano Mover." O's intent was to attract some of the customers P had formerly served. When the wagon was put into use, P was designated as its driver. About half a year later, P without authority sold the wagon to B who honestly thought that P owned the wagon. P absconded with the money, and O sued B to recover possession.

By having P's name on the wagon, O made it easy for P to mislead B as to ownership. Thus, as a matter of policy, O's title was deemed to be cut off by the sale, and O could not recover from B.

POSSESSOR IS OWNER'S AGENT

When the owner of certain goods turns them over to an agent, a remote party dispute will sometimes arise between the owner and a person with whom the agent deals. Most such disputes are settled by the rules of agency law discussed in Chapter 12. Thus it is clear that the owner is bound by any transaction which comes within his agent's actual or apparent authority, whether the principal is disclosed or undisclosed. It is equally clear that if the remote party knows that he is dealing with an agent, the owner is not bound by any transaction which is outside his agent's actual or apparent authority. More difficulty arises when an agent acts in an unauthorized way for an undisclosed principal. Even then the agency rules will usually be applied, holding that a principal is not bound by an agent's unauthorized act. However, there are some situations in which the law feels, as a matter of policy, that the scales of justice should tip the other way—against the undisclosed principal, even though the agent's act is unauthorized, especially if the agent is a selling agent. Two of the most common selling agent situations involve 1) factors statutes and 2) consignments.

Factors Statutes

Many states have statutes which extend some protection to creditors (and sometimes to buyers) who deal with factors (selling agents) in the mistaken belief that the factors are the owners of the goods in their possession. Under such statutes if a creditor, mistakenly believing that a factor owns certain goods, enters into a pledge transaction with the factor, loaning money to the factor and receiving the goods as security for the factor's repayment of the loan, the creditor will be deemed to have a valid claim against the goods for the amount of the loan. In other words, the creditor has a lien enforceable against the true owner of the goods even though the factor was not authorized to borrow on the goods. Some statutes extend similar protection to a buyer who, unaware of the factor's agency, buys and receives goods from the factor; under these statutes, such a buyer is given a lien enforceable against the true owner for the amount of the purchase price paid by the buyer to the factor, even though the factor's sale was outside his authority.

Consignments

Suppose that a creditor has the sheriff levy on goods in his debtor's possession, and then learns that the debtor is merely an agent holding the goods for their true owner. Generally the creditor's attachment will be subject to the interest of the true owner; in other words, the attaching creditor will acquire no better claim against the goods than the agent-debtor had. This is a fair result when the possessor is actually serving as a bona fide agent for the true owner. Sometimes, however, persons attempt to disguise a secured transaction in agency garb. For example, suppose that a manufacturer is making a credit sale of goods to a dealer, and wants to be able to reclaim the goods should the dealer become insolvent and fail to pay. As explained in Chapter 18, the proper way to accomplish this is for the manufacturer to reserve a security interest in the goods, *and* protect his interest from the claims of other creditors by filing a written description of his security interest (called a "financing statement") in the proper public office. To avoid the necessity of filing, a manufacturer will sometimes ship goods on consignment and, until the goods are paid for, attempt to protect his interest by claiming that the dealer is merely a selling agent. Because of the likelihood of unfairly misleading the dealer's other creditors, the Uniform Commercial Code requires[4] that the arrangement be treated as a security transaction if it actually is one. In setting guidelines for this policy rule, the Code provides that regardless of what the parties call their transaction, it is a secured transaction under the Code if all of the following circumstances are present:

1. The agent-possessor to whom the owner delivers the goods is a dealer in goods of the kind involved.

2. The name under which the agent's business is carried on does not include the name of the owner of the goods.

3. The agent-possessor is not generally known to be engaged in selling goods belonging to other persons.

4. Either a) The parties do not comply with a statute (if the state has such a statute) requiring that the true owner's interest be evidenced by a sign, or b) As is true in many states, there is no such sign statute.

If the case fits the above four-point description, the owner must protect his interest like any other secured party—by filing a financing statement as a public record of his interest (as explained in Chapter 18). If no financing statement is filed, the goods are deemed to be subject to the claims of the agent-possessor's creditors.

Possessor Is a Merchant

Rights of a Purchaser

The Code states:

> Any entrusting of possession of goods to a merchant who deals in goods of that kind gives him power to transfer all rights of the entruster to a buyer in ordinary course of business. . . .
>
> "Entrusting" includes any delivery and any acquiescence in retention of possession regardless of any condition expressed between the parties to the delivery or acquiescence and regardless of whether the procurement of the entrusting or the possessor's disposition of the goods have been such as to be larcenous under the criminal law.[5]

For a person to be a buyer in ordinary course of business,[6] he must buy in good faith and without knowledge that a sale to him violates the rights of any other person. The principal type of buyer who is not in ordinary course of business is a bulk buyer, discussed later in this chapter.

Example: An owner delivered his watch to a jeweler for repair. The jeweler's business included selling new and used watches. The jeweler wrongfully sold the owner's watch to a buyer in ordinary course of business.

[4] U.C.C. Sec. 2-326.
[5] U.C.C. Sec. 2-403.
[6] U.C.C. Sec. 1-201.

The owner's title would be cut off. Even if he could trace the watch, he could not recover it from the innocent buyer. The owner's only right would be against the jeweler, who, of course, would be liable for the tort of conversion (and the crime of embezzlement or larceny by bailee).

Rights of a Lien Creditor

The Code provision quoted above gives a superior right to a buyer in ordinary course of business; a merchant-possessor's lien creditor will not acquire any better right than the possessor himself has.

Possessor Retains Possession After Selling

After making a purchase, a buyer will sometimes temporarily leave the purchased goods in his seller's possession. He may do this for any of a variety of legitimate reasons. For example, the buyer may be unprepared to transport the goods or to use them, and for that reason may request the seller to keep the goods for a time. If while the seller is still in possession of the goods he wrongfully resells and delivers them to an innocent second buyer, or if a creditor of the seller, unaware of the transaction with the prior buyer, attaches the goods, a remote-party dispute will arise between the prior buyer and the second buyer, or between the prior buyer and the seller's lien creditor. The relative rights of these remote parties depend, first of all, on how much of an ownership interest had already passed to the prior buyer. The possibilities, as discussed in Chapter 16, can be classified as follows:

1. Legal title to the goods had passed to the prior buyer before the interest of the later remote party (second buyer or lien creditor) arose.

2. Although no legal title had passed to the prior buyer before the interest of the remote party arose, (a) The prior buyer had acquired a special property interest in the goods, or (b) The prior buyer had acquired a security interest in the goods. Security interests are discussed in the next chapter and will not be further discussed here.

3. The prior buyer had acquired no property interest in any specific goods. If a prior buyer leaves goods in his seller's possession and has not yet acquired any property interest at all, there is certainly no reason to prefer him over a later, innocent second buyer or lien creditor. For what the prior buyer has already paid, he would be in no better position than any other unpaid, general creditor.

Title Passed to Buyer

Since early common-law days an unpublicized or secret transfer of title, without any change in possession, has been viewed by the courts with great suspicion—and rightly so. Secret transfers have frequently been used in attempts to defraud third parties, and even when made innocently, a secret transfer can be especially misleading to a third party. When an owner delivers certain goods into the possession of someone else, only this one act on the part of the owner tends to mislead later parties into thinking that the new possessor owns the goods. While sometimes this factor will be sufficient to justify cutting off the owner's title in favor of a later innocent party (depending upon the purpose of the delivery and the status of the one to whom delivered, as, for example, when the owner delivers to a merchant who sells in the ordinary course of his business), nevertheless basically there is only the one misleading factor—the transfer of possession. On the other hand, if a person in possession of certain goods is known to be the owner of those goods and then sells and transfers his ownership but continues in possession, two factors combine to mislead third parties into thinking that the possessor is the owner—his possession, and in addition to possession, his former ownership. In other words, the appearance of ownership that results from the possession of certain goods is especially strong when the possessor at one time owned the goods and there has been no apparent change in his relationship to the goods. Many times this misleading appearance of continued ownership has been used in attempts to defraud third parties, as illustrated in the following examples:

Example: S sells and delivers certain goods to P for $1,000, which P pays to S. S thereupon disappears and B enters the scene with evidence that he had previously purchased the same goods from S, paid S for them, and innocently trusted S to hold the goods until B came to take them away.

Unless the law intervenes, P will lose the goods or be required to pay their value to B. B could then disappear and meet S at a prearranged place where they could share the profits from the scheme.

Example: S, operating a fully equipped business establishment in a rented building, appears to have a profitable business and induces C to extend credit. When S fails to pay, C obtains a judgment against S and has the sheriff levy on the equipment in S's establishment. S then disappears, and B shows up with the same story as in the preceding example.

If B is successful in proving his story and C is not otherwise protected, C's levy will be dissolved. Later B could meet S and share the proceeds of their fraudulent scheme.

While the courts in England and in the United States unanimously agree that a seller's retention of possession should be viewed with great suspicion, they do not entirely agree on the degree of protection which should be given to third persons. Some favor the complete protection of giving automatic priority to a third person who is innocently misled by the seller's retention of possession; others feel that the partial protection, afforded by closely scrutinizing the alleged prior sale is sufficient. Courts using the "close scrutiny" approach will favor the later third party, unless the evidence clearly shows that the prior buyer bought for value, in good faith, and without any *actual* intent to hinder, delay, or defraud third parties. Many courts have taken a middle position, affording automatic priority to later buyers and close scrutiny but not automatic priority in favor of later lien creditors. This appears to be the modern trend, and seems quite fair. On the one hand a later buyer pays or contracts to pay new consideration for the goods which the first buyer is also claiming, while on the other hand a lien creditor is not making any new investment, but is only attempting to collect for a prior extension of credit. Complete protection in favor of later buyers has been written into the English Sale of Goods Act, the American Uniform Sales Act, and the Uniform Commercial Code. The Uniform Sales Act provides:

> Where a person having sold goods continues in possession of the goods, or of negotiable documents of title to the goods, the delivery or transfer by that person, or by an agent acting for him, of the goods or documents of title under any sale, pledge, or other disposition thereof, to any person receiving and paying value for the same in good faith and without notice of the previous sale, shall have the same effect as if the person making the delivery or transfer were expressly authorized by the owner of the goods to make the same.[7]

Protection under the Uniform Commercial Code appears to be the same. The Code expressly protects a second buyer who innocently purchases in the ordinary course of the seller's business,[8] and the courts will probably hold that the Code extends somewhat the same protection to all innocent buyers, whether the seller is a merchant or not.[9]

Although the overwhelming trend of judicial opinion favors absolute protection for later buyers, judicial opinion is more divided in respect to protecting later lien creditors. Thus the Uniform Sales Act left this protection to be determined by each state, the Commissioners on Uniform State Laws explaining:

> The law in this country as to the effect of retention of possession on the rights of creditors is in such conflict and the different rules

---

[7] Unif. Sales Act Sec. 25.

[8] U.C.C. Sec. 2-403.

[9] U.C.C. Sec. 1-103 provides: "Unless displaced by the particular provisions of this Act, the principles of law and equity, including the law merchant and the law relative to capacity to contract, principal and agent, estoppel, fraud, misrepresentation, duress, coercion, mistake, bankruptcy, and other validating or invalidating cause shall supplement its provisions."

are locally so firmly fixed that it seemed unwise to try to provide a uniform rule. All states, however, agree that if the retention is fraudulent in fact, the sale is void as to creditors. The draft [of the Uniform Sales Act], therefore, so provides, and as to other cases— cases of constructive fraud—adopts the locally prevailing rule.[10]

With the matter thus left to local option, many states give later lien creditors the same automatic priority over a prior buyer that is enjoyed by later innocent buyers, while many other states closely scrutinize the prior transaction but give priority to the seller's later lien creditors only if the transaction between the seller and the prior buyer shows actual fraud. Feeling that the latter view represents the better policy for sales by merchant-sellers, the authors of the Code have provided[11] that a prior buyer's title is superior to the interest of the seller's later lien creditor if the seller's retention of possession after selling to the prior buyer 1) does not exceed a reasonable time, 2) is in good faith, and 3) is consistent with the regular course of the seller's business. For sales by nonmerchants or when otherwise a seller's retention of possession fails to meet these three conditions, the Code leaves to the policy of each state the determination of the relative rights of prior buyers and later lien creditors.

Special Property Interest (but no title) Passed to Buyer

As discussed in Chapter 16, a buyer who has not yet acquired title to goods will nevertheless acquire a special property interest if the goods are designated or set aside for the contract. If the seller thereafter wrongfully sells, delivers, and thereby passes title to a later buyer, the prior buyer who did not previously acquire title himself will have no grounds at all to claim priority over the later innocent buyer who does obtain title. The picture changes, however, in regard to the seller's later lien creditors. It is not unusual that a buyer's order for a prompt or current shipment of certain goods will be accompanied by a partial or full payment. Until the goods are segregated for shipment, no property interests arise which can reasonably be protected. But after the goods have been set aside for shipment, it seems fair to give some priority to the prepaying buyer over the seller's lien creditors, especially if the seller has become insolvent—so long as the transaction is one which is considered "current" in the usual, commercial sense. For this type of case the authors of the Code pick ten days as the limit of what should be considered a "current" transaction. Thus under the Code,[12] if a seller becomes

[10] Commissioners' Note to Sec. 26.
[11] U.C.C. Sec. 2-402.
[12] U.C.C. Secs. 2-402, 2-502.

insolvent within ten days after the buyer has made a payment, and if goods have been segregated for the buyer (thus passing a special property interest), the buyer has the same preference over the seller's lien creditors that a buyer with title would have. Note that the buyer's protection depends upon a very restrictive condition, the seller "*becoming*" insolvent within the ten-day period; apparently the buyer would not be protected if, within the ten-day period, he learned of an insolvency which actually had begun prior to that period.

If a buyer pays in advance for other than a current shipment (as for example when a buyer finances the seller's manufacturing process), he should protect his investment by contracting for a security interest and filing a public record that he has such an interest, as described in the next chapter.

POSSESSOR IS A MERCHANT SELLING IN BULK

With the exception of dealers selling very costly items (such as motor vehicles, house trailers, yachts, major appliances, and the like) retail merchants customarily purchase merchandise from a number of different suppliers, usually on short-term credit, in moderate amounts, and with rapid turnover. When such credit purchases are made by established retailers, suppliers usually do not find it necessary or convenient to reserve security interests. Instead, the typical supplier will sell on open account, trusting entirely the established retailer's solvency and honesty in the normal operation of his store. Certainly, if a clothing retailer fails to pay for a shipment of shirts, the unpaid supplier does not expect to have an enforceable claim against a retail customer who purchases one of the shirts. But if the retailer unexpectedly sells out his business or sells most of the merchandise in his store in one lump or bulk sale, the credit picture is completely changed, introducing risks which the supplier did not anticipate. To protect such suppliers state legislatures have adopted bulk-sale statutes. As the authors of the Code explain:

> Their [bulk sales laws] central purpose is to deal with two common forms of commercial fraud:
> (a) The merchant, owing debts, who sells out his stock in trade to a friend for less than it is worth, pays his creditors less than he owes them, and hopes to come back into the business through the back door some time in the future.
> (b) The merchant, owing debts, who sells out his stock in trade to any one for any price, pockets the proceeds, and disappears leaving his creditors unpaid.[13]

[13] Comment to U.C.C. Sec. 6-101.

While the first of these commercial frauds is a fraudulent conveyance,[14] it is frequently difficult and sometimes impossible for creditors to prove the fraud unless they are alerted before the transfer is made. And as the authors of the Code indicate, even if the transferee pays full value, creditors are considerably prejudiced by the retailer's unexpectedly converting his fairly immovable store and merchandise into highly mobile money—with which he can easily and quickly disappear.

In modernizing the protection afforded by bulk-sales statutes, the Code provides:

> (1) A "bulk transfer" [with a few stated exceptions] is any transfer in bulk and not in the ordinary course of the transferor's business of a major part of the materials, supplies, merchandise or other inventory . . . of an enterprise subject to this Article. . . .
>
> (3) The enterprises subject to this Article are all those whose principal business is the sale of merchandise from stock, including those who manufacture what they sell.[15]

The Code prescribes in considerable detail the procedure which must be followed in making a bulk sale. The chief purpose of the required procedure is to give creditors advance notice that a bulk transfer is going to be made. To accomplish this, the Code requires:[16]

1. That the transferee obtain from the transferor a sworn list of his creditors and the amounts owing to each, and

2. That at least ten days before the bulk transfer is made the transferee give to each creditor on the list a notice of the proposed bulk transfer. The creditors can then protect themselves by verifying in advance the bona fides of the proposed transfer.

Many of the prior bulk-sales statutes afforded additional protection by further requiring a transferee to assure that the money he pays for a bulk transfer is applied to the transferor's debts. By writing alternate provisions,[17] the authors of the Code enable state legislatures to adopt this further protection if desired. Thus, for example, the Code as adopted in Pennsylvania includes this additional feature, while the Massachusetts Code does not.

Note that the initiative in following bulk-sales procedure is on the *transferee*. If he fails to follow the prescribed procedure, he is liable to the transferor's creditors and can be sued by them anytime within the next six months following the bulk transfer. On the other hand, if the transferee carefully follows bulk-sales procedure, he is not liable, even

---

[14] A fraudulent conveyance, more fully discussed in Chapter 19, is 1) a transfer not for fair value, 2) which leaves the transferor insolvent or unable to pay his debts.

[15] U.C.C. Sec. 6-102.

[16] U.C.C. Secs. 6-104, 6-105.

[17] U.C.C. Sec. 6-106.

though a creditor was omitted from the transferor's sworn list, for, as the Code provides:

> Responsibility for the completeness and accuracy of the list of creditors rests on the transferor, and the transfer is not rendered ineffective by errors or omissions therein unless the transferee is shown to have had knowledge.[18]

SELLER HAS POWER TO DIVERT SHIPPED GOODS

When goods conforming to a buyer's order are shipped f.o.b. shipping point, title passes to the buyer at the time and place of shipment. If a shipment is made by a straight bill of lading, the Code gives[19] the seller-consignor the power to divert the shipment by requesting the carrier either to return the shipment, or to deliver it to a person other than as stated in the bill of lading. The seller has this power even though the straight bill names the buyer as the consignee. If a seller diverts and has goods delivered to another person who takes them as a buyer in the ordinary course of the seller's business, the title of the first buyer will be cut off and a good title will pass to the second buyer. The first buyer will have no recourse against the carrier, but of course he can recover damages from the seller. For this reason a buyer who pays on a straight bill of lading prior to receiving the goods should realize that he is trusting the business good faith of his seller. On the other hand, with a shipment by an order bill of lading, only the holder of the bill of lading (that is, the indorsee, or the bearer if so deliverable) has the power to divert the shipment.

The power of a consignor to divert is personal. If he does not request the carrier to divert the goods, his creditors have no power to divert the goods in his name and thus recapture goods while they are in transit to a buyer.

An interstate shipment comes under Federal law. Under the present Federal Bills of Lading Act, if the title to goods shipped on a straight bill of lading has passed to the buyer, the seller-consignor has no power to divert the shipment and thereby defeat the consignee's title.

PROBLEMS

1. Calling his establishment the S Stables, S carried on the business of boarding and training horses for various owners, and also buying and selling horses. X, the owner of a valuable racehorse, delivered the horse to S for training. Y was another owner of a valuable racehorse. A thief who carried on business as a horse dealer stole Y's horse and sold it in the ordinary course

---

[18] U.C.C. Sec. 6-104.
[19] U.C.C. Secs. 7-303, 7-504.

of business to P who bought innocently and for value. P delivered this horse to S for training. Although S had no authority or right to sell either of the horses left with him by X and P, S wrongfully sold and delivered both horses to B who bought in the ordinary course of S's business and paid fair value, honestly and reasonably thinking that S owned both horses and had every right to sell them. After considerable difficulty, X and Y succeeded in tracing the two horses and conclusively proved the above facts. As between B, X, and Y, respectively, who had the better right to the horses? Explain.

2. B, a retail appliance dealer, ordered from S, a wholesaler, five refrigerators of a certain specified make and model. The agreed terms for the transaction included the following: the refrigerators were shipped to B on consignment; B was to place them in stock in his store and sell them at the list price of $195.50 apiece; after sixty days B was to remit $125 to S for each refrigerator sold and return at S's expense the unsold refrigerators; ownership was to remain in S until sale by B. One week after B received the refrigerators, a creditor with a judgment against B and ignorant of B's agreement with S, had the sheriff levy on various items in B's store, including these five refrigerators. As between S and the attaching creditor, who would have the superior interest in the refrigerators? Explain.

3. In S's lumber yard, lumber was stacked in various separate piles according to size and kind, and each pile was identified by a lettered sign in front of the pile. On April 1 S entered into a written contract with B, a builder, for the sale and purchase of all the lumber in the pile designated "F." The contract provided that 1) B was to pay S the full purchase price of $3,000 at the time the agreement was formed; 2) as B needed lumber in his building operations, he was to load the lumber on his own trucks anytime during the normal business hours when the yard was open; 3) all of the lumber in pile "F" was to be thus removed before the expiration of the next three months. B paid the full price and by April 15 B had removed about one-tenth of the lumber from pile "F."

a) On April 15 a fire in S's yard, not the fault of either B or S, destroyed considerable lumber including all that remained in pile "F." Pile "F" was not covered by fire insurance. Assume that under the circumstances it was not negligent for S to fail to have insurance coverage. B demanded that S repay $2,700 and when S refused, B sued S. What result?

b) On April 15 the market price of such lumber advanced so that the market value of the lumber remaining in pile "F" was $3,500. When S refused to permit B to remove any more lumber, B sued to obtain possession of the lumber in pile "F." What result?

c) On April 15 a creditor with a judgment against B had the sheriff levy on the lumber remaining in pile "F." What result?

d) On April 15 a creditor with a judgment against S and knowing nothing of the contract between S and B had the sheriff levy on the lumber in the yard, including that in pile "F." What result? (Modified from A.I.C.P.A., May 51-2.)

4. B bought a floor lamp from S, a furniture retailer, and paid to S $25, the purchase price of the lamp. B had other shopping to do and asked S to allow him to leave the lamp in S's store until B returned for it. S agreed and placed a "SOLD" tag on the lamp. The tag fell off and a clerk in S's store sold the lamp to P who paid for it and took it with him when he left the store. Both the clerk and P were unaware of the previous sale to B.

a) Did B or P have the better right to the lamp? Explain.

b) Other facts remaining the same, assume that B left the lamp in the store to be delivered to B's home by S's delivery truck. How would this change of fact affect the relative rights of B and P? Explain. (Modified from A.I.C.P.A., Nov. 52-8a.)

5. S, a minor planning to enlist in the armed forces, sold and delivered his portable TV set to a neighbor, B, for $100. About a week later B won a costly floor-model TV set in a church raffle and thereupon sold the portable set to another neighbor, P, for $75. Both B and P were adults, both knew that S was a minor, and P knew of B's purchasing the portable set from S. S changed his mind about enlisting, notified B and P that he disaffirmed the contract by which he had sold the portable TV set, and sued P to recover possession of the TV set. What result?

6. O deposited two rings with P for safekeeping. P sold them for a valuable consideration to B who did not know of the bailment. Would O or B have the better right to the rings? (Modified from A.I.C.P.A., May 47-10d.)

7. On June 4 a retail appliance dealer bought from a wholesaler a TV set, a refrigerator, a stove, and a washer, for $100 each. The agreed terms were cash, nothing was said between the dealer and the wholesaler about title or security interest, and no public record was filed relating to the transaction. The dealer signed and gave to the wholesaler a check for the agreed purchase price of $400, naming the wholesaler as payee. After delivering the purchased items to the dealer who placed them in his salesroom, the wholesaler deposited the check in his bank. On June 8 the check was returned to the wholesaler unpaid, with a notation that the dealer had no account in the bank. On investigation, the wholesaler learned that the dealer had had no account in any bank for the past month. On June 7 the dealer left for South America, taking all of his money with him. In each of the following, the wholesaler desired to collect as much as he legally could, in goods or money.

a) On June 5 the dealer sold and delivered the TV set to a barber who paid the dealer the usual retail price in cash without knowledge of the circumstances under which the dealer had obtained the TV set. The barber installed the set in his barber shop for use in connection with his barbering business. On June 11 the wholesaler demanded return of the TV set from the barber. Assuming that the wholesaler made no attempt to recover anything from any other party, what or how much, if anything could the wholesaler recover from the barber? Explain.

b) On June 5 the dealer delivered the refrigerator to the community hospital as an unrestricted, complete gift. The hospital had no knowledge of the circumstances under which the dealer had obtained the refrigerator. Assuming that the wholesaler made no attempt to recover anything from any other party, what or how much, if anything, could the wholesaler recover from the hospital? Explain.

c) On June 5 a judgment creditor of the dealer had the sheriff levy on and take possession of the stove. The judgment creditor had no knowledge of the circumstances under which the dealer had obtained the refrigerator. Assuming that the wholesaler made no attempt to recover anything from any other party, what right, if any, would the wholesaler have against the attaching creditor and sheriff? Explain.

d) On June 6 the dealer sold his business and stock in trade to P, a newcomer in business, who paid the dealer $8,000 in cash, a fair price, and took possession. The dealer volunteering no information about outstanding obligations, P assumed that there were none and never asked the dealer about any debts. P had no knowledge of the circumstances under which the dealer had obtained the washer which was still in the salesroom. Assuming that the wholesaler made no attempt to recover anything from any other party, what or how much, if anything, could the wholesaler recover from P? Explain.

chapter *18*

Personal-Property Financing Transactions

Part 1   INTRODUCTION

From an overall view, the predominant features of modern business consist of volume production, diversification into numerous kinds and styles of goods, and specialization, both as to the kinds of goods handled by particular business units and also as to the function or role played by each unit.   Typically, manufacturers rely on other agencies for financing and marketing, wholesalers usually rely on outside financing and sell to independent retailers, retailers usually rely on outside financing and do not themselves produce what they sell.   Note the repeated need for outside financing in the chain from production to consumption. Credit serves as a sort of catalytic agent without which most of the modern, economic, "chain reaction" from production through distribution to consumption could not take place.   Truly, "Credit is essential to the economic development attained in the modern world."[1]

Basically, two types of credit exist—secured and unsecured.   When credit is extended without security, the creditor obtains nothing more than his obligor's promise to pay.   Such a creditor is trusting entirely in his obligor's honesty, business good faith, and solvency.   If the obligor fails to pay, the unsecured creditor's only recourse in almost all cases is the usual, protracted, legal procedure—suing and obtaining a judgment against the obligor, and then having the sheriff attach or levy on property belonging to the obligor, sell it at a sheriff's sale, and pay the proceeds to the creditor up to the amount of the judgment.   An unsecured creditor usually has no right to seize or claim any of his obligor's property without first obtaining a judgment.   Even if a credit obligation arises from the sale and delivery of certain goods, the seller usually cannot reclaim or repossess those goods without first obtaining a judgment, when the seller has nothing more than the buyer's unsecured promise to pay. Moreover, an unsecured seller runs the risk of being completely blocked out by another creditor.   The creditor who first obtains a judgment and order for the sheriff to levy on or attach a specified item has first claim

[1] *Encyclopedia of the Social Sciences,* vol. IV, p. 549.

on the attached item and on the proceeds realized from the ensuing sheriff's sale. Or if an obligor is adjudged insolvent, a court-appointed receiver (or other representative of creditors) takes possession of all of the obligor's property (including the unpaid-for goods) for the benefit of *all* creditors.

Example: A manufacturer sold and delivered a refrigerator to a retail appliance dealer on open account, the manufacturer obtaining nothing more than the dealer's promise to pay the purchase price of $500 in one month. Three weeks later, to the complete surprise of most of his creditors, the dealer was adjudged insolvent and a court-appointed receiver took possession of all of the dealer's assets, including this particular refrigerator. Upon learning of the dealer's insolvency, the manufacturer attempted to reclaim possession of the refrigerator from the receiver. Assume that the dealer's assets were so depleted that the receiver would be able to pay creditors only 30 percent of their claims.

Not having retained a security interest in the refrigerator, the manufacturer would have no preferential rights. The manufacturer would have to stand by while the refrigerator was sold with the dealer's other assets, and be content with $150 (30 percent of the $500 debt) as all that he could collect from the insolvent debtor. (If the dealer later became solvent again, the manufacturer could collect the unpaid balance, unless the insolvency proceeding was a Federal bankruptcy proceeding, in which case the unpaid balance of this type of debt would be declared canceled and uncollectible—as discussed in Chapter 19.)

Suppose that the insolvency adjudication occurred less than ten days after the manufacturer delivered the refrigerator to the dealer. This would not change the result. Note that, as discussed on page 544, an unsecured seller's right to reclaim goods from an insolvent buyer is cut off by the intervention of an attaching creditor (or representative of creditors).

Suppose the manufacturer could prove that in order to purchase the refrigerator on one-month's credit, the dealer, fully aware of his own insolvency, deliberately lied, stating to the manufacturer that he was solvent. Even this would not change the result. Ordinarily a person who has been induced by fraudulent misrepresentations to enter into a contract has the right to cancel the contract and the voidable title which the buyer acquired, and recover what he delivered under the contract. However, for sales-of-goods transactions, the authors of the Code feel[2] that since a seller can so easily retain a security interest in goods which he is delivering to his buyer, a seller who does not so protect himself should not be entitled to priority over other innocent creditors, even though the buyer did fraudulently misrepresent his solvency.

If a creditor is unwilling to take a chance on his obligor's honesty, good faith, and solvency, he will refuse to extend credit without obtain-

[2] U.C.C. Sec. 2-702.

ing some security. He will require, in exchange for extending credit, that he be given an assignment of some right owned by the obligor, or that he obtain a "security interest" in certain of the obligor's property. If a creditor has a security interest in goods, he has the legal right to take the specified goods from the obligor's possession and sell them without the necessity of a lawsuit and judgment, and also he has priority in case another creditor attaches those goods while they are still in the obligor's possession. In many cases a security interest will also give the creditor an interest superior to that of an innocent buyer who may subsequently purchase the goods from the obligor.

As modern business gradually evolved after the Industrial Revolution, various stages in the business chain expanded at different speeds and at different times. These expansion periods were always accompanied by —indeed often stimulated by—various devices for securing credit which were designed from time to time by business and legal technicians. Most of these devices were based upon common-law principles, and until the drafting of the Uniform Commercial Code, these security devices and the statutes which were later passed to implement them followed the common-law view that interests in property must be based on either possession or on title. The chief common-law security devices which thus developed were 1) pledges, 2) consignments, 3) chattel mortgages, 4) conditional sales and hire-purchase or bailment lease contracts, and 5) assignments of accounts receivable. In more recent times the common-law approach, with the emphasis on possession or title became too restrictive for the needs of business, and two statutory innovations were adopted in many states, 1) trust receipts, and 2) factors' inventory liens.

The essential features of the pre-Code security devices are summarized in the following several paragraphs. Note that these are very brief summaries, omitting the additional provisions and greater detail which were incorporated into the actual contracts.

Pledge. To secure payment of a debt, a debtor transferred possession of certain property to his creditor. The creditor retained possession until the debt was repaid, and in case of default, the creditor had the right to sell the property and apply the proceeds thereby received to the unpaid debt. Until default and sale by the creditor, title remained in the debtor, the creditor had possession, and the creditor's security was his possession and right to sell.

Consignment. A manufacturer consigned goods to a retailer on credit, specifying that title was to remain in the manufacturer until the retailer paid the agreed purchase price. The retailer was authorized to display the goods for sale, to sell them for a stated price, and upon making a sale to receive payment of the purchase price. The retailer then remitted the purchase price to the manufacturer less an agreed compensation for the retailer's services. Until the retailer made an authorized sale, title remained in the manufacturer, possession was in the retailer, and the manufacturer-creditor's security or protection, while the goods were in the retailer-debtor's possession, arose from the manufacturer's retention of title.

Chattel Mortgage. To secure payment of a debt, a debtor transferred the title of certain property to his creditor. The debtor remained in possession and when he satisfied his obligation, the transfer became void. If the debtor defaulted, the creditor could have the property attached and sold. Title was in the creditor (although some states used more modern terminology and called this a mortgage lien instead of title), possession was in the debtor, and the creditor's security was his title (or mortgage lien) and consequent right to have the property attached and sold. Pre-Code statutes in many states required each chattel mortgage to be recorded in a designated public office, in order for a creditor's security interest to be valid against third persons.

Conditional Sale. A seller sold and delivered certain goods to a buyer but retained title until the buyer paid the stated price at specified times. If the buyer defaulted, the seller could retake the goods and dispose of them elsewhere. Title was in the seller-creditor, possession was in the buyer-debtor, and the seller's security was his retained title and consequent right to repossess the conditionally sold goods and sell them elsewhere. Pre-Code statutes in many states required each conditional sale contract to be recorded.

Bailment Lease (also called hire-purchase in some jurisdictions). A dealer leased and delivered certain goods to a lessee who had the right to use the goods and was to pay a certain amount as rent. The total of the rental payments equaled the usual purchase price of the goods, and upon making the last rental payment, the lessee had the right to purchase the goods for a specified, nominal consideration—frequently $1. If the lessee defaulted in making the rental payments, the dealer could repossess the goods. Title was in the dealer-creditor, possession was in the lessee-debtor, and the dealer's security was his retention of title and consequent right to repossess.

Note that the only difference between conditional sale and bailment lease agreements was the difference in terminology. If the agreement called the parties seller and buyer, the transaction a sale, and the money to be paid the purchase price, the transaction was a conditional sale. If, on the other hand, the parties were referred to as lessor and lessee (or tenant), the transaction as a lease, and the money to be paid as rent, the transaction was a bailment lease. Many courts gave no weight to this difference in terminology and called both transactions conditional sales. Other courts, which had earlier decided, as a matter of policy that a conditional seller's rentention of title was not effective against innocent third parties, joined in this game of words and treated the two transactions differently. These courts were not gullible, lacking in perception, or engaging in unsound semantical jurisprudence; rather they were recognizing and giving effect to a desired social need.

Assignment of Account Receivable. This security device differs from those previously described in that what was transferred to the creditor was not tangible property, but instead only an intangible right to collect money from someone else. Suppose that on April 1 a manufacturer shipped certain goods on open account to a dealer who was to pay $2,000 by June 1. The manufacturer's right to collect from the dealer was recorded in the manufacturer's accounting records as an account receivable. Suppose further that the manufacturer then borrowed $1,500 from a bank, promised to repay the loan by May 29, and as collateral security transferred the account receivable, that is, assigned to the bank the manufacturer's right to collect the $2,000 from the dealer. If the manufacturer defaulted in repaying the $1,500 loan, the bank could, on June 1, collect the $2,000 obligation owed by the dealer, retain $1,500 for the loan plus whatever additional sum was owed by the manufacturer for interest and costs, and remit the remainder to the manufacturer. Pre-Code statutes in some states required the assignor's accounting records to be marked in order for the assignment to be effective against third parties; statutes in some other states required a public notice to be filed telling of the assignment.

Trust Receipt. After making appropriate arrangements with his bank, a dealer ordered certain goods from a manufacturer. The manufacturer consigned the goods to the bank which paid the full price for them. The bank then released possession of the goods to the dealer upon his agreement to pay the price advanced by the bank (plus interest), and his acknowledgment that he held and would display and sell the goods as a trustee for the bank. The bank had a security interest in the goods and in anything the dealer received upon selling the goods. Possession was in the dealer-debtor; the bank-creditor's security was not a complete title but rather was a limited title or security interest, which was sufficient to enable the bank to realize from the entrusted goods what was owed, and also to assure that the bank's claim to the entrusted goods would have priority over other creditors. For the bank's trust-receipt interest to be effective against third parties, the Uniform Trust Receipts Act (which has been superseded by the Code) required the bank and dealer to file a public notice stating their intent to engage in trust receipt financing and specifying the types of goods to be thus financed.

Factors' Liens. Before the drafting of the Code, many states passed statutes authorizing so-called factors' liens. In such statutes the term "factor" was not used in its older sense as meaning a selling agent; rather the term referred to a financing institution which provided certain financing services to businesses. In order to purchase certain raw materials a manufacturer borrowed from a bank and agreed that the bank was to have a lien on such materials; the bank's lien attached as soon as the manufacturer acquired raw materials of the type described, carried over to the finished product manufactured from those materials and to the proceeds received from selling the finished product, and further carried over to new acquisitions of the same type of raw materials. The manufacturer-debtor had possession of the secured property; the bank-creditor's security was its limited title or security interest, which was sufficient to assure that the bank's claim would have priority over other creditors. Some pre-Code statutes required a notice of this type of financing to be filed in a public office; some also required a sign to the same effect to be posted on the manufacturer's premises.

As previously indicated, the primary purpose of any security or financing transaction is to expedite the collection of certain obligations, especially by assuring that a secured creditor will have some degree of protection or priority over other creditors. On the whole, the pre-Code security devices, because of their complicating technicalities and haphazard and incomplete coverage, were quite inadequate to meet the needs of modern business. Graphically illustrating this inadequacy, the authors of the Code have briefly sketched some of the legal complexities which plagued the entire field of pre-Code financing transactions, writing:

> Existing law [referring to the law which prevailed *before* general adoption of the Code] recognizes a wide variety of security devices, which came into use at various times to make possible different types of secured financing. Differences between one device and another persist, in formal requirements, in the secured party's rights against the debtor and third parties, in the debtor's rights against the secured party, and in filing requirements, despite the fact that today many of those differences no longer serve any useful function. Thus an unfiled chattel mortgage is by the law of many states "void" against creditors generally; a conditional sale, often available as a substitute for the chattel mortgage, is in some states valid against all creditors without filing, and in states where filing is required is, if unfiled, void only against lien creditors. The recognition of so many separate security devices has the result that half a dozen filing systems covering chattel security devices may be maintained within a state, some on a county basis, others on a state-wide basis, each of which must be separately checked to determine a debtor's status.
> Nevertheless, despite the great number of [pre-Code] security devices there remain gaps in the structure. In many states, for example, a security interest cannot be taken in inventory or a stock in trade although there is a real need for such financing. It is often baffling to try to maintain a technically valid security interest when financing

a manufacturing process, where the collateral starts out as raw materials, becomes work in process and ends as finished goods. . . .

The cases are many in which a security transaction described by the parties as a conditional sale or a trust receipt has been later determined by a court to be something else, usually a chattel mortgage. The consequence of such a determination is typically to void the security interest against creditors because the security agreement was not filed *as a chattel mortgage* (even though it may have been filed as a conditional sale or a trust receipt). . . .

The growing complexity of financing transactions forces us to keep piling new statutory provisions on top of our inadequate and already sufficiently complicated nineteenth-century structure of security law. The results of this continuing [pre-Code] development are, and will be, increasing costs to both parties and increasing uncertainty as to their rights and the rights of third parties dealing with them.

The aim of this Article [Article 9 of the Code which deals with financing transactions] is to provide a simple and unified structure within which the immense variety of present-day secured financing transactions can go forward with less cost and with greater certainty.

Under this Article the traditional distinctions among security devices, based largely on form, are not retained; the Article applies to all transactions intended to create security interests in personal property and fixtures, and the single term "security interest" substitutes for the variety of descriptive terms which has grown up at common law and under a hundred-year accretion of statutes. . . .

This Article does not determine whether "title" to collateral is in the secured party or in the debtor and adopts neither a "title theory" nor a "lien theory" of security interests. Rights, obligations and remedies under the Article do not depend on the location of title. . . . The location of title may become important for other purposes—as, for example, in determining the incidence of taxation—and in such a case the parties are left free to contract as they will. In this connection the use of a form which has traditionally been regarded as determinative of title (e.g., the conditional sale) could reasonably be regarded as evidencing the parties' intention with respect to title to the collateral.

Under the Article distinction based on form (except as between pledge and non-possessory interests) are no longer controlling. For some purposes there are distinctions based on the type of property which constitutes the collateral—industrial and commercial equipment, business inventory, farm products, consumer goods, accounts receivable, documents of title and other intangibles—and, where appropriate, the Article states special rules applicable to financing transactions involving a particular type of property. Despite the statutory simplification a greater degree of flexibility in the financing transaction is allowed than is possible under . . . [pre-Code] law.

The scheme of the Article is to make distinctions, where distinctions are necessary, along functional rather than formal lines.

This has made possible a radical simplification in the formal requisites for creation of a security interest.

A more rational filing system replaces the . . . [pre-Code] system of different files for each security device which is subject to filing requirements. Thus not only is the information contained in the files made more accessible but the cost of procuring credit information, and, incidentally, of maintaining the files, is greatly reduced.[3]

The Code's approach to financing transactions involves classifying in the following way the various property interests which can form the basis for security or financing transactions (in other words, things of value in which interests may be given to secure obligations to pay, or intangible rights which may be used to raise money):

1. Goods, documents of title (bills of lading and warehouse receipts), and corporate securities (stock and bond certificates). These may be further subdivided according to the location of the item involved: a) The item may be in the creditor's possession or control until the obligor completes payment, or b) The item may be in the obligor's possession, at least until he defaults in a payment.

Example of Collateral Delivered to Creditor: An obligor borrows $1,000 from a creditor, promises to repay in one month with interest, and, as security for the obligation, delivers to the creditor certain shares of stock owned by the obligor. The creditor is to hold the stock until the obligation is repaid. Should the obligor default, the creditor has the right to realize what is owed to him by selling the stock.

Example of Collateral Retained by Obligor: An obligor borrows $1,000 from a creditor, promises to repay in one month, and as security gives the creditor an interest in the delivery truck owned by the obligor and used in his business. The obligor retains possession of the truck and continues to use it. Should the obligor default, the creditor has the right, because of his security interest, to take possession of the truck and by selling the truck, realize what is owed to him. Further, if he has done what is procedurally necessary to protect his security interest, the creditor, during the term of the debt, has an interest superior to that of any other claimant who might have the sheriff levy on the truck, and an interest superior to that of any innocent person who might buy the truck from the obligor.

2. Rights to receive or collect money from others. Suppose that a creditor is owed $1,000 due in six months. By selling or assigning to someone else this intangible right to receive $1,000 six months from now, the creditor can raise money now. The creditor's right may be evidenced by any of the following:

a) *Chattel Paper.*[4] This term is used to refer to a writing signed by the obligor, which, 1) evidences a monetary obligation, and also 2) states

[3] Comment to U.C.C. Sec. 9-101.
[4] U.C.C. Sec. 9-105.

that the obligation is secured by an interest in certain described goods. Most of the pre-Code security devices already described (conditional sale, bailment lease, chattel mortgage, trust receipt, and factor's lien contracts) fit this definition and therefore under the Code are chattel paper contracts. A much simpler form, such as the following is also sufficient:

Example: "[Date]. S. Smith hereby sells and delivers to B. Brown who hereby buys an RCA TV set Model 123, receipt of which B. Brown hereby acknowledges. As the purchase price for this set, B. Brown agrees to pay S. Smith $400, as follows: $100 with the signing of this contract, the receipt of which S. Smith hereby acknowledges, and $50 on the first of each month following the date of this agreement. Until the purchase price is paid, title [or a security interest] in the above-described TV set will remain in S. Smith. (signed) S. Smith, (signed) B. Brown."

While this is sufficient to be a legally effective agreement, the contract forms in common use are usually longer, containing additional provisions regarding acceleration of maturity, location of the collateral, insurance, risk of loss, and other matters.

b) *Promissory Note.* This is a readily transferable document in which an obligor promises to pay a sum of money without referring to any security interest in goods. Promissory notes are covered in Chapter 14 and will not be further discussed here.

c) *Account Receivable.*[5] Both chattel paper and promissory notes are types of written agreements which are customarily delivered to transferees upon the transfer of the obligations which the writings evidence. An account receivable is different; any writing which evidences an account receivable obligation is not the type of writing which is customarily delivered when the obligation is assigned.

Example: A seller sells and delivers goods to a buyer for $1,000 payable in one month. The buyer's obligation is not evidenced by any note or chattel paper. The only writing may be the buyer's order for the goods, and there may not even be that if the order is verbal. The buyer nevertheless owes the seller the agreed $1,000 and the seller so records in his books of account, as a receivable. Even if the purchase contract is in writing, the written contract is not the type of document which would be transferred should the seller afterwards sell the obligation or borrow on it.

Example: A builder and the owner of a plot of land enter into a written contract under which the builder agrees to construct a building on the owner's land in accordance with certain plans and specifications, and the owner agrees to pay $100,000 at stated intervals. Immediately after this contract is formed, the builder has a contract right to receive payments at the agreed times, conditioned upon his constructing according to the contract. Even

[5] U.C.C. Sec. 9-106.

before the builder does any work, he may sell or borrow on this contract right. Although the contract between the builder and owner is in writing, it is not the type of writing which would customarily be delivered upon the builder's selling or assigning his contract right to receive money.

The Code subdivides accounts receivable into 1) accounts and 2) contract rights. If goods or services have not yet been sold or rendered, the contingent right to receive payment is termed a "contract right," while if the goods or services have already been sold or rendered, the right to receive payment is termed an "account."

The purpose of the present chapter is to present an overall picture of the common financing devices under the Code. *Note that since this book is not intended as a practitioner's manual, no attempt is made to include the considerable procedural detail which is contained in the Code.*

Part 2 GOODS, DOCUMENTS OF TITLE, OR CORPORATE SECURITIES IN CREDITOR'S POSSESSION OR CONTROL

FACT SITUATION

A typical fact situation can be stated as follows: A creditor loans money to a debtor who promises to repay according to stated terms. As collateral security for repayment of the loan, the debtor either 1) gives his creditor possession of certain goods or of certain corporate securities; or 2) indorses and delivers to his creditor a warehouse receipt (or bill of lading) covering certain goods owned by the debtor and stored in the warehouse (or in transit on the carrier) which has issued the document. This is the same as the common-law pledge transaction. For the present discussion, the debtor can be referred to as the "obligor" and the creditor, as the "secured party."

FORMAL REQUIREMENTS[6]

All that is required to give the secured party an enforceable interest is delivery of the collateral (goods, corporate security, or document of title) to the secured party.

RIGHTS AND DUTIES OF SECURED PARTY AS TO GOODS AND OBLIGOR

INCIDENTAL RIGHTS AND DUTIES

Along with other details, the Code specifies the following:

(1) A secured party must use reasonable care in the custody and preservation of collateral in his possession. In the case of an instru-

[6] U.C.C. Sec. 9-203.

ment [such as a promissory note] or chattel paper reasonable care includes taking necessary steps to preserve rights against prior parties unless otherwise agreed.

(2) Unless otherwise agreed, when collateral is in the secured party's possession. . . .

(b) the risk of accidental loss or damage is on the debtor to the extent of any deficiency in any effective insurance coverage;

(c) the secured party may hold as additional security any increase or profits (except money) received from the collateral, but money so received, unless remitted to the debtor, shall be applied in reduction of the secured obligation . . .[7]

Rights upon Obligor's Default[8]

If the obligor fails to pay his obligation when it comes due, the secured party has the legal right to sell the collateral. The sale must be commercially reasonable, and advance notice must be given to the obligor—unless, for certain reasons specified in the Code, the giving of notice would be unreasonable or unnecessary.

The proceeds realized from the sale are applied first to compensate the secured party for his reasonable expenses, then second to the secured debt, with the balance being paid to or for the benefit of the obligor. If the sale fails to produce sufficient funds to satisfy the secured debt, the secured party can recover any deficiency from the obligor.

Unless the secured party has agreed otherwise, he has no duty to dispose of the collateral within any particular period of time. For example, if the market price of pledged corporate stock is declining and upon maturity the obligor requests the secured party to sell, the secured party will usually sell in order to realize what he can; however, unless otherwise agreed, he usually has no duty to do so. If after default the secured party retains pledged goods longer than is reasonable and storage charges accumulate, the secured party cannot collect for the unnecessary storage charges, but his delay does not reduce his right to collect the principal of the obligation.

Instead of disposing of the collateral, the secured party may decide that he wishes to retain it in full satisfaction of the obligor's obligation—perhaps with the hope of disposing of the collateral at some time in the future. If the secured party gives the obligor written notice of his desire to retain the collateral in satisfaction of the obligation, the obligor is assumed to agree to such a settlement and to have no further rights unless he objects within thirty days after receiving the secured party's notification. If there has been no such agreement for a settlement, then so long as the secured party retains the collateral, the obligor may at any time

[7] U.C.C. Sec. 9-207.
[8] U.C.C. Secs. 9-501, 9-502, 9-504–506.

(at least within the period of the statute of limitations) redeem and reclaim the collateral by tendering to the secured party the amount of the debt plus reasonable costs and expenses.

RIGHTS OF SECURED PARTY AS TO THIRD PERSONS[9]

After an obligor has given a secured party an interest in certain collateral, some third person, acting in good faith and without knowledge of the secured party's interest, may also at a later date acquire an interest in the same collateral. Possible third persons include: 1) the obligor's lien creditor, 2) a subsequent secured party to whom the obligor dishonestly transfers an interest in the same collateral, and 3) a buyer to whom the obligor dishonestly sells the collateral.

Example: When O, the owner of certain goods, stored them in W's warehouse, he received a nonnegotiable warehouse receipt for the goods. O thereupon, 1) borrowed a sum of money from First Bank, 2) signed a written agreement promising to repay the loan within a stated time and transferring to the bank an interest in the goods as security for repayment, and 3) delivered to the bank the warehouse receipt. Thereafter:

First Possibility: A creditor obtained a judgment against O. Unaware of First Bank's interest, the creditor had the sheriff levy on O's goods stored in W's warehouse.

Second Possibility: O was adjudged insolvent, and the court appointed a receiver who took over all O's assets. (Such a receiver would have the same rights as an innocent attaching creditor if at least one of the creditors represented had no knowledge of First Bank's interest at the time the receiver was appointed.)

Third Possibility: O borrowed an additional sum of money from Second Bank, and by written agreement, gave Second Bank a security interest in the goods in W's warehouse, as security for Second Bank's loan. The latter bank was unaware that a warehouse receipt had been issued or that First Bank had been given an interest in the goods, and O wrongfully said nothing about First Bank's interest.

Fourth Possibility: O sold the goods to a buyer and wrongfully said nothing about the warehouse receipt or about First Bank's interest. O gave the buyer a written bill of sale together with a written order for W to deliver the goods to the buyer, and the buyer in good faith paid full value, unaware of First Bank's interest in the goods.

Any third person who acquires an interest in collateral with actual knowledge of a secured party's effective prior interest will be subject to the prior interest. However, if a third person has no actual knowledge of a prior interest, he will take free from the prior interest, unless the secured party has taken proper steps to protect or perfect his security

---

[9] U.C.C. Secs. 9-301, 9-305.

interest. In general, what a secured party is, as a matter of policy, required to do to protect his security interest depends upon the location and type of collateral.

GOODS OR CORPORATE SECURITIES IN POSSESSION OF SECURED PARTY

For this type of collateral, the secured party's possession sufficiently protects his interest against subsequent third parties from the time the secured party takes possession of the collateral.

GOODS IN POSSESSION OF AN INDEPENDENT BAILEE

If goods held by a bailee are represented by a negotiable warehouse receipt or bill of lading, a secured party's possession of the document sufficiently protects his interest against subsequent third parties from the time the secured party takes possession of the document. If the bailee has issued a nonnegotiable document of title, notice to the bailee is required to protect the secured party's interest against subsequent innocent third parties.

So long as a bailee who is in actual possession of the goods is independent from the obligor, the location of the bailee's place of storage is immaterial. The storage of goods on or substantially near an obligor's premises is commonly called "field warehousing." In a typical field warehousing situation, the obligor leases a portion of his premises to a warehouseman who is wholly independent from the obligor's control; the area is enclosed, signs are posted, and the warehouseman's custodian is left in charge; the obligor then delivers goods to the custodian who checks them in and issues a warehouse receipt. In this way the parties accomplish a transfer of possession effective for a valid pledge of the warehouse receipt and still keep the goods available for withdrawal, fabrication, and redeposit or deposit of substitute goods, without excessive transportation and handling expenses. The secured party in possession of the warehouse receipt should realize that he is protected against the obligor's lien creditors (or other innocent third persons) *only if*, at the time his interest is challenged, the secured party can show that the field warehouse is being properly conducted—that is, that the goods in question are definitely not in the possession of the obligor. Sometimes after lawyers properly set up a field warehouse plan, their efforts are thwarted by employees who fail to comply with the prescribed procedure. If to save time and inconvenience, the warehouse attendant neglects to maintain effective supervision and permits the obligor's employees to come and go with goods just as if there were no field warehouse arrangement, a court might decide that the obligor still retained or had resumed possession of the stored goods.

Part 3 GOODS, DOCUMENTS OF TITLE, AND CORPORATE SECURITIES IN OBLIGOR'S POSSESSION

A pledge (the security device previously discussed) is classified as a *possessory* security device because the collateral (goods, document of title, or corporate security) is in the possession of the secured party. In a *nonpossessory* security device, much the more common type of secured transaction, the collateral is not in the secured party's possession but rather is delivered to or left in the possession of the obligor. In most such nonpossessory security transactions the collateral consists of goods. Any desire to separate a security interest from possession when collateral consists of a document of title or a corporate security is infrequent, and then only for a very short time and for a limited purpose. Therefore, except for a brief discussion of nonpledge security interests in negotiable documents of title on page 605, the present discussion will be limited to transactions in which the collateral consists of goods.

FACT SITUATION

The basic fact situation for this type of financing transaction can be outlined as follows: To assure or secure payment of his obligation, a debtor gives to his creditor (or acknowledges that there is in the creditor) a security interest in certain described goods. Until he defaults in his obligation, the debtor remains in possession of the goods, using them as if he owned them absolutely. In the present discussion, the parties will be called the "obligor" and the "secured party."

The Code subdivides the great variety of nonpossessory security transactions according to 1) the nature of the security interest (namely either "purchase money" or "nonpurchase money"), and 2) the nature of the goods and of the obligor's use of them.

Purchase Money Security Interest

The Code states:

A security interest is a "purchase money security interest" to the extent that it is

(a) taken or retained by the seller of the collateral to secure all or part of its price; or

(b) taken by a person who by making advances or incurring an obligation gives value to enable the . . . [obligor] to acquire rights in or the use of collateral if such value is in fact so used.[10]

Example: A dealer sells and delivers a TV set to a buyer who promises to pay the price in specified installments. To assure that the buyer pays as promised, the dealer retains a security interest in the TV set.

[10] U.C.C. Sec. 9-107.

The dealer's security interest is "purchase money."

Example: A dealer sells and delivers a TV set to a buyer for an agreed price payable in cash. The buyer pays the dealer with money borrowed for that stated purpose from a bank, and promises to repay the bank loan in specified installments. To secure this promise, the buyer gives the bank a security interest in the TV set.

The bank's security interest is "purchase money."

Example: A person is the absolute owner of a TV set. Needing money for medical expenses, he borrows from a bank, and to secure his promise to repay the loan, gives the bank a security interest in the TV set.

The bank's security interest is *not* "purchase money."

CLASSIFICATION OF GOODS[11]

The Code divides most goods into four general classes—consumer goods, farm products, inventory, and equipment. In addition, certain goods (goods to be attached to other property and titled goods) which would otherwise fall into one of these classes are segregated and specially dealt with. The result is six mutually exclusive classes of goods, which can be briefly defined as follows:

1) Consumer Goods. This class consists of goods used primarily for personal, family, or household purposes.

2) Farm Products. This class consists of crops, livestock, and their products, while still in an unmanufactured state and still in the possession of a farmer—meaning a person who is engaged in farming operations. Also included are supplies which are used or produced by a farmer in connection with his farming operations. The term "farming operations" includes not only the raising of livestock and crops, but also fattening and grazing.

3) Inventory. This class consists of 1) raw materials, work in process, and finished products which are in the possession of a businessman (either a manufacturer or distributor) for sale or lease, 2) materials used or consumed over a relatively short period in the operation of a business, and 3) goods in the possession of a serviceman or repairman, who will furnish or utilize them in the performance of a service contract.

4) Equipment. This class consists of 1) goods used primarily in the operation of an organization or enterprise (including farming, the professions, nonprofit organizations, and government agencies), and also 2) goods not falling into any of the preceding three classes. Compared with "inventory," the use or consumption of goods classed as "equipment" will extend over a relatively long period of time.

[11] U.C.C. Secs. 9-109, 9-302, 9-313, 9-314.

5) Goods to Be Attached to Other Property. Such goods are further subdivided into fixtures and accessions.

a) A "fixture" is an item of personal property which is affixed to real estate in such a manner that it will usually be considered a part of the real estate (for example, a furnace in a building); however, it does not become such an integral part of the real estate as thereafter to be considered inseparable from it. Building materials, (lumber, brick, cement, glass, or metalwork) forming an integral part of a building, are not considered fixtures and are expressly excluded from the Code. Whether or not goods become fixtures is expressly left by the Code to the law of each state.

b) An "accession" is a separate item of personal property which becomes so affixed to another item of personal property that it will thereafter usually be considered as a part of the other item (for example, a replacement picture tube in a TV set).

6) Motor Vehicles and Other Goods (such as aircraft and railway rolling stock) for which some statute other than the Code provides for the filing of ownership interests.

FORMAL REQUIREMENTS[12]

For a nonpossessory security interest to come into existence and be enforceable against anyone (even for it to be enforceable against the obligor himself), the secured party must obtain a written agreement which:

1. Describes or reasonably identifies the secured goods.

2. Names the secured party and states that he has an interest in the described goods.

3. Is signed by the obligor.
A land description should, of course, be included if the goods are related to particular land, as when the secured goods are crops, oil, gas, or minerals. Even though the secured item has a serial number, copying the number into the security agreement is not necessary; however, if convenient, the secured party may wish to include the serial number in order to avoid a future dispute as to the exact identity of the secured item. A description in general terms is sufficient (for example, "an RCA TV set, Model 123"). A blanket description is also sufficient and may include goods not yet acquired by the obligor (for example, "all electric ranges now in the obligor's possession or hereafter acquired by him"). When a security agreement thus includes after-acquired property,

[12] U.C.C. Secs. 9-110, 9-203, 9-204.

the secured party's "floating" interest will attach automatically at the future time when the obligor acquires rights in the described goods.[13] In explaining the Code's recognition and validation of "floating" or "shifting" liens or charges, the authors of the Code write:

> The widespread nineteenth-century prejudice against the floating charge was based on a feeling, often inarticulate in the opinions, that a commercial borrower should not be allowed to encumber all his assets present and future, and that for the protection not only of the borrower but of his other creditors a cushion of free assets should be preserved. That inarticulate premise has much to recommend it. This Article decisively rejects it not on the ground that it was wrong in policy but on the ground that it has not been effective. In the past fifty years there has been a multiplication of security devices designed to avoid the policy: field warehousing, trust receipts, "factor's lien" acts and so on. The cushion of free assets has not been preserved. In almost every state it is now possible for the borrower to give a lien on everything he has or will have. There have no doubt been sufficient economic reasons for the change. This Article, in expressly validating the floating charge, merely recognizes an existing state of things. The substantive rules of law set forth in the balance of the Article are designed to achieve the protection of the debtor and the equitable resolution of the conflicting claims of creditors which the old rules no longer give.[14]

RIGHTS OF SECURED PARTY AGAINST GOODS AND OBLIGOR

When an obligor defaults, the secured party has two types of remedies: 1) he can proceed against the secured goods to enforce his security interests; 2) he can proceed against the obligor to enforce the obligation.

Enforcing the Security Interest

To enforce or realize on his security interest, the secured party usually starts by obtaining possession of the secured goods.

Method of Obtaining Possession[15]

With heavy equipment which would be difficult to move, a secured party can accomplish the equivalent of taking possession by obtaining control over the item (for example, by chaining and padlocking or other-

---

[13] A policy limitation written into Sec. 9-204 prohibits (for most purposes) a security interest in crops if it is to arise more than one year after the signing of a security agreement, and also prohibits creation of a security interest in consumer goods (except accessions) that may be acquired by the obligor more than ten days after the secured party has given value.

[14] Comment to U.C.C. Sec. 9-204.

[15] U.C.C. Sec. 9-503.

wise rendering the item unusable). With readily movable goods, the secured party will usually take actual possession—without a lawsuit if he can do so without a breach of the peace, otherwise by bringing a lawsuit to obtain possession.

Very often secured goods are located inside a building which is occupied by the obligor. In order to repossess such goods without a lawsuit, the secured party must be able 1) to gain entrance and 2) to remove the repossessed goods, both without a breach of the peace.

In order to enter lawfully, a secured party must obtain present permission from the obligor. Permission previously given in the security agreement itself will justify the secured party in coming onto the obligor's land, but *present* permission must be obtained to enter a building. Usually the secured party's entry will be considered illegal if (without present permission from the occupant) the secured party breaks in, gains entrance with a passkey, or pushes open a partially-opened door. Even if the obligor is temporarily out, the secured party's entering the building without present permission will usually be considered illegal. Although the opposite view has been expressed by courts in some states, there are creditable and reasonable authorities which hold that permission to enter is valid and effective even though obtained by the secured party's tricking or deceiving the obligor (for example, by saying that he has come to adjust or repair when actually the secured party intends to repossess as soon as he is permitted to enter). After a secured party has lawfully gained entrance and taken possession of secured goods, many courts have held that he must also be able to remove the goods without using or threatening physical force against the obligor. Since a jury can be expected to sympathize with a bruised obligor who claims that he was physically assaulted by the secured party and his burly helpers, it is certainly wise for the secured party to refrain from trying to fight his way out with the goods, even if permitted to do so by his state law. If the obligor physically resists removal, the secured party should usually give up the attempt and bring legal action to obtain possession—recovering money damages also for the obligor's wrongful refusal to permit repossession without a lawsuit.

In cases involving accessions or fixtures (goods which have been attached to and become a part of other goods or of real estate), dismantling and repossessing a secured item may result in some damage or injury to the other goods or to the premises. Such injuries may be of two types, 1) actual damage (for example broken plaster, holes in walls, holes in other goods, and the like) and 2) diminution in overall value through the absence of the item removed (for example, decrease in value of a building as a result of the secured party's removing the heating system). If the obligor and the secured party are the only persons involved, the secured party has the right to repossess any secured accession or fixture, so long as he does so in a reasonable manner, regardless of how much damage or injury may unavoidably result. When an obligor defaults after agreeing to a security interest in this type of goods, he can expect such injuries, and is considered to have consented to them. On the other hand, as between a secured party and a third person who has acquired an interest in the total goods or the real estate involved, while the secured party will still have the right to repossess the secured accession or fixture (provided he has protected his interest against third persons in the manner explained later), the secured party must reimburse the third person for damages of the first type mentioned above—and the third person can refuse to permit removal until he is adequately assured of reimbursement. However, the third person cannot look to the secured party for compensation for damages of the second type mentioned above (diminution in overall value); a third person who acquires property subject to a security interest in an accession or fixture, can expect such a loss and is assumed to have consented to it.

The criminal law may aid a secured party in pressuring his obligor to pay, or at least to account for secured goods. For example, as mentioned in Chapter 3, a provision of the Pennsylvania Penal Code declares that if an obligor in possession of goods subject to a security interest "maliciously or fraudulently sells, injures, destroys, conceals, abandons, or defaces identifying marks on such goods, or otherwise disposes of such goods under claim of full ownership . . ." he is guilty of a misdemeanor, punishable by not exceeding a $500 fine, one year imprisonment, or both. A secured party may be able to induce some action from a dishonest obligor by directing his attention to such a statute. However, the secured party's letter should be carefully worded, preferably by his lawyer; otherwise, the secured party may be guilty of compounding the crime or of extortion, or liable for malicious prosecution.

Procedure After Repossession[16]

Except for one specialized situation discussed in the next paragraph, the secured party has no obligation to resell repossessed goods promptly, or at all, unless he has expressly agreed to do so. The details of any resale, the obligor's rights as to goods not yet disposed of (that is, to pay the obligation and redeem the goods), and the distribution of proceeds realized from the secured party's sale (surplus returned to the obligor, the obligor liable for any deficiency) are the same as previously discussed in Part 2 of this chapter.

In one specialized situation the secured party has an obligation to

[16] U.C.C. Sec. 9-504–506.

resell the secured goods within ninety days after taking possession. The secured party has this obligation if all of the following elements are present:

1. The secured item consists of goods bought or used primarily for personal, family, or household purposes (including a motor vehicle or a fixture, as well as other goods classed by the Code as consumer goods).

2. The obligor has paid at least 60 percent of the obligation.

3. After default, the obligor has not signed a statement renouncing or modifying his right in the goods.

A secured party who fails to make this prompt resale is liable to the obligor for actual damages or for a penalty of 10 percent of the secured debt, whichever is greater.

Enforcing the Obligation[17]

Even though a creditor holds a security interest in certain goods and can repossess and resell the goods should the obligor default, this is not the secured party's sole remedy. Sometimes secured goods are destroyed, or depreciate in value to such an extent that repossessing them would be fruitless. Other times even though a secured party acts diligently and reasonably in repossessing and reselling secured property, the money thus realized nets less than the unpaid balance of the original obligation. If a secured party, although acting properly, fails to realize from the secured property the full amount due on the obligation, the secured party can avail himself of the remedy accorded by the law to any creditor—namely, to sue and obtain a judgment, and then to have the sheriff levy on any property belonging to the obligor and sell it at sheriff's sale.

RIGHTS OF SECURED PARTY AS TO THIRD PERSONS

When an obligor is in possession of the secured goods and making full use of them, it is especially easy for a third person to be misled into thinking that the obligor is the absolute owner of the goods. Accordingly, one of the chief tasks of the law in connection with nonpossessory security devices is to protect third persons, but at the same time to avoid unduly hindering the granting of this essential type of secured credit. Possible third persons who must be considered including the following:

1. The obligor's lien creditor.

2. A subsequent secured party to whom the obligor dishonestly attempts to transfer a new security interest identical to the existing security interest.

3. A buyer who purchases the secured goods from the obligor.

[17] U.C.C. Secs. 9-501, 9-502.

4. The obligor's landlord (in states which still recognize a common-law landlord's lien), and a bailee with a possessory lien effective against the obligor. Bailee's liens and landlord's liens enjoy a preferred status, the Code leaving to each state the determination of how much protection, if any, a secured party can obtain against bailees and landlords.

With respect to possible landlords' liens, the Code very simply states[18] that it will have no effect on any lien which the law of a particular state gives to landlords. In some states the common-law remedy known as the landlord's "distress" or "distraint" is still available. This remedy gives a landlord with a claim for past-due rent the right, without a lawsuit, to levy or distrain upon goods on the rented premises. The landlord thereby obtains a lien on the distrained goods, under which he can have the goods sold, receiving the proceeds up to the amount of the overdue rent. Since the early common-law theory of renting considered the land itself as owing the rent, the landlord's right to enter the land and distrain upon any personal property in the tenant's possession, included property not actually owned by the tenant. Because of the ease with which a tenant could otherwise collude with a third person to defraud the landlord, some states continue to permit a landlord to distrain upon property even though it is not entirely owned by the tenant—with however numerous exceptions, some of which have arisen under the common law, many of which have been added by various statutes.

With respect to possible bailees' liens: as is briefly mentioned in Chapter 15, if a bailor delivers goods to a bailee and contracts for the bailee to perform certain services for a stated compensation payable upon return of the goods, the bailee has the right to retain possession of the goods until the bailor pays or tenders payment. Recognizing that it is sound policy to give preference to a bailee whose work or services have enhanced or preserved the value of secured property, the Code states:

> When a person in the ordinary course of his business furnishes services or materials with respect to goods subject to a security interest, a lien upon goods in the possession of such person given by statute or rule of law for such materials or services takes priority over a perfected security interest unless the lien is statutory and the statute expressly provides otherwise.[19]

The chief examples of this type of lienholder are repairmen and warehousemen. Under this Code provision, if an obligor delivers secured goods to a repairman or warehouseman and then defaults, the secured party will usually have to pay the amount of the repairman's or warehouseman's claim against the obligor before having a right to obtain possession of the secured goods.

[18] U.C.C. Sec. 9-104.
[19] U.C.C. Sec. 9-310.

With the exception of these special types of third persons (repairmen, warehousemen, and landlords) the rights of secured parties and what they must do to protect their interests are prescribed in detail by the Code. In general, the Code provides that many types of security interests will not be effective against innocent third persons unless the secured party files in an appropriate public office a written notice of the existence of his security interest. The Code calls this filed statement a *financing statement*. Briefly, a financing statement identifies 1) the obligor, 2) the secured party, and 3) either the specific item or the type of item in which the secured party has a security interest. Financing statements will be more fully discussed in Part 6 of this chapter.

The fee for filing a financing statement varies in different states, from a low of 50 cents in some states to as much as $3 in other states. When a secured party enters into a large number of financing transactions, the preparation and filing of numerous financing statements is a substantial expense. However, in all but a few situations, the social advantage resulting from public filing is considered as outweighing this burden and expense. In only a few situations, therefore, is any protection given without filing.

The basic approach of the Code (after segregating specialized fact situations involving motor vehicles, fixtures, and accessions) is to differentiate between the financing of business goods and the financing of nonbusiness goods. Financing transactions involving equipment, inventory, and farm products are all associated in some way with the business use of the secured goods by the obligor, while consumer financing is just the opposite. On the whole, business-goods financing usually tends to involve larger sums of money, goods of greater value, and either longer credit terms or repeated extensions of credit on the same goods or types of goods. These differences directly affect both the need and burden of filing financing statements. For example, suppose that a bank is financing the inventory of an appliance dealer whose usual practice is to purchase several TV sets at a time, put them on display in his store, and eventually sell them. As each set is acquired, a security interest is intended to vest in the bank, and the bank's interest is intended to continue until the dealer sells the set. Over a period of time the turnover of even a small appliance business may easily total 200 sets. However, since the parties and type of goods remain the same, only one financing statement will have to be filed to protect the bank's "floating" security interest in the succession of TV sets. On the other hand, suppose that the bank is also financing the customers who purchase the TV sets from the dealer. If the bank were required to file a financing statement to protect its security interest in the TV sets after they became consumer goods in the possession of the customers, the bank would have to file 200 financing statements, one for each of the 200 different customer-obligors. For consumer financing, therefore, it is desirable that some protection be given without filing.

As a result of balancing the various policy factors that affect the conflicting interests of secured parties and third persons (including the burden and expense of filing, the risk of third parties being misled into thinking the obligor owns the collateral in his possession, the different types of possible third parties, etc.), the authors of the Code have worked out the following pattern for the protection of nonpossessory security interests in goods and negotiable documents of title:

1) Security Interests in Motor Vehicles.[20] Many states require owners of motor vehicles to obtain state-issued certificates of title as soon as the vehicles cease to be inventory in the hands of dealers and are put into use. Under many registration statutes, incumbrances are noted on the state records and on the certificates of title. In such states the Code requires that a security interest be noted as an encumbrance on the obligor's certificate of title, and provides that such a notation will protect the secured party's interest against any innocent third person (with the exception, depending upon local law, of repairmen, warehousemen, and landlords). In states which do not note incumbrances on certificates of title, a security interest in a motor vehicle is protected in the same way as security interests in either consumer goods or equipment, depending upon the obligor's use of the vehicle.

2) Security Interests in Fixtures and Accessions.[21] To protect a security interest in fixtures, the secured party must file a financing statement describing not only the goods but also the real estate to which the goods are affixed. The place of filing is the same office in which, under the law of the particular state involved, real estate mortgages are filed.

To protect a security interest in an accession, the secured party must take whatever steps would be necessary to protect a security interest in the item to which the accession is affixed. Often this will require filing a financing statement, or, with a motor vehicle, having an interest noted on the certificate of title.

The Code expressly leaves to the law of each state (either legislative law or, quite commonly, decisional law) the determination of whether a particular item affixed to real estate is a fixture, that is, whether it should be considered as part of the real estate. For example, a machine installed in a factory might be classed either as a fixture and therefore part of the building, or instead as equipment and not part of the building, depending upon the particular circumstances and the court rulings of the

[20] U.C.C. Sec. 9-302.
[21] U.C.C. Secs. 9-313, 9-314.

state involved. The distinction is important since a financing statement pertaining to equipment is not filed with real estate records; thus if the secured party assumes that the machine is a fixture and files in the real estate record office, the filing will not be adequate to protect his interest if the machine is actually not a fixture. In doubtful cases the secured party should file his interest both ways and thus be protected whether the machine is a real estate fixture or equipment.

The same type of question can arise when an item is affixed to other goods. For example, many courts have held that a new set of tires are not accessions to the motor vehicle upon which they are installed. Under such rulings the tires would be ordinary goods (either consumer goods or equipment, depending upon the obligor's use) and a notation on the certificate of title would *not* give sufficient protection to the secured party.

3) Security Interests in Equipment.[22] As a matter of policy, moderate-costing farm equipment (not over $2,500 in the official version of the Code—as approved by the American Law Institute and the Commissioners on Uniform State Laws—but lowered in some states to $500) is considered quite similar to consumer goods and subject to the same rules, discussed under Item 6 below. Except for such farm equipment, a security interest in equipment is not protected against innocent third parties unless the secured party files a financing statement pertaining to his interest. If the secured party files, he is fully protected against all third parties (with the exception, depending upon local law, of a repairman, warehouseman, or landlord).

4) Security Interests in Inventory.[23] There being no reason to relax the general policy of requiring notice to third persons, a secured party must file a financing statement to protect his security interest in inventory. If he does not file, he has no protection against innocent third parties. If he does file, he is fully protected against all third persons, with the exception (depending upon local law) of a repairman, warehouseman, or landlord, and also with the further exception of a buyer in the ordinary course of the obligor's business. As a matter of policy, such a buyer is preferred because a secured party who leaves inventory in an obligor-dealer's possession usually intends that the dealer display and sell the secured goods in the customary operation of his business. It is fair to consider the secured party bound by the sale unless he actually places restrictions on the dealer, *and also* brings the restrictions to the attention of the dealer's customers. As the authors of the Code point out:

> This Section provides that such a buyer takes free of a security interest, even though perfected, and although he knows the security interest exists. . . . [Such a buyer] takes free if he merely knowns that

[22] U.C.C. Secs. 9-302, 9-307.
[23] U.C.C. Secs. 9-302, 9-307.

there is a security interest which covers the goods but takes subject if he knows, in addition, that the sale is in violation of some term in the security agreement not waived by the words or conduct of the secured party.[24]

5) Security Interests in Farm Products.[25] A secured party can be protected against innocent third persons only by filing a financing statement. If he does not file, he has no protection; if he files, he is fully protected against all third persons (except, depending upon local law, a warehouseman or landlord).

6) Security Interests in Consumer Goods.[26]

a) *Purchase Money Security Interests.* If a secured party with a purchase money secured interest in consumer goods does not file a financing statement, he is nevertheless protected against all third persons, with the exception (depending upon local law) of a repairman, warehouseman, or landlord, and with the further exception of a particular type of buyer, namely a buyer who purchases the secured goods from the obligor 1) for value, 2) without actual knowledge of the security interest, and 3) for his own personal, family, or household purposes. For protection against this type of buyer the secured party must file a financing statement. In other words, if a secured party does not file, he is nevertheless protected against the consumer-obligor's insolvency and also against his dishonest sale of the secured property for business purposes; if the secured party wants protection against the obligor's dishonest sale of the secured property for personal purposes, he must file.

b) *Nonpurchase Money Security Interests.* The secured party can be protected against innocent third parties only by filing a financing statement. If he does not file, he has no protection; if he files, he is fully protected against all third persons (except, depending upon local law, a repairman, warehouseman, or landlord).

Example: This example involves a TV set and a home freezer.

TV Set. On August 1 a dealer sold and delivered the TV set to a householder, who signed a written agreement promising to pay the specified price in monthly installments, and stating that a security interest would remain in the dealer until the total price was paid. (The dealer thereby acquired a purchase money security interest.)

Freezer. For some time the householder had owned a home freezer, free and clear of all claims. On August 2 the householder borrowed a sum of money from a bank and signed a written agreement promising to repay the loan in specified monthly installments and stating that a security interest in the described freezer was given to the bank until the total loan was repaid.

[24] Comment to U.C.C. Sec. 9-307.
[25] U.C.C. Sec. 9-302.
[26] U.C.C. Secs. 9-302, 9-307.

(The bank's interest would be classed as a nonpurchase money security interest.)

The householder defaulted upon both agreements. Assume that each of the following is a separate fact situation.

Attaching Creditor: A creditor with a judgment against the householder had no knowledge of the secured parties' interests, and had the sheriff levy on both the TV set and the freezer. If neither secured party had filed a financing statement, then: as to the *TV set;* the dealer would have a superior interest; as to the *freezer,* the attaching creditor would have an interest superior to the bank's security interest. If the bank had filed a financing statement, the bank's interest would have been superior.

Buyer: The householder sold the TV set to a buyer who paid fair value, without knowledge of the interest of the dealer.

a) The buyer was a barber who put the TV set in his barber shop for the entertainment of his customers. The dealer's interest would be superior to that of the buyer, even though the dealer did not file a financing statement.

b) The buyer bought the TV set for use in his home. The buyer's interest would be superior to that of the dealer, unless the dealer had filed a financing statement.

7) Security Interests in Negotiable Documents of Title.[27] Suppose that an obligor borrows a sum of money, promises to repay by a stated time, and by written agreement gives his lender a security interest in a negotiable document of title (bill of lading or warehouse receipt) belonging to the obligor. Usually in such a transaction, the secured party will take possession of the document. If the secured party leaves the document in the obligor's possession, the secured party will be protected against the obligor's lien creditors for twenty-one days. To extend his protection against lien creditors beyond that time, the secured party must file a financing statement pertaining to his interest.

Notice that the secured party's protection is only against the obligor's lien creditors. As the Code states:

> Nothing in this Article limits the rights of a holder in due course of a negotiable instrument [commercial paper] . . . or a holder to whom a negotiable document of title has been duly negotiated . . . or a bona fide purchaser of a [corporate] security . . . and such holders or purchasers take priority over an earlier security interest even though perfected. Filing under this Article does not constitute notice of the security interest to such holders or purchasers.[28]

In other words, the secured party is protected against the obligor's subsequent insolvency, but not against his subsequent dishonesty. If the obligor transfers the document to a buyer who purchases for value, in regular course of business, and without knowledge of the secured

[27] U.C.C. Sec. 9-304.
[28] U.C.C. Sec. 9-309.

party's interest, the buyer will acquire the document free from the secured party's interest. Likewise, if the obligor borrows on the document and pledges it by delivering it to an innocent second secured party, the latter will take free from the interest of the first secured party. Of course, if the document itself is marked with notice of the first secured party's interest, any subsequent buyer or lender will take with notice of such interest and therefore will be subject to it.

Example: A dealer ordered certain refrigerators from a manufacturer for $1,000, the terms being stated as, "sight draft, bill of lading attached, cash against documents." In his order the dealer stated that he had financing arrangements with the First Bank. The manufacturer shipped the goods on order bill of lading, drew a draft on the dealer, and sent the bill of lading with draft attached to the First Bank. Upon receiving the documents, the First Bank notified the dealer. The dealer came to the bank and signed an agreement promising to repay to the bank at a stated time $1,000 plus interest, and giving the bank an interest in the bill of lading and the refrigerators it represented until the dealer repaid his $1,000 (plus interest) obligation. The bank then gave the dealer the bill of lading, and sent its own check for $1,000 to the manufacturer. Thereafter at the time stated below the dealer was adjudged insolvent and a receiver was appointed who took over all of the dealer's assets. Since the refrigerators had not yet arrived, the bill of lading representing them was among the dealer's assets which were taken over by the receiver. At least one of the creditors represented by the receiver had no knowledge of the bank's interest until after the receiver was appointed.

1. The receiver was appointed fifteen days after the dealer and the bank signed the above agreement. As between the receiver and the bank, the bank would have superior interest in the bill of lading and the goods it represented.

2. The receiver was appointed twenty-five days after the dealer and the bank signed the above agreement. If the bank had not filed a financing statement pertaining to its interest in the bill of lading, then as between the receiver and the bank, the receiver would have a superior interest. If the bank had filed an appropriate financing statement, the bank would have a superior interest. As is explained in Part 6 of this chapter, one filing is sufficient for security interests in any number of items of the general type involved. Since the bank was regularly financing the dealer's purchases, the bank could file a statement as to its interest in bills of lading (as well as its interest in refrigerators), and the statement would be effective for any bills of lading in which the dealer gave the bank a security interest for the next five years—the effective duration of a filed financing statement.

GRACE PERIOD FOR FILING[29]

Generally, a financing statement will give protection only from the date it is filed. If a time lag occurs between the day the secured party

[29] U.C.C. Sec. 9-301.

acquires his interest and the day he files, and an innocent third person acquires an interest during that time lag, the third person will usually have priority.

There is a limited exception to this. If the secured party's interest is a purchase money interest, and if the secured party files within ten days after extending the credit which his interest secures, his protection relates back to the date he extended credit, thus giving him priority over any intervening lien creditor or bulk buyer. If another type of innocent person is involved (for example, a buyer other than in bulk or another secured party), the filing will not relate back.

Part 4 CHATTEL PAPER

FACT SITUATION

As explained in Part 3 of this chapter, in order for a secured party to obtain an enforceable security interest in goods which are to remain in an obligor's possession, the secured party must obtain the obligor's signature to an appropriate security agreement. This security agreement, which the Code calls "chattel paper," can in turn be used by the secured party as a second financing device, to raise money for his own benefit. In using the chattel paper to raise money, the secured party will either borrow and assign the chattel paper as collateral security for the loan, or sell and assign the chattel paper as a complete transfer of his rights to the paper and the obligation which it evidences. The parties involved can be called the *obligor* (the debtor of the original obligation which the chattel paper evidences and secures), the *assignor* (the original secured party who raises money by assigning the chattel paper), and the *assignee* (the one to whom the original secured party assigns the chattel paper). When chattel paper is assigned, it is entirely up to the assignor and assignee whether the paper is retained by the assignor in his own possession, or instead is delivered into the possession of the assignee. As the authors of the Code explain:

> Arrangements where the chattel paper is delivered to the . . . [assignee] who then makes collections, as well as arrangements where the . . . [assignor], whether or not he is left in possession of the paper, makes the collections, are both widely used, and are known respectively as notification (or "direct collection") and non-notification (or "indirect collection") arrangements. In the automobile field, for example, when a car is sold to a consumer buyer under an installment purchase agreement and the resulting chattel paper is assigned, the assignee usually takes possession, the obligor is notified of the assignment and is directed to make payments to the assignee. In the furniture field, for an example on the other hand, the chattel paper may be left in the

dealer's hands or delivered to the assignee; in either case the obligor is usually not notified, and payments are made to the dealer-assignor who receives them under a duty to remit to his assignee. The widespread use of both methods of dealing with chattel paper is recognized by the provisions of this Article which permit perfection of a chattel paper security interest either by filing or by taking possession.[30]

FORMAL REQUIREMENTS[31]

For an assignment of chattel paper to be effective, the minimum requirement is either that the chattel paper be delivered to the assignee, or that the assignor give to the assignee a separate written assignment, which describes the chattel paper involved and states that it is assigned to the assignee. In most cases the parties are not content merely to meet this minimum requirement. Even when an assignee is taking possession of the assigned chattel paper, he will usually want the assignor also to sign a written assignment. If a number of chattel-paper contracts are assigned in a single transaction, the parties will in most cases use a single, written, assignment instrument. Such an instrument need not specifically describe each chattel-paper contract; a blanket description will suffice, and, if the parties wish, the assignment can include future chattel paper. Thus the following would be an effective description: "All chattel paper now held by the assignor, or to be acquired by him in the future." With such an assignment, the assignee will obtain an interest in each chattel-paper contract as soon as it comes into existence, without any further act of assignment.

RIGHTS OF ASSIGNEE AGAINST OBLIGOR

The assignee of chattel paper becomes the new secured party, owning both the obligation and the security interest which the chattel paper evidences, and suceeding to the rights and remedies which the original secured party (the assignor) had against the obligor. Being a secured party, the assignee can[32] (in the manner discussed in Part 3 of this chapter) 1) realize on the security interest in the secured goods, and/or 2) enforce the obligation against the obligor.

As is true of an assignee of any nonnegotiable contract right (as discussed in Chapter 10) the assignee of chattel paper is considered as standing in the shoes of the assignor. Thus not only does the assignee have the same rights which the assignor had, but also the assignee is subject to the same defenses. As the Code states:

[30] Comment to U.C.C. Sec. 9-308.
[31] U.C.C. Sec. 9-203.
[32] U.C.C. Sec. 9-501.

(1) Unless an . . . [obligor] has made an enforceable agreement not to assert defenses or claims arising out of a sale [such agreements not to assert defenses will be discussed shortly] . . . the rights of an assignee are subject to

(a) all the terms of the contract between the . . . [obligor] and assignor and any defense or claim arising therefrom; and

(b) any other defense of claim of the . . . [obligor] against the assignor which accrues before the . . . [obligor] receives notification of the assignment.

❋　❋　❋　❋　❋

(3) The . . . [obligor] is authorized to pay the assignor until the . . . [obligor] receives notification that the account has been assigned and that payment is to be made to the assignee. A notification which does not reasonably identify the rights assigned is ineffective. If requested by the . . . [obligor] the assignee must seasonably furnish reasonable proof that the assignment has been made and unless he does so the . . . [obligor] may pay the assignor. . . .[33]

Example: A dealer and a customer entered into a written agreement under which, 1) the dealer sold and delivered a described TV set to the customer, 2) the customer agreed to pay the purchase price in stated monthly installments, 3) the dealer retained a security interest in the set until the full price was paid, and 4) the dealer warranted one-year trouble-free operation of the set. The day after the agreement was signed and the set was installed in the customer's home, the dealer assigned the chattel-paper contract to a bank, receiving in return the total amount of the obligation less the bank's discount fee. The bank notified the customer of the assignment and instructed the customer to make all payments to the bank. About two weeks later the TV set became totally inoperative through no fault of the customer, and the customer promptly notified the dealer. The dealer failed to repair or replace the set, and the customer notified the bank that he would pay nothing on the installments until the dealer satisfactorily performed his warranty. Before anything further could be done the dealer was adjudged insolvent, and his business was liquidated. The bank sued the customer for payments due under the chattel-paper contract.

The bank could not recover. The bank held the contract subject to all defenses that could have been raised against the dealer. Since the customer had a breach of warranty defense that would have been good against the dealer, the defense would be equally good against the bank.

Example: A manufacturer and an oil refiner entered into a written contract under which the manufacturer sold and delivered to the refiner certain portable machinery. According to the written contract (chattel paper) the refiner was to pay $2,000 in sixty days and title to the machinery was to remain in the manufacturer until the full price was paid. About three weeks later, the manufacturer sold and assigned the chattel paper to a bank, receiving $2,000 less the bank's discount fee. According to the arrangement between the manufacturer and the bank, no notice of the assignment was given to the refiner.

[33] U.C.C. Sec. 9-318.

One week after the assignment the refiner sold and delivered to the manufacturer $1,000 worth of oil on an open account which was payable in thirty days. The manufacturer defaulted on this $1,000 obligation, whereupon the refiner refused to pay the full $2,000. At this point the bank claimed $2,000 from the refiner. When the bank made this demand, the refiner for the first time learned of the assignment. The bank refused the refiner's offer of $1,000 as full settlement and sued the refiner for $2,000.

The bank could recover only $1,000 from the refiner. If the manufacturer had still owned the chattel-paper obligation, the refiner would have had the right to set-off what was owed to him against what he owed the manufacturer. The refiner would have the same right of set-off against the bank.

Suppose that immediately after the assignment, the bank had notified the refiner of the assignment. From that moment on, the refiner would know that the assigned obligation was no longer available to be used as a set-off in any new transaction between the manufacturer and the refiner. The refiner might accordingly refuse to extend credit to the manufacturer. If the refiner did extend $1,000 credit and the manufacturer defaulted, the refiner would nevertheless be obliged to pay $2,000 to the bank.

Sometimes a chattel-paper contract will contain a provision by which the obligor expressly waives all defenses which he might otherwise have against an assignee. Various states differ as to the validity and effect which, as a matter of policy, should be accorded to such a waiver, especially when it is made by the buyer of consumer goods. Since this is a point upon which different policy views will not unduly affect overall uniformity of commercial laws, the Code states:

> Subject to any statute or decision which establishes a different rule for buyers or lessees of consumer goods, an agreement by a buyer or lessee that he will not assert against an assignee any claim or defense which he may have against the seller or lessor is enforceable by an assignee who takes his assignment for value, in good faith and without notice of a claim or defense, except for defenses of a type which may be asserted against a holder in due course of a negotiable instrument under the Article on Commercial Paper (Article 3) [discussed in Chapter 14]. A buyer who as part of one transaction signs both a negotiable instrument and a security agreement makes such an agreement.[34]

RIGHTS OF ASSIGNEE AGAINST ASSIGNOR[35]

Recall from Chapter 14 that an unqualified indorser of negotiable commercial paper impliedly guarantees that, if the holder exercises proper diligence, the obligor will pay the transferred obligation when it comes due; even though such an indorsement states no express guar-

[34] U.C.C. Sec. 9-206.
[35] U.C.C. Sec. 9-502.

anty, the indorser is liable on this implied "indorser's promise." No such implied guaranty accompanies the transfer of nonnegotiable contract claims not coming under the Commercial Paper Article of the Code. Therefore, in case the obligor of assigned chattel paper fails to pay, the assignee will have a right to collect from the assignor only if one of the following three situations is present:

1) *Breach of Express Guaranty.* Although an assignor makes no implied guaranty when he assigns chattel paper, he will sometimes include in his assignment an express guaranty of payment. If he does so and the obligor later fails to pay the assigned claim, the assignee will have a right to collect from the assignor by virtue of this express guaranty.

2) *Breach of Implied Warranty.* Although the assignor of chattel paper does not impliedly guaranty payment, he does impliedly warrant (note the similarity to an implied warranty of title which is presumed to accompany the sale of goods, discussed in Chapter 7):

a) That the chattel paper is genuine and that the obligation it evidences actually exists.

b) That the obligation is not subject to any defenses except those which are disclosed by the assignor at the time of assignment.

c) That the assignor will do nothing to prevent, hinder, or impair the assignee's collection of the assigned obligation.

3) *Default on Debt Owed by Assignor to Assignee.* The assignment of chattel paper may be intended as a complete sale of the paper, or instead merely as collateral security for a loan made by the assignee to the assignor. When a loan is secured by anything at all (stock, goods, etc.), the fact that the collateral depreciates or even becomes worthless does not (unless agreed otherwise) affect the debtor's obligation to repay the loan. Therefore, if chattel paper is assigned as collateral security for a loan which the assignee is making to the assignor, the obligor's subsequent default and failure to pay his chattel-paper obligation will not affect the assignor's obligation on this loan, and the assignee will still have a right to recover the amount of the loan from the assignor.

RIGHTS OF ASSIGNEE AS TO THIRD PERSONS

The types of third persons who might attempt to assert claims which conflict with the interest of an assignee of chattel paper are, 1) a lien creditor of the assignor, and 2) a subsequent assignee to whom the assignor might wrongfully attempt to make a second assignment of the same chattel paper.

Example: After a dealer sold and delivered certain goods to a customer whose obligation to pay was evidenced by chattel paper, the dealer assigned the chattel paper to the First Bank as collateral security for a loan. The arrangement between the dealer and the bank was that the dealer should continue to collect payments from the customer, and for this purpose the chattel paper was left in the dealer's possession. Thereafter:

Lien Creditor (through Attachment). A creditor obtained a judgment against the dealer. Knowing of the debt which the customer owed to the dealer but unaware that it had been assigned, the creditor had the sheriff levy on this obligation by handing an attachment paper to the customer, notifying him that the money which he owed to the dealer was attached by the creditor.

Lien Creditor (through Receivership). The dealer was adjudged insolvent and a receiver was appointed who proceeded to collect all debts which were owed to the dealer, including that of the customer. At least one of the creditors represented by the receiver had no knowledge of the assignment at the time the receiver was appointed.

Second Assignee. The dealer wrongfully sold, assigned, and delivered the chattel paper to the Second Bank which gave value, in good faith, and without knowledge of the first assignment.

What the assignee must do to protect his interest depends upon whether, under the arrangement between the parties, the chattel paper is delivered to the assignee, or instead is left in the possession of the assignor.

If the chattel paper is delivered to the assignee, his possession sufficiently protects his interest against subsequent third persons from the time he takes possession of the paper.[36] On the other hand, if the assignee permits the assigned chattel paper to be retained by the assignor, then:

1. To protect his interest against a later innocent lien creditor of the assignor, the assignee must file a financing statement pertaining to the assignment.[37]

2. To protect his interest against the assignor's dishonestly reassigning and transferring the chattel paper, the assignee must clearly note or stamp on the chattel paper itself a statement that the paper has already been assigned.[38] Filing a financing statement (necessary to protect against lien creditors) will *not* suffice to protect against a second assignee; the Code expressly gives a second assignee priority over a first assignee if the second assignee, 1) in the ordinary course of his business, 2) either buys the chattel paper from the assignor or loans him money on it, and 3) in doing so, takes possession of the chattel paper, 4) without actual knowledge of the prior assignment. The only way to prevent a second assignee from gaining this priority is to inform

[36] U.C.C. Sec. 9-305.
[37] U.C.C. Secs. 9-301, 9-302.
[38] U.C.C. Sec. 9-308.

him of the first assignment, and the surest way to do this is to note the assignment on the paper itself. A later assignee is supposed to examine the chattel paper being assigned to him, and will be presumed to have knowledge of whatever is noted on the paper itself.

Sometimes, after filing an appropriate financing statement, an assignee not only will permit the assignor to retain possession of assigned chattel paper and to collect payments from obligors, but also the assignee will permit the assignor to use for his own purposes the money thus collected. Since this arrangement accomplishes a useful social purpose, the Code expressly provides[39] that an assignment is not invalidated by the assignor's continuing to have complete control over the assigned chattel paper.

Example: A manufacturer customarily sold goods on credit to various buyers, each obligation being evidenced by chattel paper. To finance his operations, the manufacturer borrowed a large sum of money from a bank, signed a note promising to pay certain interest at stated intervals and to repay the amount of the loan after three years, and as security for the obligation, gave the bank a written assignment covering all chattel paper acquired by the manufacturer. Thereafter, by operation of this blanket or floating assignment, whenever the manufacturer made a sale and acquired chattel paper, the bank immediately and automatically became the assignee of the paper. Since the manufacturer was to have use of the amount of the loan for the three-year loan period and was to pay the bank no more than the agreed interest during that period, no notice of assignment was given to any of the chattel-paper obligors. Instead, as chattel paper matured, the obligors paid their obligations to the manufacturer who retained the money thus received and used it for his further business operations.

Two years after the loan was made the manufacturer was adjudged insolvent, and a receiver was appointed. The bank would have priority over the receiver as to all unpaid chattel-paper obligations, and therefore would have the right to give notice to the obligors and to collect from them all sums due, up to the amount of the bank's loan. After the bank realized the full amount of its loan, the receiver could then collect for the benefit of all other creditors any chattel-paper obligations remaining.

The Code recognizes[40] that, unlike nonpossessory transfers of tangible collateral, intangible claims which are evidenced by chattel paper or accounts receivable may frequently be assigned for other than financing purposes. As a matter of policy, therefore, nonfinancing assignments are excluded from the filing requirement. Nonfinancing assignments include 1) an assignment for collection purposes only, and 2) an assignment which is made as a part of the sale of the assignor's entire business.

[39] U.C.C. Sec. 9-205.
[40] U.C.C. Sec. 9-104.

Part 5   ACCOUNTS RECEIVABLE

The term "accounts receivable" is usually associated with business accounts or claims which arise from the sale or lease of goods or from the performance of services.   Accounts receivable financing is a relative newcomer in the financing field.   Dr. Clyde William Phelps has written:

> For more than a quarter of a century, the growth of this type of financing was slow.   But since World War II, the use of accounts receivable financing has become widespread in practically all lines of manufacturing, servicing, processing and wholesaling where sales are made to business firms on open account terms, and, more recently, in some lines of retailing.   The annual volume of such financing currently being provided by specialized financial institutions has risen to about ten billion dollars.[41]

The Code expressly[42] limits its coverage to "financing assignments" of accounts receivable.   "Nonfinancing assignments" to which the Code does not apply include, 1) an assignment for collection only, 2) an assignment in connection with the sale of a business, 3) an isolated assignment involving an insignificant amount, 4) an assignment of wages or salary, and 5) an assignment made in connection with the transfer of an unperformed contract (e.g., an assignment made by a contractor who, after agreeing to build for $50,000, transfers the contract to another builder, delegating the duty to construct along with assigning the right to the money).

A business is able to raise money on its accounts receivable in one of two ways: either 1) by borrowing and assigning its accounts receivable as collateral security for the loan, or 2) by making an outright sale and transfer of its accounts receivable.   The parties involved can be called the *obligor* (the debtor of the original obligation which is being assigned), the *assignor* (the creditor of the original obligation who assigns it to a lender or purchaser), and the *assignee* (the lender or purchaser to whom the account is transferred).

Sometimes when an account is assigned the obligor is immediately notified and directed to make payments to the assignee.   More commonly, however, no notice of assignment is given to the obligor, and the assignor continues to collect payments from the obligor, at least so long as the assignor remains financially sound.   In explaining "notification" and "nonnotification" receivables financing, Dr. Phelps writes:

> In this connection it may be mentioned . . . that, when accounts receivable financing began in the first decade of the present century,

---

[41] Clyde William Phelps, *Accounts Receivable Financing as a Method of Securing Business Loans* (2d ed.; Baltimore: Commercial Credit Company, 1962), p. 11.

[42] U.C.C. Secs. 9-104, 9-302.

it was not customary in lines other than the textile trade for business firms to make payment to third parties in settlement of purchases.

In these other lines, at that time, payment to third parties usually occurred only when accounts of business firms were placed in the hands of a collection agency or when a firm became involved in financial difficulties. Outside of the textile industry, therefore, payments in those earlier days to a third party quite naturally could then be interpreted' as an indication of financial weakness on the part of the firm concerned or even of the possibility that it might be on the road to bankruptcy. Consequently, the non-notification procedure was developed originally to avoid giving rise to false opinions about firms that were basically sound but in need of additional operating cash.[43]

Some contracts expressly state that they are nonassignable. A restriction on the easy transfer of a money claim is considered against public policy and (for assignments to which the Code applies) is declared by the Code[44] to be ineffective. Thus even though the contract which gives rise to an account expressly prohibits assignment, the account can nevertheless be assigned. As the authors of the Code explain:

> It is only for the past hundred years that our law has recognized the possibility of assigning choses in action [intangible contract claims against others]. . . .
> There can be no doubt that a term prohibiting assignment of proceeds was effective against an assignee with notice through the nineteenth century and well into the twentieth. . . .
> That rule of law has been progressively undermined by a process of erosion. . . .
> This gradual and largely unacknowledged shift in legal doctrine has taken place in response to economic need: as accounts and contract rights have become the collateral which secures an ever increasing number of financing transactions, it has been necessary to reshape the law so that these intangibles, like negotiable instruments and negotiable documents of title, can be freely assigned.
> [This Code provision] . . . thus states a rule of law which is widely recognized in the cases and which corresponds to current business practices. It can be regarded as a revolutionary departure only by those who still cherish the hope that we may yet return to the views entertained some two hundred years ago by the Court of King's Bench.[45]

The general pattern of rights and obligations which the Code follows for assignments of accounts receivable, closely parallels the pattern followed with regard to assignments of chattel paper. Thus:

1) *Formal Requirements.*[46] An assignment of an account receivable

[43] Phelps, *op. cit.*, (fn. 41), p. 22.
[44] U.C.C. Sec. 9-318.
[45] Comment to U.C.C. Sec. 9-318.
[46] U.C.C. Secs. 9-110, 9-203, 9-204.

is not effective, even between the assignor and assignee, unless the assignment is in writing and signed by the assignor. Sometimes the parties will transfer only one or more specifically described accounts, other times, their written assignment will be phrased generally, transferring all of the assignor's accounts, future as well as present.

2) *Rights of Assignee Against Obligor.*[47] One obvious difference between chattel paper and an account arises from the fact that, by definition, an account is not supported by a security interest in goods. Thus, unlike an assignee of chattel paper, the assignee of an account will have no claim against any specific goods; however, his right to collect money from the obligor is the same—and is subject to the same defenses—as the right of an assignee of chattel paper.

3) *Rights of Assignee Against Assignor.*[48] These are the same as for chattel paper.

4) *Rights of Assignee as to Third Persons.*[49] Since by definition an account is not evidenced by a transferable document, the interest acquired by the assignee of an account receivable is nonpossessory in every sense of the word. As with most other nonpossessory security devices under the Code, filing a financing statement is required to protect the interest of the assignee against a later, innocent lien creditor of the assignor, or against a later, innocent assignee to whom the assignor dishonestly attempts to assign a previously-assigned account.

Part 6 FINANCING STATEMENTS

PREPARING A FINANCING STATEMENT[50]

A financing statement is a writing that:

1. Contains the signatures and addresses of both the one obtaining a security interest or assignment, and the one giving it—the assignee and assignor in respect to an account or chattel paper, the secured party and obligor in respect to goods, and

2. States the type or types of property interest which is or will be transferred.

Although the security agreement or assignment entered into by the parties must adequately describe the particular property interest being transferred to the assignee or secured party, the financing statement need not be this specific. A financing statement is not intended to supply detailed information as to outstanding interests, rather its purpose is

[47] U.C.C. Sec. 9-318.
[48] U.C.C. Sec. 9-502.
[49] U.C.C. Secs. 9-301, 9-302.
[50] U.C.C. Sec. 9-402.

only to warn a later person that there *may* be an outstanding interest in some particular item.

Example: A dealer borrowed a sum of money from First Bank and signed a written agreement promising to repay the loan at a certain time and stating:

"As collateral security for this obligation, the undersigned dealer hereby assigns and transfers to First Bank security interests in the following:

1. All accounts of the dealer with Jones Company as the obligor, now existing or hereafter to come into existence;

2. All Westinghouse electric ranges now in the dealer's possession or hereafter to be acquired by him; and

3. One GE refrigerator, Model 123, Serial Number 12345."

(This is an unusual combination of collateral and is used here only for illustrative purposes.)

Upon entering into the written agreement with the dealer, First Bank promptly filed a financing statement which, with proper signatures and addresses, stated: "This financing statement covers the following types of property: accounts, electric ranges, electric refrigerators." The financing statement would be sufficient to protect First Bank's interests. If the dealer later wished to borrow from Second Bank and use other accounts, other stoves, or other refrigerators as collateral security, Second Bank would have the record searched, and, upon finding the financing statement, would request the dealer and First Bank to prepare an itemized list of the specific accounts, stoves, and refrigerators in which First Bank actually owned an interest. Second Bank could then safely loan with other accounts, stoves, or refrigerators as collateral. Second Bank would thus be warned to make further inquiry which is all that the filed statement is intended to accomplish.

FILING A FINANCING STATEMENT

The Code states:

(1) Presentation for filing of a financing statement and tender of the filing fee or acceptance of the statement by the filing officer constitutes filing under this article. . . .

❅ ❅ ❅ ❅ ❅

(4) A filing officer shall mark each statement with a consecutive file number and with the date and hour of filing and shall hold the statement for public inspection. In addition the filing officer shall index the statements according to the name of the . . . [obligor or assignor] and shall note in the index the file number and the address of the . . . [obligor or assignor] given in the statement. . . .[51]

PLACE OF FILING[52]

The proper place for filing financing statements pertaining to fixtures is the office (usually at the county level) where, under the law of

[51] U.C.C. Sec. 9-403.
[52] U.C.C. Sec. 9-401.

the particular state involved, real estate mortgages are filed. With other types of collateral (whether goods, chattel paper, or accounts) experts in the field of financing transactions differ. As the authors of the Code point out:

> Under chattel mortgage acts, the Uniform Conditional Sales Act and other conditional sales legislation the geographical unit for filing or recording was local: the county or township in which the mortgagor or vendee resided or in which the goods sold or mortgaged were kept. The Uniform Trust Receipts Act used the state as the geographical filing unit: under that Act statements of trust receipt financing were filed with an official in the state capital and were not filed locally. The state-wide filing system of the Trust Receipts Act has been followed in many accounts receivable and factor's lien acts.
>
> Both systems have their advocates and both their own advantages and drawbacks. The principal advantage of state-wide filing is ease of access to the credit information which the files exist to provide. Consider for example the national distributor who wishes to have current information about the credit standing of the thousands of persons he sells to on credit. The more completely the files are centralized on a state-wide basis, the easier and cheaper it becomes to procure credit information; the more the files are scattered in local filing units, the more burdensome and costly. On the other hand, it can be said that most credit inquiries about local businesses, farmers and consumers come from local sources; convenience is served by having the files locally available and there is not great advantage in centralized filing.
>
> This Section does not attempt to resolve the controversy between the advocates of a completely centralized state-wide filing system and those of a large degree of local autonomy. Instead the Section is drafted in a series of alternatives; local considerations of policy will determine the choice to be made.[53]

Under the alternative provisions (for other than fixtures) the Code permits a state to choose either, 1) central filing in a single statewide office, or 2) a combination of local and central filing, local for consumer goods and collateral pertaining to farming, central for other collateral (plus, if desired by the state legislature, local also if the obligor or assignor concerned does business in only one county).

For states adopting the combined local and central filing option, another choice between two alternatives is offered by the Code, to apply if the secured goods or the assignor move to another county in the same state. Under one choice, any required filing remains effective after the goods or assignor move to another county. Most of the states which have adopted the Code have picked this choice. Under the other choice (adopted in some states, including Pennsylvania and Oklahoma) any required local filing is effective for four months after the secured goods or assignor move to another county, and then a local filing must be

[53] Comment to U.C.C. Sec. 9-401.

made in the new county. Under the latter system especially a secured party or assignee should periodically verify the location of the secured goods or assignor.

Multistate Transactions[54]

A financing transaction will frequently affect interests of persons in more than one state. In such a case the question will arise as to where the secured party or assignee should file to protect his interest against third persons.

Example: A Pennsylvania manufacturer financed his operations through a Pennsylvania bank, giving the bank as collateral security a written assignment covering any accounts acquired by the manufacturer, and the bank filed a financing statement in Pennsylvania. Later the manufacturer sold and delivered certain goods on open account to a buyer residing in Massachusetts. Thereafter one of the manufacturer's creditors obtained a judgment against the manufacturer, and, learning of the recent credit sale to the buyer but unaware of the floating assignment, the creditor attempted to attach the obligation owed by the buyer to the manufacturer by having the appropriate attachment paper served on the buyer in Massachusetts. The question would arise whether, as a matter of policy, the Pennsylvania filing should be considered as sufficient to protect the bank's interest as an assignee of the account owed by the Massachusetts obligor.

Such a transaction might involve persons in any number of states. Suppose that the assignee bank was a New York bank, that the manufacturer made the sale to the Massachusetts buyer by shipping goods from a West Virginia warehouse, and that the judgment creditor was an Illinois resident who obtained his judgment in an Illinois court—through having the summons served on the manufacturer while he was attending a business convention in Chicago (thus giving the Illinois court jurisdiction over the manufacturer).

In general, the law which governs the protection of a security interest in personal property is the law of the state where the property is located. This rule applies to most tangible property and also to the type of intangible property interests which are generally considered as inseparable from the paper evidencing or representing the interest, such as documents of title and chattel paper. Security interests involving such paper are governed by the law of the state where the paper is physically located. The general rule is of little help, however, in the case of intangible acounts receivable, and is inadequate for some types of tangible property, particularly 1) titled goods, 2) mobile equipment and mobile, for-hire inventory, and 3) other incoming secured goods. *Warning:* It should be noted that only a very brief picture of the Code is presented

[54] U.C.C. Sec. 9-103.

here, with no attempt to cover all possible situations and details. Furthermore, it should be noted that if one or more states which have not adopted the Code are involved, it will be necessary for a secured party or assignee to check the law (legislative and decisional) of such other states, in addition to satisfying the Code rule.

Accounts Receivable. The state where an assignor maintains his accounting records is the state whose law governs the protection of an assignee's interest.

To repeat the warning of the last paragraph: Even if an assignor is located in a Code state, if he does business in some state or is incorporated in some state which has not adopted the Code, it may be necessary for the assignee to check the law of that other state.

Titled Goods. This term refers to goods such as motor vehicles for which certificates of title are issued under governmental auspices. As to such goods, the Code provides:

> . . . if personal property is covered by a certificate of title issued under a statute of this state or any other jurisdiction which requires indication on a certificate of title of any security interest in the property as a condition of perfection [that is, protection against innocent third persons], then the perfection is governed by the law of the jurisdiction which issued the certificate.

Mobile Equipment and Mobile For-Hire Inventory. Equipment and for-hire inventory (meaning inventory which is held for business leasing to others) are classed as "mobile" if they are the type of goods which are normally used in more than one state. The most common example is machinery used for road building, construction, or commercial harvesting. Trucks and other motor vehicles are also included if titled in a state which does not require a notation of a security interest on a certificate of title. For such goods, protection of a security interest is governed by the law of the state in which the obligor has his chief place of business. (To repeat the prior warning: if an obligor is sending a power shovel into a state which has not adopted the Code, the secured party will want to check the law of that state to be assured that his security interest is protected.)

Other Incoming Encumbered Goods. This classification pertains primarily to goods which do not come under either of the two preceding classifications. For convenience in this discussion, the state in which a security interest first arises will be called the "export state" and the state into which the goods are taken, the "import state." When goods which come under this classification are moved into another state, then:

1. If at the time the security interest arose, the secured party and the obligor both contemplated removal to the import state and the goods are

imported within thirty days, any protection of the security interest will be governed by the law of the import state.

2. If both parties did not contemplate removal to another state when the security interest arose, the law of the export state will govern protection of the security interest for the period of four months after the goods are moved to the import state; after the four-month period, the law of the import state will govern protection of the security interest.

Part 7 PROCEEDS REALIZED FROM COLLATERAL[55]

The following are two commonly occurring fact situations:

Situation Number 1. An obligor owed a dealer $500 on an open account, the dealer assigned the account to an assignee, and the latter filed a financing statement pertaining to the assignment. Thereafter a creditor obtained a $1,000 judgment against the dealer, and then:

1. *Before* the obligor made any payment on the account, the judgment creditor had an attachment paper served on the obligor, attempting to attach the $500 obligation.

As discussed in Part 4 of this chapter, the assignee would be protected by the financing statement and would have a right, superior to that of the attaching creditor, to collect from the obligor the $500 due on the assigned account.

2. Instead of Part 1 above, assume that before the judgment creditor made any move against the obligor, the latter, not instructed otherwise, paid the dealer-assignor the $500 due on the account, and the dealer deposited the payment in his bank account. After this payment was made, the judgment creditor attempted to attach the dealer's bank account which contained this $500 deposit and nothing more. *Question*: Should the assignee's interest in the account receivable, protected as it is by the financing statement, carry over and also give the assignee priority as to the proceeds realized from the assigned account?

Situation Number 2. A secured party held a security interest in TV sets which were in a dealer's possession as part of his inventory, and the secured party's interest was protected by an appropriate financing statement. The dealer sold and delivered one of the TV sets to a buyer who signed chattel paper promising to pay the dealer $500 at stated times and acknowledging that a security interest would remain in the dealer until the full price was paid. Thereafter a creditor obtained a $1,000 judgment against the dealer and had an attachment paper served on the buyer, attempting to attach the $500 obligation which the buyer owed to the dealer. *Question:* Should the secured party's interest in inventory, protected by the financing statement, carry over and also give the secured party a priority interest in the buyer's obligation evidenced by the chattel paper?

[55] U.C.C. 9-306.

In approaching such questions as these, the Code first of all defines and classifies proceeds in the following way:

> "Proceeds" includes whatever is received when collateral or proceeds is sold, exchanged, collected or otherwise disposed of. . . . Money, checks and the like are "cash proceeds". All other proceeds are "non-cash proceeds".

The Code then prescribes rules to cover various possible situations. To repeat the warning frequently given in the present chapter, no attempt is made here to discuss all of the details of the Code or to cover all possible fact situations for which the Code prescribes rules. The *overall* picture which the Code presents in respect to proceeds realized from secured or assigned interests consists of a general rule, followed by several special rules which apply particuarly to insolvency proceedings, to chattel paper proceeds from sales of inventory, and to returned or repossessed items.

GENERAL RULE

Certainly for a secured party or an assignee to have any basis at all for claiming a priority interest in proceeds, he will have to prove that the proceeds he claims actually came from the goods, account, or chattel paper in which the secured party or assignee held an interest. This may be quite difficult, if the secured party or assignee's interest covers only a limited number of goods or accounts. On the other hand, if a secured party has a security interest in *all* of a dealer's inventory, and if the dealer's only source of income is the sale of inventory, tracing or identifying the source of proceeds will obviously be quite easy.

In general, if proceeds can be identified as having come from the item (goods, account, chattel paper, etc.) in which the secured party or assignee held a protected interest, the secured party or assignee's interest carries over to such proceeds and continues for a period of nine days after the proceeds are received by the obligor or assignor. On the tenth day the secured party or assignee will lose his priority unless the original financing statement expressly states that it includes proceeds, or unless the secured party or assignee takes additional action to protect his interest in proceeds—usually either by filing another appropriate financing statement or by taking possession of the proceeds.

Example: Refer back to Part 2 of Situation Number 1 (page 621). If the creditor's attachment of the dealer's bank account occurred within the first nine days after the dealer received the $500 payment from the obligor, then as between the assignee and the attaching creditor, the assignee would have a superior interest in the $500. If on the other hand the creditor's attachment was made ten or more days after the dealer received the $500 payment, then

a) Assume that the filed financing statement read: "This financing statement covers the following type of property: Accounts." As between the assignee and the attaching creditor, the latter would have a superior interest to the bank account containing the $500.

b) Assume that the filed financing statement read: "This financing statement covers the following types of property: Accounts and Proceeds therefrom." Now, as between the assignee and attaching creditor, the assignee would have the superior interest.

The question asked in Situation number 2 on page 621 would be answered in the same way.

SPECIAL RULES

INSOLVENCY PROCEEDINGS

In the example just discussed the dispute was between an assignee and the assignor's attaching creditor. If a dispute over the right to proceeds involves an assignee or secured party on one side and, on the other side, a receiver (or other representative of creditors) appointed by a court in an insolvency proceeding, the authors of the Code feel that for bank accounts it is better policy to follow a different rule. For indentifiable noncash proceeds, and for indentifiable cash proceeds not commingled with other money or deposited in a bank, the previously discussed general rule will apply. In regard to bank accounts, a secured party or assignee with a protected interest in proceeds will have a priority claim on the account itself (regardless of the source of the money in the account) up to the amount of proceeds actually received within ten days before institution of the insolvency proceeding—less, however, the amount of proceeds received during that period and already paid over to the secured party or assignee.

Example: A dealer assigned all of his existing and future accounts receivable to an assignee, and the assignee filed a financing statement covering "accounts and proceeds therefrom." On June 1 the dealer received a $1,000 payment on one of the accounts receivable and deposited the money in First Bank. This was the only deposit the dealer ever made in First Bank. On June 15 the dealer received a $2,000 payment on another account and deposited the money in Second Bank. On June 16, on a check drawn by the dealer, Second Bank paid out $1,500 of the $2,000 deposit. On June 17 the dealer received a loan of $3,000 from his uncle and deposited this money in Second Bank. On June 20 a court proceeding was begun against the dealer, he was adjudged insolvent, and a receiver was appointed. The First Bank account had a balance of $500, all that was left of the $1,000 deposited by the dealer on June 1, and the Second Bank account had a balance of $3,500 ($500 left from the June 15 deposit of $2,000, plus the later deposit of $3,000). Assume that during the ten days preceding June 20, the dealer made no payments to the assignee.

Although the money in the First Bank checking account was identifiable as proceeds from an assigned account receivable, the assignee would (probably[56]) have no preferred claim to this amount. However, the assignee would have a priority claim to $2,000 of the Second Bank account, although only $500 represented proceeds.

CHATTEL-PAPER PROCEEDS FROM INVENTORY SALES

The Code states:

> A purchaser of chattel paper who gives new value and takes possession of it in the ordinary course of his business has priority over a security interest in chattel paper which is claimed merely as proceeds of inventory subject to a security interest . . . even though he knows that the specific paper is subject to the security interest.[57]

This provision recognizes that under some financing arrangements, a bank (or other financing institution) intends to finance a dealer's inventory only and will permit him to transfer his chattel paper to some other institution if he so wishes. Such an arrangement, however, is not common. As Carl W. Funk points out:

> Most banks will not lend money to a dealer on a floor plan basis [that is, for inventory financing] unless they also handle his chattel paper. Those that are willing to limit themselves to his inventory can protect themselves only by making certain that new goods to which their security interest attaches go into the dealer's stock as rapidly as sales are made, or that their loans are reduced by payments on account as the dealer's inventory is sold.[58]

Example: First Bank was financing a dealer's inventory of TV sets under an agreement which gave the bank a security interest in the TV sets. To protect its interest, First Bank filed a financing statement covering "TV sets and proceeds therefrom." Later the dealer sold and delivered one of the TV sets to a customer who signed chattel paper to evidence his obligation to pay the price of $500. The dealer then assigned and delivered the chattel paper to Second Bank for value.

Under the above-quoted Code rule, as between First Bank and Second Bank, the latter would have the better right to collect the $500 from the customer. Second Bank would be preferred even though it was actually aware of First Bank's interest in the dealer's inventory and knew of the financing statement covering inventory and proceeds.

---

[56] Such a conclusion is reached by Carl W. Funk in *Banks and the Uniform Commercial Code* (Philadelphia: Philadelphia Clearing House Association, 1962).

[57] U.C.C. Sec. 9-308.

[58] Funk, *op. cit.*, fn. 56, p. 67.

On the other hand, if the security agreement between the dealer and First Bank stated that the bank's collateral was to include not only the TV sets but also chattel paper, then First Bank as an assignee of chattel paper would have priority over the later assignee who received the paper with knowledge of the First Bank's interest.

DEALER REOBTAINING POSSESSION

Sometimes, after a dealer sells and delivers an item of inventory in which a secured party has an interest, the dealer later reacquires possession and ownership of the sold item, either through the buyer returning and canceling his purchase, or the dealer repossessing. Two of the most common fact situations can be classified as follows:

1. Assume that there is no outstanding chattel paper received by the dealer as a proceed from the sale. The secured party's interest will reattach to the item.

2. Assume that the dealer received chattel paper upon sale of the item and assigned the chattel paper to an assignee who was not the same person as the secured party. Since the assignee's interest is superior to any interest the secured party may claim as to chattel paper proceeds, the assignee will also have a superior interest in the goods when reacquired by the dealer.

PROBLEMS

1. a) Carter loaned Davis $1,000, and Davis signed the following note and gave it to Carter, together with the stock certificate described in the note:

> New York, N.Y. [Date]
> One year after date I promise to pay to the order of C. Carter $1,000 with interest. To secure payment of this note I have hereto attached as collateral security a certificate for 15 shares of $100 par value common stock of the Porter Manufacturing Company of Chicago, Ill., and hereby authorize the holder hereof, on default of this note, to sell said collateral.
>
> (signed) D. Davis

The market value of the 15 shares of stock was $2,000 when the note was signed, $1,500 two months before the due date, $1,100 on the due date, and $500 four months after the due date. At all times there was a ready market for Porter Company stock at the market price. D failed to pay the note when it came due and four months later C sold the stock for its then market value and sued D for the balance of the obligation. What result?

b) Same facts as in Part (a) plus the following: Two months before the due date, D requested C to sell the stock immediately since the market price was declining. C agreed to do so but did not make the sale until four months after the due date. Would this additional fact affect the outcome of the lawsuit of C against D? Explain.

c) Same facts is in Part (b) except that the due date was the date of D's request and C's agreement. Answer the same question asked in Part (b).

d) Same facts as in Part (c) plus the following: When D signed the note, C orally agreed that he would sell the stock at any time upon D's request if the proceeds would be sufficient to pay the debt. Answer the same questions asked in Part (c).

2. On June 1 B, an appliance dealer, ordered 20 refrigerators of a specified model from S, to be shipped by motor truck, f.o.b. shipping point, the purchase price of $2,000 to be paid within 60 days. On June 3 S shipped the described refrigerators by the T Truck Company, receiving a straight bill of lading naming B as consignee, which S mailed to B. On June 4 B borrowed $1,600 from the First Bank, delivered the T Company bill of lading to the bank, and signed and gave the Bank an agreement promising to repay the loan on demand and giving the First Bank a security interest in the described 20 refrigerators until the loan was repaid. On June 5 when T Company notified B of arrival of the refrigerators, B directed that they be stored in the T Company warehouse and received from T Company a nonnegotiable warehouse receipt. On June 6 B borrowed $1,500 from the Second Bank, delivered the T Company warehouse receipt to the Second Bank, and signed and gave the bank an agreement promising to repay the loan on demand and giving the Second Bank a security interest in the described 20 refrigerators until the loan was repaid. On June 7 B applied to the Third Bank for a $1,400 loan, offering to give a security interest in the stored 20 refrigerators as collateral security for the loan. After verifying that the refrigerators were stored in the warehouse, the Third Bank made the loan to B, and B signed and gave to Third Bank an agreement promising to repay the loan to Third Bank on demand and giving Third Bank a security interest in the described 20 refrigerators. Third Bank promptly notified T Company of the security transaction which was the first T Company knew of B's transactions with any bank concerning the 20 refrigerators. On June 10, upon petition by some of B's creditors, the court adjudged B insolvent and appointed a receiver to take over all of B's assets. B absconded, and on June 12 B's receiver and the three banks for the first time learned of B's transactions with the others. The receiver, the three banks, and S each claimed the 20 refrigerators still in the T Company's warehouse. What result?

3. By written contract a dealer agreed to sell to a customer a large refrigerator for $1,200, which amount the customer agreed to pay in stated installments, title to remain in the dealer until the full price was paid. After the customer paid a total of $700, he failed to make further contract payments and, after giving proper notice, the dealer resold the refrigerator elsewhere, realizing the amount stated below, exclusive of costs.

a) Assume that when the customer defaulted, the dealer, as provided by the agreement, was still in possession of the refrigerator. What would be the rights of the parties if the resale netted 1) $800; 2) $300? Explain.

b) Assume that the customer had possession of the refrigerator when he defaulted and that the dealer repossessed the refrigerator. What would be the rights of the parties if the resale netted 1) $800; 2) $300? Explain.

4. On October 1 an obligor borrowed $1,500 from a bank and signed and gave the bank a written agreement promising to repay the bank in three months with 6 percent interest, and giving the bank security interests in a described TV set and a described freezer. On December 26 the obligor sold and delivered the TV set to a buyer who paid the obligor fair value in full. The buyer's purpose in buying and his knowledge of the bank's interest were as stated below. On December 26 a creditor with a $1,000 judgment against the obligor had the sheriff levy on the freezer in the obligor's possession. In the questions below, assume that a sheriff's sale under the levy had not yet been held, that at the time of the levy, the creditor had *no* actual knowledge of the bank's security interest, and that the obligor paid nothing on his obligation to the bank. On December 27 the bank first learned of the obligor's selling the TV set and of the creditor's attaching the freezer.

a) As he told the bank he would, the obligor used the money the same day it was borrowed to buy and pay for in full the TV set and freezer described in the agreement. 1) Assume that from October 1 to December 26, as the bank knew, the two units were installed in the obligor's home and used by the obligor and his family. (a) The bank did not file a financing statement pertaining to its transaction with the obligor. Answer the following questions: (1) Assume that the buyer bought and used the TV set for his own personal home enjoyment, without having knowledge of the bank's interest. As between the bank and the buyer, which had the superior interest in the TV set? Explain. (2) Assume that the buyer bought and installed the TV set in his barber shop, for business use, without having knowledge of the bank's interest. As between the bank and the buyer, which had a superior interest in the TV set? Explain. (3) As between the bank and the attaching creditor, which had a superior interest in the freezer? Explain. (b) On October 1 the bank filed a financing statement pertaining to its transaction with the obligor. Answer the following questions: (1) Assume that the buyer who bought from the obligor, bought and used the TV set for his own personal home enjoyment, without having knowledge of the bank's interest. As between the bank and the buyer, which had a superior interest in the TV set? Explain. (2) As between the bank and the attaching creditor, which had a superior interest in the freezer? Explain. 2) Assume that from October 1 to December 26, as the bank knew, the two units were new, unused merchandise, displayed in the obligor's retail appliance store for sale to customers. (a) The bank did not file a financing statement pertaining to its transaction with the obligor. As between the bank and the attaching creditor, which had a superior interest in the freezer? Explain. (b) On October 1 the bank filed a financing statement pertaining to its transaction with the obligor. Answer the following questions: (1) Assume that the buyer who bought from the obligor bought and installed the TV set in his barber shop, for business use, *without* having knowledge of the bank's interest. As between the bank and the buyer, which had a superior interest in the TV set? Explain. (2) Assume that the buyer bought from the obligor and installed the TV set in his barber shop, for business use, *with* knowledge of the bank's interest at the time he bought. As between the bank and the buyer, which had a superior interest in the TV set? Explain. (3) As between the bank and the attaching creditor, which had a superior interest in the freezer? Explain. 3) Assume that from October 1 to December 26, as the bank knew, the two units were installed in and used in the operation of the obligor's restaurant. The bank did not file a financing statement pertaining to its transaction with the obligor. Answer the following questions: (a) Assume that the buyer bought from the obligor and installed the TV set in his barber shop, for business use, without having knowledge of the bank's interest. As between the bank and the buyer, which had a superior interest in the TV set? Explain. (b) As between the bank and attaching creditor, which had a superior interest in the freezer? Explain.

b) As he told the bank he would, the obligor used the borrowed money for a vacation trip. Before giving security interests to the bank, the obligor owned clear title to the TV set and the freezer described in the agreement. From October 1 to December 26, as the bank knew, the two units were installed in the obligor's home and used by the obligor and his family. Answer the following questions: 1) the bank did not file a financing statement pertaining to its transaction with the obligor. As between the bank and the attaching creditor, which had a superior interest in the freezer? Explain. 2) On October 1, the bank filed a financing statement pertaining to its transaction with the obligor. As between the bank and the attaching creditor, which had a superior interest in the freezer? Explain.

5. Pursuant to written orders, without any other written agreement, a manufacturer shipped goods to various buyers on 60-days' credit. On June 1, three separate buyers, A, B, and C, each owed the manufacturer $500 for goods thus received, their obligations all being due July 15. On June 1 by written assignment the manufacturer sold the claims against A and B to First Bank for value in the ordinary course of business. On June 2 the manufacturer by written assignment sold the claim against C to Second Bank for value in the ordinary course of business. First Bank immediately filed a financing statement pertaining to the transaction; Second Bank did not file any statement. Notices of the assignments with directions to pay to the respective banks were given to B and C on June 2 and to A on July 17.

a) On July 15 the obligors paid their obligations in full, making payment to the manufacturer. The manufacturer failed to turn over to the banks the money received, and on July 17 the banks sued the obligors to collect. 1) Could First Bank recover from A? Explain. 2) Could First Bank recover from B? Explain. 3) Could Second Bank recover from C? Explain.

b) The goods shipped by the manufacturer to A and to B were not of contract quality and were reasonably worth to A and to B only one-half the contract price. A and B each gave proper notice of the defective quality and of his decision to retain the goods and to pay only as legally obliged, A giving the manufacturer such notice on June 5, and B giving such notice to the manufacturer and to First Bank on June 6. On July 17 neither A nor B having paid anything, First Bank sued each for $500. How much could the bank recover 1) from A; 2) from B? Explain.

6. On June 1 S. Smith, a manufacturer sold and delivered a freezer case to a retailer, B. Brown. When installed in B's store, the case did not become a part of the real estate. Nothing was said between the parties as to title or security interest. Of the $450 purchase price, B paid $50 down and orally agreed to pay the balance by July 15. On June 1 S assigned the obligation to a bank by the writing quoted below, which was delivered to the bank.

a) The assignment read as follows: "[Date]. For $395 paid me, receipt of which is hereby acknowledged, I hereby sell, assign, and transfer to the Centerville National Bank all my right and interest to the $400 obligation owed to me by B. Brown, which is payable July 15 of this year. (signed) S. Smith." On June 1 the bank notified B of the assignment and directed him to pay the bank. By July 20 B had not paid any portion of the $400. 1) On July 20 did the bank have a legal right to repossess the freezer case? Explain. 2) On July 20 did the bank have a legal right to collect money from B, and if so, how much? Explain. 3) On July 20 did the bank have a legal right to collect money from S, and if so, how much? Explain.

b) The assignment read as follows: "[Date]. On July 15 of this year, for value received, I hereby promise to pay to the Centerville National Bank $400. As collateral security for this note, I hereby assign and transfer to the bank all my right and interest to the $400 obligation owed to me by B. Brown, which is payable July 15 of this year. (signed) S. Smith." By July 20, neither B nor S had paid any portion of the obligations, and the bank notified B of the assignment and directed him to pay the bank. 1) On July 20, did the bank have a legal right to repossess the freezer case? Explain. 2) On July 20, did the bank have a legal right to collect money from S, and if so, how much? Explain.

c) The assignment read as follows: "[Date]. For $395 paid to me receipt of which is hereby acknowledged, I hereby sell, assign, and transfer to the Centerville National Bank, all my right and interest to the $400 obligation owed to me by B. Brown, which is payable July 15 of this year, and guaranty payment thereof. (signed) S. Smith." On June 1 the bank notified B of the assignment and directed him to pay the bank. By July 20 B had not paid any portion of the $400. Answer the same questions asked in Part (b) above.

7. In separate transactions a manufacturer sold and shipped certain goods to A and certain other goods to B. The only written evidence of the contract with A consisted of an order form signed by A, describing the goods and agreeing to pay the price of $500 in sixty days. The order form said nothing as to title or interest in the goods. The transaction with B was evidenced by a contract form signed by the manufacturer and B, describing the goods, and stating that B would pay $600 in sixty days and that a security interest in the goods would remain in the manufacturer until full payment of the price. Assume that the manufacturer filed financing statements, if necessary, to protect his rights. A few days after entering into the two transactions, the

manufacturer in writing sold and transferred to First Bank the manufacturer's rights under the two contracts, and, with the assignments, delivered to First Bank the order form signed by A and the contract form signed by the manufacturer and B. First Bank purchased the claims for fair value, in ordinary course of its business, but did *not* file a financing statement pertaining to the transfer of either claim. In answering the following questions, assume that neither A nor B has yet paid anything on either obligation.

A month after the transfers to First Bank, the manufacturer was adjudged insolvent and a receiver was appointed who took over all the manufacturer's assets. 1) Assume that the same day that the claims were transferred to First Bank, A and B each received a notice of transfer with direction to pay First Bank. As between First Bank and the receiver, which would have a superior interest in the claim against A; in the claim against B? Explain. 2) Assume that no notice of the transfers was given to A or to B until after the receiver was appointed. Answer the same question asked in Part (1) above.

b) A month after the transfers to First Bank, the manufacturer wrongfully signed a separate agreement selling and transferring to Second Bank the manufacturer's claims against A and B. Second Bank entered into the agreement in ordinary course of its business, for fair value and without knowledge of the prior assignments of the same claims to First Bank. Second Bank immediately filed financing statements pertaining to the transfers. One month after the transfers to Second Bank A and B for the first time each received a notice of the transfer to Second Bank with direction to pay Second Bank. 1) Assume that the same day the claims were transferred to First Bank, A and B each received a notice of transfer with direction to pay First Bank. As between First Bank and Second Bank, which would have a superior interest in the claim against A; in the claim against B? Explain. 2) Assume that no notice of the transfers to First Bank was given to A or B until one week following the transfers to Second Bank. Answer the same questions asked in Part (1) above.

8. A manufacturer of paper products entered into a written contract with a distributor of such products for the sale by the manufacturer and purchase by the distributor of the entire output of the manufacturer's plant for one year. Since, regardless of the size of paper to be ultimately shipped, the paper would first be produced in large rolls of uniform size, the parties agreed that the contract price be a stated sum for each such roll, payable twenty days after billing date. The other details of the contract provided as follows: as the manufacture of each large roll of paper was completed, it would be stored on the premises in the manufacturer's warehouse; the manufacturer would contract for fire insurance on the paper as stored, the insurance being payable to the distributor; the manufacturer would bill the distributor for the paper as stored and for the fire insurance premiums; later as the distributor would receive orders from customers for paper of certain sizes, the distributor would send the orders to the manufacturer who would remove from his warehouse a sufficient number of large rolls to fill the orders, cut and package the paper as required in the orders, ship to the customers

named in the orders, and bill the distributor for the freight charges. After the parties operated under this contract for nine months, the manufacturer was adjudged insolvent and a receiver was appointed to take over and liquidate all of the manufacturer's assets. Up to that time the manufacturer had produced paper for which the distributor had paid the manufacturer $36,000. Of this paper, $5,000 worth had already been cut, packaged, and shipped to various of the distributor's customers. Another $1,800 worth of paper was in the manufacturer's plant, cut, packaged, and ready for shipment to one of the distributor's customers, and the remaining $29,200 worth of paper was still in large rolls in the manufacturer's warehouse. Since the distributor had already paid for all of the paper on the premises, he demanded the paper from the receiver.

a) Who had title to the $1,800 worth of paper; to the $29,200 worth? Explain.

b) If title was still in the manufacturer, would the distributor have a right to obtain possession of the paper from the receiver? Explain.

c) If title was in the distributor, would he have a right to obtain possession from the receiver? Explain.

d) Would field warehousing be a desirable plan for the manufacturer and distributor to have followed? Explain.

e) What would be the best plan for the parties to have followed? Explain.

chapter 19

Survey of Unsecured Creditors' Rights and Bankruptcy Proceedings

RESTRICTIONS ON CREDITORS' COLLECTIONS

As noted in the preceding chapter, the usual legal remedy of an unsecured creditor consists of suing and obtaining a judgment against the debtor. If the debtor ignores the judgment, the creditor will usually, as his next step, attempt to realize on the judgment by an attachment proceeding—that is, by having the sheriff levy on and sell various items of the debtor's property. However, it is not always sound public policy for a creditor to be able to collect immediately or completely everything that may be owed to him. For a number of reasons the overall interests of society require that certain restrictions be placed on attachment and collection proceedings. Some of these reasons include the following:

1. A sheriff's auction sale is a forced sale, as distinguished from a voluntary sale between parties who are free to bargain as to price and refuse to deal at all if either is dissatisfied with the other's proposal. Therefore prices bid at sheriffs' sales will frequently be substantially less than the actual value of the items being sold.

2. The services of a debtor's employees contribute directly to the value of his assets. Thus when a creditor attaches and takes a debtor's assets, he is to some extent appropriating the benefit of the employees' services. If the employees have not been paid for their recent services, it becomes somewhat unfair for society to permit a creditor to appropriate the debtor's assets entirely for himself.

3. If a creditor is permitted either literally or figuratively to "take the shirt off his debtor's back," the debtor may be rendered completely destitute and become a burden on public charity. When this happens, a creditor is not collecting from his debtor alone, he is also collecting from society as a whole—to the extent that public charity and relief must then be given to the debtor and his dependents. This certainly gives society a voice in saying just how much a creditor should be permitted to collect.

Of course, society also has an interest in creditors being able to collect promptly all that is owed to them. When this interest is outweighed by the undesirable results threatened by a particular collection, society places restraints on the collection process. Thus all states have statutory or constitutional provisions limiting the rights of creditors to realize on certain property interests. The principal limitations include the following:

1. Delay provisions, which sometimes force a creditor to wait a certain period of time after the maturity of an obligation or after obtaining a judgment, thus giving the debtor some additional time within which to make payment.

2. Exemption provisions, exempting certain of a debtor's property from creditors' claims.

3. Priority provisions, giving certain other claimants priority over the claim of the attaching creditor who first initiates the collection proceeding.

DELAY PROVISIONS

The general scope and details of delay provisions vary widely. Some states, for example, permit a debtor to obtain a short delay from attachment if he owns real estate or gives other court-approved security for eventual payment of the creditor's judgment. Federal statute provides for a delay when a debtor's being called into military service drastically reduces his income and thus interferes with his ability to pay his debts.

EXEMPTION PROVISIONS

Many states give a blanket exemption covering all real or personal property belonging to a debtor, up to a certain (fairly low) statutory value, for example, $300 in Pennsylvania. In addition, various statutes declare certain particular property interests wholly or partially exempt from the claims of creditors. Some of the principal types of property which are exempt in some (but not all) states, include the following:

1. Wearing apparel of the debtor and his family. Statutes in the various states differ widely, some states including all apparel, some states apparel up to a certain value, and some states apparel which can be classed as necessary.

2. Bibles and school books in use in the debtor's family.

3. Unpaid wages and salaries of laborers or employees. In states which have this exemption, some exempt all unpaid wages and salaries, some only a stated amount or percentage.

4. The debtor's life insurance, especially if the named beneficiary is the debtor's wife, child, or other dependent relative. States which give this exemption frequently do so even though a policy gives the insured debtor a right to change the beneficiary.

5. Various other specified property interests which are considered vital to the welfare of a debtor and his family, including, for example

(but varying among the states), certain specified trade tools, certain specified household furnishings, and sometimes even the debtor's homestead.

PRIORITY PROVISIONS

Generally the creditor who first has a certain item of a debtor's property attached will thereby obtain priority over other creditors in realizing his claim from the attached property. However, statutes frequently give certain classes of creditors (especially landlords and employees) priority over an attaching creditor.

Example: The only assets of D, the proprietor of a small department store, consisted of personal property. D borrowed $1,000 from a bank and signed a promissory note for its repayment. When the note came due and was not paid, the bank obtained a judgment against D for $1,200 (the debt, interest, and costs) and had D's store assets attached and sold by the sheriff. Claims filed with the sheriff prior to the sale, in addition to the $1,200 judgment, were: $800 owed to the landlord for overdue rent on the store premises at the rate of $50 per month; $500 owed to a manufacturer on open account for goods sold to D on credit; $750 owed to D's employee for unpaid wages at the rate of $250 per month. Also prior to the sale D filed a claim for his statutory exemption. The sheriff's sale netted $2,000.

The distribution of the $2,000 would vary according to the statutes of the different states. Under Pennsylvania statutes, for example, the $2,000 would be distributed as follows:

$2,000
− 300—to D as his debtor's exemption
$1,700
− 200—to the employee, this being the limit of his statutory priority
$1,500
− 600—to the landlord, this being the limit of his statutory priority
$ 900—to the bank as the attaching creditor

Note two points illustrated here:

1. The creditor who initiates a collection proceeding and attaches assets exceeding in value the amount of his claim will not always be paid in full, after exemption and priority statutes are applied.

2. An attachment and sheriff's sale is one creditor's individual collection proceeding. Except for priority claimants, no other creditor can dip into the proceeds. Only if this were an insolvency or bankruptcy proceeding could other unsecured, unpreferred creditors (like the manufacturer with his $500 claim) be able to obtain a proportional share in the distribution.

FRAUDULENT CONVEYANCES

Although a person has substantial assets, he is nevertheless classed as insolvent if he is unable to pay his debts as they come due. Insolvent debtors have often been tempted to conceal some of their assets to save them from creditors' attachments. From an early date in England, as law and commerce developed, the courts and legislatures have condemned such attempts to defraud creditors. Proof of actual intent to defraud creditors is often difficult. However in almost any type of fact situation, it is fair to presume that a person intends the usual or probable consequences of what he does. Based upon this assumption, rules of law have developed concerning fraudulent conveyances. Many of these rules of law have been codified by the Uniform Fraudulent Conveyance Act, which has been adopted in a number of states.

DEFINITION OF FRAUDULENT CONVEYANCES

Every transfer or conveyance which is injurious to a creditor at the time it is made, and which is made with an *actual* intent to hinder, delay, or defraud creditors, is fraudulent.

Without regard to actual intent, every transfer or conveyance made without fair consideration is fraudulent:

1. As to existing creditors, if the transferor is insolvent, is thereby rendered insolvent, or has been involved in an incident which will probably result in liability greater than his remaining assets; or

2. As to existing and future creditors, if the transferor is about to engage in an undertaking for which his remaining assets are unreasonably small.

REMEDIES OF CREDITORS

If the fraudulently transferred assets are not in the possession of an innocent purchaser who has paid full value, a creditor can:

1. Bring an action to have the transfer canceled; or

2. Have the sheriff levy on or attach the transferred assets as though there had been no transfer.

If the transferee has disposed of the fraudulently transferred assets to an innocent purchaser for full value, the transferor's creditor can hold the immediate transferee liable for the net value of the fraudulently transferred assets.

BANKRUPTCY PROCEEDINGS

The chronology of a typical, liquidation-type bankruptcy proceeding can be summarized as follows:

1. A petition is filed against a debtor and the court adjudges him bankrupt. If necessary, a receiver is appointed to take temporary custody of the debtor's assets.

2. The debtor files lists of his assets and of his debts.

3. The creditors are notified of the bankruptcy adjudication.

4. The creditors then, or sometime within the next six months, file claims for the money owed to them by the debtor.

5. With the approval of court the creditors select a person (or corporation) to serve as the trustee in bankruptcy.

6. The trustee liquidates the debtor's assets, and makes distribution to the creditors.

7. The proceeding is terminated and the debtor is discharged from the unpaid balance of most of his debts.

Adjudication of Bankruptcy

As indicated above, a bankruptcy proceeding begins with the filing of a petition in the appropriate Federal district court which has territorial jurisdiction over the debtor. The petition alleges certain facts and requests the court to declare or adjudge that the debtor is bankrupt.

In a *voluntary* proceeding, the debtor is the petitioner. He need not allege or prove insolvency. All that is required is that the petitioning debtor owe a debt, and be the type of debtor eligible for voluntary bankruptcy. For a bankruptcy liquidation proceeding (as distinguished from a corporate reorganization proceeding) any person or organization may become a voluntary bankrupt, except a municipal, railroad, insurance, banking, or building and loan corporation.

An *involuntary* bankruptcy proceeding does not require the debtor's consent. If the proper facts are proven, the defendant-debtor can be forced into a bankruptcy proceeding even over his vigorous objections. A liquidation type of proceeding can be initiated 1) against any natural person (that is, an actual person as distinguished from a corporation) except a wage earner whose compensation does not exceed $1,500 a year, or a farmer, or 2) against any moneyed or business corporation except those not eligible for voluntary bankruptcy. For a debtor to be adjudged an involuntary bankrupt, all of the following facts must be alleged in the petition and either admitted by the debtor or proved in court:

1. That the debtor has debts of $1,000 or more.

2. That the creditor or group of creditors filing the petition has a substantial interest in the debtor's financial affairs. If the debtor has less than twelve creditors, one creditor with an unsecured claim of at least $500 is sufficient. If the debtor has twelve or more creditors, three creditors with unsecured claims totaling altogether at least $500 must join in the petition.

3. That a fact situation exists (called an *act of bankruptcy*) which threatens possible injury to creditors or which otherwise makes a bank-

ruptcy proceeding desirable, if the proper number of creditors so wish. Insolvency does not of itself justify adjudging a person an involuntary bankrupt. Involuntary bankruptcy will be adjudged if, within the four-month period preceding the date of the petition, any one of the following occurred: 1) the debtor made a fraudulent conveyance and is insolvent on the petition date; 2) while insolvent, the debtor made a preferential transfer; 3) through court action or by landlord's distraint, a creditor obtained a lien against any assets of the insolvent debtor; 4) the debtor made a general assignment of assets for the benefit of his creditors; 5) a state court appointed a receiver for the assets of the insolvent debtor; 6) the debtor stated in writing his inability to pay his debts as they matured *and* his willingness to be adjudged bankrupt.

Insolvency as defined in the Bankruptcy Act is an ingredient of the first, second, and third acts of bankruptcy; insolvency in either the bankruptcy or the equity sense is necessary for the fifth act of bankruptcy. A debtor is insolvent in the bankruptcy sense if the total of his assets at a fair valuation is less than the total of his debts. This is sometimes called a "balance sheet" definition. For other than bankruptcy proceedings, the customary (equity) meaning of insolvency is inability to pay debts as they mature. Since a forced sale frequently brings less than fair value, it is possible for a debtor to be insolvent in the equity sense and still not bankrupt insolvent.

The term "transfer" used in the first and second acts of bankruptcy includes: 1) the debtor's transferring title to any of his property interests (either real or personal, including intangible property interests such as accounts receivable); and also 2) the debtor's granting or agreeing to a lien or security interest in any of such property interests. For example, if a buyer purchasing goods on credit agrees to his seller's retaining a security interest in the purchased property, the buyer is making a "transfer" of a security interest in the purchased goods.

Fraudulent Transfers

Since most of the provisions of the Uniform Fraudulent Conveyance Act are written into the Bankruptcy Act, any transfer defined as fraudulent under the Uniform Act is fraudulent under the Bankruptcy Act.

In addition, a debtor's transfer (of title or security interest) is fraudulent even if the transferee pays fair value, if the transferor 1) is insolvent, and 2) makes the transfer a) within the four-month period preceding the petition date, b) in contemplation of liquidation (either voluntary or involuntary) of all or a majority of his assets, and c) with the intent known to the transferee to use the consideration received from the transfer to make a preferential payment to a creditor.

It is not fraudulent for a debtor to realize on or take advantage of the exemptions which the legislature of his state feels it is sound policy for him to have. Therefore, a debtor's use of nonexempt money (or other property) to buy exempt property is not of itself fraudulent, even if done shortly before a bankruptcy proceeding initiated by the debtor himself or anticipated by him. For the transfer to be fraudulent, additional facts showing the debtor's bad faith would have to be proved, such as the debtor secretly accumulating assets to make the purchase and then purchasing more than a reasonable amount of exempt property.

If an insolvent debtor gives away *exempt property* (upon which his creditors could not have levied anyway) his transfer is *not* fraudulent. Thus, in a state recognizing tenancies by entireties, if an insolvent husband joins with his critically ill wife in transferring entireties property without consideration, the husband's creditors cannot successfully charge him with fraud, either then or a short time later when the wife dies. On the other hand, if a husband, the sole owner of a home (or of any other real or personal property) transfers title to himself and his wife as tenants by entireties, at a time when the husband is insolvent or is thereby made insolvent, the transfer is fraudulent since not for fair value, and the property remains subject to the claims of the husband's creditors. A different question is raised if the husband is solvent when the entireties title is created, but is insolvent when he later makes payments on the home (or other property). Valid arguments can be made on either side of the question (compare Chapter 10). It is understandable, therefore, that in the few states in which the question has been litigated (chiefly Pennsylvania and Michigan) the courts have reached opposite conclusions. In Pennsylvania, the status of the property is determined by the husband's financial condition at the time the entireties title is created. If the husband is solvent then, the property is immune from the claims of his individual creditors even though he is insolvent when he makes payments. Since the Bankruptcy Act contains its own fraudulent conveyance provisions, however, a Federal court is not bound to follow either the Pennsylvania or the Michigan view.

Preferential Transfers

The most commonly alleged act of bankruptcy is that the debtor made a preferential transfer. A debtor's transfer (of title or of a security interest) is preferential if all of the following features are present:

1. It is made within the four-month period preceding the petition date;

2. It is made on account of a preexisting debt;

3. The debtor is insolvent;

4. The transfer will enable the transferee-creditor to obtain a greater percentage of his debt than some other creditor of the same class.

If a buyer purchases and pays for goods on delivery, he is not making a preferential transfer even if he is insolvent at the time. His assets are not depleted, but merely changed from one type (money) to another type (goods) of equal value. On the other hand, if a buyer purchases and receives goods *on credit,* his debt arises at the time of the purchase, so that later, when he makes the agreed payment, he is paying a preexisting obligation. Even if the buyer is insolvent and makes the deferred payment within the four-month period, his payment is not a preferential transfer unless the fourth feature (listed above) is also present. If in the original contract the seller retained title or a security interest until the price was paid, then the buyer's later payment is not a preferential transfer. In exchange for his payment, the buyer receives title or a release of the seller's security interest. Like the cash purchase, this is value for value and does not deplete assets available for other creditors. On the other hand, if the purchase was made on open account, or if otherwise the buyer received full, unencumbered possession and title when he contracted to pay, then his later payment would be a preferential transfer.

Certain types of property transactions are not effective against innocent third persons until recorded or filed. If a debtor borrows and signs a security agreement in which he 1) promises to repay the loan and 2) gives a security interest in certain described property to assure his payment, clearly the security agreement is given for present consideration. If, however, the applicable state law requires such a security interest to be recorded or filed, and the secured party delays in filing, there are two possible theories as to when the transfer is made: 1) the transfer of the security interest is made on the agreement date (that is, when the agreement is signed and given to the creditor), and, therefore, is given for a present consideration; 2) the transfer is made on the filing date (that is, when the security agreement is recorded or filed) and since the obligation is in existence from the date of the agreement, the transfer should be classified as being made for a preexisting obligation. The Bankruptcy Act adopts the latter theory, but to make the rule reasonable and workable, allows the secured party a period of grace for filing. State filing statutes sometimes allow a period of grace. Under such statutes, a filing any time within the specified period relates back and is effective as if filed on the agreement date. The provisions of the Bankruptcy Act may be summarized in the following manner.

If the applicable state statute requires filing (to protect a real estate interest against a subsequent innocent purchaser for value, or to protect an interest other than real estate against a subsequent lien creditor), then:

1. If the state statute allows a period of grace for filing, not exceeding twenty-one days,

a) A security agreement filed within the specified grace period is effective from the agreement date; b) A security agreement filed after expiration of the grace period is effective from the filing date.

2. If the state statute allows a period of grace longer than twenty-one days, or does not provide any grace period,

a) A security agreement filed within twenty-one days is effective from the agreement date;

b) A security agreement filed more than twenty-one days after the agreement date is effective from the filing date.

Note that the Uniform Commercial Code[1] gives a grace period of ten days for purchase money security interests in goods.

THE BANKRUPT ESTATE

In a liquidation type of bankruptcy proceeding, the person appointed as trustee in bankruptcy takes over the assets of the bankrupt, converts them into cash, and under supervision of the court distributes the proceeds among creditors. The total property interests which the trustee has a right to take are frequently referred to as the *bankrupt estate*. In general:

1. The trustee is vested with all rights and remedies which, on the petition date,

a) Are vested in the bankrupt; and also

b) Would be vested in a creditor obtaining a lien on the petition date, whether or not such a creditor actually exists.

2. Any transfer or lien is void as to the trustee if, under applicable state law, it is fraudulent as to or voidable by any actual creditor of the bankrupt.

Example: On June 1 a barber purchased a TV set for use in his barber shop, and signed an agreement with the dealer promising to pay a stated price and giving the dealer a security interest in the set until the full price was paid. On August 1 one of the barber's judgment creditors, unaware of the dealer's interest, had the TV set levied on. On August 2 the dealer filed a financing statement pertaining to his assignment. On petition filed August 5, the barber was adjudged bankrupt. The barber had been insolvent within the meaning of the Bankruptcy Act since July 1, but there was no evidence that on August 2 the dealer had any reason to know of the barber's insolvency. The dealer, the attaching creditor, and the trustee each claimed a superior interest in the TV set which had not yet been sold under the creditor's attachment.

[1] U.C.C. Sec. 9-301.

The relative rights of the three claimants can be summarized in the following manner, and are further explained in the succeeding paragraphs.

1. The trustee would have all of the barber's rights. However, as between the dealer and the barber, the dealer's lien was valid from the date of the agreement.

2. The trustee would have the rights of a creditor obtaining a lien on the petition date. Since the dealer had filed his interest before that date, the dealer's lien would be valid against a creditor obtaining a lien on the petition date.

3. Although the dealer's lien constituted a preferential transfer made on August 2 (and therefore would qualify as an act of bankruptcy), it would not be a *voidable* preference, in the absence of evidence that the dealer on that date had reason to know of the barber's insolvency.

4. The TV set would be classified as equipment and filing would be necessary to protect the security interest against later attaching creditors. Since the dealer failed to file before the attachment (on August 1), the dealer's lien would be invalid as to the attaching creditor—and, therefore, would be void as to the trustee. This would eliminate the dealer as a secured claimant.

5. Since the lien of the attaching creditor was obtained within the four-month period preceding the petition date and at a time when the barber was insolvent., this lien would in turn be invalid as to the trustee.

Result: The trustee would take the TV set free from all liens. Both the dealer and the attaching creditor would be relegated to the status of general creditors.

Exempt Property

Whatever property interests are exempt from creditors' claims under the law of the bankrupt's state are also exempt in the bankruptcy proceeding. Of course, exempt property set aside at the bankrupt's request would be subject to the claim of any creditor with whom the bankrupt had made a valid waiver of exemptions.

Property Interest Owned by the Bankrupt

Entireties Property. In many states, assets which are properly held by a husband and wife as tenants by the entireties, cannot be effectively levied on by a creditor with a claim against only one of the co-owners. Therefore such assets would not become a part of the bankrupt estate of only one of the co-owners—unless the creation of the entireties title itself involved a fraudulent conveyance.

Encumbered Property. If on the petition date, an item of the bankrupt's property is subject to a valid lien, the lienholder is entitled to realize his claim fully from that property. Only the balance remaining after the lienholder's full satisfaction would become a part of the bankrupt estate. Liens which are *not* valid against the trustee include the following:

1) As to a Judgment Lien. A judgment lien is not valid 1) if obtained within the four-month period preceding the petition date, *and* 2) if the bankrupt was insolvent when the lien was obtained. Whether or not the creditor obtaining the lien was aware of the bankrupt's insolvency would be immaterial.

2) As to a Security Interest Lien (a mortgage or other security interest given by the bankrupt to secure his promise to pay an obligation). Such a lien is not valid against the trustee:

a) If it constitutes a fraudulent transfer or a preferential transfer made under the circumstances discussed below (see "Fraudulently Transferred Property" and "Preferentially Transferred Property"); or

b) If it would be inferior to the claim of a creditor obtaining a lien on the petition date (whether or not such a creditor actually exists is immaterial); or

c) If it is fraudulent or voidable as to an actual lien creditor. For example, suppose that between the time a debtor gave a $10,000 non-purchase money real estate mortgage to a bank and the time the bank recorded the mortgage, another creditor, while unaware of the mortgage, obtained a $500 judgment lien against the mortgaged property. Since the mortgage lien would be ineffective as to the judgment lien, the mortgage lien would be completely canceled as to the trustee. The real estate would come into the bankrupt estate subject only to the $500 judgment lien. If the judgment lien was obtained within the prior four months and at a time when the debtor was insolvent, the judgment lien would also be invalid as to the bankrupt estate. This would not prevent the trustee's using the judgment lien to invalidate the mortgage lien. The court would order that the judgment lien be preserved for the benefit of the bankrupt estate, and the trustee would take the place of the judgment lienholder.

Fraudulently Transferred Property

A fraudulent transfer made by the bankrupt within the one-year period preceding the petition date is voidable, and the trustee can recover the transferred property (or its value) from the transferee. The trustee can avoid a fraudulent transfer made earlier than this one-year period if a creditor obtaining a lien on the petition date could do so under the applicable state law.

Preferentially Transferred Property

If a transfer of property is a preferential transfer under the Bankruptcy Act *and also* if, when the transfer becomes effective, the transferee has reasonable cause to believe that the transferor is insolvent, the trustee can recover the property or its value from the transferee—less, however, the amount of any new unsecured credit the transferee extends to the transferor upon receiving the preference or afterwards.

Claims of the Bankrupt Against Others

A bankrupt's assets frequently include rights to collect money (or other property) from other persons. Except for nonassignable claims (for example, certain personal tort claims), all claims held by the bankrupt on the petition date, whether matured or not, are automatically assigned to the trustee and become part of the bankrupt estate. As is true with any assignee, the trustee's right to collect from the bankrupt's obligors is subject to defenses or claims which the obligors have against the bankrupt—with, however, some limitation on an obligor's right of set-off.

Set-off. Sometimes an obligor who owes money to the bankrupt, also has a claim against the bankrupt arising from some other transaction entered into by the bankrupt either with the obligor himself or with some other person who then assigns his rights to the obligor. The possible fact situations can be classified as follows:

1) Transaction Between Bankrupt and Obligor. If the obligor's claim against the bankrupt arises from a transaction between the obligor and the bankrupt, the date of the transaction in relation to the petition date, the bankrupt's financial status on the transaction date, and the obligor's knowledge or belief as to the bankrupt's status are all immaterial. The only requirement is that a claim used as a set-off be provable in the bankruptcy proceeding. Even an unmatured, contingent claim can be used as a set-off and the obligor would be required to pay to the bankrupt estate only the difference, if any.

2) Transaction Between Bankrupt and Obligor's Assignor. If the claim held by the obligor arises from a transaction between the bankrupt and some third person who has assigned his right to the obligor, the obligor cannot use the claim as a set-off if he acquired the claim 1) within the four-month period preceding the petition date, and 2) with knowledge of the bankrupt's insolvency or act of bankruptcy.

Life Insurance. A bankrupt's right to cash in his life insurance policy is an asset belonging to the bankrupt. In most states, however, certain life insurance policies are exempt from creditors' claims. As previously noted, the exemptions provided by the law of the state in which the bankrupt resides apply in the bankruptcy proceeding. If a bankrupt has life insurance which is not exempt, the cash surrender value as of the petition date becomes part of the bankrupt estate. The bankrupt is permitted to keep the policy alive by paying to the trustee an amount equal to the cash surrender value. In order to to this, the bankrupt is sometimes able to raise the required money by borrowing (from the insurance company) on the policy itself.

After-Acquired Property

Generally property interests which a bankrupt acquires after the petition date do not become a part of his bankrupt estate. However, suppose that an insolvent debtor, who knows that he is the principal beneficiary of his wealthy uncle's will, learns that his uncle has suffered a stroke and is in a coma. The debtor might be tempted to hurry and file a voluntary petition in bankruptcy before his uncle dies, so that the property he is to inherit will be immune from the claims of his creditors. To prevent a person from thus taking unfair advantage of the bankruptcy law, the statute provides that certain property interests which vest in a bankrupt within six months *after* the petition date will nevertheless pass to the trustee as part of the bankrupt estate. The most important of such interests are:

1. Property interests inherited by the bankrupt; and
2. Entireties property interests held by the bankrupt and spouse on the petition date, and which, within the six-month period, become transferable solely by the bankrupt—for example, upon the death of the bankrupt's spouse, or upon divorce which under the law of most states converts a tenancy by entireties into a tenancy in common.

PROVABLE CLAIMS

Creditors who are entitled to file claims and share in the distribution of the bankrupt estate include:

1. Persons holding matured and definite claims.
2. Persons holding definite claims "absolutely owing at the time of the filing of the petition by or against him [the debtor], whether then payable or not, with any interest thereon which would have been recoverable at that date or with a rebate of interest upon such as were not then payable and did not bear interest. . . ."[2]
3. Persons holding claims on open account or on any other contract, express or implied.
4. Persons holding contingent contractual claims, if the amount

---

[2] Bankruptcy Act, Sec. 63a.

of the claim can be satisfactorily determined or estimated without unduly delaying the bankruptcy proceeding.

DISTRIBUTION OF ASSETS

The order in which assets are paid to claimants is prescribed by the Bankruptcy Act. In general, claims are paid in the following order:

1. The costs of the bankruptcy proceeding.

2. Wages (not including the salary of managerial or supervisory employees) accruing within the three months preceding the petition date, but not exceeding $600 for each claimant.

3. Taxes owed by the bankrupt to any taxing authority.

4. Debts owed to the United States Government, and the claim of the bankrupt's landlord (providing state law would give the landlord priority in a state insolvency proceeding) for rent for not more than the three months preceding the petition date.

5. General creditors.

DISCHARGE IN BANKRUPTCY

The general theory of the Bankruptcy Act is that the petition date signifies the end of the bankrupt's former financial life and the start of a new financial life. In general, therefore (except as previously noted for inheritances and the like within six months after the petition date), any property which a bankrupt acquires after the petition date will be immune from the claims of most of his former creditors.

To obtain a discharge in bankruptcy, a debtor must show good faith. For any of several reasons (including dishonest dealings, refusal to cooperate in the bankruptcy proceeding, a previous discharge within the prior six years) a debtor will be refused a discharge in the bankruptcy proceeding. If so, his former debts will all continue as collectible obligations.

Even when a debtor is discharged in bankruptcy, certain obligations remain, including taxes, wages accruing during the three months preceding the petition date, and damages for any willful and malicious tort. These obligations continue to be enforceable against the debtor.

PROBLEMS

1. A manufacturer of printing machinery sold and delivered a printing press for $35,000, and the buyer, a printer, signed a promissory note for that amount, agreeing to pay $1,000 on the first of each month thereafter until the full $35,000 was paid. Although saying nothing about title or security interest the note did state, "This note is given for the purchase price of a printing press Model 123, Serial Number 4567." After almost two and a half years

of making the agreed payments, the printer had paid $28,000, leaving a balance of $7,000 still to be paid in the succeeding seven months. At that time the printer entered into a contract to sell and deliver the press to a purchaser for $25,000, delivery to be made in two weeks, payment to be made by the purchaser to the printer at the rate of $500 per month. Learning of this contract before the printer delivered the press to the purchaser, the manufacturer sued the printer for an injunction restraining him from disposing of the press until the remainder of the $35,000 note was paid in full. In the lawsuit the manufacturer proved that the press was the major part of the printer's equipment. What would be the result of the lawsuit?

2. The City Traction and Transit Company was organized and incorporated in 1920 to (as stated in the charter) "own, maintain, and operate a public transit system, by means of electric street cars and/or other suitable means of public conveyance, to construct and maintain street railway tracks, to construct and maintain waiting and information sheds and booths, and to do all other things reasonably associated with owning, maintaining, and operating a public conveyance system in [the specified city]." Up to the present time, under appropriate state Utility Commission permits, the company has been the only public conveyance system operating in that city. In 1930 the company began replacing some of the street cars with motor buses; by 1940 the company had completely converted to the use of buses and had removed all street car tracks from the streets. For the past several years the company has sustained a net operating loss. Some of the directors are considering possible corporate reorganization plans, but the directors have not yet reached a decision and nothing has yet been done to accomplish any reorganization. One group of creditors opposes any reorganization plan and files a petition to have the company adjudged bankrupt. Three unsecured creditors with claims totaling $5,000 join in the petition alleging and proving insolvency, debts in excess of $50,000 and several acts of bankruptcy (namely preferential payments) within the prior four months. Should the company be adjudged bankrupt? Explain.

3. D owned and operated a retail clothing store. On July 13 S, one of D's regular suppliers, received from D an order for various described goods for $400, at the usual terms of net in 30 days, 2 percent off in 10 days. A prior order in the amount of $800 at the same terms had been shipped by S to D on the previous January 23, and was not yet paid for. Upon receiving the July 13 order, S obtained from Dun & Bradstreet a report stating that various of D's suppliers had complained of their accounts (totaling $3,200) being three and more months overdue. After some correspondence with D, S shipped the July 13 order on July 27, upon D's payment of $800 plus one-half of the price of the July 13 order. From then on, the few purchases that D made were from suppliers other than the ones with whom he usually dealt and were all c.o.d. On the following October 7 three of D's creditors, with claims totaling $3,000, filed a petition to have D adjudged bankrupt. The evidence showed the above facts and further that D had been insolvent within the meaning of the Bankruptcy Act since the beginning of February of that year. On the above facts alone, would D be adjudged bankrupt? Explain.

4. On April 1 S sold and delivered certain goods to B for $800, payable in three months. By the following July 15 S was still unpaid, several requests for payment having gone unanswered. On that date S obtained from Dun & Bradstreet a credit report on B which stated: 1) that B had a total of seven creditors (other than S); 2) that five of them had complained of accounts being from two to four months overdue and still unpaid; 3) that another creditor with a two-month overdue claim of $500 had, by threatening lawsuit, finally obtained payment in full on June 1; and 4) that this was the only payment B had made on any obligation since May 1. S thereupon had his lawyer write demanding payment and threatening lawsuit. On July 24, in a replying letter, B wrote, "I am unable to pay S's account now. However, market conditions in my business are improving, and I know I shall be able to pay all my outstanding accounts in about a month." B was unable to make any payments to any of the eight creditors and on October 11 S filed a petition to have B adjudged bankrupt. S proved the above facts, and also proved that B's total debts were $5,000 and that B had been insolvent in the bankruptcy sense since May 1 of that year. Would the court adjudge B bankrupt? Explain.

5. D obtained a $20,000 policy of life insurance and named a grandson as beneficiary, reserving the right to change the beneficiary. D later became a bankrupt and the trustee desired to obtain the cash surrender value of the policy for the benefit of creditors. Could he do so? Explain. (Modified from A.I.C.P.A., Nov. 51-12:3.)

6. D, owner and operator of a small business, became insolvent through the ruthless competition of three large concerns, and was forced into bankruptcy. D had not yet received a discharge in bankruptcy when the following incident occurred.

a) Two months after D was adjudged bankrupt, he received $10,000 from his rich uncle with the note: "I had intended to give you this in my will, but I've just heard of your business misfortune and figure you have more use for it now." The trustee claimed the $10,000. What result?

b) Two months after D was adjudged bankrupt, his rich uncle died, leaving a will with a bequest of $10,000 to D. The trustee claimed the $10,000. What result?

7. Refer to Problem 3. Assume that B was adjudged a voluntary bankrupt on a petition filed October 7. What right would the trustee have against S? Explain.

8. Refer to Problem 4. Assume that B was adjudged a voluntary bankrupt on a petition filed October 11. What right would the trustee have against the creditor who was paid $500 on June 1? Explain.

9. D owned a store building in which he carried on a retail appliance business. D sustained financial reverses, became insolvent in the bankruptcy sense on May 1, remained insolvent thereafter, and was adjudged a voluntary bankrupt on a petition filed October 20.

a) On June 1 S, one of D's regular suppliers, received from D an order for certain TV sets for $400 on the usual terms of 2/10 net 30. At this time S had reason to believe that D was insolvent. 1) S refused to sell to D except for cash. D agreed and on June 24, S delivered the TV sets to D, and D paid S the agreed $400. What right would the trustee have against S? Explain. 2) S refused to sell to D without some security. D agreed and on the date stated below S delivered the TV sets to D, and D dated, signed, and gave S a writing promising to pay S $400 in 30 days and stating that a security interest in the described TV sets would remain in S until the full price was paid. When D was adjudged bankrupt, he had not paid S and still had in stock in his store the TV sets received from S. (a) The security agreement was dated June 2. S filed a financing statement the same day. As between the trustee and S who would have superior interest in the described TV sets? Explain. (b) The security agreement was dated July 5. S filed a financing statement the same day. Answer the same question as in (a) above. (c) The security agreement was dated June 2. S filed a financing statement on July 5. Answer the same question as in (a) above.

b) On April 15 S, one of D's regular suppliers delivered certain TV sets to D for $400 payable 2/10 net 30. When D did not pay, S sued and obtained a judgment against D. 1) S obtained the judgment against D on June 10, but did nothing further. After the bankruptcy adjudication of October 20, what would be the status of this judgment if, when S obtained the judgment, (a) he had no reason to know that D was insolvent? (b) he knew that D was insolvent? Explain. 2) S obtained the judgment against D on June 24, but did nothing further. Same additional facts as immediately above. Answer the same questions.

10. D owned and operated a small plant manufacturing industrial chemicals. D was a better chemist than business executive, and his business became hopelessly insolvent. A $2,000 note signed by D came due; the bank owning the note obtained judgment, and threatened a levy unless D paid promptly. D had a good chance to obtain an excellent job with a large chemical manufacturer and decided to liquidate his business. However, fearful of jeopardizing his job opportunity, he did not want his business forced to close for several months. He explained the entire situation to F, his father-in-law. At F's suggestion, F loaned D the $2,000 necessary to pay the bank, and D gave F a demand note secured by a written statement giving F a security interest in certain described movable equipment. F promptly filed a financing statement pertaining to his interest, and D paid the bank in full on its claim. One week later another creditor learned of the payment to the bank, initiated a bankruptcy action, and D was adjudged an involuntary bankrupt. There was no clear proof that the bank had reason to know of D's insolvency at the time D paid the note. The trustee sought to have F's security interest in the equipment declared of no effect. What result?

11. D borrowed $1,000 from C, signing and giving C a note promising to repay within two years with interest at the rate of 6 percent per year. At the time of the loan G signed the note as guarantor. Six months later, G was adjudged bankrupt. Could C file a claim against G's bankrupt estate, and if so, for how much? Explain.

12. You are setting up the accounts for R who is operating a retail business. He is desirous of having all true liabilities shown. He recently received a discharge in bankruptcy but the following proved claims were unpaid, because of lack of funds. Which of them, if any, would you consider to be enforceable claims against his new estate? Determine whether "enforceable," "not enforceable," or "partially enforceable." If "partially enforceable" determine for what amount.

a) Sales tax of $1,500 owed to the state.

b) A judgment of $3,500 in favor of P for injuries received because of R's negligent operation of his business auto for business purposes.

c) A judgment of $800 in favor of B for damages suffered from R's fraudulent misrepresentation inducing B to purchase goods from R.

d) A judgment of $4,000 against R in favor of C for breach of a sales contract through failure to deliver goods.

e) Claims of $1,000 each by X and Y for wages earned within three months immediately prior to bankruptcy. (Modified from A.I.C.P.A., May 50-9a.)

13. A bankrupt's employee earning $300 per month had not been paid for the five months preceding the bankruptcy adjudication. The employee claimed and received the amount to which he was entitled as a priority payment, and claimed the balance of what was owed him as a general creditor. Each general creditor received 10 percent of his filed claim. After the debtor received a bankruptcy discharge, would the employee still have an enforceable claim against the debtor, and if so, for how much? Explain.

14. (Assume that all of the given dates are for the same year.) On April 1, a manufacturer sold to an oil refiner certain portable machinery. According to the written agreement (chattel paper) the refiner was to pay $4,000 in six months, and title to the machinery was to remain in the manufacturer until the full price was paid. On the following day, the manufacturer by written instrument assigned to a bank all chattel paper on hand or thereafter acquired. The fact of assignment was noted on the chattel paper but, pursuant to the arrangement between the manufacturer and the bank, the manufacturer retained possession of the chattel paper, and no notice of the fact of assignment was given either publicly or to the refiner. About three weeks later the manufacturer ordered a quantity of oil products from the refiner in the amount of $1,000 payable in sixty days. The refiner's routine credit inquiry disclosed that the manufacturer became insolvent in the bankruptcy sense around the middle of April. The manufacturer remained insolvent thereafter. Nevertheless, on April 30 the refiner delivered oil products as ordered for $1,000 payable in sixty days. Thereafter the refiner purchased the following claims held by various creditors against the manufacturer: 1) On May 15 an $800 claim due on July 1, for which the refiner paid $400; 2) On May 30 a $1,000 claim due on July 1, for which the refiner paid $400; 3) On June 15 a $900 claim due on August 1, for which the refiner paid $300; 4) On July 15 a $1,000 overdue claim for which refiner paid $300. On September 25 the bank learned of the manufacturer's insolvency. The bank thereupon promptly filed a financing statement pertaining to its interest in chattel paper held by the manufacturer, and gave to each chattel paper obligor (including the refiner) personal notice of the bank's interest. On petition filed October 3 the manufacturer was adjudged a voluntary bankrupt. None of the above mentioned claims were paid. Both the bank and the trustee tried to collect from the refiner, and the refiner in turn filed a claim again the bankrupt estate. Assume that upon final settlement the bankrupt estate would pay 10 percent to all general claimants entitled to share. As to the above claims, who would collect how much from whom? Explain.

15. On February 1 D borrowed $1,000 from C, and signed and gave to C a one-month note for that amount with interest at the rate of 6 percent per year. The note contained the following provision: "I hereby waive the benefits of the present and any future bankrupt law that may be passed by the United States." On the following April 1 D was adjudged bankrupt. In final settlement of the bankruptcy proceeding all general creditors, including C, received 10 percent on their filed claims, and D received a discharge in bankruptcy. Seven months after completion of the bankruptcy proceeding, D inherited a large sum of money. C thereupon sought to collect the balance of the note from D, and upon D's refusal to pay, sued D.

a) How much, if anything, could C collect? Explain.

b) Other facts remaining the same, assume that one month after completion of the bankruptcy proceeding, D orally promised C that he would pay C the balance of the note within six months. How much, if anything, could C collect in his lawsuit against D? Explain.

book *V*

Survey of Basic Property Principles

chapter 20

Real Estate

Part 1 CONTRACTS TO SELL REAL ESTATE

Under the statutes of frauds in the various states, a contract to sell real estate is not fully enforceable against the seller unless sufficiently evidenced by a writing signed by the seller or by his agent whose authority is in writing.

As soon as an enforceable agreement to sell real estate is entered into, a property interest in the described real estate passes to and vests in the buyer. Since legal title is still vested in the seller, the property interest which vests in the buyer is frequently referred to as an *equitable* title or ownership. The exact nature of the respective legal and equitable interests varies somewhat among the states. In many states:

1. Sufficient real estate interest vests in the buyer so that, after formation of the contract but before its performance (that is, before transfer of legal title to the buyer):

a) Should either or both parties die, the seller's interest passes to his personal property heirs, the buyer's interest to his real estate heirs.

b) Should either or both parties marry, the seller's newly acquired spouse has no potential dower (or curtesy) interest in the property. In many states, the buyer's newly acquired spouse likewise has no potential dower (or curtesy) interest, until the buyer obtains full legal title.

c) Should the property be accidentally damaged or destroyed through no fault of either party, the loss falls on the buyer. Any casualty insurance the seller may be carrying is held for the benefit of the buyer.

d) Should a judgment be entered against the buyer, the judgment creditor obtains a lien against the property in the amount of purchase price paid at that time. This lien, like any other judgment lien, will continue for the statutory period and then expire unless the judgment creditor renews the judgment on the record.

2. Sufficient real estate interest remains in the seller so that, in the absence of an express agreement to the contrary, the seller's right either to possession or to rents and profits continues until the seller transfers full legal title to the buyer.

Usually the transfer of any interest in land becomes effective:

1. As between the parties—when the transfer agreement is entered into;

2. As to a later third person (acquiring an interest for value without actual knowledge of the prior interest)—when something is done on the land (for example, the transferee assuming exclusive and readily apparent occupancy of the land) or on the public record affecting land titles, sufficient to give notice of the first transferee's interest.

The practice in many states is for most land-purchase contracts to be performed within a fairly short time; therefore, they are usually not recorded. However, if the buyer pays a substantial sum before he is to receive legal title under the contract, or if the buyer distrusts the seller's honesty or solvency, the buyer should consult his lawyer about having the land-purchase contract recorded, especially if the buyer is not immediately assuming exclusive and readily apparent occupancy of the land.

Part 2   TRANSFERS OF TITLE

A transfer of the legal title to real estate is accomplished by a written instrument called a "deed."

A sale of real estate does not always include a warranty or guaranty of title by the seller. This differs from the law regarding sales of goods. Through his act of selling *goods*, a seller is considered as impliedly warranting that he is transferring clear title to the buyer. No such warranty is implied from the act of transferring *land*. If a warranty of title is to accompany the transfer of land, it must arise from appropriate language expressly used in the deed. The deed may expressly state the terms of a warranty, or may instead contain language which some statute declares gives rise to a warranty.

A warranty to defend title is the most common warranty used in modern real estate conveyancing. There are two types of such warranties, general and special.

General Warranty. A standard form of this warranty commonly used in some states reads:

> And the said grantor, his heirs, executors and administrators, does hereby covenant and agree to and with the said grantee, his heirs and assigns, that the said grantor, his heirs and assigns, all the above, together with the above mentioned and described premises, unto the said grantee, his heirs and assigns, against the said grantor and his heirs and assigns, and against all and every other person or persons whomsoever lawfully claiming or to claim the same shall and will warrant and forever defend by these presents.

Special Warranty. A standard form reads as above with the last few lines changed to read, ". . . person or persons whomsoever lawfully claiming or to claim the same by, through, or under him, shall and will warrant and forever defend by these presents."

By making this promise to warrant and defend, the grantor promises to pay for any loss suffered by the grantee or any later owner of the property, as a result of a prior claim which arose,

1. (Special warranty) while the grantor owned the property; or
2. (General warranty) while the grantor owned the property and also at any time before the grantor owned the property.

Statutes in some states provide that if a deed uses the word "grant" or the word "convey," either word is considered as stating what amounts to a special warranty.

If a deed states no express warranty, and does not include a statutory equivalent of a warranty, then no warranty accompanies the transfer of the property. A common form for a deed making no warranty at all (commonly called a "quitclaim deed") reads in part:

> The said grantor, for and in consideration of the sum of One Dollar lawful money of the United States, to him in hand paid by the said grantee, at and before the ensealing and delivery of these presents, the payment and receipt whereof is hereby acknowledged, has remised, released, and quit claimed, and by these presents does remise, release, and quit claim unto the said grantee and to his heirs and assigns forever, all that certain piece of land situated in the City of _____, County of _____, in the State of _____, more particularly described as follows: . . ."

A grantee should promptly record his deed, in order to protect his interest against third persons who deal with the grantor in the justified belief that the grantor still owns the property.

Part 3   REAL ESTATE LIENS

A "lien" is a claim held by one person against the property or property interest of another person. The most important liens which may exist against real estate are: 1) mortgage liens, 2) judgment liens, and 3) mechanics' liens.

MORTGAGE AND JUDGMENT LIENS

MORTGAGE DEFINED

A creditor desiring security for payment of an obligation may obtain from his debtor ownership, title, or a security interest in certain of the debtor's property until the obligation is paid. Generally in such an arrangement the parties intend that the debtor remain in possession at least until he defaults under the obligation. Such a transfer or pledge of title as security for an obligation is a *mortgage*. A *chattel mortgage* is a security interest in personal property, and is covered by the Uniform Commercial Code (see Chapter 18). When the term "mortgage" is used alone, it usually refers to a real estate mortgage.

Mortgages may be classified as *purchase money* and *nonpurchase money*. A purchase-money mortgage secures credit extended to enable the debtor to purchase the property which is the subject of the mortgage. A purchase-money mortgage usually has certain priorities over other liens.

The document forms used in a mortgage transaction vary in different states. In some states, forms similar to those developed at early common law are still used. The common-law instruments are the result of early common-law history, and nowadays are not considered by the courts as meaning literally what they say. A cardinal rule for many modern lawyers in drafting legal papers is to write exactly, clearly, and briefly what is meant. The common-law mortgage forms disregard this rule entirely. Nevertheless, since the forms have been working satisfactorily for hundreds of years (over which time they have been thoroughly litigated), and since procedural statutes have been drafted according to these forms, a practicing lawyer has very little inducement to attempt to simplify them on his own initiative.

The common-law forms for a mortagage transaction consist of two instruments. One evidences the obligation and is usually called the "bond" or "judgment bond." The other instrument, termed the "mortgage," creates a security interest in the real estate which is the subject of the mortgage transaction. The mortgage instrument is recorded to protect the security interest of the mortgage holder.

The common-law bond and mortgage forms for a $5,000, five year, 6 percent mortgage may be briefly outlined as follows. (It should be emphasized that these are only *outlines*; the forms in actual use are considerably longer and contain a number of additional provisions not included or referred to here. Note that, as is the practice in some states, the bond is for double the actual amount of the mortgage debt.)

BOND

D. Davis, as debtor, is bound to C. Carter, as creditor, in the sum of $10,000, signed and sealed this date.

The condition of this obligation is that if the debtor shall pay to the creditor, five years from date, the sum of $5,000 together with interest at the rate of 6 percent per year, then this bond shall cease and be forever void; otherwise it shall remain in full force and effect.

[A confession of judgment provision is usually included in states where valid.]

(signed) D. Davis SEAL

MORTGAGE

Whereas D. Davis, as debtor, by bond of this date is bound to C. Carter, as creditor, in the sum of $10,000, conditioned for the payment five years from date of $5,000 together with interest at the rate of 6 percent per year.

In consideration of and to secure said debt, the debtor grants and conveys to the creditor the following described land: [then is written a description of the mortgaged land, copied from the debtor's deed]

Provided nevertheless that if the debtor pay the creditor according to the conditions of the above mentioned bond, then these presents shall cease and be null and void.

(signed) D. Davis SEAL

DURATION OF LIEN

In general, a mortgage lien becomes effective between the parties as soon as they sign their agreement to that effect, and remains effective until barred by a statute of limitations. As to a third person who acquires an interest in a piece of land without actual knowledge of a prior mortgage, the mortgage is usually effective only from the date it is recorded. A properly recorded mortgage lien usually continues effective as to the mortgaged land until the mortgage holder receives payment or agrees to release that land from the mortgage lien. On the other hand, while a judgment lien also becomes effective from the date entered on the record, it will continue as an effective lien for only a limited time—namely the statutory period (for example five years in Pennsylvania)—after which it expires as a lien unless renewed on the record. Usually, if renewed before expiration of the statutory period, the lien continues from the time originally obtained; if renewed after expiration of that period, the lien is effective only from the date of renewal. This limited span of life refers to the judgment's *lien* on real estate. Usually no statute of limitations applies to the judgment itself; it continues as a collectible obligation until paid.

MULTIPLE LIENS

If a mortgage is already on record when a judgment becomes a lien against the debtor's real estates, the judgment is, of course, secondary in claim to the mortgage. The mortgage-holder has the right to realize on his lien unhampered by the judgment, while any attempt by the judgment creditor to realize on his judgment will be subject to the prior mortgage. A sheriff's sale on a prior lien will divest (that is, remove as a claim against the property) any later lien against the real estate (except real estate taxes which usually remain liens until paid). In most states, a sheriff's sale on a later lien will not affect a prior lien.

Remedies of Mortgage Holder

State statutes prescribe the remedies available to the creditor when the debtor fails to pay his mortgage obligation. Usually a creditor has one or more of three possible remedies:

1. Sometimes a creditor has the right to obtain possession or control of the mortgaged premises. The creditor then applies the net rents and profits to the mortgage debt and when the obligation is fully paid, restores the property to the debtor.

2. The creditor can obtain a judgment against the debtor on the obligation which the mortgage secures, that is, on the note or bond. Once the creditor obtains a judgment he may proceed like any other judgment creditor with a levy and sheriff's sale. The judgment is a lien on the mortgaged property from the effective date of the mortgage lien, and is a lien on other realty owned by the debtor in that county from the date the judgment is obtained.

3. The creditor can foreclose the mortgage. He does this by suing and obtaining a judgment for foreclosure which is then followed by a sheriff's sale of the mortgaged property. This is a limited type of judgment, effective as to the mortgaged property only; entry of judgment for foreclosure does not give the creditor a lien or right to levy on any other of the debtor's property. After the mortgaged property is sold at sheriff's sale, the debtor's interest in the property is completely cut off (foreclosed). If the foreclosure sheriff's sale fails to realize the full amount of the mortgage obligation, the creditor can usually still avail himself of the second remedy described above.

Deficiency Judgment Statutes

A sheriff's attachment and sale under any real estate lien results in the sale of the attached property to the highest bidder, regardless of how small the bid is. Therefore, the attaching creditor should be present or represented at the sheriff's sale to prevent another person's buying the property for too low a price. Since the proceeds from the sale (after payment of taxes and costs—and employees if entitled to priority) are paid to the attaching creditor, up to the amount of his claim, the creditor can bid up to that amount and (with the above exceptions) not have to make an actual payment. If no other bids are received, the creditor can buy the property for taxes and costs and the sale will be recorded as yielding nothing toward satisfaction of the creditor's judgment. Many states have statutes affording a debtor some protection against an overly greedy creditor. Such statutes usually apply when the judgment creditor, who initiates an attachment and sheriff's sale of his debtor's real estate, bids for and buys the property himself for less than the amount of his judgment. Under some statutes, the creditor's judgment is nevertheless considered fully paid and satisfied unless within a certain time (e.g., six months) after the sale, the creditor initiates a proceeding to have the court determine and declare the fair value of the realty as of the time of sale to the creditor. Although the sheriff's sale did not actually realize the amount of the court-declared fair value, this amount will be credited to the judgment. If the fair value is less than the amount of the judgment, the creditor may proceed with a levy and sheriff's sale to collect from other of the debtor's property. If the fair value equals the amount of the judgment, the creditor's judgment is considered fully paid and satisfied. If the court-declared fair value exceeds the amount of the judgment, the creditor usually has no obligation to pay the amount of the overage to the debtor since such an excess was not actually realized at the sheriff's sale.

TRANSFER OF MORTGAGED PROPERTY

Title Acquired by Grantee

When a debtor sells property upon which there is a properly recorded mortgage, the title acquired by the grantee is subject to the mortgage. That the grantee has no personal knowledge of the mortgage is immaterial.

Liability of Grantee

Especially if the mortgaged property has depreciated so that upon foreclosure it does not realize the amount of the obligation, a question may arise as to whether the creditor can recover the deficiency from the grantee. The answer depends upon the contract between the debtor and the grantee, which is usually evidenced by the type of mortgage-reference provision contained in the deed. The two principal types of mortgage-reference provisions are 1) a statement that the transfer is subject to the mortgage, and 2) a statement that not only is the transfer subject to the mortgage but also that the grantee is assuming and agreeing to pay the mortgage. The usual effect of such provisions can be summarized as follows:

1. If the grantee expressly assumes personal liability:

a) *Right of the creditor against the grantee.* The creditor, as a third party beneficiary of the debtor-grantee contract, can recover the full amount of the obligation from the grantee.

b) *Right of the creditor against the debtor.* The mortgage is security for an obligation personally incurred by the debtor, and no matter what happens to the mortgaged property, the debtor remains liable until the creditor receives full payment for the obligation, or until the creditor (by a legally enforceable agreement) expressly releases the debtor. As with the assignment of contracts generally (see Chapter 10), a delegation to the grantee of the duty of performance does not release the original obligor even though the creditor acquires the alternative right to collect from the grantee.

c) *Right of the debtor against the grantee.* Whatever amount of the mortgage obligation the debtor is forced to pay, the debtor can in turn recover from the grantee by virtue of their agreement.

2. If the grantee does not expressly assume personal liability:

a) *Right of the creditor against the grantee.* The grantee has no personal liability to the creditor.

b) *Right of the creditor against the debtor.* As explained above, the debtor's personal obligation to the creditor is not affected by whether or not the grantee assumes the mortgage obligation.

c) *Right of the debtor against the grantee.* Even though the grantee does not expressly assume the obligation (and therefore incurs no personal liability to the creditor), if the debtor and grantee take the amount of the mortgage obligation into account and deduct it in determining the selling price, the grantee has an implied obligation to reimburse the debtor for whatever of the mortgage obligation the creditor collects from the debtor.

MECHANICS' LIENS

Practically all states have statutes authorizing mechanics' liens. The term "mechanic" is somewhat of a misnomer, since such statutes apply to real estate only. Mechanic's-lien statutes assume that if a person's labor or material has improved or added to the value of land, it is fair that he should have a claim against the land for his compensation. In theory, therefore, the claim is against the land itself rather than against the owner of the land personally.

Although there is considerable variation among the states as to details, mechanic's-lien statutes fall into two general classes, known respectively as the "New York system" and the "Pennsylvania system." In general, under a New York system statute, the lien which may be obtained against real estate is limited to the amount which the owner still owes under his construction or repair contract. The lien obtainable under a Pennsylvania system statute is not so limited; a lien may be obtained even though the owner of the land has fully paid the price due under the construction or repair contract.

Statutes vary as to persons having a right to obtain mechanics' liens. Such persons may include:

1. An architect with whom the owner of land contracts for overseeing or supervising contruction or repair of a building.

2. A builder with whom the owner contracts for construction or repair of a building on his land.

3. A subcontractor with whom the builder in turn contracts for performance of a portion of the construction or repair contract.

4. A materialman or supplier who furnishes either to the owner or to the builder, supplies or materials used in the construction or repair of a building.

An authorized person may obtain a mechanic's lien against certain real estate by filing a claim in the proper public office. The right to obtain a mechanic's lien may be waived by agreement. In some states, the right of any person (including subcontractors and materialmen) to obtain a mechanic's lien may be barred by an express agreement to that effect entered into by the owner of the land and the builder, if 1) the subcontractor or materialman has actual notice of the agreement, or 2) the agreement is properly recorded before the start of work on the premises or otherwise within the period specified in the statute. It may seem strange that an agreement between the owner and builder can affect a subcontractor or materialman who is not a party to the agreement, and prevent either of them from obtaining a mechanic's lien. However, this is no more strange than the remainder of the Pennsylvania system statute, which permits a subcontractor or materialman 1) to obtain a lien without a lawsuit, 2) against the property of a person who is not otherwise the lienor's debtor.

Part 4   LANDLORDS AND TENANTS

In any discussion of the rights and duties of landlords and tenants, two legal principles predominate: 1) for a person to become a tenant of certain premises, he must have an agreement or contract with the landowner (landlord), and 2) such an agreement grants to the tenant a real estate interest in the rented premises.

Since the landlord-tenant relationship is contractual, the usual contract rules apply, including those pertaining to offer and acceptance, excuse or nonexcuse, etc. Except as otherwise required by the statute of frauds, the contract (commonly called a "lease") may be express or implied, oral or written. As is discussed in Chapter 9, most statutes of frauds require a lease for longer than a specified duration to be evidenced by a signed writing in order to be enforceable. When the parties use a written lease, frequently they choose a standard printed form suitable for their state. Such printed forms are usually prepared by or for landlords and lean heavily in their favor.

Because a tenant has a real estate interest, he is quite like an owner of the rented premises for the duration of the lease. However, because his ownership interest is limited in duration, he must refrain from causing permanent injury to the premises, or otherwise harming the premises in any way that will continue to affect the premises after expiration of the leasehold period. Such harmful conduct by a tenant is called "waste."

A roomer in a rooming house or a guest in a hotel is a lodger rather than a tenant. The parties to a lodging agreement do not intend to vest in the lodger a right of exclusive possession, one of the chief attributes of a real estate interest.

If an entire building is leased to a tenant, his interest includes not only the building but also the land upon which it stands. If an apartment or an office in a building is leased, the tenant has a real estate interest in that portion of the building but no interest in the land. It would be impractical to consider that occupants of different portions of a single building have interests in sections or slices of the land upon which the building stands, or interests in portions of the air space over the surface of the land.

The legal theory that a landlord-tenant relationship is both a contract relationship and a land relationship is especially apparent in the common-law rules concerning possession, condition of premises, and remedies.

RIGHT OF POSSESSION

By the act of leasing, a landlord impliedly warrants (unless expressly stated otherwise) that the tenant will have exclusive possession of the leased premises, uninterrupted either by the landlord himself or by a third person having a claim or interest enforceable against the landlord.

If some third person has a properly recorded title or interest which at the time of leasing is effective against the landlord, that interest will also be effective against the tenant and superior to his interest. In turn, the tenant will have a breach of warranty claim against the landlord for any damages resulting from the tenant's being disturbed or dispossessed by the superior interest—unless at the time of leasing the landlord disclosed the existence of the third person's interest and expressly stated that he was leasing subject to that interest.

Unless the lease provides otherwise, the landlord himself may not disturb the possession of the tenant except to inspect for waste. If the landlord unjustifiably disturbs the tenant, the landlord is liable for damages. If the landlord's intrusion is sufficient to interfere with the tenant's beneficial use of the premises, the tenant has the right to move out and terminate his obligation to pay rent. In many states a tenant thus evicted by conduct of the landlord can recover damages in addition to terminating his rent obligation; in other states the tenant thus evicted is excused from paying rent, but he has no right to recover damages unless, in addition, the landlord is guilty of fraud or contractual bad faith (for example, by causing the tenant's eviction with a deliberate intent to disaffirm the lease and resume possession).

A landlord may expressly reserve in the lease a right of entry for certain stated purposes. Printed-form dwelling leases frequently contain a provision such as the following:

> The right to label said premises for sale or rent, as also the right of the landlord to enter upon any portion of the same at all times (accompanied by other parties, if so desired by the landlord) to examine into their condition or for the purpose of making repairs or improvements or showing the premises with the view of renting or selling the same, is expressly conceded by the tenant.

If a tenant is disturbed by a third person who does not have a superior interest and does not represent the landlord, the tenant can recover damages from the intruder but not from the landlord.

DETERIORATION, DAMAGE, OR DESTRUCTION OF PREMISES

BEFORE COMMENCEMENT OF THE LEASEHOLD TERM

If, between the time of contracting and the time for commencement of the leasehold term, the premises are substantially damaged or destroyed through no fault of either party, the ordinary contract rule as to excuse applies, and both parties are excused from the contract.

AFTER COMMENCEMENT OF THE LEASEHOLD TERM

Lease of Entire Building

Landlord's Obligation. Under the common-law rules, a landlord, through the act of renting, does not impliedly warrant that a building is usable for the tenant's purposes or for any purpose, nor impliedly warrant that the building is tenantable or will remain so. In general, unless expressly agreed otherwise, the only obligation of the landlord as to condition of the premises is to warn the tenant of any weaknesses or defects 1) which constitute an unreasonable risk of personal injury to the tenant or to some other person on the premises with permission from the tenant, *and* 2) which are actually known to the landlord at the time of leasing, *and* 3) which the landlord can reasonably expect will not be discovered by the tenant upon ordinary inspection. All three conditions must be present for the landlord to be held liable.

Tenant's Obligation. *1) Obligation to Pay Rent.* If a rental building deteriorates, is damaged, is destroyed, or is otherwise not useable by the tenant, the tenant still has the land interest for which he has agreed to pay the rent stated in the lease. Therefore, under the common-law rules which are still followed in many states, a casualty to the premises will not excuse a tenant from his obligation to pay rent. That the landlord receives reimbursement from his casualty insurance and refuses to repair or rebuild is usually immaterial; that the casualty resulted from a concealed defect in the building (for example, defective wiring causing a fire) is usually immaterial, unless the defect was actually known to the landlord at the time of leasing. Note that this is little more than an application of the ordinary contract rule, to the effect that a person will usually not be excused from his contract merely because an unforeseen event reduces the value of what he has obtained under the contract or even renders it worthless for his purposes (see Chapter 11).

2) Obligation to Repair or Rebuild. A tenant is obliged to make ordinary repairs of a minor nature such as are necessary to prevent greater damage to the rented building. For example, the tenant must replace a broken window or at least cover over the opening, but he would not have to replace a faulty roof, because, unless he agrees otherwise, a tenant is not obliged to rebuild or to repair major damage—although he must continue to pay rent.

A tenant may be obligated to make major repairs if he so agrees in the lease. A provision similar to the following is often included in printed leases:

> The tenant agrees to keep and preserve the premises in good order, and at the expiration of the term of this lease, to peaceably and quietly surrender and yield up the premises in as good order and condition as the same shall be in at the time of taking possession—reasonable use and wear only excepted.

In many states such a provision is construed as obligating the tenant to make repairs no matter how major, and even to rebuild in case of total destruction. If so obligated, the tenant has the benefit of any casualty insurance held by the landlord. If the lease exceptions are expanded to include an "act of God," the tenant is still not adequately protected. He will be liable for destruction caused by an accidental fire not the fault of either party, unless the fire resulted from an unexpected natural force, like a bolt of lightning. If the landlord is agreeable, the tenant should have the exception further expanded to include "reasonable use, wear, and damage from fire or other agency not caused by the tenant." Or the tenant should realize the magnitude of his obligation and take out his own casualty insurance.

Lease of an Apartment

If an entire building is not leased to a certain tenant, the landlord is considered as impliedly promising to keep in reasonably safe condition the portions of the building not leased (such as the roof, common corridor and stairway, and outside walls). The tenant may recover damages resulting from the landlord's negligent failure to maintain or repair these portions, and a casualty sufficient to prevent the tenant's beneficial use of the portion leased to him will free the tenant from further payment of rent. However, in many states, the landlord has no obligation concerning a condition of disrepair arising *within* an apartment after leasing—unless (as is especially true in larger cities), a city ordinance requires a landlord to maintain multiple-tenanted premises in a certain specified state of repair.

HOLDING OVER

If a tenant continues in possession after expiration of his lease, he is said to be "holding over." Generally, regardless of the tenant's actual intent or what he says, his act of holding over constitutes an offer to the landlord to extend or renew the lease. The landlord can if he wishes reject the offer and have the tenant evicted, or he can accept the offer. If by words or conduct the landlord indicates acceptance, a new contract is formed renewing the lease.

The duration and continuity of the renewed lease may differ from that of the expired lease. Otherwise (except for such that clearly do not apply) all of the terms, agreements, conditions, and waivers contained in the expired lease also apply to the renewed lease.

DURATION

If the expired lease is for one year or for longer than one year, the renewed lease is usually considered as being for one year. If the expired lease is for a period shorter than a year, generally the renewed lease is for an equal period.

CONTINUITY

States differ as to whether the renewed lease is a definite term lease or a continuously renewing lease (usually called a "periodic lease"). In many states, holding over with the consent of the landlord creates a continuously renewing or periodic lease (unless the original lease provides otherwise). The chief difference is that upon expiration of a definite term lease (unless expressly agreed otherwise), the tenant's right to occupy the leased premises terminates, even though the landlord gives the tenant no advance notice to that effect. On the other hand, a periodic lease (year-to-year, month-to-month, etc.) is effective and binding on the parties for the leasehold term, and in addition, renews automatically for another term, unless the landlord gives the tenant proper advance notice to leave, or (in most states) the tenant gives the landlord previous notice of his intent to move.

A periodic tenancy, discussed here as arising when the tenant holds over with the landlord's consent, may also be created by an express agreement of the parties, by an oral lease extending longer than the statute-of-frauds period, or by a lease which fails to specify any duration. In the latter case, the term of the periodic tenancy equals the time interval used by the parties in stating the rent obligation.

Example: L leased certain described premises to T, effective July 20, 1953. The lease agreement said nothing concerning notice to quit or notice of intent to leave, and said nothing as to duration. Assume that the applicable state law required three-months' notice to terminate a year-to-year tenancy, and thirty-days' notice to terminate a periodic tenancy shorter than year-to-year, and that holding over created a periodic tenancy.

1. The agreed rent was $50 per month, payable in advance.

a) Assume that on August 17, 1953, L decided he wished T to move out, or T decided he wished to move. T's right to occupy would end at midnight August 19, 1953, without any prior notice to quit. Likewise if T quit the premises before midnight August 19, 1953, he would have no further obligation to pay rent, even though he gave no prior notice of his intent to leave.

b) Assume that T continued to occupy and pay rent without any new arrangement, and that on April 28 of the present year, L decided he wished T to move out, or T decided he wished to move. The earliest L could end T's right to occupy would be midnight June 19, and L would have to give T thirty-days' notice before that date. Likewise (in most states) T would be obligated to pay rent until midnight June 19; to end his obligation on that date T would have to move out by then, after giving L thirty-days' prior notice of his intent to leave.

2. The agreed rent was $600 per year payable in monthly installments in advance.

a) Assume that on July 12, 1954, L decided he wished T to move out, or T decided he wished to move. T's right to occupy would end at midnight July 19, 1954, without any prior notice to quit. Likewise, if T quit the premises before that time, he would have no further obligation to pay rent, even though he gave no advance notice of his intent to leave.

b) Assume that T continued to occupy and pay rent without any new arrangement, and that on April 28 of the present year L decided he wished T to move out or T decided he wished to move. The earliest L could end T's right to occupy would be at midnight July 19 of *next year*, and L would have to give T three-months' notice before that date. Likewise (in most states) T would be obligated to pay rent until midnight July 19 of next year; to end his obligation on that date, T would have to move out by then after giving L three-months' prior notice of his intent to leave.

EVICTION

That a tenant's legal right to occupy certain premises has expired, does not necessarily mean that the tenant will promptly leave the premises. If a tenant holds over after a lease for a definite term (and the lease does not expressly require notice to quit), the tenant's legal right to occupy ends upon expiration of the term. If the tenant holds under a periodic tenancy, his right to occupy ends upon expiration of his current term if the landlord has given the required notice before then. If a tenant refuses to leave even though his right to stay has terminated, the landlord must take additional steps to have the tenant removed. The landlord may bring the type of lawsuit (usually called ejectment) available to any owner of real estate when another person is wrongfully in possession. This type of lawsuit is available whether the wrongful possessor is a former tenant or instead is a trespasser who never had permission to occupy. However, such a lawsuit, requiring a full-scale trial, is usually too slow and costly to be a fully adequate remedy for a landlord. Many states have statutes which provide special landlord dispossession actions, speedier and less costly than a standard ejectment lawsuit. Sometimes standard form leases contain a provision authorizing entry of a judgment by confession in an action of ejectment. In states where judgment by confession is valid, this is the simplest and speediest remedy; in many such cases the landlord can have the sheriff forcefully remove the tenant about a week after the start of the proceeding.

COLLECTION OF OVERDUE RENT

As the law of landlord and tenant slowly evolved following the abolition of the feudal system, two kinds of remedies gradually arose under which a landlord could collect overdue rent: 1) a contract lawsuit against the tenant to enforce his lease agreement to pay, and 2) a proceeding relating to the real estate itself, under which the landlord could take possession of any goods on the premises, even goods belonging to persons other than the tenant. The latter remedy (known as "distress," "distraint," or "landlord's levy") has been abolished or modified by statute in most states, but is still retained in some states.

PROBLEMS

1. S and B entered into a written contract under which S agreed to sell and B to buy a certain, described house and lot for $20,000, payable $1,000 with the signing of the agreement, the balance on the settlement date one month later, at which time S was to give B a deed for the property. S had fire insurance on the property in the amount of $12,000. S made no assignment of this insurance to B and the agreement between S and B contained nothing relative to damage or destruction of the premises. Two days later, through no fault of either party, an accidental fire completely destroyed the house. S collected $12,000 from the insurance company but made no attempt to rebuild the house. On the settlement date, S tendered to B a deed for the premises and demanded the balance of the purchase price. B in turn demanded return of the $1,000 he had paid upon signing of the agreement. S sued B, and B counterclaimed against S. What result?

2. S entered into a written contract with B for sale by S and purchase by B of certain premises for $25,000, payable in stated installments, B to have the right of possession immediately and to obtain a deed upon completion of the contracted payments. No public recording was made of the contract. B took up residence on the premises and was still living there six months later when C obtained a judgment against S for $10,000. By this time B had paid $20,000 on the purchase price. When C had the sheriff levy on the premises, he learned for the first time about the contract of sale. What right would C have against the premises? Explain.

3. J obtained a judgment against A who owned and occupied certain premises, but J did nothing further to enforce the judgment until later. One year after J obtained his judgment, A sold and transferred the property to B using a special warranty deed with no exceptions. One year later B sold and transferred the property to C using a special warranty deed with no exceptions, and a year later C in turn sold and transferred to D using a general warranty deed with no exceptions. Each purchaser paid full value and recorded his deed the same day he bought the property. Assume that under the applicable state law, judgment liens were valid for five years. Four years after obtaining the judgment, J had the sheriff levy on the premises. This was the first that B, C, and D knew of J's judgment. J released the property from the levy when D paid J $3,000, the amount then owing on the judgment. Would D have a legal right to collect $3,000 from A; from B; from C? Explain.

4. On February 1 X obtained a $2,000 judgment against B. Thereafter, on March 1, B entered into a written contract with S agreeing to purchase a large tract of potentially oil-bearing land owned by S. Upon signing the contract B paid S $1,000 and contracted to pay S $4,000 more on the settlement date two weeks later and to give S a six-month mortgage for $20,000, the balance of the price. The parties carried out the contract and the new deed and mortgage were recorded on March 15. Thereafter on April 1 B sold and transferred the property to C by special warranty deed which stated that the transfer was "under and subject to a $20,000 mortgage given to S on March 15 of this year." On April 15 Y obtained a $7,000 judgment against C. On May 1 C sold and transferred the property to D by special warranty deed which stated that the transfer was "under and subject to a $20,000 mortgage given to S on March 15 of this year, which the grantee hereof assumes and agrees to pay." By the time S's mortgage came due on September 1, drilling for oil had been abandoned as hopeless. When the mortgage was not paid, S instituted foreclosure proceedings and the property was sold at sheriff's sale for $5,000, its then fair value.

a) When the foreclosure proceedings were instituted, a dispute arose among X, Y, and S as to who held a valid lien against the land, and if more than one lien existed, what the order of priority was. How would the dispute be settled? Explain.

b) For the portion of the mortgage remaining unpaid, would S have a right to collect from B; from C; from D? Explain.

c) From whom could Y collect the unpaid portion of his judgment? Explain.

5. On April 1 S, the owner of a lot, contracted with a builder for construction of a house on S's lot, according to certain plans and specifications, the builder to supply, perform, and supervise all labor, materials, and landscaping, and complete the house ready for occupancy. By the contract S agreed to pay the builder $20,000 at stated intervals as the word progressed. The builder completed construction on August 1, on which date S made the final contract payment and moved into the house. On August 3 S received a surprise promotion and transfer to another state. S immediately engaged a real estate broker to negotiate a sale of the home, for a commission of 5 percent. The broker's efforts induced B to buy. On August 10 S and B signed a contract for the sale and purchase of the home for $23,000, and B engaged a lawyer to search the title. Nobody told the lawyer that the building was of recent construction. The lawyer gave B a written certificate dated August 20, stating that he had searched the records of title and found a good record title in S. On the same day B paid S the agreed purchase price, S signed and gave B a special warranty deed and paid his broker the agreed commission, B's lawyer had the deed recorded, and B moved into the house. On August 25 S and B each received from a supplier a letter stating that the builder still owed $4,000 for materials purchased for and used in construction of the house, and demanding payment. Shortly thereafter the builder was adjudged a voluntary bankrupt, and on September 1, the supplier filed a mechanic's-lien claim against the property. With considerable vehemence, arguments raged concerning liabilities to the supplier and to each other of S, B, B's lawyer, and the real estate broker. Who could recover how much from whom? Explain.

6. O, the owner of a business building, mortgaged the premises to a bank as security for a $20,000 loan payable in five years, and the bank promptly recorded the mortgage. Three years later T was looking for a suitable location for his business. Liking O's building, T entered into a written agreement with O, leasing the premises for ten years. The lease did not mention the mortgage, and T had no actual knowledge of it. T went into possession and spent over $5,000 redecorating and fixing up the premises in a way suitable for T's busi-

ness. T expected to recoup this amount from his business profits during the next ten years. Two years later the mortgage came due, and when O failed to pay, T and the bank each for the first time learned of the other's interest. The bank started foreclosure proceedings on the mortgage. What were the relative rights of the bank and T as to each other and as to O? Explain.

7. By written agreement L leased to T a certain house and lot for one year, beginning April 1, at a yearly rental of $600 payable in monthly installments in advance. T took possession and on August 20, a fire not the fault of L or T destroyed the house and T moved elsewhere. T's last rental payment was made according to the lease on August 1, for that month. Neither L nor T had fire insurance.

a) There was no provision in the lease pertaining to damage to or destruction of the premises. 1) L made no effort to have the house rebuilt, but in April of the following year, L sued T for rent. State how much, if anything, L was entitled to recover from T. Explain. 2) Upon L's demand, T refused to have the house rebuilt. L rebuilt it to its previous condition and sued T for the expense. Was L entitled to recover? Explain.

b) The only provision in the lease pertaining to damage to or destruction of the premises read: "At the end of the term the premises shall be delivered up in as good condition as at the commencement of the term, ordinary wear and tear and unavoidable damage by fire, tempest, and lightning excepted." 1) and 2) Same additional facts and questions as in (1) and (2) above.

c) The only provision in the lease pertaining to damage to or destruction of the premises read: "T shall keep the premises in repair and at the expiration of the term of this lease, T shall return the premises in as good order and condition as the same shall be in at the time of taking possession, reasonable use and wear excepted." 1) and 2) Same additional facts and questions as in (1) and (2) above.

8. L leased to T an apartment in an apartment building, for one year, at a stated rental, and T moved in. Three months later the tenant occupying the apartment directly above T's reported to the landlord that the drain was partially clogged and draining very slowly. The landlord said that he would have the drain fixed. However, he failed to do so and shortly the drain became completely clogged. Water overflow leaked through the ceiling in T's apartment, causing a large section of plaster to come loose and fall, damaging some of T's furniture. What rights would T have as to the damaged furniture and as to the unsightly condition of the ceiling? Explain.

9. By written agreement, L leased to T a certain house and lot for a term of one year from November 1, 1954, at a yearly rental of $1,200 payable in monthly installments in advance. The written lease provided: "T will take good care of the premises while occupying the same, surrendering the premises, without notice, to L at the end of the term or any extension thereof, in as good condition as he received the premises, reasonable wear and tear and accidental damage or destruction excepted; should T remain in the rented premises by consent of L, after expiration of the term, or any extension thereof, said term shall be presumed to have been extended or further extended for a period of one year and so on from year to year, upon and under the same terms, conditions, and limitations as are herein provided and expressed." On August 15 of the present year L sold the premises to B and assigned to B all right, title, and interest in the lease, together with rentals due on and after September 1. T was notified of the sale, and, beginning September 1, paid rent to B. On October 1 B notified T to quit at the expiration of his current term. T refused to move and on November 2, B sued to recover possession. Would B be entitled to recover? Explain.

chapter *21*

Gifts and Inheritance

One way in which property is frequently transferred, or property interests created, is by gift, made either during the lifetime of the transferor or upon his death (through inheritance). A decedent's heir who inherits certain property interests receives what might be called a "deathtime" gift. Making a death gift by means of a last will and testament is, of course, quite different from making a lifetime gift. A bequest or legacy in a will does not become effective or vest any right in the legatee until the testator (the signer of the will) dies, and the will can be revoked by the testator anytime before he dies. On the other hand, an unrestricted living gift during the donor's lifetime is usually made with an intent to vest a right in the donee immediately, or in the near future, and once it is made, it cannot be revoked.

Part 1   GIFTS

Although there is considerable difference between a contract to transfer property and a gift of the property, there is also a marked policy similarity. If a person expresses an intent to transfer something of value to another—whether he intends the transfer to be made now or later —the law will not enforce the intent unless there is "something" in addition to the bare intent. In the case of a contractual promise, this "something" is consideration or a legally recognized equivalent of consideration (see Chapter 6). In the case of a gift, this "something" is delivery or a legally recognized equivalent of delivery. It is a rule of policy, therefore, that for a gift to be legally effective and enforceable, two elements are required, 1) a present intent to make a gift, and 2) a delivery of the subject matter of the gift, or a legally recognized equivalent of delivery.

PRESENT INTENT

To make a valid gift, the donor must intend that ownership or an interest in the subject matter of the gift is to vest in the donee immediately. An intent that ownership is to pass at some future time either forms a contractual promise—which is not enforceable in the absence of consideration or its equivalent—or is a will, which (for most purposes) must be in writing, and is not effective until the donor dies.

Example: On March 29, a woman who owned some valuable diamond jewelry was taken from her home to a hospital where she died on April 1. As she was leaving her house, the woman said to an impartial witness: "I have given my diamonds to Nancy, my niece, and if anything happens to me, she is to have them." After the woman's death, the court appointed an administrator to pay her debts and distribute her property to her heirs. The administrator demanded the diamonds from Nancy and, when she refused to surrender them, sued to recover possession.

The administrator would recover. The intent expressed by the owner was not to make a present gift but rather for ownership to vest in Nancy in the future. Therefore no valid gift was made. This was an oral will which in most states is not valid or effective to transfer valuable property.

DELIVERY OR ITS EQUIVALENT

An actual physical transfer of the subject matter of the gift is obviously an effective delivery.

Legally recognized equivalents of delivery include:

1. The donor's delivering to his intended donee (or to some third party to turn over to the donee) possession of something, which to some extent gives the donee (and to the same extent deprives the donor of) control over the subject matter of the gift.

2. The donor's making a contract with a third person (or institution) for the benefit of the donee, sufficient to vest an enforceable interest in the donee.

Written Instrument Evidencing an Obligation or Interest. If an obligation owed to a creditor is evidenced by a written instrument signed by the debtor, the creditor can usually make a valid gift of the obligation (presuming he manifests an intent to make a present gift), by delivering the written instrument to the donee or to someone for the donee. Valid gifts of promissory notes and corporate bonds are often made in this way. Likewise, the delivery of a stock certificate to the donee or to someone for the donee (with intent to make a present gift) accomplishes an effective gift.

Valuables Stored in a Safe-deposit Box. Generally, if the subscriber to a safety-deposit box delivers the key to another person with the intent to make a present gift of the contents, an effective gift is made. If the subscriber has another key and thus retains access to the box, some courts have said that delivering one of two keys will not make an effective gift of the contents of the box. Sometimes these courts base their conclusion on insufficiency of delivery; sometimes, the conclusion is more accurately based on the lack of a clear manifestation of an intent to make a present gift. If the evidence shows that nothing more was said or done by the subscriber, his delivering one of his two keys is more indicative of his appointing the recipient of the key as his agent than of making an outright gift.

Money in a Bank Account. Usually the presentation of the deposit book issued by a bank is required to make withdrawals from a savings account but not from a checking account. Generally, therefore, delivery of a savings deposit book, with donative intent, makes a gift of the amount in the account, while delivery of a checking account deposit book does not accomplish a gift. If a donor makes a gift of a check drawn on his checking account, even if the check is drawn for the entire balance in the account, the donor nevertheless still has power to stop payment on the check. Therefore no effective gift of money takes place until the check is paid by the bank, or until the check is transferred to a holder in due course. Much litigation has arisen involving joint bank accounts. Suppose that Arthur Adams opens a joint bank account in the names of Arthur Adams and Bernard Brown, or Adams changes his one-name account to a joint account by adding Brown's name—in either case Adams being the source of all the money deposited in the account. Frequently such a joint account has a survivorship provision—the money is to be paid to the survivor of the two parties. Generally, Adams will maintain a joint account for one of two reasons: 1) to enable Brown as Adams' agent to have access to the funds for the benefit of Adams or his estate; or 2) to make a gift to Brown of one-half of the money that Adams deposits in the account, and, upon Adams' death, of all of the money. Courts in the various states differ as to the factors relied upon in determining whether an agency or a gift is intended. In some states, the courts have said that (continuing the Adams-Brown example) Adams' designating the account as a joint account merely indicates that Brown is Adams' agent. In this connection, it is usually immaterial whether the account is an "and" or an "or" account. However, the same courts are inclined to say that if, in addition, Adams and Brown both sign a signature card clearly stating that the account goes to the survivor, an effective gift is made to Brown.

Part 2 INHERITANCE

Inheritance of property is entirely statutory. As the United States Supreme Court stated a number of years ago:

> While the laws of all civilized States recognize in every citizen the absolute right to his own earnings, and to the enjoyment of his own property, and the increase thereof, during his life, except so far as the State may require him to contribute his share for public expenses, the

right to dispose of his property by will has always been considered purely a creature of statute and within legislative control. . . . Though the general consent of the most enlightened nations has, from the earliest historical period, recognized a natural right in children to inherit the property of their parents, we know of no legal principle to prevent the legislature from taking away or limiting the right of testamentary disposition or imposing such conditions upon its exercise as it may deem conducive to public good.[1]

The general objectives of inheritance statutes are 1) *primarily*, to accomplish the distribution of a decedent's property through a practical and workable system, and in conformity with the public interest; and 2) *secondarily*, so long as consistent with the primary objective, to make distribution in accordance with a decedent's expressed desire or in a way that approximates what the decedent would probably have desired had he expressed an intent. In order that a decedent's wishes can be accurately determined, inheritance statutes are vigilant against the risk of forged and fraudulently altered wills, and accept as valid only what can be clearly shown to be a genuine expression of the decedent's intent.

A will is an effective direction given by an owner of property, stating how his property is to pass upon his death. The maker of a will is referred to as the *testator;* when he dies, he is said to have died *testate.* A person dying without a valid will dies *intestate.* A person may be testate as to some of his property and intestate as to other; in other words a will may be valid although it does not include all of a testator's property. Frequently when a bank account is opened, the card which the depositor is requested to sign contains a statement naming the person to whom the account is to be paid upon the depositor's death. Often, this is an effective will for the amount remaining in the account when the depositor dies.

Usually, soon after the testator's death, his will is submitted to the proper judicial officials together with satisfactory evidence that it is the testator's genuine and valid will. Such evidence usually consists of the testimony of persons who saw the decedent sign the will, or who are acquainted with the testator's signature and believe that the signature on the offered will is genuine. If the document which is offered as a will is challenged or contested, its validity must be determined by a court trial. Upon satisfactory proof that an offered will is genuine and valid, a decree to that effect is issued. The will is then said to be proved or "probated." Frequently, a testator will name in his will the person (or institution, such as a bank) by whom he desires his estate to be administered. Upon probate of the will the testator's nominee will be appointed executor. Under supervision of the court, the executor gathers together the testator's

[1] *United States* v. *Perkins,* 163 U.S. 625, 16 S. Ct. 1073, 41 L. Ed. 287 (1896).

assets, pays his debts, and distributes the balance of the estate to the proper parties. Statutes provide a certain order of priority for payment of creditors when estates are insolvent.

If a decedent dies intestate and court administration of his property is desirable or necessary, a party having a proper interest in the decedent's property can request the court to appoint an administrator for the decedent's estate. The administrator's duties are much the same as those of an executor.

Obviously the appointment of an administrator is not necessary for every person who dies. If nothing is to be gained or accomplished through the administration of a decedent's estate, there is no need to incur the expense. Settlement by agreement among a decedent's family will sometimes suffice, for example, with a small estate consisting of property easily transferred by delivery. If a decedent leaves goods of more than nominal value, or real estate, it is usually wise for his survivors to consult a lawyer as to the necessity of formal administration of the estate. If the lawyer considers administration unnecessary, the parties should enlist the lawyer's services to properly accomplish a family settlement. Participants in a family settlement must be sure that funeral and burial expenses, all other enforceable debts, and inheritance taxes are paid before dividing the decedent's property. Heirs are not personally liable for a decedent's debts. However, if there is no formal administration of a decedent's estate, each heir who receives a share thereby becomes liable for any of the decedent's unpaid debts, up to the value of the property received.

Statutes in many states provide for short and inexpensive administration of small estates. Also, when wages or salary are owed to a decedent, statutes frequently permit the employer to make payment to certain designated survivors, without the necessity of any administration proceedings.

Since the settlement of estates usually takes a year or longer, statutes in most states provide for some sort of a monetary allowance to the family of a decedent. In theory, a family allowance is a gratuity given by the law to assist the decedent's family to obtain its needs without waiting for complete administration of the estate. Usually, therefore, the right to a family allowance is not affected by whether the decedent dies testate or intestate, or whether his estate is solvent or insolvent. Apparently to further expedite payment of the allowance, some statutes 1) do not require proof of need, 2) grant the allowance to either a surviving husband or wife if a member of the same household with the decedent at the time of his death, and 3) if no spouse who was a member of the same household survives the decedent, grant the family allowance to the decedent's child or children who were members of the same household as the decedent—regardless of the age, dependency, or marital status of the child. With the exception of a family allowance, only the net amount of a decedent's estate, after payment of all costs of administration, debts, and taxes, can pass to the heirs.

In order to prevent too much delay in settling estates, statutes in many states give a decedent's creditors a certain period of time within which to file claims. If a creditor fails to claim within the specified time (for example, one year after advertisement of the appointment of the executor or administrator), then while the creditor's claim is still enforceable against any of the decedent's property not yet distributed, the creditor has no rights against the decedent's representative personally or against heirs to whom the decedent's property has already been distributed. In some states this rule applies to a creditor whose claim is unmatured, contingent, or both, and whether or not the creditor has actual knowledge of the decedent's death.

If a property owner and one of his heirs both sustain fatal injuries in an accident, the descent of property will depend upon which one survives the other, even for only a moment. If both die before someone arrives at the scene, an attempt to determine the respective times of the deaths may involve highly speculative medical guesses. A number of states have avoided the problem by adopting the Uniform Simultaneous Death Act. A few of the provisions of this act may be summarized as follows:

> When the title to or inheriting of property depends upon priority of death, and there is no sufficient evidence that the persons died otherwise than simultaneously, the property of each person is disposed of as if he had survived, except as otherwise provided by will.
>
> When there is no sufficient evidence that two joint tenants or tenants by the entireties have died otherwise than simultaneously, the property so held is distributed, one-half as if one had survived, and one-half as if the other survived. With an appropriate change of the fraction, the same formula applies if property is owned by three or more joint tenants.

Although the inheritance statues of the various states differ widely in many details, there is considerable uniformity in the general pattern they follow. As an example of one state's inheritance pattern, some of the chief provisions of the Pennsylvania statutes (and court decisions interpreting them) will be summarized. No attempt is made here to cover all of the details and exceptions that make up the Pennsylvania inheritance scheme. It cannot be too strongly emphasized that the entire subject of wills and decedent's estates is complex. Writing a will, even a simple one, should, if at all possible, be left to skilled legal technicians.

Example: When Andrew Brown died, a metal file box was found in his office containing various insurance policies, receipts, and a will dated about twenty years before Andrew's death. The will had been written by an attorney and signed at the end by Andrew Brown in the presence of the attorney and his secretary, both of whom signed as witnesses. As originally written and signed, the chief portion of the will read: "I give, devise, and bequeath unto my beloved brother Charles Brown, his heirs and assigns forever, all my property, real, personal, and mixed, of what nature or kind soever, and wherever the same may be found at the time of my death." When the will was found after Andrew's death, the words, "brother, Charles," had been crossed out in ink and immediately above the deletions, in ink of the same shade as that used to make the deletions and apparently in Andrew's handwriting, were written the words, "nephew, David." Andrew had never married and his parents were both dead. At one time Andrew had a brother Charles and a sister Evelyn. About ten years before Andrew's death, Charles died, survived by his widow and son, David. Andrew had been very close to Charles and his family, had made his home with them, and continued to do so after Charles's death. As the boy David grew up, Andrew took him into the trucking business which Andrew owned and operated. Andrew's sister Evelyn was married, lived in a distant part of the country, and for the past fifteen years before Andrew's death, the only contact between Evelyn and Andrew was the mutual exchange of Christmas cards. Presumably, Andrew made the above-quoted changes in his will after Charles' death. When Andrew died, Evelyn claimed one-half of Andrew's estate.

Was the will as changed a valid will? Clearly not. After a person dies, the law must protect his estate against forged and altered wills. The way to prove the genuineness of a will is either through a witness who saw the testator proclaim and sign the document as his will, or through recognition of the testator's handwriting. When handwriting is in question, the way to prove its authorship is to compare the questioned writing with writing admitted to be genuine. The most individual part of a person's writing is his signature. The signature, therefore, is taken as the best test of the genuineness of a will. The changes in Andrew's will *could* have been made by someone else. The best test—a signature—was not added after the changes. Therefore, the document as changed was not a valid will.

Was the will as originally written still in effect? This question involves a very arguable and complex legal concept. In the case upon which this example is based, the court said that apparently Andrew lined out the words in the will with an intent to cancel them. Therefore, the will as originally written was canceled and no longer in effect.

Conclusion: Andrew died without a valid will, and under the intestacy statutes his property would be divided into two parts, one part passing through the deceased Charles to David, the other half passing to Evelyn.

Irony: While the death of a will-beneficiary before the testator will usually cancel any provision in favor of the deceased beneficiary, statutes frequently provide that a will provision will not lapse if the named beneficiary was a close relative of the testator and leaves a child or children. If Andrew had kept his inexperienced fingers off the will, David would have inherited everything. But when Andrew tried, *without expert advice*, to change the will, he completely defeated his intent.

OUTLINE OF PENNSYLVANIA INHERITANCE SCHEME

DISTRIBUTION BY WILL

Who May Make a Will

Any person of sound mind, twenty-one years of age or older (eighteen for military personnel and mariners) may make a will.

Form and Execution of a Will

Oral Will. The provisions concerning oral wills are so restrictive that a valid oral will is rare. It is of little use even if valid since an oral will attempting to dispose of personal property worth more than $500, or of real estate, is wholly void.

Written Will. Except for an oral will, every will must be in writing and signed by the testator at the end. Any writing after the testator's signature is not part of the will and does not affect it. The statute specifies procedures for signing by mark if the testator is unable to sign his name, and for someone signing for the testator, if the testator is unable to make a mark.

In addition to the testator's signature, most states require the signatures of two (or sometimes three) witnesses. Such signing or "subscribing" witnesses need not read the will or be familiar with its contents; they merely observe the testator sign the document after he tells them that it is his will.

Revocation of a Will

A *codicil* is a change which is added to an existing will; to be valid, the testator must sign at the end of the codicil.

A will or codicil in writing cannot be revoked or altered otherwise than: 1) by some other will, codicil, or other writing signed at the end and provable in the same manner as a will; or 2) by being burnt, torn, canceled, obliterated, or destroyed, with the intent and for the purpose of revocation, either by the testator himself, or if by another person, at the testator's direction and in the presence of two other persons.

Modification by Circumstances

New Charitable Legacy. Any bequest or devise for religious or charitable purposes, written and signed not more than thirty days before the death of the testator, is invalid, unless all who would benefit by its invalidity agree that it shall be valid, or unless the bequest or devise in question merely continues a gift provided by a prior will (more than thirty days old) which is still in existence and can be produced.

Divorce. If a testator is divorced after making a will, all provisions in the will in favor of or relating to his spouse become ineffective for all purposes.

Marriage. If a testator marries after making a will, the surviving spouse will receive his or her intestate share unless the will provides for a greater share.

Spouse's Dissent. Except for his (or her) surviving spouse, a testator may disinherit any heir. No matter how closely related the parties are, it is not necessary that the testator specify any nominal amount for the disinherited person, nor mention the one being disinherited, nor give any reason. In fact, it is usually better for the testator not to state any reason in the will. A testator who is considerably aggravated with the ne'er-do-well he is disinheriting and proceeds to say why in his will may lay his estate open to a libel suit when the will is published.

A testator cannot disinherit his (or her) spouse. The spouse is entitled to take a certain share, in spite of the will (commonly called "taking against the will"). The share received by a spouse who takes against a will is described later as part of the topic, "Distribution Not by Will."

Birth or Adoption. If a testator fails to provide in his will for his child born or adopted after making the will, the failure may be intentional, or instead (as so often is the case) may be the result of the testators delay in modifying his will. If it does not appear from the will that the omission was intentional, the legislatures of many states feel it to be sound policy to assume that the testator procrastinated and to modify his will accordingly. Under the Pennsylvania formula, the testator's property which passes to his or her surviving spouse (taking either under or against the will) is first deducted. Then, if any of the testator's estate remains, the after-born (or after-adopted) child receives from this property the share he would receive if the testator had died unmarried and intestate. A child in existence when the will was made takes only the share (if any) provided in the will.

Rules of Interpretation

The following are some of the rules which help to determine the meaning of words used in a will.

In construing a bequest or devise to a person described by relationship to the testator rather than by name: 1) any person adopted before the death of the testator is considered the child of his adopting parent and not the child of his natural parent; 2) an illegitimate person is considered the child of his mother and not of his father unless the parents later marry and thus legitimate the child.

Ordinarily if a beneficiary dies before the testator, any devise or bequest in favor of the beneficiary is considered to have lapsed. However, even though a beneficiary (whether named or indicated by relationship) dies before the testator's death: 1) a devise or bequest to a child or other issue of the testator will not lapse, if the indicated beneficiary leaves issue surviving the testator; 2) if the property in question would not otherwise pass to the testator's spouse, a gift to the testator's brother, sister, or child thereof will not lapse, if the indicated beneficiary leaves issue surviving the testator. In either of these situations the gift for the indicated beneficiary, instead of lapsing, will pass to his or her issue.

Unless the contrary is stated or implied in the will in question,

1. If a beneficiary is not named but rather is designated as "child" or "children" (of the testator or of some other person), the gift is presumed to be intended for whoever fits that designation at the time the bequest or devise vests or is to be paid.

2. If a beneficiary is not named but is designated as "wife" (of the testator or of some other person), the gift is presumed to be intended for the person who was wife at the time the will was written.

If after the family allowance and debts are paid, insufficient property remains to pay all devises and bequests, the testator's heirs take in the following order:

1. Any specific devise or bequest to the testator's spouse is paid.

2. Then if property remains, any specific devise or bequest to the testator's issue is paid. If all within this class cannot be paid in full, payment is prorated.

3. Then if property remains, payment is made on any specific devise or bequest in favor of someone other than the testator's spouse and issue. Payments are prorated if necessary.

4. Then if property remains, any general devise or bequest is paid with payment prorated if necessary.

DISTRIBUTION NOT BY WILL

The term "issue" includes *all* lineal descendants—child, grandchild, great-grandchild, etc., while the term "child" is limited to the first degree of descendancy.

Share of Surviving Spouse

1. As to real and personal property interests owned by a decedent at the time of death:

a) If not included in a will, the share of the surviving spouse is as follows: 1) One-third, if the decedent is survived (a) by more than one child, or (b) by one or more children and the issue of a deceased child, or (c) by the issue of more than one child. 2) One-half, if the decedent is survived (a) by one child only, or (b) by no child but by the issue of one deceased child. 3) The first $10,000 and one-half of the remainder, if the decedent is survived by no issue but is survived by other close relatives. If a decedent leaves a will as to part of his property and is intestate as to the remainder, any amount the surviving spouse receives under the will is applied toward this $10,000 allowance. The term "close relatives" as used here includes only the following: parent, brother, sister, child of brother or sister ("child" rather than "issue" and therefore grandchild of a brother or sister is not included), grandparent, uncle, or aunt. 4) All of the estate, if the decedent is not survived by any issue or other close relative (as defined above).

b) If included in decedent's will, but his or her surviving spouse chooses to take against the will, the share of the surviving spouse is as follows: 1) One-third, if the decedent is survived by the heirs listed in (1) above. 2) One-half, in all other cases.

2. As to interests transferred by decedent during marriage:

a) If the decedent retained a power to revoke or use all or part of what he (or she) transferred, to that extent, the surviving spouse may treat the transfer as a testamentary disposition (that is, like a will) and take against it. There is an exception: the spouse has no right to take against any contract of life insurance purchased by the decedent.

b) As to real estate transferred by decedent during marriage: If a surviving spouse did not join in the deceased spouse's conveyance of real estate, then upon the decedent's death, an ownership interest in the transferred real estate will vest in the surviving spouse. The ownership interest which thus vests is equal to the surviving spouse's intestate share in real estate owned by the deceased spouse at the time of death— that is, from a one-third ownership interest to a total interest, depending upon the type and number of other heirs.

Forfeiture of Spouse's Right. A surviving spouse is barred from 1) taking against decedent's will or other testamentary disposition, and/or 2) taking an intestate share of a decedent's property, if, for at least one year prior to the death of the decedent:

1) As to a Surviving Husband. He willfully neglected or refused to provide for his deceased wife or intentionally and without justification deserted her.

2) As to a Surviving Wife. She intentionally and without justification deserted her husband.

Share of Others than Spouse

The share of decedent's estate to which the surviving spouse is not entitled, or the entire estate if there is no surviving spouse, descends:

1. To the issue of the decedent. If no issue survives the decedent, then

2. To the decedent's parents, or to his parent if only one is still living. If no parent survives the decedent, then

3. To the issue of each of the decedent's parents. If no issue of either of the decedent's parents survives the decedent, then

4. If at least one parent of either the decedent's mother or father is living, then half of the property goes to that grandparent (or if the other grandparent on that same side also still lives, to both), and the other half of the property goes to the grandparent or grandparents on the other side; or, if both are dead, to decedent's uncles, aunts, or their children on that other side. If none of these survive, this half goes with the first half. If no grandparent survives the decedent, then

5. To the decedent's uncles, aunts, or their children. If none of the above described persons survives the decedent, then

6. To the Commonwealth of Pennsylvania.

Degree of Relationship. If the heirs (other than a spouse) who are entitled to inherit are all in the same degree of relationship to the decedent, all share equally. If the heirs (other than a spouse) entitled to inherit the decedent's property are in different degrees of relationship to the decedent, the living heir in the nearest degree of relationship to the decedent fixes the level at which distribution is calculated. The decedent's estate is then equally divided by the number of lines of heirs at that level, either living, or if dead survived by issue. A share passes to each living heir at that level; for any heir at that level who is dead, his share passes to his issue. If any deceased heir has more than one issue in the same degree of relationship, they divide equally the share that comes down the line of the deceased heir.

Half Blood. No distinction is made between heirs of the whole and those of the half blood.

Tenancy Taken. When real or personal property is inherited by a husband and wife together, they take as tenants by the entireties.

PROBLEMS

1. One paragraph of a will, signed in 1934, read: "I bequeath to the Chicago Trust Company the sum of $50,000, in trust to invest and to pay the income monthly to my nephew, Nathan, for and during the term of his natural life, and upon his death, to pay the principal amount of said trust to

his wife and children share and share alike." From 1930 to 1936 Nathan was living with his wife, Ivy, and their two children, Andrew and Betty. In November, 1936, Nathan and Ivy were divorced, Nathan retaining custody of the children. In 1940 Nathan married Jane and at the time of his death some years later, he was survived by his widow Jane, by Andrew and Betty, and also by Carol and David, children of Nathan and Jane. Ivy also remarried shortly after the divorce and when Nathan died, was living in a distant community. How should the trust fund be distributed? Explain.

2. When D died, he left to survive him the persons listed below. His net estate for distribution to heirs (after payment of all costs, debts, taxes, and allowances) was $30,000. For each of the following, determine how this amount should be distributed:

a) D's survivors: widow, brother, two nieces (daughters of D's deceased sister) and a daughter-in-law (widow of D's deceased son).

b) D's survivors: all specified in Part (a) plus D's father.

c) D's survivors: all specified in Part (b) plus a son.

d) D's survivors: all specified in Part (c) plus two grandchildren (children of D's deceased daughter).

e) D's survivors: widow and one cousin (son of D's deceased uncle).

3. Andrew White, seriously ill and advised by his doctor that he was about to die, called to his bedside in his home an old friend and neighbor, and his housekeeper, neither of whom was related to Andrew. In the presence of disinterested witnesses Andrew handed his friend a corporate bond having a value of $4,000, saying, "This is yours." Then Andrew gave his housekeeper the key to his safe-deposit box saying, "'When I die, the contents of the box will belong to you." Andrew died the following day. The safe-deposit box contained $8,000 in cash. In addition to the bond and cash, Andrew left other personal property of the value of $24,000, after deducting costs, debts, and taxes. Andrew died intestate, survived by: Bernard White, an adopted child of one of Andrew's deceased brothers; Carrie White, Bernard's mother; David White, the illegitmate child of Andrew's deceased sister; Edward White, a half-brother; Frank and George White, sons of another of Andrew's deceased brothers; and Hanna White, the mother of Frank and George. How should Andrew's estate be distributed? Explain.

4. When Andrew White died, he left a will dated 1957 which read in part: "I devise and bequeath to my wife, Alice, such portion of my estate which is required by law but no more. The balance of my estate I devise and bequeath to my children and their heirs." In 1958, the only child of Andrew and Alice died in infancy. In 1959, Andrew and Alice adopted Bernard White, Andrew's adult brother, as their child. In 1960, Charles White was born to Andrew and Alice. Bernard died in 1961, survived by his widow Dona. When Andrew died, he was survived by Alice, Charles, and Dona. At the time of Andrew's death, he and Alice had $10,000 in a joint bank account which they held as tenants by entireties. Andrew's other property, after liquidation and payment of all costs, debts, taxes, and

family allowance, amounted to $30,000. How should Andrew's estate be distributed? Explain.

5. When Harry Smith died, a paper was found in his safe-deposit box. It was written in the decedent's handwriting and, in its entirety, read:

> "Last Will and Testament, December 1, 1945. I, Harry Smith, give and bequeath unto my wife, Mary Smith, the sum of $10,000 and to my son, Robert Smith, the rest, residue, and remainder of my estate."

In 1948, Harry and Mary were divorced. In 1950, Harry married Janet, but in 1951 Janet left Harry without good reason and never returned. At the time of Harry's death several years later, his former wife, Mary, was alive. He was survived by his widow, Janet; his son, Robert; a daughter, Ruth; and two grandchildren, Samuel and June, children of a son, Archie, who had predeceased Harry. The grandchildren lived with their mother, Sara, the widow of Archie. All of decedent's children were born prior to 1945. The estate of Harry consisted entirely of personal property. After all allowances, administration expenses, debts, and taxes were paid there was a balance for distribution of $45,000.

a) Should the writtten instrument quoted above be probated? Explain.

b) Other facts remaining the same, assume that decedent died intestate. How should his estate be distributed? Explain.

c) Other facts remaining the same, assume that decedent left a valid will reading the same as the above-quoted instrument. How should his estate be distributed? Explain.

d) Other facts remaining the same, assume that decedent left a valid will reading the same as the above-quoted instrument except that it did not contain the name "Mary Smith." How should his estate be distributed? Explain.

e) Other facts remaining the same, assume that decedent left a valid will dated 1950, reading the same as the above-quoted instrument with Janet as the named wife. How should his estate be distributed? Explain.

Table of Citations to the Uniform Commercial Code

687

Index